About Pearson

Pearson is the world's learning company, with presence across 70 countries worldwide. Our unique insights and world-class expertise comes from a long history of working closely with renowned teachers, authors and thought leaders, as a result of which, we have emerged as the preferred choice for millions of teachers and learners across the world.

We believe learning opens up opportunities, creates fulfilling careers and hence better lives. We hence collaborate with the best of minds to deliver you class-leading products, spread across the Higher Education and K12 spectrum.

Superior learning experience and improved outcomes are at the heart of everything we do. This product is the result of one such effort.

Your feedback plays a critical role in the evolution of our products and you can contact us at reachus@pearson.com. We look forward to it.

TWELFTH EDITION

HUMAN RELATIONS
INTERPERSONAL JOB-ORIENTED SKILLS

Andrew J. DuBrin

College of Business
Rochester Institute of Technology

To Melanie, once again

Original edition, entitled *Human Relations: Interpersonal Job-Oriented Skills*, 12th Edition, by DuBrin, Andrew J. published by Pearson Education Limited, Copyright © 2015.

Indian Subcontinent Reprint
Copyright © 2019 Pearson India Education Services Pvt. Ltd

ISBN 978-93-530-6696-3

First Impression

This edition is manufactured in India and is authorized for sale only in India, Bangladesh, Bhutan, Pakistan, Nepal, Sri Lanka and the Maldives. Circulation of this edition outside of these territories is UNAUTHORIZED.

Published by Pearson India Education Services Pvt. Ltd, CIN: U72200TN2005PTC057128.

Head Office: 15th Floor, Tower-B, World Trade Tower, Plot No. 1, Block-C, Sector 16, Noida 201 301, Uttar Pradesh, India.
Registered Office: 4th Floor, Software Block, Elnet Software City, TS 140, Block 2 & 9, Rajiv Gandhi Salai, Taramani, Chennai 600 113, Tamil Nadu, India.
Fax: 080-30461003, Phone: 080-30461060
Website: in.pearson.com; Email: companysecretary.india@pearson.com

Printed in India by Pushp Print Services.

BRIEF CONTENTS

CONTENTS

Chapter 3   Building Self-Esteem and Self-Confidence   72

Chapter 11   Motivating Others   274

Chapter 14   Customer Satisfaction Skills   348

Chapter 15

Enhancing Ethical Behavior 374

Chapter 16

Stress Management and Personal Productivity 398

Welcome to the 12th edition of *Human Relations: Interpersonal Job-Oriented Skills*. Success in any position involving interaction with people requires two broad sets of competencies: functional skills and generic skills. *Functional skills* refer to knowledge of one's discipline (or organizational function), technical skills, specialty skills, or simply details of the job. *Generic skills* refer to competencies important in a variety of jobs. Among these generic skills are interpersonal skills, good work habits and time management, information technology skills, and ethical behavior. Among other skills presently in demand by employers emphasized in this book are verbal communication, teamwork, and group problem solving, along with high self-motivation.

My purpose in writing this book is to help readers enhance their interpersonal skills, including ethical behavior, in the workplace. By enhancing interpersonal skills, a person has a better chance of capitalizing upon his or her other skills. Two primary approaches are used in this text to achieve the lofty goal of improving interpersonal skills. First, basic concepts are introduced to enhance understanding of key topics in interpersonal relations in organizations.

Second, skill-building suggestions, exercises, self-assessment quizzes, and cases are presented that are designed to improve interpersonal skills related to the topic. Chapter 6, for example, presents general information about the nature of teamwork, followed by suggestions for improving teamwork. The chapter also includes several exercises or experiential activities and two case problems—all designed to improve teamwork skills.

Third, examples and box inserts provide insight into how a particular skill is applied on the job. For example, Chapter 8 describes how call center operators learn another culture so that they can relate effectively to their customers.

CHANGES IN THE NEW EDITION

The new edition of *Human Relations* focuses on updating content throughout the text, as well as replacing most case problems and introductory cases and introducing more role-plays. In several places throughout the text, we add a third level of heading to better organize the information for the student. We have added three new skill-building exercises, five new self-quizzes, and fifteen new role-playing exercises. New information, research findings, and examples appear throughout the text. Twelve of the chapter openers and 24 of the cases are new. Material that may have lost some of its relevance has been selectively pruned. The new topics in the text are as follows:

- Revised and simplified discussion about practical intelligence (Chapter 2)
- Consequences of self-esteem divided into positive and negative (Chapter 3)
- Self-assessment quiz about core self-evaluations (Chapter 3)
- Getting help from others to boost self-esteem (Chapter 3)
- Description of self-compassion (Chapter 3)
- Guidelines for detecting lying through nonverbal communication (Chapter 4)
- Communication problems caused by converting too many nouns into verbs (Chapter 4)
- The interpersonal consequences of nomophobia, the fear of being without a mobile phone (Chapter 5)

- Interpersonal skill consequences of telepresence (an advanced form of videoconferencing) (Chapter 5)
- Communicating frequently and assertively to enhance teamwork (Chapter 6)
- New version of nominal group technique (NGT) (Chapter 7)
- Recognition of one's own cultural and demographic biases (Chapter 8)
- Drama as a source of conflict in the workplace (Chapter 9)
- Task versus relationship conflict (Chapter 9)
- Authenticity as a key leadership trait and behavior (Chapter 10)
- Interacting frequently with team members to enhance teamwork (Chapter 10)
- Work engagement and motivation (Chapter 11)
- Expanded discussion of e-mentoring (Chapter 12)
- Etiquette for working in open-seating arrangements in the office (Chapter 13)
- Conforming to a manager's work style to build a good relationship (Chapter 13)
- Focusing on a customer's problem rather than his or her emotions for dealing with customer dissatisfaction (Chapter 14)
- Moral disengagement as a source of unethical behavior (Chapter 15)
- Motivated blindness as a source of unethical behavior (Chapter 15)
- Engaging in unethical behavior to benefit the company (Chapter 15)
- Seeing the big picture to facilitate ethical behavior (Chapter 15)
- High reactivity as a personality factor contributing to being stressed (Chapter 16)
- Figure showing New Dietary Guidelines for Americans developed by the US Department of Agriculture (Chapter 16)
- Strategies for enhancing energy by engaging in job-related and positive activities (Chapter 16)
- Internet addiction disorder as a contributor to time wasting (Chapter 16)
- Go where the jobs are as a job-search technique (Chapter 17)
- A figure showing business-related and health-related industries with growth possibilities through 2020 (Chapter 17)
- The job résumé in the form of a tweet (Chapter 17)
- Prosocial motivation as a strategy of career advancement (Chapter 17)
- Expanded discussion of proactive personality (Chapter 17)

AUDIENCE FOR THE BOOK

The primary audience for this book is people taking courses that emphasize the development of interpersonal skills. Such courses typically include the term *human relations*. Because interpersonal relations contribute so heavily to effective leadership, the text is suited for participants in leadership and supervisory training courses that emphasize interpersonal skills rather than leadership theory and research.

FRAMEWORK FOR THE BOOK

The book is a blend of current and traditional topics dealing with interpersonal relations in organizations with a heavy component of skill development and self-assessment. The information is organized into chapters, all emphasizing interpersonal relations between two or more people. Chapter 1, "A Framework for Interpersonal Skill Development," sets the stage for improving one's interpersonal skills on the job. Chapter 2, "Understanding Individual Differences," presents information that is the foundation of effective interpersonal relations. Chapter 3, "Building Self-Esteem and Self-Confidence," describes how to develop self-esteem and self-confidence both for oneself and to improve relationships with others. Chapter 4, "Interpersonal Communication," deals with skills in sending and receiving messages.

Chapter 5, "Interpersonal Skills for the Digital World," describes how interpersonal skills can enhance the use of digital devices, as well as how these devices lend themselves to poor interpersonal skills, such as cell phone abuse. Chapter 6, "Developing Teamwork Skills," sensitizes the reader to a vital set of skills in the workplace. Chapter 7, "Group Problem Solving and Decision Making," provides additional skill in collaborative effort. Chapter 8, "Cross-Cultural Relations and Diversity," is about developing cross-cultural skills in a diverse workforce. Chapter 9, "Resolving Conflicts with Others," helps the reader develop skills in finding constructive solutions to differences of opinion and disputes with others.

Four consecutive chapters deal with exerting influence over others: Chapter 10, "Becoming an Effective Leader," presents information relevant to exercising leadership in the workplace; Chapter 11, "Motivating Others," emphasizes skills in getting others to work hard to achieve goals; Chapter 12, "Helping Others Develop and Grow," is about coaching, counseling, and teaching others; and Chapter 13, "Positive Political Skills," describes how to use power and influence for constructive purposes.

Chapter 14, "Customer Satisfaction Skills," describes several approaches to enhancing skills in satisfying customers, and thus lies at the heart of the importance placed on pleasing customers. Chapter 15, "Enhancing Ethical Behavior," translates ethical principles into usable skills. The rationale is that an ethical base is important for achieving career-long effectiveness in interpersonal relations. Chapter 16, "Stress Management and Personal Productivity," supports development of interpersonal skills by showing that productive people who have stress under control can relate more effectively to others. Chapter 17, "Job Search and Career Management Skills," includes information about the application of interpersonal skills (such as networking) to enhance one's career.

EXPERIENCE THE DUBRIN TOTAL LEARNING SYSTEM

Human Relations: Job-Oriented Skills 12e is not just a textbook. The twelfth edition includes a wealth of experiential exercises, including new cases and self-assessment quizzes that can be completed in class or as homework.

CHAPTER OPENING CASES SET THE STAGE

Following a listing of the chapter learning objectives, all chapters begin with a case scenario that deals with the chapter topic and sets the stage for the chapter narrative.

PEDAGOGICAL FEATURES RELATE CONCEPTS TO WHAT'S HAPPENING TODAY, PERSONALLY AND IN THE WORKPLACE

- **Self-Assessment Quizzes** give students the opportunity to explore their own opinions, feelings, and behavior patterns related to chapter topics. All chapters include one or more self-assessment quizzes.

- **Job-Oriented Interpersonal Skills in Action** in selected chapters illustrate a human relations business practice in today's business world.

- **Skill-Building Exercises** provide students with opportunities to apply concepts at the point at which they are being discussed in the textbook.

ASSIGNMENT MATERIAL REINFORCES CONCEPTS AND BUILDS SKILLS

End of chapter assignment material has been reorganized and expanded into two sections: **Concept Review and Reinforcement,** featuring exercises that focus on concept retention and developing critical thinking skills, and **Developing Your Human Relations Skills,** focusing on developing skills that can be used immediately in life and on the job.

Concept Review and Reinforcement	**Key Terms** reviews the key vocabulary covered in the chapter.
	The **Summary** provides an excellent detailed review of key chapter concepts.
	Questions for Discussion and Review objectively review key chapter topics.
	The **Web Corner** provides informational Web sites and asks students to use the power of the Web in researching outside resources.

Developing Your Human Relations Skills	**Interpersonal Relations Case Studies** put students into a realistic scenario so that they can practice making decisions in tough situations.
	Interpersonal Skills Role-Play exercises provide students with the opportunity to develop personal insight through interactive exercises.

SUPPLEMENTAL MATERIALS

RESOURCES FOR INSTRUCTORS:

At the Instructor Resource Center, www.pearsoned.co.in/prc/home, instructors can access a variety of print, digital, and presentation resources available with this text in down-loadable format. Registration is simple and gives you immediate access to new titles and new editions. As a registered faculty member, you can download resource files, and receive immediate access to and instructions for installing course management content on your campus server.

The following supplements are available for download to adopting instructors:

- **Instructor's Resource Manual and Test Bank**—The Instructor's Resource Manual contains chapter outlines and lecture notes, answers to case problems, and comments about the exercises. The Test Bank contains multiple-choice and true/false test questions followed by their correct answers and the learning objectives and AACSB categories they tie to.

- **PowerPoint Presentation**—A full set of PowerPoint slides is provided. The chapter files contain the relevant material from each chapter and are suitable for leading class lectures and discussion.

ACKNOWLEDGMENTS

My appreciation goes to the many people who contributed to the development and production of this book. Special thanks to Robert A. Herring III at Winston–Salem State University and Nancy Kriscenski at Manchester Community College for their insightful comments on this revision. Appreciation is also expressed to the outside reviewers who made suggestions for shaping this and previous editions of the text: Abhirjun Dutta, Bainbridge College; Robert G. DelCampo, University of New Mexico; David W. Robinson, Malaspina University College; Tim Blood, Lane Community College; Jane Bowerman, University of Oklahoma; John Adamski II, Ivy Tech State College; Patricia Lynn Anderson, Valdosta State University; Judy Bowie, DeVry Institute of Technology; Robert A. Herring III, Winston–Salem State University; H. Frederick Holmes, Ogeechee Technical Institute; Ruth V. Kellar, Ivy Tech State College; Diane Paul, TVI Community College; Lou Jean Peace, Valdosta Technical Institute; Gary W. Piggrem, PhD, DeVry Institute of Technology; Dean Weeden, Utah Career College; and James E. Wetz, Central Florida Community College.

My family members give me an additional reason for writing, so I extend my appreciation to Drew, Douglas, Melanie, Gizella, Will, Rosie, Clare, Camila, Sofia, Eliana, Julian, Carson, and Owen. I thank Stefanie for her contribution to my well-being.

Andrew J. DuBrin
Rochester, New York

CHAPTER 1

A Framework for Interpersonal Skill Development

When Marissa Mayer was 24 years old, she joined Google as employee number 20. While at Google, she ran the company's search group and worked on successful products such as Gmail. Her last position with the company was vice president, local, maps, and location services, placing her just below Google's top-executives suite. At age 37, Mayer joined Yahoo! as chief executive and president, the company's seventh CEO. Her mission was to turn around a company that had lost ground as perhaps the best-known search and content company on the Internet.

At once, the vivacious, glamorous, and super-intelligent Mayer became a celebrity CEO, receiving worldwide publicity. At Stanford University, Mayer majored in symbolic systems, a course of studies that includes psychology, linguistics, philosophy, and computer science. The aim of the program is to understand how people learn and reason, and to endow computers with human-like behavior. A dorm-mate of Mayer's who later became an information technology

Digital Vision/Thinkstock

After reading and studying this chapter and completing the exercises, you should be able to

1. Explain how interpersonal skills are learned.
2. Explain the model for interpersonal skills improvement, including how to set goals effectively.
3. Pinpoint your needs for improvement in interpersonal relations.
4. Describe potential opportunities for developing interpersonal skills on the job.

executive said that although Mayer was shy, she was not a loner. He claims that Mayer stood out because she had unusual balance along with a deep understanding of people and how to relate to them effectively.

Mayer was a standout at high school, too being captain of the debate club and the pom-pom team. She was known for scheduling long pom-pom practices to make sure that everyone was synchronized. She was also recognized for her exceptional talent in choreography as well as her fairness; she made sure the best dancers made the team.

At Google, Mayer was obsessively driven, working 90 hours per week when necessary to complete a key project. She developed a reputation for being brusque with people and quick to criticize team members when she disagreed with their ideas. Yet at the same time, Mayer respected others' talents and had many positive personal qualities that helped her attain popularity. At Google, Mayer became a leader who motivated individuals because she nurtured talent.

Part of Mayer's leadership style is to empower employees and urge them to make constructive changes. In her first few months at Yahoo!, she personally approved every new hire to help assure that talented and well-motivated people were joining the company. One of her first moves at the company to please employees was to provide free food in the company cafeteria and free smartphones for all employees.

Mayer's interest in employees also includes establishing a connection with Yahoo!'s programmers by engaging them in regular e-mail exchanges with software engineers who report to other managers in the company. She also initiated weekly "FYI" meetings every Friday in which employees are able to ask her questions, and new hires are announced.[1]

One of the several themes in this story about the famous Internet executive is that even at the highest level in an organization, skill in human relations facilitates success. Mayer may be work-obsessed and technology-obsessed, but at the same time she relates well to many people and has a deep concern for the welfare and development of others. The Dale Carnegie organization explains that because the workplace today emphasizes collaboration, motivation, and leadership, outstanding interpersonal skills are quite important.[2]

Effective interpersonal relations must be combined with technical knowledge and good work habits to achieve success in any job involving interaction with people. Workers at all levels are expected not only to solve problems and improve processes (how work is performed), but also to interact effectively with other employees.[3] Two employment specialists found that being enjoyable to work with is the most important indicator of employability. Joyce Hogan and Kimberly Brinkmeyer analyzed the content of employment ads across the United States. Of the total positions advertised, 47 percent required strong interpersonal skills. The same skills were identified as essential for 71 percent of the positions involving client contact and 78 percent of the positions requiring coworker interaction.[4].

The viewpoint of Bob McJury, the vice president for sales of a graphics company, places the importance of interpersonal skills on a more personal and less statistical basis. He observes that the basics of being courteous to people are very important for the success of his company.[5]

Furthermore, the lack of good interpersonal skills can adversely affect a person's career. A study found that 90 percent of firings result from poor attitudes, inappropriate behavior, and problems in interpersonal relationships, rather than substandard technical skills.[6] An example of poor interpersonal relations that led to job loss was a receptionist at a boat dealer who told several potential customers something to this effect: "Are you just here to look? You don't look like you could afford one of our speedboats."

Another way of looking at the importance of interpersonal skills is that they enable you to connect with others, thereby being more successful in business. Author Susan Scott observes that the next frontier for growth in business lies in the area of human connectivity.[7]

This chapter explains how people develop interpersonal skills and presents a model that can serve as a foundation for improving your interpersonal skills. In addition, the chapter explains how the workplace can be a natural setting for developing interpersonal skills.

PLAN OF THE BOOK

LEARNING OBJECTIVE 1

This entire book is devoted to many different ways of improving interpersonal relations in organizations. A three-part strategy is presented for achieving the high level of effectiveness in interpersonal relations required in today's workplace.

First, each chapter presents key concepts required for understanding a particular aspect of interpersonal relations, such as resolving conflict. Second, the chapter provides specific suggestions or behavioral guidelines for improvement in the aspect of interpersonal relations under consideration. Third, a variety of exercises give you the opportunity to work on and improve your skills. Among these exercises are self-assessment quizzes, skill-building exercises, and cases for analysis. In addition, the questions at the end of each chapter give you an opportunity to think through and apply the key ideas in the chapter. Figure 1-1 illustrates the plan of the book.

interpersonal skills training

The teaching of skills for dealing with others so that they can be put into practice.

Much of this book is concerned with **interpersonal skills training**, the teaching of skills for dealing with others so they can be put into practice.

Interpersonal skills training is referred to as *soft-skills* training to differentiate it from technical training. (Technical skill training is referred to as *hard-skills* training.) Soft-skills training builds interpersonal skills, including communication, listening, group problem solving, cross-cultural relations, and customer service. In recent years, business schools have pushed the teaching of soft skills such as accepting feedback with grace and speaking

FIGURE 1-1   Plan for Achieving Effectiveness in Interpersonal Relations

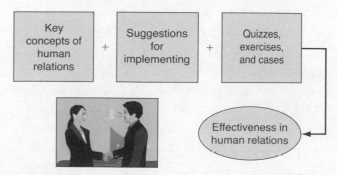

with respect to subordinates. The reason is that many corporate executives think that these skills are essential for future business leaders.[8] Several other specific competencies related to soft skills are as follows:

- Effectively translating and conveying information
- Being able to accurately interpret other people's emotions
- Being sensitive to other people's feelings
- Calmly arriving at resolutions to conflicts
- Avoiding negative gossip
- Being polite[9]
- Being able to cooperate with others to meet objectives (teamwork)
- Providing leadership to others in terms of the relationship aspects of leadership

Soft-skills training is more important than ever as organizations realize that a combination of human effort and technology is needed to produce results. Multiple studies have shown that soft skills can compensate somewhat for not having superior cognitive (or analytical) intelligence. For example, a supervisor with good interpersonal skills might perform well even if he or she is not outstandingly intelligent.

Soft skills are often the differentiating factor between adequate and outstanding performance because dealing with people is part of so many jobs.[10] Assume that a company establishes an elaborate social networking site to enable employees to exchange work-related information with each other. The system will not achieve its potential unless employees are motivated to use it properly and develop a spirit of cooperation. The employees must also be willing to share some of their best ideas with each other. Consider this example:

Sonya, a newly hired intake receptionist in a cardiac clinic, notices that too often the patients present incomplete or inaccurate information, such as omitting data about their next of kin. Sonya spends considerable amounts of time reworking forms with the patients, until she begins using soft skills more effectively. With coaching from her supervisor, Sonya learns that if she attempts to calm down a patient first, the patient is more likely to complete the intake form accurately.

Well-known executive coach Marshall Goldsmith reminds us that building relationships with people is important for workers at every level in the organization, including the CEO. An example of an interpersonal skill that can help build relationships is demanding good results from others and showing them respect at the same time.[11]

The following Job-Oriented Interpersonal Skills in Action box can jumpstart a person's career.

A MODEL FOR IMPROVING INTERPERSONAL SKILLS

Acquiring and improving interpersonal skills is facilitated by following a basic model of learning as it applies to changing your behavior. Learning is a complex subject, yet its fundamentals follow a five-part sequence, as shown in Figure 1-2. To change your behavior,

FIGURE 1-2   A Model for Improving Interpersonal Skills

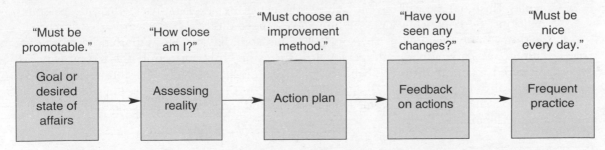

"Must be promotable." → Goal or desired state of affairs

"How close am I?" → Assessing reality

"Must choose an improvement method." → Action plan

"Have you seen any changes?" → Feedback on actions

"Must be nice every day." → Frequent practice

Jeremy Gets Rewarded for His Interpersonal Skills

Jeremy works as an electronics technician for Event Planners, a company that specializes in setting up exhibits for companies and trade associations at business meetings and conventions. Jeremy's work is highly specialized and requires installing and uninstalling electronics in compressed periods of time. All of the electronics have to work well, including panel displays, television sets, and computers. The planned events usually take place over a three-day to one-week time period, leaving little time to make repairs if the displays are set up incorrectly.

While returning home from a convention in Chicago, Jeremy received a text message from Katie, his manager: "Can you make a Monday 9 a.m. meeting in my cubicle? Have good news for you." Jeremy thought, "If Pamela wants to meet with me in person rather than virtually, this must be big." Jeremy sent back a text message immediately that he would make the meeting.

At the meeting, Pamela offered Jeremy a promotion to the position of team leader. The present team leader was moving to another position in the company, creating the vacancy. Jeremy would still have some responsibility for installing the electronic parts of exhibit booths, but his primary role would be as a team leader (also known as a crew supervisor). Jeremy's salary would be immediately increased by 10 percent.

With a big smile on his face, Jeremy said, "Wow, Pamela, that's a great offer, and I accept immediately. I love Event Planners, and I really want more responsibility. But why did you choose me? A few of the other members of the team have more experience than me, and they are very good workers."

Pamela replied, "My boss and I both chose you for the same reason. In addition to your good technical qualifications, you work great with people. You are polite and friendly, and from what I hear, you give your coworkers encouragement when they need it the most. When the pressure is enormous, you help others stay calm."

"Thank you for your encouragement, Pamela," said Jeremy. "I can't wait for our next exhibit installation."

Questions

1. To what extent is Pamela justified in promoting Jeremy to team leader over other, more experienced workers just because he has good people skills?
2. From the few statements made by Jeremy above, which good interpersonal skills are you able to detect?

and therefore improve, you need a goal and a way to measure your current reality against this goal. You also need a way to assess that reality and a way to obtain feedback on the impact of your new actions.[12]

Goal or Desired State of Affairs

Changing your behavior, including enhancing your interpersonal relations, requires a clear goal or desired state of affairs. Your goal can also be regarded as what you want to accomplish as a result of your effort. A major reason having a specific goal is important is that it improves performance and increases personal satisfaction. With a goal in mind, you keep plugging away until you attain it, thereby increasing personal satisfaction and improving your performance. Goals are also important because if people perceive that they have not attained their goal, they typically increase their effort or modify their strategy for reaching the goal.[13]

Having a goal helps provide motivation and makes it possible to exercise the self-discipline necessary to follow through on your plans. In short, the goal focuses your effort on acquiring the improvements in behavior you seek.

Here we turn to Sean, a credit analyst who is being blocked from promotion because his manager perceives him as having poor interpersonal skills. After a discussion with his manager, Sean recognizes that he must improve his interpersonal relations if he wants to become a team leader.

Sean's goal is to be considered worthy of promotion to a leadership position. To achieve his goal, he will have to achieve the general goal of improving his interpersonal relations. By conferring with the human resources director, Sean learns that his broad goal of "improving my interpersonal relations" will have to be supported by more specific goals. Having poor interpersonal relations or "rubbing people the wrong way" is reflected in many different behaviors. To begin, Sean selects one counterproductive behavior to improve: He is exceptionally intolerant of others and does not hide his intolerance. Sean's goal is to become less intolerant and more patient in his dealings with others on the job.

FIGURE 1-3 Guidelines for Goal Setting

> 1. State each goal as a positive statement.
> 2. Formulate specific goals.
> 3. Formulate concise goals.
> 4. Set realistic goals as well as stretch goals.
> 5. Set goals for different time periods.

Fine Points about Goal Setting.   So far, we have made goal setting seem easy. A truer description of goal setting is that it involves several fine points to increase the probability that the goal will be achieved. Key points about setting effective goals are outlined in Figure 1-3 and described next.

1. State Each Goal as a Positive Statement: To express your goals in positive statements is likely to be more energizing than focusing on the negative.[14] An example of a positive statement would be, "During the next year when I am attending networking events, I will create a positive, professional impression with everybody I meet." The negative counterpart would be, "During the next year, I will avoid making a fool of myself when I am attending networking events." Despite this suggestion, there are times when a negative goal is useful, such as in reducing errors.

2. Formulate Specific Goals: A goal such as "attain success" is too vague to serve as a guide to daily action. A more useful goal would be to state specifically what you mean by success and when you expect to achieve it. For example, "I want to be the manager of patient services at a large medical clinic by January 1, 2018, and receive above-average performance reviews."

3. Formulate Concise Goals: A useful goal can usually be expressed in a short, punchy statement; for example: "Decrease input errors in bank statements so that customer complaints are decreased by 25 percent by September 30 of this year." People new to goal setting typically commit the error of formulating lengthy, rambling goal statements. These lengthy goals involve so many different activities that they fail to serve as specific guides to action.

4. Set Realistic as Well as Stretch Goals: A realistic goal is one that represents the right amount of challenge for the person pursuing the goal. On the one hand, easy goals are not very motivational; they may not spring you into action. On the other hand, goals that are too far beyond your capabilities may lead to frustration and despair because there is a good chance you will fail to reach them. The extent to which a goal is realistic depends on a person's capabilities.

An easy goal for an experienced person might be a realistic goal for a beginner. **Self-efficacy** is also a factor in deciding whether a goal is realistic. (The term refers to the confidence in your ability to carry out a specific task.) The higher your self-efficacy, the more likely you are to think that a particular goal is realistic. A person with high self-efficacy for learning Chinese might say, "I think learning two new Chinese words a day is realistic."

Several goals that stretch your capability might be included in your list of goals. An extreme stretch goal might be for a store manager trainee to become the vice president of merchandising for Target within four years. Another type of stretch goal is striving for a noble cause. A Home Depot supervisor might not get excited about having the store associates load lumber onto the steel shelves, but she might get excited about the lumber being used to build homes, schools, and hospitals.

5. Set Goals for Different Time Periods: Goals are best set for different time periods, such as daily, short range, medium range, and long range. Daily goals are essentially a to-do list. Short-range goals cover the period from approximately one week to one year

self-efficacy
The confidence in your ability to carry out a specific task.

into the future. Finding a new job, for example, is typically a short-range goal. Medium-range goals relate to events that will take place within approximately two to five years. They concern such things as the type of education or training you plan to undertake and the next step in your career.

Long-range goals refer to events taking place five years into the future and beyond. As such, they relate to the overall lifestyle you wish to achieve, including the type of work and family situation you hope to have. Although every person should have a general idea of a desirable lifestyle, long-range goals should be flexible. You might, for example, plan to stay single until age 40. But while on vacation next summer, you might just happen to meet the right partner for you.

Short-range goals make an important contribution to attaining goals of longer duration. If a one-year career goal is to add 25 worthwhile contacts to your social network, a good way to motivate yourself is to search for two contacts per month for 11 months, and search for three in the remaining month. Progress toward a larger goal is self-rewarding.

Assessing Reality

The second major requirement for a method of changing behavior is to assess reality. Sean needs a way to assess how far he is from his goal of being eligible for promotion and how intolerant he is perceived to be. Sean has already heard from his manager, Alison, that he is not eligible for promotion right now. Sean might want to dig for more information by finding answers to the following questions:

"If I were more tolerant, would I be promoted now?"
"How bad are my interpersonal relations in the office?"
"How many people in the office think I rub them the wrong way?"
"How many deficiencies do my manager and coworkers perceive me to have?"

A starting point in answering these questions might be for Sean to confer with Alison about his behavior. To be more thorough, however, Sean might ask a friend in the office to help him answer the questions. A coworker is sometimes in an excellent position to provide feedback on how one is perceived by others in the office. Sean could also ask a confidant outside the office about his intolerance. Sean could ask a parent, a significant other, or both about the extent of his intolerance.

An Action Plan

The learning model needs some mechanism to change the relationship between the person and the environment. An **action plan** is a series of steps to achieve a goal. Without an action plan, a personal goal will be elusive. The person who sets the goal may not initiate steps to make his or her dream (a high-level goal) come true. If your goal is to someday become a self-employed business owner, your action plan should include saving money, establishing a good credit rating, and developing dozens of contacts.

Sean has to take some actions to improve his interpersonal relations, especially by reducing his intolerance. The change should ultimately lead to the promotion he desires. Sean's action plan for becoming more tolerant includes the following:

- Pausing to attempt to understand why a person is acting the way he or she does. An example is attempting to understand why a sales representative wants to extend credit to a customer with a poor credit rating.
- Learning to control his own behavior so that he does not make intolerant statements just because he is experiencing pressure.
- Taking a course in interpersonal skills or human relations.
- Asking Alison to give him a quick reminder whenever she directly observes or hears of him being intolerant toward customers or workmates.

A fundamental reason that action plans often lead to constructive changes is the "do good, be good" method. It capitalizes on the well-established principle that our attitudes and beliefs often stem from our behaviors rather than precede them.[15] If Sean, or anybody else, starts being tolerant of and accepting toward people, he will soon believe that tolerance is important.

In addition to formulating these action plans, Sean must have the self-discipline to implement them. For example, he should keep a log of situations in which he was intolerant and those in which he was tolerant. He might also make a mental note to attempt to be cooperative and flexible in most of his dealings at work. When a customer does not provide all of the information that Sean needs to assess his or her creditworthiness, Sean should remind himself to say, "I want to process your credit application as quickly as possible. To do this, I need some important additional information." Sean's previous reflex in the same situation had been to snap, "I can't read your mind. If you want to do business with us, you've got to stop hiding the truth."

Ryan McVay/Getty Images

Feedback on Actions

The fourth step in the learning model is to measure the effects of one's actions against reality. You obtain feedback on the consequences of your actions. When your skill-improvement goal is complex, such as becoming more effective at resolving conflict, you will usually have to measure your progress in several ways. You will also need both short- and long-term measures of the effectiveness of your actions. Long-term measures are important because skill-development activities of major consequence have long-range implications.

To obtain short-range feedback, Sean can consult with Alison to see whether she has observed any changes in his tolerance. Alison can also collect any feedback she hears from others in the office. Furthermore, Sean will profit from feedback over a prolonged period of time, perhaps one or two years. He will be looking to see whether his image has changed from an intolerant person who rubs people the wrong way to a tolerant person who has cordial interactions with others.

You will often need to be persistent and encouraging to obtain useful feedback from others. Many people are hesitant to give negative feedback because of a conscious or pre-conscious recognition that the recipient of the negative feedback might become hostile and retaliate.[16] The recipient of the negative feedback might appear hurt and respond with a statement such as, "I'm not perfect, and neither are you."

Frequent Practice

The final step in the learning model makes true skill development possible. Implementing the new behavior and using feedback for fine-tuning is an excellent start in acquiring a new interpersonal skill. For the skill to be long lasting, however, it must be integrated into your usual way of conducting yourself.

In Sean's case, he will have to practice being tolerant regularly until it becomes a positive habit. After a skill is programmed into your repertoire, it becomes a habit. This is important because a skill involves many habits. For example, good customer service skills include the habits of smiling and listening carefully. After you attempt the new interpersonal skills described in this book, you will need to practice them frequently to make a noticeable difference in your behavior. Changes may appear unnnatural at first, but with practice they become ingrained behavioral tendencies and a means of relating to other people.[17]

A sports analogy is appropriate here. Assume that Ashley, a tennis player, takes a lesson to learn how to hit the ball with greater force. The instructor points out that the reason she is not hitting with much force is that she is relying too much on her arm and not enough on her leg and body strength. To hit the ball with more force, Ashley is told that she must put one foot out in front of her when she strikes the ball (she must "step into" the ball).

Under the watchful eye of the coach, Ashley does put a foot out in front when she strikes the ball. Ashley is excited about the good results. But if Ashley fails to make the same maneuver with her feet during her tennis matches, she will persist in hitting weakly. If Ashley makes the effort to use her legs more effectively on almost every shot, she will soon integrate the new movement into her game.

In summary, the basics of a model for learning skills comprise five steps: goal or desired state of affairs → assessing reality → an action plan → feedback on actions → frequent practice. You must exercise self-discipline to complete each step. If you skip a step, you will be disappointed with the results of your interpersonal skill-development program.

IDENTIFICATION OF DEVELOPMENTAL NEEDS

LEARNING OBJECTIVE 3

An important concept in skill development is that people are most likely to develop new skills when they feel the need for change. A person might reflect, "Hardly anybody ever takes my suggestions seriously, in either face-to-face or electronic meetings. I wonder what I'm doing wrong?" This person is probably ready to learn how to become a more persuasive communicator.

As you read this book and complete the experiential exercises, you will probably be more highly motivated to follow through with skill development in areas in which you think you need development. A specific area in which a person needs to change is referred to as a **developmental need**. For instance, some people may be too shy, too abrasive, or too intolerant, and some may not give others the encouragement they need.

developmental need

A specific area in which a person needs to change or improve.

To improve interpersonal skills, we must be aware of how we are perceived by people who interact with us. Developmental needs related to interpersonal skills can be identified in several ways. First, if you are candid with yourself you can probably point to areas in which you recognize that change is needed. You might reflect on your experiences and realize that you have had repeated difficulty in resolving conflict. Second, a related approach is to think of feedback you have received. If there has been consistency in asking you to improve in a particular area, you could hypothesize that the feedback has merit. Perhaps five different people have told you that you are not a good team player. "Becoming a better team player" might therefore be one of your developmental needs.

A third approach to assessing developmental needs is to solicit feedback. Ask the opinion of people who know you well to help you identify needs for improvement with respect to interpersonal skills. Present and previous managers are a valuable source of this type of feedback. (As mentioned earlier, you may have to be persistent to obtain feedback because many people are hesistant to provide negative feedback.)

A fourth approach to pinpointing developmental needs is closely related to the previous three: feedback from performance evaluations. If you have worked for a firm that uses performance evaluations to help people develop, you may have received constructive suggestions during the evaluation. For example, one manager told his assistant, "You need to project more self-confidence when you answer the phone. You sound so unsure and vague when you talk on the telephone. I have noticed this, and several customers have joked about it." The recipient of this feedback was prompted to participate in assertiveness training in which she learned how to express herself more positively.

Self-Assessment Quiz 1-1 gives you the opportunity to identify your developmental needs. The same exercise is a first step in improving your interpersonal relations on the job because identification of a problem is the first—and most important—step toward change. For example, if you cite improving your relationships with people from cultures different from your own, you have planted the seeds for change. You are then more likely to seek out people from other cultures in the workplace or at school and cultivate their friendship.

Now that you (and perhaps another person) have identified specific behaviors that may require change, you need to draw up an action plan. Proceed with your action plan even though you have just begun studying this text, but peek ahead to relevant chapters if you wish. Describe briefly a plan of attack for bringing about the change you hope to achieve for each statement that is checked. Ideas for your action plan can come from information presented anywhere in this text, from outside reading, or from talking to a person experienced in dealing with people. A basic example would be to study materials about customer service and observe an effective model if you checked "I feel awkard dealing with a customer."

UNIVERSAL NEEDS FOR IMPROVING INTERPERSONAL RELATIONS

We have just described how understanding your unique developmental needs facilitates improving your interpersonal skills. There are also areas for skill improvement in interpersonal relationships that are shared by most managerial, professional, technical, and sales personnel. These common areas for improvement are referred to as **universal training needs**. Almost any professional person, for example, could profit from enhancing his or her negotiation and listening skills.

This book provides the opportunity for skill development in a number of universal training needs. In working through these universal training needs, be aware that many of them will also fit your specific developmental needs. A given universal training need can be an individual's developmental need at the same time. It is reasonable to expect that you will be more strongly motivated to improve skills that relate closely to your developmental needs.

universal training need

An area for improvement common to most people.

What Are Your Developmental Needs?

This exercise is designed to heighten your self-awareness of areas in which you could profit from personal improvement. It is not a test, and there is no score; yet your answers to the checklist may prove helpful to you in mapping out a program of improvement in your interpersonal relations.

Directions: Following are many specific aspects of behavior that suggest a person needs improvement in interpersonal skills. Check each statement that is generally true for you. You can add to the validity of this exercise by having one or two other people who know you well answer this form as they think it describes you. Then compare your self-analyses with their analyses of you.

Place check mark in this column.

1. I'm too shy. _____
2. I'm too overbearing and obnoxious. _____
3. I intimidate too many people. _____
4. I have trouble expressing my feelings. _____
5. I make negative comments about people too readily. _____
6. I have a difficult time solving problems when working in a group. _____
7. I'm a poor team player. _____
8. Very few people listen to me. _____
9. It is difficult for me to relate well to people from different cultures. _____
10. When I'm in conflict with another person, I usually lose. _____
11. I hog too much time in meetings or in class. _____
12. I'm very poor at office politics. _____
13. People find me boring. _____
14. It is difficult for me to criticize others. _____
15. I'm too serious most of the time. _____
16. My temper is too often out of control. _____
17. I avoid controversy in dealing with others. _____
18. It is difficult for me to find things to talk about with others. _____
19. I don't get my point across well. _____
20. I feel awkward dealing with a customer. _____
21. I am a poor listener. _____
22. I don't get the importance of ethics in business. _____
23. My attempts to lead others have failed. _____
24. I rarely smile when I am with other people. _____
25. I don't get along well with people who are from a different ethnic or racial group than mine. _____
26. I multitask when people are talking to me. _____
27. I insult too many people on social networking sites. _____
28. _____ (Fill in your own statement.) _____

The major universal training needs covered in this text are as follows:

1. **Understanding individual differences:** To deal effectively with others in the workplace, it is necessary to recognize that people have different capabilities, needs, and interests.

2. **Self-esteem and self-confidence:** To function effectively with people in most work and personal situations, people need to feel good about themselves and believe that they can accomplish important tasks. Although self-esteem and self-confidence are essentially attitudes about the self, they also involve skills such as attaining legitimate accomplishments and using positive self-talk.

3. **Interpersonal communication:** Effective communication with people is essential for carrying out more than 50 percent of the work conducted by most professional and managerial workers.

4. **Behaving appropriately when using digital devices:** Digital devices are integrated into most facets of our work and personal lives. Knowing how to use various electronic devices and systems, including e-mail, cell phones, and smartphones, in a positive and constructive way instead of being uncivil and unproductive can be a major contributor to building your interpersonal relationships.

5. **Developing teamwork skills:** The most sweeping change in the organization of work in the last 40 years has been a shift to teams and away from traditional departments. Knowing how to be an effective team player therefore enhances your chances for success in the modern organization.

6. **Group problem solving and decision making:** As part of the same movement that emphasizes work teams, organizations now rely heavily on group problem solving. As a consequence, being an above-average contributor to group problem solving is a key part of effective interpersonal relations on the job. In addition to solving the problem, a decision must be made.

7. **Cross-cultural relations:** The modern workplace has greater cultural diversity than ever before. Being able to deal effectively with people from different cultures, from within and outside your own country, is therefore an important requirement for success.

8. **Resolving conflicts with others:** Conflict in the workplace is almost inevitable as people compete for limited resources. Effective interpersonal relations are therefore dependent upon knowing how to resolve conflict successfully.

9. **Becoming an effective leader:** In today's organizations, a large number of people have the opportunity to practice leadership, even if on temporary assignment. Enhancing one's leadership skills is therefore almost a universal requirement.

10. **Motivating others:** Whether you have the title of manager or leader or are working alone, you have to know how to motivate the people who you depend on to get your work accomplished. Given that few people are gifted motivators, most people can profit from skill development in motivation.

11. **Helping others develop and grow:** As power is shared in organizations among managers and individual contributors (nonmanagers) alike, more people are required to help each other develop and grow. To carry out this role, most of us need skill development in coaching and mentoring.

12. **Positive political skills:** Whether you work in a small or large firm, part of having effective interpersonal relationships is being able to influence others in such a way that your interests are satisfied. Positive political skills help you satisfy your interests without being unethical or devious.

13. **Customer service skills:** The current emphasis on customer satisfaction dictates that every worker should know how to provide good service to customers. Most people can benefit from strengthening their skills in serving both external

and internal customers. (Internal customers are the people with whom you interact on the job.)

14. **Enhancing ethical behavior:** Although most workers know right from wrong in their hearts, we can all sharpen our ability to make ethical decisions. By consistently making highly ethical decisions, people can improve their interpersonal relations.

15. **Stress management and personal productivity:** Having your stress under control and having good work habits and time-management skills contributes to relating well to others, even though they are not interpersonal skills themselves. By having your stress under control and being efficient and productive, you are in a better position to relate comfortably to others. Coworkers enjoy relating to a person who is not visibly stressed and who does not procrastinate.

16. **Job search and career-management skills:** Finding an outstanding job for yourself, holding onto the job, and moving ahead are not specifically interpersonal skills. However, both finding the right job for yourself and managing your career rely heavily on good interpersonal skills. Two basic examples are conducting yourself well in an interview and developing a network of contacts that can help you advance.

DEVELOPING INTERPERSONAL SKILLS ON THE JOB

LEARNING OBJECTIVE 4

The primary thrust of this book is to teach interpersonal skills that can be applied to the job. As part of enhancing your skills, it is essential to recognize that opportunities also exist in the workplace for developing interpersonal skills. This dual opportunity for learning soft skills is similar to the way hard skills are learned both inside and outside the classroom. Studying a text and doing laboratory exercises, for example, will help you learn useful information technology skills. On the job, one day you might be asked to optimize your company's presence on the Internet. ("Optimize" in this sense means that your company's Web site appears higher on Internet searches.) Having never performed this task before, you may search appropriate Web sites, ask questions of coworkers, telephone tech support, and use trial and error. Within a few days, you have acquired a valuable new skill. The information technology skills you learned in the course facilitated learning new computer tasks, yet the actual work of learning how to optimize your company's URL in Web site searches was done on the job.

Here we look at two related aspects of learning interpersonal skills on the job: informal learning and specific developmental experiences.

Informal Learning

Business firms, as well as nonprofit organizations, invest an enormous amount of money and time into teaching interpersonal skills. Teaching methods include paying for employees to take outside courses, conducting training on company premises, using videoconferencing or Web-based courses, and reimbursing for distance learning courses on the Internet. Workers also develop interpersonal skills by interacting with work associates and observing how other people deal with interpersonal challenges.

informal learning
The acquisition of knowledge and skills that takes place naturally outside of a structured learning environment.

Informal learning is the acquisition of knowledge and skills that takes place naturally outside a structured learning environment. In the context of the workplace, informal learning takes place without being designed by the organization. Learning can take place informally in ways such as speaking to the person in the next cubicle, asking a question of a coworker while in the hall, or calling the tech support center.

A study conducted by the American Society for Training Directors found that informal learning is part of how employees learn. Nearly one-half of the 1,104 respondents said that informal learning is occurring to a high or very high extent in their organizations. E-mail emerged as the top-ranked informal learning tool, with accessing information from an Intranet a close second.[18]

Learning interpersonal skills informally can take place through such means as observing a coworker, manager, or team leader deal with a situation. A newly hired assistant store manager couldn't help seeing and overhearing a customer screaming at the store manager about a defective space heater. The manager said calmly, "It appears you are pretty upset about your heater that caused a short circuit in your house. What can I do to help you?" The customer calmed down as quickly as air is released from a balloon. The assistant store manager thought to herself, "Now I know how to handle a customer who has gone ballistic. I'll state what the customer is probably feeling, and then offer to help."

Informal learning can also occur when another person coaches you about how to handle a situation. The store manager might have said to the new assistant manager, "Let me tell you what to do in case you encounter a customer who goes ballistic. Summarize in a few words what he or she is probably feeling, and then offer to help. The effect can be remarkable." (This incident is classified as informal learning because it takes place outside a classroom.)

Formal and informal learning of interpersonal skills are useful supplements to each other. If you are formally learning interpersonal skills, your level of awareness for enhancing your interpersonal skills will increase. By formally studying interpersonal skills, you are likely to develop the attitude, "What hints about dealing more effectively with people can I pick up on the job?" You may have noticed that if you are taking lessons in a sport, you become much more observant about watching the techniques of outstanding athletes in person or on television.

Specific Developmental Experiences

Another perspective on developing interpersonal skills in the workplace is that certain experiences are particularly suited to such development. Coping with a difficult customer, as previously suggested, would be one such scenario. Morgan W. McCall Jr. has for many years studied ways in which leaders develop on the job. Contending with certain challenges is at the heart of these key learning experiences. Several of the powerful learning experiences McCall has identified are particularly geared toward developing better interpersonal skills.[19]

- **Unfamiliar responsibilities:** The person has to handle responsibilities that are new, very different, or much broader than previous ones. Dealing with these unfamiliar responsibilities necessitates asking others for help and gaining their cooperation. For example, being assigned to supervise a group doing work unfamiliar to you would put you in a position of gaining the cooperation of group members who knew more about the work than you.
- **Proving yourself:** If you feel added pressure to show others that you can deal effectively with responsibilities, you are likely to develop skills in projecting self-confidence and persuading others.
- **Problems with employees:** If you supervise employees or have coworkers who lack adequate experience, are incompetent, or are poorly motivated, you need to practice skills such as effective listening and conflict resolution in order to work smoothly with them.
- **Influencing without authority:** An excellent opportunity for practicing influence skills is being forced to influence coworkers, higher management, company outsiders, and other key people over whom you have no formal control. Team leaders typically face the challenge of needing to influence workers over whom they lack the authority to discipline or grant raises. (The reason is that a team leader usually does not have as much formal authority as a traditional manager.)
- **Difficult manager:** If you and your manager have different opinions on how to approach problems, or if your manager has serious shortcomings, you will have to use your best human relations skills to survive. You will need to develop subtle

skills such as using diplomacy to explain to your manager that his or her suggestion is completely unworkable.

The general point to be derived from these scenarios is that certain on-the-job challenges require a high level of interpersonal skill. Faced with such challenges, you will be prompted to use the best interpersonal skills you have. Formal training can be a big help because you might remember a skill that should be effective in a particular situation. Assume that you are faced with an overbearing manager who belittles you in front of others. You might be prompted to try a conflict-resolution technique you acquired in class.

Concept Review and Reinforcement

Key Terms

interpersonal skill training 24
self-efficacy 27

action plan 28
developmental need 30

universal training need 31
informal learning 34

Summary

Effective interpersonal relations must be combined with technical knowledge to achieve success in any job involving interactions with people. This book presents a three-part strategy for achieving a high level of interpersonal skill. Each chapter presents concepts related to an area of interpersonal skill, behavioral guidelines, and experiential exercises. Interpersonal skill training is also referred to as soft-skills training to differentiate it from technical training.

A five-part model of learning can be applied to improving interpersonal skills. First, state a goal or desired state of affairs. Second, assess the reality of how far you are from your goal. Third, develop an action plan to change the relationship between the person and the environment. Self-discipline is required to implement the action plan. Fourth, solicit feedback on actions to measure the effects of your actions against reality. Fifth, continue to practice your newly learned skill.

To use the learning model effectively, it is useful to understand the goal-setting process. The guidelines offered here for goal setting are to (1) state each goal as a positive statement, (2) formulate specific goals, (3) formulate concise goals, (4) set realistic as well as stretch goals, and (5) set goals for different time periods.

People are most likely to develop new skills when they feel the need for change. A developmental need is the specific area in which a person needs to change. Identifying your developmental needs in relation to interpersonal relations can be achieved through self-analysis and feedback from others. You can also solicit feedback and make use of the feedback you have received in performance appraisals.

Universal training needs are those areas for improvement that are common to most people. The major topics in this text reflect universal training needs because they are necessary for success in most positions involving interaction with people.

Opportunities exist in the workplace to develop interpersonal skills. A general approach to developing these skills is informal learning, whereby you acquire skills naturally outside of a structured work environment. Informal learning of interpersonal skills often takes place through means such as observing a coworker, manager, or team leader cope with a situation. Certain workplace experiences are particularly well suited to developing interpersonal skills. These include unfamiliar responsibilities, proving yourself, having problems with employees, influencing without authority, and having a difficult manager.

Questions for Discussion and Review

1. Your friend says, "I'm such a great techie that I don't have to worry about interpersonal skills." What advice do you have for your techie friend?

2. Why is goal setting in the workplace so important when you want to change your behavior?

3. What would be a suitable method of assessing your own development needs?

4. Why is informal learning needed in addition to formal learning?

5. How does a person know whether or not the feedback he or she receives from another person is accurate?

6. How could doing a thorough job on Self-Assessment Quiz 1-1 have a major impact on a person's career?

7. A statement frequently made in business is, "If you are obnoxious, you need to be very talented to succeed."

How does this conclusion relate to the learning of interpersonal skills?

8. Based on what you have learned so far in this book, and your own intuition, how would you respond to the statement, "You can't learn how to get along with people from reading a book"?

9. Give an example of a skill you might have learned informally at any point in your life.

10. Give an example of how a small-business owner needs good interpersonal skills to survive.

The Web Corner

www.interpersonalskillsonline.com/about

www.wikihow.com/Develop-interpersonal-skills
(Interpersonal skill development)

www.infed.org
(Informal learning)

Internet Skill Builder: The Importance of Interpersonal Skills

One of the themes of this chapter and the entire book is that interpersonal skills are important for success in business. But what do employers really think? To find out, visit the Web sites of five of your favorite companies, such as Starbucks.com or Apple.com. Go to the employment section, and search for a job that you might qualify for now or in the future. Investigate which interpersonal or human relations skills the employer mentions as a requirement, such as, "Must have superior spoken communication skills." Make up a list of the interpersonal skills you find mentioned. What conclusion or conclusions do you reach from this exercise?

Developing Your Human Relations Skills

Interpersonal Relations Case 1.1

Tyler Likes Tyler

Tyler is an inventory control specialist at a company that manufactures fiber-optic cables for the telecommunications industry. Among the users of fiber-optic cables are telephone companies and cable television companies. Tyler enjoys his position within the company and believes that he has a promising future in an industry that will most likely continue to grow.

During his lunch break one day, Tyler sat down next to Isabella, another inventory specialist. "Wow, I have some very exciting news to tell you," said Tyler. "I dented my SUV a week ago, and I thought I would have about a $700 repair bill not covered by insurance. Instead, I tried one of these paint-free dent specialists. The guy took out the dent for $150, and my SUV looks as good as new."

Isabella replied, "Oh yes." Tyler, then said, "Everything is good with you isn't it?" Before Isabella responded, Tyler continued, "You will be very excited to know that this summer I am going on a four-day hike in the Colorado Rockies. Isn't that really something?"

Isabella glanced up briefly at Tyler, and said, "See you later. I have an appointment."

Later that day, Tyler sat down next to Noah, a sales representative during the afternoon break. Noah began the conversation by saying, "Hey, Tyler, you might be interested in knowing about a big sale I have pending with a regional telephone company."

Tyler said in response, "I have even bigger news. My supervisor Mindy said that I am doing an outstanding job of controlling the inventory and that I might be eligible for an above-average salary increase."

Noah said, "Tyler, I'll see you later. I just remembered that I have a couple of important calls to make back at my cubicle."

Tyler began to wonder what was going on with his coworkers. He thought, "That's twice today that my coworkers have been acting a little bit uninterested in me. I wonder if they are under too much pressure."

Case Questions

1. What developmental needs does Tyler appear to have?
2. To what extent do you think Isabella and Noah were being rude toward Tyler?
3. What would you recommend that Tyler do to obtain feedback on his needs for development?

Interpersonal Skills Role-Play

Tyler Wants to Improve His Interpersonal Skills

Tyler, in the case just presented, comes to recognize that perhaps he has some problems in the way he conducts conversations, and that if he focused more on his coworkers and less on himself, he might get along better with his coworkers. This role-play is divided into two parts. In the first part, one student plays the role of Tyler, who meets up with Isabella on another day to engage her in conversation. Isabella thinks that Tyler met with her again for the purpose of talking more about himself. In the second part, one student plays the role of Tyler, who meets up with Noah again. Noah is a little discouraged with Tyler because he thinks that Tyler is looking for another opportunity to brag about his own accomplishments.

Run the role-play for about six minutes, while other class members observe the interactions and later provide feedback about the interpersonal skills displayed by Tyler in relation to his interaction with both Isabella and Noah. Also, rate Isabella and Noah. Observers rate the role players on two dimensions, using a 1-to-5 scale from very poor (1) to very good (5). One dimension is "effective use of human relations techniques." The second dimension is "acting ability." A few observers might voluntarily provide feedback to the role players in terms of sharing their ratings and observations. The course instructor might also provide feedback.

Interpersonal Relations Case 1.2

Betty Lou Sets Some Goals

Betty Lou is a marketing specialist at Pasta Mucho, the biggest pasta maker in her region. Over two years in the position, she contributed to the success of the Pasta Mucho product line. Although Betty Lou admits that a recession has contributed to the upswing in pasta sales nationwide, she believes that more than luck is involved. "After all," she says, "I contributed to the marketing campaign that showed that preparing pasta at home makes you cool."

Betty Lou's boss, Garth, is pleased with her job performance; but as part of the performance evaluation process, he has encouraged Betty Lou to prepare a goal sheet, mapping out her plans for the upcoming year. "Make it impressive," said Garth, "because my boss will be reviewing your goals also." Three days later, Betty Lou sent Garth an e-mail laying out her goals as follows:

1. Help make Pasta Mucho one of the great brands on the planet, much like Coca-Cola, Mercedes, and Microsoft.

2. Become the best marketing executive I can be.
3. Help the company develop some other wildly successful brands.
4. Get in good with more buyers at supermarket chains.
5. Get Pasta Mucho all over Facebook, Twitter, and Tumblr.

After reading the set of goals, Garth thought to himself, "What can I tell Betty Lou without hurting her feelings?"

Case Questions

1. If you were Garth, what would you tell Betty Lou about her goals without hurting her feelings?
2. What suggestions can you offer Betty Lou to improve her goal statement?
3. How might interpersonal skills contribute to Betty Lou attaining her goals?

References

1. Original story created from facts and observations in the following sources: Amir Efrati and Jessica E. Vascellaro, "Yahoo's Profit Lags: New CEO Faces Scores of Problems as Financial Woes Mount," *The Wall Street Journal*, July 18, 2012, p. B7; Michelle V. Rafter, "Yahoo's Recruiter-in-Chief," *Workforce Management*, November 2012, pp. 20–22; Amir Efrati and Jon Letzing, "Google's Mayer Takes Over as Yahoo Chief," *The Wall Street Journal*, July 17, 2012, pp. B1, B2; Patricia Sellers, "Marissa Mayer: Ready to Rumble at Yahoo," *Fortune*, October 29, 2012, pp. 118–128; Brad Stone, "Reading the Mind of Marissa Mayer," *Bloomberg Businessweek*, July 23–July 29, 2012, pp. 30–31; Gianpiero Petrigilieri, "Marissa Mayer Is Not the Exception—She Is the Norm," http://www.forbes.com/sites/insead, July 20, 2012, pp. 1–3; Joann S. Lublin and Leslie Kwoh, "For Yahoo CEO, Two New Roles," *The Wall Street Journal*, July 18, 2012, pp. B1, B6; Amir Efrati, "A Makeover Made in Google's Image," *The Wall Street Journal*, August 9, 2012, pp. B1, B6.

2. *Dale Carnegie Training Brochure*, Spring–Summer 2005, p. 12.
3. Joanne Lozar Glenn, "Lessons in Human Relations," *Business Education Forum*, October 2003, p. 10.
4. "Unleashing the Power of the New Workforce: Interpersonal Skills in the Modern Workplace," *Hogan Assessment Systems*. (Printed in *Workforce Management*, November 2011, p. S3).
5. Cited in Diana Louise Carter, "A Picture of Success: Graphics Company Has Shown Steady Growth," *Democrat and Chronicle (Roc Business)*, July 9, 2012, p. 6B.
6. Cited in Donna Nebenzahl, "Turning the Page on Corporate Leadership," *thestar.com (The Toronto Star)*, September 19, 2009, p. 2, http://www.thestar.com.
7. Based on Susan Scott, *Fierce Conversations: Achieving Success at Work & In Life, One Conversation at a Time* (New York: Random House, 2009).
8. Melissa Korn and Joe Light, "On the Lesson Plan: Feelings," *The Wall Street Journal*, May 5, 2011, p. B6.

9. George B. Yancey, Chante P. Clarkson, Julie D. Baxa, and Rachel N. Clarkson, "Example of Good and Bad Interpersonal Skills at Work," http://www.psichi.org/pubs/articles/article_368.asp, p. 2, accessed February 2, 2004.

10. Edward Muzio, Deborah J. Fisher, Err R. Thomas, and Valerie Peters, "Soft Skill Quantification (SSQ) for Project Manager Competencies," *Project Management Journal,* June 2007, pp. 30–31.

11. Marshall Goldsmith, "How Not to Lose the Top Job," *Harvard Business Review,* January 2009, p. 77.

12. The model presented here is an extension and modernization of the one presented in Thomas V. Bonoma and Gerald Zaltman, *Psychology for Management* (Boston: Kent, 1981), pp. 88–92.

13. Gary P. Latham, "The Motivational Benefits of Goal-Setting," *Academy of Management Executive,* November 2004, pp. 126–127.

14. Susan B. Wilson and Michael S. Dobson, *Goal Setting: How to Create an Action Plan and Achieve Your Goals,* 2nd ed. (New York: American Management Association, 2008).

15. Kirsten Weir, "Revising Your Story," *Monitor on Psychology,* March 2012, p. 28.

16. Karen Wright, "A Chic Critique," *Psychology Today,* March/April 2011, p. 56.

17. "Unleashing the Power of the New Workforce," p. S3.

18. Andrew Paradise, "Informal Learning Overlooked or Overhyped?" http://www.astdf.org/Publications, July 1, 2002, pp. 1–2.

19. Morgan W. McCall Jr., *High Flyers: Developing the Next Generation of Leaders* (Boston: Harvard Business School Press, 1998).

Understanding Individual Differences

wavebreakmedia/Shutterstock

US Airways Captain Chesley "Sully" Sullenberger III, the hero of the January 2009 airline ditching in the Hudson River, told investigators that he determined in a matter of seconds that only the river was "long enough, wide enough, and smooth enough" to put down the crippled jetliner. Testifying before the National Transformation Safety Board, Sullenberger said that when both engines of his Airbus 320 lost power at about 2,700 feet after sucking in birds, he quickly decided that the plane was losing speed and altitude, and that returning to New York's LaGuardia Airport was "problematic." After spotting a flock of birds that were very large and filled the entire windscreen of the jet, Sullenberger noticed a dramatic drop in thrust. Disregarding air traffic controller suggestions to return to LaGuardia or try to swoop into another nearby airport, he set his sights on the surface of the Hudson. With the plane's flaps out, speed dwindling fast, and splashdown barely seconds away, Sullenberger asked his first officer, "Got any ideas?" Copilot Jeff Skiles instantly replied, "Actually not."

Once the plane settled in the water, and the crew realized the fuselage remained intact, Sullenberger turned to his first officer and both instinctively blurted out at the same instant, "That wasn't as bad as I thought." Responding to questions about the lessons to be learned from the landing, Capt. Sullenberger mentioned training to help pilots work together as a team and additional efforts to improve emergency evacuations. His comments repeatedly swung back to the notion of an airline culture that stresses safety and respects the judgment of experienced pilots. "The captain's authority is a precious commodity that cannot be denigrated," he said. The captain's testimony also highlighted the importance of relying on experience and memory, rather than rigidly using checklists to deal with unexpected emergencies. With both pilots in the cockpit clocking an impressive 20,000 hours of total flight time, Captain Sullenberger said, "Teamwork and experience allowed us to focus on the high priorities without referring to written checklists."[1]

The story about the hero pilot "Sully" illustrates several of the key topics about differences among people that will be

After reading and studying this chapter and completing the exercises, you should be able to

1. Make adjustments for the individual differences among people in dealing with them on the job.
2. Develop insight into how your personality, mental ability, emotional intelligence, and values differ from others.
3. Respond to personality differences among people.
4. Respond to mental ability differences among people.
5. Respond to differences in values among people.

described in this chapter. Native intelligence, including the capacity to memorize details, practical intelligence (wisdom and common sense), and emotional control all play an important role in job performance. The major theme of this chapter deals with how people vary in a wide range of personal factors. **Individual differences** exert a profound effect on job performance and behavior. Such differences refer to variations in how people respond to the same situation based on personal characteristics. One of hundreds of possible examples is that some people can concentrate longer and harder on their work, thereby producing more and higher quality work, than others.

This chapter describes several of the major sources of individual differences on the job. It also gives you the chance to measure your standing on several key dimensions of behavior and helps you develop skills in responding to individual differences. Knowing how to respond to such differences is the cornerstone of effective interpersonal relations. To be effective in human relations, you cannot treat everybody the same.

individual differences

Variations in how people respond to the same situation based on personal characteristics. Mental processes used to perceive and make judgments from situations.

PERSONALITY

"We're not going to promote you to department head," said the manager to the analyst. "Although you are a great troubleshooter, you've alienated too many people in the company. You're too blunt and insensitive." As just implied, most successes and failures in people-contact jobs are attributed largely to interpersonal skills. And personality traits are major contributors to interpersonal, or human relations, skills.

Personality refers to those persistent and enduring behavior patterns that tend to be expressed in a wide variety of situations. A person who is brash and insensitive in one situation is likely to behave similarly in many other situations. Your personality is what makes you unique. Your walk, your talk, your appearance, your speech, and your inner values and conflicts all contribute to your personality.

Here, we illustrate the importance of personality to interpersonal relations in organizations by describing eight key personality traits and personality types related to cognitive styles. In addition, you will be given guidelines for dealing effectively with different personality types.

LEARNING OBJECTIVE 1

LEARNING OBJECTIVE 2

personality

Persistent and enduring behavior patterns that tend to be expressed in a wide variety of situations.

Eight Major Personality Factors and Traits

Many psychologists believe that the basic structure of human personality is represented by five broad factors, known as the Big Five: neuroticism, extraversion (the scientific spelling of *extroversion*), openness, agreeableness, and conscientiousness. Three more key personality factors—self-monitoring of behavior, risk taking and thrill seeking, and optimism—are also so important for human relations that they are considered here.

All eight factors have a substantial impact on interpersonal relations and job performance. The interpretations and meanings of these factors provide useful information because they help you pinpoint important areas for personal development. Although these

FIGURE 2-1   Eight Personality Factors Related to Interpersonal Skills

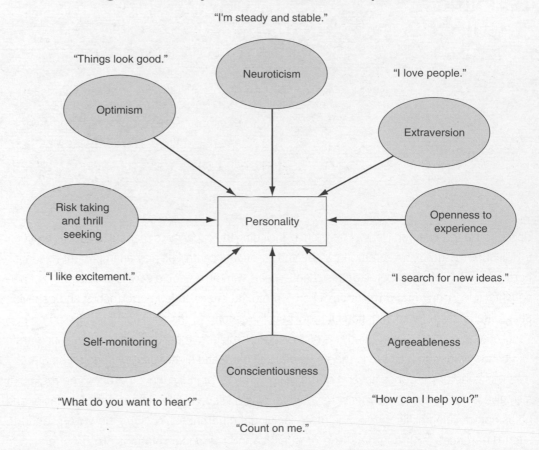

factors are partially inherited, most people can improve them provided they exert much conscious effort over a period of time. For example, it usually takes at least three months of effort before a person is perceived to be more agreeable. The eight factors, shown in Figure 2-1, are described in the following list.

1. *Neuroticism* reflects emotional instability and identifies people who are prone to psychological distress and to coping with problems in unproductive ways. Traits associated with this personality factor include being anxious, insecure, angry, embarrassed, emotional, and worried. A person of low neuroticism—or high emotional stability—is calm and confident, and usually in control.

2. *Extraversion* reflects the quantity or intensity of social interactions, the need for social stimulation, self-confidence, and competition. Traits associated with extraversion include being sociable, gregarious, assertive, talkative, and active. An outgoing person is often described as extraverted, whereas introverted persons are described as reserved, timid, and quiet. Introverts tend to prefer the inner world of their own mind, whereas extraverts tend to prefer the outer world of sociability.[2] A study conducted with more than 4,700 people found a positive relationship between extraversion and the tendency to be an entrepreneur.[3] This finding makes sense, because being an entrepreneur requires considerable reaching out to people to start the business, including fund raising.

3. *Openness* reflects the proactive seeking of experience for its own sake. Traits associated with openness include being creative, cultured, intellectually curious, broadminded, and artistically sensitive. People who score low on this personality factor are practical, with narrow interests.

4. *Agreeableness* reflects the quality of one's interpersonal orientation. Traits associated with the agreeableness factor include being courteous, flexible, trusting, good-natured, cooperative, forgiving, softhearted, and tolerant. The other end of the continuum includes disagreeable, cold, and antagonistic people.

5. *Conscientiousness* reflects organization, self-restraint, persistence, and motivation toward attaining goals. Traits associated with conscientiousness include being hardworking, dependable, well organized, and thorough. The person low in conscientiousness is lazy, disorganized, and unreliable.

6. *Self-monitoring* of behavior refers to the process of observing and controlling how we are perceived by others. Self-monitoring involves three major and somewhat distinct tendencies: (1) the willingness to be the *center of attention*, (2) *sensitivity* to the reactions of others, and (3) ability and willingness to a*djust* behavior to induce positive reactions in others. High self-monitors are pragmatic and even chameleonlike actors in social groups. They often say what others want to hear. Low self-monitors avoid situations that require them to adapt to outer images. In this way, their outer behavior adheres to their inner values. Low self-monitoring can often lead to inflexibility. Take Self-Assessment Quiz 2-1 to measure your self-monitoring tendencies.

7. *Risk taking and thrill seeking* refers to the propensity to take risks and pursue thrills. Persons with high standing on this personality trait are sensation seekers who pursue novel, intense, and complex sensations. They are willing to take risks for the sake of such experiences. The search for giant payoffs and daily thrills motivates people with an intense need for risk taking and thrill seeking.[4] Taking prudent risks can be important for the success of a business. Jim Donald, CEO of Extended Stay of America, encouraged employees to take risks, because the company had emerged from bankruptcy, and employees were still in the survival mode. They avoided decisions that might cost the company money, such as repairing the property or accommodating an angry guest with a free night's stay. Donald's solution was to hand out about 9,000 miniature "Get Out of Jail Free" cards to employees. When employees took a big risk for the company, they could use a card free, with no questions asked.[5]

   Take Self-Assessment Quiz 2-2 to measure your propensity for risk taking and thrill seeking.

8. *Optimism* refers to a tendency to experience positive emotional states and to typically believe that positive outcomes will be forthcoming from most activities. The other end of the scale is *pessimism*—a tendency to experience negative emotional states and to typically believe that negative outcomes will be forthcoming from most activities. Optimism versus pessimism is also referred to in more technical terms as positive affectivity versus negative affectivity and is considered a major personality trait.

   A person's tendency toward having positive affectivity (optimism) versus negative affectivity (pessimism) also influences job satisfaction. Being optimistic, as you would suspect, tends to enhance job satisfaction.[6]

   A potential downside of optimism is that it can lead a person to not fear risks, such as the possibility of being fired for poor performance. Also, being a little pessimistic about the future can sometimes help us reduce anxiety about potential worst-case scenarios.[7] For example, a job seeker might land a position with a start-up company that has earned hardly any revenue. Thinking about the problems of working for a company that never gets off the ground, such as not getting paid, may help that person be less anxious about the prospects of failure.

   Martin Seligman, director of the Positive Psychology Center at the University of Pennsylvania, places the need for balance between optimism and pessimism in these words: "The idea that optimism is always good is a caricature. It misses realism, it misses appropriateness, it misses the importance of negative emotion."[8]

A high standing on a given trait is not always an advantage, and a low standing is not always a disadvantage.[9] For example, a person who is highly extraverted might spend so much time interacting with coworkers that he or she does not spend enough time on analytical work. Also, a person who is a low self-monitor might give people such honest feedback—rather than telling them what they want to hear—that he or she helps others to grow and develop.

The Self-Monitoring Scale

Directions: The statements ahead concern your personal reactions to a number of different situations. No two statements are exactly alike, so consider each statement carefully before answering. If a statement is TRUE or MOSTLY TRUE as applied to you, **circle the "T"** next to the question. If a statement is FALSE or NOT USUALLY TRUE as applied to you, **circle the "F"** next to the question.

		True	False
1.	I find it hard to imitate the behavior of other people.	❏	❏
2.	My behavior is usually an expression of my true inner feelings, attitudes, and beliefs.	❏	❏
3.	At parties and social gatherings, I do not attempt to do or say things that others will like.	❏	❏
4.	I can only argue for ideas in which I already believe.	❏	❏
5.	I can make impromptu speeches even on topics about which I have almost no information.	❏	❏
6.	I guess I put on a show to impress or entertain people.	❏	❏
7.	When I am uncertain how to act in a social situation, I look to the behavior of others for cues.	❏	❏
8.	I would probably make a good actor.	❏	❏
9.	I rarely seek the advice of my friends to choose movies, books, or music.	❏	❏
10.	I sometimes appear to others to be experiencing deeper emotions than I actually am.	❏	❏
11.	I laugh more when I watch a comedy with others than when alone.	❏	❏
12.	In groups of people, I am rarely the center of attention.	❏	❏
13.	In different situations and with different people, I often act like very different persons.	❏	❏
14.	I am not particularly good at making other people like me.	❏	❏
15.	Even if I am not enjoying myself, I often pretend to be having a good time.	❏	❏
16.	I'm not always the person I appear to be.	❏	❏
17.	I would not change my opinions (or the way I do things) in order to please someone else or win their favor.	❏	❏
18.	I have considered being an entertainer.	❏	❏
19.	In order to get along and be liked, I tend to be what people expect me to be rather than anything else.	❏	❏
20.	I have never been good at games like charades or improvisational acting.	❏	❏
21.	I have trouble changing my behavior to suit different people and different situations.	❏	❏
22.	At a party, I let others keep the jokes and stories going.	❏	❏
23.	I feel a bit awkward in company and do not show up quite as well as I should.	❏	❏
24.	I can look anyone in the eye and tell a lie with a straight face (if for a good cause).	❏	❏
25.	I may deceive people by being friendly when I really dislike them.	❏	❏

Scoring and Interpretation: Give yourself one point each time your answer agrees with the key. A score that is between 0–12 would indicate that you are a relatively low self-monitor; a score that is between 13–25 would indicate that you are a relatively high self-monitor.

1. F		10. T		19. T	
2. F		11. T		20. F	
3. F		12. F		21. F	
4. F		13. T		22. F	
5. T		14. F		23. F	
6. T		15. T		24. T	
7. T		16. T		25. T	
8. T		17. F			
9. F		18. T			

Source: Mark Snyder, "Self-Monitoring of Expressive Behavior," *Journal of Personality and Social Psychology,* 4 (October 1974): 528–537.

The Eight Factors and Traits and Job Performance

Depending on the job, any one of the preceding personality factors can be important for success. The evidence of the contribution of the Big Five traits stems from the self-ratings of the people taking the test, as well as ratings by persons who know the test taker well. An analysis of a large number of studies found that ratings of the Big Five traits were more closely related to the job performance of the people rated than were self-ratings of personality.[10] One explanation for personality being tied to performance is that a particular personality trait gives us a bias or positive spin toward certain actions.[11] A person high in conscientiousness, for example, believes that if people are diligent they will accomplish more work and receive just rewards.

Conscientiousness relates to job performance for many different occupations, and has proven to be the personality factor most consistently related to success. As explained in the discussion above, each of the Big Five factors is composed of more narrow or specific traits. With respect to conscientiousness, the specific trait of *dependability* may be the most important contributor to job performance.[12]

Extraversion. Another important research finding is that extraversion is associated with success for managers and sales representatives. The explanation is that managers and salespeople are required to interact extensively with other people.[13] When referring to the association between extraversion and sales performance, it is helpful to consider which type of selling is involved. For example, particularly in selling complicated products and services, the sales representative is expected to be a problem solver who quietly reflects on the problem. Such behavior tends more toward introversion than extraversion, even though the sales representative still recognizes the importance of relationship building.

Self-Monitoring. For people who want to advance in their careers, being a high self-monitor is important. An analysis was made of the self-monitoring personality by combining 136 studies involving 23,101 people. A major finding was that high self-monitors tend to receive better performance ratings than low self-monitors. High self-monitors were also more likely to emerge as leaders and work their way into top management positions.[14] Another advantage to being a high self-monitor is that the individual is more likely to help out other workers, even when not required to do so. An example is helping a worker outside of your department with a currency exchange problem even though this is not your responsibility. Self-monitors are also much more likely to *click* with other workers and to succeed in the workplace. The "clicking" may lead to good relationships that facilitate performing well.[15]

Organizational Citizenship Behavior. The willingness to go beyond one's job description without a specific reward apparent is referred to as **organizational citizenship behavior**. We mention organizational citizenship behavior here because it is linked to other traits. Agreeableness and conscientiousness are frequently found to be associated with citizenship behavior. Recent evidence indicates that emotional stability, extraversion, and openness to experience are also linked to such behavior.[16]

Organizational citizenship behavior has many components or sub-behaviors. Two particularly important components for human relations are found in the distinction between *affiliation-oriented* and *challenge-oriented* citizenship behaviors. Affiliation-oriented behaviors are are interpersonal and cooperative, and tend to solidify or preserve relationships with others.[17] How about going out of your way to calm down a coworker who has to make a presentation to management in a couple of hours? Challenge-oriented behaviors are change-oriented and come with the risk that that they could hurt relationships with others because they criticize the status quo. How about going out of your way to tell management that in-person meetings should be replaced by video conferences to save time and money?

Good organizational citizens are highly valued by employers. An analysis of studies based on a total of more than 50,000 employees highlights the importance of organizational citizenship behavior in understanding how a willingness to help others contributes to both individual and organizational success. Among the findings were that being a good organizational citizen leads to better performance ratings by supervisors, higher salary increases, and less turnover and absenteeism. Organizational citizenship behavior also contributes to higher productivity, reduced costs, and better customer satisfaction.[18]

Another perspective on organizational citizenship behavior is that an employee will make a short-term sacrifice that leads to long-term benefits to the organization.[19] An example is an employee voluntarily working from home to deal with customer confusion about a product recall, which can lead to more loyal and appreciative customers.

Self-Assessment Quiz 2-3 gives you an opportunity to think through some of your own tendencies toward organizational citizenship behavior.

Turnover and Personality. A synthesis of studies suggests that personality can be linked to turnover. Employees who are emotionally stable are less likely to plan to quit, or to actually quit. Employees who score higher on the traits of conscientiousness and agreeableness are less likely to leave voluntarily. Another finding of note is that workers who are low on agreeableness and high on openness to experience are likely to quit spontaneously.[20] (Maybe the grouchy, intellectually curious employee may jump on a sudden opportunity for another job.)

Optimism and Pessimism. Optimism and pessimism also can be linked to job performance. Optimism can be quite helpful when attempting such tasks as selling a product or service or motivating a group of people. Yet psychologist Julie Normen has gathered considerable evidence that pessimism can sometimes enhance job performance. Pessimists usually assume that something will go wrong, and will carefully prepare to prevent botches and bad luck. A pessimist, for example, will carefully back up computer files or plan for emergencies that might shut down operations.[21]

The margin note:

organizational citizenship behavior

The willingness to go beyond one's job description without a specific reward apparent.

My Tendencies toward Organizational Citizenship Behavior

Describe whether each of the statements in the quiz ahead is mostly true or mostly false about you. If you have not experienced the situation, estimate whether it would be most likely true or most likely false about you.

No.	Statement about Organizational Citizenship Behavior	Mostly True	Mostly False
1.	I have helped a coworker with a work problem without being asked.	_____	_____
2.	I pick up litter in the company parking lot or outside of the building, and then dispose of the litter properly.	_____	_____
3.	Helping others is an important part of my job, even if I am not a manager.	_____	_____
4.	I make a special effort to say thank you and smile when somebody helps me in any way on the job.	_____	_____
5.	I volunteer to do a nonglamorous task when nobody in particular has responsibility for the task.	_____	_____
6.	If I found an apparently intoxicated person sleeping on the ground outside my workplace, I would call for help rather than leaving him or her lying there.	_____	_____
7.	I am pretty good at putting myself in another worker's place and understanding his or her perspective.	_____	_____
8.	I do my best to give effective comforting messages to other workers in distress.	_____	_____
9.	I am able to initiate, maintain, and terminate casual conversations with coworkers.	_____	_____
10.	During group meetings, I listen carefully to whomever is speaking to the group without performing another task such as looking at a smartphone placed on my lap.	_____	_____
11.	If my company faced an emergency such as a flood or hurricane, I would tell my supervisor that I will be on call 24 hours per day to help out.	_____	_____
12.	I have covered for workers who were absent or out on a break.	_____	_____
13.	I check with others before doing something that would affect their work.	_____	_____
14.	Even if I disliked a coworker, I would help him or her with a difficult problem.	_____	_____
15.	I help people outside my work group when I have the right knowledge or skill.	_____	_____
16.	I am willing to do work not in my job description, even if the effort means that I will have to work a couple of extra hours.	_____	_____
17.	I am willing to point out things the work group might be doing wrong, even if others disagree with me.	_____	_____
18.	I am willing to risk disapproval in order to do what is best for the company.	_____	_____
19.	I challenge work procedures and rules that seem to be nonproductive.	_____	_____
20.	I have tried to resolve person-to-person conflicts between workers in my department or unit.	_____	_____
21.	I do what I can to raise the spirits of coworkers who are having problems on the job.	_____	_____
22.	If I pick up some new job-related knowledge, I will share it with team members for whom the knowledge is useful.	_____	_____
23.	When I think of something that will help the entire company, I will share that knowledge with my manager and/or company leadership.	_____	_____
24.	I have politely voiced my concerns about something I think the company is doing wrong.	_____	_____

(Continued)

Combination of Standing on Several Personality Traits. A combination of personality factors will sometimes be more closely associated with job success than one factor
alone. A study about personality and job performance ratings was conducted with diverse
occupations, including clerical workers and wholesale appliance sales representatives. A
key finding was that conscientious workers who also scored high on agreeableness performed better than conscientious workers who were less agreeable.[22] (Being agreeable
toward your manager helps elevate performance evaluations!)

Personality Types and Cognitive Styles

People go about solving problems in various ways. You may have observed, for example,
that some people are more analytical and systematic, while others are more intuitive.
Modes of problem solving are referred to as **cognitive styles**. According to this method of
understanding problem-solving styles, your personality traits influence strongly how you
approach problems, such as being introverted pointing you toward dealing with ideas.
Knowledge of these cognitive styles can help you relate better to people because you can
better appreciate how they make decisions.

One of the best-known methods of measuring personality types is the Myers-Briggs
Type Indicator (MBTI®), a self-report questionnaire designed to make the theory of psy-
chological types developed by psychoanalyst Carl Jung applicable to everyday life.[23]
Another leading method of measuring types is the Golden Personality Type Profiler.[24]
Jung developed the theory of psychological types, but did not develop the two measuring
instruments just mentioned.

As measured by the Golden instrument, four separate dichotomies direct the typical
use of perception and judgment by an individual. The four dichotomies can also be considered a person's cognitive style.[25]

1. **Energy flow: extraversion versus introversion.** Extraverts direct their energy primarily toward the outer world of people and objects. In contrast, introverts direct
   their energy primarily toward the inner world of experiences and ideas.

2. **Information gathering: sensing versus intuition.** People who rely on sensing focus
   primarily on what can be perceived by the five primary senses of touch, sight,
   sound, smell, and taste. People who rely on intuition focus primarily on perceiving patterns and interrelationships.

3. **Decision making: thinking versus feeling.** People who rely primarily on thinking
   base conclusions on logical analysis, and emphasize objectivity and detachment.

cognitive styles

Modes of problem solving.

People who rely on feelings base conclusions on personal or social values, and focus on understanding and harmony.

4. **Lifestyle orientation: judging versus perceiving.** Individuals high on judging tend to orient their lives in a deliberate and planned manner. Individuals high on perceiving tend to orient their lives in a spontaneous and open-ended manner.

Combining the four types with each other results in 16 personality types, such as the ESFP, or "The Entertainer." ESFP refers to extraverted/sensing/feeling/perceiving. It is believed that approximately 13 percent of the population can be classified as the ESFP type. People of this type are optimistic and are skilled at living joyfully and entertaining others. ESFPs are effective at communicating their good-natured realism to others.

You might want to take the Golden Personality Type Profiler. Here our concern is with how your personality influences your cognitive style. Figure 2-2 presents 4 of the 16 personality types, along with the implications for each one with respect to cognitive style.

Far too many people perceive personality types as being definitive indicators of an individual's personality, and they therefore think they know exactly how to classify that person in terms of personality. The developers of the Golden point out that the instrument is an accurate and dependable measure of the aspects of personality measured. However, it is up to the person taking the Golden to determine if the report's description of him or her is accurate.[26] If the results are completely out of line with what you believe to be true about yourself, or what others have told you about your personality type, the results of the Golden (or another type indicator) should not be a cause for concern.

An interpersonal skills application of understanding the Golden personality types is to help people get along better within a work group. All the group or team members would

FIGURE 2-2   Four Cognitive Styles of the Golden Personality Types

Personality Type	Highlights of Type
ENFP (The Proponent) Extraverted/ iNtuitive/ Feeling/Perceiving	Lives continually in the realm of the possible. When absorbed in their latest project, they think of little else. Filled with energy, they are tireless in their pursuit of goals. Have an almost magnetic quality that enables them to have fun in almost any setting. The combination of Extraversion, Intuition, and Perceiving is well suited for leadership.
ENFJ (The Communicator) Extraverted/ iNtuitive/ Feeling/Judging	Chief concern is fostering harmony and cooperation between self and others. Has strong ideals and a potent sense of loyalty, whether to a mate, a school, a hometown, or a favorite cause. Usually good at organizing people to get things done while keeping everyone happy. At work, well armed to deal with both variety and action. Typically patient and conscientious, make a concerted effort of sticking with a job until finished.
INFP (The Advocate) Introverted/iNtuitive/ Feeling/Perceiving	Capable of immense sensitivity and has an enormous emotional capacity that is guarded closely. Has to know people well before displaying warmth, letting down the guard, and displaying warmth. Interpersonal relationships are a crucial focus. Has powerful sense of faithfulness, duty, and commitment to the people and causes he or she is attracted to. Able to express emotion and move people through his or her communication. A perfectionist on the job. Prefers a quiet working environment and, despite attraction for human companionship, will often work best alone. Will work at best only in job he or she truly believes in.
INFJ (The Foreseer) Introverted/ iNtuitive/ Feeling/Judging	Imaginative, inspired, tenacious, creative, and inward looking. Also stubborn, easily bored by routine work, and often pays little attention to obstacles. Makes decisions easily. Lives in a world of ideas, and will have a unique vision. Pours all own energy into achieving his or her goal. Trusts own intuition. Can express emotion and move people through written communication. Although cherishes the companionship of people, prefers a quiet working environment, and working alone. Perfectionist about quality. Creativity is his or her hallmark.

Code: E = Extraverted, N = iNtuitive, F = Feeling, P = Perceiving, I = Introverted, J = Judging

Source: Karen A. Deitz and John P. Golden, *Boundless Diversity: An Introduction to the Golden Personality Type Profiler* (San Antonio, Texas: Pearson TalentLens, 2004).

have their types assessed using the Golden instrument, and all members would be made aware of each other's type or working style. Knowing your type among the 16 types and the type of the other group members would give you some clues for working together smoothly.

To illustrate, I will use a couple of the types shown in Figure 2-2. Visualize yourself as a member of a work group. You know that Nick is a forseer (INFJ). The group has an assignment that calls for creating something new, so you consult with Nick to capitalize on his imaginative thinking, determination to attain goals, and fine written communication skills. Yet you know that you and Margot are proponents (ENFP), so you two will play a heavy role in helping translate Nick's plan into action. And you, Nick, and Margot know that Jason is an advocate (INFP), so you will have to work slowly with him to get him to believe in the new project so that he can make good use of his tendencies toward perfectionism. You will also not discourage Jason from spending some time working alone, so that he can be at his best.

Guidelines for Dealing with Different Personality Types

LEARNING OBJECTIVE 3 A key purpose in presenting information about a sampling of various personality types is to provide guidelines for individualizing your approach to people. As a basic example, if you wanted to score points with an introvert, you would approach that person in a restrained, laid-back fashion. In contrast, a more gregarious, lighthearted approach might be more effective with an extravert. The purpose of individualizing your approach is to build a better working relationship or to establish rapport with the other person. To match your approach to dealing with a given personality type, you must first arrive at an approximate diagnosis of the individual's personality. The following suggestions are therefore restricted to readily observable aspects of personality:

1. When relating to a person who appears to be emotionally unstable, based on symptoms of worry and tension, be laid back and reassuring. Attempt not to project your own anxiety and fears. Be a good listener. If possible, minimize the emphasis on deadlines and the dire consequences of a project's failing. Show concern and interest in the person's welfare.

2. When relating to an extraverted individual, emphasize friendliness, warmth, and a stream of chatter. Talk about people more than ideas, things, or data. Express an interest in a continuing working relationship.

3. When relating to an introverted individual, move slowly in forming a working relationship. Do not confuse quietness with a lack of interest. Tolerate moments of silence. Emphasize ideas, things, and data more heavily than people.

4. When relating to a person who is open to experience, emphasize information sharing, idea generation, and creative approaches to problems. Appeal to his or her intellect by discussing topics of substance rather than ordinary chatter and gossip.

5. When relating to a person who is closed to experience, stick closely to the facts of the situation at hand. Recognize that the person prefers to think small and deal with the here and now.

6. When relating to an agreeable person, just relax and be yourself. Reciprocate with kindness to sustain a potentially excellent working relationship.

7. When relating to a disagreeable person, be patient and tolerant. At the same time, set limits on how much mistreatment you will take. Disagreeable people sometimes secretly want others to put brakes on their antisocial behavior.

8. When relating to a conscientious person, give him or her freedom and do not nag. The person will probably honor commitments without prompting. Conscientious people are often taken for granted, so remember to acknowledge the person's dependability.

9. When relating to a person of low conscientiousness, keep close tabs on him or her, especially if you need the person's output to do your job. Do not assume that because the person has an honest face and a pleasing smile, he or she will deliver as promised. Frequently follow up on your requests, and impose deadlines if you have the authority. Express deep appreciation when the person does follow through.

Personality Role-Plays

The Extravert: One student assumes the role of a successful outside sales representative who has just signed a $3 million order for the company. The sales rep comes back to the office elated. The other student assumes the role of a member of the office support staff. He or she decides this is a splendid opportunity to build a good relationship with the triumphant sales rep. Run the role-play for about seven minutes. The people not involved in the role-play will observe and then provide feedback when the role-play is completed. (These directions regarding time, observation, and feedback also apply to the two other role-plays in this exercise and throughout the book.)

Openness: One student plays the role of an experienced worker in the department who is told to spend some time orienting a new co-op student or intern. It appears that this new person is open to experience. Another student plays the role of the co-op student who is open to experience and eager to be successful in this new position.

Organizational Citizenship Behavior: One student plays the role of a strong organizational citizen who wants to help other people, going beyond what is found in his or her job description. The strong organizational citizen is thinking, "What can I do today to help somebody?" As the student walks down the row of cubicles, he or she spots a person who is staring at the computer with an agonized, perplexed look. The good organizational citizen thinks, "Maybe I've just found a good opportunity to be useful today." The other student plays the role of the perplexed worker who might need help with a specific problem facing him or her at the moment.

For the three scenarios, observers rate the role players on two dimensions, using a 1-to-5 scale from very poor (1) to very good (5). One dimension is "effective use of human relations techniques." The second dimension is "acting ability." A few observers might voluntarily provide feedback to the role players in terms of sharing their ratings and observations. The course instructor might also provide feedback.

10. When dealing with a person whom you suspect is a high self-monitor, be cautious in thinking that the person is truly in support of your position. The person could just be following his or her natural tendency to appear to please others, but not really feel that way.

11. When relating to a person with a high propensity for risk taking and thrill seeking, emphasize the risky and daring aspects of activities familiar to you. Talk about a new product introduction in a highly competitive market, stock options, investment in high-technology startup firms, skydiving, and race car driving.

12. When relating to a person with a low propensity for risk taking and thrill seeking, emphasize the safe and secure aspects of activities familiar to you. Talk about the success of an established product in a stable market (like pencils and paperclips), investment in US Treasury bonds, life insurance, camping, and gardening.

13. When dealing with a sensation type of information gatherer, emphasize facts, figures, and conventional thinking without sacrificing your own values. To convince the sensation type, emphasize logic more than emotional appeal. Focus on details more than on the big picture.

14. When dealing with an intuition type of information gatherer, emphasize feelings, judgments, playing with ideas, imagination, and creativity. Focus more on the big picture than details.

To start putting these guidelines into practice, do the role-plays in Skill-Building Exercise 2-1. Remember that a role player is an extemporaneous actor. Put yourself in the shoes of the character you play, and visualize how he or she would act. Because you are given only the general idea of a script, use your imagination to fill in the details.

COGNITIVE ABILITY

Cognitive ability (also referred to as mental ability or intelligence) is one of the major sources of individual differences that affects job performance and behavior. **Cognitive Intelligence** is the capacity to acquire and apply knowledge, including solving problems. Intelligent workers can best solve abstract problems. In an exceedingly simple job, such as packing shoes into boxes, having below-average intelligence can be an advantage because the employee is not likely to become bored.

Understanding the nature of intelligence contributes to effective interpersonal relations in the workplace. Your evaluation of a person's intelligence can influence how you relate to that person. For example, if you think a person is intelligent, you will tend to seek his or her input on a difficult problem. If you realize that different types of intelligence

cognitive intelligence

The capacity to acquire and apply knowledge, including solving problems.

exist, you are more likely to appreciate people's strengths. You are thus less likely to judge others as being either good or poor problem solvers.

Four important aspects of cognitive ability include (1) the components of traditional intelligence, (2) practical intelligence, (3) multiple intelligences, and (4) emotional intelligence. (This fourth type of intelligence can also be regarded as personality, not cognitive ability.) Knowledge of the four aspects will enrich your understanding of other workers and yourself.

Components of Traditional Intelligence

g (general) factor

A factor in intelligence that contributes to the ability to perform well in many tasks.

s (special) factors

Specific components of intelligence that contribute to problem-solving ability.

Intelligence consists of more than one component. A component of intelligence is much like a separate mental aptitude. Evidence suggests that intelligence consists of a **g (general) factor** and **s (special) factors** that contribute to problem-solving ability. Scores of tests of almost any type (such as math, aptitude for spatial relations, or reading skill) are somewhat influenced by the g factor. The g factor helps explain why some people perform well in so many different mental tasks. Substantial evidence has accumulated over the years that workers with high intelligence tend to perform better. The relationship between g and job performance is likely to be strongest for those aspects of jobs involving thinking and knowledge, such as problem solving and technical expertise.[27]

Over the years, various investigators have arrived at different special factors contributing to overall mental aptitude. The following seven factors have been identified consistently:

1. **Verbal comprehension.** The ability to understand the meaning of words and their relationship to each other and to comprehend written and spoken information.

2. **Word fluency.** The ability to use words quickly and easily, without an emphasis on verbal comprehension.

3. **Numerical acuity.** The ability to handle numbers, engage in mathematical analysis, and perform arithmetic calculations.

4. **Spatial perception.** The ability to visualize forms in space and manipulate objects mentally, particularly in three dimensions.

5. **Memory.** Having a good rote memory for symbols, words, and lists of numbers, along with other associations.

6. **Perceptual speed.** The ability to perceive visual details, pick out similarities and differences, and perform tasks requiring visual perception.

7. **Inductive reasoning.** The ability to discover a rule or principle, apply it in solving a problem, and to make judgments and decisions that are logically sound.

Being strong in any of the preceding mental aptitudes often leads to an enjoyment of work associated with that aptitude. The reverse can also be true; enjoying a type of mental activity might lead to the development of an aptitude for the activity.

Attempts to improve cognitive skills, or intelligence, have become an entire industry, including both brain-stimulating exercises and food supplements. Common wisdom suggests that staying in shape mentally by such activities as doing crossword puzzles, surfing the Internet, or studying a foreign language can slow the decline of an aging brain. Brain-imaging studies support the idea that mental workouts help preserve **cognitive fitness**, a state of optimized ability to remember, learn, plan, and adapt to changing circumstances. Acquiring expertise in such diverse areas as playing a cello, juggling, speaking a foreign language, and playing video games and computer games expands your neural systems and helps them communicate with one another. This means that by learning new skills you can alter the physical makeup of the brain even in later life. Engaging in play also enhances brain functioning that helps explain the link between creativity and play.[28]

cognitive fitness

A state of optimized ability to remember, learn, plan, and adapt to changing circumstances.

Training people in memory skills (still an important part of intelligence) has been shown to be successful in many experiments. For example, research with seniors showed that training with a computer game that involved executive control skills improved performance in a variety of memory tasks.[29] Considerable evidence exists that aerobic exercise helps maintain cognitive intelligence, particularly for the elderly. It is possible that the exercise results in a better flow of oxygen to the brain, thereby boosting its capability, at least in the short term.[30]

The contribution of food supplements to enhancing or maintaining cognitive ability is debatable, yet at least promising. Nevertheless, a balanced, healthy diet contributes to the propering functioning of the brain, as well as any other organ of the body. In recent years, several energy drinks have appeared on the market that contain citicoline, an organic molecule that is said to boost the production of neurotransmitters that are necessary for brain functioning. A review of 14 experiments found that cicitcoline has a positive effect on memory and behavior, at least in the medium term.[31] So go ahead and purchase a medically approved brain booster at a pharmacy, knowing that it *could* help you conquer your next big cognitive challenge.

Practical Intelligence

Many people, including psychologists, are concerned that the traditional way of understanding intelligence inadequately describes mental ability. An unfortunate implication of intelligence testing is that intelligence as traditionally calculated is largely the ability to perform tasks related to scholastic work. Thus, a person who scored very high on an intelligence test could follow a complicated instruction manual, but might not be street smart.

The *practical* type of intelligence is required for adapting your environment to suit your needs. **Practical intelligence** is an accumulation of skills, dispositions, and knowledge, plus the ability to apply knowledge to solve every day problems.[32] The idea of practical intelligence helps explain why a person who has a difficult time getting through school can still be a successful businessperson, politician, or athlete. Practical intelligence incorporates the ideas of common sense, wisdom, and street smarts.

practical intelligence

An accumulation of skills, dispositions, and knowledge, plus the ability to apply knowledge to solve everyday problems.

A person with high practical intelligence would also have good **intuition**, an experience-based way of knowing or reasoning in which the weighing and balancing of evidence are done automatically. Examples of good intuition include a merchandiser who develops a hunch that a particular style will be hot next season, a basketball coach who sees the possibilities in a gangly youngster, and a supervisor who has a hunch that a neighbor would be a great fit for her department. Intuition is also required for creative intelligence.

intuition

An experience-based way of knowing or reasoning in which the weighing and balancing of evidence are done automatically.

An important implication of practical intelligence is that experience is helpful in developing intellectual skills and judgment. At younger ages, raw intellectual ability, such as that required for learning information technology skills, may be strongest. However, judgment and wisdom are likely to be stronger with accumulated experience. This is why people in their 40s and older are more likely to be chosen for positions such as the CEO of a large business or a commercial airline pilot. Poor judgment is *sometimes* associated with inexperience and youth, and the frequent impulsiveness of young people is often referred to as the *teenage brain*.

A study conducted with more than 300 printing industry CEOs and founders of early-stage printing and graphics businessess demonstrated that practical intelligence is associated with business success. Practial intelligence was measured by having the participants solve problems revealed in three printing-business scenarios. Among the many findings of the study was that practical intelligence is important for business success, measured in terms of new venture growth in an entrepreneurial setting.[33]

One major reservation some have about practical intelligence is the implication that people who are highly intelligent in the traditional sense are not practical thinkers. In truth, most executives and other high-level workers score quite well on tests of mental ability. These tests usually measure analytical intelligence.

Multiple Intelligences

Another approach to understanding the diverse nature of mental ability is the theory of **multiple intelligences**. According to Howard Gardner, people know and understand the world in distinctly different ways and learn in different ways. Individuals possess the following eight intelligences, or faculties, in varying degrees:

multiple intelligences

A theory of intelligence contending that people know and understand the world in distinctly different ways and learn in different ways.

1. **Linguistic.** Enables people to communicate through language, including reading, writing, and speaking.
2. **Logical-mathematical.** Enables individuals to see relationships between objects and solve problems, as in calculus and statistics.

3. **Musical.** Gives people the capacity to create and understand meanings made out of sounds and to enjoy different types of music.

4. **Spatial.** Enables people to perceive and manipulate images in the brain and to recreate them from memory, as is required in making graphic designs.

5. **Bodily kinesthetic.** Enables people to use their body and perceptual and motor systems in skilled ways, such as dancing, playing sports, and expressing emotion through facial expressions.

6. **Intrapersonal.** Enables people to distinguish among their own feelings and acquire accurate self-knowledge.

7. **Interpersonal.** Makes it possible for individuals to recognize and make distinctions among the feelings, motives, and intentions of others, as in managing or parenting.

8. **Naturalist.** Enables individuals to differentiate among, classify, and utilize various features of the physical external environment.

Your profile of intelligences influences how you best learn and to which types of jobs you are best suited. Gardner believes that it is possible to develop these separate intelligences through concentrated effort. However, any of these intelligences might fade if not put to use.[34] The components of multiple intelligences might also be perceived as different talents or abilities. Having high general problem-solving ability (g) would contribute to high standing on each of the eight intelligences.

Two books in recent years have emphasized that having natural abilities of the type just described is not as important as hard work in developing talent. According to the 10,000-hour rule proposed by Malcolm Gladwell, no one gets to the top without 10,000 hours of practice in a field.[35] Guided practice does indeed help, but a person still needs some basic talent to attain high-level success in such fields as finance, foreign languages, and sports. Recognize also that many teenagers achieve outstanding success in information technology, science, sports, and music without having practiced 1,000 hours per year for 10 years.

The three types of intelligence mentioned so far (cognitive, practical, and multiple) all contribute to but do not guarantee our ability to think critically. Critical thinking is the process of evaluating evidence and then, based on this evaluation, making judgments and decisions. Through critical thinking, we find reasons to support or reject an argument. Personality factors contribute heavily to whether we choose to use the various types of intelligence. For example, the personality factor of openness facilitates critical thinking because the individual enjoys gathering evidence to support or refute an idea. Conscientiousness also facilitates critical thinking because the individual feels compelled to gather more facts and think harder.[36]

Emotional Intelligence

How effectively people use their emotions has a major impact on their success. **Emotional intelligence** refers to qualities such as understanding one's own feelings, having empathy for others, and regulating one's emotions to enhance living. The intelligence aspect focuses on the ability to engage in complex information processing about your own emotions and those of others. At the same time, you use this information as a guide to thought and behavior.[37] A person with high emotional intelligence would be able to engage in such behaviors as sizing up people, pleasing others, and influencing them. Four key factors included in emotional intelligence are as follows:[38]

1. **Self-awareness.** The ability to understand your moods, emotions, and needs as well as their impact on others. Self-awareness also includes using intuition to make decisions you can live with happily. A person with good self-awareness knows whether he or she is pushing other people too far. Imagine that Amanda is an assistant to the food service manager at a financial services company. Amanda believes strongly that the cafeteria should ensure that no food served on company premises contains trans fats. However, the food services manager seems lukewarm to the idea. Instead of badgering the manager, Amanda decides to fight her

battle bit by bit by presenting facts and reminders in a friendly way. Eventually, the manager agrees to have a meeting on the subject, with a nutritionist invited. Amanda's self-awareness has paid off.

2. **Self-management.** The ability to control one's emotions and act with honesty and integrity in a consistent and acceptable manner. The right degree of self-management helps prevent a person from throwing temper tantrums when activities do not go as planned. Effective workers do not let their occasional bad moods ruin their day. If they cannot overcome the bad mood, they let coworkers know of their problem and how long it might last. A person with low self-management would suddenly decide to drop a project because the work was frustrating.

Imagine that Jack is an assistant to the export sales manager, and today is a big day because a company in Russia appears ready to make a giant purchase. The export sales manager says, "Today we need peak performance from everybody. If we nail down this sale, we will exceed our sales quota for the year." Unfortunately, Jack is in a grim mood. His favorite sports team was eliminated from the playoffs the night before, and his dog has been diagnosed as having a torn abdominal muscle. Jack would like to lash out in anger against everybody he meets today, but instead he focuses his energy on getting the job done, and does not let his personal problems show through.

3. **Social awareness.** Includes having empathy for others and having intuition about work problems. A team leader with social awareness, or empathy, would be able to assess whether a team member has enough enthusiasm for a project to assign him to that project. Another facet of social skill is the ability to interpret nonverbal communication, such as frowns and types of smiles.[39] A supervisor with social awareness, or empathy, would take into account the most likely reaction of group members before making a decision that affects them.

Imagine that Cindy has been working as an assistant purchasing manager for six months. Company policy prohibits accepting "lavish" gifts from vendors or potential vendors attempting to sell the company goods or services. Cindy has been placed in charge of purchasing all paper toweling for the company. Although most of the purchasing is completed over the Internet, sales representatives still make the occasional call. The rep from the paper towel company asks Cindy if she would like an iPhone as a token gift for even considering his company. Cindy badly wants an iPhone, and it is not yet in her budget. After thinking through the potential gift for five minutes, Cindy decides to refuse. Perhaps an iPhone is not really a lavish gift, but her intuition tells her it would look like a conflict of interest if she accepted the iPhone.

4. **Relationship management.** Includes the interpersonal skills of being able to communicate clearly and convincingly, disarm conflicts, and build strong personal bonds. Effective workers use relationship management skills to spread their enthusiasm and solve disagreements, often with kindness and humor. A worker with relationship management skills would use a method of persuasion that is likely to work well with a particular group or individual.

The current interest in emotional intelligence in the workplace appears to be related to a growing acceptance of emotional expressiveness, including occasional crying on the job for both men and women. A national study conducted by crying expert Anne Kreamer found that 69 percent of respondents believed that when a person gets more emotional on the job, it makes that person seem more human. Also, 93 percent of women and 83 percent of men believed that being sensitive to others' emotions at work is an asset.[40] Furthermore, a study of 212 professionals from a variety of industries found that emotional intelligence was associated with teamwork effectiveness and job performance. This finding was true mostly when the professional's job had some managerial work demands because responding to the emotions of others requires emotional capabilities.[41]

Much of this book is about relationship management, but here is yet another example. Donte is an information technology specialist. His assignment for the first six months is to visit users at their workplace to help them with any IT problems they might be experiencing. In discussing his role with his supervisor, Donte begins to realize that helping with technical problems is not his only job. He is an ambassador of good will for the IT department. He and his manager want to build a network of support for the efforts of the department. So when Donte visits the various departments, he is courteous and friendly, and asks about how an IT rep could make work easier for the person in question.

Emotional intelligence thus incorporates many of the skills and attitudes necessary to achieve effective interpersonal relations in organizations. Most of the topics in this book, such as resolving conflict, helping others develop, and possessing positive political skills, would be included in emotional intelligence. It is therefore reasonable to regard emotional intelligence as being a mixture of cognitive skills and personality.

Guidelines for Relating to People of Different Levels and Types of Intelligence

LEARNING OBJECTIVE 4

Certainly you cannot expect to administer mental ability and emotional intelligence tests to all your work associates, gather their scores, and then relate to associates differently based on their scores. Yet it is possible to intuitively develop a sense for the mental quickness of people and the types of mental tasks they perform best. For example, managers must make judgments about mental ability in selecting people for jobs and assigning them to tasks. The following are several guidelines worth considering for enhancing your working relationships with others.

1. If you perceive another worker (your manager included) to have high cognitive skill, present your ideas in technical depth. Incorporate difficult words into your conversation and reports. Ask the person challenging questions.

2. If you perceive another worker to have low cognitive skill, present your ideas with a minimum of technical depth. Use a basic vocabulary, without going so far as to be patronizing. Ask for frequent feedback about having been clear. If you have supervisory responsibility for a person who appears to be below average in intelligence, give the person the opportunity to repeat the same type of task rather than switching assignments frequently.

3. If you perceive a work associate to relish crunching numbers, use quantitative information when attempting to persuade that person. Instead of using phrases such as "most people," say "about 65 percent of people."

4. If you perceive a work associate to have high creative intelligence, solicit his or her input on problems requiring a creative solution. Use statements such as "Here's a problem that requires a sharp, creative mind, so I've come to you."

5. If you perceive a work associate to have low emotional intelligence, explain your feelings and attitudes clearly. Make an occasional statement such as "How I feel about his situation is quite important" to emphasize the emotional aspect. The person may not get the point of hints and indirect expressions.

To start putting these guidelines into practice, do the role-plays in Skill-Building Exercises 2-2 and 2-3.

VALUES AS A SOURCE OF INDIVIDUAL DIFFERENCES

value

The importance a person attaches to something.

Another group of factors influencing how a person behaves on the job is that person's values and beliefs. A **value** refers to the importance a person attaches to something. Values are also tied to the enduring belief that one's mode of conduct is better than another mode of conduct. If you believe that good interpersonal relations are the most important part of your life, your humanistic values are strong. Similarly, you may think that people who are not highly concerned about interpersonal relations have poor values.

Values are closely tied in with **ethics,** or the moral choices a person makes. A person's values influence which kinds of behaviors he or she believes are ethical. Ethics convert values into action. An executive who strongly values profits might not find it unethical to raise prices higher than needed to cover additional costs. Another executive who strongly values family life might suggest that the company invest money in an on-site childcare center. Ethics is such an important part of interpersonal relations in organizations that the topic receives separate mention in Chapter 15.

ethics

The moral choices a person makes. Also, what is good and bad, right and wrong, just and unjust, and what people should do.

Classification of Values

An almost automatic response to classifying values is that people have either good or bad values, with bad values meaning those that are quite different than yours. To the person with a strong work ethic, an individual who took a casual approach to work might have "bad values." To the person with a weak work ethic, the person who was work obsessed might have "bad values." Shalom H. Schwartz, a professor from the Hebrew University of Jerusalem, has developed a method of classifying values that is particularly useful because it points to how we establish goals to fit our values.[42] For example, as shown in Table 2-1, people who value power are likely to set the goals of attaining power, strength, and control. And those who value benevolence are likely to establish the goals of being kind, being charitable, and showing respect for others. The link between values and goals has extensive research support.

Generational Differences in Values

Differences in values among people often stem from age, or generational, differences. Workers above 50 years of age, in general, may have different values than people who are much younger. These age differences in values have often been seen as a clash between Baby Boomers and members of Generation X and Generation Y. The category of Baby Boomers is so broad that part of the Baby Boomer generation is said to include Generation Jones, the younger boomers born between 1954 and 1964. This group comprises one-fourth of the US population. Members of Generation Jones are typically entering the peak of their careers and are not yet thinking much about retirement.[43]

TABLE 2-1 A Classification of Values and Associated Goals

Value	Goals Associated with Each Value
Power	power, strength, control
Achievement	achievement, ambition, success
Hedonism	luxury, pleasure, delight
Stimulation	excitement, novelty, thrill
Self-direction	independence, freedom, liberty
Universalism	unity, justice, equality
Benevolence	kindness, charity, mercy
Tradition	tradition, custom, respect
Conformity	restraint, regard, consideration
Security	security, safety, protection

Source: Anat Bardi, Rachel M. Calogero, and Brian Mullen, "A New Archival Approach to the Study of Values and Value-Behavior Relations: Validation of the Value Lexicon," *Journal of Applied Psychology,* May 2008, pp. 483–497. Based on Shalom. H. Schwartz, "Universals in the Content and Structure of Values: Theoretical Advances and Empirical Tests in 20 Countries," in *Advances in Experimental and Social Psychology,* ed. Mark P. Zanna (New York: Academic Press, Vol. 25, 1992), 1–65.

According to the stereotype, Baby Boomers see Generation Xers and Yers as disrespectful of rules, not willing to pay their dues, and being disloyal to employers. Generation Xers and Yers see Baby Boomers as worshipping hierarchy (layers of authority), being overcautious, and wanting to preserve the status quo. Members of Generation X and Generation Y are likely to believe even more strongly than Baby Boomers in the imporance of sustainability, or preserving the physical environment. Sustainability also refers to the idea of meeting the needs of the present without creating environmental problems that will block future generations from satisfying their needs.[44]

Table 2-2 summarizes these stereotypes with the understanding that massive group stereotypes like this are only partially accurate because there are literally millions of exceptions. For example, many Baby Boomers are fascinated with technology, and many Generation Yers like hierarchy.When the Traditionalists (pre-Baby Boomers) are included, four different generations converge in today's workplace—sometimes leading to conflict as described in Chapter 9.

How Values Are Learned

People acquire values in the process of growing up, and many values are learned by the age of four. Many of our values are influenced by the cultural experiences of our childhood.[45] An example is that many people who grew up during the Internet generation believe that information should be freely exchanged and come without a fee. Whereas in the past the family was the most important environment for shaping values, attitudes, and beliefs, today children are exposed via television and the Internet to many more role models, values, ways of thinking, and choices than ever before.[46] Models can be teachers, friends, brothers, sisters, and even public figures. If we identify with a particular person, the probability is high that we will develop some of his or her major values. For example, if a parent valued helping less fortunate people, the child might place a high value on helping people in need later in life.

Another major way values are learned is through the communication of attitudes. The attitudes that we hear expressed directly or indirectly help shape our values. Assume that using credit to purchase goods and services was considered an evil practice among your family and friends. You might therefore hold negative values about installment purchases. Unstated but implied attitudes may also shape your values. If key people in your life showed no enthusiasm when you talked about work accomplishments, you might not

TABLE 2-2 Value Stereotypes for Several Generations of Workers

Baby Boomers (1946–1964) including Generation Jones (1954–1965)	Generation X (1961–1980)	Generation Y (1981–2002) Millenials
Uses technology as a necessary tool, but not obsessed with technology for its own sake	Tech-savvy	Tech-savvy, and even questions the value of standard IT techniques such as e-mail, with a preference for communications on a Web site
Appreciates hierarchy	Teamwork very important	Teamwork very important, highly team focused
Tolerates teams but values independent work	Dislikes hierarchy	Dislikes hierarchy, prefers participation
Strong career orientation	Strives for work–life balance, but will work long hours for now; prefers flexible work schedule	Strives for work–life balance, and may object to work interfering with personal life; expects flexible work schedule
More loyalty to organization	Loyalty to own career and profession	Loyalty to own career and profession, and feels entitled to career goals
Favors diplomacy and tact	Candid in conversation	Quite direct in conversation
Seeks long-term employment	Will accept long-term employment if situation is right	Looks toward each company as a stepping stone to a better job in another company
Believes that issues should be formally discussed	Believes that feedback can be administered informally, and welcomes feedback	Believes that feedback can be given informally, even on the fly, and craves feedback
Somewhat willing to accept orders and suggestions	Often questions why things should be done in certain way	Frequently asks why things should be done in a certain way, and asks loads of questions
Willing to take initiative to establish starting and completion dates for projects	Slight preference for a manager to provide structure about project dates	Prefers structure on dates and other activities based on childhood of structured activities
Regards rewards as a positive consequence of good performance and seniority	Expects frequent rewards	Feels strong sense of entitlement to rewards, including promotions
Will multitask in front of work associates when it seems necessary	Feels comfortable in multitasking while interacting with work associates	Assumes that multitasking, including listening to music on earphones while dealing with work associates, is acceptable behavior
Prefers working at desk in company office	Eager to have the option of working from anywhere at any time.	Prefers working from anywhere at any time; feels constrained when having to work in company office full time
Believes that sustainability (protecting the environment) should be balanced with its economic costs, including job generation	Wants employers to take a positive stand in terms of protecting the environment	Thinks that sustainability is as important as profitability, and only wants to work for a "green" employer

Note: Disagreement exists about which age bracket fits Baby Boomers, Generation X, and Generation Y, with both professional publications and dictionaries showing slight differences.

Sources: The majority of ideas in this table are from Adrienne Fox, "Mixing It Up," *HR Magazine*, May 2011, pp. 22–27; Ron Alsop, *The Trophy Kids Grow Up: How the Millenial Generation is Shaking Up the Workforce* (San Francisco: Jossey-Bass/Wiley, 2008); Alsop, "Schools, Recruiters Try to Define Traits for Future Students," *The Wall Street Journal*, February 14, 2006, p. B6; Kathryn Tyler, "Generation Gaps: Millennials May Be Out of Touch with the Basics of Workplace Behavior," *HR Magazine*, January 2008, pp. 69–72; Lindsay Holloway, "Stick Together," *Entrepreneur*, March 2008, p. 30; Martha Irvine, "Recession Intensifies Gen X Discontent at Work," *The Detroit News* (*www.detnews.com*), November 16, 2009; Chris Penttila, "Talking about My Generation," *Entrepreneur*, March 2009, pp. 53–55; Cindy Krischer Goodman, "Meeting in the Middle: Generations X and Y," *The Miami Herald* (http://www.miamiherald.com), August 18, 2010, pp. 1–3; and Susan Berfield, "Levi's Has a New Color for Blue Jeans: Green," *Bloomberg Businessweek*, October 26–October 28, pp. 26–28.

place such a high value on achieving outstanding results. If, however, your family and friends centered their lives on their careers, you might develop similar values. (Or you might rebel against such a value because it interfered with a more relaxed lifestyle.) Many key values are also learned through religion and thus become the basis for society's morals. For example, most religions emphasize treating other people fairly and kindly. To "knife somebody in the back" is considered immoral both on and off the job.

Although many core values are learned early in life, our values continue to be shaped by events later in life. The media, including the dissemination of information about popular culture, influence the values of many people throughout their lives. The aftermath of Hurricane Katrina intensified a belief in the value of helping less fortunate people. Volunteers from throughout the United States and several other countries invested time, money, and energy into helping rebuild New Orleans and several other Gulf Coast cities. Influential people, such as NBA players, were seen on television building houses for Katrina victims. Such publicity sent a message that helping people in need is a value worth considering.

The media, particularly through advertisements, can also encourage the development of values that are harmful to a person intent on developing a professional career. People featured in advertisements for consumer products, including snack food, beer, and vehicles, often flaunt rudeness and flagrantly incorrect grammar. The message comes across to many people that such behavior is associated with success.

Changes in technology can also change our values. As the world has become increasingly digitized, more and more people come to value a *digital lifestyle* as the normal way of life. Many people would not think of spending time away from the house without their electronic gadgets, even while participating in or watching sports. Being part of the digital lifestyle is therefore an important value for many people of all ages.

Company values can also influence or shape individual values, such as an organization emphasizing total respect for the rights of customers. Several business firms also strongly emphasize the value of spirituality, which could awaken such values with many employees. A strong example is Tyson Foods, Inc. which employs 120 chaplains. The head chaplain, Richard McKinnie, explains the value in these terms: "It's not about Chistianity or Islam. It's the spiritual side of what people are."[47]

Clarifying Your Values

The values that you develop early in life are directly related to the kind of person you are and to the quality of the relationships you form.[48] Recognition of this fact has led to exercises designed to help people clarify and understand some of their own values. Self-Assessment Quiz 2-3 gives you an opportunity to clarify your values.

The Mesh between Individual and Job Values

Under the best of circumstances, the values of employees mesh with those required by the job. When this state of congruence exists, job performance is likely to be higher. Suppose that Jacquelyn strongly values giving people with limited formal education an opportunity to work and avoid being placed on welfare. So she takes a job as a manager of a dollar store that employs many people who would ordinarily have limited opportunity for employment. Jacquelyn is satisfied because her employer and she share a similar value.

A group of researchers attempted to discover why congruence between individual and organizational values leads to positive outcomes such as low turnover and high performance. The major factor creating positive outcomes appears to be employees trusting managers based on the congruence. Communication also plays a role because when communication is regular, open, and consistent, trust is enhanced. For example, trust is enhanced when management explains the reasons behind major decisions. Good communication also enhances interpersonal attraction between managers and employees. Goal congruence also came about to a lesser extent because employees liked the managers. Liking, in turn, was enhanced by managers communicating well with employees.[49]

person–role conflict

The situation that occurs when the demands made by the organization clash with the basic values of the individual.

When the demands made by the organization or a superior clash with the basic values of the individual, he or she suffers from **person–role conflict**. The individual wants to obey orders, but does not want to perform an act that seems inconsistent with his or her

Clarifying Your Values

Directions: Rank from 1 to 20 the importance of the following values to you as a person. The most important value on the list receives a rank of 1; the least important a rank of 20. Use the space next to "Other" if the list has left out an important value in your life.

_____ Having my own place to live

_____ Having one or more children

_____ Having an interesting job and career

_____ Owning a car

_____ Having a good relationship with coworkers

_____ Having good health

_____ Spending considerable time on social networking Web sites

_____ Being able to stay in frequent contact with friends by cell phone and text messaging

_____ Watching my favorite television shows

_____ Participating in sports or other pastimes

_____ Following a sports team, athlete, music group, or other entertainer

_____ Being a religious person

_____ Helping people less fortunate than myself

_____ Loving and being loved by another person

_____ Having physical intimacy with another person

_____ Making an above-average income

_____ Being in good physical condition

_____ Being a knowledgeable, informed person

_____ Completing my formal education

_____ Other

1. Discuss and compare your ranking of these values with the person next to you.

2. Perhaps your class, assisted by your instructor, can arrive at a class average on each of these values. How does your ranking compare to the class ranking?

3. Look back at your own ranking. Does it surprise you?

4. Are there any surprises in the class ranking? Which values did you think would be highest and lowest?

values. A situation such as this might occur when an employee is asked to produce a product that he or she feels is unsafe or of no value to society.

Guidelines for Using Values to Enhance Interpersonal Relations

Values are intangible and abstract, and thus not easy to manipulate to help improve your interpersonal relations on the job. Despite their vagueness, values are an important driver of interpersonal effectiveness. Ponder the following guidelines:

LEARNING OBJECTIVE 5

1. Establish the values you will use in your relationships with others on the job, and then use those values as firm guidelines in working with others. For example, following the Golden Rule, you might establish the value of treating other people as you want to be treated. You would then not lie to others to gain personal advantage, and you would not backstab your rivals.

2. Establish the values that will guide you as an employee. When you believe that your values are being compromised, express your concern to your manager in a tactful and constructive manner. You might say to your manager, "Sorry, I choose not to tell our customers that our competitor's product is inferior just to make a sale. I choose not to say this because our competitor makes a fine product. But what I will say is that our service is exceptional."

3. Remember that many values are a question of opinion, not a statement of right versus wrong. If you believe that your values are right, and anybody who disagrees is wrong, you will have frequent conflict. For example, you may believe that the most important value top managers should have is to bring shareholders a high return on their investment. Another worker believes that profits are important, but providing jobs for as many people as possible is an equally important value. Both of you have a good point, but neither is right or wrong. So it is better to discuss these differences rather than hold grudges because of them.

4. Respect differences in values and make appropriate adjustment when the value clash is reasonable. If you are an older person, recognize that you may have to win the respect of a younger coworker rather than assume that because you are more experienced, or a manager, that respect will come automatically.[50] If you are a younger person, recognize that an older person might be looking for respect, so search for something you can respect right away, such as his or her many valuable contacts in the company.

5. Recognize that many people today are idealistic about their jobs, and want to have an impact on the lives of others.[51] In the meantime, you might feel that you need that person's cooperation to get an important task done right now, such as fulfilling a larger order. Invest a couple of minutes into helping that person understand how an ordinary task might be having an impact on the lives of others—such as earning money to feed a hungry baby at home!

To help you put these guidelines into practice, do Skill-Building Exercise 2-4. Remember, however, that being skilled at using your values requires day-by-day monitoring.

Concept Review
and Reinforcement

Key Terms

individual differences 43
personality 43
organizational citizenship
behavior 48
cognitive styles 50

cognitive intelligence 53
g (general) factor 54
s (special) factors 54
practical intelligence 55
intuition 55

multiple intelligences 55
emotional intelligence 56
value 58
ethics 59
person–role conflict 62

Summary

Individual differences are among the most important factors influencing the behavior of people in the workplace. Knowing how to respond to such differences is the cornerstone of effective interpersonal relations.

Personality is one of the major sources of individual differences. The eight major personality factors described in this chapter are neuroticism, extraversion, openness, agreeableness, conscientiousness, self-monitoring of behavior, risk taking and thrill seeking, and optimism. Depending on the job, any one of these personality factors can be important for success, and they also affect interpersonal relations. Conscientiousness relates to job performance for many different occupations, and has proven to be the personality factor most consistently related to success.

Personality also influences a person's cognitive style, or modes of problem solving. According to the Golden Personality Profiler, four separate dichotomies direct the typical use of perception and judgment by the individual as follows: (a) energy flow: extraversion vs. introversion, (b) information gathering: sensing vs. intuition, (c) decision making: thinking vs. feeling, and (d) lifestyle orientation: judging vs. perceiving. Combining the four types with each other results in 16 personality types, such as being a proponent, communicator, advocate, or enforcer. For example, the proponent (ENFP) scores high on extraversion, intuition, feeling, and perceiving.

Mental ability, or intelligence, is one of the major sources of individual differences that affects job performance and behavior. Understanding the nature of intelligence contributes to effective interpersonal relations in organizations. For example, understanding that different types of intelligence exist will help a person appreciate the strengths of individuals.

Intelligence consists of many components. The traditional perspective is that intelligence includes a general factor (g) along with special factors (s) that contribute to problem-solving ability. A related perspective is that intelligence consists of seven components: verbal comprehension, word fluency, numerical acuity, spatial perception, memory, perceptual speed, and inductive reasoning.

To overcome the idea that intelligence involves mostly the ability to solve abstract problems, the triarchic theory of intelligence has been proposed. According to this theory, intelligence has three subtypes: analytical, creative, and practical (street smarts included). Another approach to understanding mental ability contends that people have multiple intelligences, or faculties, including linguistic, logical-mathematical, musical, spatial, bodily kinesthetic, intrapersonal, interpersonal, and naturalist.

Emotional intelligence refers to factors other than traditional mental ability that influence a person's success. The four components of emotional intelligence are (1) self-awareness, (2) self-management, (3) social awareness, and (4) relationship management. Emotional intelligence is a skill through which employees treat emotions as valuable information when navigating a situation.

Values and beliefs are another set of factors that influence behavior on the job, including interpersonal relations. Values are closely tied in with ethics. A useful way of classifying values points to how we establish goals to fit our values, as shown in Table 2-1. Differences in values among people often stem from age, or generational, differences.

People acquire values in the process of growing up and modeling others, and the communication of attitudes. Later life influences such as the media also shape values.

The values a person develops early in life are directly related to the kind of adult he or she becomes and to the quality of relationships formed. Values-clarification exercises help people identify their values.

When the values of employees mesh with those required by the job, job performance is likely to be higher. **Person–role conflict** occurs when the demands made by an organization or a superior clash with the basic values of an individual.

Questions for Discussion and Review

1. Provide an example of how you have successfully taken into account individual differences in dealing with people. In what way did your approach make a difference in the outcome of the interaction with that person?

2. Suppose you found out from a reliable source that a coworker of yours is a high self-monitor. What precautions (if any) would you take in dealing with that person?

3. Identify three job situations (or entire jobs) in which being optimistic might be an asset.

4. Why might employees demonstrate a low level of organizational citizenship behavior?

5. Identify two business occupations for which a high propensity for risk taking and thrill seeking would be an asset. Also, identify two business occupations for which risk taking and thrill seeking might be a liability.

6. Imagine yourself going about your job in your field, or intended field. Give an example of how you might use the five primary senses of touch, sight, sound, smell, and taste to gather information.

7. Name three types of jobs that may benefit from a high level of emotional intelligence?

8. How could you use the concept of multiple intelligences to raise the self-esteem of people who did not consider themselves to be very smart?

9. Which aspect of personality, cognitive ability, or values would best help explain why so many actors, actresses, sports figures, politicans, and business executives damage their careers through such means as drunk driving, shoplifting, sexual harassment, or physically assaulting others?

10. How do you think your own personal values have been shaped?

The Web Corner

http://myskillprofile.com
(This site provides many self-quizzes, including emotional intelligence, sports mental skills, and spiritual intelligence. Several of the tests are free.)

http://www.queendom.com
(This site provides many tests and quizzes related to cognitive factors, personality, and emotional I.Q.)

http://www.annekreamer.com/its-always-personal/weep-survey
(Customized evaluation of your emotional style at work.)

Internet Skills Builder: Boosting Your Mental Ability

Do you want to be smarter? Thousands of specialists think they have developed intelligent ways of making people more intelligent. You will find at least 110 million Web sites that provide information about improving brain functioning through such methods as practice in problem solving and taking food supplements. Try out one of these sites. Evaluate the suggestions for plausibility. You might even try the exercises for a couple of weeks and observe whether you become smarter. Ask somebody close to you if have become smarter. You might also see if you do better on tests with the same amount of study and classroom attentiveness.

Developing Your Human Relations Skills

Interpersonal Relations Case 2.1

The Big Stakes Repo Men at International Recovery

The key players at the International Recovery Group are high-stakes repossession specialists, or "repo men" as they are commonly known. Their repossession targets are expensive properties such as $250,000 yachts or private planes worth $1 million. Banks and other lenders hire these repo specialists for the same reason they hire them to take back autos and trucks of more modest value; the loan holders have fallen way behind on their payments and have shown no good intention to catch up.

According to its owner, Ken Cage, business at International Recovery surges during a recession because many wealthy people, such as real estate developers, suffer a big loss in income. Senior repossession specialist and former professional wrestler, Randy Craft (formerly "Rockin' Randy"), says that carrying out "repos" can be dangerous. He says that he has been threatened with a snow shovel, run over by a car, and chased down a river by an enraged boat owner. (Craft has left the company to pursue other interests.)

When the business first started, Cage used to repossess mostly small airplanes and boats. As the business grows, he and his group seize much larger items, including multi-million dollar jets and yachts. International Recovery also repossesses race horses and exotic cars.

Cage and his colleagues use detective-like techniques to track down the property they are seeking, including asking disarming questions: "We were sent here to pick up this boat [while displaying a clear photo]. By any chance, have you seen it?" Cage has also developed a network of people who feed him the information he needs. Among these people are marine captains, tow-boat operators, jet-terminal workers, and aircraft pilots.

On a representative seizure, four repo men enter a marina in a truck. The group stays hidden in tall grass as they sight their target boat. One specialist quickly moves next to the target yacht, while the others stand lookout on the dock. Craft is especially skilled at lock picking, so he is the first inside the yacht. Cage unties the boat from the dock. A captain, who is part of the team, fires up the twin diesel engines. The yacht is then on its way to another marina, to be reclaimed by the bank and eventually resold.

Cage is cagey. He changes his natural Philadelphia regional accent to sound like a person from the region in which he is working, such as Florida, when he makes phone calls or interviews people face to face.

Case Questions

1. Which personality traits does Cage, as well as his coworkers, most likely demonstrate?
2. How much cognitive skill is probably required to be a repossession specialist at International Recovery Group?
3. How might practical intelligence contribute to success as a high-end repo specialist?
4. How might being a former professional wrestler be a contributing factor to success in this type of work?

Source: Original case created from facts presented in in the following sources: Robert Frank, "Cries of 'Hey, That's My Jet!' Don't Deter High-End Repo Men," *The Wall Street Journal*, March 20, 2010, pp. A1, A6; Matthew Teagure, "The Luxury Repo Men," *Bloomberg Businessweek* (http://www.businessweek. com), October 25, 2012, pp. 1–8; "Downturn Sees Rise in Repossessions of Yachts, Private Planes," *Voice of America* (http://www.voanews.com), November 2, 2009, pp. 1–2; Peter Howe, "A Day in the Life of a Luxury Repo Man," http://www. necn.com, 1–2, July 20, 2010.

Interpersonal Relations Case 2.2

A Values Clash at the Hearing Center

Jessica, a recent graduate in health administration, was delighted to be hired by the Brandon Hearing Centers as an office administrator for one of the two center locations. Her responsibilities included record keeping, dealing with vendors, accepting payments, bill paying, and monitoring the hearing center Web site, as well as fill-in responsibility as a receptionist. Brandon was operated by a husband-and-wife team of audiologists, who divided their time between the two locations.

Jessica enjoyed her new position for two key reasons. First, she was acquiring valuable ground-floor experience as a health administrator. Second, she felt she was making a contribution to helping people with hearing problems. Yet, she was concerned about one feature of her job; she had to receive and make so many phone calls to patients. Jessica thought that the Center's reliance on phone calls was both old-fashioned and a productivity drain. Jessica hinted at the problem several times to the Brandon couple, but her complaints were politely dismissed.

Several months into her position, Jessica asked to meet with Ted and Lucille Brandon about her concerns in relation to the communication mode used at the center. "I think we are in the communication dark ages around here," said Jessica. "I know that most of our patients are middle-aged or older, but still, they would probably prefer to send e-mails and text messages back and forth than make all these phone calls. Our Web site doesn't even indicate an e-mail address for our hearing center."

"Jessica, I think that you are confusing personal communication with business communication," said Lucille. "A few years ago we did give out an e-mail address for our patients, and the results were horrendous. Patients would send us e-mails day and night, and some of them would send six e-mails a day. So we turned back to telephone communication also."

"I agree with Lucille," said Ted. "And to take it one step further, I think I see a youth problem here. You probably think that texting is cool and the natural way to communicate. Especially with the assistance we provide, most of our patients prefer to use the phone because appointments with us are serious business. Text messages are more for social life and goofing around."

"I accept your reasoning for now," said Jessica. "But as a professional health administrator, I think we have to modernize communication at the Brandon Hearing Centers."

Questions

1. In what way does this case represent a problem of differences in generational values?
2. Why might excluding e-mails and text messages to and from patients lower productivity at the Brandon Hearing Center?
3. What do you think Jessica should do to change the opinions of the Brandons in relation to the communication mode? Or do you think Jessica should just drop the issue and try to understand the Brandons' point of view?

Interpersonal Relations Role-Play

Dealing with a Difference in Values

One student plays the role of Jessica, who wants to stay employed as the office administrator at the Brandon Hearing Center. However, she wants to remain true to her professional values of modernizing her workplace. Two other students play the roles of Lucille and Ted Brandon, who are meeting briefly with Jessica to listen to her thoughts about upgrading the electronic communications in the office. Ted and Lucille Brandon are becoming annoyed with Jessica's insistence on making changes in communicating with patients at the hearing center. Jessica is convinced she is right. Run the role-play for about seven minutes, with observers providing feedback about how well the differences in values are headed toward resolution.

References

1. Tom Belden, "Winging It: Sullenberger Touts the Value of Training," *Philly.com*, October 5, 2009; "Security Tape Shows Plane's Hudson Landing," *The Associated Press*, January 23, 2009; Andy Pastor, "Hero Pilot 'Sully' Stars at Hearing," *The Wall Street Journal*, June 10, 2009, p. A2.

2. Laurie Helgoe, "Revenge of the Introvert," *Psychology Today*, September/October 2010, p. 56.

3. Scott Shane, Nico Nolaou, Lynn Cherkas, and Tim D. Spector, "Genetics, the Big Five, and the Tendency to be Self-Employed," *Journal of Applied Psychology*, November 2010, pp. 1154–1162.

4. Marvin Zuckerman, "Are You A Risk Taker?" *Psychology Today*, November/December 2000, p. 53.

5. Leslie Kwoh, "Memo to Staff: Take More Risks," *The Wall Street Journal*, March 20, 2013, p. B8.

6. Remus Ilies and Timothy A. Judge, "On the Heritability of Job Satisfaction: The Mediating Role of Personality," *Journal of Applied Psychology*, August 2003, pp. 750–759.

7. Oliver Burkeman, "The Power of Negative Thinking," *The Wall Street Journal*, December 8–9, 2012, p. C3.

8. Quoted in Annie Murphy Paul, "The Uses and Abuses of Optimism (and Pessimism)," *Psychology Today*, November/December 2011, p. 63.

9. Daniel Nettle, "The Evolution of Personality Variation in Human and Other Animals," *American Psychologist*, September 2006, p. 622.

10. In-Sue Oh, Gang Wang, and Michyael K. Mount, "Validity of Observer Ratings of Five-Factor Model of Personality Traits: A Meta-Analysis," *Journal of Applied Psychology*, July 2011, pp. 762–773.

11. "Which Traits Predict Job Performance?" *APA Help Center, http://www.apahelpcenter.org/articles/article.php?id=33*, accessed March 22, 2005.

12. Nicole M. Dudley, Karin A. Orvis, Justin E. Lebiecki, and José M. Cortina, "A Meta-Analytic Investigation of Conscientiousness in the Prediction of Job Performance: Examining the Intercorrelations and the Incremental Validity of Narrow Traits," *Journal of Applied Psychology*, January 2006, p. 51.

13. Gregory M.Hurtz and John J. Donovan, "Personality and Job Performance: The Big Five Revisited," *Journal of Applied Psychology*, December 2000, pp. 869–879.

14. David V. Day, Deidra J. Scheleicher, Amy L. Unckless, and Nathan J. Hiller, "Self-Monitoring Personality at Work: A Meta-Analytic Investigation of Construct Validity," *Journal of Applied Psychology*, April 2002, pp. 390–401.

15. Gerald L. Blakely, Martha C. Andrews, and Jack Fuller, "Are Chameleons Good Citizens? A Longitudinal Study of the Relationship Between Self-Monitoring and Organizational Citizenship Behavior," *Journal of Business and Psychology,* Winter 2003, pp. 131–144; research synthesized in Ori Brafman and Rom Brafman, "To the Vulnerable Go the Spoils," *Bloomberg Business Week*, June 14–June 2, 2010, p. 72.

16. Dan S. Chiaburu, In-Sue Oh, Christopher M. Berry, Ning Li, and Richard G. Gardner, "The Five-Factor Model of Personality Traits and Organizational Citizenship Behaviors: A Meta-Analysis," *Journal of Applied Psychology*, November 2011, pp. 1140–1166.

17. Scott B. Mackenzie, Philip M. Podsakoff, and Nathan P. Podsakoff, "Challenge-Oriented Organizational Citizenship Behaviors and Organizational Effectiveness: Do Challenge-Oriented Behaviors Really Have an Impact on the Organization's Bottom Line?" *Personnel Psychology*, Number 3, 2011, p. 560.

18. Nathan P. Podsakoff, Whiting, S.W., Podsakoff, P.M., and Blume, B.D, "Individual- and Organizational-Level Consequences of Organizational Behaviors: A Meta-Analysis, *Journal of Applied Psychology*, January 2009, pp. 122–141.

19. Jeff Joireman, Dishan Kamdar, Denise Daniels, and Blythe Duell, "Good Citizens to the End? It Depends: Empathy and Concern with Future Consequences Moderate the Impact of a Short-Term Time Horizon on Organizational Citizenship Behaviors," *Journal of Applied Psychology*, November 2006, p. 1315.

20. Ryan D. Zimmerman, "Understanding the Impact of Personality Traits on Individuals' Turnover Decisions: A Meta-Analytic Path Model," *Personnel Psychology*, Summer 2008, pp. 309–348.

21. Cited in David Stripp, "A Little Worry Is Good for Business," *Fortune*, November 24, 2003, p. 68.

22. L. A. Witt, Lisa A. Burke, Murray R. Barrick, and Michael K. Mount, "The Interactive Effects of Conscientiousness and Agreeableness on Job Performance," *Journal of Applied Psychology*, February 2002, pp. 164–169.

23. Isabel Briggs Myers, *Introduction to Type,* 6th ed. (Mountain View, CA: CPP, Inc., 1996), p. 10. (Revised by Linda K. Kirby and Katharine D. Myers.)

24. John Patrick Golden, *Golden Personality Type Profiler Technical Manual* (San Antonio, TX: Pearson TalentLens, 2005).

25. Golden, *Golden Personality Type Profiler*, p. 27.

26. Golden, *Golden Personality Type Profiler*, p. 24.

27. Brian S. Young, Winfred Arthur, Jr., and John Finch, "Predictors of Managerial Performance: More than Cognitive Ability," *Journal of Business and Psychology*, Fall 2000, pp. 53–72.

28. Roderick Gilkey and Clint Kitts, "Cognitive Fitness," *Harvard Business Review*, November 2007, pp. 53–66.

29. Richard E, Nesbitt et al., "Intelligence: New Findings and Theoretical Developments," *American Psychologist*, February–March 2012, p. 130.

30. Nesbitt, et al., "Intelligence," p. 139.

31. Evidence reviewed in Laura Johannes, "An Energy Shot for the Brain," *The Wall Street Journal*, January 24, 2012, p. D3.

32. J. Robert Baum, Barbara Jean Bird, and Sheetal Singh, "The Practical Intelligence of Entrepreneurs: Antecedents and a Link with New Venture Growth," *Personnel Psychology*, Number 2, 2011, p. 39.

33. Baum, Bird, and Singh, "The Practical Intelligence of Entrepreneurs," pp. 397–425.

34. Howard Gardner, *Intelligence Reframed: Multiple Intelligence in the 21st Century* (New York: Basic Books, 1999); Mark K. Smith, "Howard Gardner and Multiple Intelligences," in *The Encyclopedia of Informal Education* (http://www.infed.or/thinkers/gardner.htm), © Mark K. Smith, 2002, 2008.

35. Malcolm Gladwell, *Outliers: The Story of Success* (Boston: Little, Brown, 2008). See also Geoff Colvin, "Why Talent is Over-Rated," *Fortune*, October 27, 2008, pp. 138–147.

36. Sharon Begley, "Critical Thinking: Part Skill, Part Mindset and Totally up to You," *The Wall Street Journal*, October 20, 2006, p. B1.

37. John D. Mayer, Peter Salovey, and David R. Caruso, "Emotional Intelligence: New Ability or Eclectic Traits?" *American Psychologist*, September 2008, pp. 503–515.

38. Daniel Goleman, Richard Boyatzis, and Annie McKee, "Primal Leadership: The Hidden Driver of Great Performance," *Harvard Business Review*, December 2001, pp. 42–51.

39. David A. Morand, "The Emotional Intelligence of Managers: Assessing the Construct Validity of a Nonverbal Measure of 'People Skills,'" *Journal of Business and Psychology*, Fall 2001, pp. 21–33.

40. Study reported in Anne Kreamer, "Go Ahead—Cry at Work," *Time*, April 4, 2011, p. 55.

41. Crystal I. C. Chien Farh, Myeong-Gu Seo, and Paul E. Tesluk, "Emotional Intelligence, Teamwork Effectiveness, and Job Performance: The Moderating Role of Context," *Journal of Applied Psychology*, July 2012, pp. 890–900.

42. Shalom H. Schwartz, "Universals in the Content and Structure of Values: Theoretical Advances and Empirical Tests in 20 Countries." In Mark P. Zanna, ed., *Advances in Experimental and Social Psychology* (New York: Academic Press, vol. 25, 1992), pp. 1–65.

43. Jeff Payne, "Generation Jones, Still Striving," *HR Magazine*, December 2008, p. 15. (From Readers section.)

44. Helen M. Haugh and Alka Talwar, "How Do Corporations Embed Sustainability Across the Organization?" *Academy of Management Learning and Education*, September 2010, p. 385.

45. Adrienne Fox, "Mixing It Up," *HR Magazine*, May 2011, p. 22.

46. 2008 Annual Report of the APA Policy and Planning Board, "How Technology Changes Everything (and Nothing) in Psychology, *American Psychologist*, July–August 2009, p. 454.

47. Fara Warner, "With their Blessing." *Workforce Management*, April 2011, p. 20.

48. David C. McClelland, "How Motives, Skills, and Values Determine What People Do," *American Psychologist*, July 1985, p. 815.

49. Jeffrey R. Edwards and Daniel M. Cable, "The Value of Value Congruence," *Journal of Applied Psychology*, May 2009, pp. 654–677.

50. Jean M. Twenge, *Generation Me* (New York: The Free Press, 2006).

51. "Get Ready for 'Millennials' at Work," *Manager's Edge*, January 2006, p. 1.

Building Self-Esteem and Self-Confidence

"My career began in the purchasing department of a large company," says John, a real-estate professional. "I felt stifled by how long it would take me to get promoted. I left the company to become a sales representative for a small real estate company. Soon I was performing so well that I was lured away to a larger, more prestigious company, Holloway Properties. I started out with a bang, and kept up the fast pace. Don Holloway, the owner, kept praising me and telling me how I was going to enable him to retire early.

Granger Wootz/Getty Images

After studying the information and performing the exercises in this chapter, you should be able to

1. Describe the nature, development, and consequences of self-esteem.
2. Explain how to enhance self-esteem.
3. Describe the importance of self-confidence and self-efficacy.
4. Pinpoint methods of enhancing and developing your self-confidence.

"One day Don asked me if I would be interested in purchasing the company. I told him that I was interested, but had limited funds. He told me he would lend me the money to buy his firm. Against the advice of my friends, I bought the business. The agreements between Don and me were spoken rather than written. The business was going very well for three years. I was beginning to see a bright future when the bottom fell out. Don had encountered some hard times and wanted the business back. He had gone through all the payments I made to him for his company. I was devastated! When I tried to fight him through a lawsuit, I had only spoken agreements to offer as proof.

"I lost all my savings, my house, and was forced to file for bankruptcy. I had reached what I thought was the darkest and most humiliating point in my life. I was filled with a sense of worthlessness and despair. I wondered what I could have done to deserve this.

"After several months of feeling sorry for myself, I visited a career counselor and got his recommendations about making a new start. His first recommendation was to make a list of my strengths and weaknesses. Second, he suggested that I ask myself what I really like to do. He also suggested that I should list goals that I wanted to attain and a prioritized plan of how I hoped to accomplish them.

"I was advised to make positive steps and improve both my morale and my self-image through the sense of achievement that comes from accomplishing these goals. With the help of my wife and the counselor, I began getting back on track. My early accomplishments included such positive steps as reducing my intake of wine and updating my résumé. Two months later I found a position as an assistant manager in a real estate firm that dealt with both commercial and residential properties. I was also given the opportunity to sell part time. Finally, I felt that my comeback was unfolding."

The story about the real-estate agent illustrates that a person can take steps to rebuild lowered self-confidence and self-esteem. Many other people you will meet in this book score high in self-esteem and self-confidence—otherwise they would never have been so successful. In this chapter, we focus on two of the biggest building blocks for more effective human relations: the nature and development of self-esteem and self-confidence. The development of both self-esteem and self-confidence includes refining certain skills.

THE MEANING OF SELF-ESTEEM, ITS DEVELOPMENT AND CONSEQUENCES

Understanding the self from various perspectives is important because who you are and what you think of yourself influence many different facets of your life both on and off the job. A particularly important role is played by **self-esteem,** the overall evaluation people make about themselves—whether positive or negative.[1] A useful distinction is that our

LEARNING OBJECTIVE 1

self-concept is what we *think* about ourselves, whereas self-esteem is what we *feel* about ourselves.[2] People with positive self-esteem have a deep-down, inside-the-self feeling of their own worth. Consequently, they develop a positive self-concept. Before reading further, you are invited to measure your current level of self-esteem by doing the Human Relations Self-Assessment Quiz 3-1. We look next at the development of self-esteem and many of its consequences.

HUMAN RELATIONS SELF-ASSESSMENT QUIZ 3-1

The Self-Esteem Checklist

Indicate whether each of the following statements is mostly true or mostly false as it applies to you.

	Mostly True	Mostly False
1. I am excited about starting each day.	_____	_____
2. Most of any progress I have made in my work or school can be attributed to luck.	_____	_____
3. I often ask myself, "Why can't I be more successful?"	_____	_____
4. When my manager or team leader gives me a challenging assignment, I usually dive in with confidence.	_____	_____
5. I believe that I am working up to my potential.	_____	_____
6. I am able to set limits to what I will do for others without feeling anxious.	_____	_____
7. I regularly make excuses for my mistakes.	_____	_____
8. Negative feedback crushes me.	_____	_____
9. I care very much how much money other people make, especially when they are working in my field.	_____	_____
10. I feel like a failure when I do not achieve my goals.	_____	_____
11. Hard work gives me an emotional lift.	_____	_____
12. When others compliment me, I doubt their sincerity.	_____	_____
13. Complimenting others makes me feel uncomfortable.	_____	_____
14. I find it comfortable to say, "I'm sorry."	_____	_____
15. It is difficult for me to face up to my mistakes.	_____	_____
16. My coworkers think I am not worthy of promotion.	_____	_____
17. People who want to become my friends usually do not have much to offer.	_____	_____
18. If my manager praised me, I would have a difficult time believing it was deserved.	_____	_____
19. I'm just an ordinary person.	_____	_____
20. Having to face change really disturbs me.	_____	_____
21. When I make a mistake, I have no fear of owning up to it in public.	_____	_____
22. When I look in the mirror, I typically see someone who is attractive and confident.	_____	_____
23. When I think about the greater purpose in my life, I feel like I am drifting.	_____	_____
24. When I make a mistake, I tend to feel ashamed and embarrassed.	_____	_____
25. When I make a commitment to myself, I usually stick to it with conviction and await the rewards that I believe will come from it.	_____	_____

Scoring and Interpretation: The answers in that indicate high self-esteem are as follows:

1. Mostly True	5. Mostly True	9. Mostly False	13. Mostly False
2. Mostly False	6. Mostly True	10. Mostly False	14. Mostly True
3. Mostly False	7. Mostly False	11. Mostly True	15. Mostly False
4. Mostly True	8. Mostly False	12. Mostly False	16. Mostly False

(Continued)

How Self-Esteem Develops

Part of understanding the nature of self-esteem is to know how it develops. Self-esteem develops and evolves throughout our lives based on interactions with people, events, and things.[3] As an adolescent or adult, your self-esteem might be boosted by a key accomplishment. A 44-year-old woman who was studying to become licensed practical nurse (LPN) said that her self-esteem increased when she received an A in a pharmacology course. Self-esteem can also go down in adulthood because of a negative event such as being laid off and not being able to find new employment.

Early life experiences have a major impact on self-esteem. People who were encouraged to feel good about themselves and their accomplishments by family members, friends, and teachers are more likely to enjoy high self-esteem. Early life experiences play a key role in the development of both healthy self-esteem and low self-esteem, according to research synthesized at the Counseling and Mental Health Center of the University of Texas.[4] Childhood experiences that lead to healthy self-esteem include

- being praised,
- being listened to,
- being spoken to respectfully,
- getting attention and hugs, and
- experiencing success in sports or school.

In contrast, childhood experiences that lead to low self-esteem include

- being harshly criticized,
- being yelled at or beaten,
- being ignored, ridiculed, or teased,
- being expected to be "perfect" all the time,
- experiencing failures in sports or school, and
- often being given messages that failed experiences (losing a game, getting a poor grade, and so forth) were failures of their whole self.

A widespread explanation of self-esteem development is that compliments, praise, and hugs alone build self-esteem. Yet many developmental psychologists seriously question this perspective. Instead, they believe that self-esteem results from accomplishing worthwhile activities and then feeling proud of these accomplishments. Receiving encouragement, however, can help the person accomplish activities that build self-esteem.

Martin Seligman argues that self-esteem is caused by a variety of successes and failures. To develop self-esteem, people need to improve their skills for dealing with the world.[5] Self-esteem therefore comes about by genuine accomplishments, followed by praise and recognition. Heaping undeserved praise and recognition on people may lead to a temporary high, but it does not produce genuine self-esteem. The child develops self-esteem not from being told he or she can score a goal in soccer, but from scoring that goal.

In attempting to build the self-esteem of children and students, many parents and teachers give children too many undeserved compliments. Researchers suggest that inappropriate compliments are turning too many adults into narcissistic praise junkies. As a result, many young adults feel insecure if they do not receive compliments regularly.[6]

As mentioned previously, experiences in adult life can influence the development of self-esteem. David De Cremer of the Tilburg University (Netherlands) and his associates conducted two studies with Dutch college students about how the behavior of leaders and fair procedures influence self-esteem. The focus of the leader's behavior was whether he or she motivated the workers/students to reward *themselves* for a job well done, such as a self-compliment. Procedural fairness was measured in terms of whether the study participants were given a voice in making decisions. Self-esteem was measured by a questionnaire somewhat similar to the Human Relations Self-Assessment Quiz 3-1 in this chapter. The study questionnaire reflected the self-perceived value that individuals have of themselves as organizational members.

The study found that self-esteem was related to procedural fairness and leadership that encourages self-rewards. When leadership that encouraged rewards was high, procedural fairness was more strongly related to self-esteem. The interpretation given of the findings is that a leader/supervisor can facilitate self-esteem when he or she encourages self-rewards, and uses fair procedures. Furthermore, fair procedures have a stronger impact on self-esteem when the leader encourages self-rewards.[7] A takeaway from this study would be that rewarding yourself for a job well done, even in adult life, can boost your self-esteem a little.

The Consequences of Self-Esteem

Extremely high as well as extremely low self-esteem has many consequences for people, as outlined in Table 3-1.

Career Success.   A major consequence of having high self-esteem is that you have a better chance of attaining career success, as mentioned at the beginning of this section and supported by long-term research. The study in question was known as the National Longitudinal Survey of Youth, involving over 12,000 young men and women. The group was studied over a 25-year period beginning in 1979. The Human Relations Self-Assessment Quiz 3-2 gives you the opportunity to take the same survey used in the study to measure core self-evaluations.

The components of core self-evaluations include high self-esteem, self-efficacy (an aspect of self-confidence described later in this chapter), beliefs in personal control over events, and emotional stability. Individuals with high core self-evaluations are better motivated, perform better on the job, tend to hold more challenging jobs, and have higher job satisfaction.

TABLE 3-1   Several Consequences of Extremes in Self-Esteem

Positive Consequences	Negative Consequences
1. Career success including a high income	1. Narcissism
2. Organizational prosperity	2. Envying too many people
3. Good mental health	3. Romance problems
4. Profiting from feedback	
5. Serves as a guide for regulating social relationships	

National Longitudinal Survey of Youth Measure of Core Self-Evaluations

No.		True	False
1.	I have little control over the things that happen to me.	❑	❑
2.	There is little I can do to change many of the important things in my life.	❑	❑
3.	I feel that I am a person of worth, on an equal basis with others.	❑	❑
4.	I feel that I have a number of good qualities.	❑	❑
5.	All in all, I am inclined to feel that I am a failure.	❑	❑
6.	I feel I do not have much to be proud of.	❑	❑
7.	I wish I could have more respect for myself.	❑	❑
8.	I've been depressed.	❑	❑
9.	I've felt hopeful about the future.	❑	❑
10.	What happens to me in the future depends on me.	❑	❑
11.	What happens to me is of my own doing.	❑	❑
12.	When I make plans, I am almost certain to make them work.	❑	❑

Scoring and Interpretation: The answers that indicate high core self-evaluation are as follows:

1.	False	4.	True	7.	False	10.	True
2.	False	5.	False	8.	False	11.	True
3.	True	6.	False	9.	True	12.	True

Although there are no specific categories for scores, the more statements you answered in the direction of high core self-evaluations, the more likely it is that you have the type of core self-evaluations that will facilitate career success.

Questions:

1. How does your score on this quiz match your evaluation of your self-evaluation?
2. How does your score on this quiz compare to your score on Self-Assessment Quiz 3-1?
3. How can you explain the fact that responses to the preceding statements were found to be related to long-term career success?

Sources: The statements are from the National Longitudinal Survey of Youth (NLSY79), a study commissioned and operated by the Bureau of Labor Statistics, US Department of Labor. The statements are also reported in Timothy A. Judge and Charlice Hurst, "How the Rich (and Happy) Get Richer (and Happier): Relationship of Core Self-Evaluations to Trajectories in Attaining Work Success," *Journal of Applied Psychology*, July 2008, p. 863.

Among the many results of the study were that people with higher core evaluations performed better in their first jobs. Furthermore, over time, those people with high core evaluations increase their career success at a faster pace than those with below-average core evaluations. Over a 25-year span, the career success they have over others doubles. Success was measured in terms of job satisfaction, pay, and holding a higher-status position.[8] A practical conclusion to take away from this study is that if you have high core self-evaluations, it will pay impressive career dividends.

Later research suggests that people with high core self-evaluations are more likely to have high job performance when they combine positive attitudes toward the self with a concern for the welfare of others. (Consistently good job performance enhances career success.) For example, call-center employees with positive core self-evaluations tended to perform better when they worried about letting other people down. The call-center work involved telemarketing to generate funds to support new jobs at a university.[9]

Organizational Prosperity.   The combined effect of workers having high self-esteem helps a company prosper. Self-esteem is a critical source of competitive advantage in an information society. Companies gain the edge when, in addition to having an educated workforce, employees have high self-esteem, as shown by such behaviors as the following:

- Being creative and innovative
- Taking personal responsibility for problems

- Having a feeling of independence (yet still wanting to work cooperatively with others)
- Trusting one's own capabilities
- Taking the initiative to solve problems[10]

Behaviors such as these help you cope with the challenge of a rapidly changing workplace in which products and ideas become obsolete quickly. Workers with high self-esteem are more likely to be able to cope with new challenges regularly because they are confident that they can master their environments.

Good Mental Health.   One of the major consequences of high self-esteem is good mental health. People with high self-esteem feel good about themselves and have a positive outlook on life. One of the links between good mental health and self-esteem is that high self-esteem helps prevent many situations from being stressful. Few negative comments from others are likely to bother you when your self-esteem is high. A person with low self-esteem might crumble if somebody insulted his or her appearance. A person with high self-esteem might shrug off the insult as simply being the other person's point of view. If faced with an everyday setback, such as losing keys, the high self-esteem person might think, "I have so much going for me, why fall apart over this incident?"

Positive self-esteem also conributes to good mental health because it helps us ward off being troubled by feelings of jealousy and acting aggressively toward others because of our jealousy. Particularly with adolescents, lower self-worth leads to jealousy about friends liking other people better.[11]

Profiting from Negative Feedback.   Although people with high self-esteem can readily shrug off undeserved insults, they still profit well from negative feedback. Because they are secure, they can profit from the developmental opportunities suggested by negative feedback. Workers with high self-esteem develop and maintain favorable work attitudes and perform at high levels. These positive consequences take place because such attitudes and behaviors are consistent with the personal belief that they are competent individuals. Mary Kay Ash, the legendary founder of beauty products company Mary Kay, put it this way: "It never occurred to me I couldn't do it. I always knew that if I worked hard enough, I could." Furthermore, research has shown that high-self-esteem individuals value reaching work goals more than do low-self-esteem individuals.[12]

Serves as a Guide for Regulating Social Relationships.   Another positive consequence of self-esteem is that you can use it as a guide in regulating social relationships. According to Mark Leary, director of social psychology at Duke University, self-esteem provides a gauge of performance during social interactions: "Self-esteem rises and falls, acting as an internal barometer of how well you're faring, telling you to fix this problem here, and helping you understand that you don't have to worry about it there."[13]

Following this reasoning, fluctuations in self-esteem provide information that is useful in working your way through social relationships. For example, if you are talking and the person you are talking to yawns, your self-esteem drops, signaling you to change the topic. When you tell a joke, and people laugh, your self-esteem climbs rapidly. If we did not feel bad when we bored or offended others, or satisfied when we delighted them, we would not be inclined to change course.[14]

Potential Negative Consequences.   Both high and low self-esteem can sometimes have negative consequences. Three reasons for this problem are described next.

1. **Exaggerated levels of self-esteem can lead to narcissism.** Self-esteem can elevate to a level whereby the individual becomes self-absorbed to the point of having little concern for others, leading to narcissistic attitudes and behaviors. **Narcissism** is an extremely positive view of the self, combined with limited empathy for others. Quite often extreme narcissism can hamper success because the narcissist irritates

and alienates others in the workplace. A frequent human relations problem with office narcissists is that they are poor listeners because they attempt to dominate conversations by talking about themselves. Yet the right amount and type of narcissism can at times facilitate success because the narcissist appears to be self-confident and charismatic.[15]

2. **Envying too many people.** A potential negative consequence of low self-esteem is envying too many people. If you perceive that many individuals have much more of what you want and are more worthwhile than you, you will suffer from enormous envy. To decrease pangs of envy, it is best to develop realistic standards of comparison between you and other people in the world.

    If high school basketball player Joshua measures his self-esteem in terms of how well he stacks up with basketball superstar and super-millionaire LeBron James, young Joshua will take a lot of blows to his self-esteem. However, if Joshua compares himself to other players on his team and in his league, his self-esteem will be higher because he has chosen a more realistic reference group. For example, Joshua might think that Kent, the starting point guard on his team, has a good chance of winning a basketball scholarship to college, speaks intelligently, and is well groomed. Joshua works hard to develop the same potential and behaviors. When he believes he has succeeded, Joshua will experience a boost in self-esteem.

    Kristin Neff, a professor of educational psychology at the University of Texas at Austin, supports the idea that making social comparisons can lead to problems with self-esteem. She explains that in American culture, people tend to acquire a sense of self-worth from feeling special. A musician who compares herself to a musician of less talent will feel superior, and even have a boost in self-esteem. But if she compares herself to a more talented musician, she will feel a decrease in self-esteem even if her talent and skills have not diminished.[16]

3. **Poor romantic relationships when self-esteem is low.** Low self-esteem can have negative consequences for romantic relationships because people with self-doubts consistently underestimate their partners' feelings for them. People with low self-respect distance themselves from the relationship—often devaluing their partner—to prepare themselves for what they think will be an inevitable breakup. (**Self-respect** refers to how you think and feel about yourself.) John G. Holmes, a psychologist at the University of Waterloo in Ontario, Canada, says, "If people think negatively about themselves, they think their partner must think negatively about them—and they're wrong."[17]

ENHANCING SELF-ESTEEM

Improving self-esteem is a lifelong process because self-esteem is related to the success of your activities and interactions with people. The following are approaches to enhancing self-esteem that are related to how self-esteem develops. (See Figure 3-1.) Each of these approaches has a skill component, such as learning to avoid situations that make you feel incompetent. In addition to working on skills to enhance self-esteem, it is helpful to maintain a constructive attitude. A representative statement to keep in mind as you work on self-esteem enhancement is as follows:[18]

LEARNING OBJECTIVE 2

"I am a very special, unique, and valuable person. I deserve to feel good about myself."

Attain Legitimate Accomplishments

To emphasize again, accomplishing worthwhile activities is a major contributor to self-esteem (as well as self-confidence) in both children and adults. Social science research suggests this sequence of events: Person establishes a goal; person pursues the goal; person achieves the goal; person develops esteem-like feelings.[19] The opposite point of view is this sequence: Person develops esteem-like feelings; person establishes a goal; person pursues the goal; person achieves the goal. Similarly, giving people large trophies for mundane

FIGURE 3-1 Methods of Enhancing Self-Esteem

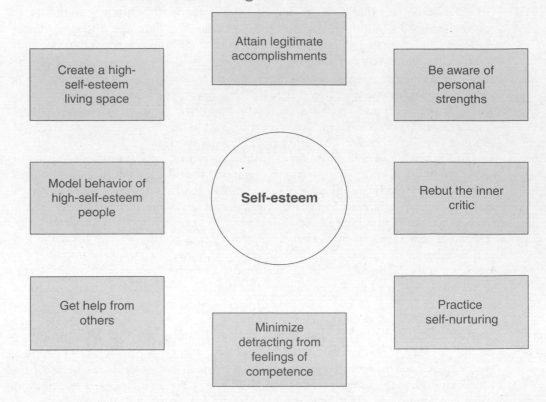

accomplishments is unlikely to raise self-esteem. More likely, the person will see through the transparent attempt to build his or her self-esteem and develop negative feelings about the self. What about you? Would your self-esteem receive a bigger boost by (1) receiving an A in a course in which 10 percent of the class received an A or by (2) receiving an A in a class in which everybody received the same grade?

Bragging about legitimate accomplishments will often give a modest boost to self-esteem. Social media posts are a natural place for bragging, with statements such as "Just aced an advanced statistics exam," or "Yesterday I received the maximum possible rating in my performance evaluation. I feel great." Although such bragging can annoy some people, it can increase our self-esteem (as well as narcissism!).[20]

Legitimate accomplishments are more effective in raising self-esteem when the legitimacy of these accomplishments is not dependent on what others think about them. *Contingent self-esteem* refers to feelings of self-worth that depend on outside praise in a realm that matters to a person.[21] An example of non-contingent self-esteem would be redecorating your work area and feeling proud because it is aesthetically pleasing. Contingent self-esteem would be not feeling proud about your redecorated cubicle until somebody else complimented the result. Keep in mind, however, that we cannot exclude outside validation as a source of self-esteem unless we are delusional. If several people who walked by your redecorated cubicle laughed at the design, it might be difficult to think you had made a legitimate accomplishment.

Be Aware of Personal Strengths

Another method of improving your self-esteem is to develop an appreciation of your strengths and accomplishments. A good starting point is to list your strengths and accomplishments in a word-processing document or on paper. This list is likely to be more impressive than you expected.

You can sometimes develop an appreciation of your strengths by participating in a group exercise designed for such purposes. A group of about seven people meet to form a support group. All group members first spend about 10 minutes answering the question,

Reinforcing a Positive Self-Image

To do this exercise, you will need a piece of paper and a pencil or pen, or a word processor, and a timer or clock. Set a timer for 10 minutes or note the time on your watch, smartphone, or a clock. Write your name across the top of the document. Then write everything positive and good you can think of about yourself. Include special attributes, talents, and achievements. You can use single words or sentences. You can write the same things over and over if you want to emphasize them. Your ideas do not have to be well organized. Write down whatever comes to mind. You are the only one who will see this document. Avoid using any negative words. Use only positive ones.

When the 10 minutes are up, read the document over to yourself. You may feel sad when you read it over because it is a new, different, and positive way of thinking about yourself. Your document will contradict some of the negative thoughts you have had about yourself. Those feelings will diminish as you reread this document. Read the document over again several times. Print the document if you used a computer, and put it in a convenient place, such as in your pocket, purse, wallet, or on your bedside table. Read it over at least once a day to keep reminding yourself of how great you are! Find a private space and read it aloud. If you have a good friend or family member who is supportive, read it to that person. Maybe your confidant can think of a positive attribute that you have missed.

Source: Adapted from "Building Self-Esteem: A Self-Help Guide," http://store. samhsa.gov/product/Building-Self-Esteem-A-Self-Help-Guide/SMA-3715, accessed July 22, 2013.

"What are my three strongest points, attributes, or skills?" After each group member records his or her three strengths, the person discusses them with the other group members.

Each group member then comments on the list. Other group members sometimes add to your list of strengths or reinforce what you have to say. Sometimes you may find disagreement. One member told the group, "I'm handsome, intelligent, reliable, athletic, self-confident, and very moral. I also have a good sense of humor." Another group member retorted, "And I might add that you're unbearably conceited."

Skill-Building Exercises 3-1 and 3-2 provide additional ways of developing self-esteem, both of which focus on appreciation of strengths.

Rebut the Inner Critic

Another early step in attaining better self-esteem is to rebut your inner critic—the voice inside you that sends negative messages about your capabilities. Rebutting critical statements

The Self-Esteem Building Club

You and your classmates are invited to participate in one of the most humane and productive possible human-relations skill-building exercises, membership in the "self-esteem building club." Your assignment is for three consecutive weeks to help build the self-esteem of one person. Before embarking upon the exercise, review the information about self-esteem development in this chapter. One of the most effective tactics would be to find somebody who had a legitimate accomplishment, and give that person a reward or a thank you. Record carefully what the person did, what you did, and any behavioral reactions of the person whose self-esteem you attempted to build. An example follows, written by a 46-year-old student of human relations:

Thursday night two weeks ago, I went to the athletic club to play racquetball. Different than usual, I had a date after the club. I wanted to look good, so I decided to wear my high school class ring. The ring doesn't have much resale value, but I was emotionally attached to it, having worn it for special occasions for 28 years. I stuffed the ring along with my watch and wallet in my athletic bag.

When I was through with racquetball, I showered, and got dressed. My ring was missing from my bag even though my wallet and watch were there. I kind of freaked out because I hate to lose a prized possession.

I shook the bag out three times, but no luck. Very discouraged, I left my name, telephone number, and e-mail address at the front desk just in case somebody turned in the ring. I kept thinking that I must have lost the ring when I stopped at the desk to check in.

The next morning before going to class, I got a phone call from a front-desk clerk at the club. The clerk told me that Karl, from the housekeeping staff, heard a strange noise while he was vacuuming near the front desk. He shut off the vacuum cleaner immediately, and pulled out my ring. To me Karl was a hero. I made a special trip to the club that night to meet with Karl. I shook his hand, and gave him a ten-dollar bill as a reward. I also explained to Karl what a difference he had made in my mood. I told him that honest, hardworking people like him who take pride in their work make this world a better place. It made my day when Karl smiled and told me it was a pleasure to be helpful.

Your instructor might organize a sharing of self-esteem building episodes in the class. If the sharing does take place, look for patterns of what seemed to work in terms of self-esteem building. Also, listen for any patterns in failed attempts at self-esteem building.

about you might also be considered another way of appreciating your strengths. Two examples of rebutting your inner critic follow:[22]

> Your unfairly harsh inner critic says: "People said they liked my presentation, but it was nowhere as good as it should have been. I can't believe no one noticed all the places I messed up. I'm such an imposter."

> Your reassuring rebuttal: "Wow, they really liked it. Maybe it wasn't perfect, but I worked hard on that presentation and did a good job. I'm proud of myself. This was a great success."

> Your harsh inner critic makes leaps of illogic: "He is frowning. He didn't say anything, but I know it means that he doesn't like me!"

> Your rebuttal that challenges the illogic: "Okay, he's frowning, but I don't know why. It could have nothing to do with me. Maybe I should ask."

The above statements are examples of the type of putdowns we often hear from our inner critic. To boost your self-esteem in spite of such criticism, you need to develop the skill of rebuttal by rebutting your inner critic frequently.

Practice Self-Nurturing

Although you may be successful at pointing to your strengths and rebutting the inner voice that puts you down, it is also helpful to treat yourself as a worthwhile person. Start to challenge negative experiences and messages from the past by nurturing and caring for yourself in ways that show how valuable, competent, deserving, and lovable you really are. Self-nurturing is often referred to as treating yourself well or spoiling yourself. Here are two suggestions for self-nurturing, both of which involve a modest amount of skill development.

- **Administer self-rewards for a job well done.** When you have carried out an activity especially well in relation to your typical performance, reward yourself in a small, constructive way. You might dine at a favorite restaurant, take an afternoon off to go for a nature walk, or spend an hour at a Web site you usually do not have the time to visit.
- **Take good care of yourself mentally and physically.** Make sure that you get enough sleep and rest, eat nutritious foods, avoid high-bacteria environments such as a public keyboard or doornob unless you use a bacteria spray, and participate in moderate physical exercise. Even taking an extra shower or bath can give you a physical and mental boost. The suggestions just mentioned are also part of stress management.

Real estate agent Laura provides a helpful example of how self-nurturing can help bolster self-esteem. While watching Todd, her son, play soccer at four in the afternoon, she was asked by another soccer parent, "How's business?" Laura replied, "I haven't made a deal in two weeks, but I know times will get better. So for now, I'm enjoying myself watching Todd play his little heart out. Afterwards we are going for pizza, and a few video games. My soul will be energized again."

Minimize Settings and Interactions That Detract from Your Feelings of Competence

Most of us have situations in our work and personal lives that make us feel less than our best. If you can minimize exposure to those situations, you will have fewer feelings of incompetence. The problem with feeling incompetent is that it lowers your self-esteem. Suppose, for example, that Sally is a very poor golf player, and intensely dislikes the sport. She is better off excusing herself from a small group of people at the office who invite her to a golf outing. A problem with avoiding all situations in which you feel not fully competent is that it might prevent you from acquiring needed skills. Also, it boosts your self-confidence and self-esteem to become comfortable in a previously uncomfortable situation. In Sally's case, perhaps she can eventually learn to play golf better, and then she will be mentally prepared to participate in golf outings.

Get Help from Others

Self-esteem is strongly shaped by how others perceive us, so getting help from others is a major step a person can take to improve his or her self-esteem. However, getting help from others can also be difficult. People with low self-esteem often do not ask for help because they may not think they are worthy of receiving help. Yet help from others is effective in overcoming the negative messages received from others in the past.

Asking for support from friends can include such basic steps as these: (1) Ask friends to tell you what they like about you or think that you do well. (2) Ask someone who cares about you to listen to you complain about something without offering a solution to your problem. (3) Ask for a hug. (4) Ask someone who loves you to remind you that he or she does.

Getting help from teachers and other helpers can include these steps: (1) Ask professors or tutors for help with work you find challenging. (2) If you lack self-confidence in certain areas, take classes or attempt new activities to increase your competence. An increasing number of retired people today are taking classes in such subjects as social media utilization and digital photography to help catch up with younger people whose skills have challenged their self-esteem.[23]

Another way of getting help from others is to talk and socialize frequently with people who can boost your self-esteem. Psychologist Barbara Ilardie says that the people who can raise your self-esteem are usually those with high self-esteem themselves. They are the people who give honest feedback because they respect others and themselves. Such high self-esteem individuals should not be confused with yes-people who agree with others just to be liked. The point is that you typically receive more from strong people than weak ones. Weak people will flatter you but will not give you the honest feedback you need to build self-esteem.[24]

For many people with low self-esteem, casual help with others will not increase self-esteem. In these situations, discussing low self-esteem with a mental health specialist might be the most effective measure.

Model the Behavior of People with High Self-Esteem

Observe the way people who you believe to have high self-esteem stand, walk, speak, and act. Even if you are not feeling so secure inside, you will project a high self-esteem image if you act assured. Eugene Raudsepp recommends, "Stand tall, speak clearly and with confidence, shake hands firmly, look people in the eye and smile frequently. Your self-esteem will increase as you notice encouraging reactions from others."[25] (Notice here that self-esteem is considered to be about the same idea as self-confidence.)

Choose your models of high self-esteem from people you know personally, as well as celebrities you might watch on television news and interview shows. Observing actors on the large or small screen is a little less useful because they are guaranteed to be playing a role. Identifying a teacher or professor as a self-esteem model is widely practiced, as is observing successful family members and friends.

Create a High Self-Esteem Living Space

A panel of mental health specialists recommends that to enhance your self-esteem you should make your living space the kind that honors the person you are.[26] Whether you live in a single room, a small apartment, or a large house, make that space comfortable and attractive for you. If you have a clean, inviting living space, others are likely to treat you with more respect, which will contribute to your self-esteem. If you share your living space with others, dedicate some space just for you—a place where you can keep your things and know that they will not be disturbed and that you can decorate any way you choose.

Your living space is part of your self-image, so you may want to ask yourself if your living space projects the right self-image. Also, if you arrange your living space to fit your preferences you will feel better about yourself.

THE IMPORTANCE OF SELF-CONFIDENCE AND SELF-EFFICACY

Although self-confidence can be considered part of self-esteem (or almost its equivalent), it is important enough to study separately. Self-efficacy is confidence in your ability to carry out a specific task in contrast to generalized self-confidence. Various studies have shown that people with a high sense of self-efficacy tend to have good job performance, so being self-confident is important for your career. They also set relatively high goals for themselves.[27] Self-confidence has also long been recognized as a trait of effective leaders. A straightforward implication of self-efficacy is that people who think they can perform well on a task do better than those who think they will do poorly.

As with other traits and behaviors, there is an optimum level of self-confidence. When self-confidence is too low, a person will appear weak and unsure. When self-confidence is too high, the person will come across as arrogant. Staying a little humble helps prevent a person from becoming arrogant. Business consultant Jason Mendelson explains that the difference between arrogance and confidence is awareness of the other person's needs.[28]

Research by college professors and psychological consultants George P. Hollenbeck and Douglas T. Hall suggests that our feelings of self-confidence stem from five sources of information.[29] The first source is the *actual experience, or things we have done*. Having done something before and succeeded is the most powerful way to build self-confidence. If you successfully inserted a replacement battery into your watch without destroying the watch, you will be confident to make another replacement.

The second source of self-confidence is the *experiences of others, or modeling*. You can gain some self-confidence if you have carefully observed others perform a task, such as resolving conflict with a customer. You might say to yourself, "I've seen Tracy calm down the customer by listening and showing sympathy, and I'm confident I could do the same thing." The third source of self-confidence is *social comparison, or comparing yourself to others*. If you see other people with capabilities similar to your own perform a task well, you will gain in confidence. A person might say to himself or herself, "If that person can learn how to work with enterprise software, I can do it also. I'm just as smart."

The fourth source of self-confidence is *social persuasion, the process of convincing another person*. If a credible person convinces you that you can accomplish a particular task, you will often receive a large enough boost in self-confidence to give the task a try. If the encouragement is coupled with guidance on how to perform the task, your self-confidence gain will be higher. So the boss or teacher who says, "I know you can do it, and I'm here to help you," knows how to build self-confidence.

The fifth source of information for making a self-confidence judgment is *emotional arousal, or how we feel about events around us and manage our emotions*. We rely somewhat on our inner feelings to know if we are self-confident enough to perform a task. Imagine a person standing on top of a high mountain, ready to ski down. However, he or she is trembling and nauseous with fear. Contrast this beginner to another person who simply feels mildly excited and challenged. Skier number one has a self-confidence problem, whereas skier number two has enough confidence to start the descent. (Have your emotional sensations ever influenced your self-confidence?)

The more of these five sources of self-confidence are positive for you, the more likely your self-confidence will be positive. A subtle point about self-confidence is that being too low in self-confidence is a problem, yet being too high is also a problem. The overly self-confident person may not listen carefully to the suggestions of others, and may be blind to criticism.

The Human Relations Self-Assessment Quiz 3-3 provides some insight into your level of self-confidence. The accompanying insert describes a leader who appears to have high self-esteem and self-confidence.

TECHNIQUES FOR DEVELOPING AND ENHANCING YOUR SELF-CONFIDENCE

LEARNING OBJECTIVE 4

Self-confidence is generally achieved by succeeding in a variety of situations. A confident civil engineering technician may not be generally self-confident unless he or she also achieves success in activities such as forming good personal relationships, navigating complex software, writing a letter, learning a second language, and displaying athletic skills.

Although this general approach to self-confidence building makes sense, it does not work for everyone. Some people who seem to succeed at everything still have lingering self-doubt. Low self-confidence is so deeply ingrained in this type of personality that success in later life is not sufficient to change things. The following are seven specific strategies

UAW Vice President Cindy Estrada Capitalizes on her Self-Esteem and Self-Confidence

Cindy Estrada was elected a UAW (United Auto Workers) vice president in June, 2010, her fifteenth year of service to the union. Age 43 at the time, she was the UAW's first Latina vice president. Insiders hinted that she might someday become the union's first female president. Estrada's previous position was director of the Union's National Organizing Department.

Estrada developed her fascination with the labor movement while growing up listening to stories from her grandparents and other family members about their days in the fields as farm workers, and also as factory workers. Estrada's earliest recollection of learning about the labor movement was when, as a seven-year old, she washed glasses at her father's bar in Detroit, Michigan that served many GM production workers.

While still a college student, she moved to Mexico to become fluent in Spanish. Later she organized tomato and strawberry pickers in California, with coaching from the famous migrant worker organizer, Cesar Chavez. Although fiercely pro-union, Estrada has made concessions in negotiations about contracts for public service workers in Michigan.

A former auto-parts executive said that "Cindy brings a little bit of fire with her—old-school fire." UAW President Bob King praises Estrada's "tremendous passion and ability and courageous leadership." Arturo Rodriguez, president of the United Farm Workers of America, who worked with Estrada in the early part of her career, noted that working with Mexican farm workers can be intimidating because they are often suspicious of outsiders. Yet Estrada was fearless. She had the ability to get workers to trust her, and get them to change old ways of doing things. When Estrada speaks to a large audience, she does so in a calm, deliberate manner, and usually hammers home the message that the labor movement is important to the future of manufacturing.

Questions:

1. What evidence do you find in this excerpt that Cindy Estrada probably has high self-esteem and self-confidence?
2. What does the fact that Estrada went to live in Mexico to become fluent in Spanish suggest about her self-confidence and self-esteem?

Sources: Original story created from facts in the following sources: Paul Egan, "UAW Vice President Cindy Estrada Shows 'Old-School Fire,'" *http://www.ufw. org*, retrieved January 14, 2012; "UAW Vice President Cindy Estrada," *http:// www.uaw.org*, © Copyright 2012 UAW; "Cindy Estrada," *Latina Style Magazine* (http://latinastyle.com/magazine), No. 4, 2012, pp. 1-2; "UAW Vice President Cindy Estrada Part of Panel at White House Event to Highlight the Auto Industry's Successful Recovery, Jobs and Innovation," *http://region1d.uaw.org*, June 27, 2012; "15 Elite Women to Watch in the Year Ahead: Cindy Estrada, Vice President, United Auto Workers," *Hispanic Business*, April 2011, p. 30.

HUMAN RELATIONS SELF-ASSESSMENT QUIZ 3-3

How Self-Confident Are You?

Indicate the extent to which you agree with each of the following statements. DS = disagree strongly, D = disagree, N = neutral, A = agree, and AS = agree strongly.

		DS	D	N	A	AS
1.	I frequently say to people, "I'm not sure."	5	4	3	2	1
2.	I perform well in most situations in life.	1	2	3	4	5
3.	I willingly offer advice to others.	1	2	3	4	5
4.	Before making even a minor decision, I usually consult with several people.	5	4	3	2	1
5.	I am generally willing to attempt new activities for which I have very little related skill or experience.	1	2	3	4	5
6.	Speaking in front of the class or another group is a frightening experience for me.	5	4	3	2	1
7.	I experience stress when people challenge me or put me on the spot.	5	4	3	2	1
8.	I feel comfortable attending a social event by myself.	1	2	3	4	5
9.	I'm much more of a winner than a loser.	1	2	3	4	5
10.	I am cautious about making any substantial change in my life.	5	4	3	2	1

Total score: _____

Scoring and Interpretation: Calculate your total score by adding the numbers circled. A tentative interpretation of the scoring is as follows:

45–50: Very high self-confidence with perhaps a tendency toward arrogance

38–44: A high, desirable level of self-confidence

30–37: Moderate, or average, self-confidence

10–29: Self-confidence needs strengthening

Questions:

1. How does your score on this test fit with your evaluation of your self-confidence?
2. What would it be like working for a manager who scored 10 on this quiz?

FIGURE 3-2 Boosting Your Self-Confidence

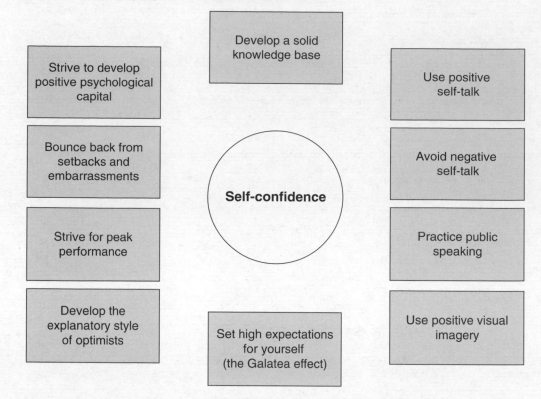

and tactics for building and elevating self-confidence, as outlined in Figure 3-2. They will generally work unless the person has deep-rooted feelings of inferiority. The tactics and strategies are arranged approximately in the order in which they should be tried to achieve best results.

Develop a Solid Knowledge Base

A bedrock strategy for projecting self-confidence is to develop a knowledge base that enables you to provide sensible alternative solutions to problems. Intuition is very important, but working from a base of facts helps you project a confident image. Formal education is an obvious and important source of information for your knowledge base. Day-by-day absorption of information directly and indirectly related to your career is equally important. A major purpose of formal education is to get you in the right frame of mind to continue your quest for knowledge. In your quest for developing a solid knowledge base to project self-confidence, be sensitive to abusing this technique. If you bombard people with quotes, facts, and figures, you are likely to be perceived as an annoying know-it-all.

A solid knowledge base contributes to self-confidence also because the knowledge facilitates engaging in conversation with intelligent people. A weak counterargument is that having information stored in your brain is no longer important because information is so accessible online. When in a gathering of people, you could then use a smartphone to access some facts to talk about. Such behavior is unlikely to help a person project a confident, intelligent image.

Use Positive Self-Talk

A basic method of building self-confidence is to engage in **positive self-talk,** saying positive things about yourself. The first step in using positive self-talk is to objectively state the incident that is casting doubt about your self-worth.[30] The key word here is *objectively*. Terry, who is fearful of poorly executing a report-writing assignment, might say, "I've been asked to write a report for the company, and I'm not a good writer."

The next step is to objectively interpret what the incident *does not* mean. Terry might say, "Not being a skilled writer doesn't mean that I can't figure out a way to write a good report or that I'm an ineffective employee."

Next, the person should objectively state what the incident *does* mean. In doing this, the person should avoid put-down labels, such as "incompetent," "stupid," "dumb," "jerk," or "airhead." All these terms are forms of negative self-talk. Terry should state what the incident does mean: "I have a problem with one small aspect of this job."

The fourth step is to objectively account for the cause of the incident. Terry would say, "I'm really worried about writing a good report because I have very little experience in writing along these lines."

The fifth step is to identify some positive ways to prevent the incident from happening again. Terry might say, "I'll get out my textbook on business communications and review the chapter on report writing" or "I'll enroll in a course or seminar on business report writing."

The final step is to use positive self-talk. Terry imagines his boss saying, "This report is really good. I'm proud of my decision to select you to prepare this important report."

Positive self-talk builds self-confidence and self-esteem because it programs the mind with positive messages. Making frequent positive statements or affirmations about the self creates a more confident person. An example would be, "I know I can learn this new equipment rapidly enough to increase my productivity within five days."

Business coach Gary Lockwood emphasizes that positive self-talk is also useful for getting people past difficult times. "It's all in your head," he said. "Remember you are in charge of your feelings. You are in control of your attitude." Instead of berating yourself after making a mistake, learn from the experience and move on. Say to yourself, "Everyone makes mistakes," "Tomorrow is another day," or "What can I learn from this?"[31]

Positive self-talk is included in **self-compassion**, or treating yourself kindly. Self-compassion can be useful in boosting self-confidence beause you view yourself in positive terms, and therefore feel more confident of your abilities. A series of studies by Mark Leary, a professor of psychology and neuroscience at Duke University, have found that self-compassionate people are happier. They also are more likely to accept the challenge of public speaking because they do not condemn themselves for looking foolish.[32] Self-compassion also includes regularly making lists of all the positive things you have done lately, as well as compliments you have received.

Despite the many advantages of positive self-talk, as with optimism, there can be times when thinking too positively can create problems. Negative thoughts are often useful in alerting us to potential problems, and prompting us to develop a plan of correction. Imagine that Lisa is job hunting, and that she has urgent need of employment. She has a promising interview, and her positive thinking prompts her to think, "There is no doubt that I will receive an offer real soon." Her positive thinking blocks her from continuing her job search. When the offer in question does not come through, Lisa has lost momentum in her job search. In the words of author John Derbyshire, we must be "vigilantly realistic" toward the potential dangers of positive thinking.[33]

Avoid Negative Self-Talk

As implied, you should minimize negative statements about yourself to bolster self-confidence. A lack of self-confidence is reflected in statements such as "I may be stupid but . . .," "Nobody asked my opinion," "I know I'm usually wrong, but . . .," and "I know I don't have as much education as some people, but. . . ." Self-effacing statements like these serve to reinforce low self-confidence.

It is also important not to attribute to yourself negative, irreversible traits, such as "idiotic," "ugly," "dull," "loser," and "hopeless." Instead, look on your weak points as areas for possible self-improvement. Negative self-labeling can do long-term damage to your self-confidence. If a person stops that practice today, his or her self-confidence may begin to increase.

Practice Public Speaking

Dale Carnegie, the original popularizer of human relations, built his empire on the foundation of the importance of public speaking in building self-confidence.[34] In the age of

Stockbyte/Thinkstock

communication technology, this basic technique holds true. If you can stand in front of an audience, even a small meeting, and deliver your thoughts effectively, you will gain in self-confidence. However, just reading PowerPoint slides to the group is not enough. You have to look at the facial expressions of the audience and speak directly to them. Making a successful presentation to the class has been a self-confidence builder for millions of students. Presentations in the workplace, to community groups, religious groups, and sports groups can also be self-confidence builders.

Use Positive Visual Imagery

Assume you have a situation in mind in which you would like to appear confident and in control. An example would be a meeting with a major customer who has told you by e-mail that he is considering switching suppliers. Your intuitive reaction is that if you cannot handle his concerns without fumbling or appearing desperate, you will lose the account. An important technique in this situation is **positive visual imagery**, or picturing a positive outcome in your mind. To apply this technique in this situation, imagine yourself engaging in a convincing argument about why your customer should retain your company as the primary supplier. Imagine yourself talking in positive terms about the good service your company offers and how you can rectify any problems.

Visualize yourself listening patiently to your customer's concerns and then talking confidently about how your company can handle these concerns. As you rehearse this moment of truth, create a mental picture of you and the customer shaking hands over the fact that the account is still yours.

Positive visual imagery helps you appear self-confident because your mental rehearsal of the situation has helped you prepare for battle. If imagery works for you once, you will be even more effective in subsequent uses of the technique.

Set High Expectations for Yourself (the Galatea Effect)

If you set high expectations for yourself and you succeed, you are likely to experience a temporary or permanent boost in self-confidence. The **Galatea effect** is a type of self-fulfilling prophecy in which high expectations lead to high performance. Similar to positive self-talk, if you believe in yourself you are more likely to succeed. You expect to win, so you do. The Galatea effect may not work all the time, but it does work some of the time for many people.

Workplace behavior researchers D. Brian McNatt and Timothy A. Judge studied the Galatea effect with 72 auditors within three offices of a major accounting firm over a three-month period. The auditors were given letters of encouragement to strengthen their feelings of self-efficacy. Information in the letters was based on facts about the auditors, such as information derived from their résumés and company records. The results of the experiment showed that creating a Galatea effect bolstered self-efficacy, motivation, and performance. However, the performance improvement was temporary, suggesting that self-expectations need to be boosted regularly.[35]

Develop the Explanatory Style of Optimists

According to the research and observations of consultant and trainer Price Pritchett, optimism is linked to self-confidence. Explaining events in an optimistic way can help preserve self-confidence and self-esteem. When experiencing trouble, optimists tend to explain the problems to themselves as temporary. Bad events are expected to be short-lived, and optimists look to the future when times will be better. Another aspect of optimists' explanatory style protects their self-confidence. Rather than condemn themselves for failures, they look for how other factors or circumstances have contributed to the problem. Optimists then do not take all the blame for a problem, but look to external factors to help explain what went wrong.

Interpreting difficulties in this way gives the optimists a sense of control. Instead of looking at the unfortunate situation as hopeless, they have faith in their ability to deal with the problem.[36] Suppose an optimist purchases a computer workstation that comes packed in a box with many parts along with directions. A problem arises in that some of the screws and dowels do not fit, and the directions are unclear. A pessimist might suffer a drop in self-confidence and self-esteem, saying "What a fool I am. I can't even assemble a piece of office furniture." In contrast, the optimist might say, "I'm doing something wrong here, and I will get a buddy to help show me my mistake. But the manufacturer can also be blamed. The instructions are terrible, and all the parts may not fit together." In this way, the optimist does not take such a big hit to self-confidence and self-esteem.

Strive for Peak Performance

A key strategy for projecting self-confidence is to display **peak performance,** or exceptional accomplishment in a given task. The experience is transient, but exceptionally meaningful. Peak performance refers to much more than attempting to do your best. Experiencing peak performance in various tasks over a long period of time would move a person toward self-actualization.[37] To achieve peak performance, you must be totally focused on what you are doing. When you are in the state of peak performance, you are mentally calm and physically at ease. Intense concentration is required to achieve this state. You are so focused on the task at hand that you are not distracted by extraneous events or thoughts. To use an athletic analogy, you are *in the zone* while you are performing the task. In fact, many sports psychologists and other sports trainers work with athletes to help them attain peak performance.

The mental state achieved during peak performance is akin to a person's sense of deep concentration when immersed in a sport or hobby. On days when tennis players perform way above their usual game, they typically comment, "The ball looked so large, I could read the label as I hit it." On the job, focus and concentration allow the person to sense and respond to relevant information coming both from within the mind and from outside stimuli. When you are at your peak, you impress others by responding intelligently to their input. While turning in peak performance, you are experiencing a mental state referred to as *flow*.

Although you are concentrating on an object or sometimes on another person during peak performance, you still have an awareness of the self. You develop a strong sense of the self, similar to self-confidence and self-efficacy, while you are concentrating on the task. Peak performance is related to self-confidence in another important way. Achieving peak performance in many situations helps you develop self-confidence.

Skill-Building Exercise 3-3 gives you the opportunity to work on enhancing your self-confidence.

Bounce Back from Setbacks and Embarrassments

Resilience is a major contributor to personal effectiveness. Overcoming setbacks also builds self-confidence, as implied from the description of the explanatory style of optimists.

HUMAN RELATIONS SKILL-BUILDING EXERCISE 3-3

Building Your Self-Confidence and Self-Efficacy

Most people can use a boost to their self-confidence. Even if you are a highly confident individual, perhaps there is room for building your feelings of self-efficacy in a particular area, such as a proud and successful business owner learning a new skill such as editing digital photos or speaking a foreign language. This skill-building exercise enhances your self-confidence or self-efficacy in the next two weeks by trying out one of the many suggestions for self-confidence building described in the text.

As part of planning the implementation of this exercise, think about any area in which your self-confidence could use a boost. A candid human relations student, who was also a confident cheerleader, said, "Face it. I'm terrible at PowerPoint presentations. I put up so many details on my slides that the audience is trying to read my slides instead of looking at me. I have to admit that my PowerPoint presentation consists mostly of my reading my slides to the audience. I'm much better at cheerleading." So this student studied information in her human relations text about making better graphic presentations. She revamped her approach to using her slides as headlines and talking points. She tried out one presentation in class, and one at her church. She received so many compliments about her presentations that now she has much higher self-efficacy with respect to PowerPoint presentations.

Your instructor might organize a sharing of self-confidence building episodes in the class. If the sharing does take place, look for patterns of what seemed to work in terms of self-confidence or self-efficacy building. Also, listen for any patterns in failed attempts at self-confidence building.

An effective self-confidence builder is to convince yourself that you can conquer adversity such as setbacks and embarrassments, thus being resilient. The vast majority of successful leaders have dealt successfully with at least one significant setback in their careers, such as being fired or demoted. In contrast, crumbling after a setback or series of setbacks will usually lower self-confidence. Three major suggestions for bouncing back from setbacks and embarrassments are presented next.

Get Past the Emotional Turmoil.   Adversity has enormous emotional consequences. The emotional impact of severe job adversity can rival the loss of a personal relationship. The stress from adversity leads to a cycle of adversity followed by stress, followed by more adversity. A starting point in dealing with the emotional aspects of adversity is to *accept the reality of your problem*. Admit that your problems are real and that you are hurting inside.

A second step is *not to take the setback personally*. Remember that setbacks are inevitable so long as you are taking some risks in your career. Not personalizing setbacks helps reduce some of the emotional sting. If possible, *do not panic*. Recognize that you are in difficult circumstances under which many others panic. Convince yourself to remain calm enough to deal with the severe problem or crisis. Also, *get help from your support network*. Getting emotional support from family members and friends helps overcome the emotional turmoil associated with adversity. Two professors of psychiatry who specialize in resiliency, Steven Southwick and Dennis Charney, believe that social support is a key factor in developing resiliency. They say that knowing someone you can count on is essential for bouncing back.[38]

Find a Creative Solution to Your Problem.   An inescapable part of planning a comeback is to solve your problem. You often need to search for creative solutions. Suppose a person faced the adversity of not having enough money for educational expenses. The person might search through standard alternatives, such as applying for financial aid, looking for more lucrative part-time work, and borrowing from family members. Several students have solved their problem more creatively by asking strangers to lend them money as intermediate-term investments. An option the investors have is to receive a payback based on the future earnings of the students.

Strive to Develop Positive Psychological Capital.   A comprehensive way of becoming more self-confident is to develop **positive psychological capital,** a positive psychological state of development in which you have hope, self-efficacy, optimism, and resilience. Note that self-efficacy and resilience have already been included in our study of self-confidence. In more detail, the components of positive psychological capital are as follows:

- *Hope* refers to persevering toward goals and, when necessary, redirecting paths to a goal in order to succeed. In everyday language, don't give up when pursuing your goals.
- *Self-efficacy* refers to having the confidence to take on and invest the necessary effort to succeed at challenging tasks. Experience is a big help here, because if you have successfully completed the same task, or a similar one, previously, you will be more confident that you can succeed.
- *Optimism* refers to making a positive attribution about succeeding now and in the future. If you are a natural pessimist, you will have to work harder at looking for the positive aspects of a given situation.
- *Resiliency* refers to dealing with problems and adversity by sustaining effort and bouncing back to attain success. Conquering a major setback would be an enormous contributor to your self-confidence.

An encouraging note about positive psychological capital is that people can develop it. An experiment conducted with 187 working adults found that a Web-based, highly-focused two-hour training program raised the average level of psychological capital. The increase in psychological capital was measured by more positive responses after training to such statements as, "If I should find myself in a jam at work, I could think of many ways to get out of it" (hope).[39] Should the participants in the study really do a better job of getting out of jams in the future, you could be even more confident about how well training improves psychological capital.

Concept Review and Reinforcement

Key Terms

self-esteem 73
self-compassion 87

positive visual imagery 88
peak performance 89

Summary

Self-esteem refers to the overall evaluation people make about themselves. People with high self-esteem develop a positive self-concept. Self-esteem develops from a variety of early-life experiences. People who were encouraged to feel good about themselves and their accomplishments by key people in their lives are more likely to enjoy high self-esteem. Of major significance, self-esteem also results from accomplishing worthwhile activities, and then feeling proud of these accomplishments. Praise and recognition for accomplishments also help develop self-esteem.

Extremes in self-esteem have many important consequences. High self-esteem often results in career success (including a high income), organizational prosperity, good mental health, and profiting from feedback, and serves as a guide for regulating social relationships. One of the links between good mental health and self-esteem is that high self-esteem helps prevent many situations from being stressful.

High self-esteem can sometimes have negative consequences such as narcissism and envying too many people. Our own reference group has the biggest impact on self-esteem. Low self-esteem can result in romantic relationship problems including distancing oneself from one's partner.

Self-esteem can be enhanced in many ways: (a) attain legitimate accomplishments, (b) be aware of personal strengths, (c) rebut the inner critic, (d) practice self-nurturing, (e) minimize settings and interactions that detract from your feelings of competence, (f) get help from others, including talking and socializing frequently with people who boost your self-esteem, (g) model the behavior of people with high self-esteem, and (h) create a high self-esteem living space.

Various studies have shown that people with a high sense of self-efficacy tend to have good job performance, so self-confidence is important for your career. There is an optimum level of self-confidence, with too much self-confidence appearing as arrogance. Our feelings of self-confidence stem from five sources of information: actual experiences, or things that we have done; experiences of others, or modeling; social comparison, or comparing yourself to others; social persuasion, the process of convincing another person; and emotional arousal, or how we feel about events around us and manage our emotions.

A general principle of boosting your self-confidence is to experience success (goal accomplishment) in a variety of situations. The specific strategies for building self-confidence described here are: (a) develop a solid knowledge base, (b) use positive self-talk, (c) avoid negative self-talk, (d) practice public speaking, (e) use positive visual imagery, (f) set high expectations for yourself (the Galatea effect), (g) develop the explanatory style of optimists, (h) strive for peak performance, (i) bounce back from setbacks and embarrassments, and (j) strive to develop positive psychological capital. Self-compassion is included in positive self-talk.

Questions for Discussion and Review

1. Why does holding an important job contribute to a person's self-esteem?

2. A study by economists indicated that workers with higher levels of self-esteem tended to be more

productive. What would be an explanation for this finding?

3. Why are people with high self-esteem to the point of being a narcissist often disliked by many other people?

4. Can you think of a situation when your self-esteem was diminished? How and why did this happen?

5. Why is self-confidence considered to be so important for being an effective leader?

6. How can you become aware of your personal strengths, apart from participating in a group exercise?

7. Why is self-esteem more important than job knowledge?

8. Many pharmaceutical firms actively recruit cheerleaders as sales representatives to call on doctors to recommend their brand of prescription drugs. The firms in question say that cheerleaders make good sales reps because they are so self-confident. What is your opinion on this controversial issue?

9. What is it about success in public speaking that tends to boost the self-confidence of the public speaker?

10. Interview a person whom you perceive to have a successful career. Ask that person to describe how he or she developed high self-esteem. Be prepared to discuss your findings in class.

The Web Corner

www.athealth.com/Consumer/disorders/self-esteem.html
(Measuring and building your self-esteem)

www.self-confidence.co.uk
(Developing your self-confidence)

www.mindtools.com/selfconf.html
(The difference between self-confidence and low self-confidence)

Internet Skills Builder: Learning More about Your Self-Esteem

The Self-Esteem Checklist in this chapter gave you one opportunity to assess your self-esteem. To gain additional insights into your self-esteem, visit www.more-selfesteem.com. Go to "quizzes" under Free Resources, and take the self-esteem test. How does your score on this quiz compare to your score on The Self-Esteem Checklist? If your level of self-esteem as measured by the two quizzes is quite different (such as high versus low), explain why this discrepancy might occur.

Developing Your Human Relations Skills

Interpersonal Relations Case 3.1

High Self-Esteem Brandy

As Brandy Barclay navigated the challenging highways toward her job interview in Los Angeles, she rehearsed in her mind the importance of communicating that she is a unique brand. "I have to get across the idea that I am special, even if my brand is not as well established as Godiva Chocolates or Dr. Pepper. [A brand is a basket of strengths that sets you apart from others.] This administrative assistant position at the hotel and resort company will be a good way to launch my career and brand. After all, I am a very special person."

An excerpt of her job interview with the hiring manager Gloria Gomez follows:

Gomez: Welcome Brandy, I am pleased that you made it through the online job application and the telephone screening interview. Tell me again why you would like to join our hotel company as an administrative assistant.

Barclay: Oh, I really don't want to join you as an administrative assistant. I would prefer a vice president job, but I have to start somewhere. (Smiling) Seriously, I like the hotel field. It fits my brand called Brandy. I am a great support person, and a great people person. I'm so unique because I'm great with details and great with people. Many people have told me that I am a very special person."

Gomez: Tell me specifically what key strengths would you bring to this job?

Barclay: As found in my brand called Brandy, I am high info tech and high touch. I'm a whiz at Microsoft Office Suite, and I'm sweet with people. Kind of catchy, don't you think? Come to think of it, have you seen my business card? It contains loads of details about my skills and strengths on the back. The card is laminated so it will last, and it contains my photo, and even is like a hologram with a 3-D look.

Gomez: Yes, Brandy, I do have your card. You gave one to the receptionist, and she gave it to me. And why do you keep referring to yourself as a brand? Is this just a gimmick to get you noticed?

Barclay: Being a brand is the modern way to tell you that Brandy Barclay is one of a kind. I've got a skill set that is hard to beat. Besides, I want to build a reputation fast that will propel me to the top as an executive in the hotel field. I am quite proud of who I am.

Gomez: On your trip to the top, what do you plan to do for us as an administrative assistant?

Barclay: I will live up to the brand called Brandy by getting the job done big time. Just ask me to do something, and it will be done. Don't forget I will be building my brand image while in this beginning assignment.

Gomez: Now let's talk about details like the job assignment, salary, and benefits.

Barclay: Fine with me. We have to deal with the mundane at some point.

Case Questions

1. How effectively is Brandy Barclay presenting herself as a brand (or a unique individual)?
2. What suggestions can you offer Barclay for presenting herself as a strong individual more effectively?
3. To what extent do you think that Brandy's high self-esteem has reached the point of narcissism?

Interpersonal Relations Case 3.2

Anthony Needs a Boost

"I'm losing my mojo," said Anthony, a salesman who sells cargo space on ocean liners to companies all over the world who want to ship goods to or from the United States. After five consecutive years of being one of the top sales reps in his company, Anthony's sales had plunged 25 percent. Quincy, his manager, was sympathetic, but he wanted to see Anthony sell more cargo space. A ship crossing the ocean with too much empty cargo space usually loses money for the shipper. Anthony explained to Quincy that he too wanted to boost sales, but you cannot force a company to ship goods he or she has not sold. Part of Anthony's problem was the fact that many manufacturers in the United States were now doing more of their manufacturing in the United States, resulting in less demand for shipments of manufactured goods from other countries.

"My personal life is in a bigger slump than my sales performance," explained Anthony. Two months ago Anthony totaled his car when he slipped off the road and hit a tree while driving 10 miles per hour beyond the speed limit. In addition to getting a speeding ticket, his insurance company raised his auto insurance premium by 25 percent. Another discouraging problem Anthony faced was that his fiancée broke off their engagement two months ago. She claimed that she suddenly felt trapped by the prospects of a committed relationship as well as marriage.

Anthony's golf game life has suffered also suffered recently. "Maybe I'm bringing too much of my outside life onto the golf course. I've been shooting about six strokes higher than my average game recently. A big part of my problem is that it is difficult for me to concentrate on golf, particularly the putting. I keep thinking about my work and personal problems when I line up the ball.

"I want to get my life back on track, but I don't know where to begin. I'm losing faith in my abilities."

Case Questions

1. To what extent is Anthony facing a self-confidence problem?
2. What do you recommend that Anthony do to regain his self-confidence?
3. How might Anthony's manager be able to help Anthony boost his self-confidence?

Interpersonal Relations Role-Play

Quincy Attempts to Boost Anthony's Self-Confidence

Quincy is worried about the loss in self-confidence that Anthony appears to be experiencing, and believes that as Anthony's manager he should attempt to be helpful. Quincy decides to conduct a one-on-one session with Anthony to do whatever he can to help the sales representative regain some of his self-confidence. Quincy believes that his knowledge of human relations should be useful in helping Anthony. Although Anthony is surprised about the meeting, he is eager to listen to any advice that could possibly help him regain his confidence.

Conduct this role-play for about seven minutes. Observers rate the role players on two dimensions, using a 1-to-5 scale from very poor to very good. One dimension is "effective use of human relations techniques." Focus on the technique Quincy uses to attempt to booses Anthony's self-confidence. The second dimension is "acting ability." A few observers might voluntarily provide feedback to the role players in terms of sharing their ratings and observations. The course instructor might also provide feedback.

References

1. Michelle K. Duffy, Jason D. Shaw, Kristin L. Scott, and Bennett J. Tepper, "The Moderating Roles of Self-Esteem and Neuroticism in the Relationships Between Group and Individual Undermining Behavior," *Journal of Applied Psychology*, September 2006, p. 1067.
2. April O'Connell, Vincent O'Connell, and Lois-Ann Kuntz, *Choice and Change: The Psychology of Personal Growth and Interpersonal Relationships*, 7th ed. (Upper Saddle River, NJ: Pearson/Prentice Hall, 2005), p. 3.
3. "Better Self-Esteem," http://www.utexas.edu/student/cmhc/booklets/selfesteem/selfest.html, 1999, p. 2.
4. Ibid.
5. Cited in Randall Edwards, "Is Self-Esteem Really All that Important?" *The APA Monitor*, May 1995, p. 43.
6. Research reported in Jeffrey Zaslow, "The Most Praised Generation Goes to Work," *The Wall Street Journal*, April 20, 2007, p. W7.

7. David De Cremer et al., "Rewarding Leadership and Fair Procedures as Determinants of Self-Esteem," *Journal of Applied Psychology*, January 2005, pp. 3–12.

8. Timothy A. Judge, Charlice Hurst, and Lauren S. Simon, "Does It Pay to Be Smart, Attractive, or Confident (or All Three)? Relationships Among General Mental Ability, Physical Attractiveness, Core Self-Evaluation, and Income," *Journal of Applied Psychology,* May 2009, pp. 742–755. The definition of core self-evaluations is from Christian J. Resick et al., "The Bright-Side and the Dark-Side of CEO Personality: Examining Core Self-Evaluations, Narcissism, Transformational Leadership, and Strategic Influence," *Journal of Applied Psychology,* November 2009, p. 1367.

9. Adam M. Grant and Amy Wrzenesniewki, "I Won't Let You Down . . . Or Will I? Core Self-Evaluations, Other-Orientation, Anticipated Guilt and Gratitude, and Job Performance," *Journal of Applied Psychology,* January 2010, pp. 108–121.

10. Nathaniel Branden, *Self-Esteem at Work: How Confident People Make Powerful Companies* (San Francisco: Jossey-Bass, 1998); Timothy A. Judge and Joyce E. Bono, "Relationship of Core Self-Evaluations Traits—Self-Esteem, Generalized Self-Efficacy, Locus of Control, and Emotional Stability—With Job Satisfaction and Job Performance: A Meta-Analysis," *Journal of Applied Psychology,* February 2001, pp. 80–92.

11. Research reported in Melissa Dittman, "Study Links Jealousy with Aggression, Low Self-Esteem," *Psychology Today,* February 2005, p. 13.

12. As quoted in Erika Casriel, "Stepping Out," *Psychology Today*, March/April 2007, p. 73.

13. Ibid.

14. Jon L. Pierce, Donald G. Gardner, Larry L. Cummings, and Randall B. Dunman, "Organization-Based Self-Esteem: Construct Definition, Measurement, and Validation," *Academy of Management Journal*, September 1989, p. 623.

15. Andrew J. DuBrin, *Narcissism in the Workplace: Research, Opinion, and Practice* (Cheltenham UK: Edward Elgar, 2012), p. 1.

16. Cited in Brown, "The Boom and Bust Ego," p. 73.

17. Cited in Julia M. Klein, "The Illusion of Rejection," *Psychology Today*, January/February 2005, p. 30.

18. "Building Self-Esteem: A Self-Help Guide," http://store. samhsa.gov/product/Building-Self-Esteem-A-Self-Help-Guide/SMA-3715, p. 2, accessed July 22, 2013.

19. Research mentioned in book review by E. R. Snyder in *Contemporary Psychology*, July 1998, p. 482.

20. Research cited in Elizabeth Bernstein, "Are We All Braggarts Now?" *The Wall Street Journal*, August 14, 2012, p. D1.

21. Research cited in Harriet Brown and Dan Winters, "The Boom and Bust Ego," *Psychology Today*, January/February 2012, p. 69.

22. "Better Self-Esteem," pp. 3–4.

23. Ibid., pp. 4–5.

24. Cited in "Self-Esteem: You'll Need It to Succeed," *Executive Strategies*, September 1993, p. 12.

25. Eugene Raudsepp, "Strong Self-Esteem Can Help You Advance," *Career Journal.com* (*The Wall Street Journal*) August 10, 2004.

26. "Building Self-Esteem: A Self-Help Guide," http://store. samhsa.gov/product/Building-Self-Esteem-A-Self-Help-Guide/SMA-3715, p. 2, accessed July 22, 2013.

27. Marilyn E. Gist and Terence R. Mitchell, "Self-Efficacy: A Theoretical Analysis of Its Determinants and Malleability," *Academy of Management Review*, April 1992, pp. 183–211.

28. Cited in Erika Napoletano, "Confidence vs. Arrogance," *Entrepreneur*, June 2011, p. 20.

29. George P. Hollenbeck and Douglas T. Hall, "Self-confidence and Leader Performance," *Organizational Dynamics*, Issue 3, 2004, pp. 261–264.

30. Jay T. Knippen and Thad B. Green, "Building Self-Confidence," *Supervisory Management*, August 1989, pp. 22–27.

31. Quoted in "Entrepreneurs Need Attitude: Power of Being Positive Can Help You to Succeed In Spite of Setbacks," *Knight Ridder*, September 16, 2002.

32. Research reported in Elizabeth Bernstein, "Self-Help for Skeptics," *The Wall Street Journal*, August 28, 2012, p. D1.

33. John Derbyshire, *We Are Doomed* (New York: Crown Forum, 2009).

34. Daniel Okrent, "The Best Salesman in Business," *Fortune*, May 3, 2010, p. 204.

35. D. Brian McNatt and Timothy A. Judge, "Boundary Conditions of the Galatea Effect: A Field Experiment and Constructive Replication," *Academy of Management Journal*, August 2004, pp. 550–565.

36. Price Pritchett, *Hard Optimism: Developing Deep Strengths for Managing Uncertainty, Opportunity, Adversity, and Change* (Dallas, TX: Pritchett, 2004), p. 16.

37. Frances Thornton, Gayle Privette, and Charles M. Bundrick, "Peak Performance of Business Leaders: An Experience Parallel to Self-Actualization Theory," *Journal of Business and Psychology*, Winter 1999, pp. 253–264.

38. Steve Southwick and Dennis Charney, *Resilience: The Science of Mastering Life's Greatest Challenges* (New York: Cambridge University Press, 2012); Julia Savacool, "Anyone Can Learn to Be More Resilient," *USA Weekend*, November 16–18, 2012, p. 4.

39. Fred Luthans, James R. Avey, and Jaime L. Patera, "Experimental Analysis of a Web-Based Training Intervention to Develop Positive Psychological Capital," *Academy of Management Learning and Education*, June 2008, pp. 209–221.

Interpersonal Communication

Maria is the director of e-commerce for a company in Brooklyn, New York, that was a reseller of a variety of specialty machines used in manufacturing. Many of the machines the company sells are new, and many refurbished. Competition from overseas manufacturers, particularly those in China, is making the sales of machines more difficult. Almost all of Maria's contacts with customers and prospective customers are over the Internet, including e-mail and Facebook.

stockyimages/Fotolia

After reading and studying this chapter and completing the exercises, you should be able to:

1. Explain the basic steps in the communication process.
2. Explain the relationship-building aspect of interpersonal communication.
3. Understand nonverbal communication and improve your nonverbal communication skills.
4. Understand barriers to communication, including gender differences, and know how to overcome them.
5. Enhance your listening skills.

Maria noticed a year ago that she had not received an order from one of the company's largest customers, a successful machine tool company in Detroit, Michigan. Maria wrote a few e-mails to her contact at the company, Larry, the chief operating officer, asking if there was any way her company could help his company. Larry basically ignored the e-mail messages, except for one response that his company was in good shape with respect to machinery.

Maria decided to telephone Larry and ask if she could visit him at his office. Larry responded, "We've done everything over the Internet so far. I had never thought of seeing you in person. But if you think the trip is worth your time and money, let's schedule a date." Maria did visit her customer in Detroit, and her visit lasted two hours. Larry proudly showed Maria how his company was expanding, and how her company's machines were being deployed. Larry also went into detail about what he liked and did not like about the machines he had bought from Maria's company.

Within three months after the visit, Maria's company received two orders for machines that would help the Detroit company expand on a new product line. Larry also wrote to Maria, explaining that it was refreshing to see an e-commerce manager in person.

The story about the e-commerce manager actually making an in-person visit to a customer illustrates that in this era of high technology, face-to-face communication still plays an important role in business. **Communication** is the sending, receiving, and understanding of messages. It is also the basic process by which managers, customer-contact workers, and professionals accomplish their work. For example, a customer service representative cannot resolve a thorny customer problem without carefully receiving and sending information. Communication is also important because communication skills are a success factor for workers in a wide variety of jobs.

The subject of this chapter is interpersonal, or face-to-face, communication rather than electronic communication, such as e-mail, instant messaging, text messaging, and videoconferencing; however, almost all principles of interpersonal communication also apply to electronic communication. Chapter 5 deals with the interpersonal aspects of communication in the digital world. Chapter 8 includes a section about coping with cross-cultural communication barriers.

The importance of face-to-face communication has increased in the age of electronic communication. Many companies have discovered that the subtle aspects of communication possible in face-to-face communication can help productivity. A key example is talking to a person to help build a good working relationship. As illustrated in the case opener, there is not yet a good substitute for face-to-face contact in building relationships. Entrepreneurship consultant Jim Blasingame reports, "There is a comfort level that is achieved when you've met the person you're doing business with."[1]

A conference held with representatives from major American manufacturing companies pointed directly to the importance of communication skills for employability. One of the key subjects at the conference was the difficulty in finding qualified job candidates. Several industry representatives said that sometimes simply finding someone who could properly answer a telephone was a challenge.[2]

The information in this chapter is aimed at reducing communication problems among people and helping you enhance your communication effectiveness. The chapter approaches these ends in two ways. First, it explains the nature of a few key facets of interpersonal communication. Second, it presents guidelines for improving your effectiveness, along with skill-building exercises. We lay particular emphasis on listening as part of achieving good communication. Keep in mind that communication underlies almost every human relations activity, as much as running supports almost every sport. You need good communication skills to get through job interviews, perform well on the job, and get promoted.

STEPS IN THE COMMUNICATION PROCESS

LEARNING OBJECTIVE 1

One way to understand how people communicate is to examine the steps involved in transmitting and receiving a message, as shown in Figure 4-1. For effective communication to take place, six components must be present: a sender, a message, a channel, a receiver, feedback, and the environment. In addition, a seventh component, noise, affects the entire communication process. To help understand the communication process, assume that a production manager in a bicycle factory wants to inform a team leader that productivity in her department slipped last month.

1. **Sender (or source):** The sender in a communication event is usually a person (in this case the production manager) attempting to send a spoken, written, sign language, or nonverbal message to another person or persons. The perceived authority and credibility of the sender are important factors in influencing how much attention the message will receive.

message

A purpose or idea to be conveyed.

2. **Message:** The heart of the communication event is the **message**, a purpose or idea to be conveyed. Many factors influence how a message is received. Among them are clarity, the alertness of the receiver, the complexity and length of the message, and how the information is organized. The production manager's message will most likely get across if he says directly, "I need to talk to you about last month's below-average productivity figures."

3. **Channel (medium):** Several communication channels, or media, are usually available for sending messages in organizations. Typically, messages are written (usually

FIGURE 4-1   A Basic Model of the Communication Process

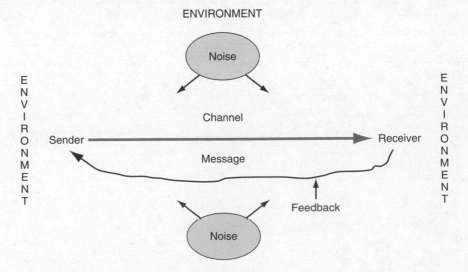

electronically), spoken, or a combination of the two. Some kind of nonverbal signal such as a smile or hand gesture accompanies most spoken messages. In the production manager's case, he has chosen to drop by the team leader's cubicle and deliver his message in a serious tone.

4. **Receiver:** A communication event can be complete only when another party receives the message and understands it properly. In the example here, the team leader is the receiver. Perceptual distortions of various types act as filters that can prevent a message from being received as intended by the sender. If the team leader is worried that her job is at stake, she might get defensive when she hears the production manager's message.

5. **Feedback:** Messages sent back from the receiver to the sender are referred to as **feedback**. Without feedback it is difficult to know whether a message has been received and understood. The feedback step also includes the reactions of the receiver. If the receiver takes action as intended by the sender, the message has been received satisfactorily. The production manager will know his message got across if the team leader says, "Okay, when would you like to review last month's productivity reports?" Effective interpersonal communication, therefore, involves an exchange of messages between two people. The two communicators take turns being receivers and senders.

6. **Environment:** A full understanding of communication requires knowledge of the environment in which messages are transmitted and received. The organizational culture (attitudes and atmosphere) is a key environmental factor that influences communication. It is easier to transmit controversial messages when trust and respect are high than when they are low.

7. **Noise:** Distractions such as noise have a pervasive influence on the components of the communication process. In this context, **noise** is anything that disrupts communication, including the attitudes and emotions of the receiver. Noise includes such factors as stress, fear, negative attitudes, and low motivation.

feedback

In communication, messages sent back from the receiver to the sender.

noise

Anything that disrupts communication, including the attitudes and emotions of the receiver.

RELATIONSHIP BUILDING AND INTERPERSONAL COMMUNICATION

Another way of understanding the process of interpersonal communication is to examine how communication is a vehicle for building relationships. According to Ritch Sorenson, Grace DeBord, and Ida Ramirez, we establish relationships along two primary dimensions: dominant–subordinate and cold–warm. In the process of communicating, we attempt to dominate or subordinate. When we dominate, we attempt to control communication. When we subordinate, we attempt to yield control, or think first of the wishes and needs of the other person. Dominators expect the receiver of messages to submit to them; subordinate people send a signal that they expect the other person to dominate.[3]

LEARNING OBJECTIVE 2

We indicate whether we want to dominate or subordinate by the way we speak and write, or by the nonverbal signals we send. The dominator might speak loudly or enthusiastically, write forceful messages filled with exclamation points, or gesture with exaggerated, rapid hand movements. He or she might write a harsh e-mail message such as, "It's about time you started taking your job seriously, and put in some real effort."

In the subordinate mode, we might speak quietly and hesitantly, in a meek tone, and be apologetic. A subordinate person might ask, "I know you have better things on your mind than to worry about me, but I was wondering when can I expect my reimbursement for travel expenses?" In a work setting, we ordinarily expect people with more formal authority to have the dominant role in conversations; however, in more democratic, informal companies, workers with more authority are less likely to feel the need to dominate conversations.

The *cold–warm dimension* also shapes communication because we invite the same behavior that we send. Cold, impersonal, negative messages evoke similar messages from others. In contrast, warm verbal and nonverbal messages evoke similar behavior from others. Getting back to the inquiry about the travel-expense check, here is a colder versus warmer response by the manager:

Colder: Travel vouchers really aren't my responsibility. You'll just have to wait like everybody else.

Warmer: I understand your problem. Not getting reimbursed on time is a bummer. I'll follow up on the status of your expense; check sometime today or tomorrow.

The combination of dominant and cold communication sends the signal that the sender of the message wants to control and limit or even withdraw from a personal relationship. A team leader might say that she cannot attend a Saturday morning meeting because she has to go out of town for her brother's wedding. A dominant and cold manager might say, "I don't want to hear about your personal life. Everyone in this department has to attend our Saturday meeting."

Subordinate actions combined with warm communication signal a desire to maintain or build the relationship while yielding to the other person. A manager communicating in a warm and subordinate manner in relation to the wedding request might say, "We'll miss you on Saturday morning because you are a key player in our department. However, I recognize that major events in personal life sometimes take priority over a business meeting."

Figure 4-2 summarizes how the dual dimensions of dominant–subordinate and cold–warm influence the relationship-building aspects of communication. Rather than regarding these four quadrants of relationships as good or bad, think of your purposes. In some situations, you might want to dominant and be cold, yet in most situations you might want to submit a little and be warm in order to build a relationship. For example, being dominant and cold might be necessary for a security officer who is trying to control an unruly crowd at a sporting event.

Observe that the person in the quadrant *dominant–cold* has an impersonal relationship with the receiver, and the person in the *warm–subordinate* quadrant has a supportive relationship with the receiver. Being *dominant* and *warm* leads to a personal relationship, whereas being *subordinate* and *cold* leads to an accepting relationship.

FIGURE 4-2 Communication Dimensions of Establishing a Relationship

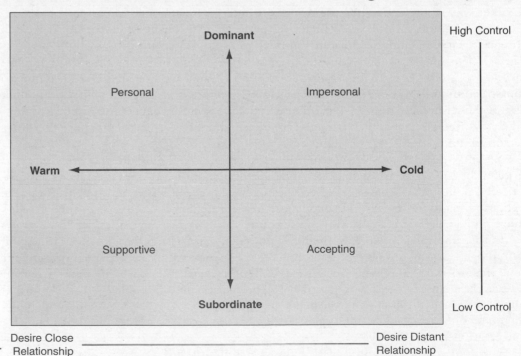

Source: Sorenson, Ritch; Debord, Grace; Ramirez, Ida, *Business and Management Communication: A Guide Book*, 4th Edition, p. 7. © 2001. Adapted by permission of Pearson Education, Inc., Upper Saddle River, NJ.

Harvard psychologist Steven Pinker adds additional insight into how warm acquaintances communicate. They go out of their way to look as if they are presuming not a dominant–subordinate relationship but instead a relationship of equals.[4] Your friend who values your relationship might say, "If you are going to the recycling center today, is there any chance you might be able to take along my old cell phone and laptop with you?"

An acquaintance not interested in maintaining a relationship with you might communicate in a cold, dominant–subordinate fashion by saying, "When you visit the recycling center today, take along my old cell phone and laptop with you."

NONVERBAL COMMUNICATION IN ORGANIZATIONS

A substantial amount of communication between people takes place at the nonverbal level. **Nonverbal communication** refers to the transmission of messages through means other than words. These messages accompany verbal messages, or sometimes they stand alone. The general purpose of nonverbal communication is to communicate the feeling behind a message. For instance, you can say no with either a clenched fist or a smile to communicate the intensity of your negative or positive feelings. Workers who rely solely on verbal messages to communicate with employees miss what the majority of what work associates are saying.[5]

Observing the nonverbal communication of others is useful in understanding whether they are sending a mixed message. In this context, a **mixed message** is a discrepancy between what a person says and how he or she acts. If teammate Rex says he is eager to contribute to a rush project, yet looks angry and distracted and slams his writing pad on the table, you may not get the cooperation you need. To clarify whether Rex is going to put forth full effort today, you might ask, "Rex, you tell us that you are going to work full force today, but you look upset. Is there anything I can do to help?"

The following paragraphs summarize the major modes of transmission of nonverbal communication and provide guidelines for improving nonverbal communication. Chapter 8, about cross-cultural relations, describes cultural differences in nonverbal communication.

Modes of Transmission of Nonverbal Communication

Nonverbal communication can be transmitted in many modes. You may be surprised that certain factors, such as dress and appearance, are considered part of nonverbal communication.

Environment. The setting or environment in which you send a message can influence how that message is received. Assume that your manager invites you out to lunch at an upscale restaurant to discuss a problem. You will think it is a more important topic under these circumstances than you would if the manager had lunch with you in the company cafeteria.

Other important environmental silent messages include room color, temperature, lighting, and furniture arrangement. A person who sits behind a large, uncluttered desk, for example, appears more powerful than a person who sits behind a small, messy desk.

Interpersonal Distance. The placement of one's body in relation to someone else is widely used to transmit messages (see Figure 4-3). In general, getting physically close to another person conveys a positive attitude toward that person. Putting your arm around someone is generally interpreted as a friendly act. (Some people, however, recoil when touched by someone other than a close friend. Touching others on the job can also be interpreted as sexual harassment.) Watch out for cultural differences in preferences for interpersonal distance, such as French people standing much closer to each other while conversing than do Americans.

Closely related to interpersonal distance is where and how you sit in relation to another person during a meeting. Sitting across the table from a person during a negotiation session creates a defensive, competitive atmosphere, often leading to each party taking a firm stand on his or her point of view. The table becomes a tangible and psychological barrier between both parties. Recognition of this observation leads many managers and salespeople to sit down with another person with either no table or a coffee

nonverbal communication
The transmission of messages through means other than words.

mixed message
A discrepancy between what a person says and how he or she acts.

FIGURE 4-3 Four Circles of Intimacy

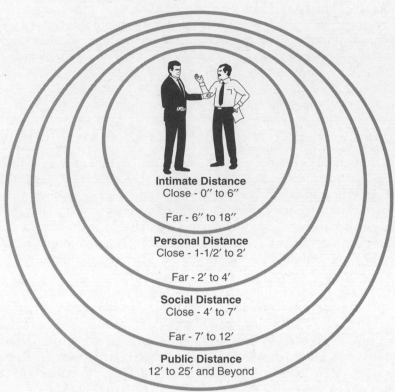

Intimate Distance
Close - 0″ to 6″

Far - 6″ to 18″

Personal Distance
Close - 1-1/2′ to 2′

Far - 2′ to 4′

Social Distance
Close - 4′ to 7′

Far - 7′ to 12′

Public Distance
12′ to 25′ and Beyond

table between the two. Even when seated on separate chairs instead of a sofa, removal of a large table or desk separating the two parties leads to a friendlier, more open negotiation or sales discussion.

Posture.   Posture communicates a variety of messages. Standing erect usually conveys the message that the person is self-confident and experiencing positive emotion. Slumping makes a person appear to be lacking in self-confidence or down in the dumps. Another interpersonal message conveyed by posture involves the direction of leaning. Leaning toward the sender suggests that you are favorably disposed toward his or her message; leaning backward communicates the opposite. Openness of the arms or legs serves as an indicator of liking or caring. In general, people establish closed postures (arms folded and legs crossed) when speaking to people they dislike.

Can you think of an aspect of your posture that conveys a specific message?

Hand Gestures.   Frequent hand movements show positive attitudes toward another person. In contrast, dislike or disinterest usually produces few gestures. An important exception is that some people wave their hands furiously while arguing. Gestures are also said to provide clues to a person's levels of dominance and submission. The gestures of dominant people are typically directed outward toward the other person. Examples include a steady, unwavering gaze and touching one's partner. Submissive gestures are usually protective, such as touching oneself or shrugging one's shoulders. A person who tucks his or her thumbs under his arms so that only the fingers are exposed is resisting what is being said.[6]

Facial Expressions and Eye Contact.   Using your head, face, and eyes in combination provides the clearest indications of interpersonal attitudes. Looking at the ceiling (without tilting your head), combined with a serious expression, almost always communicates the message "I doubt what you're saying is true." Maintaining eye contact with another person improves communication. To maintain eye contact, it is usually necessary to move your face and eyes to follow the other person. Moving your face and eyes away from the other person is often interpreted as defensiveness or a lack of self-confidence.

Kinga/Shutterstock

The face is often used as a primary source of information about how we feel. We look for facial clues when we want to determine another person's attitude. You can often judge someone's current state of happiness by looking at his or her face. The term "sourpuss" attests to this observation. Happiness, apprehension, anger, resentment, sadness, contempt, enthusiasm, and embarrassment are but a few of the emotions that can be expressed through the face.

Voice Quality. Often more significance is attached to the *way* something is said than to *what* is said. A forceful voice, which includes a consistent tone without vocalized pauses, connotes power and control. Closely related to voice tone are volume, pitch, and rate of speaking. Anger, boredom, and joy often can be interpreted from voice quality. Anger is noted when the person speaks loudly, with a high pitch and at a fast rate. Boredom is indicated by a monotone. Joy is indicated by loud volume. Avoiding an annoying voice quality can make a positive impact on others. The research of voice coach Jeffrey Jacobi provides some useful suggestions. He surveyed a nationwide sample of 1,000 men and women and asked, "Which irritating or unpleasant voice annoys you the most?" The most irritating was a whining, complaining, or nagging tone.

Jacobi notes that we are judged by the way we sound. He also notes that careers can be damaged by voice problems such as those indicated in the survey. "We think about how we look and dress," says Jacobi, "and that gets most of the attention. But people judge our intelligence much more by how we sound than how we dress."[7] Complete Self-Assessment Quiz 4-1 to apply Jacobi's findings to your development.

More recent research also supports the importance of voice quality in the workplace. The sound of a speaker's voice has an impact twice as much as the content of a message, according to a study of 120 business executives' speeches by a communication analytics company. Researchers used software to analyze the voices of speakers, then collected feedback from a panel of experts as well as 1,000 listeners. Voice quality accounted for 23 percent of listeners' evalations, whereas content accounted for 11 percent of the evaluations. Other evaluation factors were the speakers' passion, knowledge, and presence.[8] These findings do not mean that a person with a high-quality voice can speak nonsense and still make a good impression. A more accurate interpretaton is that voice quality creates a bigger impact than content, assuming that you have a worthwhile message to deliver.

Personal Appearance. Your external image plays an important role in communicating messages to others. Job seekers show recognition of the personal appearance aspect of nonverbal communication when they carefully groom for a job interview. People pay more respect and grant more privileges to those they perceive as being well dressed and neatly groomed. The meaning of being well dressed depends heavily on the situation. In an information technology firm, neatly pressed jeans, a stylish T-shirt, and clean sport shoes might qualify as being well dressed. The same attire worn in a financial services firm would qualify as being poorly dressed.

A current tendency is a return to more formal business attire, to suggest that a person is ambitious and successful. Even business casual is losing some acceptance, particularly when business casual resembles everyday casual (such as jeans and a T-shirt). The best advice for using appearance to communicate nonverbal messages is to size up the environment to figure out what type of appearance and dress connotes the image you want to project.

As you may have noticed, many men choose to shave their heads even when they are not experiencing natural baldness. A study conducted at the University of Pennsylvania's Wharton School suggests that men with shaved heads are perceived to be more dominant, and in some cases to have greater leadership potential, than their counterparts with longer hair or thinning hair.[9] For women, hair of moderate length often connotes more professionalism and leadership potential than does long, flowing hair.

Attention Paid to Other Person. The more attention paid to the other person during face-to-face interaction, the more valued and important that person feels. Paying attention to another individual includes other modes of nonverbal communication such as eye contact, an interested facial expression, and moving toward the other person. In a society that increasingly accepts and values multitasking, a natural tendency is to divide your attention between the person you are communicating and a computer screen, cell phone message, or a text message. Such multitasking is acceptable and natural to some people, yet makes many others feel unimportant and marginalized.

Research using electronic data supports the idea that the appropriate type of nonverbal communication has a positive impact on effectiveness. MIT professors Sandy Pentland and Daniel Olguín outfitted executives at a party with electronic devices that recorded data on their nonverbal signals, including tone of voice, gesticulation, and proximity to others. Five days later the same executives presented business plans to a panel of judges in a contest related to business plans. Without reading or hearing the presentations made to the judges, Pentland correctly predicted the winners, using only data collected at the party. The presence of a larger number of positive nonverbal signals was used to predict success in presenting a business plan.[10]

Guidelines for Improving Nonverbal Communication

Nonverbal communication, like verbal communication, can be improved. Here are eight suggestions to consider.

1. **Obtain feedback on your body language by asking others to comment on the gestures and facial expressions you use in conversations.** Be videotaped conferring with another individual. After studying your body language, attempt to eliminate those mannerisms and gestures that you think detract from your effectiveness. Common examples include nervous gestures such as moving knees from side to side, cracking knuckles, rubbing the eyes or nose, head scratching, and jingling coins.

2. **Learn to relax when communicating with others.** Take a deep breath and consciously allow your body muscles to loosen. Tension-reducing techniques should be helpful here. A relaxed person makes it easier for other people to relax. You are likely to elicit more useful information from other people when you are relaxed. Also, you will appear more confident and credible when you are relaxed to an appropriate degree.

3. **Use facial, hand, and body gestures to supplement your speech, but don't overdo it.** A good starting point is to use hand gestures to express enthusiasm. You can increase the potency of enthusiastic comments by shaking the other person's hand, nodding approval, or smiling.

4. **Avoid using the same nonverbal gesture indiscriminately.** If you want to use nodding to convey approval, do not nod with approval when you dislike what somebody else is saying. Also, do not pat everybody on the back. Nonverbal gestures that are used indiscriminately lose their communication effectiveness.

5. **Use role-playing to practice various forms of nonverbal communication.** A good starting point would be to practice selling your ideas about an important project or concept to another person. During your interchange, supplement your spoken messages with appropriate nonverbal cues, such as posture, voice intonation, gestures, and so forth. Later, obtain the other person's perception of the effectiveness of your nonverbal communication.

6. **Use mirroring to establish rapport.** Nonverbal communication can be improved through **mirroring**, or subtly imitating someone. The most successful mirroring technique is to imitate the breathing pattern of another person. If you adjust your own breathing rate to match someone else's, you will soon establish rapport with that individual. Another effective mirroring technique is to adopt the voice speed of the person with whom you are communicating. If the other person speaks more slowly than you typically do, slow down to mirror him or her.

mirroring
Subtly imitating someone.

You can also use mirroring by imitating a manager to win favor. Many subordinates have a relentless tendency to copy the boss's mannerisms, gestures, way of speaking, and dress. As a consequence, without realizing why, your manager may think more favorably of you.

Caution: Do not use mirroring to the extent that you appear to be mocking another person, thereby adversely affecting rapport. Do Skill-Building Exercise 4-1 to get started developing your mirroring skills.

7. **Check to see if your appearance fits the message you want to send to others in a work environment.** It may take considerable courage, but ask several people to provide you with feedback on how well your appearance fits the image you want to portray, and the message you want to send in a work setting. Obtain impressions of your clothing style, grooming, and hairstyle (baldnesss included). If your appearance is lacking, make appropriate adjustments by observing a few role models as well as seeking written and spoken advice.

8. **To appear in control and self-confident when standing, plant both feet firmly on the floor and with a distance between the feet of approximately twelve inches.** Executive coach Sharon Sayler says that any other stance could send the message that you are off balance personally or professionally.[11]

The Mirroring Technique

To practice mirroring, during the next 10 days each class member schedules one mirroring session with an unsuspecting subject. An ideal opportunity would be an upcoming meeting on the job. Another possibility would be to ask a friend if you could practice your interviewing techniques with him or her—but do not mention the mirroring technique. A third possibility would be to sit down with a friend and conduct a social conversation.

While holding an interview or discussion with the other party, use the mirroring technique. Imitate the person's breathing pattern, rate of speech, hand movements, eye movements, leg movements, or any other noticeable aspect of behavior.

After the mirroring sessions have been conducted, hold a class discussion about the results. Questions include the following:

1. Did the other person notice the mirroring and comment on the behavior of the person doing the mirroring?
2. Was the rapport enhanced (or hindered) by the mirroring?
3. How many of the students intend to repeat the mirroring technique in the future?

Guidelines for Detecting Lying through Nonverbal Communication

Another interpersonal skill related to nonverbal communication is the ability to detect lying. A conservative approach is to regard certain indicators to suggest that a person might by lying, and then to investigate further the truthfulness of certain statements. For example, an employee suspected of selling employee social security numbers to an outside party might respond to any questioning about this theft with a quick, seemingly rehearsed answer. Further investigation, perhaps using a private detective, might be warranted.

It is important to recognize that surefire behavioral indicators of deception do not exist—that the behavior of liars is not consistently revealing. A team of three researchers who reviewed the evidence about human behavior and deception detection concluded that no researcher has documented a "Pinocchio response." (The nose of the fairy tale character Pinocchio grew when he told a lie.) The finding means that there is no behavior or pattern of behavior that in all people, in all situations indicates deception.

What is known with reasonable certainty is that lying requires extra mental effort. The liar must think quite hard to cover up and create events that have not happened. The extra effort will show up in the nonverbal forms of longer pauses between thoughts, and the use of hand and head movements that accompany speech will be less frequent. Part of the extra effort stems from the liar changing his or her typical behavior.

With respect to emotions, liars do appear to be more nervous than truth tellers. The facial expressions of liars tend to be less pleasant, and also show higher vocal pitch, more tension in their voice, greater pupil dilation, and more fidgeting.[12] A related cue is that the vocal pitch suddenly going up or down is frequently associated with lying.

The scientific evidence about nonverbal indicators of lying therefore supports the generally-accepted belief that liars touch their face more, twitch more, avoid eye contact, and fidget considerably.[13]

GUIDELINES FOR OVERCOMING COMMUNICATION PROBLEMS AND BARRIERS

LEARNING OBJECTIVE 4

Communication problems in organizations are ever present. Some interference usually takes place between ideation and action, as suggested earlier by the noise factor in Figure 4-1. The type of message influences the amount of interference. Routine or neutral messages are the easiest to communicate. Interference is most likely to occur when a message is complex, emotionally arousing, or clashes with a receiver's mental set.

An emotionally arousing message deals with topics such as money or a relationship between two people. A message that clashes with a receiver's mental set requires the person to change his or her typical pattern of receiving messages. Try this experiment. The next time you visit a restaurant, order dessert first and the main meal second. The server probably will not receive your dessert order because it deviates from the normal sequence.

FIGURE 4-4   Overcoming Communication Problems and Barriers

1. Communicate honestly.
2. Understanding the receiver.
3. Minimize defensive communication.
4. Repeat your message and use multiple channels.
5. Check comprehension and feelings via verbal and nonverbal feedback.
6. Display a positive attitude.
7. Communicate persuasively.
8. Engage in active listening.
9. Prepare for stressful conversations.
10. Engage in metacommunication.
11. Recognize gender differences in communication style.

Here we will describe strategies and tactics for overcoming some of the more frequently observed communication problems in the workplace, as outlined in Figure 4-4. A useful guideline is that the communicator should take the initiative to increase the probability that his or her message will get across as intended. In the words of Jess Thomas, the chairman, president, and CEO of Molina Healthcare of Michigan, "A sobering reality in communication is that the greater burden and basis for breakdown in effective communication rests with the communicator. The communicator has to be very articulate in communicating what he or she wants."[14]

Communicate Honestly

A major reason many communicators are not taken seriously, and that their messages do not get across as intended, is because they are not trusted. When people lie, a communication barrier is erected. A similar perspective is that when people are trusted, their messages are more likely to be received. A person who communicates honestly is also more likely to receive honest communications from others. When people trust you, they are more likely to present you with accurate information.[15] For example, a team leader is more likely to be informed of a problem if the informer does not think he or she will be blamed for the problem. The subject of trust will be explored in more depth in relation to characteristics of a leader in Chapter 10.

Understand the Receiver

Understanding the person you are trying to reach is a fundamental principle of overcoming communication barriers. The more you know about your receiver, the better you are able to deliver your message effectively. Three important aspects of understanding the receiver are (1) developing empathy, (2) recognizing his or her motivational state, and (3) understanding the other person's frame of reference.

Developing **empathy** requires placing yourself in the receiver's shoes. To accomplish this, you have to imagine yourself in the other person's role and assume the viewpoints and emotions of that individual. You have to imagine how you would feel if placed in that situation. For example, if a supervisor were trying to communicate the importance of customer service to sales associates, the supervisor might ask himself or herself, "If I were a part-time employee being paid close to the minimum wage, how receptive would I be to messages about superior customer service?" To empathize, you have to understand another person. *Sympathy* means that you understand and agree.

Research suggests that subtle patterns of brain cells, called mirror neurons, help us empathize with others. These brain circuits reflect the actions and intentions of others as if they were our own. Neuroscientist Marco Iacoboni explains that the mirror system gives us an open-mindedness and a propensity to understand others and other cultures. The cells work in this manner: When another person smiles or wrinkles his or her nose in

empathy

In communication, imagining oneself in the receiver's role and assuming the viewpoints and emotions of that individual.

distaste, motor cells in your own brain linked to those expressions resonate in response like a tuning fork. As a result, you get a hint of the feeling itself. The more empathy you have, the stronger the motor neuron response.[16]

The biological component to empathy should not lead you to conclude that empathy is not a skill that can be acquired. It is conceivable that as you develop empathy, your mirror neurons grow in number or become better developed, just as your calf muscles become better defined if you run frequently.

motivational state

Any active needs and interests operating at a given time.

The receiver's **motivational state** could include any active needs and interests operating at the time. People tend to listen attentively to messages that show promise of satisfying an active need or interest. Management usually listens attentively to a suggestion framed in terms of cost savings or increased profits. A coworker is likely to be attentive to your message if you explain how your idea can lead to a better year-end financial bonus for the group.

frame of reference

The fact that people perceive words and concepts differently because their vantage points and perspectives differ.

People perceive words and concepts differently because their vantage points and perspectives differ. Such differences in **frame of reference** create barriers to communication. A frame of reference can also be considered a lens through which we view the world. A manager attempted to chastise a team member by saying, "If you continue to make these technical errors, we are going to have to assign you to a less technical role." The technician replied, "That's good news," because he was becoming frustrated with doing technical work for the entire workday. Understanding another person's frame of reference requires empathy.

On a day-by-day basis, understanding another person's frame of reference often translates into figuring out his or her mindset. A woman telephoned a tech support center located in India with a sense of frustration in her voice. She said she was instructed by her computer to "press any key to continue," and was upset that her keyboard didn't have an "any" key. The caller's mindset was that she had to search for the "any" key.[17] Of course, a more perceptive person might have noticed that the instructions did not say press *the* any key to continue, but *any key*.

Minimize Defensive Communication

defensive communication

The tendency to receive messages in such a way that our self-esteem is protected.

An important general communication barrier is **defensive communication**—the tendency to receive messages in such a way that our self-esteem is protected. Defensive communication is also responsible for people sending messages to make them look good. For example, when being criticized for low production, a financial sales consultant might blame low mortgage rates, which are encouraging many people to invest in a new home rather than in the stock market.

denial

The suppression of information we find uncomfortable.

Overcoming the barrier of defensive communication requires two steps. First, people have to recognize the existence of defensive communication. Second, they have to try not to be defensive when questioned or criticized. Such behavior is not easy because of the unconscious or semiconscious process of **denial**—the suppression of information we find uncomfortable. For example, the sales consultant just cited would find it uncomfortable to think of himself or herself as being responsible for below-average performance.

Repeat Your Message Using Multiple Channels (in Moderation)

Repetition enhances communication, particularly when different channels are used to convey the same message. Effective communicators at many job levels follow spoken agreements with written documentation. Since most communication is subject to at least some distortion, the chances of a message being received as intended increase when two or more channels are used. Many firms have a policy of using a multiple-channel approach to communicate the results of a performance evaluation. The worker receives an oral explanation from the manager of the results of the review. The worker is also required to read the form and indicate by signature that he or she has read and understands the meaning of the review. Another useful way of using multiple channels is to follow up a telephone call or in-person conversation with an e-mail or text message summarizing key facts or agreements. Such an approach helps overcome the communication problem of a person saying, "I never received your e-mail (or text message). Maybe it was placed in my junk mail."

When repeating your message or using multiple channels, use moderation to avoid contributing to the problem of **information overload**—a phenomenon that occurs when people are so overloaded with information that they cannot respond effectively to messages. Research consistently suggests that the expanding volume of information can not only create stress, but also negatively affect decision making, innovation, and productivity.[18]

Check Comprehension and Feelings through Verbal and Nonverbal Feedback

Ask for feedback to determine whether your message has been received as intended. A frequent managerial practice is to conclude a meeting with a question such as, "Okay, what have we agreed upon?" Another useful form of feedback after a meeting is to have participants post on a company Web page (such as an intranet) what message they took away from the meeting. Unless feedback of this nature is obtained, you will not know whether your message has been received until the receiver carries out your request. If the request is carried out improperly, or if no action is taken, you will know that the message was received poorly.

Obtaining feedback is important because it results in two-way communication in which people take turns being sender and receiver, thereby having a dialogue. Dialogues take time because they require people to speak more slowly and listen more carefully. Obtaining feedback also contributes to an interactional encounter between two (or among several) people. By interacting with the other person, the other person is more likely to perceive you positively and support your ideas.[19] An easy way to prompt an interaction is to ask a question. For example, the store manager might make the following statement followed by a question: "We need to get more customers signing up for our warranty program. Why do you think so many customers are not signing up for the program?"

Feedback is also important because it provides reinforcement to the sender, and few people will continue to communicate without any reinforcement. The sender is reinforced when the receiver indicates understanding of the message. When the original receiver indicates that he or she understands the message, that person becomes the sender. A nod of approval would be an appropriate type of nonverbal reinforcement for the sender to receive.

In addition to looking for verbal comprehension and emotions when you have delivered a message, check for feelings after you have received a message. When a person speaks, we too often listen to the facts and ignore the feelings. If feelings are ignored, the true meaning and intent of the message is likely to be missed, thus creating a communication barrier. Your boss might say to you, "You never seem to take work home." To clarify what your boss means by this statement, you might ask, "Is that good or bad?" Your boss's response will give you feedback on his or her feelings about getting all your work done during regular working hours.

When you send a message, it is also helpful to express your feelings in addition to conveying the facts. For example, "Our defects are up by 12 percent (fact), and I'm quite disappointed about those results (feelings)." Because feelings contribute strongly to comprehension, you will help overcome a potential communication barrier.

Display a Positive Attitude

Being perceived as having a positive attitude helps melt communication barriers. This is true because most people prefer to communicate with a positive person. Being positive helps make you appear more credible and trustworthy, whereas being consistently negative makes you less credible and trustworthy. As one coworker said about a chronic complainer in his office, "Why take Margot seriously? She finds something wrong with everybody and everything."

Communicate Persuasively

A powerful tactic for overcoming communication barriers is to communicate so persuasively that obstacles disappear. Persuasiveness refers to the sender convincing the receiver to accept his or her message. Persuasion thus involves selling to others. Hundreds of articles, books, audiotapes, and videos have been developed to help people become more persuasive. The following are 11 representative suggestions for becoming a more persuasive communicator, both in speaking and in writing.[20]

1. **Know exactly what you want and communicate directly:** Your chances of selling an idea increase to the extent that you have clarified the idea in your own mind. The clearer and more committed you are at the outset of a selling or negotiating session, the stronger you are as a persuader. After knowing what you want, you are in a position to communicate directly. Suppose you do not want to join your coworkers for lunch today because you are overloaded with work. An indrect statement would be, "It looks like the restaurants would be very crowded because it is St. Patrick's Day." You would be more persuasive if you said, "Thanks for the invitation, but I would prefer to join some other time. I am overloaded today."

2. **Never suggest an action without explaining its end benefit:** In asking for a raise, you might say, "If I get this raise, I'll be able to afford to stay with this job as long as the company likes. I will also increase my productivity because I won't be distracted by thinking about meeting my expenses."

3. **Get a yes response early on:** It is helpful to give the persuading session a positive tone by establishing a "yes pattern" at the outset. Assume that an employee wanted to convince the boss to allow the employee to perform some work at home during normal working hours. The employee might begin the idea-selling questions with "Is it important for the company to obtain maximum productivity from all its employees?"

4. **Use power words:** An expert tactic for being persuasive is to sprinkle your speech with power (meaning powerful) words. Power words stir emotion and bring forth images of exciting events. Examples of power words and expressions include consequences, impact, engagement, bonding with customers, surpassing previous profits, building customer loyalty, and sustainability. Using power words is part of having a broad vocabulary.

5. **Minimize raising your pitch at the end of sentences:** Part of being persuasive is not to sound unsure and apologetic. In English and several other languages, a convenient way to ask a question or to express doubt is to raise the pitch of your voice at the end of a sentence or phrase. As a test, use the sentence "You like my ideas." First say *ideas* using approximately the same pitch and tone as with every other word. Then say the same sentence by pronouncing *ideas* with a higher pitch and louder tone. By saying *ideas* loudly, you sound much less certain and are less persuasive.

6. **Talk to your audience, not the screen:** Computer graphic presentations have become standard practice even in small-group meetings. Many presenters rely so heavily on computer-generated slides and transparencies that they basically read the slides and transparencies to the audience. In an oral presentation, the predominant means of connection between sender and receiver should be eye contact. When your audience is frequently distracted by movement on the screen, computer sounds, garish colors, or you looking at the screen, eye contact suffers. As a result, the message is weakened, and you are less persuasive.[21] Many companies have virtually banned PowerPoint presentations because so many presenters use this technique poorly.

7. **Back up conclusions with data:** You will be more persuasive if you support your spoken and written presentations with solid data. You can collect the data

yourself or quote from a printed or electronic source. Relying too much on research has a potential disadvantage, however. Being too dependent on data could suggest that you have little faith in your intuition. For example, you might convey a weak impression if, when asked your opinion, you respond, "I can't answer until I collect some data."

8. **Minimize "wimp" phrases and words:** Persuasive communicators minimize statements that make them appear weak and indecisive. Such phrases convey the impression that they are not in control of their actions. Wimp phrases include: "It's one of those days," "I'm not sure about that," "Don't quote me on that," and "I'll try my best to get it done." (It is better to commit yourself forcibly by saying, "I'll get it done.") Wimpy words include "sort of," "hopefully," and "maybe." A word that borders on being wimpy, or that is at least not strong, is "if" in place of "when." Notice the difference between the two following statements: "If I get this report done this week, I'll send you an e-mail" and "When I get this report done this week . . . . ."

Another problem with wimp words and phrases is that they can mar your image, or make you appear not in control of your work. Three examples follow:

- "I'm too busy/I don't have time/I'm just swamped."
- "I'm having one of those days/Things are crazy here/You have caught me at a bad time."
- "We'll see how it goes/I'll try my best."[22]

Although wimp phrases and words should be minimized, there are times when they reflect honest communication, such as a team leader saying to the manager, "Maybe we can get this crash project completed by the end of the month."

9. **Avoid or minimize common language errors:** You will enhance your persuasiveness if you minimize common language errors because you will appear more articulate and informed. Here are several common language errors:

a. "Just between you and I" is wrong. "Just between you and me" is correct.

b. *Irregardless* is not a word; *regardless* is correct.

c. Avoid double negatives when you want to express the negative, despite the increasing popularity of double negatives. Common examples of double negatives are "I got no nothing from my best customer this week" and "We don't have no money in the budget for travel." If expressed with the right inflection, a double negative can be correct. For example, to say "We don't have no money" with an emphasis on *no money* means that the budget is not completely depleted. Yet in general, double negatives make the sender appear so ill-informed that they fail to persuade.

d. "Ask your guest what *they* want for lunch" is incorrect despite the widespread use of using a plural pronoun instead of the singular. "Ask your guest what *he* (or *she*) wants" is correct. A caution here is that it appears about 90 percent of Americans including the well-educated confuse the singular and plural today, so using "they" instead of "he" or "she" is not a dreadful error in grammar; however, using "themselves" instead of "him" or "her" is a dreadful error. An example of this misuse is, "I prefer a coworker who can speak up for *themselves*."

10. **Avoid overuse of jargon and clichés.** To feel "in" and hip, many workers rely heavily on jargon and clichés, such as referring to their "fave" (for *favorite*) product, or saying that "At the end of the day" something counts, or that software is "scalable" (meaning it can get bigger). Add to the list "a seamless company" to mean the various departments cooperate with one another. The caution is that if a person uses jargon and hip phrases too frequently, the person appears to be too contrived and lacking in imagination.[23]

11. **Avoid converting too many nouns into verbs:** A frequent error in the workplace and in personal life is to convert too many nouns into verbs. Many

nouns have become verbs, such as, "I will phone you tomorrow." (The noun is *phone*.) Another positive example is, "We need to hammer home this point." (The noun is *hammer*.) In contrast, a questionable communication practice is to say, "I'll Skype you tonight," or "I will W2 you tommorrow." (W2 is the statement of wages and taxes given to employees as well as the Internal Revenue Service.)

If you can learn to implement most of the preceding 11 suggestions, you are on your way toward becoming a persuasive communicator. In addition, you will need solid facts behind you, and you will need to make skillful use of nonverbal communication. If you are looking for an example of a persuasive communicator in business, check out David A. Brandon, the former CEO of Domino's Pizza. Brandon is such a great motivator and communicator that many people have encouraged him to run for public office. He is now the director of intercollegiate athletics at the University of Michigan. See if you can find a video of Brandon on the Internet.

Skill-Building Exercise 4-2 provides you with an opportunity to practice persuasive communication.

Engage in Active Listening

Persuasion deals primarily with sending messages. Improving one's receiving of messages is another part of developing better communication skills. Unless you receive messages as they are intended, you cannot perform your job properly or be a good companion. A major challenge in developing good listening skills is that we process information much more quickly than most people speak. The average speaking rate is about 130 words per minute. In contrast, the average rate of processing information is about 300 words per minute.[24] So, you have to slow down mentally to listen well. A related problem is that many people like to dominate conversations, making it difficult to listen. As expressed by investment banker Herb Allen, "It's tough to listen when you're talking."[25]

Communication consultant Connie Kieken observes that in today's time-pressed workplaces many people attempt to listen at high speed, causing their minds to fade in and fade out. To prevent this problem, focus on the other person's meaning and motivation.[26]

Listening can be even more essential than talking when engaged in face-to-face communication. Listening is a particularly important skill for anybody whose job involves troubleshooting, because one needs to gather information to solve problems. Listening is also regarded as the front-end of decision making, because you need to absorb relevant facts before making a decision.[27] Another reason that improving the listening skills of employees is important is that insufficient listening is extraordinarily costly. Listening mistakes lead to reprocessing letters, rescheduling appointments, reshipping orders, and recalling defective products. Effective listening also improves interpersonal relations because the people listened to feel understood and respected.

A major component of effective listening is to be an **active listener**. The active listener listens intensely, with the goal of empathizing with the speaker. Several important skills and behaviors associated with active listening are presented next.

Show Respect.   A cornerstone of effective listening, including active listening, is to show respect for others in the form of being eager to receive their input. To actively listen to another person is to respect him or her as well as that person's ideas. A good example is the chief operating officer of a large medical institution who was known to be an excellent listener. The executive in question said he could not run an operation as complex as a hospital without seeking input from workers at all levels, from the chief of surgery to the custodial crew.[28]

Accept the Sender's Figure of Speech.   A useful way of showing empathy is to accept the sender's figure of speech. By so doing, the sender feels understood and accepted. Also, if you reject the person's figure of speech by rewording it, the sender may become defensive. Many people use the figure of speech "I'm stuck" when they cannot accomplish a task. You can facilitate smooth communication by a response such as, "What can I do to help you get unstuck?" If you respond with something like, "What can I do to help you think more clearly?" the person is forced to change mental channels and may become defensive.[29]

Paraphrase and Listen Reflectively.   As a result of listening actively, the listener can give feedback to the speaker on what he or she thinks the speaker meant. Feedback of this type relies on both verbal and nonverbal communication. Feedback is also important because it facilitates two-way communication. To be an active listener, it is also important to **paraphrase**, or repeat in your own words what the sender says, feels, and means. Paraphrasing is also referred to as reflective listening, because the listener reflects back what the sender said. You might feel awkward the first several times you paraphrase. Therefore, try it with a person with whom you feel comfortable. With some practice, it will become a natural part of your communication skill kit. Here is an example of how you might use paraphrasing:

> **Other Person:** I'm getting ticked off at working so hard around here. I wish somebody else would pitch in and do a fair day's work.
> **You:** You're saying that you do more than your fair share of the tough work in our department.
> **Other Person:** You bet. Here's what I think we should be doing about it.

Life coach Sophronia Scott advises that, after you have paraphrased, it is sometimes helpful to ask the person you listened to whether your impression of what he or she said is correct. Your goal is not to make others repeat themselves, but to extend the conversation so that you can obtain more useful details.[30]

Minimize Distractions.   If feasible, keep papers, mobile devices, and your computer screen out of sight when listening to somebody else. Having distractions in sight creates the temptation to glance away from the message sender. Avoid answering a phone call unless you are anticipating an emergency call. At the start of your conversation, notice the other person's eye color to help you establish eye contact. (But don't keep staring at his or her eyes!)

Ask Questions.   A major technique of active listening is to ask questions rather than make conclusive statements. Asking questions provides more useful information. Suppose a teammate is late with data you need to complete your analysis. Instead of saying, "I must have your input by Thursday afternoon," try, "When will I get your input?"

Allow Sender to Finish His or Her Sentence. Be sure to let others speak until they have finished. Do not interrupt by talking about yourself, jumping in with advice, or offering solutions unless requested. Equally bad for careful listening is to finish the sentence of a receiver. Almost all people prefer to complete their own thoughts, even though there are two curious traditions that run counter to this idea. One is that business partners who have been working together for many years, and understand each other well, have a tendency to finish the other partner's sentence. Couples in personal life behave similarly. Also, have you noticed how when you start to enter a phrase into a major search engine, suddenly you are given about 10 choices that are not necessarily what you are planning to write? (Of course, this is responding to writing, and not really listening, but the overtaking of your thinking is the same.)

Use Nonverbal Communication. Another component to active listening is to indicate by your body language that you are listening intently. When a coworker comes to you with a question or concern, focus on that person and exclude all else. If you tap your fingers on the desk or glance around the room, you send the message that the other person and his or her concerns do not warrant your full attention. Listening intently through nonverbal communication also facilitates active listening because it demonstrates respect for the receiver.

Observing nonverbal communication is another important part of active listening. Look to see if the speaker's verbal communication matches his or her nonverbal communication. Suppose you ask another person if he or she would like to join your committee. If the person says "yes," but looks bored and defensive, he or she is probably not really interested in joining your committee. Quite often a person's nonverbal communication is more indicative of the truth than is verbal communication.

Minimize Words That Shut Down Discussion. A key part of listening is to keep the conversation flowing. According to executive coach Marshall Goldsmith, an especially useful approach to keep conversation going in most work situations is for the listener to minimize certain negatively toned words that frequently shut down conversation. When you say "no," "but," or "however," you effectively shut down or limit the conversation. No matter what words follow, the sender receives a message to the effect, "You are wrong and I am right." Even if you say "I agree, but . . ." the shutdown message still comes through. The other person is likely to get into the defensive mode.[31] Another way of shutting down conversation is to say, "I already know that."

After the person has finished talking, there are times it will be appropriate to say "no," "but," or "however." Assume, for example, that a worker says to the business owner that the company should donate one-third of its profits to charity each year. The owner might then reply, "I hear you, but if we give away all that money our profits will be too slim to grow the business."

Avoid the Need to Lie or Fake When You Have Not Been Paying Attention. A consequence of active listening is that you will avoid the need to pretend that you have been paying attention. Performance management coach Joe Takash suggests that you remind yourself that other people can sense if you're not listening. Force yourself to be honest and admit that you didn't catch everything that was said. That means asking the other person to repeat or requesting clarification. In this way you're being honest rather than deceitful—and deceit kills results-producing relationships fast.[32]

Specific suggestions for improving active listening skills are summarized in Figure 4-5. These suggestions relate to good listening in general, as well as active listening. Many suggestions reinforce what has already been described. As with any other suggestions for developing a new skill, considerable practice (with some supervision) is needed to bring about actual changes in behavior. One of the problems a poor listener would encounter is the difficulty of breaking old habits to acquire new ones. To practice your listening skills, do Skill-Building Exercise 4-3.

FIGURE 4-5 Suggestions for Active Listening

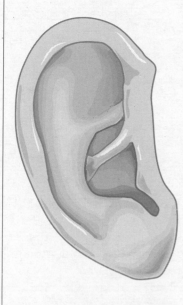

- *While your target is talking, look at him or her intently.* At the same time, maintain steady eye contact.

- *Be patient about your turn to speak.* A common barrier to effective listening is to mentally prepare an answer while another person is speaking.

- *Nod your head in agreement from time to time.*

- *Mutter "mmh" or "uh-huh" periodically, but not incessantly.*

- *Ask open-ended questions to encourage the other person to talk.* For example, you encourage more conversation by saying "What do you think of . . . ?" rather than asking "Do you agree that . . . ?"

- *Reflect your target's content or meaning.* Rephrase and summarize concisely what the other person is saying.

- *Reflect the other person's feelings.* Reflection-of-feeling responses typically begin with "You feel that . . . "

- *Keep your ratio of talking to listening down to about one to five.* In other words, spend 20 percent of your time talking and 80 percent listening to be perceived as a great listener.

- *Ask yourself whether anything the other person is saying could benefit you.* Maintaining this perspective will enable you to benefit from most listening episodes and will motivate you to listen intently.

- *Minimize chatter in your head while listening.* Thinking of other things, including conversations you would like to have while the other person is talking, detracts from carefully listening to what the other person is saying.

epare for Stressful Conversations

Communication barriers will frequently surface when two or more people are engaged in conversation fraught with emotion, such as giving highly negative performance feedback, rejecting a person for membership in your team, or firing an employee. Praising is another exchange that can make either or both parties uncomfortable. The sender might feel that he or she is patronizing the receiver, and the receiver might feel unworthy of the praise. One technique for reducing the stress in potentially stressful conversations is to prepare for them in advance.

A starting point in preparing for a stressful conversation is self-awareness about how you react to certain uncomfortable exchanges. For example, how do you feel when the receiver of the negative feedback reacts with hostility? Do you clam up, or do you become counterhostile? If you anticipate a hostile reception to an upcoming conversation, rehearse the scenario with a neutral friend. Deliver the controversial content that you will be delivering during the real event. Practice the body language you will use when you deliver a phrase such as, "As team leader, I must tell you that you have contributed almost nothing of value to our current project." Another part of the rehearsal is to practice delivering clear content—be explicit about what you mean. "Almost nothing of value to our current project" is much more explicit than "Your contribution has much room for improvement."

Also, practice *temperate phrasing*, or being tactful while delivering negative feedback. Communications specialist Holly Weeks suggests the following. Instead of snapping at someone—"Stop interrupting me"—try this: "Can you hold on a minute? I want to finish before I lose my train of thought." Temperate phrasing will take some of the sting out of a stressful conversation.[33]

Listening to a Coworker

Before conducting the following role-plays, review the suggestions for effective listening presented in the text and Figure 4-5. Restating what you hear (summarization) is particularly important when listening to a person who is talking about an emotional topic.

The Elated Coworker: One student plays the role of a coworker who has just been offered a six-month assignment to the Rome, Italy, unit of the company. She will be receiving a 30 percent pay increase during the assignment plus a supplementary living allowance. She is eager to describe the full details of her good fortune to a coworker. Another student plays the role of the coworker to whom the first worker wants to describe her good fortune. The second worker decides to listen intently to the first

worker. Other class members will rate the second student on his or her listening ability.

The Discouraged Coworker: One student plays the role of a coworker who has just been placed on probation for poor job performance. His boss thinks that his performance is below standard and that his attendance and punctuality are poor. He is afraid that if he tells his girlfriend, she will leave him. He is eager to tell his tale of woe to a coworker. Another student plays the role of a coworker he corners to discuss his problems. The second worker decides to listen intently to his problems, but is pressed for time. Other class members will rate the second student on his or her listening ability.

When evaluating the active listening skills of the role players, consider using the following evaluating factors, on a scale of 1 (low) to 5 (high):

Evaluation Factor	Rating 1 2 3 4 5
1. Maintained eye contact	
2. Showed empathy	
3. Summarize what the other person said	
4. Focused on other person instead of being distracted	
5. Asked questions	
6. Let other person speak until he or she was finished	

Engage in Metacommunication

metacommunication

To communicate about your communication to help overcome barriers or resolve a problem.

Sometimes the best way to overcome a communication barrier with another person is to describe the nature of the relationship between you two at the moment. **Metacommunication** is to communicate about your communication to help overcome barriers or resolve a problem. If you, as a team leader, are facing heavy deadline pressures, you may say to a team member, "I might appear brusque today and tomorrow. Please don't take it personally. It's just that I have to make heavy demands on you because the team is facing a gruesome deadline." A more common situation is when the person with whom you are attempting to communicate appears angry or indifferent. Instead of wasting the communication event, it would be better to say, "You do not seem receptive to listening to me now. Are we having a problem? Should I try again later?"

Recognize Gender Differences in Communication Style

A trend in organizations for many years has been to move toward gender equality. Despite this trend, substantial interest has arisen in identifying differences in communication styles between men and women. People who are aware of these differences face fewer communication barriers between themselves and members of the opposite sex. As we discuss these differences, recognize that they are group stereotypes. Please do not be offended by these stereotypes; they are exaggerations noticed by some researchers and observers. To cite one example that runs counter to the stereotype, some women dominate meetings, whereas some men focus on listening to and supporting others during a meeting. Individual differences in communication style usually are more important than group (men vs. women) differences. Here we will discuss nine major findings of gender differences in communication patterns.[34]

1. **Women prefer to use conversation for rapport building.** For most women, the intent of conversation is to build rapport and connections with people. Women are therefore more likely to emphasize similarities, to listen intently, and to be supportive.

2. **Men prefer to use talk primarily as a means to preserve independence and status by displaying knowledge and skill.** When most men talk, they want to receive positive evaluation from others and maintain their hierarchical status within the group. Men are therefore more oriented to giving a *report* while women are more interested in establishing *rapport*.

3. **Women want empathy, not solutions.** When women share feelings of being stressed out, they seek empathy and understanding. If they feel they have been listened to carefully, they begin to relax. When listening to the woman, the man may feel blamed for her problems or feel that he has failed the woman in some way. To feel useful, the man might offer solutions to the woman's problems.

4. **Men prefer to work out their problems by themselves, whereas women prefer to talk out solutions with another person.** Women look upon having and sharing problems as an opportunity to build and deepen relationships. Men are more likely to look upon problems as challenges they must meet on their own. The communication consequence of these differences is that men may become uncommunicative when they have a problem.

5. **Women are more likely to compliment the work of a coworker, whereas men are more likely to be critical.** A communication problem may occur when a woman compliments the work of a male coworker and expects reciprocal praise.

6. **Men tend to be more directive in their conversation, whereas women emphasize politeness.** Women are therefore more likely to frequently use the phrases "I'm sorry" and "Thank you," even when there is no need to express apology or gratitude. For example, a supermarket manager notices that the store has suddenly become busy. She would therefore say to a store associate unpacking boxes, "I'm sorry Pedro, but we've become busy all of a sudden. Could you please open a new lane up front? Thank you." A manager who is a stereotypical male might say, "Pedro, we need you to open a line up front, pronto. Put down the boxes and get up there."

7. **Women tend to be more conciliatory when facing differences, whereas men become more intimidating.** Again, women are more interested in building relationships, whereas men are more concerned about coming out ahead.

8. **Men are more interested than women in calling attention to their accomplishments or hogging recognition.** In one instance, a sales representative who had already made her sales quota for the month turned over an excellent prospect to a coworker. She reasoned, "It's somebody else's turn. I've received more than my fair share of bonuses for the month."

9. **Men tend to dominate discussions during meetings.** One study of college faculty meetings found that women's longest turns at speaking were, on average, of shorter duration than men's shortest turns. A possible explanation here is that women are still less assertive than men in the workplace.

How can the information just presented help overcome communication problems on the job? As a starting point, remember that these gender differences often exist. Understanding these differences will help you interpret the communication behavior of people. For example, if a male coworker is not as effusive with praise as you would like, remember that he is simply engaging in gender-typical behavior. Do not take it personally.

A woman can remind herself to speak up more in meetings because her natural tendency might be toward diffidence. She might say to herself, "I must watch out to avoid gender-typical behavior in this situation." A man might remind himself to be more complimentary and supportive toward coworkers. The problem is that although such behavior is important, his natural tendency might be to skip the praise.

A woman should not take it personally when a male coworker or subordinate is tight-lipped when faced with a problem. She should recognize that he needs more encouragement to talk about his problems than would a woman. If the man persists in not wanting to talk about the problem, the woman might say, "It looks like you want to work out this problem on your own. Go ahead. I'm available if you want to talk about the problem."

Men and women should recognize that when women talk over problems, they might not be seeking hard-hitting advice. Instead, they might simply be searching for a sympathetic ear so that they can deal with the emotional aspect of the problem.

A general suggestion for overcoming gender-related communication barriers is for men to improve communication by becoming more empathic (showing more empathy) listeners. Women can improve communication by becoming more direct.

Concept Review and Reinforcement

Key Terms

communication 97
message 98
feedback 99
noise 99
nonverbal communication 101

mixed message 101
mirroring 105
empathy 107
motivational state 108
frame of reference 108

defensive communication 108
denial 108
active listener 113
metacommunication 116

Summary

Communication is the basic process by which managers, customer-contact workers, and professionals accomplish their work. Communication is also important because communication skills are a success factor for workers in a wide variety of jobs. Communication among people is a complex process that can be divided into six components: sender or source, message, channel (or medium), receiver, feedback, and environment. Noise, or interference, can disrupt communication within any component.

Communication is a vehicle for building relationships. We establish relationships along two primary dimensions: dominant–subordinate and cold–warm. In the process of communicating, we attempt to dominate or subordinate. We indicate whether we want to dominate or subordinate by the way we speak or write or by nonverbal signals we send. The four combinations of the two primary dimensions lead to different types of relationship—dominant–cold (impersonal), cold–subordinate (accepting), subordinate–warm (supportive), and warm–dominant (personal).

Nonverbal communication plays an important part in sending and receiving messages and is especially important for imparting the emotional aspects of a message. The modes of nonverbal communication include the environment in which the message is sent, interpersonal distance, posture, hand gestures, facial expressions and eye contact, voice quality, personal appearance, and attention paid to the other person.

Nonverbal communication can be improved through such means as obtaining feedback, learning to relax, using gestures more discriminately, role-playing, and mirroring. The latter refers to subtly imitating someone. Another interpersonal skill related to nonverbal communication is the ability to detect lying, such as nonverbal indicators of extra effort including longer pauses between thoughts.

Methods of overcoming communication barriers include the following: (1) communicate honestly, (2) understand the receiver, (3) minimize defensive communication, (4) repeat your message using multiple channels, (5) check comprehension and feelings via verbal and nonverbal feedback, (6) display a positive attitude, (7) use persuasive communication, (8) engage in active listening, (9) prepare for stressful conversation, (10) engage in metacommunication (communicating about your communication), and (11) recognize gender differences in communication styles.

Skills and behaviors associated with active listening include the following: (1) show respect, (2) accept the sender's figure of speech, (3) paraphrase and listen reflectively, (4) minimize distractions, (5) ask questions, (6) allow the sender to finish his or her sentence, (7) use nonverbal communication, (8) minimize words that shut down discussion, and (9) avoid the need to lie or fake when you have not been paying attention.

Questions for Discussion and Review

1. How would you reduce the effect of noise when communicating with another person?

2. What is your opinion on the importance of face-to-face communication in the business world of today? For example, with all the new communication technology tools, is it still important to have face-to-face meetings and sales representatives calling on customers?

3. Identify several suggestions about communication contained in this chapter that you think are particularly important in communicating with deaf and hard-of-hearing coworkers.

4. What type of voice quality do you think would be effective in most work situations?

5. In what way might you have ever experienced information overload? What did you do, or what are you doing, to cope with the situation?

6. How could an appreciation of non-verbal communication be useful in an interview situation?

7. Why does giving employees training in listening often lead to increased productivity and profits?

8. Professional listeners such as counselors, psychotherapists, and life coaches often say that they are exhausted after a day of listening. Why might listening be exhausting?

9. Watch Martin Luther King's "I Have a Dream" speech on YouTube. In what way does he use techniques of persuasive communication?

10. Suppose your manager does not listen to your suggestions for job improvements. How would you metacommunicate to deal with this problem?

The Web Corner

http://www.optimalthinking.com/quiz-communication-skills.asp
(Rate your level of communication)

http://www.queendom.com
(Look for the Interpersonal Communication Skills Test)

http://nonverbal.ucsc.edu
(Explore nonverbal communications, and test your ability to read nonverbal communication)

http://center-for-nonverbal-studies.org
(Nonverbal dictionary of gestures, signs, and body language cues—includes YouTube links)

Internet Skill Builder: Practicing Listening Skills

Infoplease offers some practical suggestions for improving your listening skills that both support and supplement the ideas offered in this chapter. Infoplease divides listening into three basic steps: hearing, understanding, and judging. Visit the site at www.infoplease.com/homework/listening-skills1.html

Developing Your Human Relations Skills

Interpersonal Relations Case 4.1

Why Am I Not Getting Through to These People?

A few years ago, Laura left her position as a supervisor in a health insurance company to start a lawn care, landscaping, and snow removal business. She started the business by taking care of the lawns and snow removal for a few relatives and friends. Laura charged them approximately half price just so that she could establish the legitimacy of her business and get started seeking customers. Her first employees were a 16-year-old nephew, an 18-year-old niece, and an uncle.

After passing out hundreds of flyers in her neighborhood, and three adjoining neighborhoods, Laura finally developed a big enough customer base to start obtaining referral business. After two years running her firm, "Laura's Property Service," Laura was breaking even, including paying herself a modest salary. Her firm had grown to taking care of more than 100 customers, with three full-time and six part-time employees.

When asked about her biggest challenge in operating her business, Laura replied:

Getting through to my workers is my biggest headache, no doubt. A big money drain in my business is repairing the damage we do to people's lawn and driveway in the process of removing snow. Also, the fellows and gals sometimes bang into garages and drain pipes with our lawnmowers when they are cutting grass.

I keep telling the gang to be careful, but I am not making much of a dent in terms of reducing customer complaints about damage. The typical response I get when I deliver my message about being careful is, "Yeah, yeah, I'll be careful."

Case Questions

1. What kind of communication problem does Laura appear to be facing?
2. What do you recommend Laura do so that her employees act positively in response to her message?

Interpersonal Skills Role-Play 4.1

Getting through to a Property Specialist

One person plays the role of Laura, who is somewhat frustrated. It is early spring, and five different customers have called to complain about the damage the snow removal team did to their driveways and lawn during the winter. Laura has gathered three of her workers (Tammy, Jud, and Ben) to explain once again the need for doing less damage to customer lawns and driveways while snow plowing. Three other students play the roles of Tammy, Jud, and Ben, and are wondering why Laura is complaining because they think such damage is inevitable.

Conduct this role-play for about seven minutes. Observers rate the role players on two dimensions, using a 1-to-5 scale from very poor (1) to very good (5). One dimension is "effective use of human relations techniques." Focus on the communication skill that Laura demonstrates. The second dimension is "acting ability." A few observers might voluntarily provide feedback to the role players in terms of sharing their ratings and observations. The course instructor might also provide feedback.

Interpersonal Relations Case 4.2

Troy, the Aspiring Hotel Manager

Troy spent the first two years in his hotel management career performing entry-level responsibilities. The tasks included working the front desk and helping in the dining room during banquets provided for customers such as business groups and wedding parties. Troy was then promoted to assistant manager in another hotel within the same chain, in the same city. Six months later, Troy met with Sharon, the hotel manager, to discuss his progress as assistant manager.

Sharon opened the conversation by asking Troy how he was enjoying his work as the new assistant manager at the hotel. Troy answered, "Thanks for even asking me how I like my job. I mean, an assistant manager isn't really such an important person. I kind of like my job, even if it's not the best in the world."

"What could make this job better for you?" asked Sharon.

"I'm not exactly sure," said Troy. "Well, maybe if I didn't have so many different responsibilities to handle at once, my job could possibly be better."

"Could you possibly be more specific?" asked Sharon.

"Well, I don't exactly like to accuse anybody of anything," said Troy. "But maybe, perhaps maybe, some of the other people around here could recognize that an assistant manager can't work on five problems at the same time."

"Are you sure about that?" asked Sharon.

"Oh well, perhaps I am overstating things a little," replied Troy. "I'm sorry."

With an exasperated expression, Sharon said, "Troy, if you want to be a success in hotel management, you've got to come across with more conviction."

Case Questions

1. What evidence do you see that Troy needs to come across with more conviction?

2. What do you recommend that Troy do to become a more persuasive communicator?

Interpersonal Relations Role-Play 4.2

Troy Communicates Persuasively

One student plays the role of Troy, who has requested another meeting with Sharon to further discuss his progress as an assistant manager; however, Troy has taken quite seriously Sharon's recommendations that he communicate more persuasively. The student who plays the role of Sharon will listen attentively to and judge his ability to communicate persuasively. Conduct the role-play for about seven minutes, and provide feedback to both role players about their communication effectiveness.

References

1. Jim Blasingame, "There Are No Handshakes 'In the Clouds,'" *The Wall Street Journal* (Special Advertising Feature), October 13, 2009, B5.

2. Nick Schultz, "Hard Unemployment Truths About 'Soft' Skills," *The Wall Street Journal*, September 20, 2012, p. A15.

3. Ritch Sorenson, Grace DeBord, and Ida Ramirez, *Business and Management Communication: A Guide Book*, 4th edition (Upper Saddle River, NJ: Prentice Hall, 2001), pp. 6–10.

4. Steven Pinker, *The Stuff of Thought* (New York: Viking, a Member of Penguin Group (USA), Inc., 2007).

5. Linda Talley, "Body Language: Read It or Weep," *HR Magazine*, July 2010, p. 64.

6. Ibid., p. 65.

7. Jeffrey Jacobi, *The Vocal Advantage* (Upper Saddle River, NJ: Prentice Hall, 1996).

8. Research reported in Sue Shellenbarger, "Is This How You Really Talk?" *The Wall Street Journal*, April 24, 2013, p. D1.

9. Study reported in Rachel Emma Silverman, "Bald Is Powerful," *The Wall Street Journal*, October 3, 2012, p. B1.

10. Research presented in "We Can Measure the Power of Charisma," *Harvard Business Review*, January–February 2010, p. 34.

11. Cited in "Body Language Do's and Don'ts," McClatchy Newspapers (MCT), July 25, 2012.

12. Mark G. Frank, Melissa A. Menasco, and Maureen O'Sullivan, "Human Behavior and Deception Detection," in John G. Voeller, editor, *Handbook of Science and Technology Security, Volume 5*, (New York: Wiley, 2008), pp. 2–3.

13. Eric Benac, "Nonverbal Ways to Tell Someone is Lying," retrieved February 2, 2013, from http://ehow.com.

14. Benice Atufundwa, "The Art of Effective Communication," *Black Enterprise*, November 2009, p. 47.

15. Randy G. Pennington, "Trust Is an Action Verb," *HR Magazine*, February 2012, pp. 90–91.

16. Robert Lee Hotz, "How Your Brain Allows You to Walk in Another's Shoes," *The Wall Street Journal*, August 17, 2007, p. B1.

17. Jared Sandberg, "'It Says Press Any Key. Where's the Any Key?'" *The Wall Street Journal*, February 20, 2007, p. B1.

18. Paul Hemp, "Death by Information Overload," *Harvard Business Review*, September 2009, p. 83.

19. Marty Stanley, "Focus on Communication Interactions," *Communication Briefings* (*Briefings Bonus*), April 2011, p. 1.

20. Steve Tobak, Speak Up Without Being Kicked Out," *Communication Briefings*, June 2011, p. 8; Frank Luntz, "Words That Pack Power," *Business Week*, November 3, 2008, p. 106; Roberta H. Karapels and Vanessa D. Arnold, "Speaker's Credibility in Persuasive Work Situations," *Business Education Forum*, December 1997, pp. 24–26; Interview by Alyssa

Danigelis, "Like, Um, You Know," *Fast Company*, May 2006, p. 99; "Rid Your Speech of Weak Words," *Executive Leadership*, October 2012, p. 5.

21. Jean Mausehund and R. Neil Dortch, "Communications—Presentation Skills in the Digital Age," *Business Education Forum*, April 1999, pp. 30–32.

22. "Avoid Words That Mar Your Image," *Administrative Professional Today*, January 2009, pp. 1–2.

23. For more details, see Brian Fugere, Chelsea Hardaway, and Jon Warshawsky, *Why Business People Speak Like Idiots* (New York: Free Press, 2005).

24. Joann Baney, *Guide to Interpersonal Communication* (Upper Saddle River, NJ: Pearson/Prentice Hall, 2004), p. 7.

25. Quoted in Jessica Shambora, "Stop Talking and Start Listening," *Fortune*, November 9, 2009, p. 24.

26. Cited in "Improve Listening Skills to Boost Career," *Tribune Media Services* (http://www.chicagotribune.com), July 7, 2012, p. 3.

27. Bernard T. Ferrari, "The Executive's Guide to Better Listening," *McKinsey Quarterly*, February 2012, p. 1.

28. Ibid, p. 2.

29. Daniel Araoz, "Right Brain Management (RBM): Part 2," *Human Resources Forum*, September 1989, p. 4.

30. Cited in Matthew S. Scott "Five Keys to Effective Listening," *Black Enterprise*, March 2005, p. 113.

31. Ideas from Marshall Goldsmith cited in "Eliminate Bad Words," *Manager's Edge*, special issue, 2008, p. 5.

32. Quoted in Mimi Whitefield, "Listen Up—Your Job Could Depend on It," *Miami Herald* (http://www.miamiherald.com), April 20, 2009.

33. Holly Weeks, "Taking the Stress Out of Stressful Conversations," *Harvard Business Review*, July–August 2001, pp. 112–119. The quote is from p. 117.

34. Deborah Tannen, *Talking from 9 to 5* (New York: William Morrow, 1994); Tannen, "The Power of Talk: Who Gets Heard and Why," *Harvard Business Review*, September–October 1995, pp. 138–148; Daniel J. Canary and Kathryn Dindia, *Sex Differences and Similarities in Communication* (Mahwah, NJ: Erlbaum, 1998), p. 318; John Gray, *Men Are from Mars, Women Are from Venus* (New York: HarperCollins, 1992).

Interpersonal Skills for the Digital World

Trevor worked as a product designer for Sensor Products, based in Portland, Oregon. The company designs and manufactures electronic controls used in automobiles, trucks, and related vehicles. His wife, Rita, an executive assistant, had to relocate back to Boston because her mother and father were in poor health. So, Trevor and Rita made the decision to move to an apartment in Boston.

Rita felt confident that she could find employment in Boston, but Trevor did not want to leave his position as a senior product designer. Because of Trevor's reputation as a talented and dedicated worker, a top-level manager at Sensor agreed to let Trevor work mostly from home, spending about three days per month in Portland.

Monkey Business Images/Shutterstock

After reading and studying this chapter and doing the exercises, you should be able to

1. Describe interpersonal skills related to one-on-one interactions in the digital world.
2. Describe interpersonal skills related to social networking.
3. Describe interpersonal skills related to working with small audiences with respect to digital devices.

After several weeks of working from home in their cramped Boston apartment, Trevor began to feel uncomfortable. "I was going stir-crazy," he said. "I enjoy my technical work, but I'm also a people person. Much of my career success stems from my enjoyment of interacting with people. Doing my designs on a computer and interacting with colleagues through e-mail is not enough for me. I kind of feel starved for human interaction."

After some careful thought, Trevor modified his idea of working from home. He found a place called Galaxy Towers just 15 minutes from his apartment in Boston, where he was able to share office space, have his own desk, Internet, a conference room, and coffee and tea for $350 per month. Trevor would become what is now called a *co*-worker. His company agreed to pay the bill to keep Trevor happy and productive.

Trevor was now able to interact with other workers on occasion, even if they were working for different companies. As Trevor puts it, "Just shooting the breeze with intelligent, working adults stimulates by thinking. Our dog Lila is wonderful, but she doesn't provide the kind of warm, human presence that I need to be at my professional best. Also, I can even brainstorm a bit with a few of the other tenants at Galaxy."[1]

The story about the senior product designer illustrates one of the ways in which interpersonal skills figure into the digital age. Trevor's ability to interact positively with others stimulates his own thinking—making him productive—and also contributes to his job satisfaction. In this chapter, we examine the interpersonal skill aspects of working in the digital age, an often-neglected aspect of making good use of the communication and information technology surrounding us in the workplace. This subject increases in importance as more companies permit, or even encourage, workers to conduct company business with their mobile devices.

We organize information about interpersonal skills for the digital world into two broad categories. First, we describe interpersonal skills for using digital devices in one-on-one interaction. Second, we examine the interpersonal skill aspects of using communication technology for social networking and small audiences.

To begin thinking through interpersonal skills in relation to the digital world, you are invited to take Self-Assessment Quiz 5-1. The statements in the quiz cover many of the behaviors relevant to digitally based interactions

INTERPERSONAL SKILLS FOR ONE-ON-ONE INTERACTIONS

As with interpersonal skills in general, interactions with people one at a time create the majority of opportunities for displaying interpersonal skills related to the digital age. In this section, we describe four such settings or scenarios in which the communication is typically (not always) directed toward one person: cell phones (including smartphones) and text messaging, e-mail messages and instant messaging, webcam job interviews, and interpersonal aspects of multitasking.

LEARNING OBJECTIVE 1

The Interpersonal Skills for the Digital World Checklist

Indicate whether each of the following statements is mostly true or mostly false as it applies to you (or would apply to you if you were in the situation indicated by the statement). Even if your reaction to a particular statement is "duh," remember that all the statements reflect incidents of real behavior.

Statement	Mostly True	Mostly False
1. I get really upset if I send a coworker an instant message (IM), and I do not receive an answer within five minutes.	_____	_____
2. While being interviewed for a job, I receive and send text messages to a work associate or friend.	_____	_____
3. While working in a group, I regularly check my e-mail and text messages.	_____	_____
4. I often check Web sites such as ESPN, Facebook, Twitter, or home-shopping channels on my laptop while at a meeting.	_____	_____
5. I often eat while talking on my cell phone.	_____	_____
6. I typically check my e-mail, text messages, or a Web site while talking on my cell phone.	_____	_____
7. If I made a webcam presentation for work purposes, I would make sure that my grooming was at its best.	_____	_____
8. I would bring a pet such as a cat, dog, or parrot along to a webcam conference for business purposes.	_____	_____
9. If I were giving a presentation at a business banquet, I would keep my smart phone in my hand.	_____	_____
10. I keep my bottle of water in my hand at all times when making a PowerPoint presentation.	_____	_____
11. When making a PowerPoint presentation, I use the information on the slides as headlines for talking points rather than reading the slides to the audience.	_____	_____
12. If I attended a two-hour videoconference, I would see no problem in leaving the room from time to time just for a break.	_____	_____
13. I have posted, or would be willing to post, some outrageous videos of myself on Facebook, such as driving a vehicle with a bottle of beer in my hand.	_____	_____
14. I use, or would use, a social networking site to really blast a company whose product proved to be faulty.	_____	_____
15. For me, social networking sites are a useful place to post nasty things about people I do not like.	_____	_____
16. Older workers who are not savvy about information technology deserve nicknames like "Mr. Depends" or "Ms. Dinosaur."	_____	_____
17. I laugh when I see somebody doing something as old-fashioned as reading a newspaper or consulting a telephone book.	_____	_____
18. I have received compliments about my ability to explain how to use technology to another worker.	_____	_____
19. I am patient and polite when a tech support person cannot resolve my technology problem right away.	_____	_____
20. I have sent hand-written thank-you notes to people even if they use e-mail and text messaging.	_____	_____

Scoring and Interpretation: Give yourself one point (+1) for each statement you gave in agreement with the keyed answer. The keyed answer indicates a positive interpersonal skill for the digital world.

1. Mostly false	4. Mostly false	7. Mostly true	10. Mostly false
2. Mostly false	5. Mostly false	8. Mostly false	11. Mostly true
3. Mostly false	6. Mostly false	9. Mostly false	12. Mostly false

(Continued)

Smartphones, Cell Phones, and Text Messaging

Smartphones have become such an integrated part of life both on and off the job that many photographs in magazines and newspapers of business people show them using their phones. Television advertisements also often depict workers using a smartphone, even when the advertisement is not for phones. In the business section of most cities, it appears that approximately two-thirds of the people in business attire on the street are using a mobile device. Cell phones, and their ability to send text messages, therefore represent an enormous opportunity for displaying good, as well as poor, interpersonal skills.

Positive Interpersonal Skills While Using Smartphones. The many positive behaviors possible when using smartphones and cell phones for one-on-one interaction usually are a question of doing the opposite of negative behaviors. The behaviors in the following list illustrate how positive interpersonal skills can be demonstrated while using smartphones and text messaging during one-on-one interactions.[2]

1. **Use a standard ringtone instead of a loud, unusual tone.** In this way, if your phone rings in the presence of a work associate, your behavior will not provoke surprise or laughter.

2. **Inform the caller that you are receiving his or her call on a cell phone.** If you let the caller know that you are on a cell phone, the caller will not be surprised when the reception fades in and out, or when you are interrupted by honking horns or other background noises, including the conversations of people walking by.

3. **Inform work associates ahead of time if you are waiting for a call from a medical professional or in reference to an urgent home situation.** Assume, for example, that you and a coworker are discussing a customer problem. Let your coworker know that your conversation might be interrupted by the type of urgent call just described. In this way, accepting a call will not be interpreted as rudeness.

4. **Ask your work associate if he or she would like you to access an item of work-related information using your smartphone.** Assume that sales rep Ashley is talking with customer Todd, and Todd wants to know if her company would have a large quantity of a specific product in stock. Ashley would be displaying good interpersonal skills by saying, "Todd, would you like me to access this information on my iPhone? It will take just a minute." Todd will inevitably agree, and he will also understand why Ashley is using her iPhone in the middle of their conversation.

5. **Inform your coworker that you are shutting off your cell phone or smartphone during your conversation.** Because so many people do not think to, or refuse to, turn off their cell phones or smartphones, you can gain some psychological capital by mentioning your courteous behavior. You tell your work associate, "Our meeting is important, so just one second—I want to turn off my phone and put it out of view."

6. **For business purposes, use a fully functioning phone, and stay current with your cell phone bill.** You will appear much more professional to work associates when your cell phone call is not interrupted by a disappearing voice or reception much like you are in heavy traffic or a shower. Keeping current with your bill avoids

the unprofessional image created by a message that your phone number is "temporarily out of service" or your inability to send an outgoing message.

7. **When making calls from outside the office, search for a relatively quiet environment so that your message will be clearer, and you will not have to ask the receiver to repeat information.** Even in a busy environment like an airport, it is possible to find a relatively quiet alcove from which to make a call. The interpersonal skill link here is that you appear more professional when your communication is relatively free of environmental noise.

8. **If absolutely necessary to take a cell phone call while interacting with a work associate, excuse yourself and move at least 15 feet away to process the call.** Work associates who are themselves polite will appreciate your display of polite behavior.

9. **When you are the driver of a vehicle, explain to your work associate that for safety's sake you are putting your cell phone away.** Point out that just as you would not be the driver when you are drunk, you will not use your cell phone for voice communication or text messaging while you are driving. Although many coworkers might think you are eccentric, the data are convincing about the dangers of cell phone use while driving. On balance, your concern for the safety of your passenger will be interpreted as a positive interpersonal skill.

10. **When at work, make any personal cell phone calls on break and away from your assigned physical location, such as outside the building or in an employee lounge (but not in the restroom!).** Blocking your personal calls and making them outside your assigned work area shows that you have enough interpersonal skill to care about the need of other workers for a tranquil work environment.

Negative Interpersonal Skills While Using Smartphones and Cell Phones. The dissatisfaction with, and anger toward, people who abuse mobile phones in the workplace continues to appear in articles, books, blogs, and letters to the editor. All this negativity, however, must be placed in the proper context. If the person with whom you are interacting does not perceive a particular use of the cell phone as rudeness, then it is not rude. For example, if your coworker smiles at you while you receive a phone call in his or her presence, you are probably not being perceived as displaying negative interpersonal behavior. The following is a list of frequent smartphone and text messaging behaviors that many (not all) people will interpret as rudeness and insensitivity. As a result, the person engaging in the act will be perceived as showing negative interpersonal skill.[3]

1. **Accepting a call during a work conversation.** You communicate the fact that your coworker or other work associate is less important than the caller when you allow a call to interrupt your conversation. Some people interpret making a call as even more insensitive than receiving a call, but both behaviors are dismissive of the importance of the work associate with whom you are interacting. Customers are likely to be irritated even more so than coworkers if you interrupt your conversation to accept or make a phone call. CEOs who use their cell phones while talking to other workers are likely to be perceived as power abusers and therefore arrogant. In short, by accepting a cell phone call in the presence of others, you diminish the status of the person who is physically present—hardly an impressive interpersonal skill.

2. **Wearing a cell phone earpiece in the presence of a coworker when not on the phone.** Wearing an earpiece while interacting with a coworker suggests that you do not intend to remain fully engaged in your conversation. Also, when wearing a phone earpiece, the person in your physical presence is never sure if you are listening to another call at the same time. Building rapport with a work associate includes making him or her feel important. The fact that you appear to be ready to connect to the outside world trivializes that person.

3. **Making frequent personal calls on your phone in earshot of coworkers.** A major complaint of people who work in cubicles is that someone in an adjoining cubicle spends much of the day making calls loudly on a cell phone. The same practice

would be possible on a landline phone, but many people perceive using their cell phone for personal calls as more justified than using the office phone. Loud, personal calls made throughout the day suggest lack of consideration for others, as well as a low work ethic and an unwillingness to contribute a fair share of work.

4. **Talking loudly and shouting on the cell phone.** Whether in one-on-one interactions or in the middle of a group of work associates, talking loudly and shouting on the cell phone is widely disliked. Particularly annoying for many people is the compulsion many cell phone shouters have to repeatedly say "Okay" in a especially loud voice. Talking so loudly on the cell phone suggests insensitivity to the feelings of others as well as being egocentric.

5. **Eating while making a phone call.** Eating with the mouth open in a restaurant is a major violation of etiquette. Equally annoying and disgusting to many receivers of these messages is the sender eating while talking. Although the practice of eating while talking on the phone is widespread, its vulgarity to many people is not diminished, and will not be tolerated by many customers. On display is the negative interpersonal skill of poor etiquette.

6. **Constant handling of or looking at the cell phone, even when not in use.** Many workers have become so dependent on their mobile phones that they handle them during conversations, as well as keeping the phone in constant view. Workers have also been observed placing their smartphones on their laps while speaking with others. One manager frequently polishes his chrome-covered smartphone while talking to subordinates.

   The physical attachments just mentioned all suggest the negative trait of being so dependent on a physical device that it interferes with concentrating on others. The constant physical or visual contact with the phone also has the negative impact of making the worker appear immature. An explanation offered for the physical attachment so many people have to their cell phones is that the phones have become "electronic pets." A technology reporter observed, "You constantly see people taking their little pets out and stroking the scroll wheel, coddling them basically petting them."[4]

7. **Driving a work associate while under the influence of a smartphone, including text messaging.** A positive interpersonal skill is not using your cell phone while driving a vehicle in which a work associate is present. A negative interpersonal skill is doing the opposite, even if you live in a state, province, or country in which cell phone use is permitted for drivers. A study published in a British medical journal reported that talking on the cell phone while driving quadruples your risk of being in an accident. Using a hands-free device does little to reduce the risk of an accident.[5] Many work associates will accept driving while using a cell phone, including sending text messages, as typical and appropriate behavior. Yet others will interpret your behavior as a propensity to engage in senseless risks.

8. **Accepting and sending phone messages from restrooms.** A widely reported form of cell phone rudeness is sending and receiving cell phone calls from public restrooms. Many receivers of these calls who hear the water running from the faucets or toilets flushing will be appalled and disgusted. The restroom cell phone user will therefore be perceived as insensitive and lacking in social graces—both quite negative interpersonal skills.

Skill-Building Exercise 5-1 gives you an opportunity to practice a core skill with the use of a cell phone and text messaging in the office.

E-Mail Messages and Instant Messaging

E-mail messages and instant messages (IMs) provide another opportunity for displaying positive as well as negative interpersonal skills linked to the digital age. Many people believe that formality and careful use of language can be neglected when sending messages by e-mail, using instant messaging, and when sending text messages. Remember, however, that the way in which any message is sent tells something about the sender.

The Important Message

Two coworkers are discussing a joint assignment about preparing a spreadsheet related to product returns. The analysis needs to be completed by 5 p.m. One student plays the role of the worker who is intently focusing on the task. Another student plays the role of the worker who feels the smartphone attached to his or her belt vibrate. The worker notices a text message from the bank indicating that five checks have bounced, which appears to be a bank mistake. The worker with the text message does not want to be totally rude, yet this is an urgent problem. Run the role-play for about four minutes. Observers might provide feedback on the quality of the interpersonal skills displayed in dealing with this text message challenge.

E-mail messages should be proofread, should be sent only when necessary, and generally should be no longer than one screen—not including attachments. Although many e-mail users rely on a strikingly informal and casual writing style, such informality for business correspondence is poor etiquette. For example, avoid confirming a meeting with your CEO in these words: "C U LTR, 4 sure.☺." Overloading the company system with attachments containing space-consuming graphics is often considered rude. Text messaging, because of its limited space, can be more casual than other electronic messages.

Sending e-mails indscriminantly also contributes to stress from information overload, particularly if many people also send large numbers of unnecessary e-mail messages. The negative interpersonal skill here is that engaging in activities that create stress for coworkers is inconsiderate and rude. Here is an e-mail message sent during the workday that many people would perceive to be unessential: "Look out the window. The snow is coming down heavy."

An e-mail etiquette problem with legal implications is that company e-mail messages are the property of the company, not the sender. So avoid sending insulting, vulgar, or inflammatory comments through e-mail because even deleted e-mail messages can be retrieved. Be careful not to forward an e-mail message that has negative comments about the recipient. For example, a customer service representative sent an e-mail to a customer attempting to resolve a complaint. However, instead of beginning with a fresh e-mail, the representative included an e-mail from her boss that said, "Give this idiot what she wants to get her off our back." The customer later sued the company, then agreed to a small financial settlement.

Instant messaging has created additional challenges for e-mail etiquette. Because instant messaging allows you to intrude on coworkers anytime—and allows them to drop in on you—the opportunities to be rude multiply. Managers should not intrude upon workers through instant messaging unless it is urgent. Think before you send, and make sure the message has real value to the recipient. Suggest politely to "buddies" who are taking up too much of your time with messages that they contact you after work.

Many companies are shifting from extensive use of e-mail to having some of the written communication among people placed on intranets and internal Web sites similar to Facebook. For example, you can inform all your work associates at once that you are going on a business trip for three days and will not be able to respond to their messages. (Of course, this is a good way to invite criminals to burglarize your home.) All of the comments about the polite use of language apply to these replacement technologies for e-mail.

Figure 5-1 summarizes a large amount of information about etiquette related to e-mails and instant messaging. Following this accumulated wisdom will enhance your interpersonal skills linked to the digital age.

Webcam Job Interviews

Yet another interpersonal skill useful in the digital age is to perform well during a webcam interview. Performing well in such an interview combines interpersonal skills with those related to communication technology. On occasion, a hiring manager or human resource representative will request that an interview be conducted by webcam. The job candidate might have a webcam, or use one owned by a friend or the college placement office. (Skype is the leading software to communicate via webcam.) A challenge in being interviewed via a webcam is that some job candidates do not come across as strongly as they believe.

FIGURE 5-1   E-Mail and Messaging Etiquette

Observing the following tips will enhance your e-mail etiquette and electronic communication effectiveness, as well as enhancing your interpersonal skills.

Address and sign your e-mail messages. Many people neglect to mention a person's name in an e-mail, or sign their own name. Giving your e-mail a personal touch is a useful interpersonal micro-skill.

Keep it simple. Each message should have only one piece of information or request for action so that it's easier for the receiver to respond. However, avoid sending an e-mail with an attachment without some type of greeting or explanation. Do not allow e-mail threads longer than a couple of pages. E-mail messages longer than one screen often are filed instead of read. Brief e-mails messages show compassion for the recipient's workload.

Include an action step. Clearly outline what type of reply you're looking for as well as any applicable deadlines.

Use the subject line to your advantage. Generic terms such as "details" or "reminder" do not describe the contents of your message or whether it's time sensitive, and so the receiver may delay opening it. "Came in Under Budget" illustrates a specific (and joyful) title. Do not forward a long chain of e-mails without changing the subject; otherwise, you might have a confusing subject line, such as "RE: FW: RE: FW: RE: FW."

Take care in writing e-mails. Clearly organize your thoughts to avoid sending e-mails with confusing, incomplete, or missing information. Use business writing style and check carefully for grammatical and typographical errors. (Also, generally avoid the trend to refer to yourself as "I" in lowercase ["i"].) When in doubt, use traditional formatting rather than bright colors and unusual fonts; many people prefer standard formatting.

Inform receivers when sending e-mails from a mobile device. If you use a mobile phone, include a tagline informing people that you are using such a device; it will help explain your terseness. Without explanation, you might project an image of rudeness or limited writing skill.

Be considerate. Use "please" and "thank you" even in brief messages. Part of being considerate, or at least polite, is to begin your e-mail with a warm salutation, such "Hello Gina," rather than jumping into the subject with no greeting. Avoid profane or harsh language. Another way of being considerate is to send e-mails only when necessary, to help combat information overload. Sending copies to only recipients who need or want the information is part of being considerate.

Don't include confidential information. The problem is that e-mail is occasionally forwarded to unintended recipients. If your message is in any way sensitive or confidential, set up a meeting or leave a voice mail in which you request confidentially. Also, avoid including gossip such as negative rumors in e-mail messages because the subject of the gossip could voice a major complaint.

Do not use e-mail to blast a coworker, and send copies to others. Criticizing another person with e-mail is equivalent to blasting him or her during a large meeting.

Ask before sending huge attachments. Do not clog e-mail systems without permission.

Encourage questions and demands for clarification. E-mail functions best when it is interactive, so ask receivers to send along questions they might have about your message, including any requests for clarification.

Consider the timing of e-mail messages. An e-mail that makes a major request should be sent earlier in the day so that the person has time to process the request. Good news can be sent almost anytime. For some recipients, bad news is best sent early in the day so that they can ask for your support in dealing with the problem. However, very bad news (such as being laid off) is best delivered in person. Some people prefer to receive bad news later in the day so that it will not interrupt their entire workday.

Avoid keeing a personal e-mail account on the job unless welcomed by management. An estimated one-quarter of e-mails received at work are for personal purposes. To resist the temptation of spending too much time with personal e-mails, it is best not to have a

(Continued)

FIGURE 5-1 Continued

personal e-mail account, such as Gmail, on the office computer. You will appear more professional if you avoid the temptation to spend a lot of work time sending and receiving personal e-mails and instant messages.

Minimize "BIF" messages in the evening and on weekends. In today's demanding workplace, it is easy to send "before I forget" messages in the evening, on weekends, and during holidays. Some people will regard you as insensitive to their lifestyle if you badger them outside of regular working hours with e-mail messages. Save your urgent messages for the next workday—unless an immediate exchange of information is essential.

Instant messaging requires a few additional considerations for practicing good electronic etiquette:

Use instant messaging sparingly because it is interruptive. An instant message is likely to interrupt a person's concentration on an important task, so it should be sent infrequently. Be careful not to send an instant message to a coworker who you know is working on an analytical task. However, if the company culture encourages the use of instant messaging, you display good interpersonal skill by going with the flow.

Don't be Big Brother. Some bosses use instant messaging to check up on others, to make sure that they are seated at their computer. Never intrude on workers unless it is urgent.

Lay down the instant-messaging law. Make sure that your message has some real value to the recipient before jumping right in front of someone's face. Instant messaging is much like walking into someone's office or cubicle without an appointment or without knocking.

Take it offline. When someone on your buddy list becomes too chatty, don't vent your frustration. By phone, in person, or through regular e-mail, explain tactfully that you do not have time for processing so many instant messages. Suggest that the two of you might get together for lunch or coffee soon.

Set limits to avoid frustration. To avoid constant interruptions, use a polite custom status message, such as "I will be dealing with customers today until 4:40."

Source: "Communicating Electronically: What Every Manager Needs to Know," *Communication Solutions,* Sample Issue, 2008, p. 2; Heinz Tschabitscher, "The Ten Most Important Rules of Email Etiquette," http://email.about.com/cs/netiquettetips/tp/core_netiquette.htm, accessed September 9, 2013; Monte Enbysk, "Bosses: 10 Tips for Better E-mails," *Microsoft Small Business Center,* www.microsoft.com/smallbusiness/resources/technology/communications/bossess_10, 2006; Nancy Flynn, "50% of Bosses Ban Personal E-mail Accounts," *Workplace Communication Examiner* (http://www.examiner.com), July 28, 2009; "5 Tactics to Curb E-Mail Overload," *Manager's Edge,* June 2008, p. 6.

As webcam technology continues to improve, and more managers are familiar with the technique, the number of these computer-based interviews is likely to increase. (Unless both parties in a Skype conversation have current hardware and software, the video and audio can be poor.) Some companies use webcam interviews to reduce travel costs, and this type of interview provides more data than a phone call. Christa Foley, recruiting manager at Zappos.com, says, "If you see facial expressions and body language, you have a different sense of what a person is saying."[6] After candidates are interviewed by webcam, the strongest ones are typically invited for an in-person visit to the company. Foley says that Zappos looks for job candidates who are a little weird and fun.[7]

Above all, a webcam interview is still an interview; so review the interview suggestions in Chapter 17 to appear at your best. In addition, keep in mind the following positive suggestions, all of which imply mistakes to avoid at the same time.[8]

1. **Use even lighting.** As with all forms of photography, lighting is a big part of making a successful webcam appearance. A bright light behind you is particularly poor because your face will be in shadow. Lighting bounced off the ceiling works the best for a soft, even image, yet side lighting will often suffice. Do not place a bright light on the computer in front of you to avoid too much glare on your face, particularly if you are light skinned.

2. **Wear appropriate clothing.** Dress as if you were having an in-person interview, and minimize the color white because it comes across poorly on computer screens. Loud patterns are also distracting. Unless otherwise directed, it is best to wear a business suit or dress. Investigate what type of clothing job applicants typically wear. For example, if you were applying for a management training position at Home Depot, business casual dress might be appropriate.

3. **Do your best to appear relaxed and not overly stressed.** Light exercise and a shower about 30 minutes before the interview will help give you a refreshed look. Use your favorite stress reduction technique shortly before the webcam interview. Familiarity with the webcam technology will help you feel relaxed.

4. **Use or create an uncluttered area free of personal belongings, pets, and television sets.** Although your living quarters may be the locale of your interview, you still want to simulate the appearance of a professional office. Tidy up the interview area, and move away as much clutter as possible. Background noise, including a ringing telephone or a television set turned on, would detract from a professional image.

5. **Sit tall with good posture, and stay at approximately the same distance from the computer screen that you do for most of you computer work.** The worst posture error webcam interviewees typically make is to move the head within a few inches of the screen. A close-up shot of this nature distorts the face and looks a little bizarre to most interviewers.

6. **Rehearse so that you will be better able to implement the previous five suggestions.** Collaborate with someone in your network of contacts to interview each other on webcam. The rehearsal will familiarize you with the technology, and you can also get feedback on the adequacy of the lighting, and how natural and positive you appeared. As was often said in the early days of photography, "Smile, you're on camera."

A fundamental reason that rehearsal for a webcam interview is important is that people have a tendency to overrate the image they project on video. A webcam image is, of course, a variation of a video image. Karen Friedman, a video presentation trainer, has this to say about the importance of getting accurate feedback on the video image you project:

> People will tell you that they're perceived as dynamic, engaging, and interesting, with full command of the material. And when they see themselves on videotape or DVD and it's a rude awakening, because they see how other people really see them. You can pick up odd mannerisms you're not aware of. You may have the words down and the verbal techniques, but your body language might give away that you're nervous or unsure of yourself.[9]

Interpersonal Aspects of Multitasking

Multitasking has two meanings, and the difference is of major significance for interpersonal relationships. One meaning of multitasking is that you have two or more projects that you are working on, but you do not work on these projects at the same time. For example, a person might be responsible for investigating customer complaints as well as purchasing new furniture for the office. In the morning she works on the complaints, and in the afternoon she negotiates a furniture purchase. The other type of multitasking creates more potential interpersonal problems. With this type of multitasking, the person does two or more things simultaneously, such as visiting an office furniture Web site while talking on the phone with a dissatisfied customer.

Chapter 16 deals with the productivity problems often associated with multitasking. Also, the discussion of cell phone use described the insensitivity of accepting and sending calls while talking to another person (a frequent type of multitasking). Here we explain how multitasking might have (a) a positive influence on interpersonal relationships and (b) a negative influence on interpersonal skills.

Multitasking and Positive Interpersonal Skills. In some situations, performing two tasks at once can enhance interpersonal skills because you are helping another person.

> " Your multitasking skills are second to none. You process information at lightning speed and have the organizational skills to manage multiple projects at once. Rising to the top under pressure while managing many different initiatives will set you apart from the crowd. "
>
> —Brandi Blades, vice president of marketing at Gen Y talent acquisition agency Brill Street + Company, talking about how young professionals can use their youth to advantage during the job hunt and in the workplace[10]

Multitasking

(a) Having two or more projects that you are working on, but you do not work on these projects at the same time. (b) Doing two or more tasks simultaneously.

Imagine that Sally asks Fernando for help in inserting accents into Spanish words, such as wanting to convert "carino" into "cariño" (with caring). Fernando sits down next to Sally at her computer, and says, "Watch me, Sally. I'm moving my hand over to the Num Lock keyboard. With a finger on my left hand, I press Alt. Then with a finger on my right hand, I press 0241 in sequence. See, we have an ñ. Next, I will show you how to use the character map that will get you all the Spanish accents·you will ever need."

Fernando is indeed doing two tasks at once—manipulating the keyboard and talking to Sally. If he had not multitasked, he would not have been a good tutor. Fernando is also not being rude because he has Sally's implicit permission to multitask. A lot of coaching and tutoring requires multitasking of the nature just described.

The scenario of Sally and Fernando illustrates another key principle of using multitasking to enhance interpersonal skills. When two people are holding a conversation for purposes of joint problem solving, multitasking will sometimes enhance the problem solving, thereby creating a stronger interpersonal relationship. Visualize Mike and Tammy driving together on a business trip. Mike is driving, and his vehicle is not equipped with a GPS. Mike says to Tammy, "I think we may have missed the Liberty Road exit on this highway. It would be a nightmare to exit and find the way back. What should we do?"

"Hold on Mike," says Tammy. I'll access the GPS app on my BlackBerry and get us centered in a minute." Fifty seconds later, Tammy says to Mike while still looking at the screen on her BlackBerry, "We're good. The Liberty Road exit is 5.6 miles down the road. We'll make a right turn off the exit ramp."

Multitasking and Negative Interpersonal Skills. The major negative interpersonal skill aspect of multitasking is that it trivializes the person with whom you are interacting, as described with cell phone abuse. Imagine you are listening to a coworker who is describing a proposed solution to a problem. You shift your gaze to your computer so that you can seek who just "poked" you on Facebook. This immediately sends the message that your "poker" is more important at the moment than your coworker who wanted to discuss a legitimate work problem.

Another negative interpersonal skill associated with multitasking is more subtle. When you respond to an electronic interruption, such as an instant message or an e-mail alert, your attention is sapped for more time than it takes to read the message. You have to recover from the interruption and refocus your attention on your work associate. While you are in the recovery mode, perhaps even 30 seconds, you are paying less than full attention to the other person.[11] This inattentiveness is made obvious by the blank stare on your face or recovery murmurs such as "yeah, yeah."

Multitasking can be particularly disruptive to others when working in the open spaces used by so many companies to foster collaboration. Coworkers are subject to a constant stream of people talking on the phone while performing other tasks. The noise level alone may create stress for others, leading to strained interpersonal relationships.[12]

A major contributing factor to the negative intepersonal consequences of multitasking is that many people today suffer from **nomophobia**, the fear of being without a mobile phone. (The term stems from "no mobile.") Nomophobics feel anxious when not using or touching a smartphone or even when the phone battery is low. A lost phone can result in a panic attack. It therefore becomes difficult for many people to engage in interactions with others unless they are using a mobile gadget.

Harassment of Others

A negative consequence of communication technology in the workplace is that it is easier to harass coworkers than in the analog age. To harass coworkers in the past, it was necessary to say nasty things to them in person, telephone them in a menacing way, write them threatening notes, or send them upsetting words on paper or photographs. The Internet, including e-mail and the Web, has made it much easier to harass people.

Creating a hostile environment by displaying pornography to coworkers who do not want to see it has become one of the most frequent forms of harassment. Aside from being rude, sexual harassment through pornography has frequently been ruled as illegal. A representative example is that the 2nd Circuit Court of Appeals in New York State consistently

Nomophobia

The fear of being without a mobile phone.

has ruled that "the mere presence of pornography in a workplace can alter the 'status' of women and may be objective proof of a hostile environment."[13] (A hostile environment is one of the two forms of sexual harassment as described in Chapter 9.)

An employee can be accused of hostile environment harassment by simply leaving open a porn site on his or her desktop. Sending coworkers sexually oriented jokes by e-mail can result in similar accusations. If you work for a company that distributes adult films, pornography would be part of your job, and you therefore might be excluded from the harassment accusation.

Harassment can also deal with a person's race or ethnicity, such as making insulting comments or jokes about a person's race. Age is another demographic factor that could possibly lead to a person being harassed, such as continuous joking by e-mail that a senior worker was suffering from Alzheimer's disease.

Harassing others through communication technology is a negative interpersonal skill. A possible positive twist would be that the person who abstains 100 percent from any computer-related actions that could be interpreted as harassment is demonstrating a positive interpersonal skill. A behavioral specific would be to delete without opening an advertisement for adult videos that made its way past the company spam filter.

INTERPERSONAL SKILLS FOR SOCIAL NETWORKING AND SMALL AUDIENCES

LEARNING OBJECTIVE 2

LEARNING OBJECTIVE 3

Interpersonal skills related to the digital age are also demonstrated while interacting with large numbers of people, as well as groups. Among these settings are social networking by Internet, using laptop and netbook computers and smartphones during a meeting, making electronic presentations, videoconferencing, telecommuting, and preserving your online reputation. You will notice that a couple of these settings could be focused more on an individual than a large number of people or a group. For example, you might be sending a message on a social networking site to one person, and while telecommuting you might be interacting with one person.

Social Networking by Internet

Almost infinite knowledge exists about social networking, including its technology, application for building a personal network, and marketing.[14] Included in this abundance of information is how Twitter and Facebook have completely transformed the way we live,

PBNJ Productions/Getty Images

and how e-mail has now become obsolete because of social networking sites. Our aim here is to simply list a few of the positive and negative interpersonal skills associated with the use of social networking sites.

Positive Interpersonal Skills and Social Networking. The use of Twitter, Facebook, LinkedIn, and the like provides the serious worker with several opportunities for displaying positive interpersonal skills, as follows:

1. **Demonstrate your loyalty by posting gracious comments about your employer.** Social networking sites include a heavy component of being mini-blogs, and therefore present an open forum for your ideas about the company. You can demonstrate empathy and compassion for the mission of your company by commenting on an action taken by the company that you perceive as positive. An example: "I'm proud to work for the Jeep division of Fiat/Chrysler. My wife and our three children were caught in a snow storm. I put my Cherokee into four-wheel drive and made it through the storm until we could find a motel. There were dozens of overturned vehicles, but we made it to safety. The vehicle stabilization feature really functions."

2. **Display your compassion for people in need.** Post on the company social networking site, and also a public site, that you want to help people in need in some specific way. For example, you might state that you have a bunch of clothing that you want to give to a needy family in any way associated with the company. Or explain that you have developed your language tutoring skills, and you are willing to help for free any person who needs help in learning to read. Compassion might be considered a value, but it also translates into a skill in terms of helping people.

3. **Demonstrate professional-level communication skills.** When making entries on Twitter in particular, many people feel compelled to write carelessly, foolishly, and viciously. Demonstrate your professionalism by writing in a style suited for a printed newspaper or a term paper. Remember that many influential people regard written communication skills as a subset of interpersonal skills.

4. **Demonstrate a willingness to collaborate with others.** A major purpose of business networking Web sites is to foster collaboration and cooperation among workers.[15] A worker therefore displays positive interpersonal skills by taking the initiative to demonstrate a willingness to collaborate with others. When asked for information by another worker, respond promptly and positively. A related positive approach is to ask to collaborate, such as taking the initiative to ask to contribute when you are made aware of a project being undertaken that fits your skill set and knowledge. Assume that a person works at Godiva, the luxury chocolate maker. He notices a posting about the company getting ready to expand into Hungary. A worker whose family is from Hungary might post the following: "I know the Hungarian culture pretty well. Can I be of help in this expansion of Godiva?"

5. **Pay deserved compliments to company personnel.** The ability to compliment others in a sensible way is an advanced interpersonal skill. Complimenting a person in private may be useful, but public compliments are welcome also. An example of a Facebook post of this nature: "I want everybody to know that Tom Barnes, our facilities manager, spearheaded the planting of a garden on the office building roof. We are saving the planet, one petunia at a time."

6. **Establish meaningful contact with workers far and wide.** The major purpose of social networking is to develop valuable contacts with many people with whom it would be difficult to maintain person-to-person or phone contact. Selective use of social networking sites enables you to relate, at least on a written level, to a variety of people in your fields. You might be able to enhance your cross-cultural skills by interacting with professionals in different countries. (LinkedIn is particularly good for this purpose because virtually all of its members have a professional intent.)

7. **Display a desire to help others grow and develop.** Social networking sites afford an easy opportunity to point others toward helpful information, such as referring friends to useful Web sites and books. You can also alert people to dangers, such as

a new scam related to the sale of gold. Although the same type of alerts can be accomplished by e-mail, social networking sites do not require long distribution lists. By pointing people in the direction of useful information, you will be demonstrating part of a useful interpersonal skill of helping others grow and develop. Instead of just writing about yourself on your post, include information that will help others.

Negative Interpersonal Skills and Social Networking.   Social networking provides a setting for displaying negative as well as positive interpersonal skills. In general, all of the positive opportunities mentioned previously could be reversed to become negative. For example, instead of helping others grow and develop with postings on your site or their site, you slam and demean these people. Several adolescent suicides have been reported that appeared to have been triggered by being insulted on a teen-oriented social networking site. The following list presents a few ways in which negative interpersonal skills are sometimes displayed on social networking sites.

1. **Using social networking sites to eliminate face-to-face interactions with work associates.** As with e-mail, social networking sites provide an opportunity to avoid face-to-face interaction with coworkers, managers, and customers. However, the temptation is even greater with social networking sites because they tout the concept of being "friends" with people on your list of electronic contacts. A person might think consciously or subconsciously, "If my customer is already my friend, why should I have to talk to or personally visit him? Our relationship is already good." If all relationships could be built and maintained electronically, you would not need to be studying human relations.

2. **Showing the same casual attitude and approach on social business networks that is often used on public social networking sites.** Social networking sites for business purposes such as Salesforce.com and Yammer are designed for company-wide information sharing and collaboration. Because these Web sites have the feel and look of general social networking sites, it is easy for many workers to communicate to coworkers and managers in an overly casual, cavalier, and often offensive manner.[16] An example is this post: "Are you there? Why the _____ haven't u answered me?"

3. **Posting confidential or derogatory information about your employer.** In the words of technology writer Bridget Carey, "Employees need to realize some conversations are privileged. Just because you're in a meeting about a new product, or worse, layoffs, doesn't mean you should be broadcasting to the world."[17] Posting negative information and insults about your employer demonstrates even lower emotional intelligence. Nasty comments about the employer, even if deserved, are often made out of uncontrolled anger. Thousands of employees have been fired because of making inflammatory comments on social networking sites (particularly Facebook) about their employers.[18] Poor interpersonal skill is also displayed by joining a social networking group dedicated to destroying the reputation of your employer.

4. **Posting extremely negative online reviews about other companies because of dissatisfaction with their products or services.** It is almost inveitable that people will occasionally be frustrated with their customer experience at a given store or on the phone. The online reviews on social networks have become a natural place to post rants condemning the company that delivered a defective product or service.[19] For example, "The name of this phone service provider should be 'The Pits.' The staff is stupid and uncooperative. Avoid this company like the plague." Not only does a rant like this project rudeness toward the company in question, it might make you appear emotionally immature to your own employer (assuming the the post is viewed by a representative of your employer.) If you are job hunting, hiring managers and recruiters may not take kindly to your rants.

5. **Posting derogatory information about and photos of a coworker.** Social networking site administrators generally do not edit posts, so anybody registered on the site can post dreadful comments about another person as a mean prank or a

deliberate effort to ruin the target's reputation. YouTube can serve a similar evil purpose. Some of these negative posts reflect backstabbing because another person encourages you to engage in embarrassing behavior. He or she may quote you, or post a photo or video of you engaged in outrageous behavior.

6. **Engaging in social networking at inappropriate times.** Many "Tweeters" in particular are so habituated to visiting their favorite social networking site that they do so at inappropriate times, such as during work. Several NFL teams, including the Miami Dolphins, had to clamp down on players tweeting during practice. Many office workers access their social networking sites during meetings. The interpersonal skill deficiency of accessing a social network site for nonbusiness purposes during working hours is that it reflects insensitivity and immaturity. (Print-related distractions would also be unwelcome, such as doing crossword puzzles during a football practice or in a meeting.)

7. **Bragging too much about being an "online celebrity."** A small percentage of the workforce has so many followers, contacts, and friends on social media that they view themselves as online celebrities or as having an Internet brand of their own.[20] A person who is willing to spend endless hours at the task can usually accumulate thousands of Internet contacts. It is even possible to purchase thousands of these contacts for a few hundred dollars. The negative interpersonal skill in question is when the worker with thousands of contacts brags about being a brand as important as the employer or being an online celebrity. An example of this type of bragging is informing your coworkers, "Hooray for me. My followers on Twitter now number 10,000, and the number is growing by the hour."

Laptop and Smartphone Use during Meetings

Whether the use of laptop and netbook computers as well as smartphones during meetings enhances your interpersonal skills depends on company custom and why you are using your computer. Some companies welcome computer use during meetings, while in other companies such practice is considered distracting and inconsiderate. Laptops are widely used during meetings at the business process consulting company Accenture.

At Ford Motor Company, CEO Alan Mulally is adamant about meetings not being interrupted by people using their BlackBerrys or laptop computers or by holding side conversations.[21] Another example of a company intent on boosting the productivity of meetings by banning digital devices is Adaptive Path, a design firm in San Francisco. Meeting participants must leave their laptops on their desks, and they must place mobile phones on a counter or in a box.[22]

The practice of consulting a smartphone during a meeting has the potential to annoy, therefore detracting from the image of the smartphone user. An example is Joel L. Klein, the former New York City schools chancellor. He has gained such a negative reputation for checking his BlackBerry during meetings that some parents joke that they might be better off sending him an e-mail message.[23]

As with cell phones, when laptop computers and smartphones are used at meetings to facilitate information gathering (with permission), they can enhance interpersonal skills. If you contribute to the purpose of the meeting and are not being rude or interruptive, you are displaying good interpersonal skill. Imagine you are present at a marketing meeting of a swimsuit designer and manufacturer. The head of marketing says, "We have been thinking of finding a distributor in Alaska, but I wonder what percentage of Alaskans own a swimsuit?" You say, "If you would like, give me five minutes to search the Internet for a factual answer to your question." Particularly if you find a plausible answer, you will be perceived as constructive.

The etiquette aspect of laptops, netbooks, and smartphones at meetings has created a spirited debate. People with traditional attitudes about etiquette say the use of smartphones at meetings is as gauche as ordering out for pizza. In contrast, techno-evangelists insist that to ignore real-time text messages invites peril because so many people demand an immediate response to these messages.[24] Again, to avoid being perceived as gauche (rude), follow the corporate culture. Skill-Building Exercise 5-2 deals with this issue.

Justifying Laptop Use during a Meeting

Five students play the role of a group of workers who are developing a marketing campaign for a new energy drink, Vitalize27. Ideas are flying around the meeting room. One student plays the role of a member of the group who suddenly opens a laptop computer and begins watching the screen. By mistake the audio is turned on, and the other members of the group can easily hear that the laptop user has accessed a sports channel, ESPN.com. The laptop user gets a few frowns and some stern questioning from the team leader. The student playing the role of the laptop user must present a sensible and diplomatic excuse as to why he or she was tuned into ESPN during the meeting. Another student plays the role of the team leader, who is disappointed with the behavior he or she has observed. The other three role players might make any comments they deem to be appropriate.

Observers rate the role players on two dimensions, using a 1-to-5 scale from very poor (1) to very good (5). One dimension is "effective use of human relations techniques." The second dimension is "acting ability." A few observers might voluntarily provide feedback to the role players in terms of sharing their ratings and observations. The course instructor might also provide feedback.

Interpersonal Aspects of Presentation Technology

Presentation technology has become almost synonymous with PowerPoint and other computer graphics programs. However, presentation technology also includes laptops, data projectors, remote controls, and presentation software. The use of presentation technology provides an exceptional opportunity to display interpersonal skills—good or poor. In the words of Whitey Bluestein, an advisor to technology companies, ". . . the best presentations are based on the value of the content, the skill of the delivery, and the charisma of the speaker."[25]

The biggest challenge in using presentation technology is to maintain a human presence while still making effective use of the technology. Among the obvious indicators of good interpersonal skill during an electronic presentation are to maintain eye contact with the audience, smile, show a sense of humor, and interact with the audience. Among the potential displays of negative interpersonal skills are reading detailed slides to the audience, not maintaining eye contact, and continuous fiddling with your equipment, thereby ignoring participants at the meeting.

A practical way of maintaining a human presence is to tell a story, and use a few slides to support the story.[26] For example, a cost accountant making a PowerPoint presentation might tell a story about a pharmaceutical firm that went bankrupt because it did not carefully track how much it cost to make the drugs. The accountant might present a graph showing how costs began to outpace revenue for a drug that reduced inflammation in the joints.

All you have learned about making presentations (or public speaking) applies even though you might be tapping a key on your laptop computer while making a presentation. Self-Assessment Quiz 5-2 presents a checklist of behaviors that summarizes major points of demonstrating effective interpersonal skills during a presentation. Many people who are watching you make a presentation will be making judgments about your interpersonal and cognitive skills. One reason is that the digitized workplace has decreased other opportunities, such as visits to your work area, to form judgments about you.

Videoconferencing and Telepresence

Videoconferencing and teleconferencing place extra demands on making a good first impression and demonstrating good interpersonal skills. Telepresence is an advanced form of videoconferencing that comes closer to simulating a face-to-face meeting. Some telepresence meetings are set up in studios with a bank of high-definition screens and cameras. Others telepresence meetings are accomplished through robots containing the necessary electronics. Images are presented on giant screens, much like high-end television receivers. Keep the following considerations in mind for creating a good impression and demonstrating sensitivity to the situation at a videoconference:[27]

1. **Choose your clothing carefully.** Some participants expect the screen to display only their upper torso, and therefore wear business attire above the waist and perhaps shorts and sports shoes below. Busy patterns do not look good on camera.

The Presentation Technology Checklist of Interpersonal Behaviors

Directions: Indicate whether each of the following statements is mostly true or mostly false as it applies to you (or would apply to you if you were in the situation indicated by the statement).

Statement Number	Mostly True	Mostly False
1. I make frequent eye contact with as many members of the audience as feasible.	_____	_____
2. I like to present a large number of slides in rapid sequence just to dazzle the audience.	_____	_____
3. I tend to get irritated if a member of the audience disagrees with one of my points.	_____	_____
4. I will often attempt to loosen up the audience by telling a joke related to nationality, age, or hair color.	_____	_____
5. I attempt to pack as much information onto a slide as possible, even it requires using a 10-point font.	_____	_____
6. If somebody in the audience complains about not being able to hear me, I like to retort with a negative comment like, "Have you had your hearing checked lately?"	_____	_____
7. I smile frequently during my presentation.	_____	_____
8. I explain to the members of the audience that they can revisit my presentation on a specific Web site, or that I am willing to send them an e-mail attachment of the presentation.	_____	_____
9. At the end of the presentation, I will typically thank the audience for having watched.	_____	_____
10. I will ask the audience an open-ended question such as, "What questions do you have?" rather than a close-ended question like, "Any questions?"	_____	_____

Scoring and Interpretation: Give yourself one point (+1) for each statement you gave in agreement with the keyed answer. The keyed answer indicates a positive interpersonal skill for presentation technology.

1. Mostly true	4. Mostly false	7. Mostly true	10. Mostly true
2. Mostly false	5. Mostly false	8. Mostly true	
3. Mostly false	6. Mostly false	9. Mostly true	

9–10: You have good skills related to the interpersonal aspects of presentation technology.

1–8: You have much room for improvement in terms of your skills related to the interpersonal aspects of presentation technology.

Clothing may be more superficial than interpersonal skill, but your choice of clothing reflects on your judgment and how seriously you take the conference.

2. **Speak in crisp, conversational tones, and pay close attention.** Maintain eye contact with live participants and remote viewers; this is an important interpersonal skill, as it is with presentation technologies. Getting up to leave the room looks particularly bad on camera.

3. **Never forget the powerful reach of the video camera.** Behavior such as falling asleep or rolling the eyes in response to an executive's suggestions are readily seen by associates in the same and other locations. Such behavior is likely to be interpreted as indicative of immaturity. It is also important to stay within reach of camcorders in both videoconferencing and telepresence. A recurring problem is that when a person stands to stretch or simply to pause from sitting down, the person may appear headless—hardly a way to establish rapport with people at other sites.

4. **Avoid culturally insensitive gestures.** For example, large hand and body motions make many Asians uncomfortable. Also, extreme behaviors sometimes appear magnified on video camera, although they might be less distracting in person.

5. **Decrease nervousness about video interviews by rehearsing.** Use a camcorder to see how you appear and sound during a practice interview, engaging the help of a friend. Solicit his or her feedback about your performance. Appearing relaxed during a videoconference helps you project the important interpersonal skill of being self-confident.

Interpersonal Skills Linked to Telecommuting

As illustrated in the chapter introduction, people who work from home face challenges to their interpersonal skills related to communication. Telecommuters can communicate abundantly via electronic devices, but they miss out on the face-to-face interactions so vital for dealing with complex problems. Another communication problem telecommuters face is feeling isolated from activities at the main office and missing out on the encouragement and recognition that take place in face-to-face encounters. (Of course, many telecommuters prefer to avoid such contact.) Many telecommuters have another communications problem: Because they have very little face-to-face communication with key people in the organization, they believe that they are passed over for promotion. Most telecommuters spend some time in the traditional office, yet they miss the day-by-day contact.

Another communication problem with telecommuting is that it lacks a solid human connection. As one telecommuting marketing consultant put it, face time is critical for building empathy. "It's a human connection. It takes time, and human beings need visual cues, the symbols of being together and caring for one another."[28] To combat the problem of isolation, most companies schedule some face time with remote workers perhaps every few months. At a minimum, a supervisor might phone the teleworkers at least once a week, or hold a monthly videoconference.[29]

To display positive interpersonal skills as a worker from home or other remote location, the individual should make good use of the limited face-to-face contact he or she has with other workers. Display warmth toward and interest in work associates. Staying in touch online with a human relations twist is also important. Occasionally asking how the other person is doing is helpful, as is an occasional question about the person's interests or family life. Co-working (using shared office space) places extra demands on being cordial and friendly because the other people who rent co-working space came there in part for the opportunity to interact with other remote workers.[30] Also, because the space is so cramped, negative behaviors such as shouting on the phone and swearing in frustration should be minimized.

Many telecommuters are asked to attend an occasional company meeting. On these occasions, it is important to display high enthusiasm. To keep interpersonal skills sharp, it is good to interact with store associates and service workers such as the postal service and package delivery workers. The designer described at the chapter outset kept his interpersonal skills in use by interacting with other workers sharing the same office space.

Successful telecommuters also need the interpersonal skill of being able to work well without supervision. You also need to be able to work well in isolation, and not be dependent on frequent interaction with coworkers or a supervisor.[31] High-maintenance employees who need frequent praise and attention are much better suited for working in a traditional office than working from home.

Avoiding Damage to Your Online Reputation

Postings on the Internet, including newspaper articles, blogs, and video Web sites, can rapidly broadcast favorable or unfavorable data about your interpersonal skills and judgment. Based largely on the Internet, much more information about a person's private life has become public. Some aspects of your personal life therefore affect your professional reputation. If an Internet blog contends that a given individual was an accessory to an armed robbery, that person's job might become in jeopardy.[32]

Matt Zimmerman, senior staff attorney for the Electronic Frontier Foundation, explains the importance of having a squeaky clean reputation in these terms: "Now we have this giant megaphone of the Internet, where every little whisper about someone shows up in Google."[33]

A positive interpersonal and cognitive skill is therefore to avoid having embarrassing information or photographs linked to you accessible through search engines. A Career-Builder survey found that 65 peercent of the employers surveyed said they visited social media to investigate whether a given job candidate presents himself or herself professionally.[34] Many career-minded people who are concerned that a photograph of them posted on the Internet might damage their reputation are using a mobile application that deletes the photo within ten seconds. Such software is not designed for desktop computers.[35]

Your reputation can also be damaged by posting extreme viewpoints on the Web because these extreme viewpoints might be unwelcome by employers who want to avoid offending customers or potential customers. Two examples of extreme viewpoints are stating that (a) all people who wear fur coats should be physically attacked, and (b) all investment bankers who earn more than $2 million in an annual bonus should be sent to jail.

Another aspect of your online reputation is that you might need to distance yourself from others who share your name. If you have a LinkedIn or Facebook profile, insert a clear photo of yourself. During a job search, when you send your résumé either as a hard copy by mail or via the Internet, provide a link to your profile. Also, alert present or prospective employers if someone with the same name as yours has a negative online presence. A challenge in terms of job hunting is that an Internet search has become part of the employer's background investigation. Negative information about oneself on the Web can sometimes be removed by request or by hiring a service for such purposes.

Concept Review and Reinforcement

multitasking 133

nomophobia 134

Summary

Effective interpersonal skills help make good use of the communication and information technology surrounding us in the workplace. Interactions with people one at a time create the majority of opportunities for displaying interpersonal skills related to the digital age. Smartphones, cell phones, and text messaging represent an enormous opportunity for displaying good, as well as poor, interpersonal skills. An example of a positive skill is to ask your work associate if he or she would like you to access an item of work-related information using your cell phone. An example of a negative skill is work-related driving under the influence of a cell phone, including text messaging.

E-mail messages and instant messaging (IM) provide another opportunity for displaying positive as well as negative interpersonal skills related to the digital age. The way in which a message is sent, positive or negative, tells something about the sender. Figure 5-1 summarizes a large amount of information about etiquette related to e-mail and instant messaging.

Another interpersonal skill useful in the digital age is to perform well during a webcam interview. Performing well in such an interview combines interpersonal skills with those related to communication technology. In some situations, performing two tasks at once can enhance interpersonal skills because you are helping another person, as is often done in coaching and tutoring. The major negative interpersonal skill aspect of multitasking is that it trivializes the person with whom you are interacting.

A negative consequence of communication technology in the workplace is that it is easier to harass coworkers than in the analog age. Creating a hostile environment by displaying pornography to workers who do not want to see it has become one of the most frequent forms of harassment.

Positive interpersonal skills associated with social networking include (1) demonstrating your loyalty by posting gracious comments about your employer, (2) displaying your compassion for people in need, (3) demonstrating professional-level communication skills, and (4) demonstrating a willingness to collaborate with others.

Negative interpersonal skills associated with social networking include (a) using social networking sites to eliminate face-to-face interactions with work associates, (2) posting confidential or derogatory information about your employer, (3) engaging in social networking at inappropriate times, and (4) bragging too much about being an "online celebrity."

Whether the use of laptop and notebook computers as well as smartphones during meetings enhances your interpersonal skills depends on company custom and why you are using your computer. When laptop computers and smartphones are used at meetings to facilitate information gathering (with permission), they can enhance interpersonal skills.

The biggest challenge in using presentation technology is to maintain a human presence while still making effective use of the technology. An example of a positive interpersonal skill is maintaining eye contact with the audience; a negative skill is continuous fiddling with the equipment, thereby ignoring the audience.

Videoconferencing and telepresence place extra demands on creating a good first impression and demonstrating good interpersonal skills. A positive skill is to speak in crisp, conversational tones and pay close attention. People who work from home face challenges to their interpersonal skills related to communication. To display positive interpersonal skills, the worker from home should make good use of the limited face-to-face contact he or she has with other workers.

Protecting your online reputation is a skill. A positive interpersonal and cognitive skill is therefore to avoid having embarrassing information and photographs linked to you accessible through search engines. Many employers search social media sites to observe if a job candidate presents himself or herself professionally.

Questions for Discussion and Review

1. Why do you feel that some companies have a problem with employees sending rude or insulting e-mails?

2. Assume that you send an instant message to the company CEO stating that you enjoy working for the company. Explain whether you think the CEO is obliged to respond immediately, or at all, to your message.

3. Assume that you send some useful information to a coworker , and he or she sends back an e-mail message or text thanking you. How important is it that you send back a reply that he or she is welcome?

4. Your author posted a message on the White House Web site in 2013, suggesting that the government conduct a nationwide charity drive to help reduce the federal debt. Two months later, President Barack Obama responded with an e-mail from the White House, addressed to "Dear Friend." The e-mail contained a detailed description of the president's plans for the economy. What does the interaction just described tell you about the digital interpersonal skills of President Obama (or his staff)?

5. What should a person who is invited for a webcam job interview do if he or she does not feel telegenic (photogenic on TV) to perform well in such an interview?

6. What might you be able to do in the next several days to demonstrate on Facebook or Twitter a positive aspect of your interpersonal skills?

7. Imagine that you are attending an in-person meeting as your favorite sports team is playing a championship game in a different time zone. Explain whether you would take a quick peek at the score from time to time on your smartphone during the meeting.

8. Give an example of one of the best displays of interpersonal skills you have seen in a PowerPoint presentation by one of your professors.

9. Would you feel comfortable being interviewed by webcam? If not, what aspects would cause you problems?

10. Why do some people interpret harassment differently from others?

The Web Corner

http://www.cnn.com/2012/09/28/tech/mobile/ netiquette-eight-phone-habits/
(Avoiding smartphone rudeness.)

http://www.virginmediabusiness.co.uk/Business- needs/Outlook-Magazine/Video-conferencing-Skills/
(Presenting yourself well during a videoconference.)

http://inspirationfeed.com/articles/blogging/ how-to-develop-a-constructive-online-reputation/
(Developing a good online reputation.)

Internet Skill Builder: Interpersonal Skills of a Technology Executive

Think of a well-known information technology executive, such as the late Steve Jobs at Apple or Marissa Mayer at Yahoo!. Arrive at a judgment about his or her interpersonal skills through video research on the Internet. For example, you might find a brief video of your target executive on YouTube, Hulu, or Facebook. Based on this small sample of behavior, reach any conclusion you can about the technology executive's interpersonal skills. Two traits to judge would be rudeness and insensitivity to people, because some well-known technology executives have the reputation of treating others poorly. Forget about the opinion of others; you are the judge in this assignment.

Developing Your Human Relations Skills

Interpersonal Relations Case 5.1

Sonya Takes Chances on Yammer

Sonya is a product placement specialist for an international manufacturer and distributor of a wide variety of beverages and snack foods. As a product placement specialist, her key role is to get company products displayed in movies, on TV, in video games, on social media, and even in TV ads for other products. One example would be to have someone in a film waiting for a bus sipping one of the company's non-carbonated beverages. Another example of product placement would be an advertisement for an automobile in which people seated in the car are holding a bag of tortillas made by the company.

Six months ago Sonya's company signed on with Yammer, essentially a social network for employees. Top management thought that Yammer would enhance communication among employees, leading to more creativity. Also, employees could quickly access relevant information without having to send so many e-mails to other employees. Along with any employee she spoke to, Sonya enjoyed communicating her ideas so freely and also having quick access to the thoughts of others.

One day Bruce, the director of product placement, sent Sonya an e-mail asking her to meet with him that afternoon in his office to discuss her over-the-top use of Yammer. Two minutes into the meeting, Bruce said to Sonya, "Here is what I'm talking about. I have accessed four of your Yammer postings that I think are over the top in terms of being a little rude and unprofessional." The Yammer posts in question were as follows:

- I had a great idea this morning. Why not a product placement at an open-coffin funeral? The corpse could be holding a bag of barbeque chips and a bottle of our vitamin water.

- I'm a little worried about our vice president of finance. Have you seen her face lately? It looks like her boyfriend left her or her dog has been diagnosed with a brain tumor.

- I heard an unconfirmed rumor today that our revenues are going to take a big hit next quarter. It seems that consumers are getting tired of paying premium prices for big-brand names and are shifting a little more to store brands.

- Those penny pinchers in the finance department are questioning how much we are paying for product placements. If they knew anything about marketing, they would know that what we are doing has a tremendous return on investment.

Sonya looked at the posts and replied, "Okay, the jokes are a little edgy. But the other comments are totally honest. I thought the purpose of Yammer was for employees to engage in open communication."

Case Questions

1. What is your evaluation of the criticisms that Bruce made of Sonya's posts?
2. What suggestions can you make to Sonya to improve her interpersonal skills for the digital world? (Or, does she need any improvement based on the evidence presented in this case?)

Interpersonal Relations Role-Play

Bruce Confronts Sonya about Her Yammer Posts

Bruce decides that he needs a face-to-face meeting with Sonya to discuss her Yammer posts because she continues to write posts that many people might find objectionable. One person plays the role of Bruce, who does not want to violate Sonya's freedom of expression, but does want her to use better judgment with respect to her Yammer posts. Another student plays the role of Sonya, who believes that open criticism and playfulness is acceptable on Yammer. Run the role-play for about seven minutes, and see if the two role players can resolve this issue about the use of Yammer.

Interpersonal Relations Case 5.2

Kevin, the Twitter Guy

Kevin, a real estate agent specializing in low-priced homes in Detroit, Michigan, is an avid Twitter user. He spends approximately two hours per day checking out his followers and the people he is following. Kevin posts about six tweets a day with the hope of building his reputation as an intelligent professional, as well as obtaining referrals of potential homebuyers. The contents of 10 tweets Kevin posted last month are presented next.

1. The #Detroit Lions might be good this season. Owing a home in downtown is a good investment. Kevin@ MetroRealty.com.
2. My buddies love my barbeques. Get in touch to buy a house. Kevin@MetroRealty.com.
3. Looks like I have pinkeye today. Send along your home-hunting friends. Kevin@MetroRealty.com.
4. I tried one of those #electronic cigarettes. No thanks. Home ownership is a great investment. Kevin@ MetroRealty.com.
5. My niece sent me a Valentine's Day card saying she loves me. Kevin@MetroRealty.com.
6. Just advised my folks to get a #reverse mortgage. I told them home ownership is good. Kevin@ MetroRealty.com.
7. Keep an eye on your #BMI (body mass index). Did you know that I sell houses? Kevin@MetroRealty.com.
8. I may need a new transmission on my SUV. I'm waiting for a referral from you guys. Kevin@MetroRealty.com.
9. It's hot and my AC in the SUV is down. Home ownership is the American Dream. Kevin@MetroRealty. com.
10. Did you know that Domino's has made its pizzas spicier and tastier? Pizza goes great with a house. Kevin@MetroRealty.com.

Case Questions

1. How well is Kevin doing in terms of projecting the image of an intelligent professional?
2. What advice might you give to Kevin so that his tweeting might lead to more referrals?
3. To what extent is Kevin just wasting time with his Twitter activity?

References

1. Several of the facts in this case are from Jessica Marquez, "Corporations Footing the Bill for Co-Working," *Workforce Management*, August 11, 2008, pp. 10–11; Jeffrey Blackwell, "Shared Spaces," *RocNext, Democrat and Chronicle*, August 19, 2012, pp. 1E, 5E.
2. Many of the ideas in this list are based on the following sources: Louise Lee, "Cell? Well . . . Use Your Phone for Good, Not Evil," *Business Week Small Biz*, February/March 2009, p. 22; Catherine Hatcher, "11 Rules For Good Cell Phone Etiquette," *http://cbs1tv.com*, Accessed December 30, 2007; Amy Novotney, "Dangerous Distractions," *Monitor on Psychology*, February 2009, pp. 32–3; Elizabeth Bernstein, "The Miscommunicators," *The Wall Street Journal*, July 3, 2012, pp. D1, D3.
3. The sources in endnote 2 also apply to endnote 3. In addition are the following: Rachel Emma Silverman, "Here's Why You Won't Finish This Article," *The Wall Street Journal*, December 12, 2012, pp. B1, B6; Alex Williams, "Mind Your BlackBerry or Mind Your Manners," *The New York Times* (http://www.nytimes.com); "Cell Phone Etiquette at

the Office, *Articlesbase*, April 27, 2009; Lynette Spicer, "Civility in the Workplace," *Iowa State University Extension*, (http://www.extension.iastate.edu/mt/civility), May 4, 2009.

4. Quoted in Christine Rosen, "Our Cell Phones, Ourselves," *The New Atlantis*, p. 31.

5. Research cited in Novotney, "Dangerous Distractions," Summer 2004, p. 32.

6. Quoted in Barbara Kiviat, "Résumé? Check. Nice Suit? Check. Webcam?" *Time Magazine*, November 9, 2009, p. 50.

7. "Christa Foley, Recruiting Manager, Zappos.com," *Chequed.com* (http://www.chequed.com/hr-interview-series), April 7, 2011, p. 1.

8. Several of the suggestions for what to do and what not to do during a webcam interview are from Kiviat, "Résumé? Check. Nice Suit? Check. Webcam?" *Time Magazine*, November 9, 2009, p. 50.

9. Quoted in Abby Ellis, "Auditioning in a Video Résumé," *The New York Times* (http://www.nytimes.com), April 21, 2007, p. 3.

10. Quoted in Heather Huhman, "Use Youth to Your Advantage," *http://www.examiner.com*, accessed April 21, 2009.

11. Paul Hemp, "Death by Information Overload," *Harvard Business Review*, September 2009, p. 85.

12. Rachel Emma Silverman, "Here's Why You Won't Finish This Article," *The Wall Street Journal*, December 12, 2012, pp. B1, B6.

13. "Goes Without Saying, but Say It Anyway: No Porn at Work," *HR Specialist: New York Employment Law*, June 2008, p. 1.

14. For a useful perspective on how social networking is changing society, see Steven Johnson, "How Twitter Will Change the Way We Live." *Time*, June 15, 2009, pp. 32–37.

15. Ronald Deiser and Sylvain Newton, "Six Social-Media Skills Every Leader Needs," *McKinsey Quarterly* (http://www.mckinseyquarterly.com), February 2013, p. 2.

16. Ashlee Vance, "Trouble at the Virtual Water Cooler," *Bloomberg Businessweek*, May 2–May 8, 2011, p. 31.

17. Bridget Carey and Niala Boodhoo, "How to Deal with What Feels Like Online Identity Theft," *The Miami Herald* (*http://miamiherald.com*), April 14, 2009.

18. Matthew Miller, "Employers Get a #Boost from @NLRB's Social Media Report," *Workforce Management*, April 2012, p. 10.

19. Kim Komando, "Use Discretion with Online Reviews," *Democrat and Chronicle, RocBusiness*, June 25, 2012, pp. 5B, 6B.

20. Alexandria Samuel, "Your Employee Is an Online Celebrity. Now What Do You Do?" *The Wall Street Journal*, October 20, 2012, pp. B7, B8.

21. Alex Taylor III, "Fixing Up Ford," *Fortune*, May 25, 2009, p. 49.

22. "Go 'Topless,'" *Manager's Edge*, August 2008, p. 6.

23. Alex Williams, "Mind Your BlackBerry or Mind Your Manners," *The New York Times* (http://www.nytimes.com), June 22, 2009.

24. Ibid.

25. Quoted in Dan O'Shea, "How to Get to the Point," *Entrepreneur*, October 2011, p. 46.

26. Bob Parks, "Death to PowerPoint," *Bloomberg BusinessWeek*, September 3–September 9, 2012, pp. 83–85.

27. Joann S. Lublin, "Some Dos and Don'ts To Help You Hone Videoconference Skills," *The Wall Street Journal*, February 7, 2006, p. B1; Drake Bennett, "I'll Have My Robots Talk to Your Robots," *Bloomberg Businessweek*, February 21–February 27, 2011, pp. 52–56.

28. "Work à la Modem," *Businessweek*, October 4, 1999, p. 176.

29. "Bridge Gaps with Remote Workers," *Manager's Edge*, July 2008, p. 1.

30. Jeffrey Blackwell, "Shared Spaces," *RocNext, Democrat and Chronicle*, August 19, 2012, pp. 1E, 5E.

31. Michelle Conlin, "Telecommuting: Out of Sight, Yes. Out of Mind, No," *Businessweek*, February 18, 2008, p. 060.

32. Stephen Behnke, "Ethics in the Age of the Internet," *Monitor on Psychology*, July/August 2008, pp. 74–75.

33. Anita Hamilton, "Outsmart Your Haters," *Time*, October 6, 2008, pp. 67–68.

34. Debra Auerbach, "Employers Checking Social Sites," *CareerBuilder*, May 6, 2012,

35. Felix Gillette, "Snapchat and the Right to be Forgotten," *Businessweek*, February 11–February 17, 2013, pp. 42–47.

Developing Teamwork Skills

Aicha is proud of her position as a construction and building inspector for a large metropolitan area. She and her coworkers are responsible for ensuring that new construction, changes, or repairs comply with local and national building codes as well as contract specifications. Aicha visits many smaller sites on her own, but also participates in team inspections at larger sites.

Aicha is well liked by her teammates and her supervisor, most of all because she combines her professional and technical skills with being a cooperative and friendly team member. Don, her supervisor, explains that after Aicha makes an inspection, she typically posts information the department might be able to use in future inspections. One time, she noted that the battery used in a backup system for a building's electrical power plant was the same brand that had overheating problems at other installations. Aicha told her team members to be on the lookout for these batteries at other new buildings.

Goodluz/Shutterstock

After reading and studying this chapter and completing the exercises, you should be able to

1. Explain the difference between a traditional team and a virtual team.
2. Understand the advantages and disadvantages of teams.
3. Identify various team member roles.
4. Apply interpersonal-related tactics for effective team play.
5. Apply task-related tactics for effective team play.

Don also noted that, "Last spring, our department was overloaded because of a lot of new downtown construction. Baxter, one of our experienced inspectors, banged up his knee in a skateboarding crash, so he had to miss work for a week. Aicha told me and the team not to worry, that she would gladly take over Baxter's scheduled inspections for the week.

"To top off that kind of willingness to incovenience herself to help the team get its job done, Aicha adds a warm, human touch. Three times this year, she has brought the team cookies that she baked herself."

The attitude of the construction and building inspector just described illustrates a spirit of teamwork that can help a company prosper. The modern organization depends on teamwork throughout the company. Many firms rely more on teamwork than on individuals acting alone to accomplish work. To be successful in the modern organization, it is, therefore, necessary to be an effective team player. You have to work smoothly with other members of the team to accomplish your goals. Teamwork is more important as people work their way up through the organization; however, even at the top of the organization, members of the executive team are expected to work smoothly together.

The challenges a team member faces come to light when the true nature of a team is recognized. A **team** is a special type of group. Team members have complementary skills and are committed to a common purpose, a set of performance goals, and an approach to the task. In other words, the members of a team work together smoothly, and all pull in the same direction. A workplace team should be more like an effective athletic team than a group of individuals out for individual glory.[1]

This chapter gives you the information, insights, and preliminary practice necessary to develop effective teamwork skills. Chapter 7 continues the study of teams and groups in the context of making decisions as a group. Self-Assessment Quiz 6-1 will help you assess your current mental readiness to be a contributing team member.

team

A small number of people with complementary skills who are committed to a common purpose, set of performance goals, and approach for which they hold themselves mutually accountable.

FACE-TO-FACE VERSUS VIRTUAL TEAMS

All teams in the workplace have the common elements of people working together cooperatively and members possessing a mix of skills. No matter what label the team carries, its broad purpose is to contribute to a *collaborative workplace* in which people help each other achieve constructive goals. The idea is for workers to collaborate (a high level of cooperation) rather than to compete with or prevent others from getting their work done. To make collaboration work effectively, team members have to agree to be accountable to one another as peers, and recognize that what they are doing is a joint effort. Each team or group member is expected to commit to specific goals and to expect that each member will follow through.[2] Self-Assessment Quiz 6-2 presents a representative listing of characteristics and attitudes of people that facilitate their being effective team members.

LEARNING OBJECTIVE 1

Although many different types of teams exist, a useful distinction is between the traditional teams in which workers share the same physical space and virtual teams in which the team members rarely see each other in person.

Face-to-Face (Traditional) Teams

The best-known workplace team is a group of workers who take some of the responsibility for managing their own work. Face-to-face teams are used in a wide variety of activities, including producing motorcycles, performing complex surgery, producing a major component for a large computer, or launching a new product. Team members interact with other frequently, rather than doing their work in isolation from one another.

Members of a traditional team typically work together on an ongoing, day-by-day basis, thus differentiating it from a task force or a committee. The team is often given total responsibility for or "ownership" of an entire product or service, such as producing a video game. At other times, the team is given responsibility for a major chunk of a job, such as building an airplane engine (but not the entire airplane). Structuring work around self-managing teams has become commonplace in contemporary workplaces, as workers are expected to rely more on their own resources and less on being carefully supervised.[3]

A major hurdle in forming a true team is to help employees overcome the attitude reflected in the statement "I'm not paid to think." Teams often rely less on supervisors and more on the workers assuming more responsibilities for managing their own activities.

As with all groups, mutual trust among members contributes to team effectiveness. A study conducted with business students, however, showed that if the members trust each other too much, they may not monitor (check up on) each other's work enough. As a result, group performance will suffer. This problem of too much trust surfaces primarily when the team members have individual assignments that do not bring them into frequent contact with each other.[4] An example of an individual, or autonomous, project is preparing a statistical report to later be given to the group.

An important observation about face-to-face teams is that they typically contain subgroups, or groups within the team.[5] The larger the group, the more likely that subgroups will be present. The subgroups are often similar in some key attribute such as speciality or a demographic characteristic such as age or gender. Visualize a large product development team. A couple of subgroups might form composed of some people with an engineering background and some with a business background, including finance. Subgroups can be an asset when they solve problems well because they work smoothly together. It is also important for the various subgroups to pull together to achieve the overall group or team goal.

Virtual Teams

Some teams conduct most of their work by sending electronic messages to each other and holding videoconferences rather than conducting face-to-face meetings. A **virtual team** is a small group of people who conduct almost all of their collaborative work by electronic communication rather than by face-to-face meetings. E-mail, including instant messaging and text messaging, is the usual medium for sharing information and conducting meetings. *Groupware* is another widely used approach to conducting an electronic meeting. Using groupware, several people can edit a document at the same time, or in sequence. Company social media Web sites might also be classified as groupware.

Most high-tech companies make some use of virtual teams and electronic meetings. Strategic alliances in which geographically dispersed companies work with each other are ideally suited for virtual teams. It is less expensive for the field technician in Iceland to hold an electronic meeting with her counterparts in South Africa, Mexico, and California

virtual team

A small group of people who conduct almost all of their collaborative work by electronic communication rather than face-to-face meetings.

than it is to bring them all together in one physical location. Virtual teams are sometimes the answer to the challenge of hiring workers with essential skills who do not want to relocate. Because the members of a virtual team might be working in different countries, they are often considered to be multicultural teams.

With team members geographically dispersed, precise communications are all the more important for virtual teams. The virtual team members usually need a formal document outlining objectives, job responsibilities, and team goals. Another concern about virtual teams is that a lot of work gets accomplished because of relationships, and it is more difficult to build relationships virtually.[6] The team leader as well as team members, therefore, have to put special effort into relationship building, even if only through elecronic communication and the occasional videoconference.

Establishing trust is a major challenge in a virtual team, because the team members have to rely on people they never see to carry out their fair share of the workload and to exchange reliable information. Trust is also needed in terms of what information should be shared outside of the team. For example, if the team is behind schedule on a project, can each member be trusted not to inform outsiders about the problem? For example, one virtual team had an external communication norm (standard of conduct) that prohibited team members from conveying negative information to anyone outside of the team.[7]

Despite the efficiency of virtual teams, there are times when face-to-face (or at least telephone) interaction is necessary to deal with complex and emotional issues. Negotiating a new contract between management and a labor union, for example, is not well suited to an electronic meeting.

THE ADVANTAGES AND DISADVANTAGES OF TEAMS AND TEAMWORK

Groups have always been the building blocks of organizations. Yet groups and teams have grown in importance as the basic unit for organizing work. In an attempt to cope with numerous changes in the outside world, many organizations have granted teams increased independence and flexibility. Furthermore, teams are often required to work more closely with customers and suppliers.

The increased acceptance of teams suggests that group work offers many advantages. Nevertheless, it is useful to specify several of these advantages and also examine the potential problems of groups. Being aware of these potential pitfalls can often help a person avoid them. These same advantages and disadvantages also apply to group decision making, to be described in Chapter 7.

synergy

A situation in which the group's total output exceeds the sum of each individual's contribution.

George Doyle/Getty Images

Advantages of Group Work and Teamwork

Group work and group decision making offer several advantages over individual effort. Because so much of what is accomplished in organizations is done by groups, it may appear obvious that groups and teams have many advantages. The importance of this topic, however, warrants mentioning a few of the specific advantages of groups, teams, and group decision making.

Synergy.   If several knowledgeable people are brought into the decision-making process, a number of worthwhile possibilities may be uncovered. It is also possible to gain **synergy**, whereby the group's total output exceeds the sum of each individual's contribution. For example, it would be a rare person working alone who could build a racing car. At the same time, groups and teams are the building blocks of the larger organization.

Work Accomplishment and High Productivity.   Without groups, including teams, an organization could not get its work accomplished. Clarence Otis, Jr., the CEO of Darden Restaurants (which includes Olive Garden, Red Lobster, and Bahama

Breeze), says that the thrust of his leadership is to build the team, because the team accomplishes so much of the work.[8]

A major justification for relying on teams in the workplace is that under the right circumstances, they can enhance productivity and profitability. The right circumstances include an atmosphere that promotes teamwork and financial bonuses for high-performing teams. A classic example is American steel maker Nucor Corp. The company is committed to the spirit of teamwork, and bonuses for teams of steelworkers average 170 percent to 180 percent. Since Nucor implemented its team incentive plan in 1966, the company has been profitable each quarter through 2012 despite foreign competition. Also, the company has increased the dividend to shareholders for 37 consecutive years.[9]

A broad perspective about the advantages of groups is that because of groups and teams, large organizations can be built that provide useful goods and services to the world. For example, a company such as Coca Cola, Inc., or Volkswagen is only possible because of group effort. Furthermore, the existence of large organizations, including business firms, colleges, universities, and hospitals, helps advance civilization.

Acceptance and Commitment.   Group decision making is also helpful in gaining acceptance and commitment. The argument is that people who contribute to making a decision will feel some ownership about implementing the decision. Under these conditions, it becomes more difficult to object to a decision because your contribution is included in the decision. At times, managers will deliberately ask for input into a decision they have already made as a manipulative way of gaining acceptance for and commitment to the decision.

Avoidance of Major Errors.   Team members often evaluate each other's thinking, so the team is likely to avoid major errors. An advertising specialist was developing an advertising campaign to attract seniors to live in a retirement community. The proposed ads had photographs of senior citizens engaged in playing shuffleboard, visiting the pharmacy, and sleeping in a hammock. Another team member on the project pointed out that many seniors perceive themselves to be energetic and youthful. Ads emphasizing advanced age might, therefore, backfire. A successful advertising campaign was then developed that featured seniors in more youthful activities, such as jogging and dancing.

Increased Job Satisfaction.   Working in teams and groups also enhances the job satisfaction of members. Being a member of a work group makes it possible to satisfy more needs than working alone. Among these needs are affiliation, security, self-esteem, and self-fulfillment. (Chapter 11 provides more details about psychological needs.)

A major reason that groups and teams contribute to worker satisfaction is that many people find working in groups to be a natural way of life. In school, sports, and the community, they have been accustomed to working collaboratively and therefore feel more comfortable in groups than in individual effort.

Disadvantages of Group Work and Teamwork

Group activity has some potential disadvantages for both individuals and the organization, as described in the following paragraphs. Some of these disadvantages serve as alerts for preventing problems.

Time Wasting.   Teams and other groups often waste time because they talk too much and act too little. Committees appear to suffer from more inaction than teams. Abigail Johnson, president of Fidelity Employer Services Division, says that committees are not effective decision makers. "They have tended to be slow and overly risk averse. Even worse, I believe, they can drain an organization of talent, because the group can only be as good as the average."[10]

Pressures toward Conformity.   A major problem is that members face pressures to conform to group standards of performance and conduct, as just implied. Some teams might shun a person who is much more productive than his or her coworkers. Also, to be liked by coworkers, as well as to avoid conflict, a group member will sometimes agree with the opinion of other group or team members. Group members will often use the same jargon, whether or not it is precise. For example, workers at Microsoft refer to e-mail as "mail," thereby snubbing postal mail.

Conformity in dress and appearance is also apparent in many work groups. You might want to examine a photo of Google or Apple employees and observe how much conformity in dress you find. Conformity in dress, however, is not much of a disadvantage, except when a group member is dissatisfied because of the pressure to dress in the same manner as coworkers.

Self-Assessment Quiz 6-3 gives you an opportunity to think about your tendencies toward conformity.

Shirking of Individual Responsibility (Social Loafing). Shirking of individual responsibility is another problem frequently noted in groups. Unless work is assigned carefully to each team member, an undermotivated person can often squeeze by without contributing his or her fair share to a group effort. **Social loafing** is the psychological term for shirking individual responsibility in a group setting. The social loafer risks being ostracized (shunned) by the group, but may be willing to pay the price rather than to work hard. Loafing of this type is sometimes found in groups such as committees and project teams. Have you ever encountered a social loafer on a group project at school?

Fostering of Conflict. At their worst, teams and other groups foster conflict on the job. People within the work group often bicker about such matters as doing a fair share of the undesirable tasks within the department. Cohesive work groups can also become xenophobic (fearful of outsiders). As a consequence, they may grow to dislike other groups and enter into conflict with them. A customer service group might put considerable effort into showing up a sales group because the latter makes promises to customers that the customer service group cannot keep. For example, a sales representative might promise that a customer can get a loaner if his or her equipment needs repair, although customer service has no such policy.

Groupthink. A well-publicized disadvantage of group decision making is **groupthink**, a deterioration of mental efficiency, reality testing, and moral judgment in the interest of group solidarity. Simply put, groupthink is an extreme form of consensus. The group atmosphere values getting along more than getting things done. The group thinks as a unit, believes it is impervious to outside criticism, and begins to have illusions about its own invincibility. As a consequence, the group loses its powers of critical analysis.[11] Groupthink appears to have contributed to several of the major financial scandals of the previous decade. Members of top management got together to vote themselves huge bonuses just before filing bankruptcy for their company. Several of the executives, including a few from Enron Corporation, were later sent to prison for their outrageous decisions.

Two conditions are important for overcoming the potential disadvantages of teams and groups.[12] First, the members must strive to act like a team following some of the suggestions given in the upcoming pages. Second, the task given to the group should require collective effort instead of being a task that could better be performed by individuals. For example, an international business specialist would probably learn to conjugate verbs in a foreign language better by working alone than on a team. What is your opinion on this issue? Figure 6-1 presents more information about key factors associated with effective work teams and groups. The more of these factors that are present, the more likely it is that a given team or group will be productive.

LEARNING OBJECTIVE 3

TEAM MEMBER ROLES

A major challenge in learning to become an effective team member is to choose the right roles to occupy. A **role** is a tendency to behave, contribute, and relate to others in a particular way. If you carry out positive roles, you will be perceived as a contributor to team effort. If you neglect carrying out these roles, you will be perceived as a poor contributor. Self-Assessment Quiz 6-4 will help you evaluate your present inclinations toward occupying

---

social loafing

The psychological term for shirking individual responsibility in a group setting.

groupthink

A deterioration of mental efficiency, reality testing, and moral judgment in the interest of group solidarity.

role

A tendency to behave, contribute, and relate to others in a particular way.

The Conformity Quiz

Directions: Circle the extent to which each of the following statements describes your behavior or attitude: agree strongly (AS); agree (A); neutral (N); disagree (D); disagree strongly (DS). You may have to respond in terms of any team or group experience you have had if you are not currently a member of a work team, a class-project team, or a sports team. Consider having someone who is familiar with your behavior and attitudes help you respond accurately.

		AS	A	N	D	DS
1.	I rarely question the decision reached by the team.	5	4	3	2	1
2.	Whatever the group wants is fine with me.	5	4	3	2	1
3.	My clothing distinguishes me from the other members of the team.	1	2	3	4	5
4.	I consider myself to be one of the gang.	5	4	3	2	1
5.	I rarely express disagreement during a group discussion.	5	4	3	2	1
6.	I routinely have lunch with other members of the team.	5	4	3	2	1
7.	My teammates sometimes complain that I think too independently.	1	2	3	4	5
8.	My preference is to piggyback on the ideas of others rather than contributing ideas of my own.	5	4	3	2	1
9.	When I notice that other members of the team make the same error in speech, I will copy them rather than sound different.	5	4	3	2	1
10.	I am often the first person to get up at the scheduled ending of the meeting.	1	2	3	4	5
11.	I do almost all of my creative thinking for the team task when I'm with the team.	5	4	3	2	1
12.	I'm particularly careful not to criticize an idea submitted by the team leader.	5	4	3	2	1
13.	The number of hours I work per week corresponds closely to the number worked by my teammates.	5	4	3	2	1
14.	When I think it is necessary, I bring information to the group that conflicts with the path we are following.	1	2	3	4	5
15.	I would rather keep my mouth closed than point out weaknesses in a teammate's ideas.	5	4	3	2	1
16.	I've been called a maverick on more than one occasion by teammates.	1	2	3	4	5
17.	I encourage team members to express doubts about proposed solutions to problems.	1	2	3	4	5
18.	I invite criticism of my ideas.	1	2	3	4	5
19.	When the team laughs at a comment, I laugh too, even if I don't think the comment was funny.	5	4	3	2	1
20.	Most of my social life centers on activities with my teammates.	5	4	3	2	1

Scoring and Interpretation: Calculate your score by adding the numbers you have circled, and use the following guide:

80–100: You are a high-conforming individual who readily goes along with the team without preserving your individuality. In an effort to be liked, you might be over-compromising your thinking.

40–79: You have probably achieved the right balance between following group norms (standards of conduct) and expressing your individuality. With actions and attitudes like this, you are on your way to becoming a good team player, yet also in a position to attain individual recognition.

20–29: You are highly individualistic, perhaps to the point of not working smoothly in a team setting. Be careful that you are not going out of your way to be a nonconformist, thereby interfering with your ability to be an effective team player.

Skill Development: Examine your responses to the 20 questions, because the response might give you a clue to needed development, often possible just by making a subtle change within your control. Here are two examples: If you answered agree strongly or agree to question 8, you might work toward contributing ideas of your own. If you answered disagree or disagree strongly to question 14, you might work toward helping the team think more critically about the path it is following.

FIGURE 6-1 Key Characteristics of Effective Teams and Work Groups

- The group has collective efficacy, or a belief that it can handle the assigned task.

- The team has clear-cut goals linked to organizational goals so that group members feel connected to the entire organization; however, the group does not have so many goals that confusion results. Goals include having a mission that helps explain what the group is attempting to accomplish.

- Group members are empowered so that they learn to think for themselves rather than expecting a supervisor to solve all the difficult problems. At the same time, the group believes it has the authority to solve a variety of problems without first obtaining approval from management.

- Group members are assigned work they perceive to be challenging, exciting, and rewarding. As a consequence, the work is self-rewarding.

- Members depend on one another to accomplish tasks and work toward a common goal. At the same time, the group believes in itself and believes that it can accomplish an independent task.

- Diversity exists within the group, including differences in education, experience, and cultural background. Different backgrounds lead to more creative problem solving. Also, the differences prompt more discussion and analysis.

- Members receive extensive training in technical knowledge, problem-solving skills, and interpersonal skills.

- Members receive part of their pay related to team or group incentives, rather than strictly based on individual performance.

- Group size is generally about six people, rather than 10 or more.

- Team members have good intelligence and personality factors, such as conscientiousness and pride, that contribute to good performance.

- There is honest and open communication among group members and with other groups in the organization.

- Members are familiar with their jobs, coworkers, and the work environment. This experience adds to their expertise. The beneficial effects of experience may diminish after awhile, because the team needs fresh ideas and approaches.

- The team has emotional intelligence in the sense that it builds relationships both inside and outside the team. Included in emotional intelligence are norms that establish mutual trust among members, a feeling of group identity, and group efficacy. The emotional intelligence of group members makes group emotional intelligence possible.

- Stronger-performing group members assist weaker-performing group members accomplish their task, particularly when the performance of the "weakest link" in the group is key for group performance.

- The team or group members, as well as the leader, are authentic in the sense of being ethical and transparent.

- The leader focuses on being a *servant leader*, or being there to serve and help group members, rather than seeking individual glory or advancing his or her career.

Sources: Alexander D. Stajkovic, Dongseop Lee, and Anthony J. Nyberg, "Collective Efficacy, Group Potency, and Group Performance: Meta-Analysis of their Relationships, and Test of a Mediation Model," *Journal of Applied Psychology*, May 2009, p. 815; Sean T. Hannah, Fred O. Walumba, Louis W. Fry, "Leadership in Action Teams: Team Leader and Members' Authenticity, Authenticity Strength, and Team Outcomes," *Personnel* Psychology, Number 3, 2011, pp. 771–802; Jia Hu and Robert C. Liden, "Antecedents of Team Potentcy and Team Effectiveness: An Examination of Goal and Process Clarity and Servant Leadership," *Journal of Applied* Psychology, July 2011, pp.851–862; Stephen R. Covey, "Secrets Behind Great Teams," *USA Weekend*, July 11–13, 2008, p. 7; Crystal I. C. Chien Farh, Myeong-Gu Seo, and Paul E. Tesluk, "Emotional Intelligence, Teamwork Effectiveness, and Job Performance: The Moderating Role of Job Context," *Journal of Applied* Psychology, July 2012, pp. 890–900; Katherine W. Phillips, Katie A. Liljenquist, and Margaret A. Neale, "Is the Pain Worth the Gain? The Advantages and Liabilities of Agreeing With Socially Distinct Newcomers," *Personality and Social Psychology Bulletin*, March 2009, pp. 336–350; Claus W. Langred, "Too Much of a Good Thing? Negative Effects of High Trust and Individual Autonomy in Self-Managing Work Teams," *Academy of Management Journal*, June 2004, pp. 385–389.

Team Player Roles

Directions: For each of the following statements about team activity, check mostly agree or mostly disagree. If you have not experienced such a situation, imagine how you would act or think if placed in that situation. In responding to the statements, assume that you are taking the questionnaire with the intent of learning something about yourself.

		Mostly agree	*Mostly disagree*
1.	It is rare that I ever miss a team meeting.	_____	_____
2.	I regularly compliment team members when they do something exceptional.	_____	_____
3.	Whenever I can, I avoid being the note taker at a team meeting.	_____	_____
4.	From time to time, other team members come to me for advice on technical matters.	_____	_____
5.	I like to hide some information from other team members so that I can be in control.	_____	_____
6.	I welcome new team members coming to me for advice and learning the ropes.	_____	_____
7.	My priorities come first, which leaves me with very little time to help other team members.	_____	_____
8.	During a team meeting, it is not unusual for several other people at a time to look toward me for my opinion.	_____	_____
9.	If I think the team is moving in an unethical direction, I will say so explicitly.	_____	_____
10.	Rarely will I criticize the progress of the team, even if I think such criticism is deserved.	_____	_____
11.	It is typical for me to summarize the progress in a team meeting, even if not asked.	_____	_____
12.	To conserve time, I attempt to minimize contact with my teammates outside our meetings.	_____	_____
13.	I intensely dislike going along with a consensus decision if the decision runs contrary to my thoughts on the issue.	_____	_____
14.	I rarely remind teammates of our mission statement as we go about our work.	_____	_____
15.	Once I have made up my mind on an issue facing the team, I am unlikely to be persuaded in another direction.	_____	_____
16.	I am willing to accept negative feedback from team members.	_____	_____
17.	Just to get a new member of the team involved, I will ask his or her opinion.	_____	_____
18.	Even if the team has decided on a course of action, I am not hesitant to bring in new information that supports another position.	_____	_____
19.	Quite often I talk negatively about one team member to another.	_____	_____
20.	My teammates are almost a family to me because I am truly concerned about their welfare.	_____	_____
21.	When it seems appropriate, I joke and kid with teammates.	_____	_____
22.	My contribution to team tasks is as important to me as my individual work.	_____	_____
23.	From time to time, I have pointed out to the team how we can all improve in reaching our goals.	_____	_____
24.	I will fight to the last when the team does not support my viewpoint and wants to move toward consensus.	_____	_____
25.	I will confront the team if I believe that the members are thinking too much alike.	_____	_____

Total Score _____

(Continued)

effective roles as a team member. In this section, we describe a number of the most frequently observed positive roles played by team members.[13] We will also mention a group of negative roles. The description will be followed by an activity in which the roles can be practiced.

According to the role theory developed by R. Meredith Belbin and his group of researchers, there are nine frequent roles occupied by team members. All of these roles are influenced to some extent by an individual's personality.

1. **Creative problem solver:** The creative problem solver is imaginative and unorthodox. Such a person solves difficult problems. A potential weakness of this role is that the person tends to ignore fine details and becomes too immersed in the problem to communicate effectively.

2. **Resource investigator:** The resource investigator is extraverted, enthusiastic, and communicates freely with other team members. He or she will explore opportunities and develop valuable contacts. A potential weakness of this role is that the person can be overly optimistic and may lose interest after the initial enthusiasm wanes.

3. **Coordinator:** The coordinator is mature, confident, and a natural team leader. He or she clarifies goals, promotes decision making, and delegates effectively. A downside to occupying this role is that the person might be seen as manipulative and controlling. Some coordinators delegate too much by asking others to do some of the work they (the coordinators) should be doing.

4. **Shaper:** The shaper is challenging, dynamic, and thrives under pressure. He or she will use determination and courage to overcome obstacles. A potential weakness of the shaper is that he or she can be easily provoked and may ignore the feelings of others.

5. **Monitor-evaluator:** The monitor-evaluator is even tempered, engages in strategic (big-picture and long-term) thinking, and makes accurate judgments. He or she sees all the options and judges accurately. A potential weakness of this role occupant is that he or she might lack the drive and the ability to inspire others.

6. **Team worker:** The team worker is cooperative, focuses on relationships, and is sensitive and diplomatic. He or she is a good listener who builds relationships,

dislikes confrontation, and averts friction. A potential weakness is that the team worker can be indecisive in a crunch situation or crisis.

7. **Implementer:** The implementer is disciplined, reliable, conservative, and efficient. He or she will act quickly on ideas, and convert them into practical actions. A potential weakness is that the implementer can be inflexible and slow to see new opportunities.

8. **Completer-finisher:** The completer-finisher is conscientious and eager to get the job done. He or she has a good eye for detail and is effective at searching out errors. He or she can be counted on for finishing a project and delivering on time. A potential weakness is that the completer-finisher can be a worrier and reluctant to delegate.

9. **Specialist:** The specialist is a single-minded self-starter. He or she is dedicated and provides knowledge and skill in rare supply. A potential weakness of the specialist is that he or she can be stuck in a niche with little interest in other knowledge and may dwell on technicalities.

The weaknesses in the first nine roles point to problems the team leader or manager can expect to emerge, and therefore an allowance should be made. Belbin refers to these potential problems as *allowable weaknesses* because an allowance should be made for them. To illustrate, if a team worker has a tendency to be indecisive in a crisis, the team should not have high expectations of the team worker when faced with a crisis. Team workers will be the most satisfied if the crisis is predicted and decisions involving them are made before the pressure mounts.

Another perspective on team roles is that team members will sometimes engage in *self-oriented roles*. Members will sometimes focus on their own needs rather than those of the group. The individual might be overly aggressive because of a personal need, such as wanting a bigger budget for his or her project. The individual might hunger for recognition or power. Similarly, the person might attempt to dominate the meeting, block others from contributing, or serve as a distraction. One of the ploys used by distracters recently is to engage in cell phone conversations during a meeting, blaming it on "those people who keep calling me."

The many roles just presented overlap somewhat. For example, the implementer might engage in specialist activities. Do not be concerned about the overlap. Instead, pick and choose from the many roles as the situation dictates—whether or not overlap exists. Skill-Building Exercise 6-1 gives you an opportunity to observe these roles in action. The behavior associated with the roles just described is more important than remembering the labels. For example, remembering to be creative and imaginative is more important than remembering the specific label "creative problem solver."

Understanding team-member roles will contribute to working effectively as a member of a team; however, foundational contributors to effective team play are recognizing individual differences and having good communication skills. The same two factors are fundamental for effectiveness in any setting involving interaction between and among people. Here is an example of how recognizing individual differences and having effective communication skills can help in a team setting: Max and Beth are teammates, and Max notices that Beth is shy and somewhat sullen. (He observes individual differences.) Max gives Beth a playful fist in the air, and says, "Come on Beth, we need your contribution in the 10 o'clock meeting. You have one of the sharpest minds on the team, and you're hiding it from us." With such warm encouragement, Beth then has the courage to contribute more to the morning meeting.

GUIDELINES FOR THE INTERPERSONAL ASPECTS OF TEAM PLAY

The purpose of this and the following section is to help you enhance your effectiveness as a team player by describing the skills, actions, and attitudes required to be an effective team player. You can regard these behaviors (the collective term for skills, actions, and attitudes) as goals for personal improvement. Identify the actions and attitudes for which

LEARNING OBJECTIVE 4

Team Member Roles

A team of approximately six people is formed to conduct a 20-minute meeting on a significant topic of their choosing. The possible scenarios follow:

Scenario A: Management Team. A group of managers are pondering whether to lay off one-third of the workforce in order to increase profits. The company has had a tradition of caring for employees and regarding them as the company's most precious asset; however, the CEO has said privately that times have changed in our competitive world, and the company must do whatever is possible to enhance profits. The group wants to think through the advisability of laying off one-third of the workforce, as well as explore other alternatives.

Scenario B: Group of Sports Fans. A group of fans have volunteered to find a new team name to replace "Redskins" for the local basketball team. One person among the group of volunteers believes that the name "Redskins" should be retained because it is a compliment, rather than an insult, to Native Americans. The other members of the group believe that a name change is in order, but they lack any good ideas for replacing a mascot team name that has endured for over 50 years.

Scenario C: Community Group. A community group is attempting to launch an initiative to help battered adults and children. Opinions differ strongly as to what initiative would be truly helpful to battered adults and children. Among the alternatives are establishing a shelter for battered people, giving workshops on preventing violence, and providing self-defense training. Each group member with an idea strongly believes that he or she has come up with a workable possibility for helping with the problem of battered people.

While the team members are conducting their heated discussion, other class members make notes on which team members carry out which roles. Students should watch for the different roles as developed by Belbin and his associates, as well as the self-oriented roles. For example, students in the first row might look for examples of the creative problem solver. Use the role worksheet that follows to help make your observations. Summarize the comment that is indicative of the role. An example is noting in the shaper category: "Linda said naming the team the 'Washington Rainbows' seems like too much of an attempt to be politically correct."

Creative Problem Solver _____

Resource Investigator _____

Coordinator _____

Shaper _____

Monitor-Evaluator _____

Team Worker _____

Implementer _____

Completer-Finisher _____

Specialist _____

Self-Oriented Roles _____

you need the most improvement, and proceed accordingly with self-development. Apply the model for skill development presented in Chapter 1.

One convenient method for classifying team activities in the pursuit of goals is to categorize them as people-related or task-related. The categorization of people- versus task-related activities, however, is not entirely accurate. For example, if you are challenging your teammates with a difficult goal, are you focusing more on the people (offering them a motivational challenge) or the task (achieving the goal)? We begin first with people-related actions and attitudes (see also Figure 6-2), followed in the next section by task-related actions and attitudes.

Communicate Frequently and Assertively

Communicating frequently and assertively contributes to good team play, and both verbal and nonverbal communication are important. Allthough it is well accepted that speaking up in meetings facilitates teamwork, for many people, communicating assertively in small

FIGURE 6-2 Interpersonal Aspects of Team Play

1. Communicate frequently and assertively.
2. Trust team members.
3. Display a high level of cooperation and collaboration.
4. Recognize the interests and achievements of others.
5. Give and receive helpful criticism.
6. Share the glory.
7. Take care not to rain on another person's parade.

groups is difficult. Reasearch conducted by scientists at the Virginia Tech Carilion Research Institute helps explain why so many people say so little at meetings. The problem is that if we think others in the group are smarter, our problem-solving ability is suppressed a little. In a sense, we choke with respect to displaying intelligence. Clamming up tends to be more frequent among women and more intelligent people. The reason given for women being more subdued at meetings is that they may be more attentive than men to what others may be feeling or thinking.[14] High intelligence might also contribute to this sensitivity.

Recent research also supports the contribution of nonverbal communication to being an effective team player. Alex "Sandy" Pentland, the director of the Human Dynamics Laboratory at MIT, has collected data about teams by attaching sensors that capture people's tone of voice and body language to team members. (The sensors took the form of the standard security badges worn around the neck.) As a result, Pentland and his associates were able to observe highly consistent patterns of communication associated with productive teams for a variety of work activities.

The communication patterns identified in the study supported the importance of using effective nonverbal communication. A pleasant tone of voice was found to be effective in communicating with team members. Choosing an appropriate body position, such as standing the right distance away from the message receiver, facilitated good communication. A third key factor was body language, such as welcoming arm and hand movements. A general finding of the study was that face-to-face communication was more valuable for team purposes, with e-mail and texting being the least valuable. The most effective team players connect ther teammates with each other and spread ideas around.[15]

Trust Team Members

The cornerstone attitude of an outstanding team player is to trust team members, including the leader. Working on a team is akin to a small-business partnership. If you do not believe that the other team members have your best interests at heart, it will be difficult for you to share opinions and ideas. You will fear that others will make negative statements behind your back.

Trusting team members also includes believing that their ideas are technically sound and rational until proven otherwise. Another manifestation of trust is taking risks with others. You can take a risk by trying out one of their unproved ideas. You can also take a risk by submitting an unproved idea and not worrying about being ridiculed.

One of the goals of offsite training is to help team members trust each other. As is familiar to most readers, such trust builders include falling into each other's arms, rappelling up a wall, racing down rapids in a raft, and dangling from cables over gorges.

Display a High Level of Cooperation and Collaboration

Cooperation and collaboration are synonymous with teamwork. If you display a willingness to help others by working cooperatively with them, you will be regarded as a team player. If you do not cooperate with other team members, the team structure breaks down. Collaboration at a team level refers to working jointly with others to solve mutual problems. Good collaboration is important at teams at all levels in the organization. An extreme example is Steven Sinofsky, the former president of the Microsoft Windows division. Insiders said the key factor that prompted his departure from Microsoft was that he was an abrasive loner with a business firm that was attemping to foster high levels of cooperation and consensus.[16]

Although working with another person on a given problem may take longer than working through a problem alone, the long-term payoff is important. You have established a climate favorable to working on joint problems for which collective action is necessary. Sharing success stories with each other about what worked in the past is another useful approach to collaboration.[17]

Achieving a cooperative team spirit is often a question of making the first move. Instead of grumbling about poor teamwork, take the initiative and launch a cooperative spirit in your group. Target the most individualistic, least cooperative member of the

The Scavenger Hunt

The purpose of this teamwork exercise is to demonstrate the importance of cooperation and collaboration in accomplishing a task under pressure. The class is divided into teams of about five students. How much time you can devote to the task depends upon your particular class schedule. The instructor will supply each team with a list of items to find within a prescribed period of time—usually about 45 minutes. Given the time constraints, the group will usually have to conduct the hunt on campus. The following is a representative list of items to find in an on-campus scavenger hunt:

- A piece of chalk
- A tie or scarf

- A brick
- A cap from a beer bottle
- A pocket knife
- A flash drive

When the group returns within 30 minutes, hold a public discussion about what you learned about teamwork and what insights you acquired.

group. Ask the person for his or her input on an idea you are formulating. Thank the person, and then state that you would be privileged to return the favor.

Another way of attaining good cooperation is to minimize confrontations. If you disagree with the opinion of another team member, patiently explain the reasons for your differences, and look for a workable way to integrate both your ideas. A teammate might suggest, for example, that the team stay until midnight to get a project completed today. You have plans for the evening and are angered by the suggestion. Instead of lashing out at your teammate, you might say, "I agree we need to put in extra time and effort to get the job done, but why can't we spread out this extra effort over a few days? In this way, those of us who cannot work until midnight this evening can still contribute."

A side advantage of cooperation within the group is that the part of the brain associated with pleasure is activated when people cooperate. According to team-building specialist Anna Maravelas, "It is intrinsically rewarding for human beings to pull together."[18]

Skill-Building Exercise 6-2 is a widely used technique for demonstrating the importance of cooperation and collaboration.

Recognize the Interests and Achievements of Others

A fundamental tactic for establishing yourself as a solid team player is to actively recognize the interests and achievements of others. Let others know you care about their interests. After you make a suggestion during a team meeting, ask: "Would my suggestion create any problems for anybody else?" or "How do my ideas fit into what you have planned?"

Recognizing the achievements of others is more straightforward than recognizing interests. Be prepared to compliment any tangible achievement. Give realistic compliments by making the compliment commensurate with the achievement. To do otherwise is to compromise your sincerity. For example, do not call someone a genius just because he or she showed you how to compute an exchange rate from one currency to another. Instead, you might say, "Thank you. I am very impressed by your knowledge of exchange rates."

A technique has been developed to enable the entire team to recognize the interests and achievements of others. Playing the anonymous praise game, each team member lists what he or she admires about a specific coworker. The team leader collects the responses and sends each team member the comments made about him or her. Using this technique, team members see a compilation of praise based on how coworkers perceive them. The anonymous praise game helps overcome the hesitancy some people have to praise another person face to face.[19]

Give and Receive Helpful Criticism

The outstanding team player offers constructive criticism when needed, but does so diplomatically. To do otherwise is to let down the team. A high-performance team demands sincere and tactful criticism among members. No matter how diplomatic you are, keep your ratio of criticism to praise small. Keep two time-tested principles in mind. First, attempt to criticize the person's work, not the person. It is better to say, "The conclusion is missing from your analysis" rather than, "You left out the conclusion." (The latter statement hurts because it sounds like your teammate did something wrong.)

Another key guideline for criticism is to ask a question rather than to make a declarative statement. By answering a question, the person being criticized is involved in improving his or her work. In the example at hand, it would be effective to ask, "Do you think your report would have a greater impact if it contained a conclusion?" In this way, the person being criticized contributes a judgment about the conclusion. The person has a chance to say, "Yes, I will prepare a conclusion."

Criticism works both ways, so the effective team player is willing to accept helpful criticism, such as, "You are speaking too fast for several of our team members for whom English is their second language." Becky Blalock, the former vice president and chief information officer (CIO) of the Georgian Power and Southern Company, regards being open to feedback as one of the core principles of teamwork.[20]

Share the Glory

An effective team player shares praise and other rewards for accomplishment, even if he or she is the most deserving. Shared praise is usually merited to some extent because teammates have probably made at least some contribution to the achievement that received praise. For example, if a team member comes up with a powerful suggestion for cutting costs, it is likely that somebody else in the group sparked his or her thinking. Effective examples of sharing glory are easy to find. Think back to watching athletes and other entertainers who win a title or an award. Many of them are gracious enough to share the glory. It has become almost standard practice for an award-winning coach or player to say, "I never would have accomplished what I did if I hadn't played with such a great group of people."

Take Care Not to Rain on Another Person's Parade

As teamwork specialist Pamela Lovell observes, we all have achievements and accomplishments that are sources of pride. Belittling the achievements of others for no legitimate reason brings about tension and anger. Suppress your feelings of petty jealousy.[21] An example would be saying to someone who is proudly describing an accomplishment, "Don't take too much credit. It looks to me like you were at the right place at the right time." If you support teammates by acknowledging their accomplishments, you are more likely to receive their support when needed.

GUIDELINES FOR THE TASK ASPECTS OF TEAM PLAY

The task aspects of team play also make a key contribution to becoming an effective team player. Here we describe seven major task-related tactics (see Figure 6-3). As mentioned earlier, a task aspect usually has interpersonal consequences.

LEARNING OBJECTIVE 5

FIGURE 6-3   Task Aspects of Team Play

1. Provide technical expertise (or knowledge of the task).
2. Assume responsibility for problems.
3. See the big picture.
4. Believe in consensus.
5. Focus on deadlines.
6. Help team members do their jobs better.
7. Be a good organizational citizen.

Provide Technical Expertise (Or Knowledge of the Task)

Most people are selected for a work team primarily because of their technical expertise. *Technical* refers to the intimate details of any task, not just tasks in engineering, physical science, and information technology. The sales promotion specialist on a product development team has technical expertise about sales promotion, whether or not sales promotion requires knowledge of engineering or computers.

A key use of technical expertise to facilitate group effectiveness is to freely contribute knowledge and skills to teammates. Studies led by Philip Podsakoff indicate that helping behavior facilitates organizational effectiveness by:

- enabling teammates to solve problems and get work done faster
- enhancing group cohesion and coordination
- reducing variability in performance because of teammates being overloaded or distracted[22]

An analysis of 72 studies based on more than 17,000 individuals in a variety of work settings lends credibility to the belief that information sharing is beneficial to teams. A major finding of the analysis is that team performance is enhanced when team members share information not commonly shared by all team members. A somewhat distressing side finding of the study is that many teams do not share information when the sharing is most needed. An example of information being most needed is when the other team members are not aware of the useful information possessed by the other members.[23]

Assume Responsibility for Problems

The outstanding team player assumes responsibilities for problems. If a problem is not yet assigned to anybody, he or she says, "I'll do it." One team member might note that true progress on the team's effort is blocked until the team benchmarks (compares itself) with other successful teams. The effective team player might say, "You are right, we need to benchmark. If it's okay with everybody else, I'll get started on the benchmarking project tomorrow. It will be my responsibility." Taking responsibility must be combined with dependability. The person who takes responsibility for a task must produce, time after time.

See the Big Picture

Effective team players need to think conceptually, or see the big picture. A trap in team effort is that discussion can get bogged down in small details, and the team might lose sight of what it is trying to accomplish. The team player (including the team leader) who can help the group focus on its broader purpose plays a vital role. The following case history illustrates what it means to see the big picture.

John Rowley/Thinkstock

A group of retail sales associates and customer service representatives were sent to a one-day seminar about customer-service training. The group was sent to training because customer-service ratings at their store were below the level store executives thought was acceptable. During the lunch break, the conversation quickly turned to the fact that the coffee was not as hot as desired, the snacks were mediocre, the restrooms were too far from the meeting room, and the presenter had a phony smile and told goofy jokes. Next came a few complaints about a couple of the PowerPoint slides having too much detail.

Alyssa, an experienced sales associate, stepped in with a comment. She noted, "I think all of you have valid complaints, but your points are minor. We are here to learn how to improve customer service. If we want our store to survive, and we want to earn bigger bonuses, we have to learn what we can to help us do our jobs better. Whether or not you like our trainer's smile or jokes, he is trying to be helpful." The group returned after lunch with a more determined effort to focus on the purpose of the seminar—picking up ideas to improve customer service.

Believe in Consensus

A major task-related attitude for outstanding team play is to believe that consensus has merit. **Consensus** is general acceptance of a decision by the group. Every member may not be thrilled about the decision, yet they are unopposed and are willing to support the decision. Believing that consensus is valuable enables you to participate fully in team decisions without thinking that you have sacrificed your beliefs or the right to think independently. To believe in consensus is to believe that the democratic process has relevance for organizations, and ideal solutions are not always possible.

Focus on Deadlines

A notable source of individual differences among work group members is how much importance they attach to deadlines. Some work group members may regard deadlines as a moral contract, to be missed only in case of emergency. Others may view deadlines as an arbitrary date imposed by someone external to the group. Other work group members may perceive deadlines as moderately important. Differences in perception about the importance of deadlines influence the group's ability to meet deadlines.[24]

Keeping the group focused on the deadline is a valuable task behavior, because meeting deadlines is vital to team success. Discussing the importance of the deadlines is helpful because of the varying attitudes about deadlines that are likely to be found among group members.

Help Team Members Do Their Jobs Better

Your stature as a team player will increase if you take the initiative to help coworkers make needed work improvements. Helping other team members with their work assignments is a high-level form of cooperation. Make the suggestions in a constructive spirit rather than displaying an air of superiority. Identify a problem that a coworker is having, and then suggest alternatives he or she might be interested in exploring. Avoid saying to team members that they "should" do something, because many people become defensive when told what they should do. The term *should* is usually perceived as a moral judgment given to one person by another, such as being told that you should save money, should learn a second language, or should improve your math skills.

Be a Good Organizational Citizen

A comprehensive way of carrying out the task aspects of team play (as well as relationship aspects) is to help out beyond the requirements of your job description. As discussed in Chapter 2, such extra-role activity is referred to as organizational citizenship behavior—working for the good of the organization, even without the promise of a specific reward. As a result of many workers being good organizational citizens, the organization functions more effectively in such ways as improved product quantity and quality and high individual job performance.[25]

Good citizenship on the job encompasses many specific behaviors, including helping a coworker with a job task and refraining from complaints or petty grievances. A good organizational citizen would carry out such specific acts as quickly advising the company security department if she or he suspects a virus and turning out lights when they are not in use. He or she would also bring a reference to the office that could help a coworker solve a job problem. Most of the other team player tactics described here are related to organizational citizenship behavior.

Two experiments, one with business students and one with managers, suggested that organizational citizenship behavior is even more important when people depend on each other to accomplish a task.[26] An example is filling an order with components from different departments. Given that most tasks on a team are interdependent, organizational citizenship behavior is quite important for effective teamwork.

Habitat for Homeless People

Organize the class into teams of about six people. Each team takes on the assignment of formulating plans for building temporary shelters for homeless people. The task will take about one hour and can be done inside or outside the class. The dwellings you plan to build, for example, might be two-room cottages with electricity and indoor plumbing.

During the time allotted to the task, formulate plans for going ahead with Habitat for Homeless People. Consider dividing up work by assigning certain roles to each team member. Sketch out tentative answers to the following questions:

1. How will you obtain funding for your venture?
2. Which homeless people will you help?
3. Where will your shelters be located?
4. Who will do the actual construction?

After your plan is completed, evaluate the quality of the teamwork that took place within the group. Specify which teamwork skills were evident and which ones did not surface. Search the chapter for techniques you might use to improve teamwork. The skills used to accomplish the habitat task could relate to the team behaviors and attitudes presented in Self-Assessment Quiz 6-2, the interpersonal aspects of team play, the task aspects of team play, or some team skill not mentioned in this chapter. Here is a sampling of the many different skills that might be relevant in this exercise:

- Speaks effectively
- Listens to others
- Innovates solutions to problems
- Thinks outside the box
- Displays a high level of cooperation and collaboration
- Provides knowledge of the task
- Sees the big picture
- Focuses on deadlines

A synthesis of studies about the type of team processes described in this chapter supports the relevance of such actions by team members. (A team process is essentially an action taken by one or more team members.) A group of researchers examined the results of a variety of team member processes in 147 different samples of workers. The major conclusion reached was that teamwork processes are positively associated with both team member performance and satisfaction.[27] You can, therefore, have some assurance that if you engage in the activities described in this chapter, your efforts will help increase performance and satisfaction.

Although this chapter has been about being a good team player, a person can still be a competitive and a strong individual performer while being a productive member of the group. It is posssible to take ownership and pride in your own work, and still take the time to cooperate with teammates.[28] An analogy can be drawn to team sports in which there are stars and effective team players at the same time.

Skill-Building Exercise 6-3 will help you integrate the many suggestions presented here for developing teamwork skills.

Concept Review and Reinforcement

Key Terms

Summary

To be successful in the modern organization, it is necessary to be an effective team player. Team members have complementary skills and are committed to a common purpose. All teams have some elements in common. Teams can be broadly classified into face-to-face versus virtual types. A virtual team does most of its work electronically instead of in face-to-face meetings.

Groups and teams offer such advantages as (1) gaining synergy, (2) work accomplishment and high productivity, (3) gaining increased acceptance of and commitment to decisions, (4) avoidance of major errors, and (5) increased job satisfaction.

Groups and teams also have disadvantages, such as (1) time wasting, (2) pressures toward conformity, (3) shirking of individual responsibility, (4) fostering of conflict, and (5) groupthink. The latter refers to making bad decisions as a by-product of strong consensus. Key characteristics of effective work groups are outlined in Figure 6-1.

An important part of being an effective team player is to choose effective roles. The roles studied here are: creative problem solver, resource investigator, coordinator, shaper, monitor-evaluator, team worker, implementer, completer-finisher, and specialist. Self-oriented roles are less effective and detract from group productivity. Understanding roles does not supplant the need for recognizing individual differences and communicating well.

Guidelines for effectively contributing to the interpersonal aspects of team play include (1) communicating frequently and assertively, (2) trusting team members, (3) displaying a high level of cooperation and collaboration, (4) recognizing the interests and achievements of others, (5) giving and receiving helpful criticism, (6) sharing the glory, and (7) taking care not to rain on another person's parade.

Guidelines for effectively contributing to the task aspects of team play include (1) providing technical expertise, (2) assuming responsibility for problems, (3) seeing the big picture, (4) believing in consensus, (5) focusing on deadlines, and (6) helping team members do their jobs better.

A synthesis of research studies demonstrates that the types of teamwork processes described here are positively associated with both team member performance and satisfaction.

Questions for Discussion and Review

1. What do executives really mean when they say that "business is a team sport"?

2. Identify a few experiences most people have in high school and post-secondary school that make working in teams a natural experience for them.

3. Many futurists have predicted that soon most work will be conducted remotely (such as from homes, coffee shops, and co-working sites), with a minority of people working in company offices. What impact will this development have on teamwork?

4. How do team members know when they have achieved synergy?

5. What should the other team members do when they uncover a social loafer?

6. How can the *monitor-evaluator* role backfire for a person?

7. Assume that you are a team member. What percentage of your pay would you be willing to have based on a group reward? Explain your reasoning.

8. Suggest three ways in which trust could be established in virtual teams. Why would these three work?

9. Name two situations when groupthink contributed to a critical or dangerous situation. How did those situations develop, and why did groupthink work in such situations?

10. How would an understanding of Belbin's team roles help a team leader?

The Web Corner

http://www.timeanalyzer.com/lib/teamroles.htm
(Belbin's team roles to improve team performance)

http:/www.quintcareers.com/team_player_quiz.html
(Take the quiz, "Are You a Team Player: A Quintessential Careers Quiz")

Internet Skill Builder: Becoming a Better Team Player

The purpose of this exercise duplicates the major purpose of the chapter—finding practical suggestions for improving your teamwork skills. Visit several Web sites that deal with enhancing teamwork skills from the standpoint of the individual, not the manager. An example of such a Web site is www.confidencecenter.com. Write down at least three concrete suggestions you find, and compare these suggestions to those made in this chapter. If the opportunity arises, practice one of these skills in the next 10 days, and observe the results.

Developing Your Human Relations Skills

Interpersonal Relations Case 6.1

Leah Puts on Her Team Player Face

Leah was happy to find a position as a scanning technician at a business process outsourcing company, Expert Resource, Inc. A major part of Expert's business was converting paperwork related to human resource management into digital form. Clients would mail their forms, such as medical claims, to Expert. Scanning technicians would then insert the claim forms into large scanning machines to make the conversion to digital. Clients would then have digital instead of paper documents for health claims and other human resource records.

The scanning technicians had to interact with other employees in several ways. Many of the claims received contained illegible identifying information, so they had to be sent to a security department that attempted to obtain the proper identification for the forms. The scanning technicians were expected to help level the workload among the technicians. For example, if one of the technicians was overwhelmed, and another was caught up, the latter was supposed to help out the former. Also, the company frequently held small celebrations in the office. A typical celebration would be to hold a brunch in honor of a new employee joining the company.

Leah believed that if she performed well in her position as a scanning technician, she would be eligible for promotion to the information technology department. Eventually, being promoted to a supervisor position was also within the realm of possibility. Leah also recognized that having good skills and speed in scanning documents were not sufficient to be promoted to a supervisory position. Her size up of the situation was that being a good team player would be required to be considered for promotion. Leah then set out to develop the reputation of being a good team player.

The next Monday morning, Leah arrived at the office with a box of donuts that she placed in the break room, with a note attached that said, "Enjoy your coffee or tea this morning with a treat from your coworker Leah." Several of the other scanning technicians thanked Leah; however, one technician said to her, "Why did you bring us donuts? You're not our supervisor."

A week later, Leah implemented another tactic designed to boost her reputation as a team player. She sent an e-mail to the other technicians informing them that they were free to send her an e-mail or an IM anytime they were overloaded with documents to scan. Leah said that she would help the overloaded coworker so long as she was caught up on her own work.

A week later, Leah reflected, "I think I am developing a reputation as a good team player, but I can't give up yet. I think I know a way to really cement being regarded as a strong team player." Leah then wrote an e-mail to the other scanning technicians, as well as her supervisor. The e-mail read in part:

"We all know that it takes a village to raise a child. But did you also know that it takes a group of friendly and cooperative coworkers to get a scanning technician up to speed? I want to thank you all for your cooperation and friendliness. You have been very helpful to me."

Case Questions

1. How effective do you think Leah's initiatives are in helping her develop a reputation as a strong team player?
2. If you were Leah's supervisor, how would you react to the e-mails she sent to the group?
3. What advice might you offer Leah to help her advance her reputation as a team player?

Interpersonal Relations Case 6.2

Trevor Speaks Freely

Elizabeth is the owner of Home Healthcare Finders, a prosperous company that provides home healthcare services to individuals. Many of the clients are elderly people in need of home healthcare, but many other people in need of home healthcare are also served by the agency. Among these clients are people temporarily disabled because of illness and accident and younger people with long-term or permanent disabilities such as brain damage that began at birth. The clients also include a few people who are morbidly obese and require assistance with ordinary living.

Home Healthcare Finders has been located in the suburbs for the six years of its existence. Elizabeth is pondering whether to renew the lease for the company's present location, or move to another office. She has given serious thought to relocating Home Healthcare Finders to a loft in an old building in the city that overlooks the river, or another attractive loft. Elizabeth organized a face-to-face meeting in the conference room to discuss possible relocation. She began the meeting with an explanation that the lease for the office was up for renewal, and that she had given some preliminary thought to relocating to a loft. A partial transcript of the meeting follows:

Elizabeth: Do you folks think we should relocate? And if you do think that relocation is a good idea, what do you think of moving Home Healthcare to a city loft?

Terry: I like the idea of relocating, because we need more space. Even our waiting room is too cramped. Also, right now we are wedged between a sub shop and a dollar store. I think we could do better.

Dave: Yes, why not relocate? And it would be so cool to work in a loft.

Trevor: Would relocation really benefit us? I think we would lose a lot of clients who would not want the hassle of driving downtown. I am also concerned that relocation would mean higher rent and therefore smaller year-end bonuses for the team.

Cindy: I'm a little concerned that an old downtown building would not be so accessible for some of our clients who come to visit us with their guardians.

Trevor: Wow, Cindy, you are right on target. Can you imagine Home Healthcare being sued because we have limited accessibility for physically disabled people?

Charlene: I have always wanted to have an office in a loft. Yet I am a little concerned about spending money on parking daily, weekly, or monthly.

Trevor: You have nailed down another good argument for not moving downtown. We have to know first if Elizabeth would give us a parking allowance. Otherwise, the value of our salaries would decrease.

Julio: I like the idea of relocating to a loft by the river. Our image would be enhanced, and I could take a lunch break seated on a bench by the river.

Trevor: Yet there is a downside to what Julio likes about the riverside location. We could easily get distracted from our work because of the pleasant location.

Elizabeth: Let's not discuss the subject of relocation to a downtown loft until a meeting next week. In the meantime, let's send e-mail messages back and forth dealing with some of the issues.

Case Questions

1. What is you evaluation of Trevor as an effective team player?
2. Which team member role or roles does Trevor appear to be occupying?
3. How should Elizabeth have dealt with Trevor's objections during the meeting?

Interpersonal Relations Role-Play

Elizabeth Wants More Cooperation from Trevor

The case just presented provides the scenario for this role-play. Elizabeth has become annoyed with Trevor's negative attitude toward the office relocation to a downtown loft. Elizabeth likes the idea of obtaining input from the group about the possible relocation, but she expected less opposition. One student plays the role of Elizabeth, who wants to encourage Trevor to take on a more positive attitude about the contemplated move. Another student plays the role of Trevor, who thinks he is making an important contribution by preventing Home Healthcare Finders from making a big mistake. Four other students might play the roles of Cindy, Terry, Dave, and Julio, who might want to contribute to Trevor having a more harmonious attitude toward the relocation. Run the role-play for about seven minutes, with the observers providing feedback when the role-play is completed.

References

1. Jon R. Katzenbach and Douglas K. Smith, "The Discipline of Teams," *Harvard Business Review,* March–April 1993, p. 112.

2. Donna M. Owens, "Is Management Obsolete? Traditional Management Practices Don't Fit Today's Workplaces," *HR Magazine,* May 2012, p. 28.

3. Quinetta M. Roberson and Ian O. Williamson, "Justice in Self-Managing Teams: The Role of Social Networks in the Emergence of Procedural Justice Climates," *Academy of Management Journal,* June 2012, p. 685.

4. Claus W. Langfred, "Too Much Trust a Good Thing? Negative Effects of High Trust and Individual Autonomy in Self-Managing Teams," *Academy of Management Journal,* June 2004, pp. 385–399.

5. Andrew M. Carton and Jonathon N. Cummings, "A Theory of Subgroups in Work Teams," *Academy of Management Review,* July 2102, p. 441.

6. Achieveglobal (company name), "Leading Virtually: Inspiring Peak Performance in Long-Distance Teams," *Workforce Management,* December 2001, p. S3.

7. Arvind Malhotra, Ann Majchrzak, and Benson Rosen, "Leading Virtual Teams," *Academy of Management Perspectives,* February 2007, p. 62.

8. Cited in Adam Bryant, "Ensemble Acting, in Business," *The New York Times* (http://www.nytimes.com), June 7, 2009.

9. Matt Bolch, "Rewarding the Team," *HR Magazine,* February 2007, pp. 91–93; http://www.wikiinvest.com, December 4, 2009; "Nucor Reports Results for Second Quarter and First Half of 2012," http://nucor.com/investor, July 19, 2012.

10. Ross Kerber, "For Abigail Johnson, a Leadership Test," *The Boston Globe* (*http://boston.com*), August 21, 2007, p. 1.

11. Irving L. Janus, *Victims of Groupthink: A Psychological Study of Foreign Policy Decisions and Fiascos* (Boston: Houghton Mifflin, 1972); Glen Whyte, "Groupthink Reconsidered," *Academy of Management Review,* January 1989, pp. 40–56.

12. Martha A. Peak, "Treating Trauma in Teamland," *Management Review,* September 1997, p. 1.

13. "R. Meredith Belbin," in *Business: The Ultimate Resource* (Cambridge, MA: Perseus, 2002), pp. 966–967; Belbin, *Management Teams* (London: Elsevier Butterworth-Heinemann, 2003); Belbin® Team-Roles, *http://www.belbin.com*.

14. Research reported in Elizabeth Bernstein, "Speaking Up Is Hard to Do: Researchers Explain Why," *The Wall Street Journal,* February 7, 2012, pp. D1, D4.

15. Alex "Sandy" Pentland, "The New Science of Building Great Teams," *Harvard Business Review*, April 2012, p. 64.

16. Ashlee Vance and Dina Bass, "Microsoft: No Company for Solo Artists," *Bloomberg Businessweek,* November 19–November 25, 2012, p. 37.

17. Romanus Wolter, "Get Team-Focused," *Entrepreneur,* February 2009, p. 124.

18. Cited in "Gather Round, People!" *Entrepreneur,* September 2009, p. 21.

19. "Fly in Formation: Easy Ways to Build Team Spirit," *WorkingSMART,* March 2000, p. 6.

20. Cited in "Score a Perfect '10' on Teamwork," *Manager's Edge,* May 2006, p. 1.

21. Pamela Lovell, "Healthy Teams Display Strong Vital Signs," *Teamwork,* sample issue, the Dartnell Corporation, 1997.

22. Research reported in Adam Grant, "Givers Take All: The Hidden Dimension of Corporate Culture,: *McKinsey Quarterly* (http://www.mckinseyquarterly), April 2013, pp. 1-2.

23. Jessica R. Mesmer-Magnus and Leslie A. DeChurch, "Information Sharing and Team Performance: A Meta-Analysis," *Journal of Applied Psychology,* March 2009, pp. 535–546.

24. Mary J. Waller et al., "The Effect of Individual Perceptions of Deadlines on Team Performance," *Academy of Management Review,* October 2001, p. 597.

25. Mark G. Ehrhant and Stefanie E. Naumann, "Organizational Citizenship Behavior in Work Groups: A Group Norms Approach," *Journal of Applied Psychology,* December 2004, pp. 960–97; Nathan P. Podsakoff, Steven W. Whiting, Philip M. Podaskoff, and Brian D. Blume, Individual- and Organization-Level Consequences of Organizational Citizenship Behaviors: A Meta-Analysis," *Journal of Applied Psychology,* January 2009, pp. 122–141.

26. Daniel G. Bachrach, Benjamin C. Powell, Elliot Bendoly, and R. Glenn Richey, "Organizational Citizenship Behavior and Performance Evaluations: Exploring the Impact of Task Interdependence,"*Journal of Applied Psychology,* January 2006, pp. 193–201.

27. Jeffrey A. LePine et al., "A Meta-Analysis of Teamwork Processes: Tests of a Multidimensional Model and Relationships with Team Effectiveness Criteria," *Personnel Psychology,* Summer 2008, pp. 273–307.

28. Janet Paskin, ""Finding the 'I' in Team," *Bloomberg Businessweek,* February 18–February 24, 2013, p. 78.

Group Problem Solving and Decision Making

Craig is the president of the pet clothing and accessories division of a larger consumer products company. Several years ago he became concerned that his division was experiencing a decline in sales, even though consumer interest in pets was increasing. Craig accepted the criticism from the CEO that his division was producing few new products or ideas for new products and that the division had substantial ways to reduce costs.

Craig had encouraged his department heads to conduct brainstorming groups to develop new product ideas and ideas for cost cutting, but the ouput was modest. After reading several articles on the topic, Craig decided that the office structure needed revamping to facilitate more day-to-day exchanges of ideas and creativity. He called in a consultant from one of the better known office furniture, layout, and design firms. Among the suggestions were for the

Monkey Business Images/Shutterstock

After reading and studying this chapter and completing the exercises, you should be able to

1. Understand the difference between rational and political decision making.
2. Use the general approach to problem-solving groups.
3. Use brainstorming effectively.
4. Use the nominal group technique effectively.
5. Understand how to increase the efficiency of group problem solving through e-mail and collaborative software.
6. Pinpoint several suggestions for being an effective meeting participant.
7. Explain how national culture and organizational culture might influence the acceptance of group decision making.

division to rely less on placing workers in cubicles. Other suggestions included installing more lounge areas, tables, a larger café, and a few whiteboards and felt-tip pens in open areas. The purpose of these physical modifications was to encourage more joint decision making and the daily exchange of ideas.

Within one year, Craig noticed a difference in terms of creative contribution. More ideas were floating to the surface for both new products and cost cutting. Among the new pet accessories introduced were backpacks for dogs, team jerseys for dogs, snow galoshes for both dogs and cats, and an improved line of car seatbelts for domestic animals. One of the most effective cost-cutting ideas was to reduce the number of delivery trucks owned by the division and to rely more on delivery services.

Findings ways of organizing physical space to encourage group interaction is but one approach to facilitate group decision making and creativity. At the same time, part of having high-level interpersonal skills is the ability to work closely with others in solving problems and making decisions. This chapter will enhance your group problem-solving and decision-making skills. You will receive guidelines for applying several major group problem-solving methods, along with suggestions for being an effective contributor at meetings. As a starting point in studying these techniques, first think through your present level of receptiveness toward group problem solving by doing Self-Assessment Quiz 7-1.

RATIONAL VERSUS POLITICAL DECISION MAKING IN GROUPS

Group decision making is the process of reaching a judgment based on feedback from more than one individual. Most people involved in group problem solving may share the same purpose in agreeing on a solution and making a decision. Nevertheless, they may have different agendas and use different methods. Two such different approaches to group decision making are the rational model and the political model.

The **rational decision-making model** is the traditional, logical approach to decision making, based on the scientific method. It is grounded in establishing goals, establishing alternatives, examining consequences, and hoping for optimum results. The search for optimum results is based on an economic view of decision making: the idea that people hope to maximize gain and minimize loss when making a decision. For example, a team should choose the lowest-cost, highest-quality supplier, even though the team leader may be a good friend of the sales representative of a competitor.

LEARNING OBJECTIVE 1

group decision making

The process of reaching a judgment based on feedback from more than one individual.

rational decision-making model

The traditional, logical approach to decision making based on the scientific method.

The rational model also assumes that each alternative is evaluated in terms of how well it contributes to reaching the goals involved in making the decision. For example, if one of the goals in relocating a factory was to reduce energy costs and taxes, each alternative would be carefully examined in terms of its tax and energy consequences. A team member might say, "Setting up a factory in the Phoenix area sounds great. It's true that taxes are low, the labor market is wonderful, and we won't lose any days to snow emergencies. But did you know that the energy costs are very high because of the amount of air conditioning required?"

The **political decision-making model** assumes that people bring preconceived notions and biases into the decision-making situation. Because the decision makers are politically motivated (a focus on satisfying one's own interests), the individuals often do not make the most rational choice. The field of behavioral economics is based on the idea that many decisions are irrational or politically based. Revenge and cheating are among the irrational behaviors that underlie the behavior of many employees and customers.[1] Most computer hackers decide to create a virus or destroy computer records based on revenge, cheating, or a sadistic delight in creating misfortune for others.

People who use the political model may operate on the basis of incomplete information. Facts and figures that conflict with personal biases and preferences might get blocked out of memory or rationalized away. A team member might say, "Those air conditioning costs are exaggerated. I have heard that if you use thermal pumps in a factory, the cooling costs go way down."

political decision-making model

The approach that assumes that people bring preconceived notions and biases into the decision-making situation.

Another unintentional contributor to political decision making is **blind spots**: areas of unawareness about our attitudes, thinking, and behaviors that contribute to poor decisions. Shawn O. Utsey, a psychology professor at Virginia Commonwealth University, says that blind spots prevent us from making sound decisions by distorting vision, impairing judgment, and impairing personal and professional growth. An example of a frequent blind spot is not stopping to think, particularly when under pressure.[2] For example, a person might purchase a luxury SUV on the spot that will wind up creating a monthly negative cash flow.

blind spots

Areas of unawareness about our attitudes, thinking, and behaviors that contribute to poor decisions.

Greed and gluttony are major contributors to irrational (or political) decision making. During the mid-2000s, an astounding number of financial managers decided to invest in subprime mortgage loans and then convert these loans into equity investments. Eventually, many holders of these high-risk mortgages were unable or unwilling to make their payments.[3] As the securities collapsed in value, an enormous stock market crisis took place. The securities were based on complex mathematic models, yet were believed in because the investment bankers were looking for ways to capture millions of dollars in bonuses for themselves. (Some observers believe that the US government agencies involved in housing promoted generous lending practices that prompted many unqualified buyers to obtain mortgages.)

In the relocation example at hand, two of the members may say "Thumbs up to Phoenix" for reasons that satisfy their own needs. One team member might be fascinated with the American Indian culture so prevalent in Arizona and may, therefore, want to move to Phoenix. Another member might have retired parents living in Phoenix and be interested in living near them.

In practice, it is sometimes difficult to determine whether a decision maker is being rational or political. Have you ever noticed that hotels almost never have a 13th floor? The reason is both rational and political. The hotel manager might say rationally, "Many people are superstitious about the number 13, so they will refuse to take a room on the 13th floor. So if we want to maximize room use, the rational decision for us is to label the 13th floor as 14. In this way, we will avoid the irrational [political] thinking of guests."

Although the examples about political and irrational decision making have been related mostly to individuals, the same problems may surface in group decision making. This is true because a group decision is still based on what takes place in the brains of its members.

GUIDELINES FOR USING GENERAL PROBLEM-SOLVING GROUPS

Solving problems effectively in groups requires skill. The effort is often worthwhile because participation in group decision making frequently leads to better acceptance of the decision, and stronger commitment to the implications of the decision. For example, a group involved in making decisions about cost cutting might be more willing to carry through with the suggestions than if participants had not made the decision. Group decision making can also lead to higher quality decisions and innovations because the group collectively has more information than might individuals.[4] Similarly, the group might come up with better suggestions for cost cutting because of group members sharing information.

Keith Dannemiller/Corbis

Current research reinforces the idea that group problem solving has the potential to be quite effective. A team of researchers headed by Anita Williams Woolley of Carnegie Mellon's Tepper School of Business studied the performance of groups engaged in a wide variety of tasks, such as reading the facial expressions of others. Seven hundred people participated in the two studies. The key study result was that groups featuring the right kind of internal dynamics perform well on a variety of tasks. This finding suggests the presence of collective intelligence that goes beyond the problem-solving ability of individual members. Collective intelligence is associated with the average social sensitivity of group members, members taking turns talking, and the proportion of women in the group. Women appear to contribute to the group collective intelligence because of their relatively high social sensitivity.[5]

Here we examine three aspects of group problem solving useful in making more effective decisions: working through the group problem-solving steps, managing disagreement about the decision, and aiming for inquiry rather than advocacy.

Working through the Group Problem-Solving Steps

When team members get together to solve a problem, they typically hold a discussion rather than rely on formal problem-solving techniques. Several team members might attempt to clarify the true nature of the problem, and a search then begins for an acceptable solution. Although this technique can be effective, the probability of solving the problem well (and, hence, making the right decision) increases when the team follows a systematic procedure.

The Problem-Solving Steps.   The following guidelines represent a time-tested way of solving problems and making decisions within a group. You may recognize these steps as having much in common with the scientific method. The same steps are, therefore, ideal for following the rational decision-making model. Two other aspects of group decision making will be described here: managing disagreement and inquiry versus advocacy.

Assume that you are a team member of a small business that distributes food supplies to hospitals, nursing homes, and schools. Your business volume is adequate, but you have a cash-flow problem because some of your customers take over 30 days to pay their bills. Here is how problem solving would proceed following the steps for effective group problem solving and decision making:

Step One. *Identify the problem.* Discuss the problem, weigh the various perceptions, and reach consensus. The surface problem is that some customers are paying their bills late. Your company's ultimate problem is that it does not have enough cash on hand to pay expenses.

Step Two. *Clarify the problem.* If group members do not see the problem the same way, they will offer divergent solutions to their own individual perceptions of the problem. To some team members, late payments may simply mean the company has less cash in the bank. As a result, the company earns a few dollars less in interest. Someone else on the team might perceive the problem as mostly an annoyance and inconvenience. Another person may perceive late payers as being immoral and may, therefore, want to penalize them. The various perceptions of the problem solvers contribute to their exercising a political model of decision making. It is important to reach consensus that the ultimate problem is not enough cash in hand to run the business, as explained in Step One.

Step Three. *Analyze the cause.* Understand the cause of the each problem and find ways to overcome it, to convert what exists into what you want. Late payment of bills (over 30 days) can be caused by several factors. The customers may have cash-flow problems of their own, they may have slow-moving bureaucratic procedures, or they may be understaffed. Another possibility is that the slow-paying customers may be dissatisfied with the service and could be holding back on payments in retaliation. Research, including interviewing customers, may be needed to analyze the cause or causes.

Step Four. *Search for alternative solutions.* Remember that multiple alternative solutions can be found to most problems. The alternative solutions you choose will depend on your analysis of the causes. Assume that you did not find customers to be dissatisfied with your service, but they were slow in paying bills for a variety of other reasons. Your team then gets into a creative mode by developing a number of alternatives. Among them are offering bigger discounts for quick payment, dropping slow-paying customers, sending out your own bills more promptly, and using follow-up e-mail messages and phone calls to bring in money. For regular customers, you might try for automatic withdrawals from their checking account. Another possibility would be to set up a line of credit that would enable your firm to make short-term loans to cover expenses until your bills were paid.

Step Five. *Select alternatives.* Identify the criteria that solutions should meet; then, discuss the pros and cons of the proposed alternatives. No solution should be laughed at or scorned. Specifying the criteria that proposed solutions should meet requires you to think deeply about your goals. For example, your team might establish the following criteria for solutions: that they (a) improve cash flow, (b) do not lose customers, (c) do not cost much to implement, and (d) do not make the company appear desperate. The pros and cons of each proposed alternative can be placed on a flip chart, board, or computer screen.

For many complex problems, it is best to select an alternative solution that is based on a variety of options. The blended-options solutions will often be stronger because it contains several useful ideas.[6] At the same time, several group members will be satisfied that at least part of their suggestion was incorporated in the final solution. For example, if the problem under group discussion was choosing a theme for decorating a new office, several ideas might be selected. An advertising agency used group decision making to arrive at a dual theme for decorating the office: cool, yet affluent.

Step Six. *Plan for implementation.* Decide what actions are necessary to carry out the chosen solution to the problem. Suppose your group decides that establishing a bank line of credit is the most feasible alternative. The company president or the chief financial officer might then meet with a couple of local banks to apply for a line of credit at the most favorable rate. Your group also chooses to initiate a program of friendly follow-up telephone calls to encourage more rapid payment.

In many organizations, the group may have to present its finding to the next level of management or higher before they are authorized to implement their decision. For example, a group of product developers at Proctor & Gamble might decide that the company should launch a muscle-building food supplement; however, mangement would have the authority to reject the idea, therefore, blocking the implementation of the suggestion.

Step Seven. *Clarify the contract.* Assess what needs to be done and what deadlines to reach. The contract is a restatement of what group members have agreed to do and deadlines for accomplishment. In your situation, several team members are involved in establishing a line of credit and initiating a system of follow-up phone calls.

Step Eight. *Develop an action plan.* Specify who does what and when to carry out the contract. Each person involved in implementing alternatives develops an action plan in detail that stems logically from the previous steps.

Step Nine. *Provide for evaluation and accountability.* Reconvene to discuss progress after the plan is implemented, to hold people accountable for results that have not been achieved. In the situation at hand, progress will be measured in at least two objective ways. You can evaluate by accounting measures whether the cash-flow problem has improved and whether the average cycle time on accounts receivable has decreased.

When to Apply the Problem-Solving Steps. The steps for effective group problem solving are best applied to complex problems. Straightforward problems of minor consequence (such as deciding on holiday decorations for the office) do not require all the steps. Nevertheless, remember that virtually every problem has more than one feasible alternative. A classic example of searching for the best alternative to a problem is as follows:

Many years ago a Ritz-Carlton hotel was receiving complaints of late room service, which was unusal for such a luxury hotel. The hotel president sent out a team composed of a room-service specialist, a waiter, and a cook. All appeared fine except that the service elevator was consuming a lot of time. Engineers in charge of the elevator could find no technical problem. Team members then rode the service elevators for a week. The team observed that the elevator made several stops on the way from the first floor to the top floor. It was noted that housemen were taking towels from one floor to bring them to housekeepers on other floors. The team concluded that the Ritz-Carlton did not have a room-service problem or an elevator problem—it was experiencing a towel shortage. After a bunch of new towles were purchased, complaints about room service dropped by one half.[7]

The Importance of Collective Efficacy. How well a given group solves a problem depends on many of the characteristics of an effective work group outlined in Figure 6-1 (in the previous chapter). Of particular relevance is the group's level of confidence that it can solve the problem at hand. **Collective efficacy** is a group's belief that it can handle certain tasks. Collective efficacy influences a group to initiate action, influences how much effort it will apply to the task, and influences how long the group's effort will be sustained.[8] (Note that collective efficacy refers to confidence, whereas collective intelligence has to do with actual ability.) If the group members say spontaneously, "We can do it, let's go," they will usually be successful in solving the problem, assuming they have the necessary knowledge and talent.

For practice in using the problem steps described earlier, do Skill-Building Exercise 7-1.

Managing Disagreement about Group Decision Making

A major reason that group decision making does not proceed mechanically is that disagreement may surface. Such disagreement is not necessarily harmful to the final outcome of the decision, because those who disagree may have valid points and help prevent groupthink. For committees and other groups to work well, they should be composed of people with different perspectives and experiences who are not hesitant to speak their minds, says psychologist Richard Larrick at the Fuqua School of Business, Duke University.[9]

The idea is to manage disagreement so that the decision-making process does not break down, and the dissenters are not squelched. Conflicts about decisions were studied among 43 cross-functional teams engaged in new product development. Disagreeing about major issues led to positive outcomes for team performance (as measured by ratings made by managers) under two conditions.[10]

First, the dissenters have to feel they have the freedom to express doubt. To measure such freedom, participants in the study responded to such statements as "I sometimes get the feeling that others are not speaking up although they harbor serious doubts about the direction being taken." (Strongly disagreeing with this statement would suggest that group members had the freedom to express doubt.)

Second, doubts must be expressed collaboratively (trying to work together) rather than contentiously (in a quarrelsome way). An example of collaborative communication would be having used the following statement during decision making: "We will be working together for a while. It's important that we all feel comfortable with a solution to this problem." An example of contentious communication would be high agreement with the statement, "You're being difficult and rigid."

Another study lends strength to the idea that teams are more likely to make optimal decisions when they take the time to debate the issues and thoughtfully discuss alternative

---

SKILL-BUILDING EXERCISE 7-1

A General Problem-Solving Group

The class is divided into groups of about six people. Each group takes the same complicated problem through the nine steps for effective group decision making. Several of the steps will be hypothetical because this is a simulated experience. Pretend that you are a task force composed of people from different departments in the company. Choose one of the following possibilities:

Scenario 1: Your company wants your task force to decide whether to purchase a corporate jet for members of senior management, or require them to continue flying on commercial airlines.

Scenario 2: You are employed by Samsung, an information technology giant that manufactures and sells printers, among its many products. Data supplied by the marketing research department indicates that the consumption of Samsung inkjet cartridges by consumers worldwide is declining more rapidly than anticipated. At the same time, private label refill cartridges are selling at a pace much faster than forecasted. Your task force is asked to recommend a plan for increasing the consumption of inkjet cartridges.

solutions. A study about hiring pilots for long-distance flights found that when groups disagreed over who to hire, there was more information sharing. Also, the strong disagreement led to more intense discussions that prompted participants to repeat their reasoning in front of other group members. A debate over which candidate to hire encourages team members to focus on information that may be inconsistent with how they formed their original opinion.[11]

Part of discussing alternative solutions is to take seriously minority opinions within the group. The consideration of minority opinions when making team decisions contributes to team effectiveness.[12] For example, a minority opinion in a hypothetical muscle-building food supplement scenario might be, "I doubt that a company with the great reputation of Procter & Gamble should get involved in anything that resembles using steroids for body building."

Conflict-resolution techniques, as described in Chapter 9, are another potentially useful approach to managing disagreement about decision making.

Aiming for Inquiry versus Advocacy in Group Decision Making

Another useful perspective on group decision making is to compare the difference between group members involved in *inquiry* (looking for the best alternative) versus *advocacy* (or fighting for one position). Inquiry is an open process designed to generate multiple alternatives, encourage the exchange of ideas, and produce a well-reasoned solution. Decision makers who care more about the good of the firm than personal gain are the most likely to engage in inquiry. According to David A. Garvin and Michael A. Roberto, this open-minded approach doesn't come easily to most people.[13]

Instead, most groups charged with making a decision tend to slip into the opposite mode, called advocacy. The two approaches look similar because under either mode the group members are busily immersed in work and appear to be searching for the best alternative. Yet, the results from the two modes are quite different. Using an advocacy approach, participants approach decision making as a contest with the intent of selecting the winning alternative. One member of the group might be trying to gain the largest share of the budget and might become so passionate about winning budget share that he loses objectivity. Advocates might even withhold important information from the group, such as not revealing that their budget is big enough, considering their decreased activity.

With an advocacy approach, the disagreements that arise tend to separate the group and are antagonistic. Personality conflicts come into play, and one person might accuse the other side of not being able to see the big picture. In contrast, an inquiry-focused group carefully considers a variety of alternatives and collaborates to discover the best solution.

Conflict-resolution methods can be useful in helping the decision makers overcome the advocacy approach. As part of resolving the conflict, the group leader must make sure that everyone knows that his or her viewpoint is being carefully considered.

GUIDELINES FOR BRAINSTORMING

In many work situations, groups are expected to produce creative and imaginative solutions to problems. When the organization is seeking a large number of alternatives for solving problems, **brainstorming** is often the technique of choice. Brainstorming is a group problem-solving technique that promotes creativity by encouraging idea generation through noncritical discussion. Alex Osborn, who developed the practice of brainstorming, believed that one of the main blocks to organizational creativity was the premature evaluation of ideas.[14] The basic technique is to encourage unrestrained and spontaneous participation by group members. The term *brainstorm* has become so widely known that it is often used as a synonym for a clever idea.

Brainstorming is used both as a method of finding alternatives to real-life problems and as a creativity-training program. In the usual form of brainstorming, group members spontaneously call out alternative solutions to a problem facing them. Any member is free to enhance or "hitchhike" upon the contribution of another person. At the end of the session, somebody sorts out the ideas and edits the more unrefined ones.

Brainstorming is widely used to develop new ideas for products, find names for products, develop advertising slogans, and solve customer problems. For instance, the design firm

brainstorming

A group problem-solving technique that promotes creativity by encouraging idea generation through noncritical discussion.

Ideo uses brainstorming as standard practice for tasks such as thinking of new high-tech gadgets for children. Brainstorming has also been used to develop new organizational structures and names for companies and products, and it is widely used in developing software.

Adhering to a few simple rules or guidelines helps ensure that creative alternative solutions to problems will be forthcoming. The brainstorming process usually falls into place without frequent reminders about guidelines. Nevertheless, here are ten rules to improve the chances of having a good session. Unless many of these rules are followed, brainstorming becomes a free-for-all, rather than brainstorming in its original intent.

1. **Begin with a goal, usually stated in the the message inviting people to participate in the session.** If people know the purpose of the brainstorming session in advance, they will often give some serious thought to the suggestions they will bring to the meeting. Doing homework is a major contributor to brainstorming effectiveness.

2. **Group size should be about five to seven people.** If there are too few people, not enough suggestions are generated; if there are too many people, the session becomes uncontrolled; however, brainstorming can be conducted with as few as three people.

3. **Everybody is given the chance to suggest alternative solutions.** Members spontaneously call out alternatives to the problem facing the group. (Another approach is for people to speak in sequence.)

4. **No criticism is allowed.** All suggestions should be welcome; it is particularly important not to use derisive laughter.

5. **Freewheeling is encouraged.** Outlandish ideas often prove quite useful. It's easier to tame a wild idea than to originate one. Although freewheeling is encouraged, a few moments of silence is not counterproductive because participants may need a few pauses to think.[15]

6. **Quantity and variety are very important.** The greater the number of ideas put forth, the greater the likelihood of a breakthrough idea.

7. **Combinations and improvements are encouraged.** Building upon the ideas of others, including combining them, is very productive. Hitchhiking or piggybacking is an essential part of brainstorming.

8. **Notes must be taken during the session by a person who serves as the recording secretary.** The session can also be taped, but this requires substantial time to retrieve ideas.

9. **Invite outsiders to the brainstorming session.** Inviting an outsider to the brainstorming session can add a new perspective the "insiders" might not think of themselves. (Such is the argument for having a diverse problem-solving group.)

10. **Do not overstructure by following any of the above nine ideas too rigidly.** Brainstorming is a spontaneous group process.

Goodluz/Shutterstock

A widely accepted suggestion for brainstorming effectiveness is to have diverse group members. Diversity includes differences in age, sex, race, experience levels, and educational background, as well as functional background (e.g., marketing and information technology). The diversity contributes to different perspectives that facilitate a variety of ideas surfacing during the brainstorming session.

According to one observer, the most productive brainstorming sessions take place in physically stimulating environments, as opposed to drab conference rooms. Natural light may stimulate thinking, so work in a room with windows (or outside, if weather permits). Changing from a seated position to walking around from time to time can be mentally stimulating. Food and drink also contribute to an enhanced environment for brainstorming.[16]

As implied in the opening case to this chapter, an open physical arrangement in the workplace can encourage people to engage in brainstorming informally, outside of a formal brainstorming group. James Hackett, the CEO of furniture maker Steelcase Inc., says that customers are purchasing products such as café lounge seating and benches to encourage brainstorming.[17]

Brainstorming is an effective technique for finding a large number of alternatives to problems, particularly when the list of alternatives is subsequently refined and edited. Brainstorming in groups is also valuable because it contributes to job satisfaction for many people. Skill-Building Exercise 7-2 gives you an opportunity to practice a commercially useful application of brainstorming.

A curious feature of brainstorming is that individuals working alone typically produce more useful ideas than those placed in a group. Brainstorming by individuals working alone is referred to as **brainwriting**. Skill-Building Exercise 7-3 gives you a chance to compare brainstorming with brainwriting.

brainwriting

Brainstorming by individuals working alone.

GUIDELINES FOR THE NOMINAL GROUP TECHNIQUE

A team leader or other manager who must make a decision about an important issue sometimes needs to know what alternatives are available and how people will react to them. The leader also wants to obtain consensus on the alternative solution chosen. In such cases, group input is quite helpful. Spoken brainstorming is not ideal because the problem is still in the exploration phase and requires more than a list of alternative solutions.

LEARNING OBJECTIVE 4

A problem-solving technique called the **nominal group technique (NGT)** was developed to fit the situation. The NGT is a group problem-solving technique that calls people together in a structured meeting with limited interaction. The group is called nominal (in name only) because people first present their ideas without interacting with each other, as they would in a real group. Group discussion, however, does take place at a later stage in the process. A version of the nominal group technique developed by the Centers for Disease Control and Prevention of the US Department of Health and Human Services contains the following steps.[18]

nominal group technique (NGT)

A group problem-solving technique that calls people together in a structured meeting with limited interaction.

1. **Generating Ideas:** The moderator or group leader presents the question or problem to the group in written form and reads the question to the group. The moderator directs everyone to write ideas in brief phrases or statements and to work silently

and independently. Paper, computers, or mobile devices can be used to record suggestions and thoughts. Tablet and laptop computers are well suited for the NGT.

2. **Recording Ideas:** Group members engage in a round-robin feedback session to concisely record each idea (without discussion or debate at this point). The moderator writes an idea from a group member on a flip chart or projects the idea onto a screen and proceeds to ask for another idea from the next group member, continuing until each participant has contributed an idea. Ideas do not have to be repeated; however, if group members believe that an idea provides a different emphasis or variation, the idea can be included.

3. **Discussing Ideas:** Each recorded idea is then discussed to determine clarity and importance. For each idea, the moderator asks, "Are there any questions or comments group members would like to make about the item?" This step provides an opportunity for members to express their understanding of the logic and the relative importance of each item. The creator of the idea need not feel obliged to clarify or explain the item—any member of the group can carry out that role.

4. **Voting on Ideas:** Individuals vote privately to prioritze the ideas. The votes are tallied to identify the ideas that are ratest highest by the entire group. The moderator establishes which criteria are used to prioritize the ideas. To start, each group member selects the five most important ideas from the group list and writes one idea on each index card. Next, each member ranks the five ideas selected, with the most important receiving a rank of 5 and the least important receiving a rank of 1.

5. **Selecting the Highest-Ranking Alternative:** After members rank their responses in order of priority, the moderator creates a tally sheet on the flip chart or screen with numbers down the left-hand side of the chart, which correspond to the ideas from the round-robin. The moderator collects all the cards from the participants and and asks one member to read the idea number and number of points allocated to each one. Also, the moderator records and then adds the scores on the tally sheet. The ideas that are most favorably rated by the group are the most favored group actions or ideas in response to the idea posed by the moderator.

Figure 7-1 illustrates the ranking and tallying process in steps 4 and 5. To practice the nominal group technique, do Skill-Building Exercise 7-4.

FIGURE 7-1 The Ranking (Voting) and Tallying Process for the Nominal Group Technique

Problem: A not-for-profit tennis and swim club finds that it has a surplus of $9,571 at the end of the year. The club president meets with five board members to decide what to do with the surplus. The table below lists the alternatives, the ranking of 1-5 by board members, and the tallying of the ranks.

Table 1: Alternatives Chosen by Group Members

A. Purchase new trees for the property
B. Paint and refurbish men's and women's locker rooms
C. Build locker rooms for boys and girls
D. Trade in club pickup truck for new one
E. Donate funds to Community Chest (a charity) in our city

Table 2: Ranks by Members and Tallying (5 is highest)

Choice	Oscar	Mary	Rex	Jessica	Ted	Lori	Sum of Ranks
A	2	4	3	5	2	2	18
B	1	2	5	2	5	4	19
C	3	5	4	4	3	5	24
D	5	1	2	3	1	1	13
E	4	3	1	1	4	3	16
Row and Column Sums	15	15	15	15	15	15	90

Alternative C, build a locker room for boys and girls, is the favorite alternative.

USING STANDUP MEETINGS TO FACILITATE PROBLEM SOLVING

LEARNING OBJECTIVE 5

Problem solving and decision making can sometimes be improved by conducting meetings while standing up instead of sitting down. The general idea is that participants standing up in the problem-solving group are likely to be more alert and will come to a decision more quickly. Some people solve problems better when standing because they literally "think well on their feet." Few people would be willing to stand for several hours, so they reach a decision quickly.

Many meeting leaders who use standup meetings are pleased with the results in terms of reaching high-quality decisions rapidly. At United Parcel Service (UPS), every morning and several times a day, managers assemble workers for a required standup meeting that lasts precisely three minutes. Among the topics covered are local information, traffic conditions, and customer complaints. Each meeting ends with a safety tip. The 180-second limit helps enforce punctuality throughout UPS.[19] Many problem-solving meetings at Google are held standing up. For example, details about a new version of the Google results page were hammered out at a meeting of 10 people.[20]

Standup meetings at Atomic Object, the software developer, and other firms have been prompted by the growing use of "Agile," an approach to developing software that requires compressing development projects into short pieces. Agile demands standup meetings during which participants update their coworkers with three items: what they have accomplished since yesterday's meeting, what they plan to do today, and any barriers they see to getting work done.[21] By participating in these focused meetings, workers hone their interpersonal skills in such areas as communicating quickly and openly, interpreting the nonverbal communication of others, and resolving disagreements on the spot.

USING E-MAIL AND COLLABORATIVE SOFTWARE TO FACILITATE GROUP DECISION MAKING

The presence of so many teams in the workplace means that people must work collectively and that they must make decisions together. Collective effort usually translates into meetings. Without any meetings, people are working primarily alone and thus are not benefiting from working in teams. Yet with too many meetings, it is difficult to accomplish individual work, such as dealing with e-mail, making telephone calls, analyzing information, and preparing reports.

Appropriate use of e-mail and collaborative software (formerly referred to as groupware) can facilitate interaction among team members and group decision making, while at the same time minimizing the number of physical meetings. Such use of e-mail and other electronic tools including business social networking makes possible the virtual teams described in the previous chapter.

Using E-Mail to Facilitate Meetings

Athough e-mail in the workplace is often replaced by more modern forms of electronic communication, such as intranets and business social networking sites, it still can make an important contribution to group problem solving and decision making. Using e-mail, many small details can be taken care of in advance of the meeting. During the meeting, major items can be tackled. The typical use of e-mail is to send brief memos to people on a distribution list. A more advanced use of e-mail is to distribute word processing documents as well as spreadsheets and graphics, including photographs, as attachments. If the subject of the meeting deals with uncomplicated issues, text messaging can be used instead of e-mail.

E-mail, instant messaging, and text messages are also quite useful for following up on meetings. Instead of calling a new meeting to take care of a few items, people with additional thoughts can simply send around information for sharing or action. For example, the meeting leader might send an e-mail to all participants stating, "I found out today that if we purchase those batteries in a package of 100, we can get a 15% discount. Should we go ahead?"

Pushing the use of e-mail too far can inhibit rather than enhance group decision making and teamwork. If people communicate with each other almost exclusively by e-mail, the warmth of human interaction and facial expressions is lost. Piggybacking of ideas is possible by reading each other's ideas on a computer monitor. Nevertheless, the wink of an eye, the shared laughter, and the encouraging smiles that take place in a traditional meeting make an important contribution to team effort, including group problem solving. Also, face-to-face interaction facilitates creativity as people exchange ideas.

Using Collaborative Software and Social Platforms to Facilitate Group Problem Solving

The application of e-mail just described can be considered part of collaborative software because e-mail was used to facilitate work in groups. Electronic brainstorming also relies on collaborative software, because software is applied to facilitate group decision making. Using electronic brainstorming, as well as the other electronic approaches to group problem solving, participants are free to comment on or suggest a modification of the ideas of other contributors. Assume that Sara, a marketing assistant at a bicycle company, enters the following comment on her e-mail or Web site post: "I say, let's push for selling more adult tricycles in Florida because of the many seniors down there." Engineering technician Jason then adds to Sara's comment, "I love Sara's idea. But why limit the marketing push to Florida? Let's follow the senior crowd right into Arizona and the Carolinas."

The various electronic approaches to group decision making have been labeled social platforms because they function in the same manner as social networking Web sites. At the same time, because the group members can interact with each other frequently and comment on the posts placed by other group members, social platforms encourage collaboration.[22]

At its best, collaborative software offers certain advantages over single-user systems. Three of the most common reasons people use collaborative software are as follows:[23]

- Making communication faster, clearer, and more persuasive
- Enabling people to work from remote locations, including home.
- Reducing travel costs
- a sufficient number of people face-to-face

Another example of collaborative software is a *shared whiteboard* that allows two or more people to view and draw on a common drawing surface, even when they are at a distance. The link to group decision making is that drawing sketches and diagrams might be an important part of decision making. An example is a sales team suggesting ways of dividing a geographic territory for selling.

An advantage of virtual problem solving is that it avoids the problem of a couple of people dominating the meeting and some people making no contribution because they are timid. In-person meetings are useful for a final discussion or vote because of the exchange of ideas possible.[24] Another problem with anonymity in problem solving is that many workers want to receive credit for their good ideas.

Despite all these potential applications and benefits of collaborative software and social platforms, the system will break down unless almost all the parties involved use the software successfully. For example, all members of the virtual team must be willing to get online at the same time to have a productive meeting.

SUGGESTIONS FOR BEING AN EFFECTIVE MEETING PARTICIPANT

LEARNING OBJECTIVE 6

Except for virtual meetings such as those made possible by collaborative software, group problem solving takes place within the context of a face-to-face meeting. A major problem with most meetings is that they frustrate the participants, particularly those who are accomplishment-oriented. Steven G. Rogelberg and his associates conducted an online survey of 980 participants from the United States, Australia, and the United Kingdom. The more meetings the accomplishment-oriented workers attended, the worse they felt about their job and the lower their feelings of wellbeing. The meetings appeared to have been perceived as an interruption to the tasks these ambitious people set out to accomplish.[25] Many workers, however, do enjoy the social interaction involved in meetings, as well as a change of pace from individual work.

Meetings are not likely to be eliminated, despite their unpopularity with accomplishment-oriented workers. A possible solution is for meeting participants to conduct themselves in a professional, task-oriented manner. In this way, meetings will most likely be shorter and more productive. A few key suggestions follow for being an effective meeting participant.[26]

- Arrive at the meeting prepared, such as by having studied the support material and agenda, thought through your potential contribution, and taken care of some details by e-mail beforehand.

- Arrive on time, and stay until the meeting is completed. The meeting leader will often wait for the last participant before getting down to business. Leaving early distracts other participants.

- Do not hog the meeting or sit silently. Meetings are much more effective when the participants make balanced contributions.

- Use constructive nonverbal communication rather than slouching, yawning, looking bored and frustrated, leaving the room frequently, chewing gum, checking your smartphone or tablet computer, or engaging in similar negative behaviors.

- Converse only with others in the meeting when someone else is not speaking. Some executives will oust participants from a meeting if they engage in *sidebar conversations*.

- Be prepared to offer compromise solutions when other meeting participants and the meeting leader are haggling about a conflict of opinion.

- When possible, have data ready to support your position, such as estimating from industry data how much money your suggestion will save the company.

From studying these suggestions, you will observe that conducting yourself productively and professionally in a meeting is yet another job-oriented interpersonal skill.

Another consideration in being a productive member of a meeting is to be able to deal effectively with other participants who seem intent on creating problems for others. Chapter 12 includes a discussion of how to deal with difficult people. Four types of "meeting killers" can be identified, all of whom have to be dealt with sympathetically for their problems. At the same time, these meeting killers must receive clear feedback about how they are lowering the productivity of the meeting.

One meeting killer is the *jokester* who keeps cracking jokes whether or not they are appropriate. The *dominator* greatly overestimates the value of his or her personal views, and so the person keeps on taking up time of the group. The *naysayer* objects to all points raised and waits until consensus is almost attained to present his or her major objections. The *rambler* frequently goes off on a tangent, prompting others to wonder what point he or she is trying to make.[27]

CULTURAL FACTORS AND GROUP DECISION MAKING

LEARNING OBJECTIVE 7

Most aspects of human relations and interpersonal skills are affected by cultural factors, including both national and organizational cultures. Chapter 8 focuses on developing cross-cultural skills, and describes many national differences in culture. Here we present a couple of examples of how cultural factors can influence the acceptance of group problem solving and decision making.

Whenever differences attributed to national cultures are mentioned, it must be recognized that these are sweeping generalizations that apply to average, or typical, behaviors. The same is true for generational and gender differences. Craig L. Pearce and his associates studied three sets of cultural differences in workplace attitudes and behaviors related to how willing workers are to share decision making. Highlights of the findings are as follows.[28]

1. **Acceptance of unequal distribution of power in institutions and organizations.** Workers in societies in which workers expect managers to have more power—and in which workers accept this reality—are more hesitant to participate in group decision making. The same workers might be hesitant to contribute radical ideas to brainstorming because they think the manager is responsible for producing innovative ideas. Countries in which workers believe in managers holding most of the power include Arab countries and France. Positive attitudes toward power sharing are more common in the United States and Canada.

2. **The degree to which a country is aggressive versus nurturing.** Aggressive societies are less prone to group decision making because aggressive people prefer to dominate. People in an aggressive society are oriented toward the achievement of goals at the expense of others. Managers from a nurturing society are more likely to believe in group decision making because the process helps workers to develop. On the list of aggressive societies are Ireland and the United States.

3. **The degree to which a society is individualistic or collectivistic.** Members of an individualistic society tend to be self-reliant and value independence, whereas members of a collectivistic society are oriented toward groups. Workers from an individualistic society might not enjoy working in teams and would not be so enthusiastic about group decision making. Workers from a collectivistic society take naturally to group decision making. People from Germany and the United States tend to value individualism. This stereotype exists despite the emphasis on teamwork in the United States.

The organizational culture, or values and behaviors of most members of the organization, exerts a strong influence on the preference for group decision making. When the organizational culture emphasizes collaboration, group problem solving and decision making is prevalent and welcome. Procter & Gamble and Xerox are two examples of successful corporations that emphasize group decision making. The General Motors of old emphasized individual decision making.

Concept Review
and Reinforcement

Key Terms

Summary

An important aspect of interpersonal relations in organizations is that groups solve many key problems. Group problem solvers and decision makers often use the rational model or the political model. The rational decision-making model is the traditional, logical approach to decision making based on the scientific method. The model assumes that each alternative is evaluated in terms of how well it contributes to reaching the goals involved in making the decision.

The political decision-making model assumes that people bring preconceived notions and biases into the decision-making situation. Because the decision makers are politically motivated, the individuals often do not make the most rational choice. Instead, the decision makers attempt to satisfy their own needs. Blind spots are an unintended contributor to political decision making, as are greed and gluttony.

General problem-solving groups are likely to arrive at better decisions when they follow standard steps or guidelines for group problem solving. The steps are as follows: (1) Identify the problem, (2) clarify the problem, (3) analyze the cause, (4) search for alternative solutions, (5) select alternatives, (6) plan for implementation, (7) clarify the contract, (8) develop an action plan, and (9) provide for evaluation and accountability. The group's collective efficacy influences its ability to solve problems.

Disagreements about group decisions can be managed by giving dissenters the freedom to express doubt and by expressing doubts collaboratively rather than contentiously. Group decision making is more productive when group members are involved in inquiry, or looking for the best alternative. Advocacy, or fighting for one position, leads to poorer decisions. Research indicates that teams are more likely to make optimal decisions when they take the time to debate the issues and thoughtfully discuss alternative solutions.

When the organization is seeking a large number of alternatives to problems, brainstorming is often the technique of choice. Brainstorming is used as a method of finding alternatives to real-life problems and as a creativity-training program. Using the technique, group members spontaneously call out alternative solutions to the problem. Members build on the ideas of each other, and ideas are not screened or evaluated until a later stage. Diversity within the group facilitates brainstorming, as does the right physical environment, such as sunlight. Brainstorming by working alone, or brainwriting, is also effective in generating alternative solutions.

The nominal group technique (NGT) is recommended for a situation in which a leader needs to know what alternatives are available and how people will react to them. In the NGT, a small group of people contributes written solutions to the problem. Other members respond to their ideas later. Members rate each other's ideas numerically, and the final group decision is the sum of the pooled individual votes.

Problem solving and decision making can sometimes be improved by conducting meetings while standing up instead of sitting down. The general idea is that participants who are standing up are more likely to be alert and come to a decision quickly. An experiment with management students indicated that standup groups made decisions more quickly, but that decision makers who sat down were more satisfied.

E-mail can be used to facilitate group decision making because members can feed information to each other without having to meet as a group. Memos, spreadsheet analyses, and graphics can be distributed through the network. Too much emphasis on e-mail, however, results in losing the value of face-to-face human interaction.

Various types of collaborative software, including e-mail and electronic brainstorming, can facilitate group decision making. Also, a shared whiteboard allows two or more people to view and draw on a common drawing surface, even when they are at a distance. Facebook, or a company Web site of the same type, can also be used for group decision making. Virtual problem solving helps avoid individual domination of decision making, but face-to-face discussion is important in making a final decision.

To help avoid the frustration of many accomplishment-oriented people in meetings, participants should conduct themselves in a professional, task-oriented manner. The suggestions presented here include: arrive prepared, arrive on time and stay for the full meeting, do not hog the meeting or sit silently, use constructive non-verbal communication, avoid sidebar conversations, offer compromise solutions to conflicts, and use data to support your position.

Questions for Discussion and Review

1. Give an example of the advocacy approach in a domestic or international political situation, such as Occupy Wall Street. Comment on how practical an inquiry approach may be in your chosen situation.

2. Many successful entrepreneurs, including the late Steve Jobs at Apple Corporation, made most of the big product decisions by themselves. So why should you worry about developing skills in group decision making?

3. Which personality characteristics described in Chapter 2 do you think would help a person be naturally effective in group problem solving?

4. Give an example of how knowledge of the team member roles presented in Chapter 6 could help you be a better contributor to group problem solving.

5. Suggest a situation when brainstorming is preferable to a staged approach to problem solving.

6. What is your opinion of the importance of the physical setting (such as sunlight and refreshments) for stimulating creative thinking during brainstorming?

7. Identify two work-related problems for which the nominal group technique is particularly well suited.

8. How would you deal with a suggestion made during a brainstorming group that you thought was outrageously stupid?

9. Why are face-to-face meetings generally still considered more effective than virtual meetings?

10. How might groupthink (described in Chapter 6) interfere with the quality of decisions made in a group?

11. What annoys you the most about how some people conduct themselves in problem-solving meetings of any type? What changes in their behavior would you recommend?

The Web Corner

http://www.mindtools.com
(Techniques for group and individual problem solving and creativity.)

http://www.referenceforbusiness.com/ management/Gr-Int/Group-Decision-Making.html
(Improving group decision making. Video is included.)

Internet Skill Builder: Where Did I Put that Great Idea I Had?

Many people involved in group brainstorming hit upon useful ideas when away from the brainstorming session,

then forget the idea by the time they get to the session. So during the session, the person fails to make an outstanding contribution. Search the Internet for some cool ideas for recording your ideas. An example would be sending yourself an e-mail or voicemail message if you come up with a useful idea while hiking. You are encouraged to look widely for a couple of concrete suggestions for filing your creative ideas right on the spot. Remember that fresh ideas are the building block for all types of group as well as individual problem solving.

Developing Your Human Relations Skills

Interpersonal Relations Case 7.1

Pet Groomers on Wheels Get into a Huddle

Ted and Erin, a married couple, both loved pets, and both craved becoming small-business owners. So several years ago while still holding down corporate positions, they launched a new business, Pet Groomers on Wheels. The basic model of the business is to make house calls to groom pets at the pet owner's home.

The key services for dogs are shampoos, haircuts, nail clips, teeth polishing, and ear cleaning. Except for the shampoos, the services are similar for cats. Ted and Erin travel in a van fully equipped with their supplies, and the pet grooming is conducted in the van rather than bringing all the equipment into the customer's home. Ted and Erin started the operation part-time by making their calls at night and on weekends. Soon it appeared the business was ready to become a full-time business, so the couple both quit their corporate positions.

Operating in the prosperous North Virginia geographic area, Pet Groomers on Wheels has far exceeded the sales volume and profits projected by Ted and Erin. To successfully manage all the client demands, the couple hired two close relatives, Tanya and Nick, to make some of the calls. To help keep Tanya and Nick motivated—as well to prevent their becoming competition for Pet Groomers on Wheels—Ted and Erin made them part owners of the business.

After three years of operation, Pet Groomers on Wheels has generated $85,000 in profits beyond paying Ted, Erin, Tanya, and Nick salaries of an average of $65,000 each. In the process of preparing the income tax for Pet Groomers, Erin decided that the company was not managing its money effectively by leaving the profits in a checking account. After chatting about the situation with Ted, they both agreed that the company should manage its money more professionally. Ted said jokingly, "I guess we could run to Vegas and parlay the money into a fortune. Or, we could take a comparable risk and invest in the stock market."

Erin replied, "I have a better idea. Let's get together with Tanya and Nick, and really thrash out what to do with Pet Groomers profits. We can all have dinner together, followed by a no-holds-barred problem-solving session."

Case Questions

1. Does the problem facing the owners of Pet Groomer on Wheels seem suited for going through the steps for group problem solving? Or, what other problem-solving technique would you recommend?
2. Take the problem of what to do with Pet Groomer profits through the group problem-solving steps, even if you have to make assumptions about some of the data for the steps.
3. Compare the conclusion you reach in response to question 2 with the conclusion reached by other individuals or groups within the class.

Interpersonal Relations Role-Play

Group Decision Making at Pet Groomers on Wheels

In this group role-play, students play the roles of Ted, Erin, Tanya, and Nick, who decide to conduct a brief brainstorming session about what to do with the cash Pet Groomers on Wheels is accumulating. Let this be a no-holds-barred session. Run the session for about fifteen minutes.

Observers will rate the participants on two dimensions. One dimension is the creative output of the group. The second dimension is the quality of the suggestions arrived at by the group. A few observers might voluntarily provide feedback to the role players in terms of sharing their ratings and observations. The course instructor might also provide feedback.

Standing Up at Vogue Travel

Chelsea is the CEO of Vogue Travel, a multioffice travel agency that focuses on arranging business trips for large corporations. Vogue also plans luxury trips for individuals. As Chelsea explains, "Most ordinary travel agencies have gone the way of the typewriter and camera film. Our computer-savvy population makes almost all of its travel arrangements online. The service Vogue provides is much more complex. We pin down every detail for our clients and save them money."

Despite Chelsea's boastful statement, she recognizes that even the high-end travel agency is conducting business in a highly competitive environment. She believes that her staff should approach each day in a more fired-up frame of mind, much like an athletic team just before a challenging match. After reading an article in *Entrepreneur* about standup meetings, she thought that this type of meeting is just what her company needed. Chelsea then informed her top-level staff that at the start of each business day, the team would get into a ten-minute huddle to discuss the biggest challenges they would be facing during the day.

One month after implementing the standup meetings, Chelsea thought that they were making a contribution to team work and problem solving. For example, during one of the meetings, the team decided it would be a good idea to tell clients how to increase the chances of not becoming ill when visiting a faraway region. Yet Chelsea thought it would be helpful to ask her staff what they thought of the effectiveness of the meetings. The subject of the next standup meeting was to discuss the effectiveness of this type of meeting so far. Among the opinions expressed during the evaluation meeting were the following:

Eric: I love the fast-paced action. Because we are standing up, we jump in on problems we are facing without frittering away time.

Phyllis: Ouch, my aching feet. I mean it. I don't like the demands on my feet and legs in these standup meetings.

Karl: My feet don't hurt. But I like to have a table to put my coffee on. To me, having coffee and refreshments is part of a meeting.

Cindy: I think we could accomplish more by posting our problem-solving on a common Web page or exchanging e-mails. During our morning huddles it seems that we are just trying to impress each other.

Bob: We spend so much time in our cubicles that we hardly ever interact face-to-face. The standup meetings give me the feeling that we are really a team.

Melody: Our standup meetings are working somewhat, but I think we should meet once a week unless there is an emergency. Otherwise, we tend to be stretching to come up with good ideas for the meeting.

Chelsea: Thanks gang, I appreciate the candor. Our ten minutes are up, and I'll be processing your feedback.

Case Questions

1. Explain why you think Chelsea should continue or discontinue the standup meetings.
2. What evidence do you have that the standup meetings at Vogue Travel are contributing to (or detracting from) teamwork and problem solving?
3. How might Chelsea improve the effectiveness of these standup meetings?

References

1. Dan Ariely, "The End of Rational Economics," *Harvard Business Review,* July–August 2009, pp. 78–84.
2. Cited in Marcia A. Reed-Woodard, "What Were You Thinking?" *Black Enterprise,* January 2009, p. 87.
3. Thomas H. Davenport, "Make Better Decisions," *Harvard Business Review,* November 2009, p. 117.
4. Felix C. Brodbeck et al., "Group Decision Making under Conditions of Distributed Knowledge: The Information

Asymmetries Model," *Academy of Management Review,* April 2007, pp. 459–460.

5. Anita Williams Woolley, Christopher F. Chabris, Alex Pentland, Nada Hashmi, and Thomas W. Malone, "Evidence for a Collective Intelligence Factor in the Performance of Human Groups," *Science* (http://www.sciencemag.org), October 2010, pp. 686–688.

6. Debra Wheatman, "Problem Solving in the Workplace," *San Francisco Examiner* (http://www.examiner.com), June 28, 2009.

7. Michael Mercer, *Absolutely Fabulous Organizational Change* (Lake Zurich, IL:Castlegate, 2000); Duncan Maxwell Anderson, "Hidden Forces," *Success,* April 1995, p. 1.

8. Alexander D. Stajkovic, Dongseop Lee, and Anthony J. Nyberg, "Collective Efficacy, Group Potency, and Group Performance: Meta-Analysis of their Relationships, and Test of a Mediation Model," *Journal of Applied Psychology,* May 2009, p. 815.

9. Cited in Jason Zweig, "How Group Decisions End Up Wrong-Footed," *The Wall Street Journal,* April 25–26, 2009, p. B1.

10. Kay Lovelace, Debra L. Shapiro, and Laurie R. Weingart, "Minimizing Cross-Functional New Product Teams' Innovativeness and Constraint Adherence: A Conflict Communications Perspective," *Academy of Management Journal,* August 2001, pp. 779–793.

11. Stuart D. Sidle, "Do Teams Who Agree to Disagree Make Better Decisions?" *Academy of Management Perspectives,* May 2007, pp. 74–75. The Sidle article is a review of S. Schultz-Hardt et al., "Group Decision Making in Hidden Profile Situations: Dissent as a Facilitator for Decision Quality," *Journal of Personality and Social Psychology,* No. 6, 2006, pp. 1080–1093.

12. Guihyun Park and Richard P. DeShon, "A Multilevel Model of Minority Opinion Expression and Team Decision-Making Effectiveness," *Journal of Applied Psychology,* September 2010, pp. 824–833.

13. David A. Garvin and Michael A. Roberto, "What You Don't Know about Making Decisions," *Harvard Business Review,* September 2001, pp. 110–111.

14. Leigh Thompson, "Improving the Creativity of Work Groups," *Academy of Management Executive,* February 2003, p. 99.

15. Ross McCammon, "What's the Secret to Better Brainstorming?" *Entrepreneur,* October 2011, p. 19.

16. "Future Edisons of America: Turn Your Employees into Inventors," *WorkingSMART,* June 2000, p. 2.

17. Cited in James R. Hagerty, "Office Furniture in the Age of Smartphones," *The Wall Street Journal,* August 8, 2012, p. B5.

18. Adapted and expanded from "Gaining Consensus Among Stakeholders Through the Nominal Group Technique," *Evaluation Briefs* (Department of Health and Human Services, Centers for Disease Control and Prevention), No. 7, November 2006. pp. 1–2

19. Owen Thomas, "The Three-Minute Huddle," *Business 2.0,* April 2006, p. 94.

20. "How Google Got Its New Look," *Bloomberg Businessweek,* May 10–May 16, 2010, p. 60.

21. Rachel Emma Silverman, "No More Angling for the Best Seat; More Meetings Are Stand-Up Jobs," *The Wall Street Journal,* February 2, 2012, pp. A1, A10.

22. "Making Internal Collaboration Work: An Interview with Don Tapscott," *McKinsey Quarterly,* January 2013, p. 2.

23. "Introduction to Groupware," http://www.usabilityfirst.com/. Accessed July 18, 2013.

24. "Nail Down Decision Making," *Manager's Edge,* July 2009, p. 1.

25. Erika Packard, "Meetings Frustrate Task-Oriented Employees, Study Finds," *Monitor on Psychology,* June 2006, p. 10; Steven G. Rogelberg, Desmond J. Leach, Peter B. Warr, and Jennifer L. Burnfield, "'Not Another Meeting!' Are Meeting Time Demands Related to Employee Well-Being?" *Journal of Applied Psychology,* January 2006, pp. 83–96.

26. Several of the suggestions are based on Rachel Zupek, "Horrible, Terrible Meeting Mistakes," http://www.CNN.com, August 29, 2007, pp. 1–3.

27. Sue Shellenbarger, "Meet the Meeting Killers," *The Wall Street Journal,* May 16, 2012, p. D, D3.

28. Research described in Craig L. Pearce, "Follow the Leaders," *The Wall Street Journal,* July 7, 2008, p. R12.

Cross-Cultural Relations and Diversity

Bright Horizons Family Solutions provides childcare and dependent care services to companies, hospitals, universities, and government agencies. The childcare centers are located on-site or near-site to help employers to reduce work/family challenges for employees who are parents of young children. Bright Horizons also offers in-home and center-based care for children as well as adults in need of personal care.

The company operates 775 centers in the United States, the UK, the Netherlands, Ireland, Canada, and India. Bright Horizons has been selected as one of the 100 best companies to work for by *CNN Money*. One contributing factor to this ranking is that the company offers benefits rare for the child- and dependent-care industry, including higher pay, a generous 401(k) plan, and the opportunity for employee training and development.

Bright Solutions highly values a domestically and culturally diverse workforce and client base. To reinforce the importance of diversity (also known as inclusion), a few years ago the company diversity council sparked an initiative to challenge everyone in the organization to make a commitement to doing one thing to help advance diversity and inclusiveness at Bright Horizon. A key point of the one-thing initiative is that a corporate program alone is not sufficient to bring about a truly diverse organization; employees have to take actions themselves.

Among the many One Thing commitments by employees have been to take a new employee to lunch to make him or her feel more welcome, to hold a discussion group about Tourette's syndrome, and to read a book about diversity to gain new perspectives.[1]

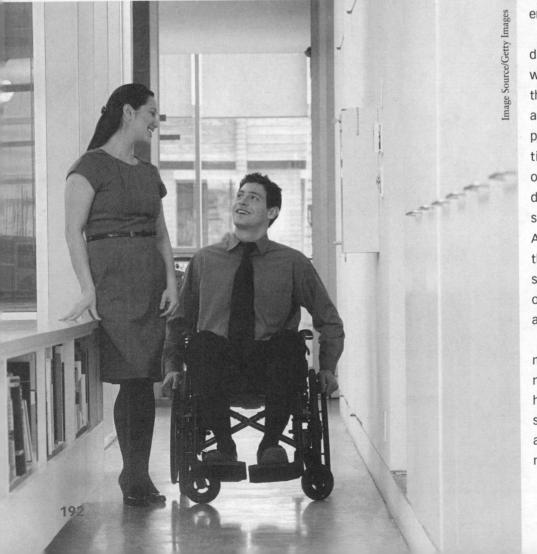

Image Source/Getty Images

LEARNING
Objectives

After reading and studying this chapter and completing the exercises, you should be able to

1. Recognize who fits under the diversity umbrella.
2. Understand cultural differences.
3. Overcome many cross-cultural communication barriers.
4. Improve your cross-cultural relations.

The One Thing initiative illustrates how employers give serious thought to strengthening diversity in their organizations. Top management at business firms continues to recognize the importance of a diverse workforce as well as diverse customers. Not only is the workforce becoming more diverse, but business has also become increasingly international. Approximately 15 percent of the US workforce is composed of people born in another country. Small- and medium-size firms, as well as corporate giants, are increasingly dependent on trade with other countries. An estimated 10 to 15 percent of jobs in the United States depend on imports or exports. Also more and more work, such as call centers and manufacturing, is subcontracted to companies in other countries.

All this workplace diversity has an important implication for the career-minded individual. To succeed in today's workplace, a person must be able to relate effectively to people from different cultural groups from within and outside his or her country. Being able to relate to a culturally diverse customer base is also necessary for success. Being skilled at cross-cultural relations is also an asset in personal life because of the diversity within the society.

This chapter presents concepts and techniques you can use to sharpen your ability to work effectively with people from diverse backgrounds. To get you started thinking about your readiness to work in a culturally diverse environment, take Self-Assessment Quiz 8-1.

THE DIVERSITY UMBRELLA

Improving cross-cultural relations includes understanding the true meaning of appreciating diversity. To appreciate diversity, a person must go beyond tolerating and treating people from different racial and ethnic groups fairly. The true meaning of valuing diversity is to respect and enjoy a wide range of cultural and individual differences. Appreciating these differences is often referred to as *inclusion* to emphasize unity rather than diversity. To be diverse is to be different in some measurable way, even if what is measurable is not visible (such as religion or sexual orientation).

LEARNING OBJECTIVE 1

To be highly skilled in interpersonal relations, one must recognize and appreciate individual and demographic (group or category) differences, as well as cultural differences. People from the same demographic group often come from many different cultures. For example, the Latino demographic group is composed of many different cultures. Some people are more visibly diverse than others because of physical features or disabilities. Yet the diversity umbrella is supposed to include everybody in an organization. To value diversity is therefore to appreciate individual differences among people.

Appreciating cultural diversity in organizations was originally aimed at assisting women and minorities. The diversity umbrella continues to include more people as the workforce encompasses a greater variety of people. For example, in recent years much attention has been paid to the rights of employees included in the group LGBT (lesbian, gay, bisexual, and transsexual). The rights of members of diverse religious groups are also receiving attention. At times, some of the religious groups may oppose the advances of the LGBT group.

A current concern among many US employers is to ensure that Muslims are both not disciminated against and welcomed as much as other ethnic, religious, and racial groups. Although Muslims constitute less than one percent of the US population, they can be a

Cross-Cultural Skills and Attitudes

Directions: Listed below are skills and attitudes that various employers and cross-cultural experts think are important for relating effectively to coworkers in a culturally diverse environment. For each of the statements, check applies to me now or not there yet.

	Applies to me now	Not there yet
1. I have spent some time in another country.	___	___
2. At least one of my friends is deaf, blind, or uses a wheelchair.	___	___
3. Currency from other countries is as real as the currency from my own country.	___	___
4. I can read in a language other than my own.	___	___
5. I can speak in a language other than my own.	___	___
6. I can write in a language other than my own.	___	___
7. I can understand people speaking in a language other than my own.	___	___
8. I would be comfortable being supervised by a person with a sexual orientation different from mine.	___	___
9. My friends include people of races different from my own.	___	___
10. My friends include people of different ages.	___	___
11. I feel (or would feel) comfortable having a friend with a sexual orientation different from mine.	___	___
12. My attitude is that although another culture may be very different from mine, that culture is equally good.	___	___
13. I am willing to eat (or have eaten) food from other countries that is not served in my own country.	___	___
14. I would accept (or have already accepted) a work assignment of more than several months in another country.	___	___
15. I have a passport.	___	___
16. I know the approximate difference in value between the US dollar and the euro.	___	___
17. I know how many hours difference there is between my time zone and at least two other overseas time zones.	___	___
18. I do not tell jokes that deal with the subjects of race or ethnic background.	___	___
19. I have purposely visited a neighborhood, store, or entertainment event at which most of the people were of a different race than mine.	___	___
20. Martin Luther King Jr. Day is just as important as other American official holidays.	___	___

Interpretation: If you answered applies to me now to 12 or more of the preceding questions, you most likely function well in a multicultural work environment. If you answered not there yet to 12 or more of the questions, you need to develop more cross-cultural awareness and skills to work effectively in a multicultural work environment. You will notice that being bilingual gives you at least four points on this quiz.

highly visible target of discrimination. Many progressive employers have worked diligently to reduce tensions among Muslim and other workers. *Islamophobia* has been fostered by terrorism and wars against Muslim nations.[2]

Efforts have increased in recent years for the inclusion of people with physical, emotional, and intellectual disabilities. Accomodations for people of physical disabilities would include such measures as wheelchair accessible workspaces and standup desks for people with back problems.[3] An accomodation for an intellectual disability would include a less noisy and distracting work space for a person with an attention-deficit disorder.

FIGURE 8-1 The Diversity Umbrella

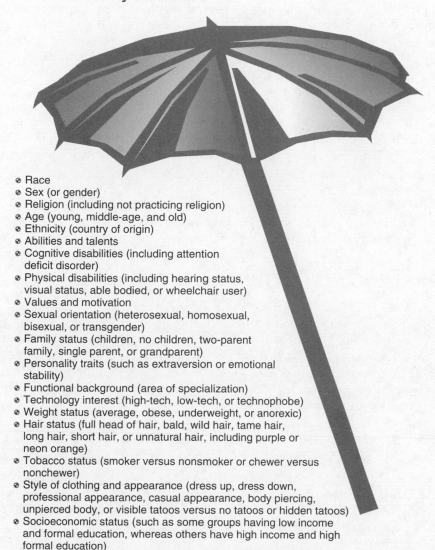

- Race
- Sex (or gender)
- Religion (including not practicing religion)
- Age (young, middle-age, and old)
- Ethnicity (country of origin)
- Abilities and talents
- Cognitive disabilities (including attention deficit disorder)
- Physical disabilities (including hearing status, visual status, able bodied, or wheelchair user)
- Values and motivation
- Sexual orientation (heterosexual, homosexual, bisexual, or transgender)
- Family status (children, no children, two-parent family, single parent, or grandparent)
- Personality traits (such as extraversion or emotional stability)
- Functional background (area of specialization)
- Technology interest (high-tech, low-tech, or technophobe)
- Weight status (average, obese, underweight, or anorexic)
- Hair status (full head of hair, bald, wild hair, tame hair, long hair, short hair, or unnatural hair, including purple or neon orange)
- Tobacco status (smoker versus nonsmoker or chewer versus nonchewer)
- Style of clothing and appearance (dress up, dress down, professional appearance, casual appearance, body piercing, unpierced body, or visible tatoos versus no tatoos or hidden tatoos)
- Socioeconomic status (such as some groups having low income and formal education, whereas others have high income and high formal education)

The goal of a diverse organization is for persons of all cultural backgrounds to achieve their full potential, not restrained by group identities such as gender, nationality, or race. Another important goal is for these groups to work together harmoniously.

Figure 8-1 presents a broad sampling of the ways in which workplace associates can differ from one another. Studying this list can help you anticipate the types of differences to understand and appreciate in a diverse workplace. The differences include cultural as well as individual factors. Individual factors are also important because people can be discriminated against for personal characteristics as well as group factors. Many people, for example, believe they are held back from promotion because of their weight-to-height ratio.

A diverse workforce is noted to have many consequences to the organization, mostly positive, but some negative. A sampling of these consequences is as follows:

- Multicultural experiences are strongly associated with creative thinking, and creative outcomes such as ideas for new products.[4] If you work with people from different cultures on the job or associate with them in personal life, your creativity is likely to be enhanced.

- A diverse workforce helps generate more profits through such means as having employees onboard who look similar to and share the same customs as their customers.[5] Allstate, Home Depot, and Walmart exemplify companies whose culturally diverse workforce helps them attract more customers.

- When employees and managers working for a large retailer perceive that a positive climate (atmosphere) for diversity exists, the store is likely to prosper. A one-year study of more than 650 store units at J. C. Penney found that the largest sales growth occurred in stores wherein subordinates and managers perceived highly pro-diversity climates. In contrast, the lowest sales growth was found in stores in which both managers and subordinates reported a less hospitable climate for diversity.[6]

- Cultural diversity within groups can sometimes lead to so much conflict and disagreement that productivity suffers. Diversity in educational background and age can also lead to conflict. However, a study in Germany found that in teams in which the need for intellectual stimulation was relatively high, team performance increased in the presence of diversity in educational experience and age.[7]

- A work environment perceived to be supportive of diversity is likely to foster more commitment to the organization, including a greater likelihood of staying with the firm. In contrast, perceived racial discrimination is negatively related to commitment to the firm and positively related to voluntary turnover. (A series of three studies with white, Latino, and black employees was the basis for these conclusions.)[8]

UNDERSTANDING CULTURAL DIFFERENCES

LEARNING OBJECTIVE 2

The groundwork for developing effective cross-cultural relations is to understand cultural differences. The information about different communication patterns between men and women presented in Chapter 4 is relevant here. Here we discuss six aspects of understanding cultural differences: (1) cultural sensitivity, including political correctness, (2) cultural intelligence, (3) respect for all workers, (4) cultural fluency, (5) dimensions of differences in cultural values, and (6) avoidance of cultural bloopers. To work smoothly with people from other cultures, it is important to become competent in all six areas.

Cultural Sensitivity and Political Correctness

In order to relate well to someone from a foreign country, a person must be alert to possible cultural differences. When working in another country, a person must be willing to acquire knowledge about local customs, and learn how to speak the native language at least passably. When working or socializing with people from different cultures, even from his or her own country, the person must be patient, adaptable, flexible, and willing to listen and learn.

cultural sensitivity

An awareness of and willingness to investigate the reasons why people of another culture act as they do.

The characteristics just mentioned are part of **cultural sensitivity**, an awareness of and willingness to investigate the reasons why individuals of another culture act as they do.[9] A person with cultural sensitivity will recognize certain nuances in customs that will help build better relationships from cultural backgrounds other than his or her own. A survey from *The Economist* showed that 73 percent of the respondents indicated that this cultural sensitivity is a top skill for global managers (those who manage in an international environment).[10]

Another aspect of cultural sensitivity is **political correctness:** being careful not to offend or slight anyone and being extra civil and respectful.[11] An effective use of political correctness would be to say, "We need a ladder in our department because we have workers of different heights who need access to the top shelves." It would be politically incorrect to say, "We need ladders because we have some short workers who cannot reach the top shelves." Carried too far, political correctness can push a person in the direction of being too bland and imprecise in language. The ultra-politically correct person, for example, will almost never mention a person's race, sex, ethnicity, or health status when referring to another worker. For example, the ultra-politically correct person would not make a statement like, "Sadie is German, so she was a natural to be our liaison with the manufacturing group." (The cultural stereotype here is that Germans are quite interested in manufacturing technology and think precisely.)

Ultra political correctness also involves using supposedly correct terms to describe people, even if a given individual rejects the label. For example, many black people are correctly referred to as "black" rather than "African-American," because they might be citizens of Africa, Haiti, England, etc. Also, the same people do not consider themselves to be African-American.

Empathy is a major trait and skill that facilitates cultural sensitivity and political correctness. You have to place yourself in the other person's perspective, and ask yourself questions like, "How would I like it if somebody snarled and said an ugly word when he or she looked at my favorite food?" Kim Oliver and Sylvester Baugh offer this insight into developing the type of empathy helpful in building cross-cultural relations in the workplace: "We want to try to develop an understanding for the majority about what it might be like to be the minority, and help the minority understand what it's like to be the majority."[12]

Cultural Intelligence

An advanced aspect of cultural sensitivity is to be able to fit in comfortably with people of another culture by observing the subtle cues they give about how a person should act in their presence. **Cultural intelligence (CQ)** is an outsider's ability to interpret someone's unfamiliar and ambiguous behavior the same way that person's compatriots would.[13] With high cultural intelligence, a person would be able to figure out what behavior would be true of all people and all groups, such as rapid shaking of a clenched fist to communicate anger. Also, the person with high cultural intelligence could figure out what is peculiar to this group, and those aspects of behavior that are neither universal nor peculiar to the group. These ideas are so abstract that an example will help clarify.

cultural intelligence (CQ)
An outsider's ability to interpret someone's unfamiliar and ambiguous behavior the same way that person's compatriots would.

> *An American sales representative for a company that manufactures large-scale earth-moving equipment was in conference in Seoul, South Korea to get final approval on additional design features that the Seoul company had demanded. The two key representatives of the company smiled and nodded their heads as the American made a PowerPoint presentation on the new features and their added cost. All went so well with his presentation that the American was surprised when the South Korean team did not agree to the terms of the new features at the end of the meeting. The South Korean representatives said they would need a few more weeks to evaluate the proposal.*
>
> *At first the American was upset that agreement was not reached depite the warm reception he was receiving. During dinner that night, the American's cultural intelligence kicked in. He thought to himself, "Maybe I went a little overboard in thinking that the South Korean team was so impressed with my presentation. I should have realized that South Korean businesspeople are polite and cordial. They don't like to appear rejecting until it comes time to sign the contract."*

Similar to emotional intelligence, cultural intelligence encompasses several aspects of behavior. The three sources of cultural intelligence relate to the cognitive, emotional/motivational, and the physical, shown in Figure 8-2, and explained as follows:[14]

1. **Cognitive (the Head):** The cognitive part of CQ refers to what a person knows and how he or she can acquire new knowledge. Here you acquire facts about people from another culture such as their passion for football (soccer in North America), their business practices, and their promptness in paying bills. Another aspect of this source of cultural intelligence is figuring out how you can learn more about the other culture.

2. **Emotional/Motivational (the Heart):** The emotional/motivational aspect of CQ refers to energizing one's actions and building personal confidence. You need both confidence and motivation to adapt to another culture. A man on a business trip to Africa might say to himself, "When I greet a work associate in a restaurant, can I really pull off kissing him on both cheeks? What if he thinks I'm weird?" With strong motivation, the same person might say, "I'll give it a try. I kind of greet my grandfather the same way back in the United States."

3. **Physical (the Body):** The body aspect of CQ is the action component. The body is the element for translating intentions into actions and desires. Kissing the same-sex African work associates on both cheeks is the *physical* aspect just mentioned.

FIGURE 8-2   The Components of Cultural Intelligence

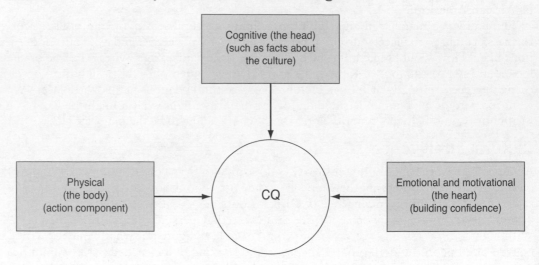

We often have an idea of what we should do, but implementation is not so easy. You might know, for example, that when entering an Asian person's home you should take off your shoes, yet you might not actually remove them, thereby, offending your Asian work (or personal life) associate.

To practice high cultural intelligence, the mind, heart, and body have to work together. You need to figure out how to act with people from another culture, you need motivation and confidence to change, and you have to translate your knowledge and motivation into action. So when you are on a business trip to London, go ahead and hold your fork in your left hand!

Respect for All Workers and Cultures

An effective strategy for achieving cross-cultural understanding is to simply respect all others in the workplace, including their cultures. Respecting people from other cultures works equally well in personal life. An example is not joking about the fact that an acquaintance of yours puts his head on the floor to pray.

An important component of respect is to believe that although another person's culture is different from yours, it is equally good. Respect comes from valuing differences. Respecting other people's customs can translate into specific attitudes, such as respecting one coworker for wearing a yarmulke on Friday or another for wearing African clothing to celebrate Kwanzaa. Another way of being respectful would be to listen carefully to the opinion of a senior worker who says the company should never have converted to voice-mail and a voice recognition system in place of assistants answering the phone (even though you disagree).

Jacobs Stock Photography/Photodisc/
Getty Images

An aspect of respecting all workers that achieves current attention is the importance of respecting the rights of majorities, particularly white males. Many of these men want to be involved in—not excluded from—bringing about cultural diversity in organizations. For example, they might want to mentor minority group members.

Company policies that encourage respect for the rights of others are likely to create a positive influence on tolerance throughout the firm. An example is that many employers have taken steps to recognize and affirm the existence of gay and lesbian workers. Among these steps are publishing formal statements of nondiscrimination and the inclusion of issues about sexual orientation in diversity training programs. A major policy change has been to grant same-sex couples the

Developing Cultural Sensitivity

Ask a few people from other countries, in-person or electronically, what they consider to be a couple of the most unusual practices from your country that they have heard about or read about. Also gently inquire as to why the practice is perceived to be unusual. Collaborate with classmates to compile the list. After the list and the explanations are compiled, reflect on how this exercise enhanced your cultural sensitivity. For your curiosity, here is an example:

A network member from Morocco, living in the United States said, "I don't understand why so many Americans speak only one language. Almost all children from educated families in Morocco grow up speaking Arabic and French, and many of us also speak English. Don't you Americans have enough time to learn another language?"

same benefits granted to opposite-sex couples. Later legislation in many states and provinces made such a policy mandatory.

Another formal (official) way of demonstrating respect for all workers is to provide for the presence of **employee network** (or **affinity**) **groups**. Such a group is composed of employees throughout the company who affiliate on the basis of group characteristics, such as race, ethnicity, gender, sexual orientation, or physical ability status. The network group provides members of the same demographic or cultural group with an avenue for sharing ideas with management. An example of such a group would be the Hispanic Employee Network at McDonald's. A study of 537 gay and lesbian employees working for a variety of organizations demonstrated that the more prevalent policies dealing with respect, the more equitably sexual minorities are likely to be treated at work. More equitable treatment, in turn, was associated with gays and lesbians being more satisfied and less likely to leave the firm.[15]

Skill-Building Exercise 8-1 is a warm-up activity for achieving cultural sensitivity and, perhaps, respect for all workers.

cultural fluency

The ability to conduct business in a diverse, international environment.

Digital Vision/Thinkstock

Cultural Fluency

A high-level goal in understanding cultural differences is to achieve **cultural fluency**, the ability to conduct business in a diverse, international environment.[16] Achieving cultural fluency includes a variety of skills, such as relating well to people from different cultures and knowing a second language. Cultural fluency also includes knowledge of the international business environment, such as how the exchange rate can affect profits. Having high cultural intelligence would contribute to cultural fluency because such intelligence makes it easier to work well with people from other cultures. If you are culturally fluent, you will also find it easier to make friends (real and virtual) from other cultures.

Dimensions of Differences in Cultural Values

One way to understand how national cultures differ is to examine their values or cultural dimensions. The formulation presented here is based on the worldwide research in 62 societal cultures and builds on previous analyses of cultural dimensions.[17] The cultural dimensions presented here are those most directly related to interpersonal skills. Keep in mind that these cultural dimensions are stereotypes that apply to a representative person from a particular culture and are not meant to insult anybody. These cultural dimensions are differences between national societies and may not be representative of a given individual. As with gender stereotypes in communication, individual differences are substantial. For example, many Americans are not asscrtive, and many French are willing to work 70 hours per week.

1. **Performance orientation** is the degree to which a society encourages, or should encourage, and rewards group members for performance improvement and excellence. Countries high on this dimension are the United States and Singapore, whereas those low on this dimension are Russia and Greece.

2. **Assertiveness** is the degree to which individuals are (and should be) assertive, confrontational, and aggressive in their relationships with one another. Countries scoring high on this dimension are the United States and Austria, whereas those low on this dimension are Sweden and New Zealand. Assertive people enjoy competition in business, in contrast to less assertive cultural groups who prefer harmony, loyalty, and solidarity.

3. **Time orientation** is the importance nations and individuals attach to time. People with an urgent time orientation perceive time as a scarce resource and tend to be impatient. People with a casual time orientation view time as an unlimited and unending resource and tend to be patient. Americans are noted for their urgent time orientation. They frequently impose deadlines and are eager to get started doing business. Asians, Mexicans, and Middle Easterners, in contrast, are patient negotiators.

4. **Humane orientation** is the degree to which a society encourages and rewards, and should encourage and reward, individuals for being fair, altruistic, caring, and kind toward others. Egypt and Malaysia rank high on this cultural dimension, and France and Germany rank low.

5. **In-group collectivism** is the degree to which individuals express, and should express, pride, loyalty, and cohesiveness in their organizations and families. Asian societies emphasize collectivism, as do Egypt and Russia. One consequence of collectivism is taking pride in family members and the organizations that employ them.

6. **Gender egalitarianism** is the degree to which a culture minimizes, and should minimize, gender inequality. European countries emphasize gender egalitarianism, and so do the United States and Canada. South Korea is an example of a country that is low on gender egalitarianism and is male dominated.

7. **Acceptance of power and authority** is the degree to which members of a society expect, and should expect, power to be distributed unequally. Individuals who accept power and authority expect the boss to make the major decisions. These same individuals are more formal; however, being formal toward people in positions of authority has decreased substantially throughout the world in recent years. Examples of societies that score high on acceptance of power and authority are Thailand, Brazil, France, and Japan.

8. **Work orientation** is the number of hours per week and weeks per year people expect to invest in work versus leisure or other nonwork activities. American corporate professionals typically work about 55 hours per week, take 45-minute lunch breaks, and two weeks of vacation. Americans tend to have a stronger work orientation than Europeans, but a weaker one than Asians. US employees average 1,797 hours of work per year, compared with 1,336 for Dutch workers and 1,392 for the French. Workers in South Korea were on the job about 2,193 hours per year.[18]

9. **Social support seeking** is the degree to which people seek out others to help them with difficult problems through such means as listening, offering sympathy, and giving advice. Asians and Asian-Americans are more reluctant to explicitly request support from close others than are European Americans. The hesitancy comes about because the Asians and Asian-Americans are more concerned about negative relationship consequences, such as disrupting group harmony or receiving criticism from the other person. Another possible reason for the hesitancy is that Asians and Asian-Americans expect social support without having to ask.[19]

An analysis of 600 studies about cultural values, stemming three decades, arrived at a few conclusions for better understanding human relations on the job.[20] First, an individual's cultural value profile is more important in understanding how that person will behave than the typical value for his or her profile. For example, South Koreans may in general have high respect for power and authority, but your coworker Helen Kim might be more egalitarian. Second, cultural values may have a stronger effect on job behavior for workers who are older rather than younger, male rather than female, and for more highly educated workers. Third, cultural values have their biggest impact on job behavior when certain emotional responses, beliefs, and attitudes are critical to the position. For example, a humane orientation would usually be helpful in customer service positions. Fourth, cultural values are more predictive of how workers behave from culturally tighter rather than looser cultures. A tight culture is more homogeneous with respect to values, whereas a loose culture is more heterogeneous. Also, social norms are stronger in a tight culture, such as India or Singapore, rather than in a loose culture, such as the United States or Canada.

How might someone use information about cultural differences to improve his or her interpersonal relations on the job? A starting point would be to recognize that a person's national values might influence his or her behavior. Assume that you wanted to establish a good working relationship with a person from a high humane-orientation culture. An effective starting point would be to emphasize care and concern when communicating with the individual.

Attitudes toward acceptance of power and authority can make a difference in establishing working relationships. A worker who values deference to age, gender, or title might shy away from offering suggestions to an elder or manager to avoid appearing disrespectful. This worker would need considerable encouragement to collaborate in decision making.[21] *Time-orientation* may create a conflict if you are committed to making deadlines and a team member has a laid-back attitude toward time. You might explain that although you respect his attitudes toward time, the company insists on getting the project completed on time.

Self-Assessment Quiz 8-2 will help you think about how cultural dimensions might be influencing your interpersonal relations in the workplace.

Cultural Bloopers

An effective way of being culturally sensitive is to minimize actions that are likely to offend people from another culture based on their values. Cultural bloopers are most likely to take place when you are visiting another country. The same bloopers, however, can also be committed with people from a different culture within your own country. To avoid these bloopers, you must carefully observe persons from another culture. Studying another culture through reading is also helpful.

E-commerce and other forms of Internet communication have created new opportunities for creating cultural bloopers. The Web site developers and workers responsible for adding content must have good cross-cultural literacy, including an awareness of how the information might be misinterpreted.

- Numerical date formats can be readily misinterpreted. To an American, 4/9/16 would be interpreted as April 9, 2016 (or 1916!). However, many Europeans would interpret the same numerical expression as September 4, 2016.
- Colors on Web sites must be chosen carefully. For example, in some cultures purple is the color of royalty, whereas in Brazil purple is associated with death.
- Be careful of metaphors that may not make sense to a person for whom your language is a second language. Examples include "We've encountered an ethical meltdown" and "Our biggest competitor is over the hill."

English has become the language of business and science throughout the world, yet communicating in a customer's native tongue has its advantages. Being able to communicate your message directly in your customer's mother tongue provides a competitive advantage. Bilingualism also has career implications. Some telemarketing, banking, engineering, and financial service companies are searching for workers with bilingual skills. The two major contributing factors are the growing immigrant population in the United States that companies are engaged more in international business.[22]

Charting Your Cultural Dimension Profile

Directions: For each of the nine cultural dimensions, circle the number that most accurately fits your standing on the dimension. For example, if you perceive yourself to be highly humane, circle 2 on the fourth dimension (item 4).

1. High performance orientation   Low performance orientation

   1   2   3   4   5   6   7

2. Low assertiveness   High assertiveness

   1   2   3   4   5   6   7

3. Urgent time orientation   Casual time orientation

   1   2   3   4   5   6   7

4. High humane orientation   Low humane orientation

   1   2   3   4   5   6   7

5. In-group collectivism   In-group individualism

   1   2   3   4   5   6   7

6. High gender egalitarianism   Low gender egalitarianism

   1   2   3   4   5   6   7

7. High acceptance of power and authority   Low acceptance of power and authority

   1   2   3   4   5   6   7

8. Work orientation   Leisure orientation

   1   2   3   4   5   6   7

9. Social support seeking   Social support avoidance

   1   2   3   4   5   6   7

Scoring and Interpretation: After circling one number for each dimension, use a pen or pencil to connect the circles, thereby giving yourself a profile of cultural values. Do not be concerned if your line cuts through the names of the dimensions. Compare your profile to others in the class. Should time allow, develop a class profile by computing the class average for each of the nine points and then connecting the points.

Furthermore, according to the research firm International Data Corporation (IDC), consumers are four times more likely to purchase a product online if the Web site is in their preferred language.[23] Many Web sites give the viewer a language choice, but seeing the site at first glance in one's native language is still generally more compelling. The translator, of course, must have good knowledge of the subtleties of the language to avoid a blooper. An English-to-French translator used the verb *baiser* instead of *baisser* to describe a program of lowering prices. *Baisser* is the French verb "to lower," whereas *baiser* is the verb "to kiss." Worse, in slang *baiser* is a verb that refers to having intimate physical relationships!

Keep two key facts in mind when attempting to avoid cultural mistakes. One is that members of any cultural group show individual differences. What one member of the group might regard as an insensitive act, another might welcome. Recognize also that one or two cultural mistakes will not peg you permanently as a boor. Skill-Building Exercise 8-2 will help you minimize certain cultural bloopers.

OVERCOMING CROSS-CULTURAL COMMUNICATION BARRIERS

LEARNING OBJECTIVE 3

We have already discussed the importance of overcoming communication barriers in Chapter 4. Cultural differences create additional barriers. Here are some guidelines for overcoming cross-cultural communication barriers.

1. **Be sensitive to the fact that cross-cultural communication barriers exist.** If you are aware of these potential barriers, you will be ready to deal with them. When you are dealing with a person in the workplace with a different cultural background than

Cultural Mistakes to Avoid with Selected Cultural Groups

EUROPE

Great Britain
- Asking personal questions. The British protect their privacy.
- Thinking that a businessperson from England is unenthusiastic when he or she says, "Not bad at all." English people understate their positive emotion.
- Gossiping about royalty.

France
- Expecting to complete work during the French two-hour lunch.
- Attempting to conduct significant business during August—*les vacances* (vacation time).
- Greeting a French person for the first time and not using a title such as "sir," or "madam," or "miss" (*monsieur, madame,* or *mademoiselle*).

Italy
- Eating too much pasta, as it is not the main course.
- Handing out business cards freely. Italians use them infrequently.

Spain
- Expecting punctuality. Your appointments will usually arrive 20 to 30 minutes late.
- Making the American sign for "okay" with your thumb and forefinger. In Spain (and many other countries) this is vulgar.

Scandinavia (Denmark, Sweden, Norway)
- Being overly rank conscious. Scandinavians pay relatively little attention to a person's rank in the hierarchy.

ASIA

All Asian countries
- Pressuring an Asian job applicant or employee to brag about his or her accomplishments. Asians feel self-conscious when boasting about individual accomplishments; they prefer to let the record speak for itself. In addition, they prefer to talk about group rather than individual accomplishment.

Japan
- Shaking hands or hugging Japanese (as well as other Asians) in public. Japanese consider these practices to be offensive.
- Not interpreting "We'll consider it" as a "no" when spoken by a Japanese businessperson. Japanese negotiators mean "no" when they say "We'll consider it."
- Not giving small gifts to Japanese when conducting business. Japanese are offended by not receiving these gifts.
- Giving your business card to a Japanese businessperson more than once. Japanese prefer to give and receive business cards only once.

China
- Not taking a business card presented to you seriously, such as quickly stuffing it in your pocket.
- Using a strong handshake instead of a limp one. Insisting on a handshake rather than a polite bow.
- Giving expensive gifts, because this may obligate the person to reciprocate with something of equal value to you. Giving a clock can sometimes backfire, because the Mandarin word for "to give clocks" resembles "to attend to a dying relative."
- Making cold calls on Chinese business executives. An appropriate introduction is required for a first-time meeting with a Chinese official.

Korea
- Saying no. Koreans feel it is important to have visitors leave with good feelings.

India
- Telling Indians you prefer not to eat with your hands. If the Indians are not using cutlery when eating, they expect you to do likewise.

Thailand
- Pointing the sole of your shoes toward another person. (It's not so cool in other countries also.) Be aware of this potential mistake when sitting.

MEXICO AND LATIN AMERICA

Mexico
- Flying into a Mexican city in the morning and expecting to close a deal by lunch. Mexicans build business relationships slowly.

Brazil
- Attempting to impress Brazilians by speaking a few words of Spanish. Portuguese is the official language of Brazil.

Most Latin American countries
- Wearing elegant and expensive jewelry during a business meeting. Latin Americans think people should appear more conservative during a business meeting.

Note: A cultural mistake for Americans to avoid when conducting business in most countries outside the United States and Canada is to insist on getting down to business quickly. North Americans in small towns also like to build a relationship before getting down to business. The preceding suggestions will lead to cross-cultural skill development if practiced in the right setting. During the next 30 days, look for an opportunity to relate to a person from another culture in the way described in these suggestions. Observe the reaction of the other person for feedback on your cross-cultural effectiveness.

Source: Two of the items about China are from Eric Spitsnagel, "Impress Your Chinese Boss," *Bloomberg Businessweek,* January 16, 2012, pp. 80–81.

yours, solicit feedback in order to minimize cross-cultural barriers to communication. Being aware of these potential barriers will help you develop cultural sensitivity.

2. **Show respect for all workers.** The same behavior that promotes good cross-cultural relations in general helps overcome communication barriers. A widely used comment that implies disrespect is to say to a person from another culture, "You have a funny accent." Should you be transposed to that person's culture, you too might have a "funny accent."

3. **Use straightforward language and speak slowly and clearly.** When working with people who do not speak your language fluently, speak in an easy-to-understand manner. Minimize the use of idioms and analogies specific to your language. For example, "tabling an idea" means rejecting an idea in some English-speaking countries, yet means putting the idea on the table for discussion in others.

4. **Observe cultural differences in etiquette.** Violating rules of etiquette without explanation can erect immediate communication barriers. A major rule of etiquette in many countries is that people address superiors by their last name unless they have worked together for a long time. Or the superior might encourage being on a first-name basis with him or her. Be aware that an increasing number of cultures are moving toward addressing each other and customers by using the first name only. Yet, it is best to err on the side of formality.

   Another key aspect of cross-cultural etiquette is to observe and implement the appropriate greeting. Among these greetings are handshakes, kisses on the cheek, hugs, and bows. Touching is also a touchy subject. Observe carefully whether it seems appropriate to touch the other person in some way, such as a back pat or a fist bump on another person's elbow or shoulder.[24]

5. **Be sensitive to differences in nonverbal communication.** Stay alert to the possibility that a person from another culture may misinterpret your nonverbal signal. Hand signals of various types, such as a thumb up or the okay sign to indicate acceptance, are the most liable to misinterpretation. Another key area of cross-cultural differences in nonverbal communication is the handshake. In some cultures, a woman is expected to extend her hand first to shake with a man. In other cultures, people hug, embrace, or bow instead of shaking hands. (With good cultural sensitivity and cultural intelligence, you can figure out what to do when meeting another person.)

   Behavioral mirroring, as described in Chapter 4, is another example of how the effectiveness of nonverbal behavior might be influenced by the other person's culture. Three experiments with bank managers required Anglos and Latinos to interact with an interviewer who was trained to mirror the behavior of the interviewee. It was found that Latino interviewees rated interviewers higher who used behavioral mirroring. Also, the Latinos experienced more anxiety when the interviewer did not mirror their behavior.[25] The intercultural explanation for these findings is that Latinos, as a group, value nonverbal behavior more than do Anglos. The implication of the experiment for cross-cultural communication is to attempt to determine if you are making appropriate use of nonverbal communication techniques when interacting with a person from another culture.

6. **Do not be diverted by style, accent, grammar, or personal appearance.** Although these superficial factors are all related to business success, they are difficult to interpret when judging a person from another culture. It is therefore better to judge the merits of the statement or behavior. A brilliant individual from another culture may still be learning your language and may thus make basic mistakes in speaking your language. Also, he or she might not yet have developed a sensitivity to dress style in your culture.

7. **Be attentive to individual differences in appearance.** A major intercultural insult is to confuse the identity of people because they are members of the same race or ethnic group. An older economics professor reared in China and teaching in the United States had difficulty communicating with students because he was unable to learn their names. The professor's defense was, "So many of these Americans look alike to me." Research suggests that people have difficulty seeing individual differences among people of another race because they code race first, such as thinking "He has the nose of an African-American." However, people can learn to search for more distinguishing features, such as a dimple or eye color.[26] In this way, individual differences are recognized.

8. **Pronounce correctly the names of people you interact with from other countries.** Communication is much smoother when you correctly pronounce the name of

another person. For many Americans, this is a challenging task because they are accustomed to names with one or two syllables that are easy to pronounce, such as Bob or Ann. A trouble spot for many people whose only language is English is that "H" and "J" might be silent in another language.[27] Suppose one of your work or personal associates has the first name "Hyuntak." After listening to his name for the first time, develop a phonetic spelling that will help you pronounce the name in the future. (How about "High-oon-tack"?)

9. **Be aware of key words that could be objectionable in another country or culture.** A challenge for the cross-cultural worker is that occasionally a key word in one's culture may be unacceptable in another culture, thereby weakening your central message. An HR (human resources) consultant was launching a program for helping employees—an employee assistance program—in Russia. Using the word "assistance" might hurt the presentation because the notion of seeking help in Russia carries a certain stigma. The HR specialist framed its services to Russian workers as "support."[28] (Note that the HR specialist sought assistance in choosing the best word to sell the assistance program.)

TECHNIQUES FOR IMPROVING CROSS-CULTURAL RELATIONS

LEARNING OBJECTIVE 4

Many training programs have been developed to improve cross-cultural relations and to help workers value diversity. All of the information presented so far in this chapter is likely to be included in such programs. In this section, we describe programs for improving cross-cultural relations, including cultural training, recognizing your own cultural biases, cultural intelligence training, language training, diversity training, and cross-cultural mentoring.

Cultural Training

For many years, companies and government agencies have prepared their workers for overseas assignments. The method most frequently chosen is **cultural training,** a set of learning experiences designed to help employees understand the customs, traditions, and beliefs of another culture. In today's diverse business environment and international marketplace, learning about individuals raised in different cultural backgrounds has become more important. Many industries therefore train employees in cross-cultural relations.

cultural training

A set of learning experiences designed to help employees understand the customs, traditions, and beliefs of another culture.

Cultural training is also important for helping people of one culture understand their customers from another culture in particular, such as Chinese people learning to deal more effectively with their American customers. For example, in one training program Chinese businesspeople are taught how to sprinkle their e-mail with English phrases like "How are you?" "It was great to hear from you," and "Can we work together?"[29]

The Job-Oriented Interpersonal Skills in Action box describes how cultural training can improve the effectiveness of establishing call centers overseas.

To practice improving your cross-cultural relations, do Skill-Building Exercise 8-3.

Recognize Your Own Cultural and Demographic Biases

A potential barrier to working smoothly with people from cultures other than our own is an almost unconscious tendency to react positively or negatively toward those people from a particular cultural or demographic group. Let us begin with a seemingly harmless example. Your positive bias toward Chinese people is that they have exceptional quantitative skills. One day at the office, you are trying to divide some fractions by other fractions (such as dividing 4/8 by 2/3) using a calculator. Your first impulse is to ask Li, a Chinese-American coworker, to help you with the calculation. An example of a negative bias is a person rejecting a job offer because his or her supervisor would be a person of about age 70. The bias might be that the applicant perceives an older person as intellectually slow, living in the past, and technology challenged.

Research conducted with customer satisfaction evaluations supports the idea that many people have biases related to workplace interactions. One study involved satisfaction

Mexican Call Center Workers Learn to Deal Effectively with Americans

In a high-rise office building, one dozen young Mexicans are studying the customs of a country most of them have never visited. One by one, the students present their conclusions about the United States. "Americans think Mexicans eat mostly tacos and drink margaritas everyday. They give big tips if they like you. Unless they are Latino-Americans, they probably speak only one language," says Maria. "People are self-centered. The average American uses a credit card even to pay for lunch in a restaurant," says Hugo.

The Mexicans, who range in age from 20 to 29, have been hired to take calls from confused or angry Americans who are having a functional problem with their prepaid cell phone or smartphone. The problem could be technical, or it could relate to a customer service problem such as their prepaid minutes not being accurately recorded or their phone being shut down. The phone company works on a slim profit margin, so it cannot afford to maintain a tech support and customer service center in the United States. The company offers a Web site for providing technical support and customer service, yet many customers feel the need to interact with a live person.

To communicate with the Americans, the Mexican workers must communicate in their second language and a culture that is foreign. "We're not saying that Mexico is better or the United States is better," says their trainer, Tanya. "We just want our tech support staff to develop cultural awareness so there is better rapport when someone calls in for help."

Call centers for inexpensive cell phone service took root in Mexico when the demand for mobile phones skyrocketed in the mid-2000s, yet many people did not have good enough credit to purchase traditional cell phone service. Large prepaid cell phone and smartphone providers like Tracfone wanted to provide the best tech support they could, yet still remain profitable.

At first, training at the tech support centers and customer service centers was simple. The centers gave employees names that were easy for Americans to understand such as Pedro, Suzie, Maria, and Bob in cases where they had names difficult for Americans to pronounce. The new hires were instructed to watch American television shows to get an idea of American pop culture. In this way, if there was a waiting period during the help session, they could make a few minutes of small talk.

Shortly after the support center was established, problems in dealing with the Americans began to surface. Although the customers were paying the minimum price possible for cell phone or smartphone service, they were often quite demanding and aggressive. One man swore at the customer service rep because he couldn't figure out how to use his phone to make a call to Ontario, Canada. Roberta, the recipient of the outrage, attempted to explain that instructions on how to telephone Canada from the United States are presented on page 8 of the manual that comes with the phone. A woman kept calling another rep a "stupid fool" because the rep couldn't understand her problem having to do with not being credited for enough minutes.

The Mexican support staff felt uncomfortable in being too firm with belligerent customers. Instead of being assertive about the company's position on a particular problem, the reps tended to be too conciliatory, often blaming the company for the problem; however, being conciliatory did not result in customers being totally satisfied. Problems were often left unresolved. As a result, the prepaid cell phone service company noticed that renewal rates were slipping. A renewal in this sense is a customer purchasing more minutes at a store or through the company Web site.

The cell phone and smartphone company hired a firm that offers cultural training to help the Mexican call center workers deal more effectively with upset American customers. (Tanya was the trainer assigned to the account.) The workers were given careful instructions on how to express sympathy, using phrases such as "I am sorry that you are having this problem. I know that your phone is important to you." When a customer is explosively angry, the call center workers were coached on how to let the customer finish the outburst, and then say, "I hear that you are upset. But let us see how we can get this problem solved."

New hires as well as experienced employees were also taught to defend the company when the company is right. For example, to fix a technical problem such as the voicemail feature not working, the caller usually has to key in a long series of numbers. A frustrated customer often has difficulty with such a task. To deal with the frustration, the call center worker is taught to say something like, "Please try entering the numbers again slowly and carefully." If the customer enters the sequence of numbers incorrectly again, the worker is coached on how to be assertive, such as "This method does work. If you want to fix your phone, you have to do it carefully."

Many customer complaints that get back to the company deal with not being able to understand the English spoken by the call center workers, so the Mexican workers are coached on how to speak key English words with a general American accent. For example, instead of saying "She-ca-go" for "Chicago," the worker is taught to say "Sha-ca-go." And the workers are coached to pronounce "nine" as "nyne" instead of "neen."

Questions

1. What do you see as a major cultural difference between Mexicans and Americans that make the call center job so challenging for Mexicans?
2. Some of the call center representatives in Mexico are instructed to identify themselves as students in Kansas City, in addition to giving them American first names. What is your take on the ethics of these disguises?

Source: Case history collected from a human resource specialist at the mobile phone company in question.

---

ratings with physicians, 38 percent of whom were women, and 11.5 percent of whom were ethnic minorities. In the survey of patients, each physician was rated by an average of 107 patients. The medical service organization, an HMO, had objective data available about the performance of physicians. No significant differences were found in performance based on physician race and gender. Another study was conducted at a large country-club organization. A third study was conducted with college students, using a simulated college bookstore. The overall results of the three studies indicated that customers tended to be less satisfied with the services provided by women and nonwhite employees in contrast to the services provided by men and white employees. The team of

SKILL-BUILDING EXERCISE 8-3

Cross-Cultural Relations Role-Play

One student plays the role of Ritu, a call center representative in New Delhi, India. Her specialty is helping customers with cell phone and smartphone problems. Another student plays the role of Todd, an irate American. His problem is that he cannot get his camera-equipped phone to transmit his photos over e-mail. He is scheduled to attend a party in two hours and wants to take loads of photos with his smartphone. Todd is impatient and, in the eyes of Ritu, somewhat overbearing. Ritu is good natured and pleasant, but feels she must help Todd solve his problem without being bullied by him. Because Ritu is instructed to spend the minimum time necessary to resolve the problem, she spends about five minutes on this problem.

The observers should make note of how well Ritu has made the necessary cross-cultural adaptations.

researchers concluded that customer satisfaction evalutations are biased because they are anonymous judgments by untrained raters who may lack an evaluation standard.[30]

We may not be able to control all our biases toward cultural and demographic groups, but awareness can lead to a reduction and control of these biases. Suppose you and your spouse or partner decided to place your house on the market for sale. Instead of choosing a real estate agent based on a bias (such as the idea that an attractive woman in her forties makes the best agent), you would choose an agent based on prior sales performance.

Self-Assessment Quiz 8-3 offers you an opportunity to think about the cultural biases you might have.

SELF-ASSESSMENT QUIZ 8-3

The Personal Biases and Prejudices Checklist

Check whether each of the attitudes, beliefs, and actions in the following list are generally true or generally false for you. Responding to this checklist is difficult, because you are required to be objective and honest about your biases and prejudices.

No.	Statement about Biases and Prejudices in Relation to People	GENERALLY TRUE	GENERALLY FALSE
1.	I can imagine a woman being an effective president of the United States.	_____	_____
2.	I would feel comfortable if my boss were four feet in height.	_____	_____
3.	I would be fearful of any woman wearing a covering over her face in an airport.	_____	_____
4.	It makes sense to charge higher interest rates for loans and mortgages to minority group members, even if their credit rating is above average.	_____	_____
5.	If I or a loved one needed brain surgery, I would want the surgery performed only by a male, Caucasian brain surgeon.	_____	_____
6.	During a major athletic contest, such as a basketball or soccer game, I would want a black person to take the game-deciding shot.	_____	_____
7.	I would prefer not to be a passenger on an airplane if the pilot were older than age 50.	_____	_____
8.	My like or dislike for President Barack Obama had (or has) nothing to do with his being African-American (or mixed race).	_____	_____
9.	When I am uncertain about a person's race or ethnic background, I often ask, "What are you?"	_____	_____
10.	If I needed a financial planner, I would never hire one who was under age 35.	_____	_____

Scoring and Interpretation: Give yourself one point for the following answers: generally true to questions 3, 4, 5, 6, 7, 9, and 10; generally false to questions 1, 2, and 8. If you scored 5 or more points, you most likely have biases and prejudices that hold you back a little from having strong cross-cultural relations. If you scored between 0 and 4, you are likely to be perceived as an unbiased person, and one whose biases and prejudices create very few problems in interpersonal relationships. Being perceived as unbiased and unprejudiced could facilitate you getting along well with coworkers and being selected for a leadership position. A caution is that it quite difficult to be honest with oneself about one's level of bias and prejudice, so perhaps take this quiz again in one week.

Cultural Intelligence Training

An advanced method assisting people to work more effectively with workers in other cultures is *cultural intelligence training*, a program based on the principles of cultural intelligence described earlier in this chapter. A key part of the training is to learn the three contributors to CQ—head, heart, and body. Instead of learning a few simple guidelines for working effectively with people from another culture, the trainee is taught strategies for sizing up the environment to determine which course of action is best. The culturally intelligent overseas worker would learn how to determine how much humor to interject into meetings, what kind of handshake is most appropriate, and so forth.[31] The following excerpt will give you a feel for what is involved in cultural intelligence training:

> *An American manager, Leah, is visiting a large food company in Tijuana, Mexico. Her goal is to work out some details in a contract for the Mexican company to supply Mexican food to the American food distributor that Leah represents. Her main contact is the marketing director, Carlos. Leah has been taught in cultural intelligence training that she must first gather facts about the Mexican business culture, such as their preference for relationship building before concluding a deal. Leah must also focus on the emotional/motivational aspect of cultural intelligence, such as being confident that she can use her limited knowledge of Spanish to add a warm note to the negotiations. Next, Leah focuses on the body (physical) aspect of conducting business with a Mexican in Mexico. Leah notes that a firm handshake followed by a respectful hug goes a long way in cementing a business relationhsip in Tiujuana. So as negotiations conclude favorably, she shakes hands with Carlos, hugs him, and adds a respectful kiss on the cheek. Olé.*

As the example illustrates, to be culturally intelligent you need to apply cognitive skills, have the right motivation, and then put your knowledge and confidence into action. Armed with such skills you would know, for example, whether to greet a Mexican worker on a business trip to Texas with a handshake, a hug, or a kiss on both cheeks.

Language Training

Learning a foreign language is often part of cultural training, yet it can also be a separate activity. Knowledge of a second language is important because it builds better connections with people from other cultures than does relying on a translator. Building connections with people is still important even if English has become the international language of business. Many workers, aside from international business specialists, also choose to develop skills in a target language. Speaking another language can help build rapport with customers and employees who speak that language. It is easier to sell to customers when using their native language, unless they prefer to conduct business in your language.

Almost all language training has elements similar to taking a course in another language or self-study. Companies invest heavily in helping employees learn a target language because it facilitates conducting business in other countries. For this reason, companies that offer language training and translation services are currently experiencing a boom. Medical specialists, police officers, and firefighters also find second language skills to be quite helpful because clients under stress, such as an injured person, are likely to revert to their native tongue. Learning a second language is particularly important when many of your customers and employees do not speak your country's official language. For example, English-speaking managers in Texas, Arizona, and California might not be able to communicate with Spanish-speaking employees regarding benefits and other issues.

As with any other skill training, investments in language training can pay off only if the trainee is willing to work hard at developing the new skill outside the training sessions. Allowing even 10 days to pass without practicing your target language will result in a sharp decline in your ability to use that language.

Skill-Building Exercise 8-4 presents a low-cost, pleasant method of enhancing your foreign language and cross-cultural skills.

Using the Internet to Help Develop Foreign Language Skills

A useful way of developing skills in another language, and learning more about another culture, is to create a computer "bookmark," "favorite," or front page written in your target language. In this way, each time you go to the Internet on your own computer, your cover page will contain fresh information in the language you want to develop.

Enter a search phrase such as "Italian newspaper" or "Spanish language newspaper" in the search probe. After you find a suitable choice, enter the edit function for "Favorites" or "Bookmarks" and insert that newspaper as your front page. For example, imagine that French is your target language and

culture. The search engine might have brought you to the site http://www.france2.fr. This Web site keeps you abreast of French and international news, sports, and cultural events—written in French, along with videos. Every time you access the Internet, you can spend five minutes on your second language in both writing and speaking, thereby becoming multicultural. You can save a lot of travel costs and time using the Internet to help you become multicultural, including developing proficiency in another language. You might be able to find an app for your smartphone for learning another language by linking to an appropriate Web site.

Diversity Training

The general purpose of cultural training is to help workers understand people from other cultures. Understanding can lead to dealing more effectively with them as work associates or customers. **Diversity training** has a slightly different purpose. It attempts to bring about workplace harmony by teaching people how to get along better with diverse work associates. Quite often the program is aimed at minimizing open expressions of racism and sexism. In recent years, diversity training has acquired the additional goal of accepting all dimensions of diversity based on the belief that enhanced business performance will result. For example, learning how to relate effectively to diverse customers can increase sales.[32]

diversity training

Training that attempts to bring about workplace harmony by teaching people how to get along better with diverse work associates.

Forms of Diversity Training. Diversity training takes a number of forms. Nevertheless, all center on increasing awareness of and empathy for people who are different in some noticeable way from oneself. Training sessions in appreciating cultural diversity focus on the ways that men and women or people of different races reflect different values, attitudes, and cultural backgrounds. These sessions can vary from several hours to several days. Training sessions can also be held over a long period of time. Sometimes the program is confrontational, sometimes not.

An essential part of relating more effectively to diverse groups is to empathize with their points of view. To help training participants develop empathy, representatives of various groups explain their feelings related to workplace issues, including how they have felt different in a way that made them feel uncomfortable. A representative segment of a training program designed to enhance empathy took the following format. A minority group member was seated at the middle of a circle. First, the coworkers listened to a Vietnamese woman explaining how she felt excluded from the in-group composed of whites and African-Americans in her department. "I feel like you just tolerate me. You do not make me feel that I am somebody important." The next person to sit in the middle of the circle was a Muslim. He complained about people treating him with suspicion. "I want people to understand that I am a Muslim-American. Everybody in my family likes our country. We are not associated with a handful of evil people thousands of miles away from here."

Another form of diversity is aimed specifically at able-bodied workers understanding the challenges faced by workers with physical disabilities. At Diversity Learning Labs one such lab simulates working with disabilities. For one hour, participants lived with a disability. One employee wore earplugs blocking out all sound, thereby simulating deafness. Another employee wore a dark blindfold to simulate not having physical vision. Someone else used a wheelchair and was assigned such tasks as navigating into a conference room and using the restroom.[33] A major point of these simulations is that it is easier to understand the challenges faced by a person with a specific disability if you have experienced the same disability, even on a trial basis.

Diversity training can also take the form of cross-generational diversity, or relating effectively to workers much older or younger than you. Cross-generational awareness training is one component in the corporate training program. The premise behind the program is that after acquiring cognitive knowledge, engaging in dialogue, and role-playing, employees will learn to accept people's differences, some of which are age driven. For example, younger employees might feel less guilty than would seniors when calling in sick just to have a day's vacation. Another part of cross-generational training would be to help older and younger generations appreciate their different preferences in communication. An example is sending e-mails versus text messages for disseminating brief bits of information.

Concerns about Diversity Training.   Diversity training has frequently improved cross-cultural relationships in the workplace. Yet such programs can also create ill will and waste time. One problem is that participants are sometimes encouraged to be too con-frontational and express too much hostility. Companies have found that when employees are too blunt during these sessions, it may be difficult to patch up interpersonal relations in the work group later on.

Another potential negative consequence of diversity training is that it sometimes results in perpetuating stereotypes about groups, such as people from Latin America not placing much value on promptness for meetings. A related problem is that diversity training might focus too much on differences instead of similarities.[34] For example, even if people are raised with different cultural values, they must all work harmoniously together to accomplish work. Although a worker believes that relationships are more important than profits, he or she must still produce enough to be a good investment for the company.

A consistent conclusion reached by diversity training program researchers is that such training is the most effective if the organization really cares about being diverse. Without such commitment, the training is likely to be quickly forgotten.[35] Also, the diversity trainee should have an attitude something to the effect, "Now that my awareness of appreciating diversity has increased, what can I do differently to bring about genuine inclusion at my place of work?"

Skill-Building Exercise 8-5 provides you with an opportunity to simulate an empathy-building experience in a diversity-training program.

Cross-Cultural and Cross-Gender Mentoring Programs

An advanced method of improving cross-cultural relations is mentoring members of tar-geted minority groups. The mentoring demonstrates the company's interest in enhancing cross-cultural relations and simultaneously enhances the minority group member's oppor-tunities for advancement. To achieve cross-culture and cross-gender mentoring, compa-nies often assign the member of the minority group a mentor who is typically an experienced manager. For example, a 24-year-old African-American woman might be mentored by a 45-year-old Caucasian middle manager. Or, a minority group member could be the mentor, such as a 45-year-old African-American woman mentoring a 24-year-old Japanese man.

SKILL-BUILDING EXERCISE 8-5

Developing Empathy for Differences

Class members come up to the front of the room one by one and give a brief presentation (perhaps even three minutes) of any way in which they have been perceived as different and how they felt about this perception. Sometimes this exercise is referred to as "When I Felt Different." The difference refers to feeling different from the majority. The difference can be of any kind, relating to characteristics such as ethnicity, race, choice of major, physical appearance, height, weight, hair color, or body piercing. After each member of the class (perhaps even the instructor) has presented, class members discuss what they learned from the exercise. It is also important to discuss how this exercise can improve relation-ships on the job.

As described in Chapter 12, mentors might help the person being mentored in such ways as making the right contacts and learning useful professional skills. A challenge noted with cross-cultural and cross-gender mentoring is a shortage of mentors with the right knowledge and interpersonal skills.

Sprint started a trial mentoring program with 50 employees at company headquarters. Although open to all employees, the program targeted minority groups. Soon the program had 500 participants. "The demand was overwhelming," says Tammy Edwards, director of inclusion and diversity, who became a mentor to several employees. She adds that the mentee (person who is mentored) pool became so large that each mentor is paired with up to five mentees.[36]

Concept Review and Reinforcement

Key Terms

Summary

Today's workplace has become more culturally diverse, and business has become increasingly international. As a result, to succeed one must be able to relate effectively to people from different cultural groups from within and outside one's country. The true meaning of valuing diversity is to respect and enjoy a wide range of cultural and individual differences. The diversity umbrella continues to include more people as the workforce encompasses a greater variety of people.

A diverse workforce brings potential advantages to the organization, including higher creativity, more profits because of a demographic match with customers, overall business prosperity, and commitment to the organization. Cultural diversity within groups can lead to conflict. Results suggest that relations-oriented diversity leads to high performance in service-industry settings.

The groundwork for developing effective cross-cultural relations is to understand cultural differences. Six key aspects of understanding cultural differences are (1) cultural sensitivity including political correctness, (2) cultural intelligence, (3) respect for all workers and all cultures, (4) cultural fluency—the ability to conduct business in a diverse and international environment, (5) differences in cultural dimensions, and (6) avoidance of cultural bloopers. Cultural intelligence is based on cognitive, emotional/motivational, and physical (taking action) factors.

Countries differ in their national values or cultural dimensions, leading to differences in how most people from a given country will react to situations. The dimensions studied here are (1) performance orientation, (2) assertiveness, (3) time orientation, (4) human orientation, (5) in-group collectivism, (6) gender egalitarianism, (7) acceptance of power and authority, (8) work orientation, and (9) social support seeking.

An effective way of being culturally sensitive is to minimize actions that are likely to offend people from another culture based on their values. These cultural bloopers can take place when working in another country or when dealing with foreigners in one's own country. Studying potential cultural bloopers is helpful, but recognize also that individual differences may be of significance.

Communication barriers created by cultural differences can often be overcome by the following: (1) Be sensitive to the fact that these barriers exist; (2) show respect for all workers; (3) use straightforward language and speak slowly and clearly; (4) observe cultural differences in etiquette; (5) be sensitive to differences in nonverbal communication; (6) do not be diverted by style, accent, grammar, or personal appearance; (7) be attentive to individual differences in appearance; and (8) pronounce correctly the names of people you interact with from other countries.

Cultural training is a set of learning experiences designed to help employees understand the customs, traditions, and beliefs of another culture. In today's diverse business environment and international marketplace, learning about individuals raised in different cultural backgrounds has become more important. Recognizing your own cultural and demographic biases can help smooth cross-cultural relations. Cultural intelligence training includes developing strategies for sizing up the environment to determine which course of action is best. Learning a foreign language is often part of cultural training, yet it can also be a separate activity.

Diversity training attempts to bring about workplace harmony by teaching people how to get along better with diverse work associates. Another goal of diversity training is to improve business performance. Most forms of diversity training center on increasing awareness of and empathy for people who are different in some noticeable way from you. Diversity training can also take the form of simulating having a physical disability.

Cross-cultural and cross-gender mentoring are advanced methods of improving cross-cultural relations. The minority group member or woman is assigned a mentor who helps the person advance in his or her career.

Questions for Discussion and Review

1. How could cultural sensitivity help with international relations between countries?

2. What benefits can a multicultural workforce bring to a company?

3. Some companies, such as Singapore Airlines, make a deliberate effort for all customer-contact personnel to be of the same ethnic group (Singapore natives). How is this practice justified in an era of cultural diversity and valuing differences?

4. A working couple visited a childcare center seeking childcare services five days a week for their three-year-old daughter. When the couple observed that one of the childcare workers was a man in his fifties, the couple decided against the center. What is your evaluation of the couple's decision in terms of inclusion, cultural sensitivity, and discrimination?

5. What have you personally observed about Asians and Asian-Americans being less likely to ask for social support when they are facing a difficult problem?

6. The majority of people under age 45 in the United States grew up being educated with, participating in sports with, and working with people from other cultures and demographic groups. To what extent do people under age 45 therefore need cultural diversity training?

7. How useful is the adage "When in Rome, do as the Romans do" for someone who wants to work in another country for a while?

8. Given that English is now the international language of business, what benefits could you gain from learning another language?

9. The cultural bloopers presented in Skill-Building Exercise 8-2 all dealt with errors people make in regard to people who are not American. Give an example of a cultural blooper a person from another country might make in the United States.

10. Many people speak loudly to other people who are deaf, blind, and those who speak a different language. Based on the information presented in this chapter, what mistakes are these people making?

The Web Corner

http://www.DiversityInc.com
(Extensive information including videos about cultural diversity in organizations)

http://www.berlitz.com
(Information about language training and cultural training in countries throughout the world—investigate in your second language to enhance the cross-cultural experience)

Internet Skill Builder: Avoiding Cultural Insensitivity

One of the most effective ways of hampering relationships with people of another culture is to be grossly insensitive. If you can avoid these gross errors, you will be on your way toward at least acceptable relationships with people from another domestic or foreign culture. Two examples of cultural insensitivity uncovered on the Internet are: In Alberta, Canada, a sign in the window of a large chain restaurant read, "No drunken Indians allowed." Walmart performed poorly in Germany because it did not recognize the cultural fact that Germans do not like to spend a lot of time shopping by walking through a giant store and waiting in line. Search the Internet for examples of cultural insensitivity. You may have to dig hard to find these nuggets of insensitivity, but the activity will help you become more culturally sensitive and aware.

Developing Your Human Relations Skills

Interpersonal Relations Case 8.1

What to Do with Shabana?

Shabana was raised in Pakistan and graduated from the University of Punjab with a major in commerce. She then moved to Chicago, Illinois, to live with her married aunt, as well as to begin a career in business in the United States. Shabana is fluent in her native Punjabi, but also has spoken and written English since the beginning of her primary education.

Having a sponsor in the United States made it possible for Shabana to enter the job market in Chicago. In addition to having a good formal education, Shabana makes a positive physical appearance that includes a warm smile and a comfortable, relaxed manner. After a two-month-long job search, Shabana found employment as a store associate in a smartphone store of one of the major mobile phone providers. She was content with this position because she thought it would be a stepping stone to store management in the field of consumer electronics.

Shabana enjoyed interacting with the other store associates as well as the customers. An important part of her role was explaining some of the intricacies of smartphones and cell phones, as well as the contracts, to customers. She willingly worked Saturday nights and Sunday afternoons, store hours unpopular with other associates.

From time to time, Shabana was perplexed as to why some customers did not understand her. With a few of the older customers, Shabana attributed their lack of understanding to limited knowledge of technology or hearing impairments. One customer looked straight at Shabana and said, "I do not understand a word you are saying."

One day Trevor, the store manager, took Shabana aside and told her, "You are a wonderful sales associate in many ways. The other associates enjoy working with you, and you get along well with many of our customers. Yet we are getting too many complaints by e-mail and phone that many of our customers cannot understand you. It seems like some of these Chicago people just can't understand English with a Pakistani accent."

"Maybe some of our customers aren't the most sophisticated, but they are still customers. And we need every dollar we can take in to meet our sales goals. You need to become better understood by all our customers, or we can't keep you as a sales associate."

A little perplexed, Shabana replied, "I am so sorry to know that I have disappointed you and some of our valued customers. Please give me several weeks to correct this situation of my not being so well understood by all our customers."

Trevor replied, "Okay, but I am going to keep close watch on your progress."

Case Questions

1. What should Shabana do to improve her ability to be understood by more customers?
2. Is the problem of language comprehension in this case really a problem of customers not being too sharp mentally?
3. What actions do you recommend that Trevor take to help Shabana improve her ability to be understood by her customers? Or should he just fire her?
4. To what extent do you think Trevor is practicing job discrimination by even hinting that he might fire Shabana if she is not better understood by a wider variety of customers?

Interpersonal Skills Role-Play 8.1

Helping Shabana Develop Better Customer Service

This role-play is basically a re-enactment of the case just presented. One student plays the role of Trevor, who wants Shabana to succeed but is skeptical that she can improve her spoken English enough to satisfy all of the customers. Another student plays the role of Shabana, who is confident she can make enough slight adjustments in her word pronunciation to satisfy almost all her customers. Also, Shabana wants to keep her job. Run the role-play for about seven minutes, followed by some observer feedback.

Interpersonal Relations Case 8.2

Pierre Keeps One Foot in Haiti

Pierre, a native of Haiti with a degree in electronic technology, was hired by a branch of a major heating, ventilation, and air-conditioning company in Florida, HVAC Service. The company specializes in the installation of heating and air-conditioning systems in new buildings, as well as replacing older equipment in existing buildings. Providing maintenance service is another important component of HVAC Service's business. Pierre was assigned to a team that maintains systems installed by HVAC.

During Pierre's first two weeks on the job, Pierre's teammates generally enjoyed his frequent references to Haiti, including its climate, food, friendly people, and national pride. But after that orientation period, a few of his teammates as well as the team leader, Suzanne, began to tire of his frequent references to Haiti. One member of the team asked Pierre one day, "If Haiti is so great, why does the economy struggle so much?" and "Why can Haiti not overcome the devastation from its last major earthquake?"

One day during a break on a client site, Suzanne pointed out to Pierre that he was well liked as a team member and that his technical contribution to team was quite good. She also reported to Pierre that he seemed to be having difficulty adjusting to the American culture. Pierre asked, "In what way, Suzanne?" Suzanne then gave him four examples of why he gave the impression of having problems adjusting to his new culture.

"A few days ago, Ted said it was a hot day in Florida. You told us that it is much hotter in Port au Prince (a major city in Haiti) than here.

"You must have told us five times that instead of eating canned food we should all eat the type of natural fruits and vegetables that are harvested in Haiti.

"You told us that people in Florida are too sensitive to the heat, but that in the tropical climate of Haiti most people use fans instead of air conditioning.

"We were kind of taken aback when you said that too many people in America are poorly educated because so many of them speak only one language. In contrast, the educated Haitians speak a minimum of two languages, French and English."

With a quizzical expression, Pierre responded, "I thought that HVAC welcomed cultural diversity."

Case Questions

1. To what extent is Pierre is having a problem adjusting to his new culture?
2. To what extent are Suzanne and the team not showing good cultural sensitivity?
3. How justified is Pierre's insinuation that HVAC does not welcome cultural diversity?

Interpersonal Skills Role-Play 8.2

Suzanne Attempts to Help Pierre Adjust to his New Culture

This role-play is a reenactment and continuation of the scenario presented in the previous case. Suzanne wants to facilitate Pierre's better adjustment to American culture, but she does not want to appear negative toward a worker from another culture. She meets alone with Pierre, who is still puzzled by the reaction to his remarks. He believes that frequent references to his native culture should be expected by others. Run the role-play for about seven minutes. Observers should look to see if Suzanne can maintain cultural sensitivity and not appear to be discriminating against Pierre.

References

1. Original story created from facts and observations presented in the following sources: Todd Henneman, "Making the Pieces Fit," *Workforce Management*, August 2011, p. 12; Chris Dieterich, "Bright Horizons Family Solutions IPO Opens Strong," *The Wall Street Journal* (http://online.wsj.co), January 25, 2013, pp. 1-2; "Diversity and Inclusion: My One Thing," *Solutions at Work* (http://blogs.brighthorizons.com), 2010, p. 1; http://solutionsatwork.brighthorizons.com, retrieved February 23, 2013; "100 Best Companies to Work For," *CNN Money* (http://money.cnn.com), 2012.

2. Robert J. Grossman, "Muslim Employees: Valuable but Vulnerable," *HR Magazine*, March 2011, pp. 22–27.

3. Inga Fond, "Disability Accommodations, Unemployed Applicants, Sustainability," *HR Magazine*, December 2011, p. 20.

4. Angela Ka-yee Leung, William W. Maddox, Adam D. Galinsky, and Chi-yue Chu, "Multicultural Experience Enhances Creativity," *American Psychologist*, April 2008, pp. 169–181.

5. Michael Bowker, "Corporate Diversity Driving Profits," *Hispanic Business*, September 2008, pp. 12, 14.

6. Patrick F. McKay, Derek R. Avery, and Mark A. Morris, "A Tale of Two Climates: Diversity Climate from Subordinates' and Managers' Perspectives and Their Role in Store Unit Sales Performance," *Personnel Psychology*, Winter 2009, pp. 767–791.

7. Eric Kearney, Diether Gebert, and Sven C. Voelpel, "When and How Diversity Benefits Teams: The Importance of Team Members' Need for Cognition," *Academy of Management Journal*, June 2009, pp. 581–598.

8. María del Carmen Triana, María Fernanda Garcia, and Adrienne Clella, "Managing Diversity: How Organizational Efforts to Support Diversity Moderate the Effects of Perceived Racial Discrimination on Affective Commitment," *Personnel Psychology*, Winter 2010, pp. 817–843.

9. Arvind V. Phatak, *International Dimensions of Management* (Boston: Kent, 1983), p. 167.

10. Cited in "Are Your People Global Ready?" Flyer from the Koazi Group, 2013.

11. Robin J. Ely, Debra Meyerson, and Martin N. Davidson, "Rethinking Political Correctness," *Harvard Business Review*, September 2006, p. 80.

12. Quoted in "Leveraging Diversity at Work," *Hispanic Business*, November 2006, p. 70.

13. P. Christopher Earley and Elaine Mosakowski, "Cultural Intelligence," *Harvard Business Review*, October 2004, p. 140.

14. P. C. Earley and E. Mosakowski, "Toward Culture Intelligence: Turning Cultural Differences into a Workplace Advantage," *Academy of Management Executive*, August 2004, pp. 154–155.

15. Scott B. Button, "Organizational Efforts to Affirm Sexual Diversity: A Cross-Level Examination," *Journal of Applied Psychology*, February 2001, pp. 17–28.

16. Charlene Marmer Solomon, "Global Operations Demand That HR Rethink Diversity," *Personnel Journal*, July 1994, p. 50.

17. Mansour Javidan, Peter W. Dorfman, May Sully de Luque, and Robert J. House, "In the Eye of the Beholder: Cross Cultural Lessons in Leadership from Project GLOBE," *Academy of Management Perspectives*, February 2006, pp. 69–70. Similar dimensions were described in Geert Hofstede, *Culture's Consequences: International Differences in Work Related Values* (Beverly Hills, CA: Sage, 1980); updated and expanded in "A Conversation with Geert Hofstede," *Organizational Dynamics*, Spring 1993, pp. 53–61; Hofstede, "Who Is the Fairest of Them All? Galit Ailon's Mirror," *Academy of Management Review*, July 2009, pp. 570–571. Dimension 8 is not included in this research. Paul J. Taylor, Wen-Dong Li, Kan Shi, and Walter C. Borman, "The Transportability of Job Information Across Countries," *Personnel Psychology*, Spring 2008, pp. 72–76.

18. Michael Morrison, "U.S. Workers Win the Average Annual Hours Worked Per Week Contest," http://www.decisionevidence.com. July 30, 2012; Steven Yoder, "16 Countries Where People Work the Longest Hours," *The 3 Fiscal Times* (http://www.thefiscaltimes.com). February 24, 2012, p. 1.

19. Heejung S. Kim, David K. Sherman, and Shelley E. Taylor, "Culture and Social Support," *American Psychologist*, September 2008, pp. 518–526.

20. Vas Taras, Bradeley L. Kirkman, and Piers Steel, "Examining the Impact of *Culture's Consequences*: A Three-Decade, Multilevel, Meta-Analytic Review of Hofstede's Cultural Value Dimensions," *Journal of Applied Psychology*, May 2010, pp. 405–439.

21. Lee Gardenswartz and Anita Rowe, "Cross-Cultural Awareness," *HR Magazine*, March 2001, p. 139.

22. Ellyn Ferguson, "Many Firms Seek Bilingual Workers," *Gannett News Service*, May 13, 2007.

23. Daren Foinda, "Selling in Tongues," *Time*, November 26, 2001, pp. B12–B13.

24. Gayle Cotton, "Global Business Etiquette: Cultural Clues, Do's and Taboos," *GaylerCotton.com*. Accessed June 13, 2013.

25. Jeffrey Sanchez-Burks, Caroline A. Bartel, and Sally Blount, "Performance in Intercultural Interactions at Work: Cross-Cultural Differences in Response to Behavioral Mirroring," *Journal of Applied Psychology*, January 2009, pp. 216–233.

26. Siri Carpenter, "Why Do 'They All Look Alike'?" *Monitor on Psychology*, December 2000, p. 44.

27. Kathleen Begley, "Managing Across Cultures at Home," *HR Magazine*, September 2009, p. 115.

28. Rebecca Vesely, "Seven Seas Change," *Workforce Management*, September 2012, p. 20.

29. Mei Fong, "Chinese Charm School," *The Wall Street Journal*, January 13, 2004, p. B1.

30. David K. Heckman et al., "An Examination of Whether and How Racial and Gender Biases Influence Customer Satisfaction," *Academy of Management Journal*, April 2010, pp. 238–264.

31. P. Christopher Earley and Randall S. Peterson, "The Elusive Cultural Chameleon: Cultural Intelligence as a New Approach to Intercultural Training for the Global Manager," *Academy of Management Learning and Education*, March 2004, p. 106.

32. Rohini Anahand and Mary-Frances Winters, "A Retrospective View of Corporate Diversity Training from 1964 to the Present," *Academy of Management Learning & Education*, September 2008, p. 356.

33. Henneman, "Making the Pieces Fit," *Workforce Management*, p. 16.

34. Gillian Flynn, "The Harsh Reality of Diversity Programs," *Workforce*, December 1998, p. 29.

35. Katerina Bezrukova, Karen A. Jehn, and Chester S. Spell, "Reviewing Diversity Training: Where We Have Been and Where We Should Go," *Academy of Management Learning and Education*, June 2012, pp. 207–227.

36. Kathryn Tyler, "Cross-Cultural Connections: Mentoring Programs Can Bridge Gaps between Disparate Groups," *HR Magazine*, October 2007, pp. 77–83.

Resolving Conflicts with Others

Karen was one of five members of a group of workers who repaired and installed desktop and laptop computers for individuals and small businesses. Her company, Elite Computers, also installed new software and repaired virus damage. Karen enjoyed the technical challenges in her work, as well as the opportunity to work directly with a variety of clients and provide them with valuable assistance.

A major challenge facing Karen and her teammates was that some of the on site repair work had to be done on Saturdays and Sundays to accommodate clients who worked on weekends as well as weekdays. When their computers were down, some clients could not wait until Monday for an Elite technician to begin the repairs.

Pixland/Jupiter Images/Getty Images

One of Karen's teammates, Charlie, seemed to often have an excuse for not making a weekend client visit when it was his turn. Several times, Charlie sent Karen an urgent text message saying that he or a family member was sick and that he needed Karen to take the service call for him. Each time, Charlie ended his message with "Please help. I'll return the favor later."

One Friday at 8 a.m. Karen received a voice message from Charlie that said, "One of our biggest clients, Silver Motor Sales, has a system breakdown, and needs help this morning. It could be a virus attack. I have to take my brother to the emergency room. Please go to Silver Motors for me, ASAP."

Karen thought, "This dependency of Charlie on me has gotten out of hand. I don't know if he is lying. But if our team screws up with Silver Motors, we will all look bad. Maybe I should call Fred (the team leader). I think Charlie is taking advantage of me. I've got to work on my problem with him."

Objectives

1. Specify why so much interpersonal conflict exists in organizations.
2. Recognize your typical method of resolving conflict.
3. Identify the five styles of handling conflict.
4. Acquire effective techniques for resolving conflict and negotiating.
5. Understand how to combat sexual harassment in the workplace.

The situation of computer repair technicians Karen and Charlie illustrates how so often it becomes imperative to resolve conflicts with a coworker to fix an intolerable problem. This chapter will help you improve your ability to resolve conflicts with people at work. The same techniques are also useful in personal life. To improve your understanding of how to resolve conflict, this chapter will present specific techniques and also explain why so much conflict exists. To get you started relating the topic of conflict to yourself, take Self-Assessment Quiz 9-1.

SOURCES OF INTERPERSONAL CONFLICT IN ORGANIZATIONS

A **conflict** is a situation in which two or more goals, values, or events are incompatible or mutually exclusive. A conflict is also a strife, quarrel, or battle, such as would be the case if computer repair technician Karen told Charlie he was a lazy jerk, and he replied that she was callous and unfeeling about his problems.

Conflict between and among people has many sources or causes. In this section, six of the leading sources are described. A seventh category, workplace violence, is both a cause and a consequence of conflict. If you understand the cause of a conflict, it can help you resolve the conflict and help prevent a similar recurrence. For example, if you learn that much conflict on the job is caused by people being uncivil toward each other, you might remind yourself to behave civilly. You can also learn how to deal with uncivil coworkers so that they treat you less rudely. Although specific sources of conflict can be identified, keep in mind an important fact: All conflict includes the underlying theme of incompatibility between your goals, values, or events and those of another person.

Competition for Limited Resources

An underlying source of job conflict is that few people can get all the resources they want. These resources include money, material, and human resources. Conflicts arise when two or more people squabble over who should get the resources. Even in a prosperous organization, resources have to be divided in such a manner that not everybody gets what he or she wants.

Assume that you believe you need to have a document scanner immediately accessible for the full workday. Yet the company has decided that 10 people must share one scanner. As a result, you are likely to enter into conflict with the coworkers sharing the scanner. The conflict will be intense if several of your coworkers also think they need full-time access to a scanner.

Role Conflict

A major source of conflict (and stress) on the job relates to being placed in a predicament. **Role conflict** stems from having to choose between two competing demands or expectations. If you comply with one aspect of a role, compliance with the other is difficult or impossible. An important example would be receiving contradictory orders from two

LEARNING OBJECTIVE 1

conflict
A situation in which two or more goals, values, or events are incompatible or mutually exclusive.

role conflict
The situation that occurs when a person has to choose between two competing demands or expectations.

SELF-ASSESSMENT QUIZ 9-1

Collaborative versus Competitive Styles of Conflict Management

Circle the number under the category that most closely matches your feelings (disagree strongly; disagree; neutral; agree; agree strongly) on each of the following statements:

	Disagree Strongly	Disagree	Neutral	Agree	Agree Strongly
1. I like to see the other side squirm when I resolve a dispute.	5	4	3	2	1
2. Winning is everything when it comes to settling conflict.	5	4	3	2	1
3. After I have successfully negotiated a price, I like to see the seller smile.	1	2	3	4	5
4. I have a "smash-mouth" attitude toward resolving conflict.	5	4	3	2	1
5. In most conflict situations, one side is clearly right, and the other side is clearly wrong.	5	4	3	2	1
6. I think there are effective alternatives to strikes for settling union versus management disputes.	1	2	3	4	5
7. The winner should take all.	5	4	3	2	1
8. Conflict on the job is like a prize fight; the idea is to knock out the opponent.	5	4	3	2	1
9. I like the idea of tournaments in which first-round losers receive another opportunity to play.	1	2	3	4	5
10. Nice guys and gals usually finish first.	1	2	3	4	5

Scoring and Interpretation: Add the point value of your scores to obtain your total. Scores of 40 and higher suggest that you prefer a *collaborative*, or *win–win*, approach to resolving conflict. You tend to be concerned about finding long-term solutions to conflict that will provide benefits to both sides. Scores of 39 and lower suggest that you prefer a *competitive* approach to resolving conflict. You want to maximize gain for yourself, with little concern about the welfare of the other side.

people above you in your company. If you comply with the wishes of one person, you will antagonize the other. A higher-ranking manager might encourage as many employees as possible to work from home a few days per week. In contrast, your own manager demands that you be on the work premises full time.

Role conflict can take various forms. You might be asked to accomplish two objectives that are in apparent conflict. If your boss asks you to hurry up and finish your work but also decrease your mistakes, you would experience the conflict of incompatible demands (plus a headache, perhaps). Another problem is when two or more people give you incompatible directions. For example, your immediate supervisor may want you to complete a crash project on time, but company policy might temporarily prohibit authorizing overtime payments to clerical help or hiring office temporaries.

Role conflict also results when two different roles that you play are in conflict. Your company may expect you to travel 50 percent of the time, whereas your spouse threatens a divorce if you travel over 25 percent of the time. To complete the picture, *person–role conflict* takes place when the role(s) your organization expects you to occupy is in conflict with your basic values. Your company may ask you to fire the bottom 10 percent of performers, but this could be in conflict with your humanistic values. Another example of person–role conflict would be a person working for a retailer who knowingly sold counterfeit (knock-off) handbags when he or she believed that such a practice is immoral and illegal.

Competing Work and Family Demands

Balancing the demands of career and family life has become a major role conflict facing the workforce. Caring about work and family responsibilities is more likely to intensify work-family conflict. The challenge is particularly intense for employees who are part of a two-wage-earner family. **Work–family conflict** occurs when an individual's roles of worker and active participant in social and family life compete with one another. This type of conflict is frequent because the multiple roles are often incompatible. Imagine having planned to attend your child's solo recital and then being ordered at the last minute to be present at an after-hours meeting. Work–family conflict can lead to interpersonal conflict because your boss or coworkers might think that you are asking them to cover for you while you attend to personal matters.

Work-to-Family and Family-to-Work Conflict. Work–family conflict can be viewed from two perspectives, with both leading to conflict and stress. A person's work can interfere with family responsibilities, or family responsibilities can interfere with work. In the above example, the person might say, "This is terrible. The meeting called for at the last minute will block me from attending my child's solo recital." Or, the same person might say, "This is terrible. My child's solo recital is going to block me from attending an important last-minute meeting."

An analysis of many scientific studies on the subject found that work demands can create some stress and low satisfaction at home, and personal demands can create some stress and low satisfaction on the job.[1] Have you ever noticed that problems at work or school can negatively influence personal life? Have you also noticed that problems in personal life can negatively influence work or school?

Another study investigated the effect of work–family conflict on the emotions of guilt and hostility among employed adults. The study also explored how work–family conflict, guilt, and hostility affected job satisfaction and marital satisfaction. It was found that work-to-family conflict and family-to-work conflict led to guilt and hostility at work and at home, respectively. A sidelight finding of interest to the study of human relations is that hostile people suffer even more conflict at home and on the job.[2]

The Issue of Work–Life Choices. A continuing debate exists over whether a person can have an equal balance between work and family life and still advance far in his or her career. If getting far in your field requires 60 hours per week of hard work, you might not be able to meet that demand and still be a full contributor to family life. Jack Welch, former GE chief executive and now business writer and educator, told participants at a human resources conference, "There are work–life choices, and you make them, and they have consequences."[3]

Another issue related to work–life choices is that when managers perceive subordinates to be experiencing family–work conflict, there is a tendency for the bosses to think that the subordinate is not a good candidate for promotion. A study with supervisors in a large transportation company found that managers tended to categorize women as experiencing greater family–work conflict even when the women did not perceive themselves to have much family–work conflict. As a result, the managers downgraded their perception of the women supervisors' fit for the job, as well as their promotability.[4] Even if the managers' perceptions were biased, the supervisors still had to deal with these misperceptions.

Making a work–life (or work–family) choice can sometimes reduce conflict. It is helpful to develop a general guideline about how much time a person wants to invest in both work and family life, and then be satisfied with the compromise. Certain types of careers have to be excluded in order to spend most evenings and weekends in family and other personal activities. For example, to be a successful small business owner or a Wall Street financial analyst typically requires working between 60 and 70 hours per week. From the opposite standpoint, certain types of social activities have to be controlled to attain career success. An adult who wants to play video games and visit social networking sites for a combined nine hours per day will not succeed in most careers. After choices are made about type of work and type of personal life activities, work–family conflict will be minimized.

Company Initiatives to Reduce Work–Family Conflict. Companies can often avoid or minimize serious work–family conflict among employees by implementing equitable time-off policies. The underlying company attitude is that all employees need a work–life balance. Encouraging such an atmosphere of goodwill among coworkers can help prevent conflicts and resentments when one employee leaves early to take care of family responsibility.[5]

Many companies offer flexible working hours to a majority of their employees. In this way, a worker might be able to meet family demands that take place during typical working hours. An example is taking the morning off to care for an ill parent and working later that same evening to make up the time. People who are exceptionally good at organizing their time and efforts will often experience less work–family conflict, by such behaviors as staying on top of work to minimize periods of time when they are completely work-centered.[6]

In addition to a company providing formal programs to reduce work–family conflict, supervisory support is helpful in reducing such conflict. Supervisor support for work–family conflict includes such behaviors as expressing sympathy for the worker's challenges and giving friendly advice. An analysis of a group of studies involving over 75,000 employees provided evidence that supportive supervisors and supportive organizations were effective methods of reducing work–family conflict.[7] A supportive organization would include the initiatives previously mentioned plus frequent statements by company executives indicating concern for family welfare.

Company initiatives, including supervisory and organizational support, can help reduce work–life conflict. At the same time, such policies contribute to the job satisfaction of workers making use of work–family initiatives or policies.[8] Support within the family is also quite important, such as an equitable division of household tasks between the working couple.[9] For example, parents should take turns leaving work to pick up a child who becomes ill at school or caring for a child who cannot attend school because of illness.

Personality Clashes and Drama

Many workplace disagreements arise because people simply dislike each other. A **personality clash** is thus an antagonistic relationship between two people based on differences in personal attributes, preferences, interests, values, and styles. A personality clash reflects negative chemistry between two people, whereas personal differences are based more specifically on a value clash. According to the research of psychologist Judith Sills, the most commonly reported office problem is the personality conflict. One of the most frequent conflicts is between the sweeping big-picture person and the cautious detail-oriented person.[10] The big-picture concern manager might say, "Give me a general idea of ticket sales for the Dixie Chicks," expecting a response like, "Might even have a full house with luck." Instead, the detail-oriented person says, "Last time I checked we had 37,431 tickets sold."

People involved in a personality clash often have difficulty specifying why they dislike each other. The end result, however, is that they cannot maintain an amiable work relationship. A peculiarity about personality clashes is that people who get along well may begin to clash after working together for a number of years. A contributing factor is that as both people change and as the situation changes, the two people may no longer be compatible.

You are probably familiar with "drama" in personal life, such as the person who demands a "drama-free" relationship or says "I'm drama-free." Drama takes the form of an obstacle to what you want to attain, and often functions like a personality clash because the dramatic person does not get along with you.[11] Instead, he or she might blame you for a problem or be so preoccupied with personal problems that working smoothly with you is extremely difficult. A coworker who introduces drama might say, "I know that we are supposed to investigate these missing funds together, but I am facing a personal emergency today. You cannot expect me to concentrate on my work with all the problems I am facing."

Bullies in the Workplace

Coworkers naturally disagree about topics, issues, and ideas. Yet some people convert disagreement into an attack that puts down other people and damages their self-esteem. As a result, conflict surfaces. **Bullies** are people who verbally, and sometimes physically, attack others frequently. Among the typical behaviors of bullies are interrupting others, ranting in a loud voice, and making threats. Joe Grimm, a professor of journalism at Michigan State University, observes that bullying is considered part of daily workplace culture and often takes the form of browbeating, intimidation, cutting people off, and loudly expressing a personal opinion.[12]

A typical attitude of a bullying boss is "My way or the highway," sending the message that the employee's suggestions are unwelcome. Bullied workers complain of a range of psychological and physical ailments, such as anxiety, sleeplessness, panic attacks, and low self-esteem.

Research suggests that the most likely victims of supervisory bullying are those workers with less power, especially those working in personal service roles, such as housekeepers, nannies, and office assistants. [13]

Online interviews with 7,740 adults conducted by the Workplace Bullying Institute found that 60 percent of bullies are male, and 40 percent are female. An estimated 37 percent of American workers have been bullied on the job. Male bullies appear to choose men and women as targets in equal number. In contrast, women choose women as their targets 71 percent of the time. According to the Bullying Institute, bullying usually results in work interference and sabotage, therefore lowering productivity.[14]

What constitutes true bullying depends somewhat on a person's perception, including cultural values. Jennifer Loh, a management professor at University of New England, Australia, and her colleagues compared Australian and Singapore employees in terms of the effects workplace bullies had on their victims. Singapore is a culture that highly respects power and authority, whereas Australians have a more egalitarian view of hierarchy. The researchers found that regardless of the two cultures, workplace bullying lowered job satisfaction, including feeling alienated from coworkers; however, the degree of distress was higher for Australians than Singaporeans. The implication is that in a culture in which managers are expected to exercise power and authority, workers will tolerate a little more bullying.[15]

Methods of dealing with bullies are described in the section in Chapter 12 about dealing with difficult people.

Incivility and Rudeness

A milder form of aggressiveness than bullying in the workplace is being rude or uncivil toward work associates. **Incivility** (or employees' lack of regard for one another) has gained attention as a cause of workplace conflict. What constitutes being uncivil or rude depends upon a person's perceptions and values.

> *Imagine two people having a business lunch together. One of them answers his cell phone during lunch and, while still eating, engages the caller in conversation. To some people this everyday incident would be interpreted as double rudeness—interrupting lunch with a cell phone call and eating while talking. Another person might perceive the cell phone incident to be standard behavior in a multitasking world.*

Rudeness also includes swearing at coworkers, a cubicle dweller shouting loudly on the phone while making a personal call, and performing other work at a meeting. Typical forms of "other work" are sorting through paper mail or surfing the Internet on a notebook computer.

A survey of workplace incivility was conducted with three different groups, including university employees, attorneys, and federal court employees. Overall, employees subjected to incivility tended to feel frustrated, annoyed, and a little bit offended. Also, when employees are subjected to coworkers or managers who yell and swear, make them the object of mean jokes, or intentionally exclude them from friendship-building activities, their morale and performance often suffers.[16] (Does this finding surprise you?) A similar study found that after being the victim of rudeness and hostility on the job, nearly two-thirds of employees said their performance declined.[17] Other negative outcomes from being treated uncivilly in the workplace include job stress, physical illness, and emotional exhaustion.[18]

Why might the rudeness of others bother us? A group of researchers at Duke University suggest that we become upset with rude behavior because the behavior violates unwritten laws of behavior referred to as *social exchange rules*. Mutually beneficial interactions are excluded when one person violates social exchange rules.[19] Two examples of

incivility

In human relations, employees' lack of regard for one another.

these rule violations are eating part of a coworker's lunch stored in the refrigerator and sleeping at a meeting (or during class).

To place rudeness and incivility in perspective, it may simply be part of modern life in which self-expression counts for everything and manners nothing. Rudeness in the workplace is therefore just a natural extension of rudeness occurring in everyday life.[20] Yet, a person who has good manners and behaves civilly can capitalize on these behaviors in his or her career.

Cross-Generational Conflict

As explained in Chapter 2, differences in values across generations lead to differences in behavior. And these value-based differences in behavior can lead to conflict, such as disputes about Gen Y workers wanting members of Gen X and Baby Boomers to be continuously logged on to instant messaging (IM) and often to send text messages instead of talking on the phone. The following list presents three examples of potential work-related conflict across generations. The illustrations presented are stereotypes that apply to a *typical* member of each generation.

- **Preferred approach to communication:** Some Gen Y members prefer abbreviated conversation rather than fully explaining what they mean. Baby Boomers prefer e-mail, cell phones, and face-to-face communication. Some Generation Y members express their discontent with something at work by sending a tweet, whereas most Baby Boomer and Generation X members would deal with the matter internally.

- **Approach to problem solving:** Gen X members prefer to form a team to brainstorm a solution, as well as to use the Internet and social networking for research. Gen Y members prefer to think up a list of solutions on their own, then call a meeting to discuss the alternative solutions. Baby boomers like to think about what has worked in the past and how it can be replicated. Then they call a meeting to discuss possible alternatives. Traditionalists (born 1922–1945) tend to be thorough and detail oriented. Gen Y (Millenials) will often multitask while solving a problem. Often they want to move quickly to another problem because of a short attention span, whereas Traditionalists and Baby Boomers may want to drag out a problem.

- **Requirement for being respected:** Gen X members want to have their ideas valued by coworkers. Gen Y members want to have their professionalism and growing knowledge valued. Baby boomers want to have their decades of work experience and input still valued.[21] Many Generation Y members want continual praise, and are hurt by criticism. Many Baby Boomers and Generation X members see no problem with deserved criticism and use praise only when deserved.[22]

Although cross-generational conflict is mild in nature, it can still lead to miscommunication and hard feelings that disrupt work.

Workplace Violence (A Cause and Effect of Conflict)

Aggressiveness in the workplace can take extreme forms, such as the shooting or knifing of a former boss or colleague by a mentally unstable worker recently dismissed from the company. Workplace violence is a cause of conflict in the sense that being the subject of violence, witnessing violence, or worrying about violence creates two opposing needs—the worker wants a peaceful environment, yet is forced to experience chaos. Conflict is also created by any physical altercation between the perpetrator and the victim. Workplace violence is an effect of conflict because as an extreme response to conflict, such as being fired, some workers strike back at their employer through physical aggression directed at the former boss and coworkers.

Violence has become so widespread that homicide is the fourth leading cause of workplace deaths, with about 500 workers murdered each year in the United States. According to the Bureau of Labor Statistics Census of Fatal Occupations, homicides account for about 10 percent of all fatal workplace injuries.[23] Homicide is the leading cause of death for women in the workplace. Most workplace deaths result from a robbery or commercial crime. Many of these killings, however, are perpetrated by a disgruntled worker or fired employee harboring an unresolved conflict. As companies have continued to reduce their workforce despite being profitable, these incidents have increased in frequency.

Workplace violence is often predictable, with the worker who may erupt into violence showing early signals, according to Lynne McClure, a specialist in managing high-risk employees.[24] Predictors of workplace violence include the following employee behaviors and verbal expressions: talk about weaponry, paranoid (highly suspicious) or antisocial behavior, reference to not being heard by management, expression of extreme desperation, history of violence, and being a loner who does not fit into the group. Multiple behaviors such as those just described might be reported to the manager or human resource professional. Yet you need to be careful about not referring a coworker who displays just one predictor of violent behavior.

Task versus Relationship Conflict

In addition to the sources of conflict, another way to understand conflict is whether it is aimed at work or personal issues. A subtle point here is that you can be involved in interpersonal conflict over both the task and the relationship. Some conflicts on the job deal mostly with disagreements over how work should be done. **Task conflict** focuses on substantive, issue-related differences related to the work itself.[25] These issues are tangible and concrete and can be dealt with more intellectually than emotionally. Two group members, for example, might argue over whether it is better to use their limited advertising budget to buy space on the outside of a bus or on Facebook.

Other conditions within the group are more people oriented. They occur because people have personality clashes, are rude to each other, or simply view problems and situations from a different frame of reference. **Relationship conflict** focuses on personalized, individually oriented issues. The conflict relates to subjective issues that are dealt with more emotionally than intellectually.[26] One symptom indicating that relationship conflict exists with the group is when during a meeting, two people say to each other frequently, "Let me finish speaking."

An analysis of many studies cautions that task conflict and relationship conflict can be equally disruptive. A little conflict may be beneficial, but this advantage quickly breaks down as conflict intensifies.[27] An example of an advantage of conflict is the stimulation of problem solving and creativity; a disadvantage is negative stress. The underlying explanation for the problems associated with all conflict is that people take differences of opinion personally, whether the issue is strictly the task or their personal characteristics.

CONFLICT-MANAGEMENT STYLES

LEARNING OBJECTIVE 3

The information presented so far is designed to help you understand the nature of conflict. Such background information is useful for resolving conflict because it helps you understand what is happening in a conflict situation. The next two sections offer more specific information about managing and resolving conflict. Before describing specific methods of resolving conflict, it is useful to present more details about five general styles, or modes, of handling conflict. You received preliminary information on two of these five styles when you completed Self-Assessment Quiz 9-1.

As shown in Figure 9-1, Kenneth Thomas identified five major styles of conflict management, with this categorizing of styles still in active use. Each style is based on a combination of satisfying one's own concerns (assertiveness) and satisfying the concerns of others (cooperativeness).[28]

Competitive Style

The competitive style is a desire to win one's own concerns at the expense of the other party, or to dominate. A person with a competitive orientation is likely to engage in power struggles in which one side wins and the other loses (an approach referred to as win–lose). "My way or the highway" is a win–lose strategy. Workplace bullies prefer the competitive style of conflict management. The competitive style works best when quick, decisive action is essential, such as in an emergency.

FIGURE 9-1 Conflict-Handling Styles According to Degree of Cooperation and Assertiveness

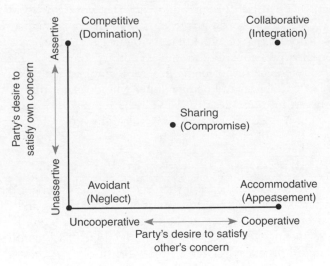

Accommodative Style

The accommodative style favors appeasement, or satisfying the other's concerns without taking care of one's own. People with this orientation may be generous or self-sacrificing just to maintain a relationship. An irate customer might be accommodated with a full refund, just to calm down the person. The intent of such accommodation might also be to retain the customer's loyalty. Accommodation sounds harmless, but can result in granting such large conscessions that they are later regretted.

Accommodation works best when you are wrong, or when the issues are more important to the other side. For example, a small business owner might take back damaged merchandise rather than going through the struggle of facing a lawsuit.

win–win

The belief that after conflict has been resolved, both sides should gain something of value.

Ryan McVay/Getty Images

Sharing Style

The sharing style is halfway between domination and appeasement. Sharers prefer moderate but incomplete satisfaction for both parties, which results in a compromise. The phrase "splitting the difference" reflects this orientation and is commonly used in such activities as purchasing a house or car. The sharing (or compromising) style is well suited to a situation in which both sides have equal power, yet are committed to mutually exclusive goals such as the buyer and the seller of the house wanting to maximize financial gain.

Collaborative Style (Win–Win)

In contrast to the other styles, the collaborative style reflects a wish to fully satisfy the desires of both parties. It is based on an underlying philosophy of **win–win**, the belief that after a conflict has been resolved, both sides should gain something of value. The use of a win–win approach is aimed at arriving at a settlement that meets the needs of both parties, or at least does not badly damage the welfare of either side. The option chosen results in a mutual gain. When collaborative approaches to resolving conflict are used, the relationships among the parties are built on and improved.

Mobile phone companies in search of antenna sites have led to win–win conflict resolution between companies and communities. Many of these companies have integrated antennas into church steeples, high-rise buildings, and other tall structures without defacing them. A mobile telephone company has sometimes constructed a new church steeple that harbors a giant antenna. The company wins by having an antenna to provide cell phone service, and community groups do not object to the sight of a freestanding antenna. At the same time, the church wins by having a new steeple.

Collaborating is particularly important when both sides must be committed to the solution, such as the situation with the hidden cell antennae. Divorcing parents also need collaboration in their division of assets, because they need to work together long term for the good of the children.

Finding win–win solutions to problems (or options for mutual gain) is one of the most important conflict-resolution skills. To obtain practice in this skill, complete Skill-Building Exercise 9-1.

Avoidant Style

The avoider is a combination of a person who is uncooperative and unassertive. He or she is indifferent to the concerns of either party. The person may actually be withdrawing from the conflict to rely upon fate. Avoiding works well when an issue is trivial, or there are more pressing issues to worry about. For example, a supervisor might not bother reprimanding workers who are a few minutes late, because the supervisor is flooded with other work.

In the following description of specific techniques for resolving conflict, attempt to relate most of them to these five key styles. For example, you will observe that the confrontation and problem-solving technique reflects the collaborative (win–win) style.

GUIDELINES AND TECHNIQUES FOR RESOLVING CONFLICTS

LEARNING OBJECTIVE 4

Interpersonal conflict in organizations is inevitable. A career-minded person must therefore learn effective ways of resolving conflict. This section describes methods of conflict resolution that you can use on your own. All are based somewhat on the underlying win–win model, or integrating the interests of both parties. Integrating both interests focuses on resolving the underlying concerns of the parties in conflict. By dealing with these concerns, it is more worthwhile for both sides to resolve the conflict than it is to have no agreement.

Suppose a woman named Molly Coors wanted to open a beer brewery and name her beer Coors. The company lawyers from Coors-Molson, which own the rights to the brand name Coors, would attempt to block her from using the same brand name—even if her family name is Coors. Molly Coors would hire her own lawyer to fight back. Two key concerns must be addressed. Molly Coors' underlying concern is that she feels her civil liberties have been violated because she cannot name a business after herself. And Molly must deal with Coors-Molson's concern about a smaller company capitalizing on its well-known name (brand equity).

Later in the chapter, you will be asked to resolve such difficult conflict. The following paragraphs describe four methods of conflict resolution.

Confrontation and Problem Solving

The ideal approach to resolving any conflict is to confront the real issue and then solve the problem. **Confrontation** means taking a problem-solving approach to differences and identifying the underlying facts, logic, or emotions that account for them. When conflicts are resolved through confronting and understanding their causes, people feel responsible for finding the soundest answer.

Confrontation can proceed gently, in a way that preserves a good working relationship, as shown by this example. Assume that Mary, the person working at the desk next to you, loudly cracks chewing gum while she works. You find the gum chewing both distracting and nauseating. If you don't bring the problem to Mary's attention, it will probably grow in proportion with time. Yet you are hesitant to enter into an argument about something that a person might regard as a civil liberty (the right to chew gum in public places).

A psychologically sound alternative is for you to approach her directly in this manner:

You: Mary, there is something bothering me that I would like to discuss with you.

She: Go ahead, I don't mind listening to other people's problems.

You: My problem concerns something you are doing that makes it difficult for me to concentrate on my work. When you chew gum, you make loud cracking noises that grate on my nerves. It may be my problem, but the noise does bother me.

She: I guess I could stop chewing gum when you're working next to me. It's probably just a nervous habit.

When resolving conflict through confrontation and problem solving, as well as other methods of conflict resolution, it is helpful to bring closure by shaking hands, repeating your individual commitments, and then saying "thank you." Following through on your commitments is also essential for effective conflict resolution.[29]

A notable point about the process of confrontation and problem solving is that an in-person meeting is preferable to using e-mail, texting, social media, or even a telephone call for the confrontation. As career counselor Deb Koen explains, in an emotionally charged situation e-mails do not work well for expressing feelings. An e-mail or social media message leaves too much room for interpretation and hides most of the nonverbal communication essential for communicating feelings.[30]

Constructive Handling of Criticism

Learning to profit from criticism is an effective way of benefiting from conflict. People who benefit from criticism are able to stand outside themselves while being criticized. It is as if they are watching the criticism from a distance and looking for its possible merits. People who take criticism personally anguish when receiving negative feedback. The following are six specific suggestions for dealing with criticism, including two methods that will often get the other party on your side.[31]

1. **See yourself at a distance.** Place an imaginary Plexiglas shield between you and the person giving the criticism. Attempt to be a detached observer looking for useful information.

2. **Ask for clarification and specifics.** Ask politely for more details about the negative behavior in question so that you can change if change is warranted. If your boss is criticizing you for being rude to customers, you might respond: "I certainly do not want to be rude. Can you give me a couple of examples of how I was rude? I need your help in working on this problem." After asking questions, you can better determine whether the criticism is valid.

3. **Decide on a response.** An important part of learning from criticism is to respond appropriately to the critic. Let the criticizer know what you agree with. Apologize for the undesirable behavior, such as saying, "I apologize for being rude to

customers. I know what I can do differently now. I'll be more patient so as not to appear rude." Apology is a highly effective method of getting the criticizer on your side. Without an apology, the attack is likely to continue.

4. **Look for a pattern in terms of other criticism.** Is the criticism you are receiving something you have heard several times before from different people? The more times you have heard the same criticism, the more likely it is to be valid. If three different supervisors have told you that you do not follow through with your promises to get work done, the criticism is most likely valid.

5. **Disarm the opposition.** An extension of point 3 is that you will often decide to agree with the criticizer because the person has a legitimate complaint about you. If you deny the reality of that person's complaint, he or she will continue to harp on that point, and the issue will remain unresolved. By agreeing with the criticism, you may set the stage for a true resolution of the problem.

   Agreeing with criticism made by a person with formal authority over you is effective because by doing so you are then in a position to ask for his or her help in improving the situation. Rational managers realize that it is their responsibility to help group members overcome problems, not merely to criticize them. Imagine that you have been chronically late with reports during the last six months. It is time for a performance evaluation, and you know that you will be reprimanded for your tardiness. You also hope that your manager will not downgrade all other aspects of your performance because of your tardy reports. Here is how disarming the opposition would work in this situation:

   Your manager: Have a seat. It's time for your performance evaluation, and we have a lot to talk about. I'm concerned about some things.

   You: So am I. It appears that I'm having a difficult time getting my reports in on time. I wonder if I'm being a perfectionist. Do you have any suggestions?

   Your manager: Well, I like your attitude. Maybe you are trying to make your reports too perfect before you turn them in. I think you can improve in getting your reports in on time. Try not to figure out everything to three decimal places. We need thoroughness around here, but we can't overdo it.

   Disarming is effective because it takes the wind out of the other person's sails and has a calming effect. The other person is often waiting to clobber you if you deny guilt. If you admit guilt, you are more difficult to clobber. Skill-Building Exercise 9-2 gives you an opportunity to practice disarming the opposition.

6. **Offer an apology if warranted.** Related to disarming the opposition is the general-purpose technique of apologizing for something you have done wrong. An apology often helps keep the criticism from escalating. For example, if a worker apologizes for publicly insulting the company on Facebook, the CEO might simply say, "Apology accepted. Just don't do it again." An effective apology includes an acknowledgement of the wrongdoing, regret, responsibility for what happened,

SKILL-BUILDING EXERCISE 9-2

Disarming the Opposition

In each of these two scenarios, one person plays the role of the person with more power in the situation. The other person plays the role of the individual attempting to disarm the criticizer.

1. A representative from a credit agency telephones you at work to inform you that you are 60 days behind schedule on your car payment. The agent wants a settlement as soon as possible. Unfortunately, the credit agent is correct. Run this happy scenario for about five minutes.

2. Your manager calls you into the office to discuss the 10-page report you just submitted. The boss says in a harsh tone,

"Your report is a piece of trash. I counted 25 word-use mistakes such as writing *whether* for *weather* and *seen* for *scene.* (Your spell checker couldn't catch these errors.) Besides that, I can't follow many of your sentences, and you left out the table of statistics. I'm wondering if you are qualified for this job."

Observers of the role-play will judge how effective the person being criticized was in reducing some of the anger directed against him or her. Look also for any changes in attitude on the part of the criticizer.

and a plan to remedy the problem.[32] The person who posted the offensive comment on Facebook might therefore say. "I did something stupid, and I regret having insulted our fine company. It was entirely my fault. Tonight I will work on getting this post removed."

Reframing

Another useful approach to resolving conflict is to reexamine or *reframe* the conflict situation by looking at it in a different light. The following are two practical approaches to reframing, one by searching for the positives in the situation, and the other by asking questions.

Reframing through Cognitive Restructuring. An indirect way of resolving interpersonal conflict is to lessen the conflicting elements in a situation by viewing them more positively. According to the technique of **cognitive restructuring**, you mentally convert negative aspects into positive ones by looking for the positive elements in a situation. How you frame or choose your thoughts can determine the outcome of a conflict situation. Your thoughts influence your actions. If you search for the beneficial elements in the situation, there will be less area for dispute. Although this technique might sound like a mind game to you, it can work effectively.

Imagine that a coworker of yours, Jeff, has been asking you repeated questions about how to carry out a work procedure. You are about ready to tell Jeff, "Go bother somebody else; I'm not paid to be a trainer." Instead, you look for the positive elements in the situation. You say to yourself, "Jeff has been asking me a lot of questions. This does take time, but answering these questions is valuable experience. If I want to become a manager, I will have to help group members with problems."

After having completed this cognitive restructuring, you can then deal with the conflict situation more positively. You might say to Jeff, "I welcome the opportunity to help you, but we need to find a mutually convenient time. In that way, I can better concentrate on my own work." To get started with cognitive restructuring, do Skill-Building Exercise 9-3.

Reframing by Asking Questions. Another way to use reframing is to step back, take a deep breath, and then ask the following questions about the conflict situation that arises within the work group:

- Do I fully understand the situation?
- Am I sure what my coworker is really saying?
- Is the person really angry with me or just worried and anxious?
- Have I missed something important?
- Do I have all the facts?
- What is the real issue here?
- How do I want to react in this situation?
- How would I want to be treated if the situation were reversed?

cognitive restructuring

Mentally converting negative aspects into positive ones by looking for the positive elements in a situation.

SKILL-BUILDING EXERCISE 9-3

Reframing through Cognitive Restructuring

The following are examples of negative statements about others in the workplace. In the space provided, cognitively restructure (reframe) each comment in a positive way.

Negative: Nancy is getting on my nerves. It takes her two weeks longer than anyone else in the team to complete her input.

Positive:

Negative: Rob is so obsessed with sports that he is hurting my productivity. Where does it say in the employee handbook that I have to spend 30 minutes on Monday listening to Rob's comments

on his team's weekend performance? Doesn't he know that I have a job to do and that I just don't care about his team?

Positive:

Negative: My boss is driving me crazy. He is forever telling me what I did wrong and making suggestions for improvement. He makes me feel like I'm in elementary school.

Positive:

By taking such a approach, you are more likely to communicate more effectively and constructively with each of your coworkers when conflict situations arise. You carefully talk through the issues rather than becoming explosive, defensive, and argumentative. A useful scenario for reframing through questioning is when a coworker accuses you of not carrying your fair share of the workload.[33]

Negotiating and Bargaining

Conflicts can be considered situations calling for **negotiating**, or conferring with another person to resolve a problem. When you are negotiating a fair salary for yourself, you are trying to resolve a conflict. At first the demands of the two parties may seem incompatible, but through negotiation, a salary figure may emerge that satisfies both. The Program on Negotiation at the Harvard Law School emphasizes a useful and human perspective about negotiation. The focus of negotiation should be on building a cooperative relationship and creating value. You might want to claim as much of that value you can for yourself, but the goal is not to squash the other side.[34]

negotiating

Conferring with another person to resolve a problem.

Another perspective on negotiation is that people are not just negotiating for the economic value of the negotiation. They are also negotiating for intangibles, such as feeling good about the negotiation process, the other party, and themselves.[35] For example, after the negotiation is complete, the individual might want to be perceived as an honest, sincere professional, rather than as a dishonest person out to maximize gain.

Managers and staff specialists must negotiate both internally (e.g., with subordinates, managers, and team leaders) and externally (e.g., with customers, suppliers, and government agencies). Considerable negotiation also takes place among coworkers. Team members, for example, sometimes negotiate among themselves about work assignments. One might say to the other, "I'm willing to be notetaker this year if there is some way I can cut back on the amount of plant visits I make this year." Eight useful negotiating tactics are presented here. Before studying them, take Self-Assessment Quiz 9-2.

Understand the Other Party's Perspective.   As in being a good listener, empathy can be an important part of negotiation. Deepak Malhotra and Max H. Bazerman observe that negotiators often channel too much effort into pushing their own position and too little into understanding the other side's perspective.[36] To obtain a good deal, or sometimes any deal at all, negotiators have to dig for information about *why* the other side wants what it demands. Inaccurate assumptions about the other side's motives can lead negotiators to propose solutions to the wrong problems, waste money, or kill a deal. How about a personal life example for dog lovers?

You have wanted a Great Dane puppy for a long time. You enter into negotiations with the owner of the puppy and his mother. The owner is asking $900, and is adamant about her demands. If you are low on empathy, you will raise such negotiating points as how much the little Great Dane is costing the owner in food, that you will pay cash, and that the little fellow is ugly and therefore is only worth $500. (You might get invited off the premises in a hurry.) In contrast, with high empathy and a detective-like mind, you recognize that the owner wants the puppy to go to a wonderful home. So, if she asks for a lot of money, the potential owner is likely to be really interested in finding someone who truly wants the dog and would therefore probably take good care of the puppy.

With this negotiating point in mind, you point out what great care you will give the Great Dane, what a spacious yard you have, how you would take him jogging every day, and how he would be your dream dog. The owner is happy, because one of her key motives is for the pup to have a wonderful home. She is touched and agrees to your offer of $600.

Another key part of understanding the other party's perspective is that you look for common ground. Your talk of care and concern about the dog's health indicates that both you and the owner share a humanitarian attitude toward dogs.

To understand the other party's perspective, you often have to prepare in advance. Obtain as much information as you can about the other party's side before the negotiation

The Negotiator Quiz

Directions: The following quiz is designed to give you tentative insight into your tendencies toward being an effective negotiator. Check whether each statement is mostly true or mostly false as it applies to you.

		Mostly true	Mostly false
1.	Settling differences of opinion is a lot of fun.	_____	_____
2.	I try to avoid conflict and confrontation with others as much as possible.	_____	_____
3.	I am self-conscious about asking people for favors they have not offered me spontaneously.	_____	_____
4.	I am generally unwilling to compromise.	_____	_____
5.	How the other side feels about the results of our negotiation is of little consequence to me.	_____	_____
6.	I think very well under pressure.	_____	_____
7.	People say that I am tactful and diplomatic.	_____	_____
8.	I have heard that I express my viewpoint clearly.	_____	_____
9.	Very few things in life are not negotiable.	_____	_____
10.	I always (or would always) accept whatever salary increase is offered to me.	_____	_____
11.	A person's facial expression often reveals as much as what the person actually says.	_____	_____
12.	I wouldn't mind taking a few short-term losses to win a long-term battle.	_____	_____
13.	I'm willing to work long and hard to win a small advantage.	_____	_____
14.	I'm usually too busy talking to do much listening.	_____	_____
15.	It's fun to haggle over price when buying a car.	_____	_____
16.	I almost always prepare in advance for a negotiating session.	_____	_____
17.	When there is something I need from another person, I usually get it.	_____	_____
18.	It would make me feel cheap if I offered somebody only two-thirds of his or her asking price.	_____	_____
19.	People are usually paid what they are worth, so there's no use haggling over starting salaries.	_____	_____
20.	I rarely take what people say at face value.	_____	_____
21.	It's easy for me to smile when involved in a serious discussion.	_____	_____
22.	For one side to win in negotiation, the other side has to lose.	_____	_____
23.	Once you start making concessions, the other side is bound to get more than you.	_____	_____
24.	A good negotiating session gets my competitive urges flowing.	_____	_____
25.	When negotiations are completed, both sides should walk away with something valuable.	_____	_____
	Total Score	_____	_____

Scoring and Interpretation: Score yourself 1 for each of your answers that agrees with the scoring key. The higher your score, the more likely it is that you currently have good negotiating skills, providing your self-assessment is accurate. It might prove useful to also have somebody who has observed you negotiate on several occasions to answer the Negotiator Quiz for you. Scores of 7 or lower and 20 or higher are probably the most indicative of weak or strong negotiating potential. Here is the scoring key:

1. Mostly true	8. Mostly true	15. Mostly true	22. Mostly false
2. Mostly false	9. Mostly true	16. Mostly true	23. Mostly false
3. Mostly false	10. Mostly false	17. Mostly true	24. Mostly true
4. Mostly false	11. Mostly true	18. Mostly false	25. Mostly true
5. Mostly false	12. Mostly true	19. Mostly false	
6. Mostly true	13. Mostly true	20. Mostly true	
7. Mostly true	14. Mostly false	21. Mostly true	

session. A basic example is that many prospective car buyers first research the fair value of a vehicle before making an offer. Knowing how long the vehicle has been sitting on the lot or in the showroom is also useful advance information, because dealers often borrow money to build inventory.

Focus on Interests, Not Positions.   Rather than clinging to specific negotiating points, keep your overall interests in mind and try to satisfy them. Remember that the true object of negotiation is to satisfy the underlying interests on both sides, as in the case of Molly Coors. Part of focusing on interests is to carefully study the other side's comments for clues to the type of agreement that will satisfy both of you.

Careful listening will help you uncover the negotiating partner's specific interests and motivations. (This is another application of understanding the other party's perspective.) Here is how this strategy works:

> You are considering accepting a job offer that will enable you to work on the type of problems you prefer and to develop your professional skills. You have a starting salary in mind that would make you very happy: 10 percent higher than you are currently making. Your negotiating position is thus your present salary plus 10 percent; however, your true interests are probably to have more discretionary income than at present. (You want to make more purchases and invest more.) You will therefore be better off negotiating for a work situation that spreads your money further. You can now accept the offer by negotiating other points in addition to a 10 percent higher salary, including (1) working in a geographic area with a lower cost of living, (2) having a better opportunity for earning a bonus, or (3) receiving a generous expense account. During the negotiations, you may discover that the other party is looking for a talented employee at a salary and with benefits the company can afford.

Compromise.   The most widely used negotiating tactic is **compromise**, settlement of differences by mutual concessions. One party agrees to do something if the other party agrees to do something else. Compromise is a realistic approach to resolving conflict. Most labor–management disputes are settled by compromise. For instance, labor may agree to accept a smaller salary increase if management will subcontract less work to other countries.

Some people argue that compromise is not a win–win tactic. The problem is that the two parties may wind up with a solution that pacifies both but does not solve the problem. One example would be purchasing for two team leaders half the new equipment each one needs. As a result, neither department really shows a productivity gain. Nevertheless, compromise is both inevitable and useful.

compromise

Settlement of differences by mutual concessions.

Begin with a Plausible Demand or Offer, Yet Allow Room for Negotiation.   The commonsense approach to negotiation suggests that you begin with an extreme, almost fanciful demand or offer. The final compromise will therefore be closer to your true demand or offer than if you opened the negotiations more realistically; however, a plausible demand is useful because it shows you are bargaining in good faith. Also, if a third party has to resolve a conflict, a plausible demand or offer will receive more sympathy than an implausible one will. An example would be an arbitrator giving only a minimum settlement to an investor who wanted $10 million in damages for having received bad advice from an investment broker. (The arbitrator thinks that a $10 million settlement would be ridiculous.)

Although it is advisable to begin with a plausible demand, one must still allow room for negotiation. A basic strategy of negotiation is to begin with a demand that allows room for compromise and concession. If you think you need $5,000 in new furniture for your department, you might begin negotiations by asking for a $7,000 layout. Your boss offers you $4,000 as a starting point. After negotiation, you may wind up with the $5,000 you need.

Make Small Concessions Gradually.   Making steady concessions leads to more mutually satisfactory agreements in most situations. Gradually, you concede little things to the other side. The hard-line approach to bargaining is to make your concession early in the negotiation, and then grant no further concession. The tactic of making small concessions is well suited to purchasing a new car. In order to reach a price you consider acceptable, you might grant concessions such as agreeing to finance the car through the dealer or purchasing a service contract.

Know Your Best Alternative to a Negotiated Agreement. The reason you would probably negotiate would be to produce something better than the result obtainable without negotiating. The goal of negotiating is thus not just to agree, but to obtain more valuable results than would otherwise have occurred. When you are aware of your best alternative to a negotiated agreement (BATNA), it sets a floor to the agreement you are willing to accept. Your BATNA becomes the standard that can protect both parties from accepting terms that are too unfavorable. It also keeps you from walking away from terms that would be beneficial for you to accept.

What might a BATNA look like in practice? Suppose you are negotiating a starting salary for a full-time, professional position. The figure you have in mind is $42,000 per year. Your BATNA is $36,500, because this is the salary your future in-laws will pay you to enter the family business. You will therefore walk away from any offer of less than $37,000—just taking salary into account.

Knowing the other side's BATNA is also important because it helps define the other participant's bargaining zone. Understanding each other's bargaining zones makes it possible to arrive at mutually profitable trade-offs. In the preceding salary negotiations, the company's BATNA might be to hire a less well-educated job candidate at $30,500 and then upgrade his or her knowledge on the job.

An underlying advantage of knowing your BATNA is that it capitalizes on the power of a positive "no." Famous negotiator William Ury reasons that being able to say "no" to a demand places you in a strong position.[37] During negotiations, a statement such as "I am not willing to make that big a concession" can bring you respect, because you are standing up for your principles. For best effect, "no" should be expressed in a friendly and firm manner.

Use Anger to Your Advantage. Master negotiators make selective use of anger as a negotiating and bargaining tool. When a person becomes genuinely angry, the anger can energize him or her to be more resourceful and creative while bargaining. If you are angry about an issue or a negotiating point, the other side may be willing to submit to your demand rather than receive more of your anger. The director of a company wellness program might say with an angry look toward top management, "Why is there money in the budget for all kinds of frills like corporate jets, when a program that is preventing millions of dollars in lost productivity has to grovel for a decent budget?"

The downside of anger is that it can degenerate into incivility and personal insults. A touch of anger can be effective, but overdone, it becomes self-defeating. You have to size up how far you can push people before damaging a work relationship—or being fired. To make effective use of anger during negotiation, it has to be used at the right time, with the right tone, and in the right amount.[38] A person who is always angry will often not be taken seriously.

Allow for Face-Saving. We have saved one of the most important negotiating and conflict resolution strategies for last. Negotiating does not mean that you should try to squash the other side. You should try to create circumstances that will enable you to continue working with that person if it is necessary. People prefer to avoid looking weak, foolish, or incompetent during negotiation or when the process is completed. If you do not give your opponent an opportunity to save face, you will probably create a long-term enemy.

Face-saving could work in this way. A small-business owner winds up paying a higher starting salary for the director of manufacturing than she wanted. The employment agency who placed the director of manufacturing says to the business owner, "I know that Derek costs more than you have budgeted, but don't worry about it; you have made a great investment. Derek will increase your manufacturing productivity so much that his salary and benefits will be a bargain for you."

Effective negotiation, as with any other form of conflict resolution, requires extensive practice and knowledge of basic principles and techniques. As a starting point, you might take one of the negotiating tactics just described and practice it when the stakes are not so high. You might attempt to negotiate the price of a consumer electronics device, or negotiate for getting a particular Friday afternoon off from work.

A major theme running through the various approaches to conflict resolution, including negotiating and bargaining, is that cooperating with the other side is usually preferable to competing. A study with 61 self-managing teams with 489 employees supports this idea of the superiority of cooperation over competition in successful conflict resolution. The style of conflict resolution was measured through questionnaires. For example, a statement geared toward cooperative behavior was, "We seek a solution that will be good for the whole team." Conflict efficacy was measured by a questionnaire indicating the extent to which team members believed that they could successfully manage different conflict situations. Group effectiveness was measured by the ratings of supervisor and team leaders on productivity, quality, and cost savings: central reasons why self-directed teams are formed.

The study found that the cooperative approach to conflict was positively related to conflict efficacy. In contrast, the competitive approach to conflict was negatively related to conflict efficacy. Equally important, conflict efficacy was strongly associated with supervisory and team-leader ratings of team effectiveness.[39]

Skill-Building Exercise 9-4 provides you with the opportunity to practice negotiating in a scenario that most people encounter at least once in their career.

COMBATING SEXUAL HARASSMENT: A SPECIAL TYPE OF CONFLICT

Many employees face conflict because a supervisor, coworker, or customer sexually harasses them. **Sexual harassment** is generally defined as unwanted sexually oriented behavior in the workplace that results in discomfort or interference with the job. The legal definition of sexual harassment is unwelcome verbal, visual, or physical conduct of a sexual nature that is severe or pervasive and affects working conditions or creates a hostile working environment. It can include an action as violent as rape or as subtle as a sexually oriented comment about a person's body or appearance. Harassment creates conflict because the harassed person has to make a choice between two incompatible motives. One motive is to get ahead, keep the job, or have an unthreatening work environment. But to satisfy this motive, the person is forced to sacrifice the motive of holding on to his or her moral value or preferences. Here we focus on the types and frequency of sexual harassment, the effects of harassment, and guidelines for dealing with the problem.

LEARNING OBJECTIVE 5

sexual harassment

Unwanted sexually oriented behavior in the workplace that results in discomfort or interference with the job.

Types of Harassment

The courts recognize two types of sexual harassment. In *quid pro quo* sexual harassment, the individual suffers job loss, or threatened loss of a job benefit, as a result of his or her responses to a request for sexual favors. The demands of a harasser can be explicit or implied. An example of quid pro quo harassment is a manager promising an employee a promotion in exchange for sexual favors and then not promoting the employee because the employee refused.

The other form of sexual harassment is *hostile environment*. It occurs when someone in the workplace creates an intimidating, hostile, or offensive working environment. An employee who is subjected to sexually suggestive comments, lewd jokes, or advances is a victim of hostile environment harassment. No tangible loss has to be suffered in this form of sexual harassment. In recent years there are more complaints about hostile enivonment harassment than quid pro quo. Quite often the complaints relate to bosses who make sexual remarks or send inappropriate e-mails and text messages ("sexting").[40]

Different Perceptions of Sexual Harassment. An analysis of many studies indicated that women perceive a broader range of social–sexual behaviors as harassing. The analysis also found that the female–male difference was larger for behaviors associated with hostile work environment harassment, derogatory attitudes toward women, dating pressure, or physical sexual contact. Men and women, however, agree closely that various types of sexual coercion, such as encounters that are made a condition of promotion, can be classified as quid pro quo harassment.[41]

In attempting to understand what constitutes sexual harassment, research and common sense suggest that not all sexually oriented behaviors such as jokes about sex and mild flirting are offensive or unwanted. Many workers perceived such behavior as enjoyable. Especially with e-mail and texting, many men and women send each other sexually oriented jokes. Sexual behavior has to be *unwanted* to be classified as sexual harassment. A surprising aspect of the research in question is that even when employees enjoyed sexually oriented behavior at work, they still experienced negative effects. The negative effects were thinking about quitting and lower psychological well-being.[42]

Sexual Harassment as Power. Sexual harassment is also regarded as an expression of power by one individual over another because the harasser often has more formal power than the harassed. The coworker who harasses another coworker may be attempting to use personal rather than formal power. Similarly, customers and clients who sexually harass a worker may be attempting to exert power. The harasser, following this logic, is a power abuser as well as a legal offender.

Frequency and Setting of Sexual Harassment

Sexual harassment is widespread in the US workplace and in other countries as well. According to one large-scale study, when conclusions are based on more scientific studies, 58 percent of women report having experienced potential harassment behaviors, and 24 percent report having experienced sexual harassment on the job. Approximately 16 percent of sexual harassment complaints made to the EEOC (Equal Employment Opportunity Commission) are from men, both against women and other men.[43] Sexual harassment directed at professional women by clients and customers is more frequent than harassment within the company. Sexist hostility, such as putting a person down because of his or her sex, was the most frequently noted type of harassment.[44]

Women in nontraditional jobs (such as welder or pressroom supervisor) are especially likely to be harassed. Similarly, a study found that women in male-dominated manufacturing plants are harassed more than women in female-dominated community service centers.[45] A possible reason is that in a male-dominated organization, men may feel that they have more power over women. Although women in nontraditional jobs run a high risk of being sexually harassed, harassment takes place in many other settings as well and at all levels in an organization.

The Adverse Effects of Sexual Harassment

Aside from being unethical, immoral, and illegal, sexual harassment is widely thought to have adverse consequences. The harassed person may experience job stress, lowered morale, severe conflict, and lowered productivity. The studies indicate that harassment negatively affects job performance, loyalty to the firm, and personal wellbeing. Note also that some women suffered posttraumatic stress disorder, almost as if they had been involved in a serious accident.[46]

Guidelines for Preventing and Dealing with Sexual Harassment

A starting point in dealing with sexual harassment is to develop an awareness of the types of behaviors that are considered sexual harassment. Often the difference is subtle. Suppose, for example, you placed copies of two photos of nude people on a coworker's desk or sent them as an attachment to an e-mail. Your coworker might call that harassment. Yet if you took that coworker to a museum to see the same photos in an exhibit, your behavior usually would not be classified as harassment. Following is a sampling of behaviors that will often be interpreted as environmental harassment.[47] Awareness of these behaviors is important because many harassers have no desire to offend or knowledge that they are offending others. Such individuals are insensitive, and often ill informed. If people refrain from doing these acts, many instances of sexual harassment will be avoided.

1. **Inappropriate remarks and sexual implications:** Coworkers, subordinates, customers, and suppliers should not be referred to as sexual beings, and their appearance should not be referred to in a sexual manner. Telling a coworker she has gorgeous feet, or he has fabulous biceps, is out of place at work.

2. **Terms of endearment:** Refrain from calling others in the workplace by names such as "cutie," "sweetie pie," "honey," "dear," or "hunk." One might argue that these terms are simply sexist (different roles for men and women) and not sexual harassment. This argument, however, has lost ground because any behavior that puts people down based on their gender can be interpreted as harassment from a legal perspective. Keep in mind also that some people find terms of

endearment to have a sexual connotation. If you felt no physical attraction toward another adult, would you call that person "beauty" or "hunk"?

3. **Suggestive compliments:** It is acceptable to tell another person that he or she looks nice, but avoid sexually tinged comments, such as mentioning that the person's clothing shows off his or her body to advantage.

4. **Physical touching:** To avoid any appearance of sexual harassment, it is best to restrict physical touching to handshakes and an occasional sideways hug. High-five handshakes or fist bumps are favored by many because they are less intimate than the traditional type. Hugging a long-term work associate is much more acceptable than hugging a new hire. Minimize such behaviors as adjusting a coworker's earring, touching someone's hair, and tweaking a person's chin.

5. **Work-related kissing:** It is best to avoid all kissing in a work context—except, perhaps, a light kiss at an office party or picnic. It is much more professional to greet a work associate with a warm, sincere handshake, including the high-five type. Cultural differences must be taken into account here; for example, many Europeans and Africans greet work associates with a peck on both sides of the face.

6. **Visual sexually oriented presentations.** Many people believe they are sexually harassed because somebody else in the workplace displays still photos, computer images, screen savers, and e-mail attachments of a sexual nature. Even photos of fully clothed people in revealing clothing might be interpeted by somebody as sexual in nature, so it is best to not display any sexually oriented visual presentations in the workplace.

Company management also plays a major role in preventing and dealing with sexual harassment. Based on the observations of dozens of human resource specialists and employment law attorneys, several actions by management are critical.[48] The cornerstone of control of sexual harassment is creating and widely disseminating a policy about harassment. The policy should carefully define harassment and state that the company has zero tolerance for such behavior. Company officials designated for hearing complaints should be specified. In addition, the company should have an open-door policy about harassment. Such a policy means that any employee with a concern about being harassed is able to go directly to a senior manager without worrying about his or her supervisor taking revenge.

Brief company training programs covering the type of information presented in this chapter are also part of a serious program to prevent and deal with sexual harassment; however, a one-time presentation of a 15-minute video about sexual harassment is not sufficient. Periodic discussion about the topic is recommended.

After sexual harassment has taken place, the victim will usually want to resolve the conflict. Two key strategies are either to use a formal complaint procedure or to resolve the conflict on your own. If you choose the latter course, you will save yourself the time of going through a lengthy investigation procedure. Figure 9-2 presents details about the two key strategies for dealing with sexual harassment. Skill-Building Exercise 9-5 offers you an opportunity to simulate the control of sexual harassment.

A major recommendation for documenting acts of sexual harassment is to keep a running diary of incidents against you. A log of the incidents is impressive to company officials, lawyers, and judges (should a lawsuit ultimately be involved). Following are examples of log entries from a woman and a man:

- January 17, 2015: Jim Quattrone, the manager of accounts payable, asked me to have dinner with him for the sixth time, and I turned him down again. I said "no," "no," "no."
- March 13, 2015: Meg Evans, my supervisor, said that I would receive a much better performance evaluation if I could come over to her house for dinner. She said her husband would be out of town, so I could stay overnight if I wanted to. I felt so uncomfortable and pressured. I made up an excuse about having an exclusive relationship.

FIGURE 9-2 How to Deal with Sexual Harassment

The potential or actual victim of sexual harassment is advised to use the following methods and tactics to deal with the problem.

Formal Complaint Procedure. Whenever an employee believes that he or she has encountered sexual harassment, or if an employee is suspected to be the perpetrator of sexual harassment, the complainant should report the incident to his or her immediate supervisor (if that person is not the harasser) or to the next higher level of management if the supervisor is the harasser. The supervisor contacted is responsible for contacting a designated company official immediately regarding each complaint. The officer will explain the investigative procedures to the complainant and any supervisor involved. All matters will be kept strictly confidential, including private conversations with all parties.

Dealing with the Problem on Your Own. The easiest way to deal with sexual harassment is to speak up before it becomes serious. The first time it happens, respond with a statement such as: "I won't tolerate this kind of talk," "I dislike sexually oriented jokes," or "Keep your hands off me."

SKILL-BUILDING EXERCISE 9-5

Combating Sexual Harassment

The two role-plays in this exercise provide practice in applying the recommended techniques for combating sexual harassment. The activities have an implied sexual content, and they are for educational purposes only. Any students offended by these role-plays should exclude themselves from participating.

Scenario 1: The Offensive Jester. One student plays the role of Max, a man who delights in telling sexually oriented jokes and anecdotes in the office. He often brings a tabloid newspaper to the office to read sexually oriented passages to coworkers, both male and female. Another student assumes the role of Maxine, a woman in the office who takes offense to Max's humor. She wants to convince Max that he is committing sexual harassment with his sexually oriented humor. Max does not see himself as committing sexual harassment.

Scenario 2: The Flirtatious Office Manager. One student assumes the role of Bertha, an office manager who is single. Another student plays the role of Bert, a married man who recently joined the company as an office assistant. Bert reports to Bertha, and she finds him physically attractive. Bertha visits Bert at his desk and makes such comments as "It looks like you have great quadriceps. I wonder what you look like in running shorts." Bert wants to be on good terms with Bertha, but he feels uncomfortable with her advances. He also wants to behave professionally in the office.

Run both role-plays in front of the class for about eight minutes. Other students in the class will observe the role-plays and then provide feedback about how well Maxine and Bert were able to prevent or stop sexual harassment. Observe if Maxine and Bert used any of the recommended techniques for dealing with harassment.

Concept Review and Reinforcement

Key Terms

conflict 219
role conflict 219
work–family conflict 221
personality clash 222

incivility 223
win–win 226
cognitive restructuring 230
negotiating 231

compromise 233
sexual harassment 235

Summary

A conflict is a situation in which two or more goals, values, or events are incompatible or mutually exclusive. Interpersonal conflicts have many sources or causes. An underlying source of job conflict is that people compete for limited resources. Another leading cause of incompatibility is role conflict, having to choose between two competing demands or expectations. Competing work and family demands represent a major role conflict. Other key sources of conflict are personality clashes and drama, aggressive personalities (including bullies, incivility, and rudeness), and cross-generational conflict. Workplace violence is both a cause and an effect of job conflict. In addition to the sources of conflict, another way to understand conflict is whether it is aimed at work or personal issues. When intense, both task and relationship conflict can by disruptive.

Five major styles of conflict management have been identified: competitive, accommodative, sharing, collaborative (win–win), and avoidant. Each style is based on a combination of satisfying one's own concerns (assertiveness) and satisfying the concerns of others (cooperativeness).

Confrontation and problem solving is the ideal method for resolving conflict. Learning to benefit from criticism is an effective way of benefiting from conflict. People who benefit from criticism are able to stand outside themselves while being criticized. Another way to deal with criticism is to disarm the opposition by agreeing with his or her criticism. Reframing a situation can be helpful in resolving conflict. Reframing through cognitive restructuring lessens conflict by the person looking for the positive elements in a situation. Asking questions such as, "How would I want to

be treated if the situation were reversed?" is another type or reframing.

Negotiating and bargaining is a major approach to resolving conflict. People negotiate for economic value and also for intangibles such as feeling good. Negotiation tactics include understanding the other party's perspective, focusing on interests rather than positions, compromising, beginning with a plausible demand or offer yet allowing room for negotiation, and making small concessions gradually. It is also important to know your BATNA (best alternative to a negotiated agreement). Using anger to your advantage can sometimes work. Allowing for face saving is also recommended.

Sexual harassment is a form of interpersonal conflict with legal implications. The two forms of sexual harassment are (1) quid pro quo (demanding sex in exchange for favors) and (2) creating a hostile environment. People have differing perceptions of what constitutes sexual harassment, and some workers enjoy sexually oriented behavior on the job. Sexual harassment is often an expression of power. Sexual harassment is widespread in the workplace. Research has pinpointed adverse mental and physical consequences of sexual harassment.

A starting point in dealing with sexual harassment is to develop an awareness of the types of behaviors it encompasses. Company policies and complaint procedures about harassment are a major part of dealing with the problem. To deal directly with harassment, the harassed person can file a formal complaint or confront the harasser when the behavior first begins. Keeping a diary of harassing events is strongly recommended.

Questions for Discussion and Review

1. What would be the best conflict resolution technique for competition over limited resources?

2. Suppose someone finds out that a coworker has an enormous collection of violent video games, leading the first person to conclude that the coworker is potentially violent. Describe whether you think the first worker should tell the supervisor that the coworker is potentially violent on the job.

3. What are the disadvantages of having an accommodative style of handling conflict?

4. Luke and Lucy are a married couple both conducting a job search after graduation. Luke receives an job offer located in Anchorage, Alaska, whereas Lucy receives an job offer in Honolulu, Hawaii; they both agree that a commuter marriage would be out of the question. How can this couple find a win–win resolution to their conflict?

5. What type of conflict resolution process is normally used in disputes between company management and trade unions?

6. How might a student use cognitive restructuring to get over the anger of having received a low grade in a course?

7. Suggest two initiatives that companies can utilize to improve work–life balance.

8. Suppose you believed that your workload was unreasonable, but you otherwise enjoyed working for your manager and your employer. Which approach to negotiation might you take to deal with the work overload problem?

9. Sexual harassment involves an unwanted sexual advance, and people at work have many different interpretations of an "unwanted sexual advance," including asking a coworker to join you for lunch. So how can a career-minded person completely avoid any behavior that might be interpreted as an "unwanted sexual advance"?

10. The vast majority of working people know that sexual harassment is both illegal and immoral. Why then is sexual harassment of both types so widely practiced in the workplace?

The Web Corner

http://www.ehow.com/how_8200614_resolve-workplace-conflicts.html
(Resolving workplace conflict)

http://www.kantola.com/Preventing-Sexual-Harassment-PDPD-47-K.aspx
(Preventing sexual harassment)

Internet Skill Builder: Finding Suggestions for Resolving Conflict on YouTube

YouTube.com often has a generous sampling of brief videos about resolving conflict that apply mostly to personal life, but some are about the workplace. Visit YouTube.com, watch a handful of videos about conflict resolution, and look for a few serious messages. Look for any similarities between the information presented in YouTube videos and in this chapter. Also, does it appear that any of the videos you find present a humorous aspect to conflict resolution?

Developing Your Human Relations Skills

Interpersonal Relations Case 9.1

Ashley Uses Passion as an Excuse

Ashley works as a price estimator in the division of a large electronics company that manufactures and sells security systems to business firms. She holds a degree in electronics technology and has extensive knowledge about security systems. In recent years her company has prospered because of heightened concerns about security. The market for security systems in her area, however, has become saturated, because virtually every firm has a security system.

New business for the division comes mostly from getting companies to switch to her company or from security system upgrades with existing customers.

As a result of the security business having stabilized in the geographic area, the atmosphere in the office has become tense. Workers have become less calm and pleasant than they were previously. Ashley, who has had a volatile personality since early childhood, has become tenser than her coworkers. During a recent project to upgrade the security system at a pharmaceutical warehouse, the sales representative accused Ashley of providing a cost estimate too high to clinch the deal. Ashley replied, "You are a sad (expletive) sales person. You will tell a prospective client anything just to bag a sale. So long as you get your commission, you don't care if the company loses money on the project." Ashley offered no apology for her outburst.

A week later at a department meeting to discuss goals for the year, Ashley said to the group, including the manager, "Goal setting for me is a dumb (expletive) idea. I will have no work to do unless this time-wasting, expense-account-hogging sales group gets off its butt and makes some sales."

Horrified, the manager said to Ashley, "You are being totally unprofessional. Please apologize to the sales group."

Ashley said, "Okay, maybe I shouldn't be so truthful in what I say. I can't help it. I'm a passionate person who wants results for the company."

Questions

1. To what extent does Ashley being "passionate" justify her expression of anger toward coworkers?
2. What do you recommend that Ashley's manager and coworkers do to resolve conflict with her in the office? Or should the manager and coworkers just ignore her?
3. What career advice might you offer Ashley? (Or does she need any advice?)

Interpersonal Skills Role-Play 9.1

Ashley Lashes Out

One student plays the role of the sales representative, who accuses Ashley of providing a cost estimate too high to clinch the deal with the pharmaceutical warehouse. Another student plays the role of Ashley, who lashes back at the sales rep. The goal of the sales representative is to be treated in a more civil manner by Ashley. The rep also wants to get Ashley more into a problem-solving mode. Ashley, in turn, thinks that the rep is more interested in bagging a sale than making money for the company.

Observers rate the role-players on two dimensions, using a 1 to 5 scale from very poor (1) to very good (5). One dimension is "effective use of human relations techniques." Focus on the rep's ability to effectively deal with Ashley's anger and hostility. The second dimension is "acting ability." A few observers might voluntarily provide feedback to the role players in terms of sharing their ratings and observations. The course instructor might also provide feedback.

The Uncomfortable Business Trip

Tammy worked diligently for two years as a marketing assistant at Biotronics, a manufacturer of electronic equipment for the health field. She was then promoted to sales representative, covering the entire state of Indiana. Tammy brought the good news home to her husband, Rick. As she explained the details of the promotion to him, Tammy noticed that Rick developed a glum expression. When asked why he was so unenthusiastic about her promotion, Rick replied:

"You may think that I'm being old fashioned, but I can see a lot of trouble ahead for you in your new job. You'll be forced into a good deal of overnight travel. In the process, you'll find yourself in some touchy situations with men from your company and also with strangers."

"Rick, I agree with one thing you said. You are being old fashioned. A woman who isn't looking to get involved with a man on a business trip will have no problem. I just read an article to that effect in a magazine for career women."

Rick and Tammy continued their discussion for 15 more minutes and then shifted to a talk about plans for the weekend. Two weeks later, Tammy's boss arranged a business trip for him and Tammy to attend a medical conference in Indianapolis. Tammy told Rick that she would be gone for three days on this important trip with "three people from the office."

Duane, Tammy's boss, invited her to have dinner with him the first night of the convention. Tammy said that she was so tired from the day's excitement that she would prefer to have a snack alone and then retire to her room. But Duane persisted, and not wanting to offend her boss, Tammy met Duane for dinner.

During dinner, Duane shifted quickly from a discussion of business topics to questions about Tammy's hobbies, personal interests, and how well she was getting along with Rick. Toward the end of the dinner, Duane extended another invitation to Tammy: "Let's you and I go dancing next. The evening is young, and we're both adults, free to do what we want. Besides that, I feel a lot of good chemistry between us. And if you and I were compatible, I would be more willing to get you assigned to some of our major customers in your territory."

Tammy felt a surge of uneasiness. She thought quickly, "What do I do now? If I turn down Duane, the trip could turn into a disaster. But if I go out with him, I'm sure I'll be facing another kind of disaster: fighting off the advances of my boss. And then if I tell Rick about this fiasco, he'll say 'I told you so' and ask me to quit my job. I've got to say something to Duane right now, but I don't know what."

Case Questions

1. Precisely what conflicts is Tammy facing?
2. What on-the-spot tactic of conflict resolution can you recommend to Tammy?
3. What should Tammy do as a long-range solution to the problem of men trying to convert business occasions into social occasions, when she wants to keep them as business occasions?
4. Explain which type of sexual harassment appears to be evident in this case.

Interpersonal Skills Role-Play 9.2

Tammy Deals with Duane's Advances

One student plays the role of Tammy, who is eager to please her boss in work-related matters and who also wants to hold on to her job. At the same time she is adamant about not wanting to be sexually harassed or unfaithful to her husband. Duane, following the scenario in the case just presented, would like to advance his romantic (or lustful) interest in Tammy as far as the situation will permit.

Run the role play for about eight minutes. Observers might provide feedback about how effective Tammy was in stopping this incident of sexual harassment, yet at the same time not creating a poor working relationship with Duane. (Or maybe some observers will think that Tammy should express anger and promise to report his behavior to the company.) Also provide feedback about how well Duane accepts the rejection of his advances without destroying his working relationship with Tammy.

References

1. Michael T. Ford, Beth A. Heinen, and Krista L. Langkamer, "Work and Family Satisfaction and Conflict: A Meta-Analysis of Cross-Domain Relations," *Journal of Applied Psychology,* January 2007, pp. 57–80.

2. Timothy A. Judge, Remus Ilies, and Brent A. Scott, "Work-Family Conflict and Emotions: Effects at Work and at Home," *Personnel Psychology,* Winter 2006, pp. 779–814.

3. Quoted in Naomi Schaefer Riley, "Work and Life—and Blogging the Balance," *The Wall Street Journal,* July 17, 2009, p. W11.

4. Jenny M. Hoobler, Sandy J. Wayne, and Grace Lemmon, "Bosses' Perceptions of Family-Work Conflict and Women's Promotability: Glass Ceiling Effects," *Academy of Management Journal,* October 2009, pp. 939–957.

5. Joyce M. Rosenberg, "Equitable Time-Off Policies Avert Staff Conflicts," Associated Press, September 3, 2007.

6. Kathryn Tyler, "Beat the Clock," *HR Magazine,* November 2003, p. 103.

7. Ellen Ernst Kossek, Shaun Pichler, Todd Bodner, and Leslie B. Hammer, "Workplace Social Support and Work-Family Conflict: A Meta-Analysis Clarifying the Influence of General and Work-Family-Specific Supervisor and Organizational Support," *Personnel Psychology,* Number 2, 2011, pp. 289–313.

8. Marcus M. Butts, Wendy J. Casper, and Tae Seok Yang, "How Important Are Work-Family Support Policies? A Meta-Analytic Investigation of Their Effects on Employee Outcomes," *Journal of Applied Psychology,* January 2013, pp. 1–25.

9. Ruth David Konigsberg, "Chore Wars," *Time,* August 8, 2011, pp. 44–49.

10. Judith Sills, "When Personalities Clash," *Psychology Today,* November/December 2006, p. 61.

11. Marlene Chism, "Drop the Curtain on Workplace Drama," *Communication Briefings,* June 2011, p. 5.

12. Cited in, "Field Guide to Office Bullies," *Bloomberg Businessweek,* November 26–December 2, 2012, p. 94.

13. Vincent J. Roscigno, Steven H. Lopez, and Randy Hodson, "Supervisory Bullying, Status Inequalities, and Organizational Context," *Social Forces,* July 2009, pp. 1561–1589.

14. Gary Namie, "(Still) Bullying with Impunity: Labor Day Survey," *Workplace Bullying* Institute, September 2009; Namie, "U.S. Workplace Bullying Survey," *Workplace Bullying Institute and Zogby International,* September 2007; Cited in "Field Guide to Office Bullying," p. 93.

15. Stuart D. Sidle, "Eye of the Beholder: Does Culture Shape Perceptions of Workplace Bullying?" *Academy of Management Perspectives,* August 2010, pp. 100–101; Jenifer Loh, Simon Lloyd D. Restubo, and Thomas J. Zagenczyk, "Consequences of Workplace Bullying on Employee Identification and Satisfaction among Australians and Singaporeans," *Journal of Cross-Cultural Psychology,* Number 2, 2010, pp. 236–252.

16. Lilia M. Cortina and Vicki J. Magley, "Patterns and Profiles of Responses to Incivility in the Workplace," *Journal of Occupational Health Psychology,* July 2009, pp. 272–288.

17. Study cited in Susan G. Hauser, "Degeneration of Decorum," *Workforce Management,* January 2011, pp. 17–18.

18. Michael P. Leiter, Heather K. Spence Laschinger, Aria Day, and Debra Gilin Oore, "The Impact of Civility Interventions on Employee Social Behavior, Distress, and Attitudes," *Journal of Applied Psychology,* November 2011, p. 1259.

19. Study cited in Elizabeth Bernstein, "Big Explosions, Small Reasons," *The Wall Street Journal,* October 16, 2012, p. D1.

20. Among the people making this comment is Merrill Markoe, "A Renaissance of Rudeness," *The Wall Street Journal,* May 21–22, 2011, p. C3.

21. Chris Pentila, "Talking about My Generation," *Entrepreneur,* March 2009, p. 55; "The Multigenerational Workforce: Opportunity for Competitive Success," *SHRM Research Quarterly,* First Quarter-2009, pp. 1–2.

22. Emilie Le Beau, "From Conflict to 'Cohorts'—When Young, Older Workers Mix," *Workforce Management,* October 2010, p. 12.

23. "Workplace Violence," *www.osha.gov,* p. 1, updated 2010.

24. Cited in Susan M. Heathfield, "Workplace Violence: Violence Can Happen; Recognizing the Potential for Workplace Violence," *About.com Human Resources,* 2009.

25. Bret H. Bradley, Bennett E. Postlethwaite, Anthony C. Klotz, Maria R. Hamdani, and Kenneth G. Brown, "Reaping the Benefits of Task Conflict in Teams: The Critical Role of Team Psychological Safety Climate," *Journal of Applied Psychology,* January 2012, pp. 151–158.

26. Carlsen K. W. De Dreu and Laurie Weingart, "Task versus Relationship Conflict, Team Performance and Team Member Satisfaction: A Meta-Analysis," *Journal of Applied Psychology,* August 2003, pp. 741–749.

27. De Dreu and Weingart, "Task versus Relationship Conflict," p. 746.

28. Kenneth Thomas, "Conflict and Conflict Management," in Marvin D. Dunnette, ed., *Handbook of Industrial and Organizational Psychology* (Chicago: Rand McNally College Publishing, 1976), pp. 900–902. Some of the information about when to use each style is from Dean Tjosvold, *The Conflict Positive Organization* (Reading, MA: Addison-Wesley, 1991).

29. "7 Steps to Conflict Resolution," *Executive Leadership*, June 2007, p. 7. As adapted from The Common Sense Guy Blog, by Bud Bilanich, *http://www.commonsenseguy.com*.

30. Deb Koen, "Face-to-Face Communication is Best for Emotionally Charged Situations," *Democrat and Chronicle*, August 2, 2011, p. 2E.

31. The first three suggestions are from Connirae Andreas and Steve Andreas, *Heart of the Mind* (Moab, UT: Real People Press, 1991). Suggestion four is from Deb Koen, "How to Handle Criticism at Work," Rochester, New York, *Democrat and Chronicle*, June 20, 2004.

32. Alina Tugend, "An Attempt to Revive the Lost Art of Apology," *The New York Times (http://nytimes.com)*, January 30, 2010, p. 1.

33. "Conquer Conflict with this Technique," *Manager's Edge*, September 2007, p. 5. As adapted from Maria Broomhower, "Dissolving Conflict through Reframing," *http://conflict911 .com*.

34. "What's Your Negotiating Style?" *Executive Leadership*, March 2010, p. 4; *Program on Negotiation*, Harvard Law School, http://www.pon.harvard.edu.

35. Jared Curhan, Hilary Anger Elfenbein, and Heng Xu "What Do People Value When They Negotiate? Mapping the Domain of Subjective Value in Negotiation," *Journal of Personality and Social Psychology*, vol. 3, 2006, pp. 493–512.

36. Deepak Malhotra and Max H. Bazerman, "Investigative Negotiation," *Harvard Business Review*, September 2007, pp. 72–78.

37. William Ury, *The Power of a Positive No* (New York: Random House, 2007).

38. Mark Diener, "Mad Skills," *Entrepreneur*, April 2003, p. 79.

39. Steve Alper, Dean Tjosvold, and Kenneth S. Law, "Conflict Management, Efficacy, and Performance in Organizational Teams," *Personnel Psychology*, Autumn 2000, pp. 625–642.

40. Jeff Green, "The Silencing of Sexual Harassment," *Bloomberg Businessweek*, November 21–November 27, 2011, p, 28.

41. Maria Rotundo, Dung-Hanh Nguyen, and Paul R. Sackett, "A Meta-Analytic Review of Gender Differences in Perceptions of Sexual Harassment," *Journal of Applied Psychology*, October 2001, pp. 914–922.

42. Jennifer L. Berdhahl and Karl Aquino, "Sexual Behavior at Work: Fun or Folly" *Journal of Applied Psychology*, January 2009, pp. 34–47.

43. Remus Ilies, Nancy Hauserman, Susan Schwochau, and John Stibal, "Reported Incidence Rates of Work-Related Sexual Harassment in the United States: Using Meta-Analysis to Explain Rate Disparities," *Personnel Psychology*, Autumn 2003, pp. 607–631; Green, "The Silencing of Sexual Harassment," p. 28.

44. Hilary J. Gettman and Michele J. Gelfand, "When the Customer Shouldn't Be King: Antecedents and Consequences of Sexual Harassment by Clients and Customers," *Journal of Applied Psychology*, May 2007, pp. 757–770.

45. Jennifer L. Berdahl, "The Sexual Harassment of Uppity Women," *Journal of Applied Psychology*, March 2007, pp. 425–437.

46. Chelsea R. Willness, Piers Steel, and Kibeom Lee, "A Meta-Analysis of the Antecedents and Consequences of Workplace Sexual Harassment," *Personnel Psychology*, Spring 2007, p. 141.

47. Kathleen Neville, *Corporate Attractions: An Inside Account of Sexual Harassment with the New Sexual Roles for Men and Women on the Job* (Reston, VA: Acropolis Books, 1992); Joanne Cole, "Sexual Harassment: New Rules, New Behavior," *HRfocus*, March 1999, pp. 1, 14–15; Jathan W. Janove, "Sexual Harassment and the Three Big Surprises," *HR Magazine*, November 2001, p. 123; "Know Your Rights: Sexual Harassment at Work," *Equal Rights Advocates*, © 2013 Equal Rights Advocates Inc.

48. Cole, "Sexual Harassment: New Rules," p. 14; "Know Your Rights: Sexual Harassment at Work."

CHAPTER 10

Becoming an Effective Leader

Patricia Elizondo holds the position of senior vice president for Global Sales Integration at Xerox Corporation, and she is therefore a business executive with enormous responsibility. Her key leadership principle focuses on how she can help other people: "Constant learning, sharing, and reaching out to help others succeed." Among the accolades she has received is recognition as a member of *Hispanic Business Magazine's* Top 25 Elite.

Elizondo believes that a key role of a leader is to make a difference one employee at a time, such as helping an employee develop new skills or get promoted. Lora J. Villarreal, executive vice president and chief people officer at Xerox, had this to say about Elizondo: "Patricia exceeds the qualities of an executive leader. She constantly demonstrates perseverance, commitment, and willingness to go beyond the call of duty in all undertakings."

mangostock/Shutterstock

Objectives

After reading and studying this chapter and completing the exercises, you should be able to

1. Identify key leadership traits for personal development.
2. Develop several attitudes and behaviors that will help you appear charismatic.
3. Develop your team leadership skills.
4. Understand how you can develop your leadership potential.

Five basic principles are the foundation of Elizondo's life, career, and approach to leading others. First, it is necessary to embrace change and be flexible because so much change takes place in organizations of all types. Second, collaborate and build bridges in order to advance your ideas and move your projects forward. Third, seek knowledge, because knowledge makes you powerful and gives you substance. Fourth, demonstrate measurable value, because knowledge alone is not as useful as achieving and accomplishing something with that knowledge. Fifth, know what you want by having your personal definition of success.

Elizondo's first professional position was as a customer service representative at the Indiana University Credit Union. She received a bachelor's degree in finance from the Kelley School of Business at Indiana University and a master's degree in business administration from Notre Dame University.[1]

As in the story just presented, effective leaders have a combination of admirable qualities, including expertise, a passion to succeed, high energy, and the ability to inspire others. In working toward improving your leadership ability, the following definition is a goal to strive for. **Leadership** is the ability to inspire support and confidence among the people who are needed to achieve company goals. A company president might have to inspire thousands of people, while a team leader is concerned with inspiring about six people. Both of these leaders nonetheless play an important role.

Leadership has also been defined in many other ways. An analysis of 221 definitions of leadership concluded that they basically all say the same thing—leadership is about one person getting one or more other people to do something.[2] The something usually refers to attaining a worthwhile company goal. In other words, the leader makes a difference.

Becoming a leader does not necessarily mean that the company has to put you in charge of others (or assign you a formal leadership position). Shortly after Sergio Marchionne became the CEO of the combined Fiat and Chrysler automotive company, he said that the company's chances for success depended in part on a culture "where everyone is expected to lead."[3] You can also rise to leadership when people come to respect your opinion and personal characteristics and are thus influenced by you. **Emergent leaders** are group members who significantly influence other group members, even though they have not been assigned formal authority.[4] You therefore can exert some leadership by being an influential coworker.

Emergent leaders

Group members who significantly influence other group members, even though they have not been assigned formal authority.

Your greatest opportunity for exerting leadership will come about from a combination of holding a formal position and exerting personal influence. An individual with appealing personal characteristics and expertise who is placed in a position of authority will find it relatively easy to exert leadership.

The purpose of this chapter is twofold. One is to make you aware of the basic concepts you need to become a leader. The other purpose is to point you toward developing skills necessary for leadership effectiveness.

KEY LEADERSHIP TRAITS TO DEVELOP

LEARNING OBJECTIVE 1

An important part of being an effective leader is to have the *right stuff*. This section and the following one about charisma describe personal attributes that help a person lead others in many situations. Recognize, however, that radically different situations require a different set of leadership characteristics. For example, a leader might have to be more assertive with group members performing distasteful work than with those whose work is enjoyable. Even if traits are but one facet of understanding leadership, they play an important role. Traits help explain individual differences in leadership.[5] For example, an assertive and self-confident leader will be able to take decisive actions.

Each of the ten leadership traits described next, and shown in Figure 10-1, can be developed. For such development to take place, you need to be aware of the importance of the personal characteristic, and then monitor your own behavior to make progress. To assist you with such development, the description of each trait is accompanied by a suggestion for improvement.

Self-Confidence and Leadership Efficacy

In virtually every leadership setting, it is important for the leader to be realistically self-confident. A leader who is self-assured without being bombastic or overbearing instills confidence in group members. Self-confidence was among the first leadership traits researchers identified. Research with leaders in many situations has continued to underscore the importance of this trait. A series of research studies have shown that increased self-confidence can bring about improvement in performance, including helping a group attain its goals.[6] Self-confidence is not only a personality trait. It also refers to the behavior a person exhibits in a number of situations. It is similar to being cool under pressure. We can conclude that a person is a self-confident leader when he or she retains composure during a crisis, such as when the company suffers flood damage during a busy season.

FIGURE 10-1   Ten Key Leadership Traits

People who possess the traits listed are usually well suited to being effective leaders; however, many other traits and behaviors are also important contributors to effective leadership.

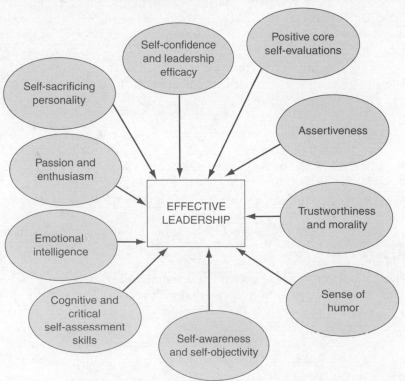

The inclusion of a feeling of efficacy in combination with self-confidence helps better pinpoint how confidence works. **Leadership efficacy** is a form of efficacy associated with confidence in the knowledge, skills, and abilities valuable for leading others. In essence, the leader is confident that he or she has the tools necessary to lead a group. Another insight into leadership efficacy is that it helps the leader step up to meet his or her challenges.[7] The confidence therefore extends beyond attitudes about the self. A leader who had been a successful racquet sports director at one athletic club might have the leadership efficacy to carry out the many aspects of that role at another club.

You can appear more self-confident to the group by using definitive wording, maintaining good posture, and making appropriate gestures such as pointing an index finger outward. Developing self-confidence is a lifelong process of performing well in a variety of situations. You need a series of easy victories to establish self-confidence. Further development of your self-confidence requires performing well in challenging circumstances. Taking risks, such as volunteering to work on an unfamiliar project, contributes to self-confidence when the risk proves to be worthwhile. As your self-confidence builds in several situations, you will also develop a strong sense of leadership efficacy.

Self-confidence and leadership efficacy make a stronger contribution to leadership effectiveness when they are combined with a sense of humility, including not being arrogant. Humility in a leader would include such actions as asking for advice from subordinates, asking for input, and apologizing for mistakes. Listening to others is therefore a key component of being humble.[8]

Positive Core Self-Evaluations

The core self-evaluations was described in Chapter 2 as closely related to self-esteem. In more detail, the core self-evaluations captures a person's self-assessment. Its four components are (1) self-esteem, (2) locus of control, (3) self-efficacy, and (4) emotional stability (low neuroticism).[9] Except for locus of control, these traits have already been defined in Chapter 2. In addition, we described how self-esteem in the form of self-confidence can be developed.

Locus of control deals with the way people look at causation in their lives. If you believe that you are controlled mostly by outside events beyond your control, you would have an external locus of control. A marketing specialist with an external control might say, "Our computer system is down today, so there is nothing constructive I can do. I'll just wait until the system is running again." With an internal locus of control, the marketing specialist might say, "The computer is down, which will slow me down. However, I'll work on whatever I can do that does not require the company computer. I can do some research on markets in Latin America with my smartphone."

An internal locus of control is better for leadership than an external locus of control. Leaders who believe that they can control events are more likely to inspire others and provide direction. High emotional stability is better for leadership than low emotional stability. Anyone who has ever worked for an unstable supervisor will attest to the importance of emotional stability as a leadership trait. Emotional stability is important for a leader because group members expect and need consistency in the way they are treated.

A useful tactic for developing an internal locus of control is to examine challenging situations, and search for what aspect of those situations might be in your control. The department leader might be informed that because of low profits, salaries will be frozen for the next year. The leader might say, "Okay, external events have created conditions for discontent in my department. However, I can still use recognition and interesting work assignments to boost morale." Emotional stability is difficult to develop, but people can learn to control many of their emotional outbursts. People who cannot control their emotions, yet still want to become leaders, should seek assistance from a mental health professional.

Assertiveness

A widely recognized leadership trait is **assertiveness**, being forthright in expressing demands, opinions, feelings, and attitudes. As a leader, is is vital to not be vague about

assertiveness

Being forthright in expressing demands, opinions, feelings, and attitudes.

what you expect from others. If you are self-confident, it is easier to be assertive with people. An assertive team leader might say, "I know that the ice storm put us out of business for four days, but we can make up the time by working smart and pulling together. Within 30 days, we will have met or surpassed our goals for the quarter." This statement reflects self-confidence in her leadership capabilities and assertiveness in expressing exactly what she thinks.

Assertiveness helps leaders perform many tasks and achieve goals and is especially important for pointing group members or team members in the right direction. In the words of Enrique Salem, the president and CEO of the computer security company Symantec, "Somebody has to make the call."[10] For example, the department head might say, "We only have so much left in our budget, so we will purchase a new couch for the lounge instead of purchasing a machine for brewing gourmet coffee."

Assertiveness also facilitates confronting group members about their mistakes, demanding higher performance, and setting high expectations. An assertive leader will also make legitimate demands on higher management, such as asking for equipment needed by the group.

To be assertive differs significantly from being aggressive or passive (or nonassertive). Aggressive people express their demands in an overly pushy, obnoxious, and abrasive manner. Passive people suppress their own ideas, attitudes, feelings, and thoughts as if they were likely to be perceived as controversial. Nonassertive people are also too accommodating. A series of three studies with a variety of workers indicated that leaders with moderate assertiveness were considered more effective than leaders low (passive) or high (aggressive) in this trait.[11]

Developing assertiveness is much like attempting to become less shy. You must force yourself to take the opportunity to express your feelings and demands. For example, if something a teammate does annoys you, make the statement, "I enjoy working with you in general, but what you are doing now annoys me." You can also practice expressing positive emotion, such as telling a coworker, "I'm happy that you and I are working on this project together, because I like your approach to work."

Expressing demands is easier for most people to practice than expressing feelings. People who do start expressing their demands are often surprised at the result. For example, if you are contemplating the purchase of an item that is beyond your budget, try this statement: "I like this product very much. Yet all I have to spend is $100 below your asking price. Can we do business?" For a reading on your own level of assertiveness, take Self-Assessment Quiz 10-1.

SELF-ASSESSMENT QUIZ 10-1

The Assertiveness Scale

Directions: Check whether each of the following statements is mostly true or mostly false as it applies to you. If in doubt about your reaction to a particular statement, think of how you would generally respond.

		Mostly true	Mostly false
1.	It is extremely difficult for me to turn down a sales representative if he or she is a nice person.	_____	_____
2.	I express criticism freely.	_____	_____
3.	If another person were being very unfair, I would bring it to his or her attention.	_____	_____
4.	Work is no place to let your feelings show.	_____	_____
5.	There's no use in asking for favors; people get what they deserve.	_____	_____
6.	Business is not the place for tact; say what you think.	_____	_____
7.	If a person looked as if he or she were in a hurry, I would let that person in front of me in a supermarket line.	_____	_____

(Continued)

8. A weakness of mine is that I'm too nice a person. ___ ___

9. I usually give other people what they want, rather than do what I think is best, just to avoid an argument. ___ ___

10. If I was trying to study in a library, and the person next to me was talking loudly on her phone, I would bring my problem to his or her attention. ___ ___

11. People would describe me as too outspoken. ___ ___

12. I am quite willing to return merchandise that I find has even a minor blemish. ___ ___

13. I dread having to express anger toward a coworker. ___ ___

14. People often say that I'm too reserved and emotionally controlled. ___ ___

15. Nice guys and gals finish last in business. ___ ___

16. I fight for my rights down to the last detail. ___ ___

17. I have no misgivings about returning an overcoat to the store if it doesn't fit me right. ___ ___

18. After I have an argument with a person, I try to avoid him or her. ___ ___

19. I insist on my spouse (or roommate or partner) doing his or her fair share of undesirable chores. ___ ___

20. If someone posted a nasty comment about me on Facebook, I would not tell him or her that I am angry. ___ ___

21. I have cried among friends more than once. ___ ___

22. If someone near me at a movie kept up a conversation with another person, I would ask him or her to stop. ___ ___

23. I am able to turn down social engagements with people I do not particularly care for. ___ ___

24. It is in poor taste to express what you really feel about another individual. ___ ___

25. I sometimes show my anger by swearing at or belittling another person. ___ ___

26. I am reluctant to speak up at a meeting. ___ ___

27. I find it relatively easy to ask friends for small favors, such as giving me a ride to work while my car is being repaired. ___ ___

28. If another person was talking very loudly in a restaurant, and it bothered me, I would inform that person. ___ ___

29. I often finish other people's sentences for them. ___ ___

30. It is relatively easy for me to express love and affection toward another person. ___ ___

Total Score ___ ___

Scoring and Interpretation: The answers for determining your assertiveness are as follows:

1.	Mostly false	9.	Mostly false	17.	Mostly true	25.	Mostly true
2.	Mostly true	10.	Mostly true	18.	Mostly false	26.	Mostly false
3.	Mostly true	11.	Mostly true	19.	Mostly true	27.	Mostly true
4.	Mostly false	12.	Mostly true	20.	Mostly false	28.	Mostly true
5.	Mostly false	13.	Mostly false	21.	Mostly true	29.	Mostly true
6.	Mostly true	14.	Mostly false	22.	Mostly true	30.	Mostly true
7.	Mostly false	15.	Mostly true	23.	Mostly true		
8.	Mostly false	16.	Mostly true	24.	Mostly false		

Scoring and Interpretation: Score yourself a +1 for each of your answers that agrees with the scoring key. If your score is 15 or less, it is probable that you are currently nonassertive. A score of 16 through 24 suggests that you are assertive. A score of 25 or higher suggests that you are aggressive. Retake this quiz about 30 days from now to give yourself some indication of the stability of your answers. You might also discuss your answers with a close friend to determine whether that person has a similar perception of your assertiveness.

Trustworthiness, Morality, and Authenticity

Group members consistently believe that leaders must display honesty, integrity, and credibility—and therefore be trustworthy. Right Management Consultants conducted a survey of 570 employees in which they found that white-collar workers value honesty and integrity in a manager more than any other trait. When asked, "What is the most important trait or attribute that the leader of your company should possess?" 24 percent of the survey participants cited honesty, and 16 percent named integrity/morals and ethics.[12] Leaders themselves believe that honesty makes a difference in their effectiveness.

It is almost an axiom in leadership studies that integrity is important for effective leadership. (Leaders who are trustworthy typically have high integrity.) Like most concepts in human relations, *integrity* has several connotations. Yet, the two key meanings of **integrity** are (a) consistency of words and deeds and (b) being true to oneself. [13] Being true to oneself refers to sticking with one's principles, such as a sales manager who preaches high ethics not giving kickbacks to customers for the purpose of closing a sale.

Being honest with team members helps build trust, which in turn leads to good cooperation and team spirit. To trust group members, the leader has to be willing to give up some control over them, such as letting group members make more decisions and not challenging their expense accounts.

Being moral is closely linked to trustworthiness because a moral leader is more likely to be trusted. A leader with high morality would perceive that he or she had an ethical responsibility to group members, as well as outsiders.[14] The moral leader would therefore not give preferential treatment to workers with whom he had an outside-of-work friendship. At the same time, the moral leader would not try to fool customers or make up false excuses for not paying bills on time to suppliers.

A highly recommended way of communicating trustworthiness is through setting a good example. Alan Deutschman, a leadership consultant, argues that leaders are most effective when they rely on the power of their example. A classic example is that Ray Kroc, the founder of McDonald's, listed cleanliness as one of the chain's three key values (along with service and quality). An employee remembered Kroc personally picking up trash around the restaurant and scraping up gum with a putty knife.[15]

Closely related to leadership trust and morality is the idea of authentic leadership. An **authentic leader** is genuine and honest about his or her personality, values, and beliefs, as well as having integrity. He or she also creates a positive ethical climate. Among the specific behaviors of an authentic leader are the following:[16]

- Clearly states what he or she means
- Shows consistency between beliefs and actions
- Admits mistakes when they occur
- Guided by his or her moral standards
- Encourages others to voice opposing points of view

A study with Army action teams suggested that authentic leaders tend to serve as attractive role models that motivate team members to emulate or model their exemplary conduct. (In an Army action team, the soldiers have specific functions to perform such as machine gunner or the individual who searches for hidden explosives.)[17] An example of authentic leadership in this context might be the squad leader making sure that no weapons were launched on defenseless people.

Chapter 15, about ethical behavior skills, provides details about honesty on the job. Being honest is an effective way of getting others to trust you. A starting point in developing a strong sense of honesty and morality is to follow a variation of the Golden Rule: Be as honest with others as you want them to be with you. Another key trust builder is to follow through on promises and commitments, because mistrust arises when a leader or manager does not do what he or she agreed to do.[18] For example, mistrust would quickly arise if the department manager did not follow through on requesting tuition reimbursements for several group members.

authentic leader

A leader who is genuine and honest about his or her personality, values, and beliefs as well as having integrity.

The Witty Leader

Students gather in problem-solving groups of about five to invent humorous comments a leader might make in the following scenarios. After the problem-solving groups have formulated their witty comments, the comments can be shared and compared. Groups also have the option of deciding that a particular scenario is too grim for humor.

Scenario 1: A store manager wants to communicate to employees that inventory slippage (merchandise stolen from the store by customers or store associates) has increased to an unacceptable level—twice the industry average.

Scenario 2: A leader has to communicate to the group that salaries have been frozen for another year due to limited business. The leader knows that group members have been eagerly awaiting news about the salary increase.

Scenario 3: The information technology head at a social media marketing firm detects that her own staff is spending an average of two hours per day accessing social media sites such as Facebook, Twitter, and Tumblr. She brings up the topic during a staff meeting.

Scenario 4: A consulting firm that specializes in helping companies downsize their workforce has seen the demand for its services decline substantially in recent months. The company must therefore downsize itself. The company founder has to announce the layoff decision to the company.

Observers might rate the attempts at humor on a 1 (low) to 10 (high) scale. Observe also if any of the role players made you laugh.

Sense of Humor

A sense of humor borders between being a trait and a behavior. However you classify it, the effective use of humor is considered an important part of a leader's role. Humor serves such functions in the workplace as relieving tension and boredom and defusing hostility. Because humor helps the leader dissolve tension and defuse conflict, it helps him or her exert power over the group. A study conducted in a large financial institution indicated that leaders who made frequent use of humor had higher-performing units. (Another interpretation is that it's easier to laugh when the group is performing well!) Among the forms of humor used by the managers were "[using] humor to take the edge off during stressful periods" and "[making] us laugh at ourselves when we are too serious."[19]

Self-effacing humor is the choice of comedians and organizational leaders alike. When you are self-effacing, nobody else is insulted or slighted, yet a point can be made. A solar heating general manager said to the tech writer, "I want you to explain the return on investment from solar panels so clearly that even a mathematically challenged person like me could follow the information."

Creativity is required for humor. Just as creativity can be enhanced with practice, so can a sense of humor. To gather some experience in making humorous comments in the workplace, do Skill-Building Exercise 10-1.

Ryan McVay/Getty Images

Self-Awareness and Self-Objectivity

Effective leaders are aware of their strengths and limitations. This awareness enables them to capitalize upon their strengths and overcome their weaknesses. A leader, for example, might realize that he or she is naturally distrustful of others. Awareness of this problem cautions the leader to not distrust people without good evidence. Another leader might realize that he or she is adept at counseling team members. This leader might then emphasize that activity in an effort to improve performance. Self-objectivity refers to being detached or nonsubjective about your perceived strengths and limitations.

According to Kevin Eikenberry, the chief potential officer of a leadership consulting group, to be an outstanding leader requires the self-awareness to know who you are and to share that knowledge with the group. A key reason is that sharing who you are helps build connections with group members.[20] Sharing who you really are tends to bring people closer to you.

Another way in which self-awareness and self-objectivity contribute to leadership effectiveness is that these traits help a person become an authentic leader. "Being yourself" thus contributes to leadership effectiveness, assuming that you have personal qualities, such as those presented in this chapter, that facilitate leadership. Patricia Elizondo, the leader described in the chapter opener, appears to be an authentic leader.

You can enhance your self-awareness and self-objectivity by regularly asking for feedback from others. You then compare the feedback to your self-perception of your standing on the same factor. You might, for example, think that you communicate in colorful, interesting terms. In speaking to others about your communication style, you might discover that others agree. You can then conclude that your self-awareness about your communication skills is accurate.

Another technique for improving self-awareness and self-objectivity is to take several self-examination exercises, such as those found in this text. Even if they do not describe you exactly, they stimulate you to reflect on your characteristics and behaviors.

Cognitive Skills Including Critical Assessments

Cognitive skills (or general mental ability), as well as personality, is important for leadership success. To inspire people, bring about constructive changes, and solve problems creatively, leaders need to be mentally sharp.

Knowledge of the Business.   A major reason that cognitive skills are important for leadership is that they enable the leader to acquire knowledge. The processing of knowledge is now considered to be the *core competence* (key ability) of organizations. The leader's role is to both originate useful ideas and collect them from smart people throughout the organization.[21] Two cognitive skills were discussed in Chapter 2: cognitive ability and the personal factor of openness to experience. Another cognitive skill of major importance is *knowledge of the business,* or technical skill. An effective leader has to be technically or professionally competent in some discipline, particularly when leading a group of specialists. It is difficult for the leader to establish rapport with group members when he or she does not know what they are doing. A related damper on leadership effectiveness is when the group does not respect the leader's technical skill.

A representative example of how knowledge of the business is helpful for occupying a leadership position took place at Wal-Mart Stores, Inc. when the company appointed Duncan Mac Naughton as chief merchandising officer. He had previously held key merchandising posts in Canada and the US. Upon being appointed, Mac Naughton explained how Walmart stores would now make better use of "action alley," referring to in-aisle displays that feature price discounts and special promotions. Stocking Walmart.com was one of the new merchandising officer's key responsibilities.[22]

Critical Assessments.   Another major reason cognitive skills are so important for leadership is that they facilitate making critical assessments, or thinking critically, about challenges facing the group or entire organization. You will recall that critical thinking refers to making a judgment after analytically evaluating a problem. Almost any course you have ever taken is supposed to improve your critical thinking ability. Making a critical assessment often boils down to sizing up a situation and analyzing how the group can profit from this situation. For example, an IT security specialist might observe that as the company permits the increased use of personal electronic gadgets in the workplace for work purposes, new security measures must be established.

Independent Decision Making.   High intelligence is particularly important for leaders when they have the opportunity to make decisions by themselves and provide direction (such as giving technical instructions) to group members. Problem-solving ability is less important when the leader delegates most of his or her responsibilities to others (or empowers them). High intelligence is important for three major aspects of the leader's job. One aspect is dealing with tasks, such as developing ideas for cost cutting. A second aspect is working with and through other people, or the human-relations focus. The third is judging oneself and adapting one's behavior accordingly as in self-awareness and self-objectivity.[23]

Increasing one's mental ability, or raw intelligence, may not be easy to accomplish. Yet, people can develop their cognitive skills by continuous study and by working on challenging problems. The mere act of keeping up with developments in your field can keep you mentally sharp. The comments about enhancing cognitive skills in Chapter 2 are also relevant here.

Emotional Intelligence

Emotional intelligence, as described in Chapter 2, refers to the ability to recognize your emotions and those of people around you. Emotional intelligence also refers to being able to work effectively with the emotions of others to resolve problems, including listening and empathizing. As such, emotional intelligence is a blend of psychological skills that enable the leader to relate effectively to people. Research conducted by Daniel Goleman in many different firms suggests that superb leaders all have one trait in common: superb emotional intelligence.[24] Many other studies suggest that emotional intelligence combined with several of the other factors mentioned in this chapter contributes to leadership effectiveness.[25] A specific example is that an effective manager or leader can often recognize the motives behind an employee's actions.

> Visualize yourself as a team leader. Vanessa, one of the team members, says to you, "I'm worried about Rick. I think he needs help. He looks like he has a drinking problem." If you have good emotional intelligence, you might think to yourself, "I wonder why Vanessa is telling me this. Is she simply being helpful? Or is she out to backstab Rick?" Therefore, you would seek some tangible evidence about Rick's alleged problem before acting. You would also seek to spend more time with Vanessa so you can better understand her motives.
>
> With much less emotional intelligence, you would immediately get in touch with Rick, accuse him of having a drinking problem, and tell him to get help or get fired.

Emotional intelligence is also reflected in a leader who incorporates the human touch into business activities, such as building personal relationships with employees and customers. An instructive example is Sherilyn S. McCoy, who was appointed as CEO of Avon Products Inc. after being a long time executive at Johnson & Johnson. McCoy had distinguished herself as having excellent strategic skills (big thinking) and knowing how to operate a business, as well as people-leadership capabilities.[26]

Leaders with emotional intelligence are in tune with their own thoughts and emotions and those of other people. The emotionally intelligent leader recognizes that emotions are contagious, such as optimists making other workers optimistic and pessimists making other workers pessimistic. At the same time, these leaders know that their own emotions are powerful drivers of their group members' moods and, ultimately, performance. [27] An experiment with Dutch business students suggested that leaders who display happiness facilitate creative performance, whereas leaders who express sadness facilitate analytical performance. The emotional contagion of the leader's mood was necessary for these results to take place.[28] (Despite this experiment, we do not recommend that readers become sad sacks in order to boost group performance on analytical tasks.)

Emotional intelligence can be developed through working on some of its components, as described in Chapter 2. It is also important to develop the habit of looking to understand the feelings and emotions of people around you. Ask yourself, "How do I feel about what's going on here?" When you have a hunch about people's motives, look for feedback in the future to see if you were right. For example, a little investigation might indicate that Vanessa and Rick are indeed rivals who have a personality clash.

Passion and Enthusiasm

A prominent characteristic of effective leaders is the passion and enthusiasm they have for their work, much like the same quality in creative people. The passion reflects itself in such ways as an intense liking for the business, the customers, and employees. Passion is also reflected in a relentless drive to get work accomplished, and an obsession for achieving company goals. Passion for their work is especially evident in entrepreneurial leaders and small-business owners who are preoccupied with growing their businesses. Many leaders use the term *love* to describe their passion for their work, business, and employees.

Digital Vision/Thinkstock

Both passion and enthusiasm contain an element of optimism that also contributes to leadership effectiveness. For example, an enthusiastic leader will often point to potential positive outcomes for the group effort such as, "If we can squeeze just five percent more out of our budget, our department will create a profit for the company." A study showed that when call center supervisors in a large travel agency service were enthusiastic about using a new technology, that enthusiasm resulted in higher motivation for the customer service representatives. Furthermore, charismatic managers were able to spread their enthusiasm more effectively than less charismatic managers.[29]

When business founders talk about their products or service, you can hear the excitement in their voices. Big company executives are often passionate about what they do. A case in point is Mark Reuss, who is in charge of the North American business of GM. In reference to the prospects of his becoming the next CEO of GM, Reuss said he did not care so much about a promotion. "If I can be around cars, touch cars, and do the job I'm doing, I can't ask for anything more," said Reuss.[30]

To display passion and enthusiasm for your work, you must first find work that creates an inner spark. The work that you choose should be equally or more exciting than your favorite pastime. If not everything about your job excites you, search for its most satisfying or intrinsically motivating elements.

Self-Sacrificing Personality

self-sacrificing personality

A tendency to be more concerned about the welfare and interests of others than those of oneself.

A final trait to be discussed here that contributes to leadership effectiveness is a **self-sacrificing personality**: a tendency to be more concerned about the welfare and interests of others than those of oneself. The self-sacrificing personality translates into a behavior while occupying a leadership role, because the leader acts in the best interest of group members. The self-sacrificing leader is often referred to as a servant leader because his or her primary focus is to serve the group.

Leaders with a self-sacrificing personality are ethical and often forgo personal interests in order to focus on the mission and purpose of the group. Such a leader would be more concerned about the group having high morale and being productive than getting a large financial bonus. Self-sacrificing leaders often engage in personally risky behaviors to benefit the group. An example is a leader taking the risk of going over-budget to purchase appropriate furnishings for the employee lounge, thereby maintaining morale. A leader with a self-sacrificing personality is typically a good role model for the group in terms of focusing more on the needs of others than being self-centered.[31] For example, a self-sacrificing leader might ask to postpone a pending promotion in order to first guide his or her present group through a difficult situation.

Another way in which leaders with a self-sacrificing personality help others is that they emphasize the development of others, much like being a good coach.[32] For example, a self-sacrificing sales manager might facilitate a subordinate closing a big sale, rather than attempt to earn the big commission by himself or herself. The sales manager coaches the rep on how to close the deal, rather than closing the deal alone.

LEARNING OBJECTIVE 2

SUGGESTIONS FOR DEVELOPING CHARISMA

charisma

A special quality of leaders whose purposes, powers, and extraordinary determination differentiate them from others. (However, people besides leaders can be charismatic.)

The study of leadership continues to emphasize the importance of inspirational leaders who guide others toward great heights of achievement. Such leaders are said to possess **charisma**, a special quality of leaders whose purposes, powers, and extraordinary determination differentiate them from others.[33] Being charismatic can make a leader's job easier, because leaders have to energize group members.

An important fact about charisma is that it reflects a subjective perception on the part of the person being influenced. Many people regard a leader such as the late Steve Jobs of Apple Inc. as being powerful and inspirational, and he is regarded as one of the key business leaders of the century. Yet he was also disliked by many people who considered him to be arrogant, prone to throwing tamper tantrums, hateful toward competitors, and a control freak. He was also involved in legally questionable ways of compensating himself and other members of his team by changing the dates on stock options, thereby guaranteeing a big payoff.

The term *charisma* is most frequently used in association with nationally and internationally known leaders. Yet first-level supervisors, team leaders, and minor sports coaches can also be charismatic. Possessing a naturally dynamic personality is a major contributor to charisma, but a person can engage in many tangible actions that also contribute to charisma. The following are 12 suggestions for behaving charismatically, all based on characteristics and behaviors often found among charismatic leaders. If you are not currently a leader, remember that being perceived as charismatic will help you become one.

1. **Communicate a vision.** A charismatic leader offers an exciting image of where the organization is headed and how to get there. A vision is more than a forecast, because it describes an ideal version of the future of an entire organization or an organizational unit such as a department. Richard Branson, the colorful British entrepreneur, has inspired hundreds of employees with his vision of the Virgin brand being a leader in dozens of fields. Among his accomplishments to reach this vision are the Virgin Atlantic airline, Virgin Megastores, and Virgin Cinema. The supervisor of paralegal services might communicate a vision such as "Our paralegal group will become known as the most professional and helpful paralegal group in Arizona." A visionary leader should also have help to implement the vision. For the paralegal supervisor, part of implementing the vision might be teaching new technology skills to the paralegals.

   An important part of communicating a vision for good effect is to be clear about what needs to be done to build a better future, even if the future is next week. Based on his study of some of the world's most successful business leaders, Marcus Buckingham concludes that the leader should define the future in vivid terms so that people can see where they are headed.[34]

   Skill-Building Exercise 10-2 will give you a chance to develop visioning skills (a buzzword in business).

2. **Make frequent use of metaphors and analogies.** To inspire people, the charismatic leader uses colorful language and exciting metaphors and analogies. Develop metaphors to inspire people around you. A metaphor commonly used after a group has suffered a setback is, "Like the phoenix, we will rise from the ashes of defeat." To pick up the spirits of her maintenance group, a maintenance supervisor told the group, "We're a lot like the heating and cooling system in a house. A lot of people don't give us much thought, but without us their lives would be very uncomfortable."

3. **Inspire trust and confidence.** Make your deeds consistent with your promises. As mentioned earlier in this chapter, being trustworthy is a key leadership trait. Get people to believe in your competence by making your accomplishments known in a polite, tactful way. The *socialized charismatic* is likely to inspire trust and confidence because such a leader is ethical and wants to accomplish activities that help others rather than pursuing personal ends such as glory and power.[35]

SKILL-BUILDING EXERCISE 10-2

Creating a Vision

The class organizes into small problem-solving groups. Each group constructs a vision for a unit of an organization or for a total organization of its choosing. Students can choose a well-known business firm, a government agency, or an organization with which they are familiar. The vision should be approximately 25 words long, and depict a glorious future. A vision is not simply a straightforward goal, such as "In 2017 our firm will gross $10 million in sales." Remember, the vision statement you draw should inspire people throughout the organization.

If class time permits, volunteers can share their visions with other class members who will provide feedback on the clarity and inspirational qualities of the visions presented.

4. **Be highly energetic and goal oriented.** Impress others with your energy and resourcefulness. To increase your energy supply, exercise frequently, eat well, and get ample rest. Closely related to being goal oriented is being optimistic about what you and the group can accomplish. People also associate optimism with energy. Being grumpy is often associated with being low on energy. You can add to an image of energy by raising and lowering your voice frequently and avoiding a slow pace.

5. **Be emotionally expressive and warm.** A key characteristic of charismatic leaders is the ability to express feelings openly. Assertiveness is therefore an important component of charisma. In dealing with team members, refer to your feelings at the time, such as "I'm excited because I know we are going to hit our year-end target by mid-October." A study with firefighters showed that leaders who were perceived to be charismatic contributed to the happiness of the group, particularly when the leader expressed positive emotion and had a positive outlook.[36]

Nonverbal emotional expressiveness, such as warm gestures and occasional touching (nonsexual) of group members, also exhibits charisma. Remember, however, that many people resent being touched when at work. Frequent smiling is another way of being emotionally expressive. Also, a warm smile seems to indicate a confident, caring person, which contributes to a perception of charisma.

6. **Make ample use of true stories.** An excellent way of building rapport is to tell stories that deliver a message. People like to hear stories about how a department or company went through hard times when it started, or how somebody climbed the corporate ladder starting at the bottom. For example, Marriott International chief executive Ed Fuller often tells the story about how he and and another senior executive began as a security guard and waiter.[37] Telling positive stories has become a widely accepted technique for building relationships with employees. Storytelling adds a touch of warmth to the teller and helps build connections among people who become familiar with the same story. Skill-Building Exercise 10-3 provides you an opprotunity to get started telling stories to add to your charisma.

7. **Be candid and direct.** Practice being direct in saying what you want, rather than being indirect and evasive. If you want someone to help you, don't ask, "Are you busy?" Instead, ask, "Can you help me with a problem I'm having right now?"

8. **Make everybody you meet feel that he or she is important.** For example, at a company social gathering, shake the hand of every person you meet. Also, thank people frequently both orally and by written notes.

9. **Multiply the effectiveness of your handshake.** Shake firmly without creating pain, and make enough eye contact to notice the color of the other person's eyes. When you take that much trouble, you project care and concern.[38]

10. **Stand up straight and use other nonverbal signals of self-confidence.** Practice good posture. Minimize fidgeting, scratching, foot tapping, and speaking in a monotone. Walk at a rapid pace without appearing to be panicked. Dress fashionably

SKILL-BUILDING EXERCISE 10-3

Creating Stories for Being a Leader

As described in the text, an effective technique for charismatic leadership is for the leader to tell true stories that reflect the values of the organization. Your task is to create stories, of about 50 words, that might inspire workers in the following settings. Perhaps students can divide up responsibility and take one setting each:

Setting 1: You are the snack food division head in a large company. You want to inspire workers based on the theme of how your company is creating a better world for people of all ages.

Setting 2: You are the owner of a hair restoration center that helps men, as well as women, become less bald. You want to

inspire your workers to understand how they are improving the lives of so many people.

Setting 3: You are the regional manager of a nationwide trash removal company that is proud of its effort toward building a greener (more environmentally friendly) country. You hear frequent mutterings from employees that it is not so glamorous working for a garbage hauler.

If class time permits, share some of your inspiring stories with other class members.

without going to the extreme that people notice your clothes more than they notice you. A fist can project confidence, power, and certainty. Waving a hand, pointing, or tapping a table can help get attention focused on you.

11. **Be willing to take personal risks.** Charismatic leaders are typically risk takers, and risk taking adds to their charisma. Risks you might take include extending additional credit to a start-up business, suggesting a bright but costly idea, and recommending that a former felon be given a chance in your firm.

12. **Be self-promotional.** Charismatic leaders are not shy. Instead, they toot their own horns and allow others to know how important they are. Without appearing self-absorbed, you too might let others know of your tangible accomplishments. Explain to others the key role that you played on your team or how you achieved a few tough goals.

An experiment was conducted with MBA students to see if charisma could be taught. The students were provided information about being charismatic, using ideas quite similar to the 12 points presented here, plus the opportunity to practice using the suggestions. Participants in the study gave speeches before and after the training in charisma. Because the students received higher ratings in being charismatic as a result of the training, it was concluded that charisma can be taught.[39]

Despite the importance of developing charisma, being excessively and flamboyantly charismatic can backfire because others may perceive you as self-serving. Therefore, the idea is to sprinkle your charisma with humility, such as admitting when you make a mistake. Also, in recent years top-level management at some companies have replaced highly charismatic, rock-star-like leaders with those who concentrate more on running the business instead of gathering publicity for themselves.

DEVELOPING TEAM LEADERSHIP SKILLS

LEARNING OBJECTIVE 3

As organizations rely heavily on teams, some of the best opportunities for practicing leadership occur as a team leader. A team leader typically reports to a higher level manager. The team leader is not a boss in the old-fashioned sense, but a facilitator or coach who shares decision making with team members. (A facilitator is a person who helps make things happen without taking control.) A team leader practices **participative leadership,** or sharing authority with the group. Being a participative leader does not mean that the leader just stays out of the way and provides no guidance or encouragement to team members. Research conducted with Norwegian companies supports the belief that danger lurks in the hands of leaders who turn over all responsibility to the group. Employees who received almost no direction from their boss suffered from role ambiguity: confusion about what needs to be done. As a result, these employees suffered from stress, and often found themselves in conflict with each other, including bullying.[40] (The conflict and bullying may have stemmed from workers in dispute over who should do what.)

participative leadership
Sharing authority with the group.

The previous discussion about developing charisma is relevant for developing team-leadership skills because when the leader is perceived as charismatic, team performance will often be enhanced.[41] The explanation is simple: Many people feel inspired to perform better when their leader is charismatic.

Self-Assessment Quiz 10-2 gives you an opportunity to gauge your attitudes toward being a participative leader. We will next discuss 10 techniques that would contribute to your effectiveness as a team leader, as outlined in Figure 10-2.

Engage in Shared Leadership

A major initiative for building teamwork is for the team leader to share, or distribute, leadership responsibilities among group members, depending on the task facing the group. The so-called *shared or collective leadership* is a reality of the modern workplace. Few leaders have enough skills to provide effective leadership in all situations.[42] The team leader might ask Ruby, who is skilled at getting budget approvals, to take leadership of the budget project. Another time the team leader might ask Eric to take leadership on a project for recapturing lost customers because he is effective at damage control.

What Style of Leader Are You or Would You Be?

Directions: Check whether each of the following questions is mostly true or mostly false, keeping in mind what you have done, or think you would do, in the scenarios and attitudes described.

	Mostly true	Mostly false
1. I am more likely to take care of a high-impact assignment myself than turn it over to a group member.	_____	_____
2. I would prefer the analytical aspects of a manager's job rather than working directly with group members.	_____	_____
3. An important part of my approach to managing a group is to keep the members informed almost daily of any information that could affect their work.	_____	_____
4. It's a good idea to give two people in the group the same problem, and then choose what appears to be the best solution.	_____	_____
5. It makes good sense for the leader or manager to stay somewhat aloof from the group so that he or she can make a tough decision when necessary.	_____	_____
6. I look for opportunities to obtain group input before making a decision, even on straightforward issues.	_____	_____
7. I would reverse a decision if several of the group members presented evidence that I was wrong.	_____	_____
8. Differences of opinion in the work group are healthy.	_____	_____
9. I think that activities to build team spirit, like the team fixing up a low-income family's house on a Saturday, are an excellent investment of time.	_____	_____
10. If my group were hiring a new member, I would like the person to be interviewed by the entire group.	_____	_____
11. An effective team leader today uses e-mail or text messaging for about 98 percent of communication with team members.	_____	_____
12. Some of the best ideas are likely to come from the group members rather than the manager.	_____	_____
13. If our group were going to have a banquet, I would get input from each member on what type of food should be served.	_____	_____
14. I have never seen a statue of a committee in a museum or park, so why bother making decisions by committee if you want to be recognized?	_____	_____
15. I dislike it intensely when a group member challenges my position on an issue.	_____	_____
16. I typically explain to group members what method they should use to accomplish an assigned task.	_____	_____
17. If I were out of the office for a week, most of the important work in the department would get accomplished anyway.	_____	_____
18. Delegation of important tasks is something that would be (or is) very difficult for me.	_____	_____
19. When a group member comes to me with a problem, I tend to jump right in with a proposed solution.	_____	_____
20. When a group member comes to me with a problem, I typically ask that person something like, "What alternative solutions have you thought of so far?"	_____	_____
Total Score	_____	_____

Scoring and Interpretation: The answers for determining what style of leader you are (or would be) are as follows:

1. Mostly false	4. Mostly false	7. Mostly true	10. Mostly true
2. Mostly false	5. Mostly false	8. Mostly true	11. Mostly false
3. Mostly true	6. Mostly true	9. Mostly true	12. Mostly true

(Continued)

Research conducted by Craig L. Pearce and his associates at the Graduate School of Management at the University of California suggests that teams that perform poorly are often dominated by the team leader. In contrast, high-performing teams have a shared leadership structure. Part of the team's success can be attributed to the team spirit stemming from the shared leadership. If the organizational or national culture does not favor shared leadership, the good results might not be forthcoming.[43] Another important contribution of shared leadership is that it helps the leader act as a servant leader who freely exchanges ideas with group members. As a result, new knowledge is generated.[44] For example, instead of the leader simply ordering workers to cut down on travel expenses, the group discusses and learns new ways of reducing travel costs without damaging morale.

Build a Mission Statement

An early point in developing teamwork is to specify the team's mission. The mission should contain a specific goal and purpose, and it should be optimistic and uplifting. A purpose is about shared values, and it answers the question of why the team exisits. Even when the purpose is obvious, it should be explained. An historic example is the 70-day rescue operation of the Chilean miners in 2010. Andre Sougarret, the senior engineer who led the

FIGURE 10-2 Developing Teamwork

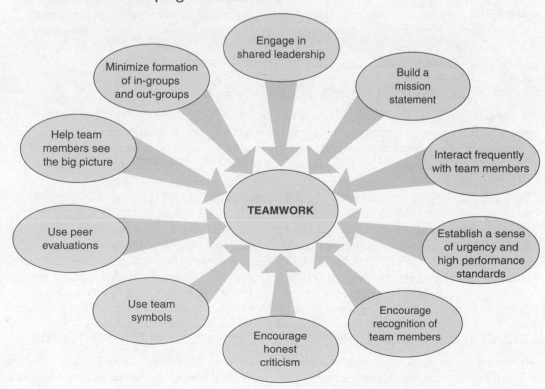

Developing a Team Mission Statement

The class organizes into teams of about six people and appoints a team leader. Each team plays the role of a specific team within a company, government agency, or hospital. An example is the customer service team at a utility company. The task is to develop a mission statement approximating the type described in the text. The team leader might also take notes for the group.

Remember that a mission statement contains a goal and a purpose, and it is uplifting and optimistic. Allow about 15 minutes for preparing the mission statements. The groups then compare mission statements. One representative from each group presents the mission statements to the rest of the class.

rescue, constantly reminded team members about the human lives they were saving.[45] Here is an example of a mission statement from a service team at a Volvo dealership:

> To plan and implement a level of automobile service and repair of the highest quality, at a competitive price, that will delight customers and retain their loyalty.

The leader can help develop the mission statement when the team is first formed or at any other time. Developing a mission statement for a long-standing team breathes new life into its activities. Being committed to a mission improves teamwork, as does the process of formulating a mission statement. Skill-Building Exercise 10-4 gives you practice in developing a mission statement for a team.

Interact Frequently with Team Members

A major strategy of being an effective team leader is to build positive relationships with team members, and relationships are built on conversations.[46] The conversations should go beyond superficialites such as discussing weekend plans or how busy the team member is. Meaningful topics would include the team member's perception of potential problems, his or her job satisfaction, and suggestions for improvement.

An effective way of interacting with team members is to hold question-and-answer sessions. The same approach demonstrates participative leadership. Both leader and members ask and answer questions, such as "How can we make an even bigger contribution to the company?" The Quality Department at Delta Dental Plan of California used question-and-answer sessions with success. The process not only boosted morale and made managers more accessible to employees, but also yielded more than 1,000 employee suggestions in the first year. The department head said, "This program totally revolutionized the company. Now employees from other divisions are eager to work in our department."[47]

Show Your Team Members That They Are Trusted

An effective leader is perceived as honest and trustworthy, and he or she trusts team members. The leader should recognize and reward ethical behavior, particularly when there is a temptation to be dishonest—such as not reporting a quality defect to a customer or cheating on tax returns. Raise expectations of honesty by telling group members you are confident that they will act in ways that bring credit to the organization.

A practical way of demonstrating trust in group members is to avoid closely monitoring their work and second-guessing their decisions about minor matters such as the best type of border for a report. A **micromanager** is one who closely monitors most aspects of group members' activities, sometimes to the point of being a control freak. As a result, the group members do not feel that the leader or manager trusts them to make even the smallest decisions. One manager checked travel Web sites himself for the best deal after a team member booked plans for a business trip. As a result, team members felt that they were not trusted to care about the financial welfare of the company.

micromanager

One who closely monitors most aspects of group members' activities, sometimes to the point of being a control freak.

Establish a Sense of Urgency and High Performance Standards

To build teamwork, members need to believe that the team has urgent, constructive purposes. A demanding performance challenge helps create and sustain the team. Team members also want to know exactly what is expected of them. The more urgent and relevant the rationale, the more likely it is that the team will perform well. Such projects are often referred to as mission-critical because the success of the team or company is at stake.[48] Based on this information, as a team leader you might project a sense of urgency and encourage setting high goals. An example is assigning the team the task of reducing reported defects in a pacemaker for the heart.

Encourage Team Members to Recognize Each Other's Accomplishments

Members of a high-spirited team look for ways to encourage and praise each other, including the traditional "high five" or fist-bump signifying an important contribution to the team. Encouragement and praise from the team leader is important, but team members also play an important role in giving positive reinforcement to each other. Team spirit develops as members receive frequent positive feedback from each other. Skill-Building Exercise 10-5 demonstrates the activity of recognizing team accomplishments.

Encourage Honest Criticism

A superficial type of camaraderie develops when team members avoid honestly criticizing each other for the sake of group harmony. Avoiding criticism can result in groupthink. As a team leader, you should therefore explain that being a good team player includes offering honest feedback on mistakes and flawed ideas. The team benefits from mutual criticism. A stronger team spirit will develop because team members realize that they are helping each other through honest feedback. An example of honest criticism took place in the customer service department at a large discount retailer. One of the team members decided to conduct an online survey of how well customers liked the restaurant lunch counter in the store. Another team member pointed out that (1) very few customers used the restaurant, and (2) it would be annoying for many customers to be asked to complete a survey about an in-store restaurant.

Use Team Symbols

Teamwork on the athletic field is enhanced by team symbols, such as uniforms and nicknames. The term "Zags," for example, deserves some credit for contributing to the mystique of the Gonzaga University men's basketball team. (The "Zags" are officially "the Bulldogs.") Symbols can also be an effective team builder in business. Trademarks, logos,

---

SKILL-BUILDING EXERCISE 10-5

Recognizing Team Accomplishments

The class organizes into teams of about six, ideally into teams or groups that already worked with each other during the course. If you have not worked with each other, you will have to rely on any impressions you have made of the other members of the team during the course. Team members will be equipped with about six 3" × 5" index cards; however, any other small-size piece of paper will work. (Or you could send e-mails, IMs, or text messages to each other.) Each member of the team thinks carefully about what other members of the team have accomplished during the course, including contribution to team problem-solving, class participation, or perhaps some accomplishment outside of class.

Assume that you have six members on the team. Prepare a card for each member by jotting down whatever accomplishments you have observed of the other team members. Each person therefore prepares five cards that will be handed to the person named on the card and then given to that person. Each team member will receive five "accomplishment cards," one from each of the other five members. Each member studies his or her accomplishment cards, consisting of statements of

accomplishments and perhaps a couple of words of praise. Here are two examples:

"I like the way you showed up on time for our study group and were prepared for action. Nice job, Ben."

"A few times you came up with great ideas in our problem-solving groups. Shauna, you are a really nice team player."

After all cards have been read carefully, discuss your feelings about the cards and their potential contribution to teamwork. Cover observations such as the following:

- How much closer to the group do you feel now?

- How much have your efforts in being a team player paid off?

- How useful a technique would this technique of accomplishment recognition be for a workplace team?

- What potential disadvantages do you see to the technique?

mottoes, and other indicators of products both advertise the company and signify a joint effort. Company jackets, caps, T-shirts, mugs, ballpoint pens, and business cards can be modified to symbolize a work unit. As a team leader, you might therefore invest part of your team's budget in an appropriate symbol. Use the opportunity to practice participative leadership. Conduct a group problem-solving session to develop a team logo to place on a T-shirt or cap.

Use Peer Evaluations

In the traditional performance-evaluation system, the manager evaluates group members at regular intervals. With peer-evaluation systems, the team members contribute to the evaluation by submitting evaluations of each other. The evaluations might consist of filling out rating forms about each other's performance. Sometimes brief essays are written about each other and then synthesized by the team leader.

Peer evaluations contribute to teamwork because team members realize that helping each other becomes as important as helping the boss. Similarly, team members recognize that pleasing each other counts as much as pleasing the boss. A potential disadvantage of peer evaluations, however, is that the group members will agree to give each other outstanding evaluations, or to get even with coworkers they do not like. In the latter case, teamwork is diminished rather than increased.

As a team leader, you might not have the authority to initiate a peer-evaluation system without first checking with your manager. Making a recommendation for peer input into evaluations might demonstrate that you are committed to participative leadership.

Help Team Members See the Big Picture

The team is likely to work together more smoothly when members have a clear understanding of how their work contributes to the company. Communicating the mission as described earlier is a good starting point. Showing the team its specific contribution to the overall organization is equally important. As the team leader you might create a flowchart that tracks an order from the time it is taken to when it is delivered. Show the team its role at each step. The team members may be aware of how they contribute to the team, but not how the team contributes to the success of the organization.[49] The team leader of a shipping department at a distribution center explains to his team regularly, "Let's keep this clearly in mind. A big factor in determining whether a customer stays with us is whether the goods arrive on time and in good shape."

Minimize Formation of In-Groups and Out-Groups

leader-member exchange model

A theory explaining that group leaders establish unique working relationships with group members, thereby creating in-groups and out-groups.

An established leadership theory, the **leader-member exchange model,** provides useful information for the aspiring team leader. According to this theory, leaders establish unique working relationships with group members. By so doing, they create in-groups and out-groups. The in-groups become part of a smoothly functioning team headed by the leader. Out-group members are less likely to experience good teamwork. Another consideration of this theory is how well group members think their relationship with the leader stacks up with the leader–member relations established by coworkers.[50] For example, Sid might have a nice relationship with the leader of the group, but he is not happy that Sue has an even better relationship. When a person believes that he or she has a better relationship with the leader than do other team members, he or she is likely to have high job satisfaction and performance. Figure 10-3 depicts the major concept of the leader-member exchange model.

The in-group may come about because the leader prefers certain group members and is therefore is motivated to form good working relationships with them. Conversely, the leader may neglect to form good relationships with people with whom he or she has limited rapport. First impressions count heavily when the leader decides on who is "in" and who is "out." Team leaders should therefore guard against the formation of out-groups just because they are not fond of a few team members, or because a given team member gives a poor first impression.

The leader-member exchange model does not mean that the team leader should avoid forming unique relationships with team members. Treating members differently based on

FIGURE 10-3 The Leader–Member Exchange Model

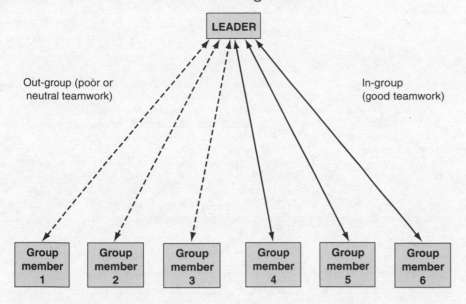

their needs and abilities makes good leadership sense. An example of a unique relationship is to give more recognition to a sales representative who craves recognition. What should be avoided is forming an out-group.

A useful perspective in understanding the importance of developing teamwork is that leaders should be judged in terms of the performance of the teams or organizations they are responsible for.[51] Good teamwork helps bring about good team performance.

DEVELOPING YOUR LEADERSHIP POTENTIAL

LEARNING OBJECTIVE 4

Much of this book deals directly and indirectly with information that could improve your leadership effectiveness. Chapter 4, on communications, is a case in point. Improving your communications effectiveness is one way to enhance your ability to lead people. Formal education and leadership development programs also contribute to enhancing leadership potential. (Many such programs include some of the activities found in this chapter.) Here we describe six strategies for developing your leadership potential, in addition to studying and participating in formal programs.

Our approach to developing leadership potential is based on the assumption that leaders are both born and made. You need some basic cognitive and personality characteristics to have the potential to be a leader, yet you need to develop these characteristics through experience and practice. A person who has good problem-solving ability and is charismatic still needs to assume leadership responsibility and engage in certain actions to become an effective leader. Among these dozens of activities would be recognizing the accomplishments of others.

Skill-Building Exercise 10-6, about maintaining a personal leadership journal, provides a start in practicing and refining leadership skills.

First-level supervisory jobs are an invaluable starting point for developing your leadership potential. It takes considerable skill to manage a rapid-service (fast-food) restaurant or direct a public playground during the summer. First-level supervisors frequently face situations in which group members are poorly trained, poorly paid, and not well motivated to achieve company objectives. Motivating and inspiring entry-level workers is one of the major challenges facing organizations. The six techniques and strategies described in the following list provide additional insight into ways of developing your leadership potential.

1. **Acquire broad experience.** Because leadership varies somewhat with the situation, a sound approach to improving leadership effectiveness is to attempt to gain supervisory experience in different settings. A person who wants to become an

executive is well advised to gain supervisory experience in at least two different organizational functions, such as marketing and operations.

Procter & Gamble, long noted for its development of leaders and managers, emphasizes broad experience. If a promising young brand assistant wants to become an executive, the company tries to give him or her as broad an experience as possible. The person might be appointed as assistant manager of Cascade detergent. Later, he or she will run laundry products in Canada, before eventually overseeing all of Northeast Asia.[52]

2. **Model effective leaders.** Another strategy for leadership development is to observe capable leaders in action, and then model some of their approaches. You may not want to copy a particular leader entirely, but you can incorporate a few of the behavior patterns into your own leadership style. For instance, most inexperienced leaders have difficulty confronting others. Observe how a skilled confronter handles the situation, and try that person's approach the next time you have unfavorable news to communicate to another person.

3. **Self-develop leadership traits and behaviors.** Study the leadership traits and behaviors described earlier in this chapter. As a starting point, identify several attributes you think you could strengthen within yourself, given some determination and perhaps combined with the right training program. For example, you might decide that with some effort you could improve your sense of humor. You might also believe that you could remember to encourage honest criticism within the team. It is also helpful to obtain feedback from valid sources (such as a trusted manager) about which traits and behaviors you particularly need to develop.

Self-development of leadership traits and behaviors is an important part of continuous learning and development. Leadership consultant Tina Smagala says that the most effective leaders continually take charge of their development, rather than waiting for their manager or the training team to push along their development.[53] For example, if you observed that more of your customers, coworkers, and subordinates were Spanish speaking, you might take the initiative to acquire some proficiency in Spanish.

4. **Become an integrated human being.** A philosophical approach to leadership suggests that the model leader is first and foremost a fully functioning person. According to William D. Hitt, mastering the art of leadership comes with self-mastery. Leadership development is the process of self-development. As a result, the process of becoming a leader is similar to the process of becoming an integrated human being. For example, you need to develop values that guide your behavior before you can adequately guide the behavior of others.[54]

Another aspect of becoming an integrated human being is to is attain self-understanding.

Suppose you discover that you feel intimidated by people who are older and more experienced than you. Armed with this self-insight, you can gradually overcome the problem, and feel more comfortable leading workers who are older and more experienced than you.

5. **Practice a little leadership.** An effective way to develop your leadership skills is to look for opportunities to exert a small amount of helpful leadership in contrast to waiting for opportunities to accomplish extraordinary deeds. The "little leadership" might involve such behaviors as mentoring a struggling team member, coaching somebody about how to use a new high-tech device, or making a suggestion about improving a product. In the words of Michael E. McGill and John W. Slocum Jr., "For those who want to stand atop the dugout, dance with the elephants, fly with the buffaloes, soar with eagles, or perform other mystical and heroic acts of large leadership, our little leadership may seem all too managerial, too modest, and too mundane."[55]

6. **Help your leader lead.** According to Michael Useem, leaders need your assistance so that they can do a good job. "If people are afraid to help their leaders lead, their leaders will fail."[56] (This idea is part of being an active participant in shared leadership.) A group member is often closer to the market and closer to how the product is used; therefore, he or she can provide useful information to the person in the formal leadership position. When you help the people above you avoid a mistake or capitalize upon an opportunity, you help the entire company. At the same time, you are developing your ability to take the initiative and lead.

Concept Review and Reinforcement

Summary

Effective leadership depends on having the right personal characteristics and taking the appropriate actions. Leadership is the ability to inspire support and confidence among the people who are needed to achieve company goals. People can exercise leadership whether or not they occupy a formal leadership position, such as being an emergent leader.

Certain traits contribute heavily to leadership effectiveness. Among them are the following: self-confidence and leadership self-efficacy; positive core self-evaluations; assertiveness; trustworthiness, morality, and authenticity; sense of humor; self-awareness and self-objectivity; cognitive skills including critical assessments; emotional intelligence; passion and enthusiasm; and self-sacrificing personality.

Although charisma depends heavily on personal characteristics, people can work toward being charismatic. Suggestions for behaving charismatically include the following:

1. Communicate a vision.
2. Make frequent use of metaphors and analogies.
3. Inspire trust and confidence.
4. Be highly energetic and goal oriented.
5. Be emotionally expressive and warm.
6. Make ample use of true stories.
7. Be candid and direct.
8. Make everyone you meet feel that he or she is important.
9. Multiply the effectiveness of your handshake.
10. Stand up straight, and use other nonverbal signals of self-confidence.
11. Be willing to take personal risks.
12. Be self-promotional.

A team leader acts as a facilitator or coach who shares decision making with team members, thus practicing participative leadership. The following are some techniques for effective team leadership:

1. Engage in shared leadership.
2. Build a mission statement.
3. Interact frequently with team members.
4. Show your team members that they are trusted.
5. Establish a sense of urgency and high performance standards.
6. Encourage team members to recognize each other's accomplishments.
7. Encourage honest criticism.
8. Use team symbols.
9. Use peer evaluations.
10. Help team members see the big picture.
11. Minimize formation of in-groups and out-groups.

In addition to participating in formal leadership development programs, six strategies for developing leadership potential are to (1) acquire broad experience, (2) model effective leaders, (3) self-develop leadership traits and behaviors, (4) become an integrated human being (a fully functioning person), (5) practice small leadership acts, and (6) help your leader lead.

Questions for Discussion and Review

1. People who were voted "most likely to succeed" in high school are frequently found in leadership positions later in life. What explanation can you offer for these predictions about success so often being true?

2. A few years ago, the Boeing Company appointed Ray Conner as the senior vice president of sales and customer support for the commerical airline division. Conner, who previously managed the company's supply chain, began his employment with Boeing as an airplane mechanic. What relevance might his experience as a mechanic have for his effectivenss as a high-level leader in the company?

3. The average age of CEOs is declining; however, what would you regard as the minimum age acceptable for a man or woman to be the CEO of a company of over 100,000 employees? Explain your reasoning.

4. How can a person demonstrate to others in the company that he or she is trustworthy enough to be considered for a leadership position?

5. Why does a leader need good emotional intelligence? Shouldn't a leader be a take-charge person focused on obtaining results like making money or building a brand?

6. Can you suggest any problems with the trait approach to leadership?

7. Suggest two situations where you may need different styles of leadership.

8. Watch a video of a top business leader or politician making a speech. How do they use language to increase their charisma?

9. How might a person in a highly specialized field, such as information technology or accounting, achieve broad experience in order to qualify for a leadership position?

10. Assume that a student obtains a part-time job as an assistant store manager. What can this person do to capitalize on this position for developing his or her leadership potential?

The Web Corner

http://www.ccl.org
(Center for Creative Leadership; includes videos)

http://www.core-edge.com
(Attaining power and charisma; includes a video)

http://www.buzzle.com
(Effective team leadership; includes an audio presentation)

Internet Skill Builder: Developing Your Charisma

One approach to developing charisma for leadership is to read brief clips about charismatic people, and look for any practical suggestions from these stories. For example, you might read that a successful charismatic leader invests time in writing hand written notes of appreciation to his or her subordinates. Search the Web for at least three brief stories about charismatic leaders. After studying these stories, arrive at least three practical suggestions for developing your charisma. Attempt to implement these suggestions during the next 12-month period and see if people react positively to your charismatic initiatives.

Developing Your Human Relations Skills

Interpersonal Relations Case 10.1

Jeb Wants to Inspire his Team

Jeb considered himself fortunate to be chosen as the team leader for one of the newly formed teams at the insurance company where he worked. The purpose of forming teams was to improve customer service. Each team now had the authority to issue policies and settle claims, within limits, for specific geographic regions. Before the shift into teams, separate departments existed for sales, underwriting, and claims. Although the company was profitable, it received too many criticisms about poor service, particulary in the time required to process a claim. Sales representatives within the company contended that the underwriting department took too long to approve and issue policies.

One of Jeb's first initiatives was to hold frequent in-person meetings to discuss how service was going to be improved. He emphasized to the team that the company had adopted the popular team concept and that teams were empowered to look for ways to improve efficiency. Jeb also emphasized that each team member had more responsibility than under the department structure. Each team member would be doing some sales, underwriting, and claims.

Team member Georgia commented during one of the meetings, "Just think of it, three jobs in one and being paid just the same as before." During the same meeting, team member Rob asked, "What's so special about calling us a team? I had a nice job in the underwriting department before these teams were formed. I enjoyed that work. Now my job is more confusing."

Jeb responded, "The company decided this was the way to go. Trust me, everything will work out fine. Just go along with the team idea for now."

Four months after the teams were formed, Jeb's boss, James, met with him to discuss progress. James said, "Your team isn't making as much progress as I would like. Policies are not being issued any faster. Customer complaints about slow claims settlements are at the same level as before we converted into teams. The other teams are making more progress. Does your team have a problem?"

"We do have a problem," said Jeb. "Everyone comes to work just as in the days before teams. They do most of the work alone, but they send e-mail messages to each other as needed. It just seems to be business as usual. So far, the idea of a high-producing team hasn't caught on."

"Are you an effective team leader?" asked James.

"I think I am," said Jeb. "I do everything I'm supposed to. I hold meetings; I post messages. I answer all questions asked of me. I try to settle problems."

"I'll be back to you in two months to discuss your team's progress. I want to see some improved results in terms of better customer service."

Case Questions

1. How can Jeb be a more effective team leader?
2. What can Jeb do to inspire his team?
3. Based on whatever information you have found in the case, what is your evaluation of Jeb's charisma?

Interpersonal Skills Role-Play

Jeb Attempts to Inspire His Team

One courageous student plays the role of Jeb, who has called a meeting late one Friday afternoon. His purpose is to inspire the team to attain higher levels of customer service and to motivate individuals to engage in more teamwork, rather than working independently. The e-mail Jeb sent a few days before the meeting just alluded to a team meeting to discuss items relevant to the team's progress. Several other students play the roles of the team members, not all of whom see much value in the team structure. Conduct this role-play for about eight minutes. Observers rate the role players on two dimensions, using a 1-to-5 scale from very poor (1) to very good (5). One dimension is "effective use of human relations techniques." Focus on how well Jeb implements effective techniqes of team leadership, development, and charisma. The second dimension is "acting ability." A few observers might voluntarily provide feedback to the role players in terms of sharing their ratings and observations. The course instructor might also provide feedback.

Interpersonal Relations Case 10.2

What Kind of Leader is Ashley?

Ashley, a department head in the assembly division of Micro Electronics, recently took a leadership development course sponsored by the company. The major thrust of the course was to teach managers and supervisors how to implement participative leadership. In the words of the course leader: "Today, almost all employees want to get involved. They want a say in all important decisions affecting them. The era of the industrial dictator has been gone for a while."

Ashley was mildly skeptical about the course leader's universal endorsement of participative leadership. Yet she decided that if this is what the company wanted, she would adopt a more participative style. Ashley took extensive notes on how to implement participative leadership.

Six months after the leadership development program was completed, the human resources department attempted to evaluate its impact. One part of the evaluation consisted of interviews with managers who had attended the program. Managers were asked how they liked the program and how it helped them. Another part of the program evaluation was to speak to employees about how the program influenced their boss's approach to supervision.

Rick, the company training director, conducted several of the interviews with employees. He spoke first with Amy, a supervisor reporting to Ashley. Rick told Amy that her answers would be confidential. He said that the purpose of these interviews was to evaluate the leadership training program, not to evaluate the manager.

Amy responded, "It would be okay with me if Ashley did hear my comments. I have nothing critical to say. I think that the leadership training program was very useful. Ashley is a much better manager now than in the past. She's much more aware that people in her group have something useful to contribute. Ashley asks our opinion on everything.

"I'll give you an example," Amy continued. "Ashley was going to order a new multi purpose printer and copier. In the past she might have just ordered the machine and told us when it would be delivered. Instead, we held three meetings to decide which multi-purpose machine to purchase. Three of us formed a committee to study the problem. We finally chose a printer/copier that everybody in the office agreed would be okay, including the office assistant."

Amy concluded, "I think that every manager at Micro should learn how to be a participative leader."

Rick then spoke to Kent, another supervisor reporting to Ashley. Kent said he appreciated the fact that interviews would be confidential; however, he hoped that the drift of his comments would get back to Ashley so long as he was not identified. Kent offered this evaluation:

"Ashley has gone downhill as a manager ever since she took your training program. She has become lazier than ever. Ashley always did have a tendency to pass off too much work to her supervisors and other employees. Now she's gone overboard. The recent purchase of the printer/copier is a good example. Too many people spent too much time deciding which machine to purchase. To make matters worse, a committee of three people was formed to research the matter. It seems to me we can make better use of our time on the job.

"If Ashley keeps up her approach to leadership much longer, she won't have a job. We will all be doing her work. How can you justify a department head's salary if other people are doing her work?"

Rick thought to himself, "I wonder if Amy and Kent are talking about the same manager. Their comments make it difficult for me to know whether the leadership development program is getting the job done."

Case Questions

1. How do you explain the different perceptions of Amy and Kent?
2. What might be wrong with the leadership development program?
3. What suggestions can you offer for making better use of participative leadership?
4. What would be the counterargument to Kent's point of view about Ashley not justifying her pay?

References

1. Original story created from facts presented in the following: Justin Fogarty, "Speakers: Pat Elizondo, Senior Vice President—Global Sales Integration, Xerox Corporation," Sales Leadership Conference, 2010 (http://www.sellingpower.com/event/conference), 2010, p. 1; "Patricia Elizondo, Xerox." *Women Worth Watching* (http://www.womenworthwatching.com/patricia-elizondo), May 20, 2006, pp. 1–3; "Patricia Elizondo, http://www.careerfocusmagazine.com, November/December 2010, pp. 22–23; "Voice of Experience: Patricia Elizondo, Senior Vice President, Eastern Operations, Xerox Corporation," *The Glass Hammer* (http://www.theglasshammer.con/news), July 6, 2009, pp. 1-3; "2010 Corporate Elite," Patricia Elizondo, SVP-Eastern Sales Operations, Xerox Corporation, *Hispanic Business*, January–February 2010, p. 32

2. E. D. Kort, "What, after All, Is Leadership? 'Leadership' and Plural Action," *Leadership Quarterly*, August 2008, p. 409.

3. Quoted in Peter Gumbel, "The Turnaround Artista," *Time*, June 29, 2009, p. 42.

4. Sankalp Chaturvedi, Michael J. Zyphur, Richard D. Arvey, Bruce J. Avolio, and Gerry Larsson, "The Heritability of Emergent Leadership: Age and Gender as Moderating Factors," *Leadership Quarterly*, April 2012, p. 219.

5. Timothy A. Judge, Ronald F. Piccolo, and Tomek Kosalka, "The Bright and Dark Sides of Leader Traits: A review and Theoretical Extension of the Leader Trait Paradigm," *Leadership Quarterly*, December 2009, p. 871.

6. George P. Hollenbeck and Douglas T. Hall, "Self-Confidence and Leader Performance," *Organizational Dynamics*, no. 3, 2004, pp. 254–269.

7. Sean T. Hannah, Bruce J. Avolio, Fred Luthans, and P. D. Harms, "Leadership Efficacy: Review and Future Directions," *Leadership Quarterly*, December 2008, pp. 669–692.

8. Bradley P. Owens and David R. Hekman, "Modeling How to Grow: An Inductive Examination of Humble Leader Behaviors, Contingencies, and Outcomes," *Academy of Management Journal*, August 2012, pp. 797–818; Erika Napoletano, "Confidence vs. Arrogance," *Entrepreneur*, June 2011, p. 20.

9. Judge, Piccolo, and Kosalka, "The Bright and Dark Sides of Leader Traits," p. 866.

10. Adam Bryant, "Want to Lead? Ask Tennyson and Shakespeare," *The New York Times*, (http://www.nytimes.com), September 4, 2011, p. 1.

11. Daniel R. Ames and Francis J. Flynn, "What Breaks a Leader: The Curvilinear Relation between Assertiveness and Leadership," *Journal of Personality and Social Psychology*, vol. 92, 2007, pp. 307–324.

12. Survey cited in "What Are the Most Important Traits for Bosses?" *Employee Recruitment & Retention*, Sample Issue, 2006.

13. Michael E. Palanski and Francis J. Yammarino, "Integrity and Leadership: A Multi-Level Conceptual Framework," *Leadership Quarterly*, June 2009, p. 406.

14. Douglas R. May, Adrian Y. L. Chan, Timothy D. Hodges, and Bruce J. Avolio, "Developing the Moral Component of Authentic Leadership," *Organizational Dynamics*, no. 3, 2003, pp. 247–260.

15. Alan Deutschman, *Walk the Walk* (New York: Portfolio, 2009).

16. Linda L. Neider and Chester A. Schriesheim, "The Authentic Leadership Inventory (ALI): Development and Empirical Tests," *Leadership Quarterly*, December 2011, p. 1149.

17. Sean T. Hannah, Fred O. Walumbwa, and Louis W. Fry, "Leadership in Action Teams: Team Leader and Members' Authenticity, Authenticity Strength, and Team Outcomes," *Personnel Psychology*, Number 3, 2011, pp. 771–802.

18. Randy G. Pennington, "Trust is An Action Verb," *HR Magazine*, February 2012, p. 90.

19. Bruce J. Avolio, Jane M. Howell, and John J. Sosik, "A Funny Thing Happened on the Way to the Bottom Line: Humor as a Moderator of Leadership Style Effects," *Academy of Management Journal*, April 1999, pp. 219–227.

20. Kevin Eikenberry, "Who Are You?" *Executive Leadership*, November 2012, p. 7.

21. Dale E. Zand, *The Leadership Triad: Knowledge, Trust, and Power* (New York: Oxford, University Press, 1997), p. 8.

22. Dick Bartels, "Wal-Mart Names Chief Merchandising Officer," Associated Press, January 28, 2011.

23. John Menkes, *Executive Intelligence: What All Great Leaders Have* (New York: Collins, 2006).

24. Daniel Goleman, "What Makes a Leader?" *Harvard Business Review*, November–December 1998, p. 92; Goleman, "Never Stop Learning," *Harvard Business Review*, January 2004, pp. 28–29.

25. Frank Walter, Michael S. Cole, and Ronald H. Humphrey, "Emotional Intelligence: Sine Qua Non of Leadership or Folderol?" *Academy of Management Perspectives*, February 2011, pp. 45–59.

26. Michelle Chapman, "J&J's McCoy New CEO at Avon," Associated Press, April 10, 2012.

27. Richard Boyatzis and Annie McKee, *Resonant Leadership* (Boston: Harvard Business School Press, 2005).

28. Victoria A. Visser, Daan van Knippenberg, Gerben A. van Kleef, and Barbara Wisse, "How Leader Displays of Happiness and Sadness Influence Follower Performance: Emotional Contagion and Creative versus Analytical Performance," *Leadership Quarterly*, February 2013, pp. 172–188.

29. Jan Wieseke, Florian Kraus, Sascha Alavi, and Tino Kessler-Thönes, "How Leaders. Motivation Transfers to Customer Service Representatives," *Journal of Social Science Research*, Number 2, 2011, pp. 214–233.

30. Tom Krisher, "GM Sees Gains as Models Refreshed," Associated Press, May 19, 2012.

31. David De Cremer, David M. Mayer, Marius van Dijke, Barbara S. Schouten, and Mary Bardes, "When Does Self-Sacrificial Leadership Motivate Prosocial Behavior? It Depends on Followers' Prevention Focus," *Journal of Applied Psychology*, July 2009, pp. 887–899.

32. Fred O. Walumbwa, Chad A. Hartnell, and Adegoke Oke, "Servant Leadership, Procedural Justice Climate, Employee Attitudes, and Organizational Citizenship Behavior: A Cross-Level Investigation," *Journal of Applied Psychology*, May 2010, p. 519.

33. Jay A. Conger, *The Charismatic Leader: Behind the Mystique of Exceptional Leadership* (San Francisco: Jossey-Bass, 1989).

34. Bill Breen, "The Clear Leader," *Fast Company*, March 2005, pp. 65–67.

35. Michael E. Brown and Linda K. Treviño, "Socialized Charismatic Leadership, Values, Congruence, and Deviance in Work Groups," *Journal of Applied Psychology*, July 2006, p. 955.

36. Amir Erez, Vilmos F. Misangi, Diane E. Johnson, Marcie A. LePine, and Kent C. Halverson, "Stirring the Hearts of Followers: Charismatic Leadership as the Transferal of Affect," *Journal of Applied Psychology*, May 2008, pp. 602–616.

37. Vickie Elmer, "How Storytelling Spurs Success," *Fortune*, December 6, 2010, p. 76.

38. Suggestions 7, 9, and 10 are from Roger Dawson, *Secrets of Power Persuasion* (Upper Saddle River, NJ: Prentice Hall, 1992), pp. 181–183, and also supported in John Antonakis, Marika Fenley, and Sue Liechti, "Learning Charisma," *Harvard Business Review*, June 2012, p. 129.

39. John Antonakis, Marika Fenley, and Sue Liechti, "Can Charisma Be Taught?" *Academy of Management Learning & Education*, September 2011, pp. 374-396.

40. A. Skogtad et al., "The Destructiveness of Laissez-Faire Leadership Behavior," *Journal of Occupational Health Psychology*, January 2007, pp. 80–92.

41. Prasad Balkundi, Martin Kilduff, and David A. Harrison, "Centrality and Charisma: Comparing How Leader Networks *and* Attributions Affect Team Performance," *Journal of Applied Psychology*, November 2011, pp. 1209–1222.

42. Christopher Hann, "We're All in This Together," *Entrepreneur*, March 2013, p. 57; Tamara L. Friedrich et al., "A Framework for Understanding Collective Leadership: The Selective Utilization of Leader and Team Expertise within Networks," *Leadership Quarterly*, December 2009, pp. 933–958.

43. Craig L. Pearce, Charles C. Manz, and Henry P. Sims, Jr., "Where Do We Go from Here? Is Shared Leadership the Key to Success?" *Organizational Dynamics*, July–September 2009, pp. 234–238.

44. Rishabh Rai and Anand Prakash, "A Relational Perspective to Knowledge Creation: Role of Servant Leadership," *Journal of Leadership Studies*, Issue 2, 2012, pp. 61-85.

45. Amy C. Edmonson, "Teamwork on the Fly," *Harvard Business Review*, April 2012, p. 78.

46. "Talking It Out: The New Conversation-centered Leadership," *Knowledge@Wharton* (http://knowledge.wharton.upenn), March 6, 2012, pp. 1–4. Article based on Alan S. Berson and Richard G. Stieglitz, *Leadership Conversations: Challenging High-Potential Managers to Become Great Leaders* (San Francisco: Jossey-Bass, 2013).

47. "Pump Up Your Leadership Style," *Manager's Edge*, March 2007, p. 3. Adapted from Patricia Fripp, "Leadership Lesson 2: 'I'm Glad You Asked'" http://www.fripp.com.

48. Michael Mankins, Alan Bird, and James Root, "Making Star Teams Out of Star Players," *Harvard Business Review*, January–February 2013, p. 77; Jon R. Katzenbach and Douglas K. Smith, "The Discipline of Teams," *Harvard Business Review*, March–April 1993, p. 118.

49. "What It Takes to Be an Effective Team Leader," *Manager's Edge*, March 2000, p. 6.

50. George Graen and J. F. Cashman, "A Role Making Model of Leadership in Formal Organizations: A Developmental Approach," in J. G. Hunt and L. L. Larson, eds., *Leadership Frontiers* (Kent, OH: Kent State University Press, 1975), pp. 143–165; Jia Hu and Robert C. Liden, "Relative Leader-Member Exchange within Team Contexts: How and When Social Comparison Impacts Individual Effectiveness," *Personnel Psychology*, Number 1, 2013, pp. 127–172.

51. Robert B. Kaiser, Robert Hogan, and S. Bartholomew Craig, "Leadership and the Fate of Organizations," *American Psychologist*, February–March 2008, pp. 96–110.

52. Mina Kimes, "P & G's Leadership Machine," *Fortune*, April 13, 2008, p. 22.

53. Tina Smagala, "Good Leaders Are Always Learning, Growing," *Democrat and Chronicle*, March 20, 2012, p. 5B.

54. William D. Hitt, *The Model Leader: A Fully Functioning Person* (Columbus, OH: Battelle Press, 1993).

55. Michael E. McGill and John W. Slocum, Jr., "A *Little* Leadership Please?" *Organizational Dynamics*, Winter 1998, p. 48.

56. Bill Breen, "Trickle-Up Leadership," *Fast Company*, November 2001, pp. 70–72.

Motivating Others

Miquel is the operations director of a firm that creates online social network style groups for doing market research. These network groups could be described as online focus groups. Such groups express their opinion about the products and services they would like to see on the market or the features they like or dislike about an existing product or service.

Miquel had read several times in management articles that few workers get enough recognition and praise to keep them happy. He also realized that the usual method of giving recognition to employees such as saying, "Great Job" in person would not be so effective because about half the staff worked from home or other remote locations. Miquel also thought that giving technically oriented workers such trinkets as coffee mugs and key chains for good performance might not be to their liking. He also reasoned that sending congratulatory e-mail messages

Pressmaster/Shutterstock

After reading and studying this chapter and completing the exercises, you should be able to

1. Understand how work engagement is related to motivation and commitment.
2. Motivate people by responding to their self-interests.
3. Make effective use of positive reinforcement to motivate people in many situations.
4. Make effective use of recognition to motivate others.
5. Apply expectancy theory as a comprehensive way of motivating others.
6. Diagnose situations to analyze the strength of motivation present.
7. Identify effective techniques for self-motivation.

might not seem particularly cool to his staff members who embraced the latest communications technology.

Miguel decided he would send tweets to his staff members when they deserved recognition and also post comments on the walls of their Facebook accounts. During the first two months of his recognition program, Miquel's posts and tweets included the following:

"Dude, you were good today. Your suggestion sent our client into orbit."

"Kathy, you found us a few outstanding social group members. Each of them has already contributed. Top job, smart lady."

"Derek, your analysis of the content of the data on the social networking group for our frozen custard client was sensational. Keep up the good work."

"Maria, great work speaks for itself, and your recent work is talking out loud."

Miquel noticed that staff members seemed quite appreciative of his tweets and posts to express appreciation. "Of course, my staff will get salary increases when possible, but in the meantime this day-to-day appreciation is really good stuff."

The experience at the social media market research firm illustrates that giving out recognition in a sensible form is a useful part of motivation. **Motivation** has two meanings: (1) an internal state that leads to effort expended toward objectives and (2) an activity performed by one person to get another to accomplish work. We often think of a manager or leader as the one attempting to motivate group members. Yet many people in the workplace have a need to motivate others. To accomplish their work, people must motivate individuals who report to them, coworkers, supervisors, or customers. Developing motivational skills will therefore help you accomplish more work than you would if you relied strictly on the good nature and team spirit of others.

This chapter first describes how worker engagement and commitment is related to motivation. The chapter then describes how to to develop motivational skills based on four related explanations of motivation. We progress from the simplest to the most complex explanation. We also describe techniques for motivating yourself. As a starting point in thinking through how to motivate others, do Self-Assessment Quiz 11-1.

motivation

An internal state that leads to effort expended toward objectives; an activity performed by one person to get another to accomplish work.

WORK ENGAGEMENT AND THE MOTIVATION OF OTHERS

A major thrust in motivation on the job is to get workers involved or engaged in their work and commited to the company as well as the work group. **Work engagement** refers to high levels of personal investment in the work tasks performed in a job.[1] As

LEARNING OBJECTIVE 1

My Approach to Motivating Others

Directions: Describe how often you act or think in the way indicated by the following statements when you are attempting to motivate another person. Circle the appropriate number for each statement using the following scale: Very Infrequently (VI); Infrequently (I); Sometimes (S); Frequently (F); Very Frequently (VF).

		VI	I	S	F	VF
1.	I ask the other person what he or she is hoping to achieve in the situation.	1	2	3	4	5
2.	I attempt to figure out whether the person has the ability to do what I need done.	1	2	3	4	5
3.	When another person is heel dragging, it usually means he or she is lazy.	5	4	3	2	1
4.	I explain exactly what I want to the person I'm trying to motivate.	1	2	3	4	5
5.	I like to give the other person a reward up front so that he or she will be motivated.	5	4	3	2	1
6.	I give lots of feedback when another person is performing a task for me.	1	2	3	4	5
7.	I like to belittle another person enough so that he or she will be intimidated into doing what I need done.	5	4	3	2	1
8.	I make sure that the other person feels treated fairly.	1	2	3	4	5
9.	I figure that if I smile nicely, I can get the other person to work as hard as I need.	5	4	3	2	1
10.	I attempt to get what I need done by instilling fear in the other person.	5	4	3	2	1
11.	I specify exactly what needs to be accomplished.	1	2	3	4	5
12.	I generously praise people who help me get my work accomplished.	1	2	3	4	5
13.	A job well done is its own reward. I therefore keep praise to a minimum.	5	4	3	2	1
14.	I make sure that I let people know how well they have done in meeting my expectations on a task.	1	2	3	4	5
15.	To be fair, I attempt to reward people similarly no matter how well they have performed.	5	4	3	2	1
16.	When somebody doing work for me performs well, I recognize his or her accomplishments promptly.	1	2	3	4	5
17.	Before giving somebody a reward, I attempt to find out what would appeal to that person.	1	2	3	4	5
18.	I make it a policy not to thank somebody for doing a job he or she is paid to do.	5	4	3	2	1
19.	If people do not know how to perform a task, motivation will suffer.	1	2	3	4	5
20.	If properly laid out, many jobs can be self-rewarding.	1	2	3	4	5

Total Score _____

Scoring and Interpretation: Add the circled numbers to obtain your total score.

90–100: You have advanced knowledge and skill with respect to motivating others in a work environment. Continue to build on the solid base you have established.

50–89: You have average knowledge and skill with respect to motivating others. With additional study and experience, you will probably develop advanced motivational skills.

20–49: To effectively motivate others in a work environment, you will need to greatly expand your knowledge of motivation theory and techniques.

Source: The idea for this quiz and a few items are from David A. Whetton and Kim S. Cameron, *Developing Management Skills,* 5th ed. (Upper Saddle River, NJ: Prentice Hall, 2002), pp. 302–303.

a result, the self is injected into the job. The engaged worker would therefore feel personally responsible for good and poor job performance, and would take pride in accomplishments. A director of marketing would likely experience engagement, but so might an amublance medic. Engagement often leads to feeling commited to the job, group, or employer. In the workplace, **commitment** refers to a perceived psychological bond that employees have with some target associated with their jobs, often another person.[2]

Workers who are both engaged and committed invest a big part of themselves into the job and employer. A wide variety of programs and actions taken by managers and employers can lead to worker engagement and commitment. Among these initiatives are paying workers well, giving them flexible working hours, assigning them meaningful work, providing them adequate health insurance, and recognizing their efforts with gifts.[3]

So how do work engagement and commitment fit into an individual attempting to motivate another person in a work setting? If you use the techniques described in this chapter, you will be motivating others and perhaps helping them become engaged and committed to the cause. Assume that you have a coworker named Bertha who is not doing her fair share in a team effort. You begin to use positive reinforcement, such as patting her on the back when Bertha does pull her weight. Under the best of circumstances, Bertha's spurt of motivation will facilitate her becoming an engaged and committed team member. Furthermore, your basic motivational technique might lead Bertha to bond with you and the entire team.

MOTIVATION SKILL BASED ON THE PRINCIPLE OF "WHAT'S IN IT FOR ME?"

LEARNING OBJECTIVE 2

The most fundamental principle of human motivation is that people are motivated by self-interest. This principle is referred to as "What's in it for me?" or WIIFM (pronounced wiff'em). Reflect on your own experience. Before working hard to accomplish a task, you probably want to know how you will benefit. If your manager asks you to work extra hours to take care of an emergency, you will most likely oblige. Yet underneath you might be thinking, "If I work these extra hours, my boss will think highly of me. As a result, I will probably receive a good performance evaluation and maybe a better-than-average salary increase."

If your instructor asks you to prepare a lengthy research paper, you might be motivated to work to the best of your ability. But before getting down to the task, it is likely that questions have raced through your mind, such as "Will this paper elevate my grade?" or "Will I pick up information that will help me in my career?"

Why Help Others? A perplexing issue is how the WIIFM principle explains why people are motivated to help others. Why would a company CEO donate gift baskets of food to homeless people? Why hire a virtually unemployable person for a nonproductive job in the mailroom? People who perform acts of social good receive the reward of feeling better about themselves. In psychological terms, they satisfy their needs to nurture (take care of) others. More cynically, helping those less fortunate leads to recognition for being a Good Samaritan.

The widespread willingness of people to contribute to Web sites that provide useful information to others gives additional insight into what satisfaction many people obtain from working for free. According to Prabhakar Raghavan, chief of Yahoo! Labs Team, approximately 4 to 6 percent of Yahoo's users contribute their energies for free in such matters as reviewing films or handling questions at Yahoo! Answers. The motivation is often pride. At other times, Internet volunteers combine their motivation to help others with the motivation to build their online presence, or *personal brand*. ThisNext is a social network in which participants exchange shopping leads, and many volunteers help run the site. Gordon Gould, the operator of ThisNext, says that volunteer workers prosper because "They can build their brands."[4] The takeaway here is that even when people do not get paid for working, they are usually obtaining an important personal benefit.

Applying the WIIFM Principle.   To use the WIIFM principle in motivating others, you have to be aware of the intensity of the person's desire. A person can be highly motivated, mildly motivated, or only slightly motivated, depending on the intensity of his or her WIIFM principle. A company might offer outstanding performers the opportunity to work at home one day per week. Employees who are intensely motivated to work at home will work virtually up to capacity to achieve a rating of outstanding performer.

To use the WIIFM principle in motivating others, you must find out what needs, desires, or motives a person is attempting to satisfy. A need acts as an internal energy force. You find out what these needs are by asking people what they want or by observing what interests them. For instance, the way a manager might motivate a recognition-hungry group member is to tell that person, "If you perform 10 percent above quota for six consecutive months, we will get you a plaque signifying your achievement to hang on the wall."

The Importance of Needs.   One of the reasons needs are so important in understanding motivation is that needs lead to behavior, or what people actually do. A person might be extraverted because of a need to affiliate with others, so that person might be motivated by the opportunity to work closely with others. Another person might be conscientious partly because of a need for achievement. This individual might be motivated by the opportunity to accomplish useful work.[5]

Employee needs have been classified in many ways, yet most of these lists overlap. According to a representative classification, 99 percent of employees are motivated by one or more of the following seven needs:

1. **The need for achievement:** Employees with strong achievement needs seek the satisfaction of completing projects successfully. They want to apply their talents to attain success, and they find joy in accomplishment for its own sake.

2. **The need for power:** Employees with a strong power need derive satisfaction from influencing and controlling others, and they aspire to become executives. These employees like to lead and persuade and be in charge of resources such as budgets.

3. **The need for affiliation:** Employees with a strong need for affiliation derive satisfaction from interacting with others, being part of a work group, and forming friendships. The same employees are motivated to avoid working alone for long periods of time.

4. **The need for autonomy:** Employees with a strong need for autonomy seek freedom and independence, such as having almost complete responsibility for a project. The same employees are motivated to avoid working in a team effort for long periods of time. Many industrial sales representatives (those who sell to companies) have a strong need for autonomy.

5. **The need for esteem:** Employees with a strong need for esteem want to feel good about themselves, and they judge their worth to a large extent based on how much recognition and praise they receive.

6. **The need for safety and security:** Employees with strong needs for safety and security seek job security, steady income, ample medical and dental insurance, and a hazard-free work environment.

7. **The need for equity:** Employees with a strong need for equity seek fair treatment. They often compare working hours, job responsibilities, salary, and privileges to those of coworkers, and they will become discouraged if coworkers are receiving better treatment.[6]

Recognizing such needs, as well as other needs and interests, helps you apply the WIIFM principle. Skill-Building Exercise 11-1 gives you the opportunity to do the preliminary work needed for applying the WIIFM principle.

USING POSITIVE REINFORCEMENT TO MOTIVATE OTHERS

A standard and widely accepted approach to motivating others is to reward them for achieving good results or behaving in a constructive manner. **Positive reinforcement** means increasing the probability that behavior will be repeated by rewarding people for making the desired response. The phrase *increasing the probability* means that positive reinforcement improves learning and motivation but is not 100 percent effective. The phrase *making the desired response* is also noteworthy. To use positive reinforcement properly, a reward must be contingent upon doing something right. Simply paying somebody a compliment or giving the person something of value is not positive reinforcement.

Positive reinforcement is easy to visualize with well-structured jobs, such as data entry or producing parts. Yet positive reinforcement is also used to encourage desired behavior in highly paid, complex jobs. An accountant who developed a new method of the company getting paid faster might be rewarded with two extra days of vacation.

Negative reinforcement (or avoidance motivation) means rewarding people by taking away an uncomfortable consequence of their behavior. Negative reinforcement is a reward because a disliked consequence is avoided or withdrawn. You are subject to negative reinforcement when you are told, "Your insurance rate will go down if you receive no traffic violations for 12 months." The uncomfortable consequence removed is a high insurance premium. Removing the undesirable consequence is contingent upon your making the right response—driving within the law.

Be careful not to make the common mistake of confusing negative reinforcement with punishment. Negative reinforcement is the opposite of punishment. It involves rewarding someone by removing a punishment or uncomfortable situation.

To use positive reinforcement effectively, certain rules and procedures must be followed, as outlined in Figure 11-1. Although using rewards to motivate people seems straightforward, positive reinforcement requires a systematic approach. The rules are specified from the standpoint of the person trying to motivate another individual, such as a team member, coworker, supervisor, or customer.

Rule 1: State Clearly What Behavior Will Lead to a Reward. The nature of good performance, or the goals, must be agreed upon by the manager and the group member. Clarification might take this form: "We need to decrease by 40 percent the number of new credit card customers who have delinquent accounts of 60 days or more."

Rule 2: Choose an Appropriate Reward. An appropriate reward is effective in motivating a given person and feasible from the standpoint of the individual or the company. If one reward does not motivate the person, try another. The importance of

positive reinforcement

Increasing the probability that behavior will be repeated by rewarding people for making the desired response.

negative reinforcement (avoidance motivation)

Rewarding people by taking away an uncomfortable consequence of their behavior.

FIGURE 11-1 Rules and Procedures for Positive Reinforcement

1. State clearly what behavior will lead to a reward.
2. Choose an appropriate reward.
3. Supply ample feedback.
4. Schedule rewards intermittently.
5. Make the reward follow the observed behavior closely in time.
6. Make the reward fit the behavior.
7. Make the reward visible.
8. Change the reward periodically.
9. Reward the group or team also.

choosing the right reward underscores the fact that not all rewards are reinforcers. A reward is something perceived to be of value by the person receiving the reward. (A supervisor might think that giving a gift certificate to a particular fast-food restaurant is a reward, but if the employee dislikes that restaurant it is not a true reward.) If the reward does not lead to strengthening a desired response (such as wearing safety goggles), it is not a true reinforcer.[7]

Figure 11-2 provides a list of factors by employees as to what would satisfy them on the job. At the same time, these factors can be translated into potential rewards for employees. For example, if employees value bonuses, a high-performing employee might be given some assurance of receiving a bonus for above-average employment. Because all of these factors are ranked as *important* job factors by employees, all of them are potentially appropriate rewards.

Rule 3: Supply Ample Feedback. Positive reinforcement cannot work without frequent feedback to individuals. Feedback can take the form of simply telling people they have done something right or wrong. Brief e-mail messages or handwritten notes are other forms of feedback. Many effective motivators, including a few technology executives, made extensive use of handwritten thank-you notes. Negative feedback by e-mail should be written tactfully to avoid resentment.

Rule 4: Schedule Rewards Intermittently. Rewards should not be given on every occasion of good performance. **Intermittent rewards** sustain desired behaviors longer and also slow down the process of behaviors fading away when they are not rewarded. If each correct performance results in a reward, the behavior will stop shortly after a performance in which the reward is not received. Another problem is that a reward given continuously may lose its impact. Also, automatic rewards for doing the right thing become perceived as entitlements. As the reward becomes almost guaranteed, the employee feels entitled to it, and the reward loses its motivational effectiveness, much like a weekly paycheck. A practical value of intermittent reinforcement is that it saves time. Few managers or team leaders have enough time to dispense rewards for every correct action by group members.

intermittent reward

A reward that is given for good performance occasionally, but not always.

FIGURE 11-2   What Workers Want from Their Jobs and Their Employers

1. Competitive salary.
2. Help in achieving financial security through employee benefits such as dental, disability, and life insurance.
3. Company-matched 401(k) investments.
4. Bonus programs.
5. Flexible schedules.
6. Compressed workweek.
7. Good relationship with the boss.
8. Recognition from employer.
9. Being treated with respect.
10. Making a contribution to the company and perhaps society.
11. Opportunity to advance in career.
12. Help from employer with financial education and planning.

Source: Table is based on a composite of information from *Metlife Study of Employee Benefit Trends*, reported in *http://*www.tlnt.com, April 14, 2012; "Listen up Employers; Employees Know What They Want This Labor Day," *http://www.kronos.com*, August 2, 2006, p. 1. The survey was conducted by Harris Interactive and sponsored by Kronos Incorporated. Factor 9 is from Timothy R. Clark, "Engaging the Disengaged," *HR Magazine*, April 2008, p. 112; "Employees Want More Recognition, Growth Opportunity," *Monitor on Psychology*, May 2011, p. 11.

Rule 5: Make the Reward Follow the Observed Behavior Closely in Time. For maximum effectiveness, people should be rewarded soon after doing something right. A built-in, or intrinsic, feedback system, such as software working or not working, capitalizes on this principle. If you are administering rewards and punishments, strive to administer them the same day they are earned. Suppose a coworker feeds you exactly the information you need to make a PowerPoint presentation for the group. Send your coworker an e-mail or text message of appreciation right that day. Or be old-fashioned, and thank him or her in person.

Rule 6: Make the Reward Fit the Behavior. People who are inexperienced in applying positive reinforcement often overdo the intensity of spoken rewards. When an employee does something of an ordinary nature correctly, simple praise such as "Good job" is preferable to "Fantastic performance." A related idea is that the magnitude of the reward should vary with the magnitude of the accomplishment.

Leadership research confirms the importance of making rewards contingent upon both doing the right thing and the magnitude of the behavior or performance. A study in six banks indicated that when leaders made rewards based on true performance, workers perceived a higher degree of fairness in their work climate (or atmosphere).[8]

Rule 7: Make the Reward Visible. Another important characteristic of an effective reward is the extent to which it is visible, or noticeable, to other employees. When other workers notice the reward, its impact multiplies because other people observe what kind of behavior is rewarded.[9] Assume that you are being informed about a coworker having received an exciting assignment because of high performance. You might strive to accomplish the same level of performance. Rewards should also be visible, or noticeable, to the employee. A reward of $10 per week for 30 weeks added to a person's paycheck might be hardly noticeable, after payroll deductions; however, a bonus check for $300 might be very noticeable.

Rule 8: Change the Reward Periodically. Rewards do not retain their effectiveness indefinitely. Employees and customers lose interest in striving for a reward they have received many times in the past. This is particularly true of a repetitive statement, such as "Nice job" or "Congratulations." It is helpful for the person giving out the rewards to study the list of potential rewards, and try different ones from time to time. A general approach relating to the previous rules is to look for creative ways to apply positive reinforcement. The creativity might be in the selection of the reward or how the reward is administered. For example, choose an especially effective employee, and at the end of the week or month have coworkers gather and clap for the person.

Rule 9: Reward the Group or Team Also. Positive reinforcement applies to groups as well as individuals in the sense that individuals within the group can be rewarded collectively. An obvious rule is that the group should receive a reward commensurate with its accomplishment; however, several of the other eight rules also apply. An example of a team reward is to implement a "Team of the Month" program.

Perform Skill-Building Exercise 11-2 to practice several of these rules for using positive reinforcement.

USING RECOGNITION TO MOTIVATE OTHERS

LEARNING OBJECTIVE 4

Motivating others by giving them recognition and praise can be considered a direct application of positive reinforcement. Nevertheless, recognition is such a potentially powerful motivator that it merits separate attention. Also, recognition programs to reward and motivate employees are standard practice in business and nonprofit firms. Examples are rewarding high-performing employees with a crystal vase (company logo inscribed) or designating them "employee of the month." Outstanding sales representatives ("beauty consultants") at Mary Kay receive recognition and rewards in the form of pink smartphones, pink Buicks, and pink Cadillacs—in the United States, as well as in China and other countries.[10] The pink, however, is just a tinge of pink to give it a modern look. In keeping with the theme of this book, the emphasis is on individual, rather than organizational, use of recognition to motivate.

Why Recognition Is an Effective Motivator

Recognition is a strong motivator because it is a normal human need to crave recognition. At the same time, recognition is effective because most workers feel they do not receive enough notice. A national survey revealed that only 46 percent of respondents agreed with the statement, "Overall, I am satisfied with the employee recognition practices of my employer."[11] Satisfying the recognition demands of employees, however, does not mean that praise is an adequate substitute for salary. Employees tend to regard compensation as an entitlement, whereas recognition is perceived as a gift. Workers, including your coworkers, want to know that their output is useful to somebody.

Recognition is also important as a motivator because it is often tied in with other motivators. Receiving a pay increase based on performance is a form of positive reinforcement. At the same time, the pay raise provides recognition for having performed well. An extensive study of call centers in the US financial and retail industries over a seven-year period provides evidence of how recognition is tied in with promotions. Call center employees were more interested in promotion than in pay increases exclusively. Promotion, as they perceived it, brought them formal recognition as well as changes in status and responsibilities.[12]

An analysis of company recognition programs indicates that the best programs boost worker engagement, reduce turnover, and usually lead to improved buisness performance. This analysis reinforces the idea that recogntion is an important motivator.[13] The obvious truth is that recognition leads employees to feel appreciated.

Approaches to Giving Recognition

To appeal to the recognition need of others, identify a meritorious behavior and then recognize that behavior with an oral, written, or material reward. E-mail, instant messaging, and text messaging are useful vehicles for providing quick recognition when in-person appreciation is not feasible. (Perhaps sending tweets can be done after working hours.) Also, sometimes people like to print a copy of the recognition they receive. Lisa Orndoff, a manager of employee relations and training at a non-profit society, says that a hand written note helps many employees feel valued. Often they retain these notes of appreciation for a long time.[14]

A growing form of recognition is a peer-to-peer recognition program in which coworkers post compliments about each other on a company social media site. A representative example is the International Fitness Holdings health-club group in Alberta, Canada. To appeal to younger workers and boost participation, the company uses a Facebook-like application that enables 1,100 employees to recognize peers by posting messages to a "team wall." Private e-mails are used for the same purpose. Employees might be recognized for such good deeds as helping a club member exercise, assisting coworkers with challenging tasks, or even pushing a coworker's car out of the snow. The program is quite popular among International Fitness employees.[15]

Some specific examples of using recognition to sustain desired behavior (a key aspect of motivation) are as follows:

- A coworker shows you how to more effectively perform an important task on the Internet. Three days later, you send her an e-mail message with a copy to the boss: "Hi, Jessica. Your suggestion about using Twitter to gain some visibility for our newest product was dynamite. I've used it five times with success since you showed me what to do." (You are reinforcing Jessica's helpful and cooperative behavior.)

- As the team leader, you receive a glowing letter from a customer about how Kent, one of your team members, solved his or her problem. You have the letter laminated and present it as a gift to Kent. (The behavior you are reinforcing is good customer service.)

Colin Hawkins/Getty Images

- One member of your department, Jason, is a mechanical engineer. While at a department lunch taking place during National Engineers Week, you stand up and say, "I want to toast Jason in celebration of National Engineers Week. I certainly wouldn't want to be sitting in this office building today if a mechanical engineer hadn't assisted in its construction." (Here the only behavior you are reinforcing is the goodwill of Jason, so your motivational approach is general rather than specific.)

As you might have inferred from the examples presented, statements of recognition tend to be more effective when they are expressed in specific, rather than general terms. "You're doing a great job" is an example of a general recognition statement. Here are a few more specific recognition statements:

"You really made a difference by . . . "
"You're right on the mark with . . . "
"We couldn't have done it without your . . . " [16]

A high-powered approach to recognizing the achievements of others is for the manager, supervisor, or team leader to hold personal celebrations of outstanding accomplishment. The celebration takes place in person in contrast to disseminating an electronic message, thereby making the celebration more personal. Such types of public recognition might be part of an employee recognition and celebration program. Personal celebrations include having a meal in a restaurant or in the workplace in honor of an outstanding accomplishment such as a major cost-saving suggestion, a major sale, or receiving a patent. Intense group recognition of this type will often boost the self-esteem of the employee who is celebrated.

A worker might conduct a personal celebration of accomplishment by honoring a coworker during a luncheon or beverage break. A warm touch would be to have a T-shirt custom-lettered to describe the accomplishment, such as "Dragon Slayer" or "Anti-Virus Queen."

Fine Points about Using Recognition to Motivate Others

An outstanding advantage of recognition, including praise, as a motivator is that it is no cost or low cost, yet powerful. Recognition thus provides an enormous return on investment in comparison to a cash bonus. Nevertheless, a challenge in using recognition effectively is that not everyone responds well to the same form of recognition. A good example is that highly technical people tend not to like general praise such as "Great job" or "Awesome." Instead, they prefer a laid-back, factual statement of how their output made a contribution. Furthermore, women are slightly more responsive to praise than are men, as revealed in a study of working adults.[17]

Giving recognition to others as a motivational tactic is more likely to be effective if a culture of recognition exists within the company. This is true because the person giving the recognition will feel that what he or she is doing fits what top management thinks is appropriate behavior. At the same time, the recipient of the recognition is likely to take it seriously.

The rules for positive reinforcement described previously also apply to giving recognition. For example, a recognition reward given too frequently either becomes stale or regarded as an entitlement. In one business firm, the CEO traditionally bought lunch for all employees every Friday to recognize their contributions. Soon, employees were asking him to be reimbursed for lunch if they ate outside of the company on a Friday.[18]

USING EXPECTANCY THEORY TO MOTIVATE OTHERS

LEARNING OBJECTIVE 5

So far we have described motivating others through applying the principle of WIIFM and positive reinforcement, including recognition. We now shift to expectancy theory, a more comprehensive explanation of motivation that includes elements of the two other approaches. Expectancy theory is given special attention here for these reasons. First, expectancy theory can help you diagnose motivational problems. Second, expectancy theory is comprehensive because it incorporates many different aspects of motivating others. Third, it gives the person attempting to motivate others many guidelines for triggering and sustaining constructive effort from group members.

Capsule Overview of Expectancy Theory

expectancy theory

A motivation theory based on the premise that the effort people expend depends on the reward they expect to receive in return.

The **expectancy theory** of motivation is based on the premise that how much effort people expend depends on the reward they expect to receive in return. (Notice the similarity to WIIFM?) Expectancy theory assumes that people are rational and logical, and the process resembles rational gambling. In any given situation, they want to maximize gain and minimize loss. The theory assumes that people choose among alternatives by selecting the one they think they have the best chance of attaining. Furthermore, they choose the alternative that appears to have the biggest personal payoff. How intensely they want that alternative is also an important consideration. Given a choice, people select an assignment they think they can handle and that will benefit them the most.

An example will help clarify the central thesis of expectancy theory. Hector, a 27-year-old credit analyst at a machine tool company, recognizes that he needs to increase his income by about $500 per month to cover his expenses. After carefully reviewing his options, Hector narrows his alternatives to the following three choices:

1. Work as a dining-room server one night a week and on most weekends, with a variable income of somewhere between $600 and $850 per month.

2. Work for an income tax preparation service about four months per year for 20 hours per week, yielding an annual income of about $7,000.

3. Work extra hard at his regular job, including taking a course in corporate finance, to improve his chances of receiving a promotion and a salary increase of $700 per month.

Hector rejects the first choice. Although he knows he can do the work, he anticipates several negative outcomes. He would much prefer to engage in extra work related to his field of expertise. The unpredictable income associated with being a dining-room server is also a concern. Hector sees merit in the second alternative because income tax preparation work relates to his accounting background. Furthermore, the outcome (amount of pay) is relatively certain. But Hector also has some concerns that working so many extra hours for four months a year could hurt his performance on his day job.

Hector decides to take a chance with the third alternative of going all out to position himself for promotion. He is confident that he can elevate his performance, but he is much less certain that hard work will lead to promotion. Yet Hector attaches such high value to being promoted and upgrading his professional credentials that he is willing to gamble.

Basic Components of Expectancy Theory

All versions of expectancy theory have the following three major components: effort-to-performance expectancy, performance-to-outcome expectancy, and valence.[19] Figure 11-3 presents a glimpse of expectancy theory.

Effort-to-performance expectancy is the probability assigned by the individual that effort will lead to performing the task correctly. An important question rational people ask themselves before putting forth effort to accomplish a task is this: "If I put in all this work, will I really get the job done properly?" Each behavior is associated in the individual's mind with a certain expectancy, or subjective hunch of the probability of success.

Expectancies range from 0 to 1.0. The expectancy would be 0 if the person thought that there was no chance of performing the task correctly. An expectancy of 1.0 would signify absolute faith in being able to perform the task properly. Expectancies thus influence whether you will even strive to earn a reward. Self-confident people have higher expectancies than do those with low self-confidence. Being well trained will also increase your subjective hunch that you can perform the task.

The importance of having high expectancies for motivation meshes well with a thrust in work motivation that emphasizes the contribution of self-efficacy, the confidence in your ability to carry out a specific task. If you have high self-efficacy about the task, your motivation will be high. Low self-efficacy leads to low motivation.[20] Some people are poorly motivated to skydive because they doubt they will be able to pull the ripcord while free falling at 120 mph.

Performance-to-outcome expectancy is the probability assigned by the individual that performance will lead to certain outcomes or rewards. When people engage in a particular behavior, they do so with the intention of achieving a desired outcome or reward.

effort-to-performance expectancy

The probability assigned by the individual that effort will lead to performing the task correctly.

performance-to-outcome expectancy

The probability assigned by the individual that performance will lead to outcomes or rewards.

FIGURE 11-3   A Basic Version of Expectancy Theory

Person will be motivated under these conditions
{
A. Effort-to-performance expectancy is high: Person believes he or she can perform the task.
B. Performance-to-outcome expectancy is high: Person believes that performance will lead to certain outcomes.
C. Valence is high: Person highly values the outcomes.

Performance-to-outcome expectancies also range from 0 to 1.0. If you believe there is no chance of receiving the desired reward, the assigned probability is 0. If you believe the reward is certain to follow from performing correctly, the assigned probability is 1.0, for example, "I know for sure that if I show up for work every day this month, I will receive my paycheck."

valence

The value, worth, or attractiveness of an outcome.

Valence is the value, worth, or attractiveness of an outcome. It signifies how intensely you want something (as described in WIIFM). In each work situation there are multiple outcomes, each with a valence of its own. Valence also gets at the idea of what people want, such as some workers striving for a work schedule to balance work and family demands, and others looking for more job challenge. Remember Hector, the credit analyst? The potential outcomes of working part time as an income tax preparer would include extra income, new experience, and interference with his day job.

In the version of expectancy theory presented here, valences range from −100 to +100. A valence of +100 means that you desire an outcome strongly. A valence of −100 means that you are strongly motivated to avoid an outcome, such as being fired. A valence of 0 means that you are indifferent toward an outcome, and it is therefore no use as a motivator. An outcome with a probable valence of 0 would be as follows: To gain the cooperation of coworkers, you promise them gold stars as a reward (or outcome).

Skill-Building Exercise 11-3 will help sensitize you to the importance of estimating valences when attempting to motivate others. A major problem faced by managers and others who attempt to motivate workers is that they have limited knowledge about the valences of their motivators (or rewards).

SKILL-BUILDING EXERCISE 11-3

Estimating Valences for Applying Expectancy Theory

Directions: Listed here are rewards and punishments (outcomes) stemming from job scenarios. Also included is a space for rating the reward or punishment on a scale of −100 to +100. Work with about six teammates, with each person rating all the rewards and punishments. Compute the mean (average) rating for each reward and punishment.

Potential Outcome	Rating (−100 to +100)
1. A 20 percent salary increase	_____
2. Profit-sharing plan in successful company	_____
3. Stock ownership in company	_____
4. Fully paid three-day leave	_____
5. A $10,000 performance bonus	_____
6. A $500 gift certificate	_____
7. Outstanding performance review	_____
8. Above-average performance review	_____
9. One-step promotion	_____
10. Two-step promotion	_____
11. Flexible working hours	_____
12. Chance to work at home one day per week	_____
13. Chance to do more of preferred task	_____
14. Take over for supervisor when the supervisor is away	_____
15. Fancy job title without change in pay	_____
16. Bigger cubicle	_____
17. Private office	_____
18. Company-paid smartphone for work and personal use	_____

19. Wall plaque indicating accomplishment	_____
20. Employee-of-the-month designation	_____
21. Warm smile and word of appreciation	_____
22. Compliment in front of others	_____
23. Threat of being suspended for a month	_____
24. One-month suspension without pay	_____
25. Demotion to undesirable job	_____
26. Being fired	_____
27. Being fired combined with promise of negative references	_____
28. Being placed on probation	_____
29. Being ridiculed in front of others	_____
30. A 30 percent pay reduction	_____

After completing the ratings, discuss the following topics:

1. Which outcomes received the most variable ratings?
2. Which outcomes received the most similar ratings?
3. Which are the three most desirable rewards?
4. Which are the three most undesirable punishments?

Another analytical approach would be to compute the class mean for all 30 outcomes. Each student could then compare his or her rating with the class average.

To apply this technique to the job, modify the preceding outcomes to fit the outcomes available in your work situation. Explain to team members that you are attempting to do a better job of rewarding and disciplining and that you need their input. The ratings made by team members will give strong clues to which rewards and punishments would be the most effective in motivating them.

How Moods Influence Expectancy Theory

Expectancy theory emphasizes the rational side of people, yet emotions still play a key role in determining the impact of expectancies, instrumentalities, and valences. Moods are relatively long-lasting emotional states that do not appear to be tied to a clear source of the emotion. For example, a person might be in a good mood despite experiencing a negative situation such as an automobile breaking down. Also, people may feel glum despite good news such as having won a prize.

Several studies have shown that moods shape people's perceptions of expectancies and valence in expectancy theory. A positive mood increases the perceived connection between effort and performance (E→P expectancy), between performance and desired outcome (P→O expectancy), and in the valence attached to those outcomes. When we are in a good mood, we are more likely to believe that we can accomplish a task, so we have more of a "can do" attitude. We are also more optimistic about the outcomes (rewards) of our effort, and the outcomes look even better to us.[21] The opposite might also be true: When we are in a bad mood, we feel less capable of task accomplishment, we are more pessimistic about getting the reward, and the reward appears less enticing.

Diagnosing Motivation with Expectancy Theory

An important potential contribution of expectancy theory to interpersonal relations is that it helps a person diagnose whether motivation is present and the intensity of the motivation. In performing your diagnosis, seek answers to the following questions:

LEARNING OBJECTIVE 6

1. Does the person I am attempting to motivate have the skills and self-efficacy to do the job? If the person feels ill-equipped to perform, he or she will be discouraged and show very little motivation.

2. What assurance does the person have that if he or she performs the work, the promised reward will be forthcoming? Does the company have a decent reputation for following through on promises? What about me? Have I established my credibility as a person who follows through on promises? (If you or the company is not trusted, motivation could be reduced to zero.)

3. How badly does the person want the reward being offered in the situation? Am I offering a reward that will make it worthwhile for the person to do what I need done? If the sum of the valences of the outcomes in the situation is close to 0 (some positive, some negative), motivation will be absent.

4. Are there any zeroes in response to the first three questions? If there are, motivation will be absent, because the expectancy theory equation is Motivation = (effort-to-performance expectancies) × (performance-to-outcome expectancies) × (the sum of the valences for all the outcomes). Remember what happens when you multiply by 0 in an equation.

5. Is the person in a reasonably good mood? Perhaps the person is poorly motivated today because of being in a bad mood.

Guidelines for Applying Expectancy Theory

The information about expectancy theory presented so far provides ideas for motivating others. Here we discuss five additional specific guidelines to improve your skill in motivating others.

Creatas/Thinkstock

1. **Train and encourage people.** If you are a manager, you should give employees the necessary training and encouragement to be confident that they can perform the required tasks. Some employees who appear to be poorly motivated simply lack the right skills and self-efficacy.

2. **Make explicit the link between rewards and performance.** Employees should be reassured that if they perform the job up to standard, they will receive the promised reward. It is sometimes helpful for employees to speak to coworkers about whether they received promised rewards.

3. **Make sure that the rewards are large enough.** Some rewards fail to motivate people because, although they are the right kind, they are not in the right amount. The promise of a large salary increase might be motivational, but a 1 percent increase will probably have little motivational thrust for most workers. An extreme approach is to give outstanding performers something luxurious or self-indulgent that they would rarely purchase for themselves even if they could afford it. An example is a three-day stay in a luxury hotel or an adventure cruise.

4. **Understand individual differences in valences.** To motivate others in the workplace effectively, you must discover individual differences in preferences for rewards. An attempt should be made to offer a worker rewards to which he or she attaches a high valence. For instance, one employee might value a high-adventure assignment; another might attach a high valence to a routine, tranquil assignment. Also keep individual differences in mind when attempting to motivate customers. One customer might attach a high valence to a volume discount, while another might favor follow-up service.

5. **Use the Pygmalion effect to increase effort-to-performance expectancies.** The **Pygmalion effect** refers to the phenomenon that people will rise (or fall) to the expectations another person has of them. Even if these expectations are not communicated explicitly, the other person will catch on to the nonverbal language. As the levels of expectation increase, so will performance. The high expectations thus become a self-fulfilling prophecy.

Pygmalion effect

The phenomenon that people will rise (or fall) to the expectations that another person has of them.

It is difficult to keep all the points made about expectancy theory in your head at the same time. Nevertheless, with practice and by referring to this book and your notes, you can apply many of the ideas. Skill-Building Exercise 11-4 will help you get started applying expectancy theory.

All of the techniques for motivating others will work well some of the time, but not all of the time. When faced with a particularly unmotivated person, you may have to repeat a given motivational technique several times. Or you may have to combine techniques such as using several rules for positive reinforcement as well as giving the person recognition and praise, and diagnosing what his or her motivational problem might be. Skill-Building Exercise 11-5 will help you think about dealing with an unmotivated (lazy) person.

TECHNIQUES FOR SELF-MOTIVATION

LEARNING OBJECTIVE 7

Many people never achieve satisfying careers and never realize their potential because of low motivation. They believe that they could perform better, but admit that "I'm simply not a high-initiative type" or "I'm simply not that motivated." Here we describe eight techniques for self-motivation.

SKILL-BUILDING EXERCISE 11-4

Applying Expectancy Theory

One student plays the role of the manager of a telemarketing firm. Another student plays the role of Terry, a telemarketing specialist who has been with the company for three months. Terry is 40 percent below target in selling magazine renewals. The manager calls Terry into the office for a discussion of the problem.

Terry goes on at length to explain how confusing the job has become. Terry makes comments, such as "I don't even know if I have the right kind of voice for this job. People I reach on the phone think

I'm just a kid." Terry also wonders what kind of money he can make in this job and whether it is a dead-end job. (The student who plays the role of Terry can improvise about more of these kinds of problems.)

The manager will apply expectancy theory to motivate Terry to achieve satisfactory performance. Other class members should jot down statements the manager makes that indicate the use of expectancy theory. Also, observe whether it appears that Terry is being helped.

Motivating an Undermotivated Coworker

You and a coworker are assigned the task of going around the company premises to make suggestions for the company being more environamentally friendly or *green*. The idea is to spot as many wasted resources as you can. For example, you might identify leaky faucets or drafty windows. Your challenge is that your work partner, Clyde, doesn't seem to be making any contribution to the project. During one of his field audits, you found him taking a nap on a company bench. You don't want to report Clyde to management, but you do want him to be more motivated on this important task.

Hold a motivational session with Clyde in which you try to motivate him to work more diligently on your joint task. Another student plays the role of Clyde, who doesn't see why he should work hard on this goofy assignment. Observers might apply feedback on the effectiveness of the motivational session.

1. **Set goals for yourself.** Goal setting is one of the most important techniques for self-motivation. If you set long-range goals and support them with a series of smaller goals set for shorter time spans, your motivation will increase.

2. **Find intrinsically motivating work.** A major factor in self-motivation is to find work that is fun or its own reward. Intrinsic motivation refers to the natural tendency to seek out novelty and challenges, to extend and use one's capacities, to explore, and to learn.[22] The intrinsically motivated person is involved in the task at hand, such as a technology enthusiast surfing the Web for hours at a time. Finding a job that offers you motivators in ample supply will help enhance your intrinsic motivation. For example, you might have good evidence from your past experience that the opportunity for close contact with people is a personal motivator. Find a job that involves working in a small, friendly department or team.

Intrinsically motivating work often takes the form of *meaningful work*, or work that has personal meaning to you based on your values and interests. One person might think that working as a store manager for the Salvation Army is meaningful. Another person might think that working as an electronics technician at a missile defense systems company is meaningful.

Based on circumstances, you may have to take whatever job you can find, or you may not be in a position to change jobs. In such a situation, try to arrange your work so that you have more opportunity to experience the reward(s) that you are seeking. Assume that solving difficult problems excites you, but that your job is 85 percent routine. Develop better work habits so that you can take care of the routine aspects of your job more quickly. This will give you more time to enjoy the creative aspects of your job.

3. **Get feedback on your performance.** Few people can sustain a high level of motivation without receiving information about how well they are doing. Even if you find your work challenging and exciting, you will need feedback. One reason positive feedback is valuable is that it acts as a reward. If you learn that your efforts achieved a worthwhile purpose, you will feel encouraged. For example, if a graphics display you designed was well received by company officials, you would probably want to prepare another graphics display.

A study conducted with management students demonstrated that participants adjusted their goals upward after receiving positive feedback and downward after negative feedback. It was also found that when the students were more emotional about the feedback, the positive and negative results were more pronounced.[23] The link here to self-motivation is that when goals are higher, motivation will be higher.

4. **Apply behavior modification to yourself.** Many people have used behavior modification to change their own behavior. (This involves rewarding yourself for attaining a goal, and punishing yourself for not attaining a goal.) Specific purposes include overcoming behaviors such as eating disorders, tobacco addiction, Internet abuse, nail biting, and procrastination. First, to boost your own motivation through behavior modification, you would have to decide what specific motivated actions you want to increase (such as working 30 minutes longer each day). Second, you would have to decide on a suitable set of rewards and punishments. You may choose to use rewards only, because rewards are generally better motivators than punishments.

5. **Improve your skills relevant to your goals.** According to expectancy theory, people hold back effort when they are not confident that their efforts will lead to accomplishments. You should, therefore, seek adequate training to ensure that you have the right abilities and skills to perform your work. The training might be provided by the employer or on your own through a course or self-study. Appropriate training gives you more confidence that you can perform the work. The training also increases your feelings of self-efficacy. By recognizing your ability to mobilize your own resources to succeed, your self-confidence for the task will be elevated. Another motivational advantage of self-efficacy is that you are likely to commit more resources, such as time and money, to attaining a goal when you feel confident that you can perform the task.[24] For example, if you had confidence in your skills to develop an eBay business, you might be willing to spend a lot of time in designing the business and money in buying products to sell on the site.

6. **Raise your level of self-expectation.** Another strategy for increasing your level of motivation is to simply expect more of yourself. If you raise your level of self-expectation, you are likely to achieve more. Because you expect to succeed, you do succeed. The net effect is the same as if you had increased your level of motivation. The technical term for improving your performance through raising your own expectations is the **Galatea effect**. High self-expectations and a positive mental attitude take a long time to develop; however, they are critically important for becoming a well-motivated person in a variety of situations.

7. **Develop a strong work ethic.** A highly effective strategy for self-motivation is to develop a strong work ethic. If you are committed to the idea that most work is valuable and that it is joyful to work hard, you will automatically become strongly motivated. A person with a weak work ethic cannot readily develop a strong one because the change requires a profound value shift. Yet if a person gives a lot of serious thought to the importance of work and follows the right role models, a work ethic can be strengthened. The shift to a strong work ethic is much like a person who has a casual attitude toward doing fine work becoming more prideful.

8. **Visualize attaining your goals and being successful.** Form images of reaching your goal, meaning that you actually develop an image of accomplishing what you want. As mysterious as this sounds, visualization helps the brain convert images into reality. The more senses you can incorporate into your visual image, the stronger its power. Imagine yourself seeing, hearing, tasting, smelling, and touching your goal. Can you imagine yourself sitting in your luxurious living quarters overlooking the ocean, eating a great meal with a loved one to celebrate the fact that the charity you have founded now helps 10 million under nourished children across the globe?

Skill-Building Exercise 11-6 provides a practical approach to self-motivation.

SKILL-BUILDING EXERCISE 11-6

Working on My Own Motivators

The focus of this chapter has been the skill of motivating others. Yet if you neglect motivating yourself, you (1) might not gain a formal position in which you can motivate others, and (2) you will not be able to motivate others by leading through example. Apply some of the concepts in this chapter to help work through this exercise.

What Motivates Me?

Think back on what situations, and factors within a situation, have prompted you to put forth your best effort and work the hardest—on the job, at community work, at school, in sports, or in other recreational activities such as being a band member. Which needs were you attempting to satisfy? Which tangible or intangible rewards were you pursuing? Here is a portion of a sample answer:

"I was lucky enough to be entered in Domino's national speed contest for making a store-usable pizza. I jumped into the situation like somebody obsessed. Here I was at 20 years old with a chance to win a national contest and be lifted up over the head of my buddies. I would have been King Pizza for a day. I didn't win, but I came close."

"Now I know that competition and recognition get my adrenaline flowing. I think that's why I will be successful in industrial sales. I need that big carrot dangling out in front of me."

What Can I Do to Capitalize on My Motivators?

It is helpful to know what motivates you, but it is even more helpful to follow up by placing yourself in situations in which you will be highly motivated. The Pizza King aspirant provides us a good example. Attempt to manage your career by placing yourself in highly motivational situations. For example, if the opportunity to work alone without supervision and the opportunity to schedule your own time motivate you, strive to work at home in the near future.

Now write down the type of situations that will most likely enable you to work at your motivated best.

Concept Review and Reinforcement

Summary

Motivation refers to an internal state that leads to effort expended toward objectives and to an activity performed by one person to get another person to work. Managers, as well as people working individually, often need to motivate others.

A major thrust in job motivation is to get workers involved, or engaged, in their work and committed to the company as well as the work group. The engaged worker feels personally responsible for good and poor job performance and takes pride in accomplishments. Workers who are both engaged and committed invest a big part of themselves into their job and employer. Using the motivational techniques described in this chapter will help workers become engaged and committed.

The most fundamental principle of human motivation is that people are motivated by self-interest, referred to as "What's in it for me?" (WIIFM). Even those who help others are simultaneously helping themselves by feeling good. In using the WIIFM principle, be aware of the intensity of a person's desire for a reward. Key employee needs that might require satisfaction include achievement, power affiliation, autonomy, esteem, safety and security, and equity.

A standard and widely accepted approach to motivating others is to reward them for achieving good results or behaving in a constructive manner—the use of positive reinforcement. Negative reinforcement, or avoidance motivation, can be used to supplement positive reinforcement. Rules for the effective use of positive reinforcement include the following:

1. State clearly what behavior will lead to a reward.
2. Choose an appropriate reward.
3. Supply ample feedback.
4. Schedule rewards intermittently.
5. Make the reward follow the observed behavior closely in time.
6. Make the reward fit the behavior.
7. Make the reward visible.
8. Change the reward periodically.
9. Reward the group or team also.

Motivating others by giving them recognition and praise is a direct application of positive reinforcement. Recognition is a strong motivator because it is a normal human need to crave recognition, and most workers feel they do not get enough recognition. Also, recognition is often tied in with other motivators, such as a promotion providing recognition to the person. To appeal to the recognition need of others, identify a meritorious behavior and then recognize that behavior with an oral, written, or material reward. Choosing when to deliver recognition can be important.

Recognition and praise are low-cost, powerful motivators. Statements of recognition tend to be more effective when they are specific. High technical people tend not to like general praise, but instead prefer a laid-back factual statement of how their output made a contribution. Recognition is more likely to be an effective motivator in a culture of recognition.

The expectancy theory of motivation assumes that people are decision makers who choose among alternatives by selecting the one that appears to have the biggest personal payoff at the time. Expectancy theory has three major components: expectancies about being able to perform, expectancies about performance leading to certain outcomes, and valence (the value attached to the reward). A positive mood state can enhance the components of expectancy theory.

Expectancy theory is useful in diagnosing whether motivation is present by examining the strength of the expectancies and the valences of the rewards. If any element is 0, motivation will not be present. Expectancy theory provides important ideas for motivating others, including the following:

1. Train and encourage people.
2. Show the link between rewards and performance.
3. Make the rewards large enough.
4. Observe individual differences.
5. Use the Pygmalion effect to increase effort-to-performance expectancies.

Techniques for self-motivation described here are as follows:

1. Set goals for yourself.
2. Find intrinsically motivating work.
3. Get feedback on your performance.
4. Apply behavior modification to yourself.
5. Improve your skills relevant to your goals.
6. Raise your level of self-expectation.
7. Develop a strong work ethic.
8. Visualize attaining your goals and being successful.

Questions for Discussion and Review

1. If people are already paid by their employer to carry out a job, why should it still be important for somebody to motivate them?
2. Suppose a worker is much more interested in personal and family life than performing well or getting promoted. What approach might the worker's supervisor use to motivate him or her toward high performance?
3. How can performance appraisals be used to increase positive reinforcement?
4. Is money always the best motivator?
5. What evidence can you suggest that some people prefer exciting and interesting work over exceptional financial rewards?

6. Identify several factors in Figure 11-1 that you think would be particularly effective in motivating managers and professional-level workers. Explain your reasoning.
7. Answer question 6 for entry-level service workers, such as supermarket cashiers.
8. How might a person's high standing on any of the personality traits described in Chapter 2 personality traits be related to how easy it would be to motivate that person?
9. Suggest two techniques for self-motivation.
10. How might cultural differences affect the valence ratings in Skill-Building Exercise 11-3?

The Web Corner

http://www.awards.com
(One-stop super-site for rewards and recognition)
http://www.ehow.com/how_4550770_self-motivation-tips.html
(Self-motivation techniques)
http://shakeoffthegrind.com
(The power of recognition for motivating others)

Internet Skill Builder: Motivating Other People

Visit www.nelson-motivation.com to watch a five-minute video clip of one of Bob Nelson's talks. After watching the video, answer the following questions: (1) What have I learned that I could translate into a skill for motivating other people as well as employees? (2) Which theory, or approach, to motivation does Nelson emphasize in his presentation?

Developing Your Human Relations Skills

Interpersonal Relations Case 11.1

How Do You Motivate a Coupon Sorter?

The R. G. Blair Company specializes in the distribution and redemption of coupons for groceries and household products sold at supermarkets, convenience stores, and discount department stores. At the heart of its operation is a huge coupon sorting department. The task of sorting coupons into appropriate boxes is performed manually by employees of different ages. Each coupon sorter is surrounded by a never-ending supply of thousands of coupons. Each day, each hour, the work is the same—sorting coupons into their appropriate boxes and sending the boxes on to the next department responsible for their processing.

One day, Jennie, manager of the coupon sorting department, was visited by Lance, her counterpart in another location of the firm. "As I mentioned over the phone," said Lance, "I am really curious about how you folks are running your coupon sorting department. You seem to be doing well, and we're having loads of trouble."

"Thanks for the compliment," said Jennie. "But what kind of trouble are you having?"

"Our problem is turnover. It's vicious. We're having a tough time keeping employees on the job for more than a few months. We have only three satisfactory employees in the department who have stayed with us over one year."

"Lance, what do you see as the basic problem?" asked Jennie.

"It must obviously be the job itself. It's a nightmare for the average person. The job isn't even clean. After a while a lot of the ink on those coupons comes off on your hands and clothing. The employees are forced to wear smocks and Latex gloves unless they want stained clothes and hands. And the coupons never stop arriving."

"What screening devices has your human resources department used in selecting employees?" inquired Jennie.

"We are trying to be as thorough as we can in terms of the type of people we hire for the job of coupon sorter. We check references. We even use psychological tests. We look for solid citizens who are fairly bright."

Jennie responded, "Lance I think I've located your problem. You are setting your problem-solving ability requirements too high. I suspect that the best coupon sorters would have average to below-average intelligence. People brighter than that would become restless sorting coupons."

Lance took Jennie's advice and did install new screening procedures for hiring coupon sorters. After eight months of using these procedures, it seemed that some of Lance's original problems were under control. Turnover was down, and the newly hired employees seemed to enjoy their work. Several of the new employees even took the initiative to thank management for having given them a job just right for them.

Lance noted, however, that productivity within the group was below company standards. Although the coupon sorters seemed to be enjoying their work, they were too relaxed. They did not seem to pay much attention to the output figures suggested by the company.

Lance paid another visit to Jennie, and said: "This time I have another tale of woe. The suggestions for lowering the problem-solving ability requirements have helped me reduce turnover. And some of the people we hired are good workers. But I think we have a bunch of contented but not highly motivated workers. They like their jobs, but they are working at a pace below what the R.G. Blair Company wants.

"What advice can you give me to get these coupon sorters to hustle a little? As you know, there are strict limits on what we can pay them."

Case Questions

1. What motivational approach do you suggest be implemented to increase the productivity of these coupon sorters?
2. Why not just fire the poor performers?
3. Putting on your information technology hat for a moment, how could the job of coupon sorter be automated? Or is this a job like that of a cake decorator or brain surgeon that cannot be automated to a large extent?

Interpersonal Skills Role-Play

Jennie Attempts to Fire Up a Coupon Sorter

Jennie, in the case just presented, decides to take a direct approach to motivating the coupon sorters one at a time. She begins by meeting with Clancy, a middle-aged man who was hired into the position a few months ago. Although a friendly person with an excellent attendance record, Clancy is barely meeting his production quota. Jennie believes that by applying the right motivational technique, she might be able to help Clancy become more productive. Clancy is happy to meet with Jennie during working hours, because this means he can get away from the tedious task of sorting coupons for about thirty minutes.

Conduct this role-play for about seven minutes. Observers rate the role players on two dimensions, using a 1-to-5 scale from very poor (1) to very good (5). One dimension is "effective use of human relations techniques." Focus on the motivational skill that Jenny demonstrates. Look to see if Clancy makes any movement troward being better motivated. The second dimension is "acting ability." A few observers might voluntarily provide feedback to the role players in terms of sharing their ratings and observations. The course instructor might also provide feedback.

Interpersonal Relations Case 11.2

The Home-Retention Consultant Blues

Alicia works in real estate as a home-retention consultant. Among the services offered by her employer, Magnum Properties, is to help people who are facing foreclosure stay in their homes. She works with clients to help them figure out a way to work with their mortgage holder to renegotiate loans and often to prevent being evicted. Alicia also works with mortgage holders to guide them through short sales, or selling homes for less than the balance on the mortgage when the property owners are way behind on their payments.

Back in 2010, the foreclosure rate in the United States was still relatively high, with 1 of 13 homeowners either 60 days behind in their mortgage payments or facing foreclosure. Alicia was earning a high income because Magnum Properties' niche in the real estate market was prospering. When asked by an old friend who located her on Facebook how she was doing in her career, Alicia responded:

> It's a mixed bag for me. I see a lot of positives in my work. I make a lot of money, and I drive a sharp car. I'm very modern because I deal with foreclosures and short sales. I am helping a lot of people because I enable some of them to keep a roof over their heads.

> My big problem is that the negatives in my work are dragging me down. Some days I can hardly muster up enough energy to follow up on leads of people in trouble to help. In some ways I feel like I'm dealing with the underbelly of humanity. A lot of people I'm trying to help have dug their own graves. They have plenty of money for beer and wine and to run up huge bills for cell phones and online video rentals, but they don't have the money to pay their mortgages.

> I need to stay pumped to keep earning a good living, but some days I just don't know how to stay motivated. Any suggestions, my friend?

Case Questions

1. What recommendations do you have for Alicia to help her increase her level of self-motivation?
2. To what extent do you think it might be advisable for Alicia to simply switch fields, such as going into traditional real estate selling, so she can stay better self-motivated?
3. What suggestions might you offer Alicia's manager at Magnum Properties to help her stay motivated?

References

1. Michael S. Christian, Adela S. Garza, and Jerel E. Slaughter, "Work Engagement: A Quantitative Review and Test of Its Relations with Task and Contextual Performance," *Personnel Psychology*, Number 1, 2011, p. 89.

2. Russell E. Johnson, Chu-Hsian (Daisy) Chang, and Liu-Qin Yang, "Commitment and Motivation at Work: The Relevance of Employee Identity and Regulatory Focus," *Academy of Management Review*, April 2010, p. 227.

3. Gary Kranz, "A Broken Engagement?" *Workforce Management*, September 2012, p. 10.

4. Quoted in Stephen Baker, "Will Work for Praise," *Business Week*, February 16, 2009, pp. 046–049; http://thisnext.com. Accessed March 20, 2013.

5. Piers Steel and Cornelius J. König, "Integrating Theories of Motivation," *Academy of Management Review*, October 2006, pp. 895–896.

6. Research summarized in "One of These Seven Things Will Motivate Any Employee in the Company," *Motivational Manager*, sample issue, 1998 (Lawrence Ragan Communications, Inc.).

7. Fred Luthans and Alexander D. Stajkovic, "Reinforce for Performance: The Need to Go Beyond Pay and Even Rewards," *Academy of Management Executive*, May 1999, p. 52.

8. Fred O. Walumbwa, Cindy Wu, and Bani Orwa, "Contingent Reward Transactional Leadership, Work Attitudes, and Organizational Citizenship Behavior: The Role of Procedural Justice Climate Perceptions and Strength," *The Leadership Quarterly*, June 2008, pp. 251, 261.

9. Steven Kerr, *Ultimate Rewards: What Really Motivates People to Achieve* (Boston: Harvard Business School Publishing, 1997).

10. Emily Glazer, "Mary Kay CEO Wants Pink Caddy in Fast Lane," *The Wall Street Journal*, (http://online.wsj.com) January 22, 2013, pp. 1–3.

11. "Employers Want More Recognition, Growth Opportunity," *Monitor on Psychology*, May 2011, p. 12.

12. Philip Moss, Harold Salzman, and Chris Tilly, "Under Construction: The Continuing Evolution of Job Structures in Call Centers, *Industrial Relations*, Vol. 47, 2008, pp. 173–208.

13. Meg McSherry Breslin, "Solid Reward Program Can Be Rewarding for Businesses," *Workforce Management*, January 2013, p. 8.

14. Cited in Kristyn Schiavone, "4 Tips to Help Make You a Great Manager," *CareerBuilder*, October 28, 2012.

15. Dave Zielinski, "Giving Praise," *HR Magazine*, October 2012, p. 77.

16. "Ten Sentences That Will Help You Retain Your Best Employees," *Employee Recruitment & Retention*, Lawrence Ragan Communications, Inc., sample issue, 2004.

17. Andrew J. DuBrin, "Self-Perceived Technical Orientation and Attitudes Toward Being Flattered," *Psychological Reports*, vol. 96, 2005, pp. 852–854.

18. Susan M. Heathfield, "Five Tips for Effective Employee Recognition," *About.com Human Resources*, August 6, 2009; http://humanresources.about.com/od/rewardrecognition/a/recognition_tip.htm. Accessed October 7, 2013.

19. The original version of expectancy theory applied to work motivation is Victor Vroom, *Work and Motivation* (New York: Wiley, 1964). A scholarly update of the theory is presented in Steel and König, "Integrating Theories of Motivation," pp. 893–895.

20. Alexander D. Stajkovic and Fred Luthans, "Social Cognitive Theory and Self-Efficacy: Going Beyond Traditional Motivational and Behavioral Approaches," *Organizational Dynamics*, Spring 1998, p. 66.

21. Steve McShane, "Getting Emotional about Employee Motivation," *Currents* (published by New York: McGraw-Hill), September 2004, p. 1; Amir Erez and Alice M. Isen, "The Influence of Positive Affect on the Components of Expectancy Motivation," *Journal of Applied Psychology*, December 2002, pp. 1055–1067.

22. Richard M. Ryan and Edward L. Deci, "Self-Determination Theory and the Facilitation of Intrinsic Motivation, Social Development, and Well-Being," *American Psychologist*, January 2000, p. 70; Mark Henricks, "Thrill and Fulfilled," *Entrepreneur*, June 2008, pp. 78–80.

23. Remus Ilies and Timothy A. Judge, "Goal Regulation across Time: The Effects of Feedback and Affect," *Journal of Applied Psychology*, May 2005, pp. 453–467.

24. Jeffrey B. Vancouver, Kristen M. More, and Ryan J. Yoder, "Self-Efficacy and Resource Allocation: Support for a Nonmonotonic, Discontinuous Model," *Journal of Applied Psychology*, January 2008, pp. 35–47.

Helping Others Develop and Grow

Lisa is the food service manager at a large HMO (health maintenance organization) in Minneapolis, employing 2,000 people. Her major responsibility is to oversee the HMO cafeteria to make sure that the meals offered employees are nutritious, healthy, uncontaminated, attractive, and reasonably priced. A small percentage of outpatients visiting the HMO also make use of the cafeteria. Lisa knows from experience that they are quick to complain about cafeteria food for the smallest of reasons, such as "the chicken parmesan was served lukewarm instead of hot."

But Lisa is facing a problem she considers to be more career threatening than a cafeteria visitor complaining about food temperature. Her boss, Tara, the director of HMO operations, has been arguing with her, even screaming at times, about how Tara must boost productivity in the cafeteria by such means as decreasing staff and purchasing food supplies at lower cost. Lisa felt that she had accomplished very little in her latest discussion with Tara about how any more

After reading and studying this chapter and completing the exercises, you should be able to

1. Understand how being a nurturing, positive person can influence the development of coworkers.
2. Specify the behaviors and skills helpful for being a mentor and role model.
3. Acquire beginning skills in coaching and training.
4. Helping difficult people on the job.

cuts in staff and food costs would lower food service and quality to the point of damaging cafeteria revenues.

During her lunch break, Lisa decided to send an e-mail to Rick, her mentor in Chicago. Rick is a restaurant manager who Lisa met at a trade association conference a few years ago. Part of Lisa's e-mail read, "Hi Rick. I know you are quite busy, but I need your good advice again. You know that Tara can be stern, but she seems to be really angry with me lately. She's leaning on me to squeeze costs beyond reason. She won't listen to me. What should I do?

"I'm in O'Hare [the major Chicago airport] right now, and my flight leaves within thirty minues. Here is my advice for now," wrote back Rick. "Go to Tara with some constructive plan, like purchasing produce from Asia and buying canned goods in bigger bulk. Let her know if a cafeteria supervisor is retiring who will not be replaced. Be positive and talk about lower costs. Get Tara to smile. Let me know what happens."

Lisa sent back an e-mail with this message. "Hi Rick. You've given me a couple of good ideas I can try. I'll let you know what happens. Thanks again for your mentoring."

The exchange between Lisa and Rick is often called e-mentoring, or mentoring via electronic messages to substitute for, or supplement, face-to-face interactions. The anecdote also illustrates the importance of people in the workplace helping each other grow and develop; however, the growth and development of workers is not the sole responsibility of managers or training specialists. Companies are placing increasing emphasis on workers training and developing each other, particularly because many companies operate with a smaller managerial and human resources staff than in previous decades.

This chapter describes the major ways in which employees help each other, and lays the groundwork for skill development in these vital activities. Learning to take the initiative to help others is particularly important because there is a natural tendency for people to be embarrassed or fearful of asking for help. The concern is that the person asking for help will be seen as deficient in some important way. Despite these concerns, a company is at an advantage when workers help each other.[1]

Among the key helping roles are nurturing others, mentoring, coaching and training, and helping difficult people become more cooperative. Do Self-Assessment Quiz 12-1 to gain preliminary insight into your attitudes toward helping others in the workplace.

BEING A NURTURING, POSITIVE PERSON

A major strategy for helping others grow and develop is to be a nourishing, positive person. A **nurturing person** promotes the growth of others. Nurturing people are positive and supportive and typically look for the good qualities in others. A **toxic person** stands in contrast to a nourishing person, because he or she dwells on the negative. Visualize the following scenario to appreciate the difference between a nurturing person and a toxic one.

LEARNING OBJECTIVE 1

nurturing person
One who promotes the growth of others.

toxic person
One who negatively affects others.

Attitudes Toward Helping Others

Directions: Describe how well you agree with the following statements by circling the appropriate letter after each statement: disagree (D), neutral (N), or agree (A).

1.	If I see a coworker make a mistake, I do not inform him or her of the mistake.	D	N	A
2.	It should be part of everybody's job to share skills and ideas with coworkers.	D	N	A
3.	The manager should have exclusive responsibility for coaching people within the work unit.	D	N	A
4.	I can think of many instances in my life when somebody thanked me for showing him or her how to do something.	D	N	A
5.	I have very little patience with coworkers who do not give me their full cooperation.	D	N	A
6.	To save time, I will do a task for another person rather than invest the time needed to show him or her how to do it.	D	N	A
7.	I would take the initiative to put an inexperienced worker under my direction.	D	N	A
8.	As a child, I often took the time to show younger children how to do things.	D	N	A
9.	Rather than ask a coworker for help, I will wait until the manager is available to help me.	D	N	A
10.	It is best not to share key information with a coworker, because that person could then perform as well as or better than me.	D	N	A
11.	"Give a person a fish and he or she will have one meal. Teach that person to fish, and he or she will eat fish for life."	D	N	A

Total Score _____

Scoring and Interpretation: Use the following score key to obtain your score for each answer, and then calculate your total score.

1. D = 3, N = 2, A = 1	5. D = 3, N = 2, A = 1	9. D = 3, N = 2, A = 1
2. D = 1, N = 2, A = 3	6. D = 3, N = 2, A = 1	10. D = 3, N = 2, A = 1
3. D = 3, N = 2, A = 1	7. D = 1, N = 2, A = 3	11. D = 1, N = 2, A = 3
4. D = 1, N = 2, A = 3	8. D = 1, N = 2, A = 3	

28–33: You have very positive attitudes toward helping, developing, and training others in the workplace. Such attitudes reflect strong teamwork and a compassion for the growth needs of others.

19–27: You have mixed positive and negative attitudes toward helping, developing, and training others in the workplace. You may need to develop more sensitivity to the growth needs of others to be considered a strong team player.

11–18: You have negative attitudes toward helping, developing, and training others in the workplace. Guard against being so self-centered that it will be held against you. Being a nurturing, positive person is a lifelong process rather than a tactic that can be used at will. Nevertheless, making a conscious attempt to be nurturing and positive can help you develop the right mindset. For example, today you might encourage a coworker or friend who is facing a work or personal problem.

Randy, a purchasing specialist, enters the office where two coworkers are talking. One person is nurturing, the other is toxic. With a look of panic, Randy says, "I'm sorry to barge in like this, but can anybody help me? I've been working for three hours preparing a spreadsheet on the computer, and it seems to have vanished. Maybe one of you can help me retrieve it."

Margot, the nourishing person, says, "I'm no computer expert, but since I'm not the one who lost the document, I can be calm enough to help. Let's go right now." Ralph, the toxic person, whispers to Margot: "Tell Randy to use the help function. If you help him now, you'll only find him at the entrance to your cubicle every time he needs help."

If you listen to toxic people long enough, you are likely to feel listless, depressed, and drained. Toxic people have been described as energy vampires because they suck all the positive energy out of you.[2] Nurturing people, in contrast, are positive, enthusiastic, and supportive. The guideline for skill development here is to engage in thoughts and actions every day that will be interpreted by others as nourishing. Three actions and attitudes that support being a nourishing person are as follows:

Stockbyte/Thinkstock

1. **Recognize that most people have growth needs.** Almost everybody has a need for self-fulfillment, although people vary widely in the extent of this need. If you recognize this need, it may propel you toward helping people satisfy the need. You might engage in interactions with coworkers, such as sharing new skills with them, forwarding relevant news articles from the Internet, or telling them about an important new specialty social media site you have discovered. You might also tell them about an exciting course you have taken that has enhanced your self-confidence.

2. **Team up with a coworker inside or outside your department so that the two of you can form a buddy system.** The buddy system is used during war combat and with children in a swimming program. You and a friend can use the same system to keep each other informed of decisions and events that could affect your careers. You might nurture your buddy by talking about growth opportunities in the company he or she might not have heard about. Your buddy would reciprocate. One person told her buddy about expanding opportunities for company employees who were fluent in both English and Spanish. The two buddies, who already knew some Spanish, worked together to become fluent.

3. **Be a role model for others.** An indirect way of being a nurturing, positive person is to conduct yourself in such a way that others will model your behavior. By serving as a role model, you help another person develop. How to become a role model for coworkers is as comprehensive a topic as learning to be successful. Among the many factors that make you role-model material are a strong work ethic, job expertise, personal warmth, good speaking ability, a professional appearance, and great ethics. Do you qualify yet, or do you need some more work?

Skill-Building Exercise 12-1 provides an opportunity to practice being a positive person.

BEING A MENTOR TO COWORKERS

In Homer's tale the *Odyssey,* Mentor was a wise and trusted friend, as well as a counselor and adviser. The term *mentor* has become a buzzword in the workplace, as well as in the community. A **mentor** is an individual with advanced experience and knowledge who is committed to giving support and career advice to a less experienced person. The less experienced person is the **protégé** (from the French word for "protected"). You may also see

---

SKILL-BUILDING EXERCISE 12-1

The Nurturing, Positive Person

One student plays the role of Pat, a worker who is experiencing difficulty on the job and in personal life. Pat approaches a coworker during lunch in the company cafeteria and says, "What a day. I just received a rotten performance review. If my work doesn't improve within a month, the company may let me go. To add to my woes, my fiancé has threatened to break off the engagement if I don't get a big raise or a promotion. My hard drive went down, taking with it

my collection of music, videos, and photos. I feel like my whole world is collapsing." The other person plays the role of Leslie, who attempts to be nurturing and positive in order to help get Pat out of the doldrums. Run the role-play for about 10 minutes.

The rest of the class provides feedback on Leslie's skill in being nurturing and helpful. Jot down specific behaviors you think are nurturing and helpful. Also be on the alert for any toxic behaviors.

the word *mentee* in reference to the person being mentored. Here we look at various characteristics of mentoring, followed by behaviors that will be useful to you in mentoring others.

Characteristics and Types of Mentoring

The term *mentoring* is used so widely and in so many contexts that it can refer to almost any type of helping relationship. From a more technically precise perspective, mentoring is characterized as:

- A unique relationship between two people
- A learning partnership that involves emotional and task-related career support
- A reciprocal helping relationship
- A frequently changing relationship between the mentor and the mentee[3]

Age and experience differences between mentor and protégé.   A mentor usually outranks the protégé and is often older. For the present purpose, however, be aware that one coworker can be a mentor to another. As long as you are more experienced and wiser than a coworker in some important aspect of the job, you can be a mentor. The term *reverse mentor* refers to a younger person who gives advice to an older person, such as a 25-year-old marketing assistant showing her 55-year-old boss how to recruit workers using Twitter.

A person who is not a manager can also be a mentor in another important way. He or she can select an entry-level person in the firm and serve as the inexperienced person's coach and adviser. Even when a person has a high-ranking person as a mentor, you can also be his or her mentor. The reason is that having more than one mentor improves a person's chances for developing job and career skills.[4]

Mentoring is more important than ever because it supports the modern, team-based organization. More people work together as equals, and they are expected to train and develop each other. Mentoring facilitates such learning and also supports the current emphasis on continuous learning.

E-mentoring.   Mentoring often takes the form of the mentor and protégé communicating by e-mail, referred to as *e-mentoring*. Many companies have established electronic matching programs that enable employees to receive mentoring from workers who are geographically distant from them. The virtual mentoring can include Web sites for matching mentors and protégés, following the model of online dating sites.[5]

A key aspect of e-mentoring is that it facilitates making quick contact with a variety of mentors or advisors who can help you with an immediate problem, as illustrated in the opening case. Career advisor and author Jeanne Meister says that today's mentorship models are more similar to Twitter conversations than to the long-term relationships of the past. The new mentoring is often short-term and informal. And the relationship can end quickly, similar to moving on from a mediocre dating relationship.[6]

As the time of corporate professionals and managers has become more scarce, e-mentoring increases in practicality. Quite often a one-minute exchange can provide a useful idea, such as texting to a coworker, "I have a salary review today with Bruce [the boss]. So should I dress business formal just for the occasion?" Also, online mentoring gives the protégé an opportunity to be mentored by a geographically distant mentor, including one who is overseas. The person being mentored might send a quick e-mail, instant message, or text message to the mentor explaining that he just received an outstanding performance review. The mentor might reply back with an encouraging message. When asked about a problem facing the protégé, the mentor might reply with advice quickly. Answers by the mentor within 48 hours are recommended to communicate an attitude of concern.[7]

How coworker mentoring takes place.   Mentoring coworkers can take place in one of two ways. With informal mentoring, the mentor and protégé come together naturally, in the same way that friendships develop. In choosing a coworker to be a mentor, a sensible approach is to ask a coworker who has valuable knowledge you need to provide you some guidance. For example, you might need help in staying on track with projects, and a coworker of yours is superbly organized and therefore someone who could be helpful to you. A suggestion is to spell out what you want, and then ask, "Will you be my mentor?"[8]

The formal approach is for the company to assign you somebody to mentor. Several studies have shown that mentoring is likely to be more effective when both the mentor and protégé have some input into the matching.[9] Measures of mentoring effectiveness include rate of promotions, salary increases, and job satisfaction. Being mentored is also a career-advancement tactic, and will be discussed in Chapter 17.

Whether the coworker mentor is assigned or chosen spontaneously, the relationship will often benefit the two people. As in the previous example, giving advice to another person about how to stay on track with an assignment can help a person refine further his or her organizational abilities.

Serving as a mentor is an excellent way of helping others on the job. Mentoring is also widely practiced off the job. Many communities have developed programs whereby working adults volunteer to serve as mentors to youths. Mentoring in these programs is designed to help adolescents and teenagers succeed at school and avoid a life of crime and substance abuse.

Specific Mentoring Behaviors

To be a mentor, a person engages in a wide range of helping behaviors, all related to being a trusted friend, coach, and teacher. To prepare you for mentoring a less experienced person, a list of specific mentoring behaviors follows:[10]

- **Sponsoring.** A mentor actively nominates somebody else for promotions and desirable positions. In some situations, one person is asked to nominate a coworker for a promotion to supervisor or team leader or for a special assignment.
- **Coaching and counseling.** A mentor gives on-the-spot advice to the protégé to help him or her improve skills. Coaching is such an important part of helping others that it receives separate mention in this chapter. Coaching as part of mentoring is quite helpful in developing the leadership potential of the mentee.[11] For example, a newly appointed supervisor might be coached on how to deal with difficult people, thereby enhancing his or her leadership skills. Counseling refers to the idea of the mentor listening to the protégé's problems and offering advice.
- **Protecting.** A mentor might shield a junior person from potentially harmful situations or from the boss. For example, the mentor might tell her protégé, "In your meeting today with the boss, make sure you are well prepared and have all your facts at hand. He is in an ugly mood and will attack any weakness."
- **Sharing challenging assignments.** One member of the team does not ordinarily give assignments to another, yet in some situations you can request that your protégé help you with a difficult task. You would then offer feedback on your protégé's performance. The purpose of these high demands is to help the protégé develop more quickly than if he or she were brought along too slowly.
- **Acting as a referral agent.** The mentor sometimes refers the protégé to resources inside and outside the company to help with a particular problem. For example, the protégé might want to know how one goes about getting the employee benefits package modified.
- **Role modeling.** An important part of being a mentor is to give the protégé a pattern of values and behaviors to emulate. Several of the specific behaviors included under being a role model were described earlier in connection with being a positive, nurturing person.
- **Giving support and encouragement.** A mentor can be helpful just by giving support and encouragement. In turn, the protégé is supposed to support the mentor by offering compliments and defending the mentor's ideas. In a team meeting, for example, the protégé might make a statement such as, "I think John's ideas will work wonders. We should give them a try."

- **Providing friendship.** A mentor is, above all, a trusted friend, and the friendship extends two ways. "Trusted" means that the mentor will not pass on confidential information or stab you in the back. (It is also possible to mentor someone who is not a friend, providing that person is interested primarily in learning business or technical skills from you.)

- **Encouraging problem solving.** Mentors help their protégés solve problems by themselves and make their own discoveries. A comment frequently made to mentors is, "I'm glad you made me think through the problem. You triggered my thinking."

- **Explaining the ropes.** A general-purpose function of the mentor is to help the protégé learn the ropes, which translates into explaining the values and do's and don'ts of the organization.

- **Teaching the right skills.** The original role of the mentor in teaching skills (such as a master teaching an apprentice) is highly relevant today. Among the many skills a mentor can help the protégé develop are those dealing with communication technology, customer service, corporate finance, achieving high quality, and thinking strategically.

- **Encouraging of continuous learning.** A major role for the modern mentor is to encourage the protégé to keep learning. Part of encouraging lifelong learning is to emphasize that formal education and an occasional workshop are not sufficient for maintaining expertise in today's fast-changing workplace. The individual has to stay abreast of new developments through courses and self-study. A specific way in which the mentor can encourage continuous learning is to ask the protégé questions about new developments in the field.

As implied by the preceding list, mentoring is a complex activity that involves a variety of helping behaviors. To develop mentoring skills, you need to offer help to several people for at least six months. Skill-Building Exercise 12-2 is a good starting point in mentoring. In preparation for more advanced mentoring, it is helpful to think of the type of person you would prefer to have as a protégé. Skill-Building Exercise 12-3 is designed to help you think through this issue. Be prepared for a potential protégé seeking you out, because many people serious about advancing their careers search for potential mentors with whom they have rapport. Similarly, if you are looking for a mentor, take the initiative to establish contact with someone you like and whom you think could help you.

Mentoring is designed to help another individual grow and develop; yet, mentoring can also help your employer at the same time. A key way in which the company benefits from coworker mentoring is that the mentor passes along, or transfers, valuable knowledge to the protégé.[12] For example, the mentor might share with the protégé a few good

SKILL-BUILDING EXERCISE 12-2

Getting Started with Mentoring

If you choose to do this skill-building exercise, it will take time outside of class, and the exercise could turn into an ongoing activity. Successful mentoring requires experience, and all mentors need to start somewhere. The task is to find somebody to mentor, and then become his or her mentor. For starters, it is usually easier to find a protégé among people younger and less experienced than you in some domain, such as math, communication technology, reading, or a sport. A source of a protégé might be a community center, a park and recreational center, a school, a church, or a temple. It is conceivable that you could find a source of people wanting mentoring in your community through an Internet search engine.

Identify the ways in which you might be able to function as a mentor, such as imparting knowledge, providing emotional support, or being a Big Brother or Big Sister. Be prepared to be subjected to a background check before being selected as a mentor.

After finding a protégé, keep a diary of your activities, including any observations about how your protégé is being helped. Identify mentoring roles that you have carried out. Record also how you are enjoying the experience. An example: "Today I was mostly a friend to Teddy. He was bummed out because the coach gave him only two minutes of playing time in Friday night's game. He was also complaining that he was the only kid on the team without an iPod. I listened carefully and then explained that patience in life is important. Teddy felt a little better and smiled. I felt wonderful for having been helpful."

Observe also any mentoring skills you need to work on to become more effective as a mentor. Also evaluate whether the mentoring appears to be having a positive impact on the life of your protégé.

Selecting a Protégé

To be a successful mentor, it is necessary to select protégés who will respond well to your advice and coaching. Since the mentor–protégé relationship is personal, much like any friendship, you must choose protégés carefully. In about 50 words (in the space provided), describe the type of person you would like for a protégé. Include cognitive, personality, and demographic factors in your description (refer to Chapter 2 for ideas). Indicate why you think the characteristics you chose are important.

My Ideal Protégé As many class members as time allows can present their descriptions to the rest of the class. Look for agreement on characteristics of an ideal protégé.

tricks for collecting money from a delinquent debtor. Workers who receive mentoring are likely to feel more satisfied about their jobs and stay with the organization longer. A study of more than 1,300 US Army officers showed that officers who were mentored felt more emotionally committed to the Army than did their nonmentored counterparts. Furthermore, mentored officers felt more likely to stay in the Army and were less likely to leave the military voluntarily.[13]

As business has become highly internationalized, mentoring people from different cultures has become more frequent. In general, to engage in cross-cultural mentoring effectively, you need to follow the principles described in Chapter 8 about cross-cultural relations.

COACHING AND TRAINING OTHERS

Two direct approaches to helping others in the workplace are coaching and training. In the traditional organization, managers have most of the responsibility for coaching and training, with some assistance from the human resources department. In the new workplace, team members share responsibility for coaching and training. High-tech companies, such as Google, Facebook, and Microsoft, heavily emphasize workers sharing knowledge with each other. Open workspaces, including the presence of whiteboards, are used to facilitate workers exchanging ideas and passing along information. Although coaching and training are described separately in the following subsections, recognize that the two processes are closely related.

coaching

A method of helping workers grow and develop and improve their job competence by providing suggestions and encouragement.

peer coaching

A type of helping relationship based on qualities such as high acceptance of the other person, authenticity, mutual trust, and mutual learning.

Coaching Skills and Techniques

Most readers probably have some experience in coaching, whether or not the activity was given a formal label. If you have helped somebody improve his or her performance on the job, on the athletic field, in a musical band, or on the dance floor, you have some coaching experience. In the workplace, **coaching** is a method of helping workers grow and improve their job competence by providing suggestions and encouragement. The suggestions for coaching are generally easier to implement if you have formal authority over the person being coached. Nevertheless, with a positive, helpful attitude on your part, coworkers are likely to accept coaching from you.

Suggestions for Coaching. Considerable workplace coaching is performed by professional coaches who specialize in helping managers improve their interpersonal skills. Our focus here is coaching by workers themselves rather than by paid professionals. **Peer coaching** is a type of helping relationship based on qualities such as high acceptance of the other person, authenticity, mutual trust, and mutual learning. Coaching other employees requires skill. One way of acquiring this skill is to study basic principles and then practice them on the job. Another way is to coach under simulated conditions, such as role-playing and modeling an effective coach. Here are 11 suggestions for effective coaching, as outlined in Figure 12-1. For the best results, combine them with the suggestions for effective listening presented in Chapter 4.

Alexander Raths/Shutterstock

FIGURE 12-1   Coaching Skills and Techniques

> 1. Build relationships.
> 2. Provide specific, constructive feedback.
> 3. Make criticism pain-free and positive.
> 4. Encourage the person you are coaching to talk.
> 5. Ask powerful questions.
> 6. Give emotional support.
> 7. Give some constructive advice.
> 8. Coach with "could," not "should."
> 9. Interpret what is happening.
> 10. Allow for modeling of the desired performance and behaviors.
> 11. Applaud good results.

1. Build relationships. A starting point in being an effective coach is to build relationships with coworkers before coaching them. Having established rapport with coworkers or subordinates facilitates entering into coaching relationships with them. A comprehensive study of coaching concludes that the relationship between two people is the most important aspect of the coaching process.[14] The suggestions ahead about giving encouragement and support are part of relationship building. Another vital aspect of relationship building is to be trusted by the people you coach.[15] For example, the person being coached has to believe that the coach is trying to help rather than undermine him or her.

2. Provide specific, constructive feedback. Instead of making generalities about an improvement area for another person, pinpoint areas of concern. A generality might be, "You just don't seem as if you're interested in this job." A specific on the same problem might be, "You neglect to call in on days that you are going to be out ill. In this way, you are letting down the team." Sometimes it can be effective to make a generalization (such as not being "interested in the job") after you first produce several concrete examples. Closely related to minimizing generalizations is to avoid exaggerating, for example, by saying such things as, "You are always letting down the team." Specific feedback is sometimes referred to as **behavioral feedback** because it pinpoints behavior rather than personal characteristics or attitudes. "Neglecting to call in" pinpoints behavior, whereas "not into the job" focuses more on an attitude.

Feedback should be positive when possible, but also negative when necessary. A balance of positive and negative feedback is usually more helpful because negative feedback helps point the person toward an area for improvement, such as, "The credit reports you have prepared are generally quite useful, but we could still use more details about credit problems you have uncovered."

3. Make criticism pain-free and positive. To be an effective coach, you will inevitably have to point out something negative the person you coach has done or is planning to do. It is helpful to come right to the point about your criticism, such as, "In our department meeting this morning, you acted so angry and hostile that you alienated the rest of the group. I know that you are generally a positive person, so I was surprised. My recommendation is that you keep your bad days to yourself when in a meeting." The positive aspect is important because you want to maintain good communications with the person you coach, whether you are the person's supervisor or coworker.[16]

4. Encourage the person you are coaching to talk. Part of being a good listener is encouraging the person being coached to talk. Ask the person you are coaching open-ended questions. Closed questions do not provide the same opportunity for self-expression, and they often elicit short, uninformative answers. Assume that you are coaching a coworker on how to use the intranet system properly. An effective open-ended question might

behavioral feedback

Information given to another person that pinpoints behavior rather than personal characteristics or attitudes.

be, "Where are you having the biggest problems using our intranet?" A closed question covering the same topic might be, "Do you understand how to use the intranet?" The latter question would not provide good clues to specific problem areas faced by your coworker. A useful technique is to begin each coaching session with a question to spark the other person's thinking.[17] An example is to ask, "What new ideas do you have for decreasing turnover among our teenage cashiers?"

5. **Ask powerful questions.** A major role for the coach is to ask *powerful* or *tough* questions that help the protégé think through the strengths and weaknesses of what he or she is doing or thinking. The powerful question is confrontational in a helpful way. The person being coached might be thinking of selling management on a program of distributing free ginkgo baloba (a food supplement believed to stimulate mental energy) to every employee to enhance productive thinking. Your powerful question might be, "What kind of figures are you going to use to support your expensive idea?"

6. **Give emotional support.** By being helpful and constructive, you provide much-needed emotional support to the person who needs help in improving job performance. A coaching session should not be an interrogation. An effective way of providing emotional support is to use positive rather than negative motivators. For example, as a team leader you might say to a team member, "If you learn how to analyze manufacturing costs, you will be eligible for an outstanding performance review." A negative motivator on the same topic might be, "If you don't learn how to analyze manufacturing costs, you're going to get zapped on your performance review."

Workers who are performing well can also profit from praise and encouragement, often so that they can perform even better. Also, even the best performers have flaws that might be preventing them from elevating their performance. As a team leader or coworker, you can therefore make a contribution by giving emotional support to a star performer.

7. **Give some constructive advice.** Too much advice-giving interferes with two-way communication, yet some advice can lead to improved performance. Assist the person being coached to answer the question, "What can I do about the problem?" Advice in the form of a question or suppositional statement is often effective. One example is, "Could the root of your problem be that you have not studied the user manual?"

8. **Coach with "could," not "should."** When instructing somebody else to improve, tell the person he or she *could* do something rather than he or she *should* do it. *Should* implies the person is doing something morally wrong, such as, "You should recycle the empty laser cartridges." *Could* leaves the person with a choice to make: to accept or reject your input and weigh the consequences.[18]

9. **Interpret what is happening.** An interpretation given by the person doing the coaching is an explanation of why the person being coached is acting in a particular manner. The interpretation is designed to give the person being coached insight into the nature of the problem. For instance, a food service manager might be listening to the problems of a cafeteria manager with regard to cafeteria cleanliness. After a while, the food service manager might say, "You're angry and upset with your employees because they don't keep a careful eye on cleanliness. So you avoid dealing with them, and it only makes problems worse." If the manager's diagnosis is correct, an interpretation can be extremely helpful.

10. **Allow for modeling of the desired performance and behaviors.** An effective coaching technique is to show the person being coached an example of what constitutes the desired behavior. A customer service representative was harsh with customers when facing heavy pressure. One way the supervisor coached the service representative was by taking over the manager's desk during a busy period. The representative then watched the supervisor deal tactfully with demanding customers.

11. **Applaud good results.** Effective coaches on the playing field and in the workplace are cheerleaders. They give positive reinforcement by applauding desired results. Some effective coaches shout in joy when the person coached achieves outstanding results; others give high-fives or clap their hands in applause.[19]

Coaching has become so ingrained into many organizational cultures that its effectiveness is rarely questioned. A frequent opinion about the benefits of coaching is that it

Characteristics of an Effective Coach

Directions: Following is a list of traits, attitudes, and behaviors of effective coaches. Indicate under each trait, attitude, or behavior whether you need to improve on it (e.g., "Yes, patience toward people"). Then, in the right column, prepare an action plan for improving each trait, attitude, or behavior that you need to develop. Sample action plans are provided.

Trait, attitude, or behavior	*Action plan for improvement*
Empathy	*Sample:* Will listen until I understand the person's point of view.
	Your own:
Listening skill	*Sample:* Will concentrate extra hard to listen.
	Your own:
Ability to size up people	*Sample:* Will jot down observations about people upon first meeting, then verify in the future.
	Your own:
Diplomacy and tact	*Sample:* Will study a book of etiquette, and/or find an app on the subject.
	Your own:
Patience toward people	*Sample:* Will practice staying calm when someone makes a mistake.
	Your own:
Concern for welfare	*Sample:* When interacting with another person, will ask self, or others, "How can this person's interests best be served?"
	Your own:
Provide constructive feedback with an I statement [22]	*Sample:* Even when upset with other person's work, I will make a suggestion, and not simply blame the person. I will say something to the effect of, "I am upset because you have been late with the customer surveys for four months in a row."
	Your own:
Self-confidence	*Sample:* Will attempt to have at least one personal success each week.
	Your own:
Noncompetitiveness	*Sample:* Will keep reminding myself that all boats with team members rise with the same tide.
	Your own:
Enthusiasm for people	*Sample:* Will search for the good in each person.
	Your own:
Work on personal development, thereby leading by example	*Sample:* Overcome projecting the attitude that people who disagree with me are really stupid.
	Your own:
Develop trust and respect[23]	*Sample:* Consistently tell the truth to people.
	Your own:

helps retain employees because being coached help builds loyalty. Being coached by a co-worker also helps the worker develop a valuable job skill, such as interpreting massive amounts of data.[20] A study with 666 call center telephone operators found that workers who received coaching tended to perform better. A key performance measure was how long it took a worker to resolve customer problems.[21]

One implication of the coaching suggestions just presented is that some people are more adept at coaching than others. Self-Assessment Quiz 12-2 provides insight into the right stuff for being an effective coach. After doing that exercise and reading the suggestions, you will be prepared for Skill-Building Exercise 12-4 about coaching.

Coaching a Mediocre Performer Role-Play

Visualize a busy sports medicine clinic and yourself as the chief administrator. You recognize that many of your patients urgently need the medical help your clinic offers because they have been injured substantially while participating in sports. Yet a good proportion of your patients are visiting the clinic for rehabilitation exercises that they can do on their own or learn from downloaded videos. As a consequence, being pleasant and hospitable is a requirement for all staff members, physicians, physical therapists, and support personnel alike. You want to keep your practice thriving through the rehabilitation patients.

One of your intake specialists, Tanya, goes about her work in a bland, mechanical manner. She makes relatively few errors in processing patient information, but she expresses very little warmth and appreciation toward patients. You have frequently observed patients appearing perplexed and displeased when Tanya deals with them. You have decided to get started coaching Tanya this afternoon toward becoming a warmer, more cheerful intake specialist.

One student plays the role of the chief administrator, and one student plays the role of Tanya, who has no clue as to why she is being coached. To her knowledge, she is a thoroughly professional sports medicine intake specialist.

For both scenarios, observers rate the role players on two dimensions, using a 1-to-5 scale from very poor (1) to very good (5). One dimension is "effective use of coaching techniques" (for the chief administrator). The second dimension is "acting ability." A few observers might voluntarily provide feedback to the role players in terms of sharing their ratings and observations. The course instructor might also provide feedback.

Training Others

A direct way of helping others in the workplace is to train them. **Training** is the process of helping others acquire a job-related skill. The emphasis on continuous learning by employees to keep up with changes in technology and work methods has helped elevate the importance of on-the-job training. For example, another training opportunity for some workers is to assist in the remedial learning of less skilled employees. According to the United States Center for Educational Statistics, one in five American adults lacks the math competency expected of an eighth grader. The problem is even more intense with respect to literacy.[24] Even if employees lacking basic skills do receive classroom instruction, they may still need the assistance from workers at a higher skill level.

Supervisors and trainers are responsible for much of the training in organizations. Yet as mentioned at the outset of the chapter, to save money, more responsibility for training has shifted to workers themselves. Also, as organizations operate with fewer managers, coworkers have more responsibility to train each other.

While training others, keep in mind certain time-tested principles that facilitate learning—and therefore training. Applying these principles consistently will increase the chances that the people you are training will acquire new skills. A considerable amount of training has shifted to e-learning (also referred to as distance learning and online learning), especially for acquiring cognitive knowledge and skills. Traditional training principles apply to e-learning, and you will still have opportunities to help the trainee. Many e-learners still need to ask a coworker a question, such as "I've been studying the metric system, and I can figure out how to convert Celsius to Fahrenheit, but I'm still having trouble going in the opposite direction. I'm doing something wrong. Can you help?" The training principles are as follows:

training

The process of helping others acquire a job-related skill.

1. **Encourage concentration.** Not much learning takes place unless the trainee concentrates carefully on what is being learned. Concentration improves the ability to do both mental and physical tasks. In short, encourage the person you are training to concentrate.

2. **Use motivated interest.** People learn best when they are interested in the problem facing them. Explain to the trainee how the skill being taught will enhance his or her value as an employee, or relate the skill to the person's professional goals. Trainees can be encouraged to look for some relationship between the information at hand and their personal welfare. With this relationship in mind, the person will have a stronger intention to learn.

3. **Remind learners to intend to remember.** We often fail to remember something because we do not intend to commit it to memory. Many executives are particularly effective at remembering the names of employees and customers. When one executive was asked how she could commit so many names to memory, she replied, "I look at the person, listen to the name, and try hard to remember." An

example of reminding a protégé to remember would be to advise him or her to memorize the company mission statement.

4. **Ensure the meaningfulness of material.** The material to be learned should be organized in a meaningful manner. Each successive experience should build on the other. In training another person how to process a customer order, you might teach the skill in terms of the flow of activities from customer inquiry to product delivery.

5. **Give feedback on progress.** As a person's training progresses, motivation may be maintained and enhanced by providing knowledge on his or her progress. To measure progress, it may be necessary to ask the trainee questions or ask for a job sample. For example, you might ask the person being trained on invoices to prepare a sample invoice.

6. **Ask the trainee to reflect on what he or she has learned.** Research indicates that if you think carefully about what you have learned, your retention of the information increases. The idea is to step back from the experience to ponder carefully and persistently its meaning to you.[25] After participating in a team development exercise involving white-water rafting, a person might reflect, "What did I really learn about being a better team player? How was I perceived by my teammates in the rubber raft? Did they even notice my contribution? Or did they think I was an important part of the team success?"

7. **Deal with trainee defensiveness.** Training is sometimes slowed down because the person being trained is defensive about information or skills that clash with his or her beliefs and practices. The person might have so much emotional energy invested in the status quo that he or she resists the training. For example, a sales representative might resist relying heavily on selling online because she believes that her warm smile and interpersonal skills have made her an excellent communicator. She is concerned that if she communicates with customers exclusively through e-mail or a company Web site, her human touch will be lost. Sensing this defensiveness, the trainer is advised to talk about e-commerce as being a supplement to, but not a substitute for, in-person communication. (However, the sales rep might also be worried that her position will be eliminated.)

8. **Take into account learning style.** Another key factor that influences training is **learning style**, the way in which a person best learns new information. An example of a learning style is passive learning. People who learn best through passive learning quickly acquire information by studying texts, manuals, magazine articles, and Web sites. They can juggle images in their mind as they read about abstract concepts such as supply and demand, cultural diversity, or customer service. Others learn best by doing rather than studying: for example, learning about customer service by dealing with customers in many situations.

learning style

The way in which a person best learns new information.

Another key dimension of learning styles is whether a person learns best by working alone or cooperatively in a study group. Learning by oneself may allow for more intense concentration, and one can proceed at one's own pace. Learning in groups through classroom discussion allows people to exchange viewpoints and perspectives.

Because of differences in learning styles, you may decide to design training to fit these differences. For example, if your trainees prefer cooperative learning, you could combine

SKILL-BUILDING EXERCISE 12-5

Designing a Training Program

The class organizes into training design teams of approximately six people. Each team sketches the design of a training program to teach an interpersonal skill to employees, such as being polite to customers or interviewing job candidates. The teams are not responsible for selecting the exact content of the training program they choose. Instead, they are responsible for designing a training program based on the principles of learning. Two examples here

would be (a) how to encourage the trainees to concentrate and (b) developing a mechanism to provide feedback to the trainee.

The activity should take about 15 minutes and can therefore be done inside or outside the class. After the teams have designed their programs, they can compare the various versions.

learning from reading books, articles, and online information with discussions in a conference room.

To start applying these principles of learning to a training situation, do Skill-Building Exercise 12-5.

HELPING DIFFICULT PEOPLE

A challenge we all face from time to time is dealing constructively with workers who appear intent on creating problems. For a variety of reasons, these difficult or counterproductive people perform poorly themselves or interfere with the job performance of others. A **difficult person** is an individual who creates problems for others, yet has the skill and mental ability to do otherwise. The difficult person may meet or exceed attendance and performance standards, yet has a toxic personality.[26] Many human resource professionals think that the number of difficult persons in the workplace is increasing partly due to the increases in workplace pressures.[27] (As you may have observed, as pressure increases, our worst personality traits and behaviors often emerge.)

Here we will discuss briefly various types of difficult people, and then emphasize methods for helping them behave more productively. To pretest your skill in dealing with and helping difficult people, do Self-Assessment Quiz 12-3.

difficult person

An individual who creates problems for others even though he or she has the skill and mental ability to do otherwise.

SELF-ASSESSMENT QUIZ 12-3

Dealing with Difficult People

Directions: For each of the following scenarios, circle the letter of what you think is the most effective way to handle the situation. Choose A or B.

No.	Difficult Behavior	A	B
1.	Coworker screams at you for having misspelled his or her name on a report. You		
	A. listen to him or her scream and then say, "You are upset today."		
	B. scream back even louder.	____	____
2.	A team member tells a gross joke during lunch, so you say,		
	A. "I am eating now, and your joke disturbs me."		
	B. "How gross. You are totally repulsive."	____	____
3.	A coworker at the next desk is talking loudly on the phone about the great concert he attended last night. You		
	A. get up from your chair, stand close to the coworker, and say loudly, "Shut up, office jerk! I'm trying to work."		
	B. slip the person a handwritten note that says, "I'm happy you attended a great concert, but I have problems concentrating on my work when you are talking so loudly. Thanks for your help."	____	____
4.	During a meeting in a cramped conference room, a coworker you do not know well puts his hand on your knee. You		
	A. yell at the offender and say he will be reported to management immediately.		
	B. say quietly, "Stop touching me right now. Your behavior is unacceptable to me."	____	____
5.	A team member who rarely carries his share of the workload asks you to cover for him this afternoon so he can take his uncle to the chiropractor. You deal with the situation by		
	A. carefully explaining that you will cover for him, providing he will take over a specified task for you.		
	B. telling him you absolutely refuse to help a person as lazy as he.	____	____
6.	You have become increasingly annoyed with another team member's ethnic, racist, ageist, and sexist jokes. During a team meeting, she tells a joke you believe is particularly offensive. To deal with the situation, you		
	A. tell the group an even more offensive joke to illustrate how this woman's behavior can get out of hand.		
	B. catch up with her later and tell her how uncomfortable her joke made you feel.	____	____

(Continued)

7. A coworker of yours regularly fails to follow through on his agreement to help with a task. Today, he is right on time to help you move some boxes into the storeroom. You say to him,

    A. "Miracles do happen. A passive-aggressive person like you actually does what he or she promised."

    B. "It is so nice of you to take the time to help me with this heavy job. Keep up your positive spirit of teamwork."   ____ ____

8. A coworker of yours is a high-maintenance type who demands so much from so many people. Today you are responsible for ordering food for a luncheon meeting in a conference room. When asked for his pizza preference, he demands four different toppings plus a rare brand of energy drink the pizza store will probably not carry. You take him aside and say,

    A. "Your pizza order is typical. You demand so much from others. Do you think you could be a little less demanding?"

    B. "Once again you are the office creep. Where do you think you get off making such a ridiculous lunch order?"   ____ ____

9. You have been placed on a task force to save the company money, including making recommendations for eliminating jobs. You interview a supervisor about the efficiency of her department. She suddenly becomes rude and defensive. You

    A. get your revenge by recommending that three jobs be eliminated from her department.

    B. politely point out how her behavior is coming across to you.   ____ ____

10. A coworker of yours sends you an average of 15 text messages and e-mails per day, almost all of no significance. You take action by

    A. explaining how responding to so many messages makes it difficult for you to accomplish your major work tasks.

    B. sending him about 25 text messages and e-mails a day for several days to see how he likes it.   ____ ____

Scoring and Interpretation: Give yourself one point for each of the following answers:

1.	A	6.	B
2.	A	7.	B
3.	B	8.	A
4.	B	9.	B
5.	A	10.	A

8–10: Your score suggests that you have good skill in dealing with a variety of difficult persons.

0–7: Your score suggests that you need to improve your skills in dealing with a variety of difficult persons.

Although you might think that the correct answers to the above scenarios are obvious, the quiz serves the important purpose of sensitizing you to the importance of dealing with difficult behavior in a tactful and sensible way in order to attain the results you want.

Types of Difficult People

Dozens of types of difficult people have been identified, with considerable overlap among the types. For example, one method of classifying difficult people might identify the dictator, while another method might identify the bully. A major challenge in classifying types of difficult people is that some of the types are manifestations of a severe underlying problem referred to as a **personality disorder**. (Such a disorder is defined as a pervasive, persistent, inflexible, maladaptive pattern of behavior that deviates from expected cultural norms.) One of these 10 different disorders is the narcissistic personality whose behavior includes being grandiose, needing admiration, and lacking empathy. As a difficult person, the narcissistic personality might be labeled a "high-maintenance person," "a me-first," or a "know-it-all expert."

Another important consideration about classifying difficult people is that most of them are a mixture and blend of various types, rather than being a pure type.[28] For example, a bully might be really a blend of a bully, a know-it-all, and an exploder. (Watch out for that guy or gal!)

personality disorder

A pervasive, persistent, inflexible, maladaptive pattern of behavior that deviates from expected cultural norms.

For our purposes, we list a sampling of the many types of difficult people found in the workplace and as customers. As you read the following list, look for familiar types.[29]

- *Know-it-alls* believe that they are experts on everything. They have opinions on every issue, yet when they are wrong they pass the buck or become defensive.
- *Blamers* are workers who never solve their own problems. When faced with a challenge or a hitch, they think the problem belongs to the supervisor or a group member.
- *Gossips* spread negative rumors about others and attempt to set people against each other.
- *Bullies* cajole and intimidate others. They are blunt to the point of being insulting, and will sometimes use harsh, vulgar language to attain their goals. Bullies constantly make demands on workmates.
- *Exploders* readily lose self-control when something important or trivial does not go their way, such as having their creative suggestion rejected by the group or being informed that their cubicle will be reduced in size. The loss of self-control frequently takes the form of a temper tantrum.
- *Repulsives* are people whose poor personal hygiene, eating habits, appearance, or foul language disrupts the tranquility of others.
- *Passive-aggressive people* appear to enthusiastically respond to another person's request or demand, while acting in a way that negatively and passively resists the request. For example, the person might agree to track down a lost shipment by tomorrow but not deliver, leaving you with an angry customer.
- *No-people* are negative and pessimistic and quick to point out why something will not work. They are also inflexible, resist change, and complain frequently.
- *Jekyll and Hydes* have a split personality. When dealing with supervisors, customers, or clients, they are pleasant, engaging people; yet, when carrying out the role of supervisors, they become tyrannical.
- *Whiners* gripe about people, processes, and company regulations. They complain about being overworked and underpaid, or not receiving assignments up to their true capabilities.
- *Backstabbers* pretend to befriend you and encourage you to talk freely about problems or personality clashes you face. Later, the backstabber reports the information— often in exaggerated form—to the person you mentioned in a negative light. Or the backstabber simply says negative things about you behind your back to discredit you to others.
- *High-maintenance types* require considerable attention from others in such forms as demanding much of the supervisor's time, making unusual requests to the human resources department, and taking the maximum number of sick days and personal days allowable. High-maintenance types are often a combination of several of the previous types described above.
- *Clods* are master procrastinators who can find plenty of excuses as to why a project has not been started. When the clod finally gets started on a project, the work proceeds so slowly that other people who need the clod's input fall behind schedule and become stressed.
- *Minimalists* are apathetic and low-performing, and do just enough work to avoid being fired. They do the bare minimum and thrive on being mediocre.
- *Office cheats* take claim for the ideas of other people and benefit from these ideas, leaving the originator of the idea without receiving deserved credit and feeling frustrated because of the stolen ideas.

Tactics for Dealing with Difficult People

How one deals most effectively with a difficult person depends to some extent on the person's type. For example, you might need more time to get through to a passive-aggressive

FIGURE 12-2   How to Be a Bully Buster

- Stand up for yourself and recognize that you have a right to be treated in a civil manner, even when a disagreement exists.

- Document every incident and every detail about the bullying, including who witnessed the act. Include information about how the bully created damage such as lowered productivity or time off from work to recover from the stress that bulllying caused.

- Explain to the bully that you are prepared to report inappropriate behavior to the manager and/or the human resources department.

- Appear calm and essentially indifferent to the bully's tactics. A bully who does not see the potential victim squirm will feel defeated and go away.

- Observe your own body language such as appearing stooped and nervous so you do not give the impression that the bully is getting his or her way. Instead, stand up straight, look the bully in the eyes, and lean forward.

- Laugh politely at the bully to show that you do not take him or her seriously.

- When the bully keeps screaming, stay calm and listen, and after the screaming has run its course, say something to the effect of, "It appears that you are upset." Such behavior will disarm the bully and make his or her tirade seem pointless.

person than to a bully. Figure 12-2 presents specific ideas for dealing with a bully. (You will recall that bullying was described in Chapter 9 as a source of workplace conflict.) The techniques ahead have wide applicability for helping difficult people change to a more constructive behavior pattern. This general approach should prove more helpful than being concerned with specific tactics for each type of difficult person you encounter. A principle to keep in mind in dealing with difficult people is that they vary in their amount of personality disturbance. Workers classified as difficult people whose behavior is propelled by a personality disorder will be the least amenable to change.

The problems difficult people (sometimes referred to collectively as *office jerks*) create have received considerable attention in recent years from managers. The precise definition of an office jerk is someone who consistently leaves people feeling demeaned, belittled, and de-energized. In addition, the office jerk typically targets people of lesser power than he or she possesses.[30] (Despite the frequent use of the term, labeling people as *jerks* tends to exclude constructive thinking about dealing with the problem and is not good human relations practice.)

Such companies as Google and Southwest Airlines have taken many of the steps described next to minimize the negative impact difficult people have on productivity and job satisfaction. Another problem is that some positive contributors will quit when forced to work permanently with a difficult person. Many difficult people are also being fired instead of counseled because of the problems they create.

Stay Calm.   A good starting point in dealing with many types of difficult people is to stay calm so that you can confront the other person in a professional manner. Staying calm also helps you think of a useful approach on the spot. Imagine that an exploder is upset because the new chair she was assigned has a broken height adjustment. You might calmly say to her, "I can imagine that having a chair that does not adjust is inconvenient, but what would you like me to do?" When you are calm, the difficult person's anger will often simmer down, and the problem that triggered the person can be solved.

Staying calm also facilitates your acting as a model of how a person should conduct himself or herself in the workplace. Freequently, one has to deal with a whiner who complains about many things. When interacting with this person, if you avoid whining and complaining and you have a positive relationship, the difficult person will sometimes follow you as a model.[31]

Give Ample Feedback.   The primary technique for dealing with counterproductive behavior is to feed back to the difficult person how his or her behavior affects you. As in other forms of feedback, be clear about what you want. Focus on the person's behavior rather than on characteristics or values. If a *repulsive type* is annoying you by constantly eating when you are working together, say something to this effect: "I have difficulty concentrating on the work when you are eating." Such a statement will engender less resentment than saying, "I find you repulsive, and it annoys me." As in coaching, it is better to avoid *should* statements because they often create defensiveness instead of triggering positive behavior. Instead of saying "You shouldn't be eating when you are working," you might try, "Could you find another place to eat when we are working together?"

Feedback will sometimes take the form of confrontation, and it is important not to lose emotional control during the confrontation. If the difficult person has criticized you unjustly in your eyes, attempt not to be defensive. Ask the difficult person exactly what he or she is upset about rather than argue. In this way, the burden of responsibility is now back on the antagonist. For example, if a bully was swearing at you during a meeting, later ask for the reason behind the outburst. Following the technique of disarming the opposition described in Chapter 9, you might agree with at least one of the bully's points. This will help establish rapport.[32] An example here would be, "Yes, I should have consulted you before making the final report. I apologize for the oversight."

Confrontation is likely to be more effective when the confronter is supportive at the same time. Express a positive intent by conveying your willingness to help and support.[33] For example, "I value your contribution as a coworker, but when you scream at me when you have a different point of view, it blocks our conversation."

Criticize Constructively.

Feedback sets the stage for criticism. It is best to criticize in private and to begin with mild criticism. Base your criticism on objective facts rather than subjective impressions. Point out, for example, that the yes-person's lack of follow-through resulted in $10,000 in lost sales. Express your criticism in terms of a common goal. For example, "We can get the report done quickly if you'll firm up the statistical data while I edit the text." When you criticize a coworker, avoid acting as if you have formal authority over the person.

An indirect form of criticism is to ask a question that indirectly criticizes the difficult person's behavior. For example, assume that a passive-aggressive person uses a voice tone that contradicts his or her intention of being willing to accept an assignment. You might say, "Is there something bothering you that we should discuss? I want to make sure we are in agreement."[34]

Help the Difficult Person Feel More Confident.

Many counterproductive employees are simply low in self-confidence and self-efficacy. They use stalling and evasive tactics because they are afraid to fail. Working with your manager or team leader, you might be able to arrange a project or task in which you know the difficult person will succeed. With a small dose of self-confidence and self-efficacy, the person may begin to complain less. With additional successes, the person may soon become less difficult.[35] Self-confidence building takes time; however, self-efficacy can build more quickly as the person learns a new skill.

Use Tact and Diplomacy.

Tactful actions on your part can sometimes take care of annoying behavior by coworkers without having to confront the problem. Close your door, for example, if noisy coworkers are gathered outside. When subtlety does not work, it may be necessary to proceed to a confronting type of feedback.

Tact and diplomacy can still be incorporated into confrontation. In addition to confronting the person, you might also point out one of the individual's strengths. In dealing with a know-it-all, you might say, "I realize you are creative and filled with good ideas. However, I wish you would give me an opportunity to express my opinion."

Use Nonhostile Humor.

Nonhostile humor can often be used to help a difficult person understand how his or her behavior is blocking others. Also, the humor will help you defuse the conflict between you and that person. The humor should point to the person's unacceptable behavior, yet not belittle him or her. Assume that you and a coworker are working jointly on a report. For each idea that you submit, your coworker gets into the know-it-all mode and informs you of important facts you neglected. An example of nonhostile humor that might jolt the coworker into realizing that his or her approach is annoying is as follows:

If there is ever a contest to choose the human being with a brain that can compete against a cloud computing backup file, I will nominate you. But even though my brain is limited to human capacity, I still think I can supply a few facts for our report.

Your humor may help the other person recognize that he or she is attempting to overwhelm you with facts at his or her disposal. You are being self-effacing and thereby drawing criticism away from your coworker. Self-effacement is a proven humor tactic.

Work Out a Deal.   A direct approach to dealing with problems created by a difficult person is to work out a deal or a negotiated solution. Workers who do not carry their load are successful in getting others to do their work. The next time such a worker wants you to carry out a task, agree to it if he or she will reciprocate by performing a task that will benefit you. For working out a deal to be effective, you must be specific about the terms of the deal. The worker may at first complain about your demands for reciprocity, so it is important to be firm.

Reinforce Civil Behavior and Good Moods.   In the spirit of positive reinforcement, when a generally difficult person is behaving acceptably, recognize the behavior in some way. Reinforcing statements would include "It's fun working with you today" and "I appreciate your professional attitude."

Ask the Difficult Person to Think Before Speaking.   Human relations specialist John Maxwell suggests that you ask the difficult person to THINK before he or she speaks, with "THINK" referring to the acronym:[36]

T   Is it True?

H   Is it Helpful?

I   Is it Inspiring?

N   Is it Necessary?

K   Is it Kind?

Although Maxwell's suggestion is aimed at difficult people, it would be a helpful rule of thumb for building relationships with people in many situations.

The tactics for dealing with the difficult people just described require practice to be effective. When you next encounter a difficult person, try one of the tactics that seems to fit the occasion. Role-plays, such as those presented in Skill-Building Exercise 12-6, are a good starting point for implementing tactics in dealing with difficult people.

SKILL-BUILDING EXERCISE 12-6

Dealing with Difficult People

In both of the following scenarios, one person plays the role of a group member whose work and morale suffer because of a difficult person. The other person plays the role of the difficult person who may lack insight into what he or she is doing wrong. It is important for the suffering person to put emotion into the role.

Scenario 1: A Bully. A bully is present at a meeting called to plan a company morale-boosting event. Several students play the roles of the group members. One student plays the role of a group member who suggests that the event center on doing a social good, such as refurbishing a low-income family's house or conducting a neighborhood cleanup. Another student plays the role of a bully who doesn't like the idea. The group member being intimidated decides to deal effectively with the bully (or dictator).

Scenario 2: A No-Person. One student plays the role of a worker with a lot of creative energy whose manager is a no-person. The energetic worker has what he or she thinks is a wonderful way for the company to generate additional revenue: conduct a garage sale of surplus equipment and furnishings. The worker presents this idea to the no-person manager, played by another student. If the manager acts true to form, the worker will attempt to overcome his or her objections.

Scenario 3: A Repulsive. Your team is so busy that you are having a working lunch today in a company conference room. This is the first time the team has had lunch with the newest member of the team. She talks loudly while eating, slurps her beverage in a loud manner, and interrupts the flow of conversation twice with vile descriptions of airplane and cruise ship lavatories being overloaded. As the team leader, you know that criticizing workers in public is poor human relations, but you have to do something to salvage the meeting that the repulsive member is interrupting.

For the three scenarios, observers rate the role players on two dimensions, using a 1-to-5 scale from very poor (1) to very good (5). One dimension is "effective use of human relations techniques." The second dimension is "acting ability." A few observers might voluntarily provide feedback to the role players in terms of sharing their ratings and observations. The course instructor might also provide feedback.

Concept Review and Reinforcement

Key Terms

nurturing person 297
toxic person 297
mentor 299
protégé 299

coaching 303
peer coaching 303
behavioral feedback 304
training 307

learning style 308
difficult person 309
personality disorder 310

Summary

Workers have a responsibility to help each other learn, grow, and develop. A major strategy for helping others grow and develop is to be a nurturing, positive person. A toxic person stands in contrast to a nurturing person because he or she dwells on the negative. Nurturing people are positive, enthusiastic, and supportive. Three actions and attitudes that support being a nurturing person are to (1) recognize growth needs in others, (2) use the buddy system, and (3) be a role model.

Being a mentor is another way to help others. As long as you are experienced and wiser than a coworker in some important aspect of the job, you can be a mentor. Mentoring often takes the form of the mentor and protégé communicating by e-mail, referred to as e-mentoring. Coworker mentoring can take place with mentors who can be selected by the company or chosen informally.

To be a mentor, a person engages in a wide range of helping behaviors. Among them are sponsoring, coaching, protecting, sharing challenging assignments, and being a referral agent. Mentors also help protégés solve problems and learn the ropes of an organization. Mentoring can sometimes help the organization by helping workers become more committed to the firm.

Coaching and training are direct helping roles. Coaching is a method of helping workers grow and develop by providing suggestions and encouragement. Suggestions for effective coaching include the following:

1. Build relationships.
2. Provide specific, constructive feedback.
3. Make criticism pain-free and positive.
4. Encourage the person you are coaching to talk.
5. Ask powerful questions.
6. Give emotional support.
7. Give some constructive advice.
8. Coach with "could," not "should."
9. Interpret what is happening.
10. Allow for modeling of the desired performance and behaviors.
11. Applaud good results.

Training involves helping people acquire job skills. To facilitate training, apply principles of learning such as the following: (1) encourage concentration, (2) use motivated interest, (3) remind learners to intend to remember, (4) ensure the meaningfulness of material, (5) give feedback on progress, (6) ask the trainee to reflect on what he or she has learned, (7) deal with trainee defensiveness, and (8) take into account learning style.

Dealing with difficult people is a major challenge in helping others. Some difficult people have a personality disorder. The many types of difficult people include know-it-alls, blamers, gossips, bullies, exploders, repulsives, yes-people, no-people, Jekyll and Hydes, whiners, backstabbers, high-maintenance types, and office cheats. Companies are concerned about the damage difficult people create and sometimes fire them.

Workers classified as difficult people whose behavior is propelled by a personality disorder will be the least amenable to change. Tactics for dealing with difficult people include (1) staying calm, (2) giving ample feedback including confrontation, (3) criticizing constructively, (4) helping the difficult person feel more confident, (5) using tact and diplomacy, (6) using humor, (7) working out a deal, (8) reinforcing civil behavior and good moods, and (9) asking the person to THINK before speaking.

Questions for Discussion and Review

1. What is your opinion on whether workers have a responsibility to help each other grow and develop?

2. What is your opinion of the potential effectiveness of the buddy system in your career?

3. Suppose one of your mentors is a highly-placed professional in his or her field. Explain whether you would you send that person tweets asking for career advice.

4. What are the main differences between mentoring and e-mentoring?

5. Should training employees be considered a cost or an investment?

6. Many career-minded workers today hire their own coach, much like a personal trainer for solving job problems and advancing. Explain whether you would be willing to invest money to hire a business coach or personal trainer for yourself.

7. What might be a problem in relying heavily on "FAQs" (frequently asked questions) to help in training employees?

8. Many feel that it is better to move difficult people to another department immediately. Comment on the effectiveness of that approach.

9. Suppose an employee notices that a water main has broken in the company parking lot, and shrugs off the incident without reporting the problem. Why should this individual's lack of action be classifed as passive–aggressive behavior?

10. How might humor help you deal with the repulsive type of difficult person? Supply an example of a witty comment you might use.

The Web Corner

http://www.jobshadow.com

(Opportunity to shadow people online who have interesting careers)

http://www.BlueSuitMom.com/career/management/difficultpeople.html

(Strategies for dealing with difficult people)

http://www.brighthub.com

(Tips for peer-to-peer coaching)

Internet Skill Builder: Mentoring Online

As mentioned in the chapter, many mentors stay in touch with the people they mentor primarily through e-mail and Web sites, including company and social networking Web sites. Such virtual networking has advantages and disadvantages. Search the Internet for three useful ideas about how to mentor effectively online. Try the search terms "virtual mentoring" and "online mentoring" as well as other terms you think might work. Think through which of these ideas you would use as an online mentor.

Developing Your Human Relations Skills

Interpersonal Relations Case 12.1

The Reality Coach

Kara was excited about her new position as Internet sales manager at a food supplement company. The company's dozens of products included pills and liquids for improving skin health, lowering blood pressure, improving digestion, and improving vision. Many of the company's sales were in bulk to supermarkets, pharmacies, and health-food stores. In addition, many orders came in over the Internet and by toll-free numbers. Kara's responsibilities included revitalizing the company Web site periodically and finding ways to direct more Internet traffic to the site.

During Kara's first week on the job, she was assigned a coach and mentor, Malcolm, the manager of order fulfillment. Malcolm was to act in the dual role of coaching and mentoring Kara, in addition to assisting in her *onboarding* (getting oriented into the company). During their first meeting, Malcolm was friendly and constructive, saying that his role was to help Kara in any feasible way.

The second meeting between Kara and Malcolm was quite brief, with Malcolm asking Kara if she were yet having any problems he could provide assistance with. Kara replied that all was going well so far.

One week later, Malcolm dropped by Kara's cubicle, and said to her, "I've noticed that Internet sales have been flat since you came on board. What is it that you are doing that is adding value to the company?" Kara replied that enhancing Internet sales takes considerable time.

Ten days later, Malcolm sent Kara an e-mail asking that she meet with him in his cubicle at 4 p.m. Malcolm asked Kara how she was doing, and then said he had some advice for her as her coach and mentor. "Quite frankly, I think you could make a more professional appearance.

Your hair is too long, and you wear too much dangling jewelry. I think that you need to tone down your appearance a little to be successful as an Internet sales manager."

Kara replied, "Nobody else has complained. Besides, most of my important interactions are over the Internet, not with customers face to face. So long hair and dangling jewelry should not be a problem."

Kara was beginning to wonder if Malcolm was really a help or just an irritant. She then devoted most of her energies the next couple of weeks into revamping and modernizing the company Web site. Her boss, as well as several coworkers, made approving comments about the new Web site. Malcolm, however, had his own opinion of the revamped Web site. He said to Kara in person, "I have heard that a few people like the changes you made to the Web site; but Kara, I am disappointed. You just tweaked the site instead of making radical changes that would increase sales substantially. I know that you can do better."

Kara replied, "Malcolm, isn't there anything I can do to please you? Are you my coach and mentor, or just my heckler?"

Malcolm retorted, "Do you think you might be too thin-skinned to succeed in business? As your coach and mentor I have to be frank. Otherwise I can't help you."

Case Questions

1. How effective do you think Malcolm is in his role as Kara's coach and mentor?
2. What suggestions can you offer Malcolm to be more effective in his role?
3. What suggestions might you offer Kara so that she can benefit more from the coaching and mentoring the company is providing her?

Interpersonal Relations Case 12.2

Paula the Petulant Paralegal

Paula enjoys her career as a paralegal in a large, successful law firm. She believes that without her keen attention to details, Internet search skills, and knowledge of relevant laws, the lawyers she supports could never get their work accomplished. Paula says, "Without me behind the scenes doing all the important detail work, our lawyers could never collect those fat hourly fees."

The attorneys and other staff members who work with Paula are quite satisfied with her legal knowledge and job performance, but working with her has its rough spots. Over a three-month period, Roger, the partner in charge of office administration and human resources, heard the following comments about Paula.

Attorney 1: I think Paula has an irresistible temptation to make little digs about people. One time at the end of a brief discussion about a case, she said to me that my tie was a terrible match for my shirt and suit. Another time Paula told me that one of our senior partners should change hair dressers because her last two hairdos made her look like she didn't care about her appearance. Just last week Paula commented to me that the newest paralegal dressed more like a rock singer than a professional working woman.

Attorney 2: Paula offers a lot to the firm because of her knowledge and dependability, but you need to take professional time to listen to her rants. One of her favorite themes is to complain about the unjust difference between the pay of attorneys and paralegals. I wonder if she wants me to give some of my salary and bonus to her.

Paralegal: Paula acts like she's the queen bee. Just because she has more experience than most of the other paralegals in the office, she acts as if she is our boss. If you make one mistake in legal terminology in front of her, she will make a sarcastic comment such as, "Are you sure you received a degree in paralegal studies?"

Office assistant: I know that Paula contributes a lot to the firm, but she should still be a little more civil and less critical. I asked her a question about a new mobile app the firm had introduced so we could do some work remotely. Paula replied in an angry tone that her ten-year-old niece knew more about technology than I do.

Case Questions

1. Which type of difficult person does Paula appear to be? Or is she a difficult person?
2. What actions should the partner in charge of office administration and human resources take to deal with the difficult behavior of Paula?
3. What should Attorney 1, the office assistant, and the paralegal have done in response to the personal criticisms made by Paula?

Interpersonal Skills Role-Play

Dealing with Petulant Paula

One person plays the role of Roger, the partner in charge of office administration and human resources. He is meeting today with Paula to discuss how she is perceived by several others in the office, particularly with respect to being so nasty. Roger's goal is to get Paula to be more civil. Roger will be particularly alert to any signs of nastiness from Paula. Another student plays the role of Paula, who believes that she is simply an open and honest person who describes the reality she sees.

Run the role-play for about six minutes, while other class members observe the interactions and later provide feedback about the interpersonal skills displayed by Roger in relation to his interaction with Paula. Also, rate Paula. Observers rate the role players on two dimensions, using a 1-to-5 scale from very poor (1) to very good (5). One dimension is "effective use of human relations techniques." The second dimension is "acting ability." A few observers might voluntarily provide feedback to the role players in terms of sharing their ratings and observations. The course instructor might also provide feedback.

References

1. Alina Tugend, "Why Is Asking for Help So Difficult?" *The New York Times* (http://nytimes.com), July 7, 2007, p. 1.
2. Jeffrey Keller, "Associate with Positive People," a supplement to the *Pryor Report*, 1994.
3. Tammy Ellen and Lillian Eby, Editors, *The Blackwell Handbook of Mentoring: A Multiple Perspectives Approach* (Malden, MA: Blackwell Publishing, 2007).
4. Monica C. Higgins and Kathy E. Kram, "Reconceptualizing Mentoring at Work: A Developmental Network Perspective,"

Academy of Management Review, April 2001, pp. 264–288.

5. Donna M. Owens, "Virtual Mentoring," *HR Magazine,* March 2006, pp. 105–107.

6. Marina Khidekel, "The Misery of Mentoring Millennials," *Bloomberg Businessweek*, March 18–March 24, 2013, p. 68.

7. Stephenie Overman, "Mentors without Borders," *HR Magazine*, March 2004, pp. 83–85.

8. Jennifer Wang, "Will You Be My Mentor?" *Entrepreneur, January 2011*, p. 22.

9. Tammy D. Allen, Lillian T. Eby, and Elizabeth Lentz, "Mentoring Behaviors and Mentorship Quality Associated with Formal Mentoring Programs: Closing the Gap between Research and Practice," *Journal of Applied Psychology,* May 2006, pp. 567–578.

10. Based mostly on Kathy E. Kram, *Mentoring at Work: Developmental Relationships in Organizational Life* (Glenview, IL: Scott Foresman, 1985), pp. 22–39; Erik J. Van Slyke and Bud Van Slyke, "Mentoring: A Results-Oriented Approach," *HRfocus*, February 1998, p. 14.

11. Stephanie T. Solansky, "The Evaluation of Two Key Leadership Development Program Components: Leadership Skills Assessment and Leadership Mentoring," *Leadership Quarterly*, August 2010, pp. 675–681.

12. Steve Trautman, *Teach What You Know: A Practical Leader's Guide to Knowledge Transfer Using Peer Mentoring* (Upper Saddle River, NJ: Prentice Hall, 2007).

13. Stephanie C. Payne and Ann H. Huffman, "A Longitudinal Examination of the Influence of Mentoring on Organizational Commitment and Turnover," *Academy of Management Journal,* February 2005, pp. 158–168.

14. Stephen Palmer and Almuth McDowall, eds., *The Counseling Relationship: Putting People First* (New York: Routledge, 2010).

15. "Coaching—One Solution to a Tight Training Budget," *HRfocus*, August 2002, p. 7; Sharon Ting and Peter Scisco, eds., *The CCL Handbook of Coaching: A Guide for the Leader Coach* (San Francisco: Jossey-Bass, 2006).

16. Editors of *Managers Edge, The Successful Manager's Guide to Giving and Receiving Feedback* (Alexander, VA: Briefings Publishing Group, 2004), p. 14.

17. Anne Fisher, "Turn Star Employees into Superstars," *Fortune*, December 13, 2004, p. 70.

18. "Coach with 'Could,' Not 'Should,'" *Executive Strategies,* April 1998, p. 1.

19. Andrew J. DuBrin, *Leadership: Research Findings, Practice, and Skills,* seventh edition (Mason Ohio: Southwestern/Cengage Learning, 2013), p. 326.

20. Nicole Long, "Organizational Benefits of Coaching & Mentoring," http://smallbusiness.chron.com, p. 1. Retrieved March 23, 2013.

21. Xiangmin Liu and Rosemary Batt, "How Supervisors Influence Performance: A Multilevel Study of Coaching and Group Management in Technology-Mediated Services," *Personnel Psychology*, Summer 2010, pp. 265–298.

22. This item is from Tina Smagala, "Having In-House Coaches Is Essential," *Democrat and Chronicle*, November 22, 2011, p. 5B.

23. This item is from John M. Ivancevich and Thomas N. Duening, *Management: Skills, Application, Practice, and Development* (Cincinnati, OH: Atomic Dog Publishing, 2006), p. 282.

24. Timothy Wall, "Program to Overcome Early U. S. Math Deficiencies Could Improve Workforce, Says MU Psychologist," *Research at Mizzou* (http://research.missouri.edu, February 4, 2013, pp. 1–2.

25. Kent W. Seibert, "Reflection in Action: Tools for Cultivating On-the-Job Learning Conditions," *Organizational Dynamics*, Winter 1999, p. 55.

26. Jathan Janover, "Jerks at Work," *HR Magazine,* May 2007, p. 111.

27. Jennifer Schramm, "The Rise of the Difficult Employee?" *HR Magazine*, June 2012, p. 144.

28. Laurence Miller, *From Difficult to Disturbed: Understanding and Managing Dysfunctional Employees* (New York: AMACOM, 2008).

29. Career Track seminar, *Dealing with Difficult People,* 2013; Fred Pryor Seminar, *How to Deal with Unacceptable* Behavior, 2007; Hara Estroff Marano, "The High Art of Handling Problem People," *Psychology Today,* May/June 2012, pp. 52–61; Jared Sandberg, "Staff 'Handfuls' and the Bosses Who Coddle Them," *The Wall Street Journal*, October 8, 2003, p. B1; Darnell Morris-Compton, "How to Unmask Workers who Cheat," *Indianapolis Star* syndicated story, March 13, 2005.

30. Leigh Buchanam, "The Bully Rulebook," *Inc. Magazine* (http://Inc.com), February 2007; Patrick White, "Sometimes Office Jerks Finish First," *Detroit News (http://detnews. com),* July 23, 2007.

31. Sue Shellenbarger, "What to Do with a Workplace Whiner," *The Wall Street Journal*, September 12, 2012, p. D1.

32. Nando Pelusi, "Dealing with Difficult People," *Psychology Today, (psychologytoday.com),* 2006.

33. Tina Smagala, "Straight Talk is Key to Changing Behavior," *Democrat and Chronicle*, January 4, 2011, p. 5B.

34. "End Passive-Aggressive Behavior," *Communication Briefings,"* December 2010, p. 1

35. "How to Deal with 'Problem' Workers," *Positive Leadership,* sample issue, distributed 2001; Martien Eerhart, "Top 7 Ideas for Dealing with Difficult Employees," http://top-7business.com/archives/personnel/050499.html.

36. John C. Maxwell, *Winning with People: Discover the People Principles That Work for You Every Time* (Nashville, TN: Nelson Books, 2004), pp. 1428–1429.

Positive Political Skills

Bonnie Marcus is the founder and principal of Women's Success Coaching. While attending the 14th Annual Wharton Women in Business Conference, she emphasized the importance of building long-term relationships. Marcus noted that while building these relationships, one should not ignore the powerful people who can influence a woman's career trajectory. She said, "We need to be authentic and so forth, but we need to make sure we understand who makes these decisions. I have learned a lot of lessons in my career, and one of them is the importance of being political."

For Marcus, that lesson came when when she was vying for a promotion. "I did everything, I thought, right. I was confident, I was competent. I had the numbers, I certainly increased the

wavebreakmedia/Shutterstock

After reading and studying this chapter and completing the exercises, you should be able to

1. Explain the importance of political skill and other human relations skills for becoming skilled at using positive political tactics.
2. Manage effectively the impression you give, including developing an awareness of the rules of business etiquette.
3. Implement political techniques for building relationships with managers and other key people.
4. Implement political techniques for building relationships with coworkers and other work associates.
5. Avoid committing political blunders.

top line and the bottom line (revenues and profits)." She even asked directly for the promotion and made sure her direct reports came forward to lobby on her behalf.

"I still didn't get the promotion. And the reason was, I didn't work the politics," she said. "I didn't build a relationship with the right decision makers." [1]

The comments just quoted from the executive emphasize the major subject of this chapter: The proper use of positive political tactics helps build good interpersonal relationships. In turn, these good relationships can facilitate achieving career goals. Recognize, however, that being competent in your job is still the most effective method of achieving career success. After skill come hard work and luck as important success factors.

A fourth ingredient is also important for success: positive political skills. Few people can achieve success for themselves or their group without having some awareness of the political forces around them and how to use them to advantage. It may be necessary for the career-minded person to take the offensive in using positive and ethical political tactics. As used here, **organizational politics** refers to gaining power through any means other than merit or luck. (Luck, of course, is what happens when preparation meets opportunity.) Politics are played to achieve power, either directly or indirectly. **Power** refers to the ability or potential to control anything of value and to influence decisions. The results of such power may take diverse forms like being promoted, being transferred, receiving a salary increase, or avoiding an uncomfortable assignment.

Organizational politics can also be regarded from the standpoint of interpersonal relationships and sizing up the environment. As described by author and speaker Donna Cardillo, office politics refers to understanding the unwritten rules of the workplace that involve getting along with others, getting recognized for one's efforts, and following the protocol of how things get accomplished.[2]

As you study this chapter, it will become evident that communication skills and team player skills are necessary for being skilled at politics. Figure 13-1 depicts the relationship among politics, power, and control and influence. Political tactics, such as developing contacts with key people, lead to power, which enables one to control and influence others.

organizational politics

Gaining power through any means other than merit or luck.

power

The ability or potential to control anything of value and to influence decisions.

FIGURE 13-1   Relationship among Politics, Power, and Influence

Political tactics, such as developing contacts with key people, lead to power, which enables one to control and influence others.

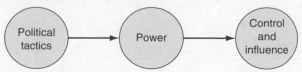

In this chapter, we approach skill development in organizational (or office) politics from several standpoints. Information is presented about such topics as managing your impression, using political tactics to improve interpersonal relationships, and avoiding hazardous political mistakes. To measure your current tendencies toward playing politics, do Self-Assessment Quiz 13-1.

SELF-ASSESSMENT QUIZ 13-1

Organizational Politics Questionnaire

Directions: For each of the following statements, check whether you mostly agree or mostly disagree, even if it is difficult for you to decide which alternative best describes your opinion.

	Mostly agree	Mostly disagree
1. The boss or the team leader is always right.	_____	_____
2. It is wise to flatter important people.	_____	_____
3. If you do somebody a favor, remember to cash in on it.	_____	_____
4. Given the opportunity, I would go out of my way to develop friendships with powerful people.	_____	_____
5. I would be willing to say nice things about a rival in order to get that person transferred from my department.	_____	_____
6. If it would help me get ahead, I would take credit for someone else's work.	_____	_____
7. Given the chance, I would offer to help my boss fix something in his or her home, including a technology problem.	_____	_____
8. I laugh heartily at my boss's humor, even if I do not think it is funny.	_____	_____
9. Dressing to create a favorable appearance is foolish. At the office, wear clothing that you find to be the most comfortable.	_____	_____
10. Never waste lunchtime by eating with somebody who can't help you solve a problem or gain advantage.	_____	_____
11. I think using e-mail to zap somebody for his or her mistake and sending copies to key people is a good idea.	_____	_____
12. If somebody higher up in the organization offends you, look for ways to get even with him or her.	_____	_____
13. Being candid is the best policy, even if it means insulting somebody.	_____	_____
14. Obtaining power for its own sake would make me feel wonderful.	_____	_____
15. If I had a legitimate gripe against my employer, I would express my views publicly (such as distributing my comments on a blog or social networking site).	_____	_____
16. I would invite my boss or team leader to a party at my home even if I didn't like him or her.	_____	_____
17. An effective way to impress people is to tell them what they want to hear.	_____	_____
18. Having a school, college, or skyscraper named after me would be an incredible thrill.	_____	_____
19. Hard work and good performance are usually sufficient for career success.	_____	_____
20. Even if I made only a minor contribution to a project, I would get my name listed as being associated with it.	_____	_____
21. I would never publicly correct mistakes made by my supervisor or team leader.	_____	_____
22. I would never use my personal contacts to gain a promotion.	_____	_____
23. If you happen to dislike a person who receives a big promotion in your firm, don't bother sending that person a congratulatory note.	_____	_____

POLITICAL SKILL AND OTHER HUMAN RELATIONS SKILLS

Political skill does not stand alone, separated from other human relations skills. Here we look at how political skill relates to awareness of one's surroundings, emotional intelligence and social intelligence, and relationship building with the leader.

LEARNING OBJECTIVE 1

Sensitivity to Your Surroundings

For starters, being sensitive to your surroundings and to other people helps make you politically aware. Cultural sensitivity, as described in Chapter 8 about cross-cultural relations and diversity, is a specific type of sensitivity to one's surroundings that deals with sizing up the cultural environment.

Stockbyte/Getty Images

Imagine that you are applying for a position at Google doing exactly the kind of work you want. You have seen photos of Google employees, and you have visited its headquarters before your interview just to see what the company looks like. No Google worker, including the founders, is ever seen in a business suit, yet this fact escapes you. You show up for your interview wearing a business suit and leather shoes as if you were applying for a position as an investment banker trainee at a Wall Street firm. Zap, you are done. The Google employees wearing jeans, casual shirts and blouses, and running shoes think you would be a poor cultural fit despite your intelligence and talent. You were not sensitive enough to the environment to choose the appropriate attire for you interview.

Emotional Intelligence and Social Intelligence

Political skill relates to emotional intelligence because you need to be able to read the emotions of others to establish rapport with them. For example, a person with good emotional intelligence would ask for a raise when the boss appeared to be in a good mood. Also, the person would avoid asking for a raise when the boss was upset, preoccupied, and in an ugly mood.

Political skill is also directly related to **social intelligence**, an understanding of how relationships with bosses and colleagues, family, and friends shape our brains and affect our bodies. (As used here, the term social intelligence does not refer to intelligence about social media.) Social intelligence is a book-length subject, yet we can take away a couple of basic lessons that are linked to positive political skill.[3] Social intelligence tells us that good relationships act like vitamins, energizing us to perform well. In contrast, bad relationships are like poison, undermining our cognitive efficiency and creativity. The person with good social intelligence would work at having positive relationships with others on the job, to be able to concentrate on the task and perform well.

Another aspect of having social intelligence would be to recognize that being arrogant or derisive toward others can cause emotional distress that impairs the brain's ability to learn and think clearly. So a good team player or a manager would relate more positively toward others in order to help attain a productive workplace.

Relationship Building with the Leader

A major purpose of organizational politics including political skill is to develop good relationships with your superior, as described later in this chapter. More specifically, strong political skills can help you develop a higher-quality leader–member exchange (LMX). A current study suggests that having good political skills can help a person develop a positive LMX even when the two parties are demographically different. Previous research had shown that LMXs tend to be more positive when the leader and group member are demographically similar, such as being the same sex or race, or similar in age.

The study in question involved 189 participants in a retail service organization. Seventy-six percent of the sample was white (Caucasian), and 56 percent was women. The average age of participants was 30. Participants all took a political skill inventory containing a few ideas similar to the inventory presented in Self-Assessment Quiz 13-1. Political skill was shown to improve relationships with racially dissimilar leaders and group members (better LMX scores). It was also found that the quality of the LMX was not due to gender or age. The researchers concluded that political skill enables subordinates who are racially dissimilar to their supervisors to get around the potential relationship problems based on these differences.[4]

IMPRESSION MANAGEMENT AND ETIQUETTE

Being an effective, responsible contributor is not always sufficient to gain the attention you deserve. It may also be necessary to make others aware of your capability. **Impression management** is a set of behaviors directed at enhancing one's image by drawing attention to oneself. Often the attention is directed toward superficial aspects of the self, such as clothing and appearance. Yet, impression management also includes doing a good job, telling people about your accomplishments, and appearing self-confident. The next subsections list specific tactics of impression management and discuss business etiquette. We discuss etiquette here because how you behave in certain situations shapes your image.

Tactics of Impression Management

Managing the impression you create encompasses hundred of specific tactics, limited only by your imagination of what will impress others. Impression management is also regarded as the process by which people control the impression others form of them. Part of your power in the organization stems from your formal position, as well as how you are perceived by others. Creating the right image is the practice of impression management.[5]

Although impression management can be used in a variety of relationships, it is most commonly found in the attempt of a worker to please the manager. For example, impression management is frequently used during performance evaluation in order to impress the manager with the worker's accomplishments. Six positive tactics of impression management are described next.

Display Organizational Citizenship Behavior. We mention organizational citizenship behavior in several places in our study of human relations because of its contribution to effective interpersonal relationships. A highly effective and meritorious way of creating a good impression is to step outside your job description to help coworkers and the company. You become admired for going beyond the call of duty.[6] Organizational citizenship behavior is generally aimed at helping others, yet it is possible that the motive underlying citizenship behavior is to foster a good impression. A prime example is that volunteering for special assignments helping others may provide workers with an opportunity to show off their talents and knowledge, leading to an enhanced image.

Impression management theorists argue that a primary human motive is to be viewed positively by others, and to avoid being viewed negatively. Engaging in organizational citizenship behavior is an effective means of being viewed positively in the sense of having positive motives for engaging in constructive behavior, such as collecting relief funds for a coworker whose apartment burned down.

Whether or not organizational citizenship behavior has an element of trying to look good, the balance of evidence is that citizenship behavior helps both individuals and the organization. On the basis of 168 studies involving more than 50,000 workers, it was found that organizational citizenship behavior helped individuals receive better performance ratings and salary increases. Organizations benefited in such ways higher productivity, lowered costs, and better customer service.[7] Another synthesis of studies found that when the level of organizational citizenship behavior in a work unit was high, work unit performance tended to be high.[8]

Perform Well, and Build Trust and Confidence. A key strategy for creating a positive impression with your immediate superior and higher ranking managers is performing well while at the same time building trust and confidence. In attempting to create a favorable impression, it is essential to remember that being a strong performer is impressive. Performing well is also the foundation for building a strong reputation.

At the same time, project the authentic impression of a person who can be trusted to carry out responsibilities faithfully and ethically. Rather than take action without permission (e.g., spending beyond budget), know the bounds of your authority and work within those bounds. Be aware that your boss has other responsibilities, so do not take more than your fair share of his or her time. You will generate an impression of confidence if you suggest alternative solutions to the problems you bring to your manager.

Be Visible and Create a Strong Presence. An essential part of impression management is to be perceived as a valuable contributor on the job. Visibility is attained in many ways, such as regular attendance at meetings and company social events, being assigned to important projects, and doing volunteer work in the community. Helping in the launch of a new product or redesigning work methods are other ways of attaining visibility and creating a strong presence. Face-to-face visibility is perhaps the best, but electronic visibility can also be effective. This includes making intelligent contributions to company intranets and blogs and sending e-mail messages of substance to the right people. Saying nice things about your company on social networking sites is valuable also. Terry Bragg observes that many employees are shocked to learn that they lost their jobs during a downsizing because upper management did not know that they were valuable contributors.[9]

Admit Mistakes. Many people believe that to create a good impression, it is best to deny or cover up mistakes. In this way, you will not appear vulnerable. A higher level of political skill is to admit mistakes, thereby appearing more forthright and trustworthy. The simple statement "I goofed" will often gain you sympathy and support, whereas an attempted cover up will decrease your social capital. For purposes of impression management, the bottom line of being wrong is to (1) admit the error, (2) request guidance, (3) step-up repair, and (4) learn from it.[10] Requesting guidance is important because it conveys the impression that you have humility and that you trust the advice and counsel of others. Here is an example of this tactic in action:

> *Cindy, a call center operator, is listening on the phone to a woman rant and rave about a $5.87 charge on her credit card that seems unwarranted. Thinking that*

she has the telephone receiver covered, Cindy says in a sigh of exasperation to a coworker, "I'm about to scream. I'm talking to the biggest jerk of year right now." Unfortunately, "the biggest jerk of the year" heard the comment and reported it to Cindy's supervisor.

During a review of the incident with her supervisor, Cindy said, "Yes indeed I made the comment," and then asked how to deal with the pressures of such an overreacting customer. Cindy offered to send a written apology to the customer. So far, Cindy has learned from her error and has not repeated the incident.

Minimize Being a Yes-Person.   A conventional view of organizational politics suggests that being a yes-person is an excellent way of developing a good relationship with higher-ups and generating the impression of a loyal and supportive subordinate. The yes-person operates by the principle, "the boss is always right." Often the boss cultivates yes-person behavior among subordinates by being intimidating and unapproachable.[11] When working for an emotionally secure and competent manager, you are likely to create a better impression by not agreeing with all the boss's ideas and plans. Instead, express constructive disagreement by explaining how the boss's plan might be enhanced, or an error might be avoided.

Assume that you work in the marketing department of the manufacturer of Jitterbug, a simplified cell phone that focuses on the senior market. Your boss suggests an advertising theme implying that even people with arthritis and those technically challenged can easily operate a Jitterbug. Your intuition tells you this theme would be a humiliating insult to seniors. So, you respond to your boss, "I know that Jitterbug targets seniors, but I suggest that we tone down the terms 'arthritis' and 'technologically challenged.' Why not be positive, and state that the keys are easy to manipulate, and the Jitterbug is as easy to operate as a landline phone?"

Create a Healthy Image.   A superficial yet important part of impression management is to project a healthy, physically fit appearance. Appearing physically fit in the workplace has gained in importance as many business firms offer workers rewards for being physically fit and avoiding smoking and obesity. Among the rewards offered by employers are electronic gadgets, discounted health insurance, and cash bonuses. As health insurance costs have steadily increased in recent years, companies have placed an even stronger emphasis on employees maintaining their physical and mental health. From an impression management perspective, being obese at health-conscious companies would be a negative.

Projecting an image of emotional fitness also contributes to a healthy image. *Emotional fitness* would include such behaviors as appearing relaxed, appropriate laughing and smiling, and a minimum of nervous mannerisms and gestures. Being physically fit helps project emotional fitness. When managing the impression you create, be mindful of the advice offered by William L. Gardner III. He urges that you be yourself. When selecting an image, do not attempt to be somebody you are not because people will see through this façade. Gardner concludes, "Make every effort to put your best foot forward—but never at the cost of your identity or integrity!"[12] Impression management is geared toward looking good, but not creating a false impression.

You need good political skills to be effective at impression management. A study of 204 employees working on environmental issues indicated that when employees with good political skill use impression management tactics, they are likely to receive higher job performance ratings from their supervisor. In contrast, individuals low in political skill who engage in impression management tend to be seen less positively by their supervisors.[13] In other words, you need a little finesse and sensitivity to people to be good at office politics.

Another essential part of impression management is to avoid creating a negative impression through such behaviors as being absent or late frequently, speaking poorly, or talking in a meeting while the presenter is speaking. The discussion of etiquette helps guide a person away from behaviors that would bring him or her negative attention.

The Elevator 30-Second Speech

A long-standing suggestion in career development and impressing higher-ups is to make a 30-second impromptu presentation when you have a chance encounter with a key person in your organization. If you work in an office tower, the chance encounter is likely to take place in an elevator—and it is generally frowned upon to have long conversations in an elevator. So the term *elevator speech* developed to describe a brief opportunity to impress a key person. Imagine that you have a chance encounter with a high-ranking executive in your area in the elevator, on the escalator, in the parking lot, during a company picnic, or at some other location. You then give that person a 30-second pitch geared to make a positive impression. Because you must boil your pitch down to 30 seconds, you will need to prepare for a long time. (Credit President Abraham Lincoln with that insight.)

About six different pairs (impresser and person to be impressed) will carry out this role-play in front of the class. The evaluators will put themselves in the role of the key person who was the target of the 30-second evaluation. Consider using the following scale, and answering the two questions:

_____ Wow, I was impressed. (5 points)

_____ I was kind of impressed with the person I ran into. (4 points)

_____ He or she left me with at least an average impression. (3 points)

_____ I found the person to be somewhat annoying. (2 points)

_____ That person I met left me with a terrible impression. (1 point)

1. What did I like about the person's 30-second pitch?

2. What did I see as possible areas for improvement?

Find a mechanism to feed back some of your observations to the role players. Volunteer to present the findings in class, give the person your comments on note paper, or send him or her an e-mail or text message.

Skill-Building Exercise 13-1 gives you an opportunity to try out a highly practical application of impression management.

Business Etiquette

A major component of managing your impression is practicing good etiquette. **Business etiquette** is a special code of behavior required in work situations. The term *manners* has an equivalent meaning. Both *manners* and *etiquette* generally refer to behaving in a refined and acceptable manner. Studying etiquette is important because knowing and using proper business etiquette contributes to individual and business success. Eliza Browning, a writer about small business, explains that etiquette is really about making people feel good and ensuring some basic social comforts.[14] For example, if you post a photo on Facebook of a coworker eating a hotdog at a picnic, will that make the person feel good?

business etiquette

A special code of behavior required in work situations.

People who are considerate of the feelings of others, and companies that are courteous toward customers, are more likely to succeed than their rude counterparts. Another perspective on etiquette is that it is a way of presenting yourself with the kind of polish that shows you can be taken seriously. So many people are rude and uncivil today that practicing good etiquette will often give you a competitive advantage.

Business etiquette includes many aspects of interpersonal relations in organizations, as described in the following discussion.[15] We have already discussed in Chapter 5 several aspects of etiquette in relation to the digital workplace. What is considered proper etiquette and manners in the workplace changes over time and may vary with the situation. At one time, addressing one's superior by his or her first name was considered brash. Today it is commonplace behavior. A sampling of etiquette guidelines is nevertheless helpful. A general principle of being considerate of the feelings of work associates is more important than any one act of etiquette or courtesy. Keep in mind also that you will find a few contradictory statements in writings about etiquette.

Etiquette for Work Behavior and Clothing. Work behavior etiquette includes all aspects of performing in the work environment, such as completing work on time, punctuality, being a good team player, listening to others, and following through. For instance, having the courtesy to complete a project when it is due demonstrates good manners and respect for the work of others.

Clothing might be considered part of general work behavior. The casual standards in the information technology field, along with dress-down days, have created confusion about proper office attire. A general rule is that *casual* should not be interpreted as sloppy, such as torn jeans or a stained sweatshirt. Many companies have moved back toward emphasizing traditional business attire, such as suits for men and women. In many work situations, dressing more formally may constitute proper etiquette.

Introductions. The basic rule for introductions is to present the lower ranking person to the higher ranking person regardless of age or sex. "Ms. Barker [the CEO], I would like you to meet my new coworker, Reggie Taylor." (Observe that the higher ranking person's name is mentioned first.) If the two people being introduced are of equal rank, mention the older one first. Providing a little information about the person being introduced is considered good manners. When introducing one person to the group, present the group to the individual. "Sid Foster, this is our accounts receivable team." When being introduced to a person, concentrate on the name and repeat it soon, thus enhancing learning. A fundamental display of good manners is to remember people's names and to pronounce them correctly. When dealing with people senior to you or of higher rank, call them by their last name and title until told otherwise. (Maybe Ms. Barker, above, will tell you, "Please call me Kathy.")

It is good manners and good etiquette to remember the names of work associates to whom you are introduced, even if you see them only occasionally. If you forget the name of a person, it is better to admit this than to guess and come up with the wrong name. Just say, "I apologize, but I have forgotten your name. Tell me once more, and I will not forget your name again."

Both men and women are expected to extend their right hand when being introduced. Give a firm, but not overpowering, handshake, and establish eye contact with the person you are greeting; however, some people are concerned about handshakes being unhygienic, so be willing to use the modern fist bump touch often used in social life and athletics. If the other person extends the fist, you do the same.

Relationships between Men and Women and between People of Different Ages. Social etiquette is based on chivalry and the gender of the person, whereas business etiquette is based on generally equal treatment for all. Women should no longer be treated differently when approaching a door, riding in an elevator, or walking in the street. According to the new rules, the person in the lead (no matter the gender or age) should proceed first and hold the door for the others following. A man should, however, still follow a woman when using an escalator. When using stairs, a man usually follows a woman going up and precedes her going down. Men no longer have to walk next to the street when walking with one or two women. Elders should still be respected, but not in such ways as holding doors open for them, helping them off with their overcoats, or getting coffee for them.

Unless you are good friends who typically hug when meeting, it is best to avoid touching others of the same or opposite sex except for a handshake. Some people believe that nonsexual touching is part of being charming and warm, yet many workers are offended when touched by another worker. The subject is controversial because public figures often drape their arms around others, and physical touching is part of the ritual of offering congratulations in sports. Of note, many athletic coaches have switched to fist bumping to say hello or offer congratulations to teenagers and young children to avoid being charged with sexually suggestive contact.

Social kissing should generally be minimzed in an American workplace, but it is welcome in Europe. Kissing in the workplace is generally regarded as rude except among close acquaintenances, yet it is more frequent in Europe; however, European kissing amounts to pecks on both cheeks or the top of the hand, never on the lips.

Dining. Etiquette surrounding meals involves planning for the meeting, making seating arrangements, bill paying, tipping, using proper table manners, and appropriate drinking of alcoholic beverages. We all know not to slurp spaghetti one strand at a time, pour ketchup over sauce, or leave a 50 cent tip. The key point is not to draw negative attention to you. Less obvious are the following guidelines:

- Arrange seating for meal meetings in advance.
- Establish with the server who will be paying the check.

- Place your napkin on your lap immediately after being seated.
- Bread should not be used to push food onto a fork or spoon.
- Attempt to pace your eating to those of others at the table.
- The wait staff, not the diners, should be responsible for moving plates around the table.
- Circulate rolls and bread to the right, not the left.
- Order an alcoholic beverage only when invited to do so by the person sponsoring the meal, and then only if he or she does. Do not get drunk or even high.

Working in a Cubicle or In an Open Seating Arrangement. Workplace cubicles were invented by fine arts professor Bob Probst in the 1960s, and they have been praised and condemned ever since. The praise generally relates to saving the company money on office space and having more open communication. The condemnation usually relates to lack of privacy, and therefore ties in directly with workplace etiquette.

Cubicles and open office spaces represent a major etiquette challenge because a variety of coworkers and superiors can observe your everyday work behavior.[16] Among the many etiquette challenges for the cubicle dweller or person working in a open space are: (1) speaking low enough into a wired phone so as not to annoy others or reveal confidential information, (2) not allowing a personal cell phone to ring during the workday, (3) not displaying material on the computer that others might find offensive, unless the subject is business related, (4) not wearing a sports cap indoors unless it is an acceptable part of the company culture, and (5) not taking care of personal hygiene such as dental flossing, hair spraying, or nail clipping (the person should do these activities at home).

Cubicle sizes have been shrunk recently or even eliminated to save on company real estate (as well as to foster face-to-face communication). As a result, people work even closer to each other physically. The etiquette challenges just mentioned have thereby intensified, particularly with respect to invading the privacy of others.[17]

Cross-Cultural Relations. What constitutes proper etiquette may differ from culture to culture. Be alert to differences in etiquette in areas such as gift giving, dining, drinking alcoholic beverages, and when and where to discuss business. A culture must be studied carefully, including asking questions, to understand what constitutes proper etiquette.

Many of these differences in customs were described in Chapter 8. Violating these customs is poor etiquette. For example, using the index finger to point is considered rude in most Asian and Middle Eastern countries. Also, people in Middle Eastern countries tend to stand as close as two or three inches from the person with whom they are talking. To back away is interpreted as an insult. An American visitor to China nearly lost a major sale because after receiving a business card from the Chinese company representative, he stuffed it in his pocket without first carefully reading the card. Proper etiquette in China is to carefully read the giver's business card, and perhaps hold it with both hands out of respect. We emphasize again that stereotypes such as those just mentioned refer to typical behavior and are accurate perhaps only about 70 percent of the time.

Suppose you are in doubt about the proper etiquette for any situation, and you do not have a handbook of etiquette readily available. As a substitute, observe how your host or a successful person in the group behaves.

Interaction with People with Physical Disabilities. Many able-bodied people are puzzled by what is proper etiquette in working with people with disabilities. Be as natural and open as you can. In addition, consider these guidelines for displaying good manners when dealing with a physical disability:

- Speak directly to a person with a disability, not to the person's companion.
- Don't assume that a person with a disability needs help. If someone is struggling, ask for permission to assist.
- When talking to a person in a wheelchair, place yourself at that person's eye level.
- When speaking to a person with impaired vision, identify yourself and anyone who may be with you. Do not shout when speaking to a blind person.

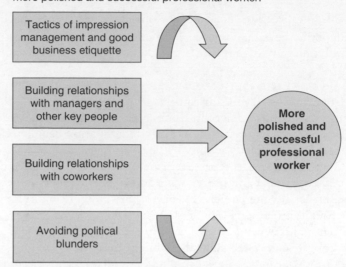

Impression management, building relationships with influential people, and avoiding political blunders all contribute to being a more polished and successful professional worker.

- To get the attention of a deaf person, tap the person's shoulder or wave your hand.
- Treat a person with a disability as you would anyone else, except for the differences noted in this list.[18]

As shown in Figure 13-2, impression management combined with managing relationships and avoiding political blunders contributes to being a more polished and successful professional worker.

Skill-Building Exercise 13-2 gives you an opportunity to practice appropriate etiquette in several situations.

BUILDING RELATIONSHIPS WITH MANAGERS AND OTHER KEY PEOPLE

LEARNING OBJECTIVE 3   The political purpose of building good relationships with managers is to gain power through such means as being recommended for promotion and key assignments. A good relationship with the boss is also important for the basic purpose of receiving a good

---

SKILL-BUILDING EXERCISE 13-2

Business Etiquette

An effective way of improving business etiquette is by using your best manners in real-life situations. Role-playing etiquette scenarios can also contribute to helping you develop the right mental set for using good etiquette.

Scenario 1: Dining Etiquette. A small group of students plan to conduct a high-etiquette meal at a local family restaurant during nonpeak hours. Pretend the stainless steel utensils are fine silver and that the glasses are crystal. Each class member uses his or her best etiquette. At the same time, each group member carefully observes the etiquette displayed by the other members.

At the conclusion of the meal, critique each other's etiquette. If you were courteous enough to invite your instructor to your high-etiquette meal, get his or her feedback.

Scenario 2: Telephone Etiquette. Two people using smartphones are separated by about six feet. Several pairs of students might conduct phone conversations covering such matters as discussing customer complaints, inquiring about a job, or asking about product availability. (*Note:* The students merely *pretend* they are using the phone, rather than waste phone minutes; however, should phone minutes not be an issue, a real phone call will add to the authenticity of the exercise.) Students not making the calls will carefully observe the callers. Look for examples of good and poor telephone etiquette. Feedback will be provided after the phone conversations are completed.

1. Network with influential people.
2. Help your manager succeed.
3. Conform to your manager's work style.
4. Understand unwritten boundaries.
5. Volunteer for assignments.
6. Flatter influential people sensibly.
7. Use information power.
8. Appear cool under pressure.
9. Laugh at your manager's humor.
10. Express constructive disagreement.
11. Present a clear picture of your accomplishments.

performance evaluation. Building these good relationships is also important because it helps create a positive, supportive work environment for you. Good relationships can also be established with managers for the nonpolitical purpose of trying to get the job accomplished. The strategies and tactics described next are outlined in Figure 13-3.

Network with Influential People

A basic success strategy is developing contacts, or **networking**, with influential people. In addition to making contacts, networking involves gaining the trust and confidence of the influential people. (Networking for job finding is described in Chapter 17.) Before you can network with influential people, you must identify who those power players are. (The executive quoted in the opening case advised about the importance of connecting with decision makers.) You might make observations of your own, such as listening for whose names are mentioned frequently by people in the company. Asking the opinions of others about which people influence decision making can be illuminating. Sometimes a person without a fancy job title might be a highly influential person. An example is that an administrative assistant might heavily influence the decisions of his or her boss.

Networking also takes place with people inside and outside the organization who are not your managers. Developing contacts with influential people is likely to pay big career dividends. A standard procedure is to create a card or computer file of the people in your network, and update it frequently. To keep your network effective, it is necessary to contact people on your list periodically. Developing a network of influential people requires alertness and planning. You have to identify influential people, and then think of a sensible reason to contact them. Here are a few possibilities:

networking

Developing contacts with influential people, including gaining their trust and confidence. Also, contacting friends and acquaintances and building systematically on these relationships to create a still-wider set of contacts that might lead to employment.

- Send an e-mail message to a high-ranking manager, offering a money-saving or revenue-producing suggestion. A related tactic is to inform the person of something of significance you did that might lie directly in his or her area of interest. Social networking sites such as Facebook, LinkedIn, and Twitter can be used for networking with influential people. An influential person who joins such a site is usually open to making new contacts. (You may find, that many influential people are not willing to become your "friend." You will, however, often be able to at least send them a message.)

- Do a standout job as a member of a task force or committee that includes a high-ranking official.

- Discuss your career plans with a neighbor who has an outstanding position.

- Take the initiative to develop a friendship with an influential person who is a member of your athletic club, YMCA, YWCA, or place of worship.

Networking is so often used—and abused—that suggestions and guidelines for networking etiquette have emerged. A starting point is to be clear, concise, and specific when making requests of networking contacts. Explain, for example, that you want to become an industry specialist and would like to acquire specific information. Be frank about the amount of time you would want from the network member, such as 15 minutes per month of e-mail and telephone contact.

After making contact with a potential network member, explain the benefit this person is likely to derive from his or her association with you. Provide a *benefit statement* for interacting with you and helping you with your career.[19] Indicate specifically how this person might benefit from you being in his or her network. (If a person is in your network, you are also in that person's network.) If the potential network member is more powerful than you, it is still possible to think of what benefit you might be able to provide. Two examples follow:

- I would like to contact you a few times a year about career concerns. In return, I would be happy to help you identify some groups on LinkedIn that might be worthwhile for our company to contact.
- In return for my receiving career advice from you from time to time, I would be happy to collect information for you about how people in my area perceive one of your products. I have lots of useful contacts in my community.

Avoid being a pest. Many influential people are bombarded with requests to be part of someone's network, so ask for a modest amount of time and assistance. Good networking etiquette is to request a collaborative relationship in which you give as much as you get. The benefit statement just mentioned will place you in a collaborative relationship with the influential person.

Help Your Manager Succeed

The primary reason you are hired is to help your manager achieve the results necessary to succeed. Avoid an adversarial relationship with your manager. Also figure out both obvious and subtle ways of ensuring the manager's success. One subtle way of increasing your manager's chances for success is to help out that person when he or she is under attack from another department. One example would be to supply information to support your manager's position on a controversial issue. Also keep in mind the cornerstone tactic of performing your job superbly. Your manager will then share in your success.

A specific relationship-building advantage of helping your manager succeed is that he or she is likely to develop loyalty toward you in such matters as recommending you for a bigger salary increase, and giving you a better performance evaluation. And during a downsizing, you are less likely to be tapped for job loss.

A contributor to helping your boss succeed is to listen carefully to what he or she expects from you.[20] When you have a clear image of what your boss expects, you know what the boss thinks is important for the work unit to suceed. For example, if you listen carefully to your boss's plea for rapid deliveries, and you faciliate rapid deliveries, you are helping him or her succeed.

Conform to Your Manager's Work Style

An advanced technique for establishing a good working relationship with a supervisor is to match your work style to his or her preferences and needs. A basic example is that your style might be to take a long time with an assignment in order to be thorough and avoid mistakes. Yet your boss is impatient and demands quick turnaround times for most assignments. To build a good working relationship with this supervisor, it would be helpful if you sacrificed some thoroughness for speed.

Leadership coach Miranda Wilcox advises professionals to be aware of a conflict in behavioral style with a manager. A frequent situation is that the superior might be detail-oriented and point out the tiniest imperfections in a subordinate's work. In contrast, the subordinate might focus on the broader purpose of an assignment and be less conscious of small details.[21] Or the situation could be reversed. To build rapport with the superior, it would therefore be best to adapt toward being detail oriented or big-picture oriented.

Another aspect of work style highly relevant is preferences with respect to communication. Some managers prefer frequent e-mails and text messages, whereas others prefer phone calls and even face-to-face conversations. To work well with the manager, it is best to accept his or her communication style. Another relevant aspect of adapting to a manager's communication style is frequency of updates on assignments. Some managers prefer almost daily progress reports, whereas others generally want to be informed about an assignment only when it is completed.

Don't worry about preserving your individuality. When you are in charge, others will have to adapt to your preferred work style.

Understand Unwritten Boundaries

A person skilled at positive organizational politics is able to read unwritten rules about who has the authority to do what. According to psychologist Judith Sills, there exist **unwritten boundaries,** or dividing lines of behavior appropriate to different roles. Many workers struggle with office problems that are boundary issues in disguise. Sills observes that boundaries for office interactions are like the rope lanes in a swimming pool. The purpose of the ropes is to enhance safety, but they can be budged or even removed depending on need, skill, and circumstance.

Unwritten boundaries deal with such issues as when it is appropriate to correct your boss, how much anger to display, which influential people you can invite to a social engagement, and whose speech or appearance you can criticize. A person with an exaggerated sense of his or her worth may have trouble that a boundary exists at all, such as one woman who felt free to protest angrily when her boss changed something in her report.[22] Two other examples of unacceptable boundary crossing are (1) a man who told a vice president that his hairpiece looked phony and (2) a woman who told her boss that she needed to upgrade her information technology skills to be a credible leader.

An example of successful boundary crossing took place when an accounts receivable specialist sent an unsolicited e-mail to the director of marketing. The young worker said that he grew up in Mexico and would be happy to provide input for the company's plans to penetrate the Mexican market. Although the accounts receivable worker was from outside of the marketing department, he was invited to participate in a focus group about expanding into the Mexican market.

Look for indicators as to whether boundaries can be crossed in your company. First, count the layers in your company's organization structure. The more layers (or more hierarchical) the company, the less welcome boundary crossing is likely to be. Look for established border crossings. Observe where people of different rank in the company mix. Among the possibilities are the fitness center, the cafeteria, and after-hours drinks. Make your first attempts at border crossing at those places.[23]

Volunteer for Assignments

An easily implemented method of winning the approval of superiors is to become a "hand raiser." By volunteering to take on assignments that do not fit neatly into your job description, you display the kind of initiative valued by employers. At the same time, you are practicing organizational citizenship behavior. Among the many possible activities to volunteer for are fundraising campaigns assigned to your company, project membership, and working overtime when most people prefer not to (e.g., on a Saturday in July). Task force and committee assignments are also useful for being noticed by key people in the organization. Offer to help coordinate a charity campaign such as the United Way. As a team member, volunteer to assume any leadership responsibility you think you can handle. If your team offers rotating leadership assignments, express an interest in taking your turn.

Flatter Influential People Sensibly

One of the most effective relationship builders is to flatter people sensibly and credibly. Despite the risk of being called obsequious or a cheap office politician, the flatterer wins.

Flattering an Influential Person

One student plays the role of a newcomer to the organization who is seeking to advance, or at least to secure, his or her position in the organization. Another person plays the role of a vice president of marketing who is visiting the newcomer's department. The company holds this vice president in high esteem because he or she recently spearheaded the introduction of a highly successful product, a *smart mattress*. The mattress adjusts to the temperature and firmness requirements of its user. In some models, the two sides of the mattress can have different settings to adapt to the heat and firmness preferences of two users sharing the same mattress.

The newcomer is asked to escort the vice president to another part of the building. The walk should take about five minutes, giving the newcomer an opportunity to work in some flattery. Fortunately, the newcomer has read the sales literature about the smart mattress, and has even tried out one in the factory showroom. Although the vice president is not naïve, he or she is proud of his or her accomplishments. The two role players conduct the five-minute walk, perhaps circling the classroom.

Observers rate the role players on two dimensions, using a 1-to-5 scale from very poor (1) to very good (5). One dimension is "effective use of flattery." The second dimension is "acting ability." A few observers might voluntarily provide feedback to the role players in terms of sharing their ratings and observations. The course instructor might also provide feedback.

A study indicated that even at the highest positions in business, flattery helps a person get ahead. Specifically, ingratiating yourself to the CEO, including flattery, was a major factor in receiving an appointment as a board of director at major companies. Not carefully monitoring (carefully scrutinizing) the CEO's activities also worked in a person's favor for obtaining a board appointment.[24] You might interpret not finding fault with a CEO to be a subtle form of flattery.

Flattery is likely to be effective because most people want to receive accolades, even if they are not completely warranted. People who pay us compliments are likely to be treated kindly in turn.[25] Recent evidence supports the idea that constructive compliments are not overblown. Descriptions of what went right are more effective than evaluative phrases, such as "magnificent" or "extraordinary." An effective, general-purpose piece of flattery is to tell another person that you are impressed by something he or she accomplished. Rather than telling an influential person that he or she is a genius, you might say to a manager after a meeting:[26] "Everyone in the meeting was listening so attentively when you gave your report. And the industry statistics you found really drove home the point."

Another way of flattering somebody is to listen attentively. If you actively listen to the other person, he or she will feel flattered. The person might think, "What I have to say is valuable. This person really cares about what I have to offer." Flattery can also take the form of quoting another person or referring to something he or she said to you earlier.

During the next two weeks, try flattering an influential person. In the interim, do Skill-Building Exercise 13-3.

Use Information Power

Power accrues to those who control vital information. At the same time, being a source of useful information will help you build constructive working relationships with managers. You will be relied on as an important contributor. Controlling vital information includes knowing how to gain access to useful information that others do not know how to retrieve. Many workers are aware of the mechanics of using the Internet, but fewer have the skills to use the Internet to retrieve commercially useful information. During a tight labor market, for example, human resource specialists can acquire power if they know how to use the Internet to find talented people who might want to join the company. These specialists have knowledge beyond using commercially available Internet recruiting services.

Information power is closely related to *expert power*, which refers to having valuable expertise. If your expertise or skill is in high demand at the moment, power will flow in your direction. Currently, an important type of expert power is being able to use social networking sites to gain publicity for products (including creating a buzz for the product) and to recruit employees.

Appear Cool Under Pressure

Showing signs of panic generally hurts your reputation with influential people. In contrast, appearing to be in emotional control when things around you are falling apart helps convey the impression that you are worthy of additional responsibility. Being cool under pressure is part of emotional stability, and it is a key leadership characteristic. Coolness under pressure is often displayed during a crisis such as a flood, hurricane, or fire. The manager who can get the operation, including store, factory, hospital, or call center, back and running within a week is perceived to work extraordinarily well under pressure. Many managers at McDonald's and Walmart enhanced their relationship with corporate executives because they responded so quickly and positively to the ravages of Hurricane Katrina. Locating and aiding displaced employees were part of the heroic efforts of these managers.

Laugh at Your Manager's Humor

When you indicate by your laughter that you appreciate your manager's sense of humor, it helps establish rapport between the two of you. An indicator of good two-way communication between people is that the two parties comprehend each other's subtle points. Most humor in the workplace deals with subtle meanings about work-related topics. To implement the tactic of laughing at your manager's jokes, do not worry excessively about having heard the joke before.

Express Constructive Disagreement

At one time the office politician thought an effective way of pleasing the boss was to be a "yes-person," as mentioned earlier. A more intelligent tactic in the modern business world is to be ready to disagree in a constructive manner when you sincerely believe that the boss is wrong. In the long run, you will probably earn more respect than if you agree with the boss just to please him or her. Constructive disagreement is based on a careful analysis of the situation and is also tactful.

The right way to disagree means not putting your manager in a corner or embarrassing your manager by confronting him or her loudly or in public. If you disagree with your boss, use carefully worded, inoffensive statements. In this way, you minimize the chances of a confrontation or hostile reaction. Remember the smart mattress mentioned in Skill-Building Exercise 13-3? Suppose the marketing vice president claims that the mattress is geared exclusively toward the senior citizen market, and you disagree. You might say, "I think that marketing our smart mattress to seniors is a breakthrough. Yet, I also see some other possibilities. There are loads of cold-sensitive young people who want a heated mattress. Also, a lot of young people with athletic injuries or orthopedic problems would welcome an adjustable mattress. Does my thinking make any sense?"

The reason constructive disagreement helps you build a good relationship with most managers is that the boss comes to respect your job knowledge and your integrity; however, if you are working with a very insecure boss, he or she may be taken aback by disagreement. In that case, you have to be extra tactful in expressing disagreement.

Present a Clear Picture of Your Accomplishments

"What have you done for me lately?" is a question on the minds of many managers. To the extent that you can clearly document what you have accomplished recently, as well as in the past, you are therefore likely to enhance your relationship with your manager. You can help your manager better understand your contributions by explaining exactly what work you are doing, problems you are solving, and the successes you are attaining. Document legitimately what you have accomplished, and communicate it in a factual, matter-of-fact manner. The occasional FYI e-mail provides useful documentation, provided you do not appear to be bragging.[27] A collection agent might report to her boss, "In March, I collected an average of $310 from my block of delinquent accounts. So far, I have collected at least something from 25 out of the 31 accounts I am currently assigned. We should be getting something from three more of these delinquent accounts."

BUILDING RELATIONSHIPS WITH COWORKERS AND OTHER WORK ASSOCIATES

Another strategy for increasing your power is to form alliances with coworkers and other work associates. You need the support of these people to get your work accomplished. Also, when you are being considered for promotion, coworkers and other work associates may be asked their opinion of you. Under a peer-evaluation system, the opinion of coworkers about your performance counts heavily. Long-term research conducted by Tom Rath of the Gallup Organization with many thousands of employees emphasizes the contribution of friendships and alliances in the workplace. Rath concludes that employees who have a best friend in the office are more productive and more likely to have positive interactions with customers, share ideas, and stay longer on the job. Also, many workers succeed or fail based on the support and involvement of best friends.[29] (The term *best* appears to imply that the contact is not simply an acquaintance or someone on your contact list on a social networking Web site.)

Another perspective on the importance of cooperation in the workplace is that cooperation enhances happiness and satisfaction. Long-term research by the University of Haifa psychology professor Richard Schuster says that it is natural for humans, as well as other animals, to want to cooperate. Schuster posits that evolution has prodded us toward enjoying the company of other people, and toward cooperation. He adds that social behavior is its own reward.[30]

Figure 13-4 lists eight strategies and techniques for developing good interpersonal relationships at or below your level. The information about developing teamwork skills presented in Chapter 6 is also relevant here.

Maintain Honest and Open Relationships

Although being honest may appear to contradict organizational politics, it is representative of the nature of positive politics. Openness and honesty also helps build trust among coworkers. Giving coworkers frank but tactful answers to their requests for your opinion is one useful way of developing open relationships. Assume that a coworker asks your opinion of an e-mail he intends to send to his supervisor. As you read it, you find it somewhat incoherent and filled with spelling and grammatical errors. An honest response to this message might be: "I think your idea is a good one. But I think your e-mail needs more work before that idea comes across clearly."

Accurately expressing your feelings, whether positive or negative, also leads to constructive relationships. If you have been singled out for good performance, let other team members know that you are happy and proud. If you arrive at work upset over a personal problem and appear obviously fatigued, you can expect some reaction. A coworker might say, "What seems to be the problem? Is everything all right?" A dishonest reply would be "Everything is fine." In addition to making an obviously untrue statement, you would also be perceived as rejecting the person who asked the question. If you prefer not to discuss your problem, an honest response would be, "Thanks for your interest. I am facing some problems today, but I think things will work out."

FIGURE 13-4 Strategies and Tactics for Developing Relationships with Coworkers and Other Work Associates

1. Maintain honest and open relationships.
2. Make others feel important.
3. Be diplomatic.
4. Exchange favors.
5. Ask for advice.
6. Share constructive gossip.
7. Minimize microinequities.
8. Follow group norms.

Another advantage of honest and open relationships is that they foster collaboration, which improves teamwork and organizational performance. Almost any successful workplace has high levels of collaboration among employees, such as the spirit of teamwork that exists at online retailer Zappos Inc. (known primarily for shoes).

One of the swiftest ways of breaking down honest and open relationships with coworkers is to **backstab**—an attempt to discredit by underhanded means, such as innuendo, accusation, or the like. The backstabber will pretend to be your friend, but will say something negative behind your back in an attempt to discredit you. For example, your rival might say to the manager, "I'm worried about the health of _____. She seems so preoccupied that it's difficult to get her attention to talk about any work problems." During times of less job security, including downsizings due to mergers, workers are more likely to say negative things about coworkers to gain advantage. Also, when a promotion is at stake, coworkers are more likely to say negative things about each other to a common boss.[31]

backstab

An attempt to discredit by underhanded means, such as innuendo, accusation, or the like.

Make Others Feel Important

A fundamental principle of fostering good relationships with coworkers and others is to make them feel important. Although the leader has the primary responsibility for satisfying this recognition need, coworkers also play a key role. One approach to making a coworker feel important would be to bring a notable accomplishment of his or hers to the attention of the group. Investing a small amount of time in recognizing a coworker can pay large dividends in terms of cultivating an ally. Expressing an interest in the work of others helps them feel important. A basic way to accomplish this end is to ask other employees questions that express an interest in their work, such as the following:

- How is your work going?
- How does the company use output from your department?
- How did you establish all the contacts you did to be so successful in sales?
- How did you develop the skills to do your job?

Expressing an interest in the work of others is also an effective tactic because so many people are self-centered. They are eager to talk about their own work, but rarely pause to express a genuine interest in others. Expressing an interest in the work of others is also effective because it is a form of recognition.

Self-Assessment Quiz 13-3 gives you an opportunity to think about your tendencies toward making others feel important.

Be Diplomatic

Despite all that has been said about the importance of openness and honesty in building relationships, most people fail to be convinced. Their egos are too tender to accept the raw truth when faced with disapproval of their thoughts or actions. Diplomacy is still an essential part of governmental and office politics. Translated into action, diplomacy often means finding the right phrase to convey disapproval, disagreement, or discontent. Here is an example of a delicate situation and the diplomatic phrase used to handle it.

> *During a staff meeting, a coworker suggests that the entire group schedule a weekend retreat to formulate a strategic plan for the department. The boss looks around the room to gauge the reactions of others to the proposal. You want to say: "What a stupid idea. Who needs to ruin an entire weekend to do something we could easily accomplish on a workday afternoon?" The diplomatic response is: "I've heard that retreats sometimes work, but would spending that much time on the strategic plan be cost effective? Maybe we could work on the plan during one long meeting. If we don't get the planning accomplished in that time frame, we could then consider the offsite."*

Exchange Favors

An important part of human interaction on and off the job is to reciprocate with others, thereby enhancing cooperation. Exchanging favors with others can make it easier for

How Important Do I Make People Feel?

Directions: Indicate how frequently you act (or would act if the situation presented itself) in the ways indicated ahead: Very Infrequently (VI); Infrequently (I); Sometimes (S); Frequently (F); Very Frequently (VF). Circle the number underneath the column that best fits your answer.

No.		VI	I	S	F	VF
1.	I do my best to correctly pronounce a coworker's name.	1	2	3	4	5
2.	I avoid letting other people's egos get too big.	5	4	3	2	1
3.	I brag to others about the accomplishments of my coworkers.	1	2	3	4	5
4.	I recognize the birthdays of friends in a tangible way.	1	2	3	4	5
5.	It makes me anxious to listen to others brag about their accomplishments.	5	4	3	2	1
6.	After hearing that a friend has done something outstanding, I shake his or her hand.	1	2	3	4	5
7.	If a friend or coworker recently received a degree or certificate, I would offer my congratulations.	1	2	3	4	5
8.	If a friend or coworker finished second in a contest, I would inquire why he or she did not finish first.	5	4	3	2	1
9.	If a coworker showed me how to do something, I would compliment that person's skill.	1	2	3	4	5
10.	When a coworker starts bragging about a family member's accomplishments, I do not respond.	5	4	3	2	1

Total Score _____

Scoring and Interpretation: Total the numbers corresponding to your answers. Scoring 40 to 50 points suggests that you typically make people feel important; 16 to 39 points suggests that you have a moderate tendency toward making others feel important; 10 to 15 points suggests that you need to develop skill in making others feel important. Study this chapter carefully.

people to accomplish their work because they are able to call on assistance when needed. The adept political player performs a favor for another employee without asking a favor in return. The favor is then cashed in when a favor is needed. Several examples of workday exchanges are as follows:

- A paralegal agrees to help another overburdened paralegal in the same law office, knowing that the other paralegal will reciprocate if needed in the future.

- A credit manager agrees to expedite a credit application for a sales representative. In reciprocation, the sales rep agrees not to commit the company to a delivery date on the next sale until the customer's credit has been evaluated.

- An assistant restaurant manager agrees to substitute for another assistant manager on New Year's Eve. A month later, the first person asks the second to take over her shift so that she can get away for the weekend.

Ask for Advice

Asking advice on technical and professional topics is a good way of building relationships with other employees. Asking for advice from another person—someone whose job does not require giving it—will usually be perceived as a compliment. Asking advice transmits the message, "I trust your judgment enough to ask your opinion on something important to me." You are also saying, "I trust you enough to think that the advice you give me will be in my best interest." Asking advice is also a subtle form of flattery because it shows that you value the person's judgment.

To avoid hard feelings, inform the person whose advice you are seeking that his or her opinion will not necessarily be binding. A request for advice might be prefaced with a comment such as, "I would like your opinion on a problem facing me. But I can't guarantee that

I'll be in a position to act on it." As with any other political tactic, asking for advice must be done in moderation. Too much advice asking can make you appear to be indecisive or a pest.

Share Constructive Gossip

An effective way of building workplace relationships is to share constructive gossip with others. Gossip has been defined in many ways, but as used here refers to talk about other people, usually assumed to be based on fact.[32] Gossip serves as a socializing force because it is a mode of intimate relationships for many employees. Workers get close to each other through the vehicle of gossip. It also serves as the lifeblood of personal relationships on the job. If you are the person supplying the gossip, people will develop positive attitudes toward you. **Constructive gossip** is unofficial information that supports others, is based on truth, and respects confidential information. Given these restrictions, here are two examples of positive gossip:

constructive gossip
Unofficial information that supports others, is based on truth, and excepts confidential information.

- "I heard that business is really picking up. If this week is any example, the company's profits for the quarter will far exceed expectations."
- "I heard yesterday that the director of public relations just got engaged to a cool guy she met on a cruise."

Minimize Microinequities

A potent way of alienating coworkers is to snub them, or put them down, in a small way without being aware of your behavior. A **microinequity** is a small, semiconscious message we send with a powerful impact on the receiver. A microinequity might also be considered a subtle slight. The inequity might take the form of ignoring another person, a snub, or a sarcastic comment. Understanding microinequities can lead to changes in one-on-one relationships that may profoundly irritate others.[33]

microinequity
A small, semiconscious message we send with a powerful impact on the receiver.

Imagine that you are in line in the company cafeteria with three coworkers. You turn around and notice an old friend from school who is visiting the company. Next, you introduce your old friend to two of the coworkers with you, but not the third. That coworker is likely to feel crushed and irritated, and it will take you awhile to patch your relationship. Looking at a microinequity from the standpoint of the receiver, a work associate might say to you, "Some computer-illiterate person sent me an e-mail this morning without the attachment he said was there." You respond, "Excuse me, but that *computer-illiterate person* was me."

To overcome giving microinequities, it is important to think through the consequences of what you are doing and saying before taking action. In the cafeteria situation described earlier, you might say to yourself, "Here comes time for an introduction, and this is not easy for me. I will remember to introduce everybody to my old friend."

Follow Group Norms

A summary principle to follow in getting along with coworkers is to heed **group norms**, the unwritten set of expectations for group members. Group norms also take the form of social cues about how to act, and they therefore contribute to the organizational culture. Representative group norms include the following: (1) help coworkers with problems if you have the right expertise, (2) do not wear formal business attire on casual dress days, (3) have lunch with your coworkers at least once a week, (4) do not complain to the boss about a coworker unless his or her negative behavior is outrageously bad, (5) do not take a sick day unless you are really sick, (6) take your turn in bringing snacks to a meeting at least once a month, and (7) side with your coworkers rather than management when there is a dispute between the two groups.

group norms
The unwritten set of expectations for group members.

Image Source/Corbis Images

If you do not deviate too far from these norms, the group will accept much of your behavior. If you do deviate too far, you will be subject to much rejection and therefore lose some of your power base. Yet if you conform too closely to group norms, higher level management may perceive you as unable to identify with management. Employees are sometimes blocked from moving up the ladder because they are regarded as "one of the gang."

Some of the relationship building described in the previous seven strategies and tactics is now being done on company social networking sites. These sites are being used to connect employees who have limited opportunity to meet face-to-face, or who simply prefer the Internet for most of their social interactions. Often the company social networking sites are supplemented with Web sites such as Facebook and Twitter because so many employees from the same firm might be members. For many workers, social networks provide a desirable way of communicating because they include photos, videos, and personal information like hobbies and music preferences, all of which are good for relationship building.

Skill-Building Exercise 13-4 provides an opportunity to practice several of the techniques for building interpersonal relationships with coworkers and other work associates.

The accompanying Job-Oriented Interpersonal Skills in Action box illustrates many of the points made so far about developing constructive workplace relationships.

AVOIDING POLITICAL BLUNDERS

LEARNING OBJECTIVE 5 A strategy for not losing whatever power you have accumulated is to refrain from making power-eroding blunders. Committing these politically insensitive acts can also prevent you from attaining power. Self-Assessment Quiz 13-4 will get you started thinking about blunders. Several leading blunders are described in the quiz.

1. **Criticizing your manager in a public forum.** The oldest saw in human relations is to "praise in public and criticize in private." Yet in the passion of the moment, you may still surrender to the irresistible impulse to criticize your manager publicly. As a result, the manager will harbor resentment toward you and perhaps block your chances for advancement.

2. **Bypassing the manager.** Many people believe that because most organizations are more democratic today, it is not important to respect the layers of authority (the chain of command). In reality, following etiquette is highly valued in most firms. Going around the manager to resolve a problem is therefore hazardous. You might be able to accomplish the bypass, but your career could be damaged and your recourses limited. It is much better to work out differences with your manager using standard methods of resolving conflict.

3. **Displaying disloyalty.** Being disloyal to your organization is a basic political blunder. Making it known that you are looking for a position elsewhere is the best-known form of disloyalty. Criticizing your company in public settings, praising the high quality of competitors' products, and writing angry internal e-mail messages about your company are others. You may not get fired, but overt signs of disloyalty may place you in permanent disfavor.

SKILL-BUILDING EXERCISE 13-4

Getting Along with Coworkers Role-Play

An inventory auditor in a department store chain decides to take action aimed at getting along better with coworkers. In each of the following two scenarios, one person plays the role of the inventory auditor. Another person plays the role of an employee whom the auditor is attempting to cultivate.

Scenario 1: Exchanging Favors. The auditor decides to strike a bargain with a store associate. (The role player decides what this exchange of favors should be.) Unknown to the auditor, the store associate is concerned about an inventory audit because he or she is worried about being accused of stealing merchandise.

Scenario 2: Expressing an Interest in Their Work. The auditor decides to express an interest in a tech fixer because he or she can be a valuable ally when conducting an inventory audit. The inventory audit is computerized, and the appropriate software is confusing and crashes frequently. The tech fixer has a heavy workload and is not prone toward small talk, but he or she does get excited talking about information technology.

For both scenarios, observers rate the role players on two dimensions, using a 1-to-5 scale from very poor (1) to very good (5). One dimension is "effective use of human relations techniques." The second dimension is "acting ability." A few observers might voluntarily provide feedback to the role players in terms of sharing their ratings and observations. The course instructor might also provide feedback.

After these scenarios have been completed, the class might discuss favors they have exchanged on the job that helped build relationships. Strive for at least five students to present examples of exchanges that enhanced their working relationships.

Ed Rosenfeld, CEO of Steve Madden Ltd., Focuses on Congenial Relationships

At age 33, Ed Rosenfeld was appointed as CEO of the popular shoe and accessories retailer and manufacturer, Steve Madden Ltd. Rosenfeld had worked with founder Steve Madden as a client. Madden invited him to join the firm as the executive vice president of strategic planning and finance because of his excellent work and consistently good attitude. Raised in Michigan and an alumni of Amherst College, Rosenfeld learned retailing in the family department store. He acquired more in-depth knowledge about retailing as an investment banker at Peter J. Solomon Company.

Madden once described Rosenfeld as having the demeanor of a "warm bath." A friend of Rosenfeld posted a comment saying she was fortunate enough to know him personally. "He is such an amazing, thoughtful man. He deserves so much credit for everything he does, and for staying down-to-earth while doing it."

When Rosenfeld visits a company store or factory, he smiles frequently, greets almost every employee he meets by name, and pauses to make small talk. He is quick to share credit when discussing the impressive success of the company with Wall Street analysts. In 2012, he was explaining the success of the company during a challenging retail environment. He said that the solid performance was ". . . a testament to the power of our brands, talent of Steve (the founder) and his design team, and the enduring strength of our business model."

Part of Rosenfeld's charm has been attributed to his use of self-effacing humor and friendliness. When asked about his greatest challenge as a young CEO of a major corporation, he responded, "Convincing people that I didn't steal my business cards from the real CEO of Steve Madden." When asked about the best part of his job, Rosenfeld said, "Working with lots of creative people." When asked about the worst part, he said, "Working with lots of creative people."

Rosenfeld's enthusiasm for the present and future of his financially successful company helps to build a spirit of optimism among employees. He mentioned at one point that the company's new handbag business is "on fire." He also talks about how effectively his company implements the creative marketing ideas developed by his staff.

Questions

1. In what way does Rosenfeld display positive political skills?
2. What does this brief sketch of Rosenfeld suggest about the relationship between company financial success and the personality of the CEO?

Source: Original story created from facts in the following sources: "Steve Madden: Ed Rosenfeld," *Question(NY)aire* (http://questionnyaire.blogspot.com/2010/04/steve-madden-ed-rosenfeld.html), April 9, 2010, pp. 1–3; "10 Most Powerful CEOs Under 40," *http://www.therichest.org*, April 5, 2011, p. 1; "Handbags 'On Fire' at Steve Madden?" *http://*www.accessoriesmagazine.com, July 27, 2012, pp. 1: Steven Madden's CEO Discusses Q2 2012 Results—Earnings Call Transcript," *Seeking Alpha* (http://seekingalpha.com), July 26, 2012, pp. 2–3; "40 under 40: The Merchant, Ed Rosenfeld, Chairman and CEO, Steven Madden," *Fortune*, November 1, 2010. p. 116.

The Blunder Quiz

Directions: Check whether you agree or disagree with the following statements.

	Agree	Disagree
1. It's fine to criticize your manager in a meeting as long as the criticism is valid.	_____	_____
2. If I objected to a decision made by top management, I would send a company-wide e-mail explaining my objection.	_____	_____
3. I am willing to insult any coworker if the insult is deserved.	_____	_____
4. I see no problem in using competitors' products or services and letting my superiors know about it.	_____	_____
5. If I thought the CEO of my company were way overpaid, I would send him or her an e-mail making my opinion known.	_____	_____
6. Never bother with company-sponsored social events, such as holiday parties, unless you are really interested.	_____	_____
7. I would not attend a company social function if I had the chance to attend another social activity of more interest to me.	_____	_____
8. I am very open about passing along confidential information.	_____	_____
9. I openly brag (or would brag) about using a competitive product or service (such as an Apple employee praising his or her Blackberry smartphone).	_____	_____
10. I avoid any deliberate attempt to please or impress coworkers or superiors.	_____	_____

Scoring and Interpretation: The greater the number of statements you agree with, the more prone you are to political blunders that can damage your interpersonal relationships and your career. You need to raise your awareness level of blunders on the job.

4. **Being a pest.** Common wisdom suggests that diligently pressing for one's demands is the path to success. This may be true up to a point, but when assertiveness is used too often it becomes annoying to many people. The overpersistent person comes to be perceived as a pest, and this constitutes a serious political blunder. An example of being a pest would be asking your manager every month when you are going to receive the raise you deserve.

5. **Being a chronic complainer.** We all have a right to express differences of opinion, and to make suggestions for improvement. Yet the chronic complainer winds up alientating superiors as well as coworkers, and will often be perceived as having a toxic personality. Expressing the occasional constructive disagreement is more effective than frequently expressing discontent with the actions of others. In the words of tech blogger Steve Tobak, ". . . those who do all the complaining are the ones who make the workplace a living hell, not the people or stuff they are always complaining about."[34]

6. **Being (or being perceived as) a poor team player.** An employee is expected to be a good team player in almost all organizations because cooperation makes collective effort possible. If you are a poor team player, or are perceived as such, your chances for promotion will diminish because you will be recognized as having poor interpersonal skills. Among the ways to be perceived as a poor team player are to engage in social loafing, miss many department meetings, take too much credit for group accomplishments, and minimize your interactions with coworkers. In short, if you ignore all the advice about team play presented in Chapter 6, you will be committing a political blunder.

7. **Burning your bridges.** A potent political blunder is to create ill will among former employers or people who have helped you in the past. The most common form of bridge burning occurs when a person departs from an organization. A person who leaves involuntarily is especially apt to express anger toward those responsible for the dismissal. Venting your anger may give a temporary boost to your emotional wellbeing, but it can be detrimental in the long run.

8. **Indiscreet behavior in private life.** Employees are representatives of the company, so their behavior off the job is considered to contribute to their performance—particularly for managers, supervisors, and professionals with visible jobs. Embarrassing the company will often lead to dismissal, combined with a negative reputation that will be difficult to shake for purposes of future employment. Indiscreet behavior in private life that can lead to dismissal includes being caught shoplifting, a citation for drunk driving, being arrested for a drug offense, charges of sexual harassment or rape, and assault and battery.

9. **Making derogatory comments about your employer on the Internet.** Large numbers of employees in recent years have been reprimanded or fired because they wrote nasty comments about their company on a blog or social networking site. (One such comment on Twitter: "Our CEO s hould hire a bodyguard. He rakes in millions yet fires thousands.") As we all know, a rant about your company or boss on a social networking site becomes a permanent record, and will almost inevitably be referred to a company executive. Even if you are not fired or severely reprimanded for your public display of hostility, you will have lost considerable political capital—even if your rant is merited.

If you want to overcome having committed a blunder, avoid defensiveness. Demonstrate that you are more interested in recovering from the blunder than in trying to share the blame for what happened. Focus on solutions to the problem rather than faultfinding. Suppose that you have been too critical of your team leader in a recent team meeting. Explain that your attempts to be constructively critical backfired and that you will choose your words more carefully in the future.

Another way to patch up a blunder is to stay poised. Admit that you made the mistake and apologize, but don't act or feel inferior. Mistakes are inevitable in a competitive work environment. Avoid looking sad and distraught. Instead, maintain eye contact with people when you describe your blunder.

Concept Review and Reinforcement

Key Terms

Summary

Positive political tactics help build good interpersonal relationships. Organizational politics refers to gaining power through any means other than merit or luck. Power refers to the ability or potential to control anything of value and influence decisions. Organizational politics can also be regarded from the standpoint of interpersonal relationships and sizing up the environment. Political skill is related to awareness of one's surroundings, emotional and social intelligence, and relationship building with the leader.

Impression management is one aspect of organizational politics. Managing the impression you create encompasses a wide range of behaviors designed to create a positive influence on work associates, including displaying organizational citizenship behavior, building trust and confidence, being visible and creating a strong presence, minimizing being a yes-person, and creating a healthy image. Also, attempt to be authentic, be aware that political skill is needed to manage one's impression, and avoid creating a negative impression.

A major component of managing the impression you create is business etiquette. The general principle of etiquette is to be considerate of the feelings of work associates, and to make others feel good. Areas of business etiquette include the following: work behavior and clothing, introductions, relationships between men and women and between people of different ages, working in a cubicle or open seating arrangement, cross-cultural relations, and interaction with people with disabilities.

(Etiquette related to the digital world was covered in Chapter 5.)

Political strategies and tactics for building relationships with managers and other key people include networking with influential people, helping your manager succeed, conforming to your manager's work style, understanding unwritten boundaries, volunteering for assignments, flattering influential people sensibly, using information power, admitting mistakes, appearing cool under pressure, laughing at your manager's humor, expressing constructive disagreement, and presenting a clear picture of your accomplishments.

Political strategies and tactics for developing relationships with coworkers and other work associates include maintaining honest and open relationships, making others feel important, being diplomatic, exchanging favors, asking for advice, sharing constructive gossip, minimizing microinequities, and following group norms.

A strategy for not losing whatever power you have accumulated is to refrain from making political blunders. Political blunders can also prevent you from attaining power. Representative blunders include criticizing your manager publicly, bypassing your manager, displaying disloyalty, being a pest, being a chronic complainer, being a poor team player and burning your bridges, indiscreet behavior in private life, and making derogatory comments about your employer on the Internet. If you want to make up for a blunder, avoid defensiveness and stay poised.

Questions for Discussion and Review

1. To what extent are office politics skills important for a person who is technically competent and hardworking?

2. Imagine you have just been employed in a new job. How do you acquire the unwritten rules of your new workplace?

3. Remember the leader–member exchange theory from Chapter 10 about leadership? What steps could you take to become part of your boss's in-group?

4. What advantages could you gain by working in a cubicle or in an open seating arrangement rather than a single person office?

5. Suggest how you could gain information power.

6. It has been observed that corporate employees who work mostly from their homes or other remote locations often put more effort into building their networks than people who work in a traditional office. Why might this be true?

7. It has been said that although most businesspeople can see through flattery, the technique still works. How would you explain this observation?

8. Give an example of a *microinequity* that you have been subjected to, or that you observed happen to another person. Explain why the incident is a microinequity.

9. In what way might being politically incorrect be a political blunder?

10. Why might the study of organizational politics seem more relevant to people with at least several years of work experience than to career beginners?

The Web Corner

http://career-advice.monster.com
(Building a solid realtionship with your boss)

http://www.ExecutivePlanet.com
(Guide to international business culture and etiquette in more than 35 countries)

http://www.techrepublic.com/blog/10-things/10-workplace-blunders-to-avoid-at-all-costs/
(10 workplace blunders to avoid at all cost)

Internet Skill Builder: Sharpening Your Compliments

An important part of being a skilled office politician, as well as a government one, is to compliment people effectively. The information about flattery contained in the chapter gave you some ideas about how to use compliments effectively. Search the Internet for a few more useful suggestions for giving compliments to others. Try out this week the best idea you find in this skill-building assignment. Observe the results of your compliment so that you can refine your technique.

Developing Your Human Relations Skills

Interpersonal Relations Case 13.1

The Talkative Boss

Suzanne, a claims adjuster, looked up from her desk as she saw her boss, Aaron, approaching. Suzanne muttered to herself, "I hope Aaron has a brief question related to my job. I don't have time to talk with him this morning. If I don't get this complicated claim processed this morning, the sales department will be screaming at me."

"Hi Suzanne," said Aaron. "It looks like another beautiful day here in Monterey. There's not a cloud in the sky. It's criminal to be inside on such a nice day. My family and I would love to be down at the beach. How are things going for you today?"

"Nothing too bad is happening," said Suzanne. "I'll be caught up with my work soon. I'm on a rush job right now. The sales department is pushing me to get this complicated claim finished by noon today."

"Suzanne, don't let the sales department hassle you. They want everything right away. Somehow the sales department doesn't realize that claims adjusting takes a lot of painful attention to detail. Better late than lousy, I always say."

"I don't disagree with you, Aaron. It's just that not getting a claim processed on time makes me a little nervous. We could lose a big customer by being late on paying this claim."

"Don't be so uptight, Suzanne. You're too young for high blood pressure or a coronary," responded Aaron.

Aaron proceeded to engage Suzanne in general conversation for another 15 minutes before he received a text message from his assistant. "Sorry we don't have enough time to finish our business," said Aaron as he left Suzanne's cubicle.

Suzanne then worked through her lunch hour and turned in her claims report one hour late. Perplexed, she telephoned Lori, a coworker in another department, and asked if she would be able to meet on a bench outside the office building after work for a few minutes.

After the two were comfortably seated, Suzanne lamented to Lori: "I just don't know what to do about Aaron. He's gobbling up my time. At least three days a week he sits in front of my desk chatting for fifteen minutes about nothing in particular. If I look like I want him to leave, he becomes annoyed. Once when I tried to politely get Aaron away from my desk, he told me that our conference was not over until he said it was."

"What really worries me is that Aaron sometimes chastises me for being late with my work, when it is he who is making me late. The whole thing has become a ridiculous problem. Any suggestions?"

Case Questions

1. To what extent should Suzanne be so concerned about Aaron taking up her time?
2. What should Suzanne do to preserve her relationship with her boss, yet still get her work accomplished on time?
3. Should Suzanne work extra hours to make up for the time she loses in small talk with Aaron?
4. What specific techniques about boss relationships apply to this case?

Interpersonal Skills Role-Play

Dealing with a Talkative Boss

One student plays the role of Suzanne, who is facing a heavy workload today, triggered by the crash of a passenger bus that resulted in a ten-vehicle pile up. She is slashing away at her computer while dealing with phone calls at the same time. Her boss, Aaron, approaches her cubicle with a smile on his face. He initiates the conversation with, "Busy day, isn't it? It could drive you crazy if you let it. The bus accident could be costly, but it's not the end of the world. Mind if I sit down and chat for a few moments?"

Suzanne's intent is to deal with the emergency the best she can, whereas Aaron wants to escape some of the pressures for a few minutes. He cannot understand why Suzanne is so stressed about the situation. Run the role-play for about six minutes, while other class members observe the interactions and later provide feedback about the interpersonal skills displayed by Suzanne in relation to his interaction with Aaron. Comment on her ability to be assertive and tactful at the same time. Also, observe the interpersonal skills that Aaron displays.

Observers rate the role players on two dimensions, using a 1-to-5 scale from very poor (1) to very good (5). One dimension is "effective use of human relations techniques." The second dimension is "acting ability." A few observers might voluntarily provide feedback to the role players in terms of sharing their ratings and observations. The course instructor might also provide feedback.

Interpersonal Relations Case 13.2

The Unpopular Office Administrator

While at a shopping mall one day, you run into Max, a former classmate of yours. Happy to see him, you comment, "Max, good to see you. How are things going? Last I heard you were promoted from administrative assistant to office administrator, like an office supervisor. How do you like your new job?"

Max answers: "Thanks for asking. That's true. I was promoted to office administrator. I work in a different department now. My boss is the director of corporate communications. The job is exciting. I'm in on a lot of important happenings, and I get to meet a lot of important people. But things in the office aren't going as well as I would like."

Your curiosity aroused, you ask: "What do you mean?"

Max continues: "I don't think the other workers in the office care too much for me. Even though I am basically the office supervisor, I feel kind of left out of things. I'm almost never asked to join the 'guys' for lunch or coffee breaks. I don't know what I'm doing wrong. Sometimes I

think it could be jealousy over my job. But that isn't such a plausible reason. Being an office administrator isn't *that* impressive. Also, I'm a few years older than most of the workers in the office. They should be glad to see that experience and hard work pay off.

"Sometimes I feel like the guy in those TV ads who loses out with friends because he needs breath freshener. That certainly isn't the case with me. I don't recall having a problem making friends either at school or in my other jobs.

"If you come up with any ideas that might help me, please let me know. I would feel awkward asking the other people in the office why they don't like me. After all, I am the office administrator."

Case Questions

1. What should Max do (if anything) to discover what might be wrong?
2. What general suggestions do you have as to how Max might become better accepted by the group?

References

1. "'More than Coffee Chats and Emails': Sustainable Networking Requires Effort, Authenticity," *Knowledge@ Wharton* (http://knowledge.whyarton.upenn), December 5, 2012, pp. 1–2.
2. Cited in Linda Noeth, "All those Unwritten Rules of the Office Also Guide Policy," *Democrat and Chronicle*, February 8, 2009, p. 2E.
3. Daniel Goleman, *Social Intelligence: The New Science of Human Relationships* (New York: Bantam, 2006); Carol Hymowitz, "Business is Personal, So Managers Need to Harness Emotions," *The Wall Street Journal*, November 13, 2006, p. B1.
4. Robyn L. Brouer, Allison Duke, Darren C. Treadway, and Gerald R. Ferris, "The Moderating Effect of Political Skill

on the Demographic Dissimilarity–Leader-Member Exchange Quality Relationship," *Leadership Quarterly,* April 2009, pp. 61–69.

5. Amos Drory and Nurit Zaidman, "The Politics of Impression Management in Organizations: Contextual Effects," in Eran Vigoda-Gadot and Amos Drory, eds., *Handbook of Organizational Politics* (Northampton, MA: Edward Elgar, 2006), p. 75.

6. Andrew J. DuBrin, *Impression Management in the Workplace: Research, Theory, and Practice* (New York: Routledge, 2011), p. 73.

7. Nathan P. Podsakoff, Steven W. Whiting, Philip M. Podaskoff, and Brian D. Blume, "Individual- and Organizational-Level Consequences of Organizational Citizenship Behaviors: A Meta-Analysis," *Journal of Applied Psychology,* January 2009, pp. 122–141.

8. Daniel S. Whitman, David L. Van Body, and Chockalingam Viswesvaran, "Satisfaction, Citizenship Behaviors, and Performance in Work Units: A Meta-Analysis of Collective Construct Relations," *Personnel Psychology,* Spring 2010, pp. 41–81.

9. Terry Bragg, "Nine Strategies for Successfully Playing Office Politics," *http://www.tbragg.addr.com,* July 15, 2005, p. 1.

10. Tamara E. Holmes, "Admitting When You're Wrong," *Black Enterprise,* May 2007, p. 124.

11. "Get Rid of 'Yes Men,'" *Manager's Edge,* Special Bulletin, Spring 2006, p. 2.

12. William L. Gardner III, "Lessons in Organizational Dramaturgy: The Art of Impression Management," *Organizational Dynamics,* Summer 1992, p. 45.

13. Kenneth J. Harris, K. Michele Kacmar, Suzanne Zivnuska, and Jason D. Shaw, "The Impact of Political Skill on Impression Management Effectiveness," *Journal of Applied Psychology,* January 2007, pp. 278–285.

14. Eliza Browning, "Business Etiquette: 5 Rules that Matter Now," *Inc.* (http://www.inc.com/eliza-browning/business-etiquette-rules-that-matter-now.html), April 17, 2012, p. 1.

15. This section of the chapter is based on "Business Etiquette: Teaching Students the Unwritten Rules," *Keying In,* January 1996, pp. 1–8; Browning, "Business Etiquette: 5 Rules that Matter Now," pp. 1–2; Letitia Baldrige, *The Executive Advantage* (Washington, DC: Georgetown Publishing House, 1999); "Culture Shock?" *Entrepreneur,* May 1998, p. 46; Blanca Torres, "Good Dining Manners Can Help Bet a Bigger Slice of the Job Pie," *Baltimore Sun* story, April 5, 2005; Erin White, "The Jungle: Focus on Recruitment, Pay and Getting Ahead," *The Wall Street Journal,* November 2, 2004, p. B8.

16. James F. Thompson, *The Cubicle Survival Guide* (New York: Villard, 2007).

17. Sarah E. Needleman, "Office Space Is Crowded Out," *The Wall Street Journal,* December 7, 2009, p. B7.

18. "Disability Etiquette," *Human Resources Forum* (a supplement to *Management Review*), June 1997, p. 3; "Helping Today's Blind Children Become the Winners of Tomorrow," American Blind Children's Council (flyer), 2002.

19. Brian Hilliard and James Palmer, *Networking Like a Pro* (Atlanta, GA: Agito Consulting, 2003,), p. 52.

20. Susan Ricker, "When the Boss Talks, Really Listen," *Career Builder,* September 30, 2012, p. 1.

21. Miranda Wilcox, "What We Don't Like May Be What We Need," *Democrat and Chronicle,* March 19, 2013, p. 5B.

22. Judith Sills, "How to Be a Rising Star," *Psychology Today,* March/April 2006, pp. 38–39.

23. Ibid, p. 39.

24. James D. Westphal and Ithai Stern, "Flattery Will Get You Everywhere (Especially If You Are a Male Caucasian): How Ingratiation, Boardroom Behavior, and Demographic Minority Status Affect Additional Board Appointments at U.S. Companies," *Academy of Management Journal,* April 2007, pp. 267–288.

25. Marshall Goldsmith, "All of Us Are Stuck on Suck-Ups," *Fast Company,* December 2003, p. 117.

26. Research reported in Jeffrey Zaslow, "The Most-Praised Generation Goes to Work," *The Wall Street Journal,* April 20, 2007, p. W7.

27. Judith Sills, "How to Improve Your Credit Rating," *Psychology Today,* March/April 2008, p. 67.

28. Quoted in Anita Bruzzese, "On-the-Job Friends Improve Workplace," *Gannett News Service,* August 21, 2006.

29. Tom Rather, *Vital Friends: The People You Can't Afford to Live Without* (New York: Gallup Press, 2006).

30. Cited in Lea Winerman, "You Rub My Fin, I'll Rub Yours," *Psychology Today,* January 2009, pp. 56–59.

31. Andrew J. DuBrin, *Political Behavior in Organizations* (Thousands Oak, CA: Sage, 2009), p. 234.

32. Lea Winerman, "Have Your Heard the Latest?" *Monitor on Psychology,* April 2006, p. 57.

33. Gary M. Stern, "Small Slights Bring Big Problems," *Workforce,* August 2002, p. 17; Joann S. Lublin, "How to Stop the Snubs That Demoralize You and Your Colleagues," *The Wall Street Journal,* December 7, 2004, p. B1.

34. Steve Tobak, "10 Workplace Blunders to Avoid at All Costs," http://www.techrepublic.com/blog/10-things/10-workplace-blunders-to-avoid-at-all-costs/, August 10, 2011, p. 3.

Customer Satisfaction Skills

During a recent day at the bank where he worked as a mortgage officer, Jared was meeting with a couple, Roger and Wanda. The couple had already completed their preliminary mortgage application online. Before making a final decision on the specific mortgage to offer the couple, Jared wanted some additional information. He congratulated Roger and Wanda for purchasing a home, then asked the couple why they were purchasing a home.

The couple said that purchasing a home represented stability in their lives, for both them and their three children. Roger and Wanda also mentioned that purchasing a home might turn out to be a good investment in contrast to renting. Jared then asked the couple why they chose to apply at the bank he represents rather than another financial institution.

Again, the couple emphasized stability, this time pointing out that Jared's employer is one of the oldest and most dependable banks in the region.

One concern the couple did express was that the mortgage Jared's bank was offering them was one-third of a percent higher than some of the rates they had seen advertised. Jared agreed that the bank's mortgage rate was higher than some competitors, but said that it was better suited to their needs. "Our bank's approach to a mortgage is different than many other morgtgage lenders. Your mortgage will stay with us after it is granted. You will not have to be concerned about us selling your mortgage to an unknown third party. In this way, you will have some peace of mind about which insitition will be providing you the customer service you need. You also won't have to worry about your mortgage rate being suddenly increased."

Roger and Wanda responded that Jared had a good point. They thought that stability and peace of mind would be essential for an obligation as big as a mortgage. Roger and Wanda asked Jared to seek final approval for their mortgage application.

BananaStock/Thinkstock

Objectives

1. Enhance your ability to satisfy customers by using general principles of customer satisfaction.
2. Create bonds with present or future customers.
3. Have a plan to manage customer dissatisfaction effectively.

The approach the mortgage officer took to dealing with the couple in question illustrates a few key points about customer satisfaction skills. Jared asked good questions and listened to the answers. In this way, he knew that stability and security was important to Roger and Wanda. Although the mortgage he offered the couple had a higher rate than some competitors might charge, the mortgage offered them the type of stability that met their needs. This chapter presents information and exercises that can enhance your ability to satisfy both external and internal customers at a high level.

External customers fit the traditional definition and include clients, guests, and patients. External customers can be classified as retail or industrial. The latter represents one company buying from another, such as purchasing steel or a gross of printer cartridges. *Internal customers* are the people you serve within the organization or those who use the output from your job. Also, everyone you depend upon is an internal customer. The emphasis in this chapter is on satisfying external customers. Much of the rest of the book deals with better serving internal customers, because improved interpersonal relationships enhance the satisfaction of work associates.

Customer satisfaction skills are necessary for all workers in contact with customers, including sales representatives, customer service representatives (those who back up sales and take care of customer problems), and store associates. Workers in a wide variety of jobs need good customer satisfaction skills. The founder of a technology consulting firm observes, "Ninety percent of the time when a client has an issue with a consultant, it's related to soft skills."[1]

Another way of understanding the importance of customer satisfaction skills is to recognize that employees who can satisfy customers contribute heavily to profits. The chief executive of a firm that surveys approximately 20 million customers a year for retail and restaurant chains concludes, "A good employee or a good sales associate might be worth 5 or 10 times an average one. We've seen that. It's unreal."[2]

Various aspects of developing customer satisfaction skills are divided into three parts in this chapter: following the general principles of customer satisfaction, bonding with customers, and managing customer dissatisfaction. As you work through this chapter, you will observe that to implement its suggestions you need many of the interpersonal skills you have been acquiring, such as communication, teamwork, motivation, and conflict resolution. To reflect on your attitudes toward satisfying customers, do Self-Assessment Quiz 14-1.

FOLLOWING THE GENERAL PRINCIPLES OF CUSTOMER SATISFACTION

Customer satisfaction is important for several reasons. To begin with, without satisfying customers, a business would cease to exist. The slogan of Tops Markets, Inc., a supermarket chain, is "Customer satisfaction is our only business." Satisfied customers are likely to tell friends and acquaintances about their satisfactory experiences, helping a firm grow its business. In contrast, dissatisfied customers—especially those with an unresolved problem—are likely to tell many people about their dissatisfaction, thus dissuading a large number of people from becoming new customers. Studies indicate that

LEARNING OBJECTIVE 1

The Customer Service Orientation Quiz

Directions: Mark each of the following statements about dealing with customers as mostly true or mostly false. The statements relate to your attitudes, even if you lack direct experience in dealing with customers. Your experiences as a customer will also be helpful in responding to the statements.

		Mostly True	Mostly False
1.	All work in a company should be geared toward pleasing customers.	_____	_____
2.	The real boss in any business is the customer.	_____	_____
3.	Smiling at customers improves the chances of making a sale.	_____	_____
4.	I would rather find a new customer than attempt to satisfy one who is difficult to please.	_____	_____
5.	Dealing with customers is more rewarding than (or as rewarding as) dealing with coworkers.	_____	_____
6.	I enjoy (or would enjoy) helping a customer solve a problem related to the use of my product or service.	_____	_____
7.	The best way to get repeat business is to offer steep discounts.	_____	_____
8.	In business, your customer is your partner.	_____	_____
9.	Dealing directly with customers is (or would be) the most boring part of most jobs.	_____	_____
10.	If you have the brand and model the customer wants, being nice to the customer is not so important.	_____	_____
11.	A good customer is like a good friend.	_____	_____
12.	If you are too friendly with a customer, he or she will take advantage of you.	_____	_____
13.	Now that individual consumers and companies can shop online, the personal touch in business is losing importance.	_____	_____
14.	Addressing a customer by his or her name helps build a relationship with that customer.	_____	_____
15.	Satisfying a customer is fun whether or not it leads to a commission.	_____	_____
16.	Working with customers is annoying because it takes me away from working with a computer or sending text messages.	_____	_____

Scoring and Interpretation: Give yourself a +1 for each of the following statements receiving a response of mostly true: 1, 2, 3, 5, 6, 8, 11, 14, and 15. Give yourself a +1 for each of the following statements receiving a response of mostly false: 4, 7, 9, 10, 12, 13, and 16.

13–16 points: You have a strong orientation toward providing excellent customer service.

8–12 points: You have an average customer service orientation.

1–7 points: You have a below-average orientation toward providing excellent customer service.

an upset or angry customer tells an average of between 10 and 20 other people about an unhappy experience. Industrial customers who are angry often switch suppliers.[3] Customer satisfaction is also highly valued because it breeds customer loyalty, which in turn is very profitable. Repeat business is a success factor in both retail and industrial companies.

Another reason for satisfying customers is the humanitarian aspect. Satisfying people enhances their physical and mental health, whereas dissatisfaction creates negative stress. Have you ever been so angry at poor service that you experienced stress?

Knowing how to satisfy customers is a subset of effective interpersonal relations in organizations. Nevertheless, there are certain general principles that will sharpen your ability to satisfy customers and thereby improve customer retention. This section presents ten key principles for satisfying customers.

FIGURE 14-1 Levels of Customer Satisfaction

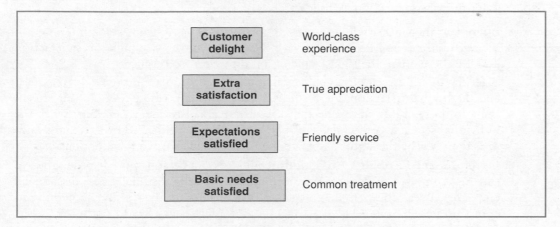

Strive for High Levels of Customer Satisfaction

In relation to developing customer satisfaction skills, keep in mind that satisfaction is considered a minimum expectation. If you do an outstanding job of satisfying customers, they will experience delight, as shown in Figure 14-1.

One of the most effective ways to provide the highest levels of customer satisfaction is to provide the customer with an unusually sensitive and warm surprise, often referred to as a "wow" experience. A daily activity at every Marriott International's Ritz-Carlton hotel around the world is the staff meeting to share "wow" stories. The stories accomplish two important ends. First, they offer workers local recognition in front of peers. Second, the wow stories reinforce the values each employee is expected to demonstrate as a Ritz-Carlton "ambassador" (being part of the hotel brand experience).[4]

A few years ago the Cadillac division of General Motors was struggling to earn a bigger share of the luxury market in the United States. One of their solutions to the problem was to bring in trainers from the Ritz-Carlton Hotel chain to show Cadillac dealers how to create a consistent sales experience at dealerships in the United States. Cadillac imitated the Ritz Carlton pocket-size "Credo" cards that explain how customers should be treated. Ritz employees are empowered to spend up to $2,000 that can be used for the purpose of compensating for a bad customer experience or surprising a guest with a better one. Cadillac dealers were told to find similar ways to wow customers. Among these approaches to pleasing customers were giving service chiefs more flexibility to provide free maintenance or even reduce service charges for unhappy customers. As a result of the training, a Cadillac dealer in Chicago gave employees $300 to $500 in "wow" money.[5]

Be Satisfied So You Can Provide Better Customer Service

Employees who are happy with their jobs are the most likely to satisfy customers. As stated by Frank DeRiso, a local president of the United Food and Commercial Workers union, "The employees are your No. 1 asset. You don't have a customer base without employees."[6] Treating employees well puts them in a better frame of mind to treat their customers well and provide better service, especially in the human interaction aspect of service.

According to consumer behavior specialist James Hazen, good service comes down to creating a positive and memorable customer experience. For example, Starbucks can command a premium price for its coffee beverages not simply because of the quality of its beans and its stylish cardboard cups, but because of the overall experience. And the employees—particularly the baristas—are part of that experience.[7] Although Starbucks has reduced many prices in recent years, its customers still have the option of purchasing lower price coffee at fast-food chains and convenience stores.

Acting alone, you cannot improve company conditions that contribute to job satisfaction. What you can control to some extent, however, is your own attitudes that are related to job satisfaction. A checklist of attitudes and beliefs related to job satisfaction, and over which you can exert some control, follows:

- **Interest in the work itself.** Job satisfaction stems directly from being interested in what you are doing. People who love their work experience high job satisfaction and are therefore in the right frame of mind to satisfy customers.

- **A feeling of self-esteem.** If you have high self-esteem, you are more likely to experience high job satisfaction. High-status occupations contribute more to self-esteem than do those of low status. Feelings of self-esteem also stem from doing work the individual sees as worthwhile. This perception is less influenced by external standards than it is by the status associated with a particular job or occupation.

- **Optimism and flexibility.** An optimistic and flexible person is predisposed to be a satisfied employee. A pessimistic and rigid person will most likely be a dissatisfied employee. Every company has its share of "pills" who always find something to complain about. Some evidence suggests that a tendency toward optimism versus pessimism is inherited.[8] If you have a predisposition toward pessimism, you can still become more optimistic with self-discipline. For example, you can look for the positive aspects of a generally unpleasant situation.

- **Positive self-image.** People possessing a positive self-image are generally more satisfied with their jobs than are those possessing a negative self-image. One explanation is that the people who view themselves negatively tend to view most things negatively. You have to like yourself before you can like your job.

- **Positive expectations about the job.** People with positive expectations about their jobs are frequently more satisfied than are those with low expectations. These expectations illustrate a self-fulfilling prophecy. If you expect to like your job, you will behave in such a way that those expectations will be met. Similarly, if you expect your job not to satisfy your needs, you will do things to make your expectations come true. Assume that a worker expects to earn low commissions in a sales job. The person's negativism may come through to customers and prospective customers, thereby ensuring low customer satisfaction and low commissions.

- **Effective handling of abuse from customers.** Customer service workers are often verbally abused by customers over such matters as products not working, merchandise returns not being acceptable, and the customer having been charged a late fee. Automated telephone-answering systems often force callers to hack through a thicket of prompts before reaching a human being. By the time a live person is reached, the customer is angry and ready to lash out at the customer service representative.[9] To prevent these oral tirades from damaging one's job satisfaction, it is essential to use effective techniques of dealing with criticism and resolving conflict as described in Chapter 9. The section on dealing with dissatisfied customers presented later in this chapter is also important. Combating sexual harassment by customers is also important for retaining emotional equilibrium.

High job satisfaction contributes to good customer service in another important way. Employees who are satisfied with their jobs are more likely to engage in service-oriented organizational citizenship behavior. As you will recall, *organizational citizenship behavior* relates to going beyond your ordinary job description to help other workers and the company. A customer service worker with high organizational citizenship behavior will go beyond ordinary expectations to find ways to solve a customer problem.[10] A member of the tech support staff in a consumer electronics store volunteered to drop by a customer's house to help him install a video recorder, even though such home visits were not required. As a result of the technician's kindness, the man purchased a $6,000 TV receiver from the store.

Understand Your Company's Expectations in Terms of Customer Service

A fundamental of good customer service is that effective communication with employees makes it possible. Dennis Snow, who launched the Disney Institute consulting firm, and who today heads his own communications firm, says that strong communications are the bedrock of strong customer service. Snow believes that a key element of good customer service is believing that "everything speaks." He cites the example of a manager who urges attention to detail, but then allows a store's displays to be dirty. The manager then sends a mixed message to the employee about the importance of details.[11]

As an employee, you need to understand how your company defines outstanding service, and the company has a responsibility to make sure you understand this definition. Managers are responsible for communicating these expectations, but the employee will often have to take the initiative to learn aobut the expectations. Among the factors you need to understand are what type of reputation the company is attempting to establish and how service levels drive that reputation. For example, the manager of a hotel that rents rooms and suites at way-below-average rates asked the owner what kind of service customers should expect. The owner said quite candidly to the manager:

> Of course you are going to receive some complaints about our TVs having a limited selection of channels, and there not being any hand-out bottles of lotion in the bathroom. At the prices we charge, the guests cannot expect perfection. We provide good value for the price, but we are not a Hilton hotel.

Knowing these expectations about customer satisfaction, the manager could then deal more realistically with minor complaints by guests. The goal of the hotel was to keep guests happy at a level commensurate with the price they were paying. Or do you think guests at a discount hotel should receive the same level of service they should expect at a Ritz Carlton?

Receive Emotional Support from Coworkers and Management to Give Better Customer Service

Closely related to the idea that satisfied workers can better satisfy customers is the finding that the emotional support of coworkers often leads to providing better customer service. According to a study, the support of coworkers is even more important than supervisory support. The participants in the study were 354 customer service workers employed in service-based facilities. Customer satisfaction surveys were collected from 269 customers. The major finding was that employees who perceived their coworkers to be supportive had a higher level of commitment to their customers.

The researchers concluded that it is important to have a supportive group of coworkers by your side to help you perform service-related duties. In this study, supervisory support was less important than coworker support in terms of bringing about a strong customer service orientation. (A *customer service orientation* includes a desire to help customers and a willingness to act in ways that would satisfy a customer.) Another important conclusion drawn from the study was that customer satisfaction was positively associated with the strength of the service worker's customer orientation.[12]

Research also supports the idea that the type of leadership sales representatives receive influences the type of relationships the reps build with customers. The study in question involved 300 pairs of sales managers and 1,400 sales people reporting directly to them. Sales managers who were charismatic and good at setting visions strongly affected the use of customer-oriented selling behaviors, such as building good relationships. Other key factors related to building good relationships with customers were the level of support the sales workers received from the organization and how much cohesiveness (closeness) they felt with coworkers.[13]

A similar study conducted in Taiwan with 450 hair stylists and 112 store managers found that charismatic and visionary leaders enhanced employee service. In turn, better service was associated with customers coming back to the salon.[14] You probably already knew that if your hair stylist gives good service, you will return—but now there is a quantitative study to support your belief.

Another key aspect of emotional support by management is the internal service the company provides workers. Internal service refers to how employees are served in their local units by the larger organization. An example of internal service would be supplying customer-contact employees with the information they need to be helpful. The widespread use of tablet computers to enable customer service workers to have immediate access to information such as product availability is an example of productive internal service. A study involving 619 employees and 1,973 customers in 326 retail branches of a bank demonstrated the impact of internal service. It was found that when corporate internal service was strong, the branches had a better climate for customer service. The improved climate at the branch level ultimately led to bank customer-contact personnel delivering superior service to customers.[15]

The major point here is that the organization plays an important role in your ability or willingness to build relationships with customers. A thought to take away is that if you perceive your manager to be charismatic, you are more likely to provide better customer service.

Understand Customer Needs and Put Them First

The most basic principle of selling is to identify and satisfy customer needs. One challenge is that many customers may not be able to express their needs clearly. To help identify customer needs, you may have to probe for information. For example, the associate in a camera and video store might ask, "What uses do you have in mind for a video camera?" Knowing such information will help the associate identify which camcorder will satisfy the customer's needs.

The concept of adding value for customers is widely accepted as a measure of satisfying customer needs. If you satisfy customer needs, you are adding value for them. A person might be willing to pay $20 more per ticket to watch an athletic event if the extra $20 brought a better view and a chair instead of a backless bench. (The better view and more comfortable back add value for the spectator.) After customer needs have been identified, the focus must be on satisfying those needs rather than the needs of oneself or the company. Assume that the customer says, "The only convenient time for me to receive delivery this week would be Thursday or Friday afternoon." The sales associate should not respond, "On Thursday and Friday our truckers prefer to make morning deliveries." Instead, the associate should respond, "I'll do whatever is possible to accommodate your request."

A major contributor to identifying customer needs is to listen actively to customers. Listening can take place during conversations with customers, and "listening" can also mean absorbing information sent by e-mail and text messages. Many improvements in customer service today stem from suggestions and complaints made in blogs or social media. For example, several dollar stores have moved into upscale shopping centers because it was suggested on social media sites that so many people today "shop down" to save money.

Focus on Solving Problems, Not Just Taking Orders

Effective selling uses sales representatives to solve problems rather than merely have them taking orders. An example is the approach taken by sales representatives for the business division of ADT Corporation. Instead of focusing on the sale of security monitoring equipment, the representatives focus on what type of security threats the potential customer might be facing, including surveillance of the ADT customers.

customer-centric sales process

A sales process emphasizing a low-pressure environment in which the sales staff acts as consultants, offering information and explaining how the product or service can help solve a customer's problem.

Consultative selling is also referred to as customer-centric. A **customer-centric sales process** emphasizes a low-pressure environment in which the sales staff acts as consultants, offering information and explaining how the product or service can help solve a customer's problem. The customer-centric approach is evident both at an Apple Store and a Container Store. At an Apple Store, customers can obtain free assistance from the Genius Bar. At a Container Store, sales associates are extensively trained to offer a light, informative touch.[16] Among the many problems discussed might be how to store clothing in a basement to avoid the risk of mold.

The focus on problem solving enables sales reps to become partners in the success of their customers' businesses. By helping the customer solve problems, the sales rep enhances the value of the supplier–customer relationship to the customer. The customer is receiving consulting services in addition to the merchandise or service being offered. In some situations, a store associate can capitalize on the same principle. If the customer appears unsure about a purchase, ask him or her which problem that the product should solve. The following scenario in a computer store illustrates this point:

> **Customer:** I think I would like to buy this computer. I'm pretty sure it's the one I want. But I don't know too much about computers other than how to use them for word processing, e-mail, forwarding articles from Web sites, and basic search.

Store associate: I am happy you would like to purchase a computer. But could you tell me what problems you are facing that you want a computer to help you solve?

Customer: Right now I feel I'm not capitalizing on the Internet revolution. I want to do more online, and get into digital photography so that I can send cool photos to friends all over. Friends and family members also want me to have a webcam. I also want to purchase music online, so I can walk around with an MP3 player like my friends do.

Store associate: To solve your problem, you will need a more powerful computer than the one you are looking at. I would like you to consider another model that is about the same price as the one you have chosen. The difference is that it has the memory you need to e-mail photos and download music from a subscription service.

A major contributor to solving customer problems is to have in-depth product knowledge, whether you are selling jet engines or domestic electronic gadgets. A few years ago, Best Buy was suffering from a sales decline. A company executive acknowledged that the chain had "let its customer-service muscle atrophy." Contributing to the problem was a perception among many customers that the store associates had limited product knowledge. The same executive then began a program of intensive sales training, including the acquisition of product knowledge.[17]

Respond Positively to Moments of Truth

An effective customer contact person performs well during situations in which a customer comes in contact with the company and forms an impression of its service. Such situations are referred to as **moments of truth**. If the customer experiences satisfaction or delight during a moment of truth, the customer is likely to return when the need for service arises again. A person who is frustrated or angered during a moment of truth will often not be a repeat customer. A moment of truth is an important part of customer service because what really matters in a service encounter is the customer's perception of what occurred.[18] Visualize a couple who has just dined at an expensive restaurant as part of celebrating their anniversary. The food, wine, and music might have been magnificent, but the couple perceives the service as poor because one of them slipped on ice in the restaurant parking lot.

You can probably visualize many moments of truth in your experiences with service. Reflect on how a store associate treated you when you asked for assistance, the instructions you received when an airplane flight was canceled, or how you were treated when you inquired about financial aid. Each business transaction has its own moment of truth, yet they all follow the same theme of a key interaction between a customer and a company employee. One way you can track moments of truth is to prepare a cycle-of-service chart, as shown in Figure 14-2. The **cycle-of-service chart** summarizes the moments of

moments of truth

Situations in which a customer comes in contact with a company and forms an impression of its service.

cycle-of-service chart

A method of tracking the moments of truth with respect to customer service.

FIGURE 14-2   A Cycle-of-Service Chart for Obtaining a Car Loan at a Bank

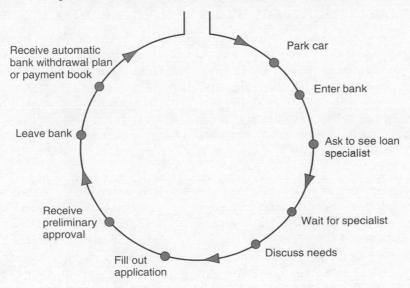

Moments of Truth

The class organizes into small groups to discuss what can go right versus what can go wrong during customer moments of truth. First refer to the cycle-of-service chart shown in Figure 14-2. Discuss what can go right or wrong at each moment of truth. Second, have the team develop its own cycle-of-service chart for another service, using its own experiences and imagination. After making the two analyses, discuss the usefulness of a cycle-of-service chart for improving customer satisfaction.

truth encountered by a customer during the delivery of a service.[19] To gain insight into these charts, do Skill-Building Exercise 14-1.

Be Ready to Accept Empowerment

empowerment

The process of managers transferring, or sharing, power with lower-ranking employees.

A major strategy for improving customer service is to empower customer contact employees to resolve problems. (The previous information about the Ritz-Carlton hotels and Cadillac dealerships included the idea of empowering employees.) **Empowerment** refers to managers transferring, or sharing, power with lower-ranking employees. In terms of customer relations, it means pushing decision making and complaint resolution downward to employees who are in direct contact with customers. The traditional method of dealing with all but the most routine customer problems is for the customer-contact worker to refer them to the manager. Many manufacturing firms and service firms now authorize customer-contact workers to take care of customer problems within limits.

Empowerment is not giving away the store, especially because limits are established to the customer-contact worker's authority. Empowerment does involve taking a reasonable risk based on company principles to provide meaningful customer service. For empowerment to work, the company must grant decision-making latitude to employees. The employees, in turn, must be willing to accept empowerment (or decision-making authority). Imagine yourself in a customer contact position. For empowerment to work effectively, you should be able to answer affirmatively to the following statements:

- I am willing to arrive at a quick decision as to whether the company or the customer is right.
- I would be willing to admit to a customer that the company has made a mistake.
- I would be willing to take the risk that at times I will lose money for the company on a given transaction.
- I would be comfortable making an out-of-the-ordinary decision about a customer problem without consulting a manager.

Enhance Customer Service through Information Technology

Much has been said and written about how information technology has depersonalized customer service, such as having customers select from a long menu of choices on a telephone. Information technology, however, also plays an important role in recording customer preferences and individualizing service. A major contribution of information technology to enhancing customer service is to develop individualized appeals to customers. With the right software in place, you can make a direct appeal to customer preferences based on past purchases and the habits of customers with similar preferences. If you have purchased online at a major e-tailer like Amazon.com or Buy.com, you may be familiar with this technology. Two examples follow:

1. Computerized information tells you immediately what the customer on the phone or online has bought in the past, so you may ask a question such as, "Two years ago you installed a centralized vacuum cleaning system. Do you need another set of bags by now?"
2. Speaking to the person, or sending an e-mail message to the customer, you may say, "Last year you purchased a heated doghouse for your Yorkshire terrier. Our

information suggests that people who own a heated doghouse are also interested in dog sweaters. Please take a moment to look at our new line of dog sweaters for the canines who appreciate warmth."

In recent years, many banks have developed mobile apps whereby customers can deposit checks by taking photos with their smartphones. Customer satisfaction is often enhanced because the customer can deposit checks immediately without having to visit the bank or an ATM. Apps are also used for such purposes as making online purchases and investigating whether a given item is in stock. Unless you are an executive in an organization, you cannot authorize such apps; however, as a worker further down the organization, you are free to make recommendations about which new apps might enhance customer service.

Developing individualized appeals to customers is likely to be included in customer relationship management (CRM) software. The complex software is used to implement a strategy of interacting with your customers to bring them more value and to bring more profits to your firm. One of its basic purposes is to make the company easier for customers to do business with, including facilitating placing orders over the Internet. As such, the individual customer service worker would not have the authority to install such a system. Yet the individual worker can always look for ways to apply the CRM system (such as that provided by Salesforce.com or SAP) in a way that best serves the customer.

A major challenge in providing good customer service when using information technology is to preserve the human touch. Here are some hints for adding a personal touch to your electronic communications to help build customer loyalty.

Using voicemail

1. Vary your voice tone and inflection when leaving messages and in your greeting to avoid sounding bored or uninterested in your job and the company.

2. Smile while leaving your message—somehow a smile gets transmitted over the telephone wires or optic fibers!

3. Use voicemail to minimize "telephone tag" rather than to increase it. If your greeting specifies when you will return, callers can choose to call again or to leave a message. When you leave a message, suggest a good time to return your call. Another way to minimize telephone tag is to assure the person you are calling that you will keep trying.

4. Place an informative and friendly greeting (outgoing message) on your voicemail. Used effectively, a voicemail greeting will minimize the number of people irritated by not talking to a person.

5. When you respond to a voicemail outgoing message, leave specific, relevant information. As in the suggestions for minimizing telephone tag, be specific about why you are calling and what you want from the person called. The probability of receiving a return call increases when you leave honest and useful information. If you are selling something or asking for a favor, be honest about your intent.

6. When leaving your message, avoid the most common voicemail error by stating your name and telephone number clearly enough to be understood. Most recipients of a message dislike intensely listening to it several times to pick up identifying information.

7. The company using computerized calls (or "robocalls") should determine if these calls are perceived as helpful or so annoying that they harm business.[20] One of the many uses of an automated calling service is to remind patients of upcoming medical and dental appointments. Some patients appreciate the reminder, whereas others slam down the phone in disgust because they expect more a more personal touch from a dental or medical office.

Using e-mail

1. Use the customer's name. Begin the greeting, "Hello, Lisa King." Most companies now greet customers by their first name only, but a minority of customers

consider this practice to be rude; however, few people are likely to be offended when you use both their first and last names.

2. Choose a human e-mail address. Marysmith@kaset.com feels more personal than an odd sequence of numbers, letters, and dashes. To enhance your credibility and professional stature, avoid cool electronic addresses, such as Steelabs@aol.com or Angellady42@gmail.com.

3. Be conversational. Mention events you have shared, such as, "I enjoyed seeing you at the company meeting."

4. Sign your name. Don't neglect your signature. "Best regards, Jim Woods."[21]

A general principle of recognizing the human aspects of information technology systems for customer service is to understand that customers might already be overloaded with instructions. Among them would be carrying out routine demands such as validating a credit card by making ten entries on the credit card company's Web site. A key finding of the Corporate Executive Board's multiple surveys of consumers and marketing executives is that customers want more simplicity in making decisions about purchases.

The single biggest driver of making customers more likely to follow through on purchases, buy repeatedly, and recommend the product or service to others was *decision simplicity*. This refers to the ease with which the customers can gather reliable information about a product or service and weigh their purchase options.[22] The speed checkout button on several online shopping sites, with Amazon.com being the leader, represents this simplicity. In short, the customer service specialist needs to sympathize with the customer having to work so hard to make a purchase. (We recognize that for some customers complex information technology instructions are natural and therefore easy to execute.)

Avoid Rudeness and Hostility toward Customers

I have reserved the most frequently violated principle of good customer service for last: Avoid being rude or hostile to customers. Although rudeness to customers is obviously a poor business practice, the problem is widespread. Rudeness by customer contact personnel is a major problem from the employer's standpoint. A widely practiced form of rudeness is for two store associates to converse with each other about nonwork matters while a customer waits for attention. Or how about a store associate making a personal phone call while waiting on you?

Rude treatment creates more lost business than does poor product quality or high prices. Several years ago McDonald's franchises were facing a downturn in sales. Surveys indicated that one of the problems facing McDonald's Corporation was the indifferent and rude behavior by many frontline workers. McDonald's then increased the training of store employees and upgraded the menu to achieve a substantial rebound in sales. Yet the problem of frontline workers being perceived as unfriendly and somewhat rude resurfaced in 2013. Company executives then renewed the emphasis on customer service, spearheaded by concerns from the newly appointed CEO, Don Thompson.[23]

Rudeness is sometimes a form of hostility, because rudeness, such as grimacing at a customer, stems from anger. Being outright hostile toward customers can be a bigger problem than rudeness, which is more subtle. The impact of service provider hostility on customer satisfaction was explored by studying 142 naturally occurring service interactions at a telephone service center of a bank. A typical interaction would be a customer phoning the bank to inquire about an account balance. (Today, such calls would only be in reference to what appeared to be inaccuracies in the online statement or the statement retrieved through the automated phone service.) Service interactions usually lasted about two minutes. Customers were later contacted to complete a quality survey about their transaction. Hostility was measured through raters' judgment of the tone of the service providers' voices.

A major finding of the study was that when the technical performance (e.g., providing the information needed) was low, hostility by the service provider lowered customer satisfaction considerably. When the technical performance of the service provider was good, hostility had a less negative impact on service quality.[24] When you get the information

Am I Being Rude?

Directions: Following is a list of behaviors that would be interpreted as rude by many customers. Check yes if you have engaged in such behavior in your dealings with customers or if you would be *likely* to do so if your job involved customer contact, and check no if you would not engage in such behavior.

		Yes	No
1.	I talk to a coworker while serving a customer.	____	____
2.	I conduct a phone conversation with someone else while serving a customer.	____	____
3.	I address customers by their first names without having their permission.	____	____
4.	I address customers as "You guys."	____	____
5.	I chew gum or eat candy while dealing with a customer.	____	____
6.	I laugh when customers describe an agonizing problem they are having with one of our company's products or services.	____	____
7.	I minimize eye contact with customers.	____	____
8.	I say the same thing to every customer, such as "Have a nice day," in a monotone.	____	____
9.	I accuse customers of attempting to cheat the company before carefully investigating the situation.	____	____
10.	I hurry customers when my break time approaches.	____	____
11.	I comment on an attractive customer's appearance in a flirtatious, sexually oriented way.	____	____
12.	I sometimes complain about or make fun of other customers when I am serving a customer.	____	____
13.	I sometimes look and act impatient if a customer fumbles around trying to locate his or her credit card, debit card, or cash.	____	____
14.	I am more attentive and friendly toward customers of my own ethnic or racial group than I am toward other customers.	____	____

Interpretation: The more of these behaviors you have engaged in, the ruder you are and the more likely it is that you are losing potential business for your company. If you have not engaged in any of these behaviors, even when faced with a rude customer, you are an asset to your employer. You are also tolerant.

you need from a service provider, you are willing to put up with a few angry tones! The overall message supports a human relations perspective: Being hostile toward customers lowers their perception of the quality of service.

To elevate your awareness level about rudeness among customer contact personnel, do Self-Assessment Quiz 14-2.

CREATING A BOND WITH YOUR CUSTOMER

Another key perspective on achieving customer satisfaction and delight is to create a bond—or emotional relationship—with customers. The rationale is that if you form warm, constructive relationships with your customers, they will keep buying. Staying focused on the importance of customers will help provide the motivation for forming such a bond. The willingness to form a bond with the customer is part of having a **strong customer orientation,** defined as "a set of basic individual predispositions and an inclination to provide service, to be courteous and helpful in dealing with customers and associates."[25] You may recall Self-Assessment Quiz 14-1 about customer orientation at the outset of the chapter. Service-oriented organizational citizenship behavior relates to the same idea of focusing on customer needs.

LEARNING OBJECTIVE 2

strong customer orientation

A set of individual predispositions and an inclination to provide service and be courteous and helpful in dealing with customers and associates.

Creating a bond is aimed at increasing sales, but it also enhances service. If the customer relies on and trusts the sales representative, the customer will perceive the service to be of high quality. Similarly, people perceive medical and legal services to be of high quality if they trust the physician or lawyer. Virtually all of the principles and techniques presented in this chapter will help form a bond with customers; however, six key principles are as follows:

1. Create a welcoming attitude, including a smile.
2. Provide exceptional service.
3. Show care and concern.
4. Make the buyer feel good.
5. Build a personal relationship.
6. Invite the customer back.

Create a Welcoming Attitude, Including a Smile

An effective starting point in creating a customer bond is to use enthusiastic expressions, including a smile, when greeting customers. Attempt to show a sincere, positive attitude that conveys to customers and prospects, "I'm here to make you happy."[26] In addition to being an effective greeting, smiling is also a natural relationship builder and can help you bond with your customer. Smile several times at each customer meeting, even if your customer is angry at your product or service. A camcorder is a useful device for getting feedback on the quality of your smile. Practicing your smile in a mirror might feel a little less natural, but it is still helpful. Smiling at customers has a potential disadvantage, despite its general effectiveness. If your smile is too friendly and inviting, the customer might think that you want to get to know him or her outside the business relationship.

Smiling is such a key part of bonding with customers that the smiles of customer service workers have been the subject of scientific study. Twenty pairs of first-year college students who were trained as coders for the experiment observed 220 employee—consumer encounters in food/coffee services. Customers were later asked to report their mood, appraisal of service quality, and encounter satisfaction. Several of the findings were as follows: Even in brief encounters, substantial smiling by employees made customers smile in return. Smiling employees were perceived as providing quality service, and the customers felt overall satisfaction with their encounters. Smiling somehow did not affect customer mood after the encounter. One interpretation of the study is that service employees should keep smiling, but not to the point that they lack authenticity.[27] Phony smiles backfire in work and personal life.

Provide Exceptional Service (or Customer Experience)

The best-accepted axiom about keeping customers is to provide exceptional service or experience. Many successful companies contend that their competitive advantage is good service. An important part of the comeback of Burger King in the mid-2000s was a subtle way of providing top service to the company's most profitable demographic group, males between the ages of 18 and 34 who visit the stores three to four times a week. These "Super Fans" want indulgent, fat-laden, high-caloric, tasty food. So Burger King served up the Enormous Omelet Sandwich. Greg Brenneman, who was CEO at the time, said he gives his customers what they want, not what others (such as nutritionists and physicians) think they should have.[28]

Exceptional service includes dozens of customer transactions, including prompt delivery, a fair-returns policy, accurate billing, and prompt attention to a customer's presence. Exceptional service also includes giving customers good advice about using the product or service. As shown in Figure 14-1, providing exceptional service leads to customer delight.

Another way of understanding the importance of exceptional customer service is to study what happens when service declines. Part of the demise of the once popular Circuit City was attributed to a decline in customer service. The CEO at the time, Phillip Schoonover, decided to reduce costs by dismissing many veteran workers and replacing them with inexperienced (and lower paid) workers. With fewer knowledgeable associates in the

Circuit City stores, many customers chose to make consumer electronic purchases at competitors. Circuit City eventually declared bankruptcy, partially because of declining revenues.[29]

Show Care and Concern

During contacts with the customer, the sales representative should show concern for the customer's welfare. The rep should ask questions such as: "How have you enjoyed the optical scanner you bought awhile back?" or "How much time and money have you saved since you installed the new system?" After asking the questions, the sales rep should project a genuine interest in the answer. Microsoft is one of many companies that asks about the quality of its service, and the inquiries are pointed and specific rather than canned. For example, a small business owner responded to an inquiry about service Microsoft provided, and he complimented "Jocelyn" for pointing him in the right direction. A team manager at Microsoft wrote back: "Thank you for taking the time to commend Jocelyn on a Job Well Done. Our primary goal at Microsoft is that our customers are very satisfied with the support they receive. I am pleased to read that we have met that goal in your case."

Make the Buyer Feel Good

A fundamental way of keeping a relationship going is to make the buyer feel good about himself or herself. In addition, the customer should be made to feel good because of having bought from the representative. Offer compliments about the customer's appearance or about a report that specified vendor requirements clearly. In retail, an effective feel-good line is to point out how well the product fits the customer, such as "It looks like Toro made that riding mower just for you." An effective feel-good line is: "I enjoy doing business with you."

Sometimes giving the customer or potential customer a small treat will make that person feel good enough to take decisive action. Key chain flash drives are often used for this purpose, because the gift is practical, yet not so lavishly expensive that it would ordinarily be considered a bribe. We caution that you need good sensitivity to the situation to avoid giving a small treat that could backfire. An example might be sending Warren Buffet (usually ranked as one of the richest people in the world) a $25 gift certificate to Macy's in order to sell to his company.

Making the buyer feel good about having made the purchase can be particularly important when selling luxury items to consumers. This helps minimize feelings of guilt for having been so extravagant. Sales consultant Jean-Marie Brücker trains store associates to sell luxury products. One training method is the *macaron* technique, which refers to the *macaron*, a sandwich-like pastry. The technique proceeds in this manner: "Madame, this timepiece [or diamond or handbag] comes from our finest workshop and has a value of $10,000. If you buy it, your children are sure to enjoy it for generations to come." The high price is sandwiched between the product's more romantic benefits. The idea is to sell the emotion of luxury. To further enhance the purchaser's emotions, Brücker insists that sales associates flatter customers by such means as complimenting the customer's own watch, even if it is made by a competitor.[30]

Build a Personal Relationship through Interaction with Customers

Interacting with customers in a personal way often enhances the customer experience, leading to repeat business. Interaction with pleasant staff members gives customers a temporary feeling of friendship that many of them value. Executives at Staybridge Suites recognize how human interaction contributes to profitability, and they use this principle as a guide for making investments in customer service. Staybridge, similar to other extended-stay hotels, provides limited services and is sparsely staffed to reduce costs. Rooms are fully cleaned only once a week, and the front desk is usually staffed by only one or two people.

Instead of providing loads of amenities, Staybridge concentrates its customer service on staff members interacting with guests. "A lot of our guests really want that personal interaction—the thing they get from home that they'd like to get from a hotel," says Rob

Stockbyte/Getty Images

Radomski, the vice president for brand management for Staybridge Suites. The conversations between guests and staff are about non-controversial subjects such as the projects they're working on and their family back home. Staybridge also offers "Sundowner receptions" on Tuesday, Wednesday, and Thursday evenings in the lobby. General managers are required to attend the receptions, in which guests are given a free meal and an opportunity to socialize. Radomski believes the meals are cost-effective in terms of developing customer loyalty.[31]

Another way of building relationships with large numbers of customers is to interact with them through company blogs or social media. The company representative is authorized to chat with hundreds of customers and potential customers by placing informal comments on the authorized company blog. The worker lets out tidbits of information to customers without betraying company confidences or making defamatory statements about the company; however, the blog entries are not usually as positive as advertisements, which help form bonds with the customers. Many customers post replies and swap ideas with the company rep.

Social media and company-approved blogs are widely used, as customers demand information presented in a more unvarnished way. A major advantage of social media Web sites and blogs is that they humanize large organizations, such as the company representative mentioning a favorite recipe as well as chatting about a new product.

Invite the Customer Back

The southern United States expression "Y'all come back, now!" is well suited for bonding with customers. Specific invitations to return may help increase repeat business. The more focused and individualized the invitation, the more likely it will have an impact on customer behavior. ("Y'all come back, now!" is sometimes used too indiscriminately to be effective.) Pointing out why you enjoyed doing business with the customer, and what future problems you could help with, is an effective technique. An industrial cleaning company supervisor might say, "Our crew enjoyed cleaning such a fancy office. Keep us in mind when you would like your windows to sparkle."

Skill-Building Exercise 14-2 gives you an opportunity to practice techniques for bonding with customers.

Despite the importance of forming a bond with your customer, getting too personal can backfire. Most customers want a business relationship with the company and are not looking for a personal relationship with a company representative. As Daniel Akst observes, "Most customers want value and service without contending with a salesman who insists that he wants to be like family to you. Chances are you've already got a family, and for most of us, one is enough."[32]

MANAGING CUSTOMER DISSATISFACTION

Most companies put honest effort into preventing customer dissatisfaction. In addition to employing many of the principles and techniques already cited, many companies routinely survey customers to detect problem areas that could lead to dissatisfaction. A representative survey used by a successful company in its field is shown in Figure 14-3. Despite all

FIGURE 14-3   A Chain Restaurant Customer Satisfaction Survey

We would like to hear about your visit and how we can improve. Thank you!

Date: _____ Time: _____ AM/PM   Which location did you visit? _____

Name: _____

Address: _____

Email: _____

Phone: _____

Check Number: _____

Please rate us:	Poor	Fair	Good	Very Good	Excellent
Host/Hostess Hospitality	1	2	3	4	5
Server's Hospitality	1	2	3	4	5
Server's Attentiveness	1	2	3	4	5
Bartender's Hospitality	1	2	3	4	5
Bartender's Attentiveness	1	2	3	4	5
Quality of Food	1	2	3	4	5
Value of Meal	1	2	3	4	5
Cleanliness	1	2	3	4	5
Likely to Return	1	2	3	4	5
Manager Visit Table?	Yes	No			

Host/Hostess' Name: _____ Hair color: _____

Server's Name: _____ Hair color: _____

Bartender's Name: _____ Hair color: _____

What did you order today or tonight? _____

Was this your first visit?   Would you like to be a Secret Shopper?
  ☐ Yes   ☐ No   ☐ Yes   ☐ No

Comments on your visit: _____
_____
_____

The information provided will be used to help us better serve you and will not be shared.

these efforts to achieve total customer satisfaction, some customer dissatisfaction is inevitable. One reason is that mistakes in serving customers are almost inevitable; for example, a piece of equipment may have a faulty component unknown to the seller. A second reason is that some customers have a predisposition to complain. They will find something to complain about with respect to any product or service. Visualize the billions of transactions that take place every year between Walmart service personnel and customers. Inevitably, some customer somewhere is going to rant and rave about poor service no matter how hard Walmart managers and store associates try to please.

An important point to remember in dealing with dissatisfied customers is that the negative personality traits of customers can bring down your level of customer service. For example, a study conducted in two major fast-food chains in Singapore found that customers who scored high on the trait of agreeableness tended to bring out positive emotion by the service personnel. In contrast, customers who scored high on negative affectivity (being disagreeable) brought out negative emotion among customer service personnel.[33] A more recent study concluded that companies might consider customer training, such as encouraging customers to say thank you and show civil behaviors toward employees. Such behavior on the part of customers will often trigger positive emotions and behavior on the part of customer service workers.[34]

A service worker cannot change the personality traits of customers, yet a little self-management of emotion is in order. The service worker might reflect, "I won't let this nasty customer get me down. I will do my best to do my job without overreacting." Be careful not to fake your emotion too frequently, because it can create stress. Instead be assertive with a comment like, "I want to help you, but might you tell me what you want in a more positive way?"

The next subsections describe five approaches to handling customer dissatisfaction: deal constructively with customer complaints and anger, involve the customer in working out the problem, focus on the customer's problems rather than his or her attitude, anticipate how to handle an unreasonable request, and maintain a realistic customer retention attitude.

Deal Constructively with Customer Complaints and Anger

In an era when customer satisfaction is so highly valued, both retail and industrial customers are likely to be vocal in their demands. When faced with an angry customer, use one or more of the following nine techniques recommended by customer satisfaction specialists.[35]

1. **Show emotional leeadership.** A major tactic for dealing with customer anger is to show emotional leadership by not reciprocating the customer's anger. When you are the target of rage or criticism, it is difficult to remain calm. Two recommended techniques are to look at the ceiling to relax your breathing and tracing figure eights in the air with your eyes. The latter technique will often relax and refocus the eye muscles, helping you calm down. After the customer calms down, the customer service worker can then begin to work on the problem.

2. **Acknowledge the customer's point of view.** Make statements such as "I understand," "I agree," and "I'm sorry." Assume, for example, that a customer says, "The accounts receivable department made a $1,000 overcharge on my account last month. I want this fixed right away." You might respond, "I understand how annoying this must be for you. I'll work on the problem right away."

3. **Avoid placing blame on the customer.** Suggesting that the customer is responsible for the problem intensifies the conflict. With the customer who claims to have been overcharged, refrain from saying, "Customers who keep careful account of their orders never have this problem."

4. **Use six magic words to defuse anger.** The magic words are *I understand* (that this is a problem), *I agree* (that it needs to be solved), and *I'm sorry* (that this happened to you). The six magic words help communicate your empathy, which is considered vital to dealing with customer problems. For example, technical support agents at Comcast are taught that they must show empathy on every call even if they have heard the same problem for 15 consecutive calls.[36]

5. **Apologize for the problems created by you or by your company.** To recover from a breakdown in customer service, it is best to acknowledge an error immediately. Apologies are most effective when stated in the first person (such as "I created the problem" or "I'm very sorry for what happened"). The corporate "we're sorry" sounds less sincere than when one specific person accepts responsibility for what went wrong. Professional workers at the Kaiser Permanente HMO receive training in how to apologize to patients for medical errors. Sincere apologies can significantly reduce the cost of settling lawsuits, and may even convince unhappy patients not to sue at all. A sincere apology includes a statement of what the apologizer is going to do to fix the problem.[37]

6. **Take responsibility, act fast, and be thorough.** This technique is a simplified framework for managing customer dissatisfaction. Many automotive recalls are handled in this manner, with the automaker admitting that the malfunction is its fault, contacting customers immediately, and ensuring that highly trained technicians at the dealer work on the problem thoroughly. Part of taking responsibility is to ask, "What can I do to make this right?"

7. **Tell the difficult customers how much you value them.** Quite often customers with problems feel unappreciated. Just before resolving the problem of a difficult customer, explain how important he or she is to your firm. You might say, "We value your business, so I want to correct this for you quickly." (Of course, you would value the customer even more after he or she becomes less difficult.)

8. **Follow up on the problem resolution.** Following up to see whether the resolution to the problem is satisfactory brings closure to the incident. The follow-up also helps the service deliverer know that he or she can rebound from an episode of customer dissatisfaction. One useful form of follow-up is to telephone or send an e-mail to the customer whose problem was solved. For example, a representative from the service department of an automobile dealership might telephone a customer whose new car required substantial warranty repairs. "Hello, this is Jill from Oak Automotive. We replaced your original transmission last month. How is the new transmission working?" The Microsoft example presented earlier in the chapter illustrates the use of e-mail for following up on problem resolution.

    A less personal, and usually less effective, form of follow-up is to send a customer satisfaction questionnaire to the person with the problem. The questionnaire will often be interpreted as a company procedure that does not reflect specific concern about the individual's problem.

9. **Do your best to make sure the problem does not happen again.** The preceding steps are all valuable in resolving the complaints of angry customers. In addition, the customer needs some assurance that the problem will not happen again. Without such assurance, repeat business is at risk. The *recovery paradox* refers to the fact that customers will sometimes be more delighted by a skillful resolution of a problem than they are by service that was failure-free to begin with. For example, a customer might be delighted that a false roaming charge of $145 was removed from a phone bill—when the customer had never visited the country in which the charge occurred.

Involve the Customer in Working Out the Problem

Mistakes and problems in serving customers are inevitable regardless of how hard service workers strive for perfection. To minimize the perception of poor service, the customer must be involved in deciding what should be done about the problem. By being involved in the solution to the problem, the customer is more likely to accept a deviation from the service promised originally. The ideal condition is for the customer service representative and dissatisfied customer to work as partners in resolving the problem. Assume that a home-improvement company installed a terrace outside a small apartment building that deviated from the agreed-upon plan. The cost of removing the old terrace and replacing it would be prohibitive for the contractor. The contractor representative might ask the building owner what type of modifications she would suggest to make the terrace acceptable. Having made these suggestions herself, the building owner is more likely to accept the modifications than if the contractor told her which modifications to accept.

Focus on the Customer's Problems, Not Emotions

The importance of focusing on the customer's problem rather on his or her expressed emotions was demonstrated in a study of 228 recorded customer service calls in a medical billing operation. The calls were recorded and evaluated by raters in terms of both problem-solving techniques used by the customer service representatives and the emotions of the customers (patients who were billed).

One problem-focused strategy in the study was for agents to do everything they could to remove, modify, or change aspects of the situation negatively affecting the customer's emotions. For example, a customer service representative (CSR) might send a replacement blood pressure monitor to a patient whose monitor was not functioning properly. The other problem-focused strategy was cognitive change, or altering the customer's perspective regarding the problem. Also, the problem could be reframed to make it subjectively less stressful. For example, a patient might complain strongly about being charged $75 for blood presssure medication while in the hospital. The CSR might explain that the cost of the medicine includes paying for the judgment of the medical staff in choosing the right blood pressure medicine.

The emotion-focused approach involved attempting to change the caller's emotions rather than dealing directly with the problem. For example, the customer service represereresentative might tell a joke or attempt to engage the customer in small talk to distract him or her.

The study showed that when situation modification was used by the CSR, the customer's negative emotions were less intense, and the customer's positive emotions were more pronounced. When cognitive reappraisal was used, the customer's negative emotions tended to be less intense at the end of the call; however, the customer would not experience enhanced positive emotions. Another key result of the study was that emotion-focused strategies resulted in more intense, negatively expressed emotions by the patients who called in with a complaint.[38]

Anticipate How to Handle an Unreasonable Request

No matter how hard the customer-contact worker attempts to provide outstanding customer service, at some point a customer comes along with an unreasonable request—or the customer may raise an unfair objection. British Airways, an airline with a positive reputation for service, nevertheless receives many unreasonable customer requests. For example, the airline sees a wide variety of luggage-related scams. An unusually high percentage of people whose bags are lost claim that their luggage was filled with furs, tablet computers, and expensive clothing. The National Retail Federation reports that among the most frequent forms of fraudulent returns are *wardrobing*, in which a shopper purchases a garment for a particular event, and then returns it when the event is over (such as a wedding or a Halloween party).[39]

Recognize that the customer who makes an unreasonable demand is usually aware of the unreasonableness. The customer may not expect to be fully granted the request. Instead, the customer is bargaining by beginning with an unreasonable demand. For example, the passengers who claim to have luggage packed with valuables are probably looking for just $100 or so more than the standard allocation for lost baggage.

Sales representatives and other customer-contact workers who stand their ground with dignity and courtesy generally will not lose customers with unreasonable requests. These suggestions will help you deal with unreasonable demands while retaining the customer's business.[40]

- Let your customers retain their dignity by stating your position politely and reasonably.
- Avoid arguing with an upset customer. As the adage says, "You never win an argument with a customer."

- Appeal to your customer's sense of fair play and integrity. Explain that your intention is to do what is right and fair.
- Be firm by repeating the facts of the situation, but keep your temper under control.
- Accept responsibility for your decision rather than blaming company policy or your manager. Making somebody else the villain may intensify the problem.
- Be willing to say "no" to a customer when it is justifiable. Saying "yes" to an outrageous demand opens the door for a series of outrageous demands.

Maintain a Realistic Customer Retention Attitude

Some customers are too unreasonable, and therefore may not be worth keeping. A realistic goal is to retain as many profitable customers as possible. At times it may be possible to retain a customer by modifying the service. For example, customers who do not pay their bills on time or at all might be changed to a prepaid service such as is done by phone companies and some Internet service providers.[41] In this way, the customers who have difficulty paying bills can still receive service.

An extreme example of a customer not worth keeping is the airline passenger who engages in *air rage*. Symptoms of air rage include (1) insisting on being served more alcoholic beverages than permissible by airline regulations, (2) sexually harassing or physically attacking flight attendants or other passengers, (3) refusing to fasten their seat belts, (4) using electronic gear such as smartphones and laptop computers when not allowed by regulations, (5) smoking in the lavatory, and (6) using the aisles for a lavatory.

It is best to set limits for unruly customers, and see if their behavior changes. If the customer insists on creating disturbances, it is best to suggest the customer never return. Another problem is that some customers require so much service, or demand such high discounts, that they are unprofitable to retain. Good service to these customers means there is less time available to respond to the needs of profitable customers.

Customers can be unreasonable and unruly also because they are late paying their bills or do not pay them. Such customers divert resources away from more loyal and profitable customers and clients. Kishau Rogers, the owner of Websmith Group LLC, is a case in point. She finally had to drop or avoid clients who are high-maintenance or habitually late paying their bills. Her clients are mostly retail stores or entrepreneurs. They often asked for discounts because of their tight budgets or an expanded level of service beyond the agreed-upon contract. Rogers said that terminating 5 percent of her clientele, ". . . was the best decision I've made, because it really reduced the level of frustration I was experiencing. It freed me up to the clients that are loyal and pay on time." [42] In this way, the service she offered to other clients improved.

Dealing diplomatically and effectively with difficult customers requires an awareness of the types of tactics described in the previous several pages. Practice on the firing line is indispensable. The type of experience provided by Skill-Building Exercise 14-3 is helpful.

SKILL-BUILDING EXERCISE 14-3

Dealing with Difficult Customers

The following scenarios require one person to play the role of the customer-contact worker and another person to play the difficult customer. As usual, the role players project their feelings into the role-play by imagining how they would behave in the situation.

Scenario 1: One person is a store associate in a high-fashion women's clothing store. A woman who bought a $2,000 gown the previous week brings back the gown today. She claims that she is returning the gown because it doesn't fit comfortably. The store associate strongly suspects the woman bought the gown originally with the intent of wearing it for a special occasion and then returning it.

Scenario 2: One person plays the role of a customer service representative in a consumer electronics store. Another person plays the role of a customer who purchased a $3,500 giant-screen television receiver three months ago. He comes up to the service rep's counter ranting about the store's ineptitude. The customer claims that the TV has broken down three times. After the first repair, the TV worked for two weeks and then broke down again. The second repair lasted two weeks, only for the TV to break down during a Super Bowl party at his house. The customer is red in the face and shouting loudly. The service rep wants to resolve the customer's problem and prevent him from bad-mouthing the store.

Concept Review and Reinforcement

Key Terms

Summary

Customer satisfaction skills are necessary for all workers in contact with customers. Internal customers must also be taken into consideration. Employees who can satisfy customers contribute heavily to profits. Dissatisfied customers, especially those with an unresolved problem, are likely to tell many people about their dissatisfaction.

Ten key principles for satisfying and delighting customers are as follows:

1. Strive for high levels of customer satisfaction.
2. Be satisfied so that you can provide better customer service. (Some of your own attitudes, such as optimism and flexibility, influence your job satisfaction.)
3. Understand your company's expectation in terms of customer service.
4. Receive emotional support from coworkers and management so that you can give better customer service.
5. Understand customer needs, and put them first.
6. Focus on solving problems, not just taking orders.
7. Respond positively to moments of truth (points at which the customer forms an impression of company service).
8. Be ready to accept empowerment. (Being empowered enables you to solve customer problems.)
9. Enhance customer service through information technology.
10. Avoid rudeness and hostility toward customers. (Rude and hostile treatment of customers creates lost business.)

Another key perspective on achieving customer satisfaction and delight is to create a bond—or emotional relationship—with customers. Almost any act of good customer service helps create a bond, but six principles are highlighted here:

1. Create a welcoming attitude, including a smile.
2. Provide exceptional service (or customer experience).
3. Show care and concern.
4. Make the buyer feel good.
5. Build a personal relationship through interaction with customers.
6. Invite the customer back.

Despite the best efforts on the company's part, some customer dissatisfaction is inevitable. Also, some customers have a predisposition to complain. One approach to managing customer dissatisfaction is to deal constructively with customer complaints and anger. Tactics for achieving this end include the following:

1. Show emotional leadership.
2. Acknowledge the customer's point of view.
3. Avoid placing blame on the customer.
4. Use the six magic words to defuse anger. (These words help communicate empathy.)
5. Apologize for the problem created by you or by your company.
6. Take responsibility, act fast, and be thorough.
7. Tell the difficult customers how much you value them.
8. Follow up on the problem resolution.
9. Do your best to make sure the problem does not happen again.

Another approach to managing customer dissatisfaction is to involve the customer in working out the problem.

Focus on the customer-problem rather than his or her emotions. The customer contact worker must sometimes deal with an unreasonable request. Remember that the customer probably recognizes that he or she is being unreasonable. Do not argue with an unreasonable customer, but at times you must say "no." Maintain a realistic customer retention attitude, meaning that as hard as you try to please, some customers are not worth keeping. Customers who delay paying bills or who do not pay divert resources away from more loyal and profitable customers.

Questions for Discussion and Review

1. Suppose your employer provides a service that customers desperately need, such as payday loans or prescription medication. Explain whether it would still be necessary to apply principles of customer satisfaction.

2. Assume that a customer at one restaurant of a well-known restaurant chain is served stale bread. How fair would it be for that customer to post an angry tweet about the incident?

3. Is paying your employees more the best way to encourage good customer service?

4. A couple walks into the showroom of a home developer with hundreds of homes for sale and asks about what type of home they should purchase. Describe how you might identify customer needs in this situation.

5. Describe several customer moments of truth you have experienced this week. What made you classify them as moments of truth?

6. What is your opinion of the impact of automated voice systems on customer service? (We refer to the use of computerized voices to replace interaction with a live company representative.) Offer at least two specifics in your answer.

7. Should customers expect lower levels of customer service from 'no frills' companies?

8. If it is really true that industrial customers tend to purchase from people they like, how might a sales representative capitalize on this fact using a couple of ideas from this chapter?

9. Imagine yourself as a marketing and sales executive at a company that sold to other business firms. What would a large customer have to do before you took the initiative to end your relationship with that customer?

10. Should empowerment mean that customers will receive higher levels of compensation for poor customer service?

The Web Corner

http://www.csmassociation.org/
(Customer Satisfaction Measurement Association)

http://www.customersatisfaction.com
(Improving customer satisfaction and retention–includes video)

http://www.customer-service.com
(Improving your customer service–includes video)

Internet Skill Builder: Building Customer Relationships

An axiom of business is that customer relationships are essential. Direct your Internet search for this assignment toward finding customer-relationship building suggestions that can be converted into specific interpersonal skills, such as making a phone call to see how things are going. An example of a Web site that offers concrete suggestions for building customer relationships related to interpersonal skills is www.sideroad.com. Walk away from this exercise with a couple of ideas you might put into practice in dealing with customers.

Developing Your Human Relations Skills

Interpersonal Relations Case 14.1

Pamela Pushes the "Wow" Experience

Pamela is a sales representative at an automotive dealership in Fort Lauderdale, Florida, that sells American-made luxury automobiles and SUVs. The dealership also sells used vehicles of many makes and models. The manufacturer the dealership represents has sponsored training programs for sales managers and sales representatives, with the intent of making the customer experience more inviting. The training includes providing a "Wow" experience to customers who enter the showroom.

The sales representatives were given some general guidelines on providing the "Wow" experience, or exceptional service, that the vehicle purchaser or potential purchaser will remember. Pamela represented her fellow sales reps when she asked the trainer to provide a list of about six routines that lead to a "Wow" experience for most customers. The trainer emphasized that a "Wow" experience should be spontaneous and geared to the moment, rather than scripted in advance. The trainer also emphasized that what makes for a "Wow" experience is often in the eye of the beholder (based on the customer's perception).

Pamela said she understood the trainer's guidelines, and that she liked what she heard. During the next several weeks, Pamela delivered what she considered to be "Wow" experiences as follows:

- A young man in hip-hop-style clothing was carefully looking at an expensive model SUV and asked about the value of his trade-in and what the monthly payments would be. To establish rapport with the likely customer, Pamela broke out into a rap song about the luxury model in question. The customer prospect smiled a little, despite a perplexed expression.

- An older woman was pondering the purchase of a full-size sedan, but she expressed concern about whether her husband who used two canes could easily get in and out of the back seat. Pamela said that if the woman went home and brought her husband back, she would give him one hour of training on how to enter and exit the vehicle, assisted by his canes. The customer prospect smiled and said, "What a lovely offer. You are so sweet. I will be back this afternoon with Henry (her husband)."

- A couple in business attire was looking warmly at a convertible and expressing interest in negotiating a price. The man said, "We like what we see, but we haven't had lunch. How late are you open this evening? Or maybe we will come back tomorrow." Pamela took the initiative to say, "Stay put, folks. There is a Taco Bell right across the street. Tell me what you want from Taco Bell, and I will get the lunch for you and bring it back. You can look over the beautiful convertible while you are waiting for me for less than fifteen minutes." The woman said, "That's asking too much. We can come back tonight."

Case Questions

1. What is your evaluation of the "Wow" experiences that Pamela is providing?
2. What suggestions might you offer Pamela about her approach to customer service?

Interpersonal Skills Role-Play

Pamela Applies the "Wow" Experience

Case 14.1 provides the three scenarios for this role-play. In each scenario one student plays the role of Pamela, who hopes to provide the "Wow" experience to the customer contemplating the purchase of a vehicle. Other students play the role of the customers. For each of the three scenarios, the students who play the role can improvise the reaction to the proposed "Wow" experience that they choose. Feedback should be directed at how effective Pamela is in delivering a "Wow" experience.

The Rumpled Claims Forms

Rob is the supervisor of scanning operations at Insurance Resource, a firm that specializes in digitizing handwritten insurance claims. The client companies mail their insurance claims in batches to Insurance Resource for processing into a digital format. In addition to scanning the handwritten documents, Insurance Resource also creates computer files for clients, and forwards the claims to the appropriate insurance company for reimbursement.

With profit margins being small in insurance claims processing, the document scanning technicians must work rapidly as well as processing a large volume of claims. One day when Rob asked Wendy to improve her speed, he received a response that he had heard many times in the past.

"How can I work fast when so many of these claims are rumpled, crumpled, and incomplete? We get some forms with missing names and addresses. The other scanning technicians say the same thing. We even have to stop to remove staples from the forms. If we are not careful, the staples get caught in the scanners, and then we have to call tech support to de-jam the machine.

"My speed problem is that some of our clients are just stupid. The speed problem is theirs, not ours. I know that we can send the documents with missing information to our research department, but that takes time from my scanning."

Rob replied, "Wendy, you have a point. Some of our clients make work difficult for us, but they are still valued customers. If we put too much pressure on them to give us claims forms that are easier to scan, they might look for another outsourcing firm.

"I'm going to get with Kim (the vice president of operations), and see if we can get a task force set up to work on this problem of difficult-to-scan documents right away."

Case Questions

1. In what way does this case deal with a customer service problem?

2. What steps do you recommend that Insurance Resource take to get clients to send the company documents that are easier to manage?

3. What suggestions can you offer Wendy and the other scanning technicians to process their work more effectively for now?

Source: Case researched by Stefanie Donaldson, Rochester, New York.

References

1. Quoted in Mark Hendricks, "Paying in Kind: How Can You Ensure Employees Give Service with a Smile?" *Entrepreneur*, February 2006, p. 82.

2. Quoted in Ryan Chittum, "Price Points: Good Customer Service Costs Money. Some Expenses are Worth It—and Some Aren't," *The Wall Street Journal*, October 30, 2006, p. R7.

3. Paul R. Timm, *Customer Service: Career Success Through Customer Satisfaction*, 2nd ed. (Prentice Hall, 2001), p. 8; Anthony Heyes and Sandeep Kapur, "Angry Customers, e-word of Mouth and Incentives for Quality Provision," *Journal of Economic Behavior & Organization*, December 2012, pp. 813–828.

4. Carmine Gallo, "Wow Your Customers the Ritz-Carlton Way," *Executive Leadership*, April 2011, p. 4.

5. Jeff Green and David Welch, "Cadillac Starts Putting on the Ritz," *Bloomberg Businessweek*, June 21–June 27, 2010, p. 24.

6. Quoted in Deborah Alexander, "Keep Tops Intact, Workers Urge," Rochester, New York, *Democrat and Chronicle*, December 1, 2006, p. 9D.

7. Quoted in Lin Grensing-Pophal, "Building Service with a Smile," *HR Magazine*, November 2006, p. 86.

8. Denise Mann, "Optimism May Be Partly in Your Genes," *WebMD Health News* (http://www.webmd.com), September 16, 2011, p. 1.

9. Sue Shellenbarger, "Domino Effect: The Unintended Results of Telling Off Customer-Service Staff," *The Wall Street Journal*, February 5, 2004, p. D1.

10. Lance A. Bettencourt, Kevin P. Gwinner, and Matthew L. Meuter, "A Comparison of Attitude, Personality, and Knowledge Predictors of Service-Oriented Organizational Citizenship Behavior," *Journal of Applied Psychology*, February 2001, pp. 29–41.

11. Philip Mann, "The Role of Communications in Customer Service: A Talk with Dennis Snow," *NY Workplace Communications Examiner* (http://www.examiner.com/), September 20, 2010, pp. 1–4.

12. Alex M. Susskind, K. Michele Kacmar, and Carl P. Borchgrevink, "Customer Service Providers' Attitudes Relating to Customer Service and Customer Satisfaction in the Customer-Server Exchange," *Journal of Applied Psychology*, February 2003, pp. 179–187.

13. Craig A. Martin and Alan J. Bush, "Psychological Climate, Empowerment, and Customer-Oriented Selling: An Analysis of the Sales Manager-Salesperson Dyad," *Journal of the Academy of Marketing Science*, No. 3, 2006, pp. 419–438.

14. Hui Lao and Aichia Chuang, "Transforming Service Employees and Climate: A Multilevel, Multisource Examination of Transformational Leadership in Building Long-Term Service Relationships," *Journal of Applied Psychology*, July 2007, pp. 1006–1019.

15. Karen Holcombe Ehrart, L. A. Witt, Benjamin Schneider, and Sara Jansen Perry, "Service Employees Give as They Get: Internal Service as a Moderator of the Service Climate-Service Outcomes," *Journal of Applied Psychology*, March 2011, pp. 423–431.

16. Jeremy Quittner, "The Art of the Soft Sell," *Business Week Small Biz*, October/November 2009, p. 50.

17. Ann Zimmerman, "Can This Former Clerk Save Best Buy?" *The Wall Street Journal*, April 20, 2013, pp. B1, B6.

18. Richard B. Chase and Sriram Dasu, "Want to Perfect Your Company's Service? Use Behavioral Science," *Harvard Business Review*, June 2001, pp. 78–84.

19. Karl Abrecht, *The Only Thing That Matters* (New York: HarperCollins, 1992).

20. Ken Belson, "For Half a Cent, a Call That Informs, and Annoys," *The New York Times* (http://nytimes.com), July 16, 2008, pp. 1–3.

21. Adapted from "For Extraordinary Service," *The Customer Service Professional*, October 1997, p. 3.

22. Patrick Spenner and Karen Freeman, "To Keep Your Customers, Keep It Simple," *Harvard Business Review*, May 2012, p. 110.

23. Julie Jargon, "McDonalds's Says 'Service is Broken,' Tackles, Repair," *The Wall Street Journal*. April 11, 2013, p. B1, B2.

24. Lorna Ducet, "Service Provider Hostility and Service Quality," *Academy of Management Journal*, October 2004, pp. 761–771.

25. D. J. Cran, "Towards the Validation of the Service Orientation Construct," *The Service Industries Journal*, vol. 14, 1994, p. 36.

26. Dot Yandle, "Helping Your Employees Give Customers What They Want," *Success Workshop* (a supplement to *Manager's Edge*), November 1998, p. 1.

27. Patricia B. Barger and Alicia A. Grandey, "Service with a Smile and Encounter Satisfaction: Emotional Contagion and Appraisal Mechanisms," *Academy of Management Journal*, December 2006, pp. 1229–1238.

28. Steven Gray, "Flipping Burger King," *The Wall Street Journal*, April 26, 2005, B1.

29. Miguel Bustillo and Ann Zimmerman, "Circuit City's Chief Executive Is Ousted," *The Wall Street Journal*, September 23, 2008, p. B1; Rachel Feintzeig, "Lessons from the Death of Circuit City," *http://blogs.wsj.com*, October 25, 2012, p. 1.

30. Christina Binkley, "How to Sell a $35,000 Watch in a Recession," *The Wall Street Journal*, July 23, 2009. p. D6.

31. Quoted in Ryan Chittum, "Price Points: Good Customer Service Costs Money: Some Expenses Are Worth It," *The Wall Street Journal*, October 30, 2006, p. R7.

32. Daniel Akst, book review of *Hug Your Customers* by Jack Mitchell (Hyperion, 2003), appearing in *The Wall Street Journal*, November 14, 2003, p. W9.

33. Hwee Hoon Tan, Maw Der Foo, and Min Hui Kwek, "The Effects of Customer Personality Traits on the Display of Positive Emotions," *Academy of Management Journal*, April 2004, pp. 287–296.

34. Eugene Kim and David J. Yoon, "Why Does Service With a Smile Make Employees Happy?" *Journal of Applied Psychology*, September 2012, p. 1065.

35. Sue Shellenbarger, "How to Keep Your Cool in Angry Times," *The Wall Street Journal*, September 22, 2010, p. D3; Chip R. Bell and Ron Zemke, "Service Breakdown—The Road to Recovery," in *Service Wisdom: Creating and Maintaining the Customer Service Edge* (Minneapolis, MN: Lakewood Books, 1992); Michel, Bowen, and Johnson, "Making the Most of Customer Complaints," pp. R4, R11; Louise Lee, "Oops," *Business Week Small Biz*, August/September 2009, p. 22.

36. Jon Yates, "Tuning In to Comcast's Customer Service," *Chicago Tribune,* November 15, 2009, Section 2, p. 1.

37. Patrick J. Kiger, "The Art of the Apology," *Workforce Management,* October 2004, p. 62.

38. Laura M. Little, Don Kluemper, Debra L. Nelson, and Andrew Ward, "More than Happy to Help? Customer-Focused Emotion Management Strategies," *Personnel Psychology,* Number 1, 2013, pp. 261–286.

39. David Segal, "Appalling Behavior, This Time by Customers," *The New York Times* (http://www.nytimes.com), July 8, 2010, pp. 1–4.

40. Matthew Dixon, Karen Freeman, and Nicholas Toman, "Stop Trying to Delight Your Customers," *Harvard Business Review,* July–August 2010, pp. 116–122.

41. Vikas Mittal, Matthew Sarkees, and Feisal Murshed, "The Right Way to Manage Unprofitable Customers," *Harvard Business Review,* April 2008, p. 102.

42. Raymond Flandez, "It Just Isn't Working? Some File for Customer Divorce," *The Wall Street Journal,* November 10, 2009, p. B7.

Enhancing Ethical Behavior

The US Food and Drug Administration, in partnership with international regulatory and law enforcement agencies, took action in one week against more than 4,100 Internet pharmacies that illegally sell potentially dangerous, unapproved drugs to consumers. Actions taken against the pharmacies included civil and criminal charges, seizure of illegal drugs, and removal of offending Web sites.

The FDA effort resulted in the shutdown of of more than 18,000 illegal pharmaacy Web sites and the seizure of about $10.5 million worth of pharmaceuticals worldwide. The goal of the annual effort, whch involves law enforcement, customs, and regulatory authorities from 100 countries, is to identify producers and distributors of illegal pharmaceutical products and medical devices, and remove these products from the supply chain.

BananaStock/Thinkstock

After reading and studying this chapter and completing the exercises, you should be able to

1. Recognize the importance of ethical behavior for establishing good interpersonal relationships in organizations.
2. Describe why being ethical is not easy.
3. Identify job situations that often present ethical dilemmas.
4. Use a systematic method for making ethical decisions and behaving ethically.

"Consumers in the United States and around the world face a real threat from Internet pharmacies that illegally sell potentially substandard, counterfeit, adulterated, or otherwise unsafe medicines," said FDA Commissioner Margaret A. Hamburg, M.D. "This week's efforts show that strong international enforcement efforts are required to combat this global public health problem. The FDA is committed to joining forces to protect consumers from the risks these Web sites present."

As a follow up to the 4,100 Web sites involved the FDA sent notices to registries, Internet Service Providers (ISPs), and Domain Name Registrants (DNRs), informing them that these Web sites were selling products in violation of US law.

Preliminary findings of the FDA showed that certain products from abroad, such as anntibiotics, antidepressants, and other drugs to treat high cholesterol, diabetes, and high blood pressure, were on their way to US consumers. Many of those products can pose health risks if taken without the supervision of a health care practitioner or if the products have been removed from the market for safety reasons.

Behind each one of the 4,100 Internet pharmacies selling drugs online, there are individuals engaged in unethical and often illegal behavior.[1] Many key people at the Internet companies also had poor enough ethics to know that the Web sites paying them advertising dollars were behaving unethically and illegally.

The federal government report about illegal selling of legal drugs, some of which are contimanated, shows that many business owners and their employees are in dire need of improvement in their ethical behavior. People performing all types of work need a good sense of ethics to be successful. Also, you often need to have an ethical reputation to get the job you want. *Ethics* refers to moral choices, or what is good and bad, right and wrong, just and unjust, and what people should do. Ethics is the vehicle for turning values into action. If you value fair play, you will do such things as giving honest performance evaluations to members of your group.

We study ethics here because a person's ethical code has a significant impact on his or her interpersonal relationships. This chapter's approach will emphasize the importance of ethics, common ethical problems, and guidelines for behaving ethically. Self-Assessment Quiz 15-1 gives you the opportunity to examine your ethical beliefs and attitudes.

WHY BE CONCERNED ABOUT BUSINESS ETHICS?

When asked why ethics is important, most people would respond something to the effect that "Ethics is important because it's the right thing to do. You behave decently in the workplace because your family and religious values have taught you what is right and wrong." All this is true, but the justification for behaving ethically is more complex, as described next.[2]

LEARNING OBJECTIVE 1

ENHANCING ETHICAL BEHAVIOR

The Ethical Reasoning Inventory

Directions: Describe how well you agree with each of the following statements, using the following scale: Disagree Strongly (DS); Disagree (D); Neutral (N); Agree (A); Agree Strongly (AS). Circle the number in the appropriate column.

No.		DS	D	N	A	AS
1.	When applying for a job, I would cover up the fact that I had been fired from my most recent job.	5	4	3	2	1
2.	Cheating just a few dollars in one's favor on an expense account is okay if a person needs the money.	5	4	3	2	1
3.	Employees should report on each other for wrongdoing.	1	2	3	4	5
4.	It is acceptable to give approximate figures for expense account items when one does not have all the receipts.	5	4	3	2	1
5.	I see no problem with conducting a little personal business on company time.	5	4	3	2	1
6.	I would blame a customer for a problem even if I knew the problem was clearly my fault.	5	4	3	2	1
7.	I would fix up a purchasing agent with a date just to close a sale.	5	4	3	2	1
8.	I would flirt with my boss just to get a bigger salary increase.	5	4	3	2	1
9.	If I received $400 for doing some odd jobs, I would report it on my income tax return.	1	2	3	4	5
10.	I see no harm in taking home a few office supplies.	5	4	3	2	1
11.	It is acceptable to read the e-mail messages and company social media postings of coworkers, even when not invited to do so.	5	4	3	2	1
12.	It is unacceptable to call in sick to take a day off, even if only done once or twice a year.	1	2	3	4	5
13.	I would accept a permanent, full-time job even if I knew I wanted the job for only six months.	5	4	3	2	1
14.	I would first check company policy before accepting an expensive gift from a supplier.	1	2	3	4	5
15.	To be successful in business, a person usually has to ignore ethics.	5	4	3	2	1
16.	If I felt physically attracted toward a job candidate, I would hire that person over a more qualified candidate.	5	4	3	2	1
17.	On the job, I tell the truth all the time.	1	2	3	4	5
18.	If a student were very pressed for time, it would be acceptable to either have a friend write the paper or purchase one.	5	4	3	2	1
19.	I would be willing to put a hazardous chemical in a consumer product if the product makes a good profit for the company.	5	4	3	2	1
20.	I would never accept credit for a coworker's ideas.	1	2	3	4	5

Total Score _____

Scoring and Interpretation: Add the numbers you have circled to obtain your total score.

90–100: You are a strongly ethical person who may take a little ribbing from coworkers for being too straitlaced.

60–89: You show an average degree of ethical awareness, and therefore should become more sensitive to ethical issues.

41–59: Your ethics are underdeveloped, but you at least have some awareness of ethical issues. You need to raise your level of awareness of ethical issues.

20–40: Your ethical values are far below contemporary standards in business. Begin a serious study of business ethics.

A major justification for behaving ethically on the job is to recognize that people are motivated by both self-interest and moral commitments. Most people want to maximize gain for themselves (remember the expectancy theory of motivation?). At the same time, most people are motivated to do something morally right. As one of many examples, vast numbers of people donate money to charity even though keeping that amount of money for themselves would provide more personal gain.

Many business executives want employees to behave ethically because a good reputation can enhance business. A favorable corporate reputation may enable firms to charge premium prices and attract better job applicants. A favorable reputation also helps attract investors, such as mutual fund managers who purchase stock in companies. Certain mutual funds, for example, invest only in companies that are environmentally friendly. Managers want employees to behave ethically because unethical behavior—for example, employee theft, wasting time on the job, and lawsuits—is costly.

Behaving ethically is also important because many unethical acts are illegal as well, which can lead to financial loss and imprisonment. According to one estimate, the cost of unethical and fraudulent acts committed by US employees totals $400 billion per year. A company that knowingly allows workers to engage in unsafe practices might be fined, and the executives may be held personally liable. In 2011, Google Inc. paid $500 million to settle the criminal probe into allowing improper online pharmacy ads on its Web site. Google later stopped running the ads, and the FDA investigation was dropped.[3]

Furthermore, unsafe practices can kill people. In recent years many people have perished in night club fires because there was only one door in operation, or unsafe pyrotechnics were on the premises. The financial scandals in recent years that resulted in major losses for millions of investors stemmed in part from financial managers making such risky investments that they were unethical. Securities were sold to the public that were based on loans to consumers with very poor credit ratings. The FDA report presented at the beginning of this chapter indicates that the unethical sale of drugs online can result in consumers ingesting dangerous substances.

A subtle reason for behaving ethically is that high ethics increases the quality of work life. Ethics provides a set of guidelines that specify what makes for acceptable behavior. Being ethical will point you toward actions that make life more satisfying for work associates. A company code of ethics specifies what constitutes ethical versus unethical behavior. When employees follow this code, the quality of work life improves. Several sample clauses from ethical codes are as follows:

- Demonstrate courtesy, respect, honesty, and fairness.
- Do not use abusive language.
- Do not bring firearms or knives to work.
- Do not offer bribes.
- Maintain confidentiality of records.
- Do not harass (sexually, racially, ethnically, or physically) subordinates, superiors, coworkers, customers, or suppliers.

To the extent that all members of the organization abide by this ethical code, the quality of work life will improve. At the same time, interpersonal relations in organizations will be strengthened.

WHY WE HAVE SO MANY ETHICAL PROBLEMS

LEARNING OBJECTIVE 2

moral intensity

In ethical decision making, how deeply others might be affected by the decision.

To become more skilled at behaving ethically, it is important to familiarize yourself with common ethical problems in organizations. Whether or not a given situation presents an ethical problem for a person depends to some extent on its **moral intensity**, or how deeply others might be affected.[4] A worker might face a strong ethical conflict about dumping mercury into a water supply but would be less concerned about dumping cleaning fluid. Yet both acts would be considered unethical and illegal. Here we first look at why being ethical is not as easy as it sounds. We then look at some data about the frequency of ethical problems and an analysis of predictable ethical temptations, and also examine the subtle ethical dilemma of choosing between rights.

Why Being Ethical Isn't Easy

As analyzed by Linda Klebe Treviño and Michael E. Brown, behaving ethically in business is more complex than it seems on the surface for a variety of reasons, as described next.[5]

Michael Stravato/AP Images

1. **Complexity of ethical decisions.** To begin with, ethical decisions are complex. For example, someone might argue that hiring children for factory jobs in overseas countries is unethical. Yet if these children lose their jobs, many would starve or turn to crime to survive. Second, people do not always recognize the moral issues involved in a decision. The home-maintenance worker who finds a butcher knife under the bed might not think that he has a role to play in perhaps preventing murder. Sometimes language hides the moral issue involved, such as when the term "file sharing" music replaces "stealing" music.

2. **Predisposition to be unethical.** A fundamental reason that being ethical is not always easy is that some people have a predisposition to be unethical. The predisposition works almost like a personality trait, compelling certain people to be devious. A person with a **utilitarian predisposition** believes that the value of an act's outcomes should determine whether it is moral.[6] A server with this predisposition might be willing to serve food that dropped on the floor, so long as no customer became sick or sued the restaurant. A small business owner with a utilitarian predisposition might be willing to sell fake luxury goods on the Internet so long as nobody complained, and he or she was not caught. When asked about why he sold imitation watches, one vendor said, "What's the difference? My watches look like the real thing, and they tell time."

3. **Self-interest.** Another major contributor to ethical problems is the same factor that motivates people to do many things—acting out of self-interest. John Bogle, the founder and former chief executive of the Vanguard Group of Mutual Funds, believes that self-interest contributed to the financial scandals of recent years. (And financial scandals of enormous proportions continue.) "But self-interest got out of hand. It created a bottom-line society in which success is measured in monetary terms. Dollars became the coin of the new realm. Unchecked market forces overwhelmed traditional standards of professional conduct, developed over centuries."[7]

Another take on self-interest is that employee fraud intensifies during difficult financial times in which workers are experiencing financial pressures in their personal lives. Among these frauds are check-forgery schemes, petty-cash thefts, and taking money from fabricated customer returns.[8] All of these schemes are illegal as well as unethical.

4. **Levels of moral development.** Another complexity in making ethical decisions is that people have different levels of moral development. At one end of the scale, some people behave morally just to escape punishment. At the other end of the scale, some people are morally developed to the point that they are guided by principles of justice and

want to help as many people as possible. The environment in which we work also influences whether we behave ethically. Suppose a restaurant owner encourages such practices as serving customers food that was accidentally dropped on the kitchen floor. An individual server is more likely to engage in such behavior to obey the demands of the owner—even though the server knows that dangerous bacteria may have attached to the food.

5. **Moral disengagement.** Closely related to moral development is that some people have a tendency to *morally disengage,* or think in such a way that avoids being moral without feeling distress. A product development specialist might morally disengage from selling a trade secret to a competitor by rationalizing that he or she is underpaid and therefore deserves supplementary income from working so hard. Workers with a strong tendency to morally disengage have been shown to engage in such behaviors as committing fraud, and self-reported lying, cheating, and stealing.[9]

6. **Goals that reward unethical behavior.** Another major reason for unethical behavior in business is that goals sometimes reward unethical behavior, such as sales representatives being rewarded for sales with less attention to how the sale is accomplished. To enhance sales, the representative might then offer a bribe (or kickback) to the customer in order to attain the sale. Another example is that a dental hygienist might be assigned a goal of increasing teeth-whitening procedures by 15 percent. She might then encourage people to have their teeth whitened whose teeth are already white enough for practical purposes.

7. **Motivated blindness.** Ethics professors Max H. Bazerman of Harvard and Ann E. Tenbrunsel at the Notre Dame University explain that another reason for poor corporate ethics is *motivated blindness.* People tend to see what they want to see and easily block out contradictory information when it is in their interest to remain uninformed.[10] A mortgage broker intent on placing a lot of mortgages may be almost unconsciously motivated to overlook certain credit red flags on a mortgage application, such as the applicant having no savings account. To find red flags in the application represents a conflict of interest between selling the mortgage to a bank and making an honest appraisal of the mortgage application.

The Extent of Ethical Problems

Ethical violations by workers at all job levels are widespread, even if decreasing from years past. According to the 2011 National Business Ethics Survey, 45 percent of US employees observed a violation of the law or ethics standards at their workplace. Sixty-five percent of employees reported wrongdoing, but one out of five employees who reported the misdeeds were retaliated against. An example of retaliation would be to receive a poor performance evalution or be denied a promotion. Here are a few findings from the survey:

- Misconduct witnessed by American workers is low in comparison to previous years, whereas reporting of the misconduct is quite high.
- Thirteen percent of employees perceived pressure to compromise standards in order to do their jobs.
- As the economy improves and employees become more optimistic about their financial futures they engage in more misconduct—most likely because they worry less about beign fired for an ethical transgression, such as taking care of personal business on the job.
- Active social networkers report many negative experiences in their workplace. At the same time, active social networkers show a higher tolerance for certain activities that could be considered questionable, such as being bullied.

Earlier surveys have indicated such specific problems as lying to employees, engaging in health and safety violations, stealing, and sexual harassment.[11] These findings might suggest that workers are observant of ethical problems and willing to note them on a survey.

FIGURE 15-1 Frequent Ethical Dilemmas

Many ethical temptations face the individual on the job, forcing him or her to think through ethical issues practically every workday.

Illegally copying software	Treating people unfairly	Sexually harassing coworkers
Facing a conflict of interest	Abusing confidential information	Misrepresenting employment or education history
Misusing corporate resources	Ethically violating computers and information technology	Wasting company time

Frequent Ethical Problems

Certain ethical mistakes, including illegal actions, recur in the workplace. Familiarizing oneself can be helpful in monitoring one's own behavior. The next subsections describe a number of common ethical problems faced by business executives as well as by workers at lower job levels.[12] Figure 15-1 outlines these problems.

Illegally Copying Software.   A rampant ethical problem is whether or not to illegally copy computer software, including downloads from the Internet. According to the Business Software Alliance, approximately 35 percent of applications used in business are illegal.[13] The rate of piracy for personal use might be higher because individuals tend to worry less about being caught than does a business enterprise.

Treating People Unfairly.   Being fair to people means equity, reciprocity, and impartiality. Fairness revolves around the issue of giving people equal rewards for accomplishing equal amounts of work. The goal of human resource legislation is to make decisions about people based on their qualifications and performance—not on the basis of demographic factors such as gender, race, or age. A fair working environment is one in which performance is the only factor that counts (equity). Employer–employee expectations must be understood and met (reciprocity). Prejudice and bias must be eliminated (impartiality).

Treating people fairly—and therefore ethically—requires a de-emphasis on political factors, or favoritism. Yet this ethical doctrine is not always easy to implement. It is human nature to want to give bigger rewards (such as fatter raises or bigger orders) to people we like.

A major contributor to treating people unfairly is cronyism, or giving jobs to people who have done personal favors for you. Often an unqualified friend is given a position even though competent and qualified candidates are available. Cronyism is often practiced in government, wherein heads of government agencies are sometimes appointed mostly because they are supporters and friends of the person in power.

Sexually Harassing Coworkers.   In Chapter 9, we looked at sexual harassment as a source of conflict and an illegal act. Sexual harassment is also an ethical issue because it is morally wrong and unfair. All acts of sexual harassment flunk an ethics test. Before sexually harassing another person, the potential harasser should ask, "Would I want a loved one to be treated this way?"

Facing a Conflict of Interest.   Part of being ethical is making business judgments only on the basis of the merits or facts in a situation. Imagine that you are a supervisor who is

> " *Follow the* Platinum Rule: *Treat people the way* they *wish to be treated.* "
>
> —Eric Harvey and Scott Airitam, authors of *Ethics 4 Everyone*

romantically involved with a worker within the group. When it comes time to assign raises, it will be difficult for you to be objective. A **conflict of interest** occurs when your judgment or objectivity is compromised. Conflicts of interest often take place in the sales end of business. If a company representative accepts a large gift from a sales representative, it may be difficult to make objective judgments about buying from the rep. Yet being taken to dinner by a vendor would not ordinarily cloud one's judgment. Another common example of a conflict of interest is making a hiring decision about a friend who badly needs a job, but is not well qualified for the position.

conflict of interest
A situation that occurs when a person's judgment or objectivity is compromised.

Blogging has created a new type of conflict of interest because many bloggers are paid for those kind, supposedly objective comments they insert on the Internet about products and services. The Federal Trade Commission now requires bloggers to clearly disclose any payments or freebies they receive from companies for publishing reviews about their products or services. Penalties include a maximum fine of up to $11,000 per violation.[14]

Abusing Confidential Information. An ethical person can be trusted by others not to divulge confidential information unless the welfare of others is at stake. Suppose a coworker tells you in confidence that she is upset with the company and is therefore looking for another job. Behaving ethically, you do not pass along this information to your supervisor even though it would help your supervisor plan for a replacement. Now suppose the scenario changes slightly. Your coworker tells you she is looking for another job because she is upset. She tells you she is so upset that she plans to destroy company computer files on her last day. If your friend does find another job, you might warn the company about her contemplated activities.

The challenge of dealing with confidential information arises in many areas of business, many of which affect interpersonal relations. If you learned that a coworker was indicted for a crime, charged with sexual harassment, or facing bankruptcy, there would be a temptation to gossip about the person. A highly ethical person would not pass along information about the personal difficulties of another person.

Misrepresenting Employment or Education History. Many people are tempted to distort in a positive direction information about their employment or education history on their job résumé, on their job application form, and during the interview. Distortion, or lying, of this type is considered to be unethical and can lead to immediate dismissal if discovered. Misrepresentation of credentials takes place at all job levels. Inflated credentials in the executive suite have been an embarrassment to many companies. A survey of 358 senior executives at 53 publicly traded companies has uncovered seven instances of inaccurate claims that an individual had received an academic degree. In recent years, misrepresentation of academic credentials has cost top corporate officials their positions at companies, including RadioShack Corp., Veritas Software Corp., Herbalife International, and Yahoo! Inc.. A former president of the US Olympic Committee resigned from her post because she lied about past college degrees.[15]

Misusing Corporate Resources. A corporate resource is anything the company owns, including its name and reputation. If Jake Petro worked for Ford Motor Company, for example, it would be unethical for him to establish a body shop and put on his letterhead and Web site, "Jake Petro, Manufacturing Technician, Ford Motor Company." (The card and Web site would imply that Ford Motor Co. supports this venture.) Other uses of corporate resources fall more into the gray area. It might be quite ethical to borrow a tablet computer for the weekend from your employer to conduct work at home; it would be less ethical to borrow the computer to prepare income taxes. In the latter case, you might be accused of using corporate resources for personal purposes. Loading personal software on company computers so that you can access your bank account and so forth also can be considered an ethical violation.

Ethically Violating Computers and Information Technology. As computers dominate the workplace, many ethical issues have arisen in addition to pirating software. One ethical dilemma that surfaces frequently is the fairness of tracking the Web sites a person visits and those he or she buys from. Should this information be sold, like a mailing list? The scams that appear on e-mail every day are another prime example of the unethical use of information technology. Another issue is the fairness of having an employee work at a keyboard for 60 hours in one week when such behavior frequently leads to repetitive motion disorder, vision problems, and back pain.

Wasting Company Time.   Many workers waste company time in the pursuit of personal interests. Among these time wasters are making personal phone calls, shopping by phone or the Internet, visiting sports and pornography sites, talking about personal matters with coworkers, daydreaming, and spending long periods of time smoking outside the building. The problem has become so severe with smartphones and text messaging that many employers forbid the use of smartphones while working. A complicating factor, however, is that many employers allow and even encourage workers to use their own electronic gadgets on the job for work purposes. The section in Chapter 16 about personal productivity presents data about time wasting on the job.

Engaging in Unethical Behavior to Benefit the Company.   A final ethical dilemma here is whether to engage in unethical behavior in order to help the company. This type of dilemma also contributes to unethical behavior in the workplace. Employees will be tempted to engage in unethical acts in order to benefit the company, in such ways as the following: (1) "cooking" numbers to boost the prediction of financial analysts' projections and stock values; (2) withholding information about the hazards of a pharmaceutical product; and (3) neglecting to give customers correct change when the amount is small, such as 25 cents.

Two studies found that workers were more likely to engage in unethical behavior when they identify with their employer, and at the same time expect they will be rewarded for such behavior.[16] An example would be receiving a favorable performance evaluation for benefiting the company with unethical behavior.

You may have observed that these common ethical problems are not always clear-cut. Aside from obvious matters such as prohibitions against stealing, lying, cheating, and intimidating, subjectivity enters into ethical decision making. Skill-Building Exercise 15-1 provides an opportunity to try out your ethical reasoning.

Choosing between Two Rights: Dealing with Defining Moments

Ethical decision making usually involves choosing between two options: one we perceive to be right and one we perceive to be wrong. A challenging twist to ethical decision making is to sort through your values when you have to choose between two rights, or two morally sound choices. Joseph L. Badaracco Jr. uses the term **defining moment** to describe choosing between two or more ideals in which we deeply believe.[17] If you can learn to work through defining moments, your ethical skills will be enhanced. Imagine the following scenario:

defining moment

Choosing between two or more ideals in which one deeply believes.

> *You work for an employer that has a policy of forbidding unauthorized personnel to stay on company premises. As you exit the office building one day through a back door, you notice a homeless-appearing person sleeping under a stairwell. The temperature outside the building is 105 degrees (F). You imagine that the sleeping visitor is attempting to escape the horrendous heat, perhaps even to survive. Do you call the security department to escort the man out the building, or do you just let him enjoy his comfortable sleeping place, thereby violating company policy?*

You may have recognized that a defining moment is a role conflict in which you have to choose between competing values. A CEO might deeply believe that she has an obligation to the stockholders to make a profit, and also believe in being generous and fair toward employees. To make a profit this year, however, she will be forced to lay off several good employees with long seniority. The CEO now faces a moment of truth. Badaracco suggests that the individual can work through a defining moment by discovering "Who am I?" You discover who you are by soul-searching answers to three questions:

1. What feelings and intuitions are coming into conflict in this situation?
2. Which of the values that are in conflict are the most deeply rooted in my life?

The Ethics Game

Many companies teach ethics by asking small teams of employees to confront difficult scenarios such as those that follow. Discuss these ethical problems in teams. As you discuss the scenarios, identify the ethical issues involved.

Scenario 1: One of your assignments is to find a contractor to conduct building maintenance for your company headquarters. You invite bids for the job. High-Performance Cleaners, a firm staffed largely by teenagers from troubled families who have criminal records, bids on the job.

Many of these teenagers also have severe learning disabilities and cannot readily find employment. High-Performance Cleaners proves to be the second highest bidder. You:

A. Advise High-Performance Cleaners that its bid is too high for consideration and that your company is not a social agency.

B. Award the bid to High-Performance Cleaners, and justify your actions with a letter to top management talking about social responsibility.

C. Falsify the other bids in your report to management, making High-Performance Cleaners the low bidder—and thus the contract winner.

D. Explain to High-Performance Cleaners that it lost the bid, but you will award the company a piece of the contract because of its sterling work with teenagers in need.

Scenario 2: You live in Texas, and your company sends you on a three-day trip to New York City. Your business dealings in the Big Apple will keep you there Wednesday, Thursday, and Friday morning. You have several friends and relatives in New York, so you decide to stay there until Sunday afternoon. Besides, you want to engage in tourist activities such as taking a boat tour around Manhattan and visiting Radio City Music Hall. When preparing your expense report for your trip, you request payment for all your business-related costs up through Friday afternoon, plus

A. Your return trip on Sunday.

B. The return trip and the room cost for Friday and Saturday nights.

C. The return trip, one-half of your weekend food expenses, and two extra nights in the hotel.

D. The return trip and your food costs for the weekend (which you justify because you ate at fast-food restaurants on Wednesday, Thursday, and Friday).

Scenario 3: You are the leader of a work team in a financial services company. The work of your team has expanded to the point where you are authorized to hire another team member. The team busily interviews a number of candidates from inside and outside the company. The other team members agree that one of the candidates (Pat) has truly outstanding credentials. You agree that Pat is a strong candidate, yet you don't want Pat on the team because the two of you were emotionally involved for about a year. You think that working with Pat would disrupt your concentration and bring back hurtful memories. You decide to

A. Tell the group that you have some negative information about Pat's past that would disqualify Pat for the job.

B. Telephone Pat and beg that Pat find employment elsewhere.

C. Tell the group that you agree Pat is qualified, but explain your concerns about the disruption in concentration and emotional hurt.

D. Tell the group that you agree Pat is right for the position, and mention nothing about the past relationship.

Scoring and Observation: Scenario 1, about High-Performance Cleaners, raises dozens of ethical questions, including whether humanitarian considerations can outweigh profit concerns. Teams that chose "A" receive 0 points; "B," 15 points; "C," −10 points; "D," 20 points. (Answer "D" is best here because it would not be fair to give the bid to the second-highest bidder; however, you are still finding a way to reward the High-Performance Cleaners for its meritorious work in the community. Answer "C" is the worst because you would be outright lying.)

Scenario 2 raises ethical issues about using company resources. Teams that chose "A" receive 20 points; "B," −10 points; "C," −15 points; "D," 0 points. (Answer "A" is fairest because the company would expect to reimburse you for your roundtrip plus the expenses up through Friday afternoon. Answer "C" is the worst because it would be unjustified for you to be reimbursed for your vacation in New York.)

Scenario 3 raises issues about fairness in making selection decisions. Teams that chose "A" receive −20 points; "B," −10 points; "C," 15 points; "D," 0 points. (Answer "C" is the most ethical because you are being honest with the group about the reason you do not wish to hire Pat. Answer "A" is the most unethical because you are telling lies about Pat. Furthermore, you might be committing the illegal act of libel.)

3. What combinations of expediency and shrewdness, coupled with imagination and boldness, will help me implement my personal understanding of what is right?

Skill-Building Exercise 15-2 gives you an opportunity to deal with defining moments. The three questions just asked could help you find answers, but do not be constrained by these questions.

GUIDELINES FOR BEHAVING ETHICALLY

Following guidelines for ethical behavior is the heart of being ethical. Although many people behave ethically without studying ethical guidelines, they are usually following guidelines programmed into their minds early in life. The Golden Rule exemplifies a

LEARNING OBJECTIVE 3

Dealing with Defining Moments

The toughest ethical choices for many people occur when they have to choose between two rights. The result is a defining moment, because we are challenged to think in a deeper way by choosing between two or more ideals. Working individually or in teams, deal with the two following defining moments. Explain why these scenarios could require choosing between two rights, and explain the reasoning behind your decisions.

Scenario 1: You are the manager of a department in a business firm that assigns each department a fixed amount of money for salary increases each year. An average-performing member of the department asks you in advance for an above-average increase. He explains that his mother has developed multiple sclerosis and requires the services of a paid helper from time to time. You are concerned that if you give this man an above-average increase, somebody else in the department will have to receive a below-average increase.

Scenario 2: You are the team leader of an e-tailing (retail selling over the Internet) group. In recent months each team member has been working about 60 hours per week, with little prospect of the workload decreasing in the future. Since the e-tailing project is still losing money, higher management insists that one person be dropped from the team. One member of the team, Mildred, is willing to work only 45 hours per week because she spends considerable time volunteering with autistic children. Mildred's work is satisfactory, but her output is the lowest in the group because of her shorter number of working hours. You must make a decision about whether to recommend that Mildred be dismissed.

guideline taught by parents, grandparents, and kindergarten teachers. In this section, we approach ethical guidelines from five perspectives: (1) developing virtuousness including honesty and integrity, (2) following a guide to ethical decision making, (3) developing strong relationships with work associates, (4) using corporate ethics programs, and (5) following an applicable professional code of conduct.

Developing Virtuousness Including Honesty and Integrity

A deep-rooted approach to behaving ethically is to have strong moral and ethical principles, or to be virtuous. A person of high virtue has good character and genuine motivation and intentions. A major problem in becoming virtuous is to agree on what values constitute virtuousness. A key component of virtuousness is **honesty**, the refusal to fake reality, a value that contributes directly to ethical behavior. Being dishonest can also be illegal, such as when a company lies to the Internal Revenue Service about expenses it incurred or hides revenue when preparing a tax report.[18] Dishonesty in terms of making false statements about the financial health of an enterprise has been one of the most frequent business frauds. Being caught lying can lead to dismissal at many employers. An example of such a lie would be blaming someone else for a mistake of your own.

honesty

The refusal to fake reality.

     Integrity means loyalty to one's rational convictions, or sticking with one's principles. If you believe that favoritism is immoral, then you would not recommend that the company hire a friend of yours who you know to be unqualified. Integrity in turn leads to being trusted, because trust stems from delivering consistently on what you promise as a manager, an employee, and a coworker.[19]

integrity

Loyalty to one's rational convictions, or sticking with one's principles.

Seeing the Big Picture

A key contributor to being ethical is to understand how the work you are doing fits into the big picture or the total consequences of your actions. To take an obvious example, the assistant pharmacist is behaving ethically when he or she concentrates totally on filling a prescription. To do otherwise might be to endanger the health of a customer by giving that person the wrong prescription or the wrong dose. R. Glenn Hubbard, dean of the Columbia Business School, believes that future leaders must connect the dots, or see the big picture instead of focusing on their area of expertise.[20] For example, if the head of finance calls for a reduction in expenses for new product development, the company may be injured in the long run. Or if the head chef uses horsemeat instead of beef in certain dishes, an exposé may result that runs the restaurant out of business. (In the examples of the financial officer and the chef, the big picture is the future of the employer, and the small picture is making an immediate dollar savings.)

Following a Guide to Ethical Decision Making

A powerful strategy for behaving ethically is to follow a guide for ethical decision making. Such a guide for making contemplated decisions includes testing ethics. **Ethical screening** refers to running a contemplated decision or action through an ethics test. Such screening makes the most sense when the contemplated action or decision is not clearly ethical or unethical. If a sales representative were to take a favorite customer to Pizza Hut for lunch, an ethical screen would not be necessary. Nobody would interpret a pizza, salad, and a beer or soft drink to be a serious bribe. Assume, instead, that the sales rep offered to give the customer an under-the-table gift of $1000 for placing a large offer with the rep's firm. The sales representative's behavior would be so blatantly unethical that conducting an ethical screen would be unnecessary.

Several useful ethical screens, or guides to ethical decision making, have been developed. A guide developed by Treviño and Nelson is presented here because it incorporates the basic ideas in other ethical tests.[21] After studying this guide, you will be asked to ethically screen three different scenarios. The eight steps to sound ethical decision making follow.

1. **Gather the facts.** When making an important decision in business, it is necessary to gather relevant facts. Ask yourself the following questions: "Are there any legal issues involved here?" "Is there precedent in our firm with respect to this type of decision?" "Do I have the authority to make this decision?" "Are there company rules and regulations governing such a decision?"

The manager of a child care center needed to hire an additional child care specialist. One of the applicants was a 55-year-old male with experience as a father and grandfather. The manager judged him to be qualified, yet she knew that many parents would not want their preschool children to be cared for by a middle-aged male. Many people perceive that a younger woman is better qualified for child care than an older man. The manager therefore had to gather considerable facts about the situation, including facts about job discrimination and precedents in hiring males as child care specialists.

Gathering facts is influenced by emotion, with the result that ethical decision making is not an entirely rational process.[22] We tend to interpret facts based upon our biases and preconceived notions. For example, if the child care center manager has heard negative information about middle-aged men who want to engage in child care, the manager might look hard for indicators that this candidate should be disqualified.

2. **Define the ethical issues.** The ethical issues in a given decision are often more complicated than a first glance suggests. When faced with a complex decision, it may be helpful to talk over the ethical issues with another person. The ethical issues might involve **character traits** such as being kind and caring and treating others with respect. Or the ethical issues might relate to some of the common ethical problems described earlier in the chapter. Among them are facing conflict of interest, dealing with confidential information, and using corporate resources.

The manager of the child care center is facing such ethical issues as fairness, job discrimination, and meeting the demands of customers at the expense of job applicants. The manager is also facing a diversity issue: Should the workforce in a child care center be culturally diverse, or do we hire only young women?

3. **Identify the affected parties.** When faced with a complex ethical decision, it is important to identify all the affected parties. Major corporate decisions can affect thousands of people. If a company decides to shut down a plant and outsource the manufacturing to a low-wage country, thousands of individuals and many different parties are affected. Workers lose their jobs, suppliers lose their customers, the local government loses out on tax revenues, and local merchants lose many of their customers. (However, many people in the other country benefit from the work being outsourced.) You may need to brainstorm with a few others to think of all the parties affected by a given decision.

The parties affected by the decision about hiring or not hiring the 55-year-old male include the applicant himself, the children, the parents, and the board of directors of the child care center. The government might also be involved if the man were rejected and filed charges of age and sex discrimination.

ethical screening

Running a contemplated decision or action through an ethics test.

character traits

Enduring characteristics of a person that are related to moral and ethical behavior.

4. Predict the consequences. After you have identified the parties affected by a decision, the next step is to predict the consequences for each party. It may not be necessary to identify every consequence, yet it is important to identify the consequences with the highest probability of occurring and those with the most negative outcomes. The problem is that many people can be harmed by an unethical decision, such as not fully describing the possible side effects of a diet program.

Both short-term and long-term consequences should be specified. A company closing a plant might create considerable short-term turmoil, but in the long term the company might be healthier. People participating in a diet program might achieve their short-term objective of losing weight. Yet in the long term, their health might be adversely affected because the diet is not nutritionally balanced.

The *symbolic* consequences of an action are important. Every action and decision sends a message (the decision is a symbol of something). If a company moves manufacturing out of a community to save on labor costs, it means that the short-term welfare of domestic or local employees is less important than profit or perhaps the company surviving.

We return to the child care manager and the job applicant. If the applicant does not get the job, his welfare will be adversely affected. He has been laid off by a large employer and cannot find work in his regular field. His family will also suffer because he will not be able to make a financial contribution to the family. Yet if the man is hired, the child care center may suffer. Many traditionally minded parents will say, "Absolutely not. I do not want my child cared for by a middle-aged man. He could be a child molester." (It may be unethical for people to have vicious stereotypes, yet they still exist.) If the child care center does hire the man, the act will symbolize the fact that the owners of the center value diversity.

5. Identify the obligations. Identify the obligations and the reasons for each obligation when making a complex decision. The manufacturer of automotive brakes has an obligation to produce and sell only brakes that meet high safety standards. The obligation is to the auto manufacturer who purchases the brakes and, more important, to the ultimate consumer whose safety depends on effective brakes. The reason for the obligation to make safe brakes is that lives are at stake. The child care center owner has an obligation to provide for the safety and health of the children at the center. She must also provide for the peace of mind of the parents and be a good citizen of the community in which the center is located. The decision about hiring the candidate in question must be balanced against all these obligations.

6. Consider your character and integrity. A core consideration when faced with an ethical dilemma is how relevant people would judge your character and integrity. What would your family, friends, significant others, teachers, and coworkers think of your actions? To refine this thinking even further, how would you feel if your actions were publicly disclosed in the local newspaper or over e-mail? Would you want the world to know that you gave an under-the-table kickback or that you sexually harassed a frightened teenager working for you? If you would be proud for others to know what decision you made when you faced an ethical dilemma, you are probably making the right decision.

The child care center manager might ponder how she would feel if the following information were released in the local newspaper or on the Internet:

> The manager of Good Times Child Care recently rejected the application of a 55-year-old man for a child care specialist position. She said that although Mr. _____ was well qualified from an experience and personality standpoint, she couldn't hire him. She said that Good Times would lose too much business because many parents would fear that Mr. _____ was a child molester or pedophile.

7. Think creatively about potential actions. When faced with an ethical dilemma, put yourself in a creative-thinking mode. Stretch your imagination to invent several options rather than thinking you have only two choices—to do or not do something. Creative thinking may point toward a third, and even fourth, alternative. Imagine this ethical dilemma: A purchasing agent is told that if her firm awards a contract to the sales representative's firm, she will find a leather jacket of her choice delivered to her door. The purchasing agent says to herself, "I think we should award the contract to the firm, but I cannot accept the gift. Yet if I turn down the gift, I will be forfeiting a valuable possession that the company simply regards as a cost of doing business."

The purchasing agent can search for another alternative. She may say to the sales rep, "We will give the contract to your firm because your products fit our requirements. I thank you for the offer of the leather jacket, but instead I would like you to give the jacket to the Salvation Army."

A creative alternative for the child care manager might be to offer the applicant the next position that opened for an office manager or maintenance person in the center. In this way, she would be offering a qualified applicant a job, but placing him in a position more acceptable to parents. Or do you feel that this is a cop-out?

8. **Check your intuition.** So far we have emphasized the rational side of ethical decision making. Another effective way of conducting an ethical screen is to rely on your intuition. How does the contemplated decision feel? Would you be proud of yourself, or would you hate yourself if you made the decision? Imagine how you would feel if you took money from the handbag of a woman sleeping in the park. Would you feel the same way if you took a kickback, sold somebody a defective product, or sold an 80-year-old man an insurance policy he didn't need? How will the manager of the child care center feel if she turns down the man for the child care specialist position? In general, experienced workers rely more heavily on intuition when making ethical choices. The reason is that intuition is based largely on experience. Rules for ethical behavior are important, yet often we have to follow our hunches. Experience and rules are not wasted because intuition includes both experience and having studied rules in the past.

You are encouraged to use the guide for ethical decision making when you next face an ethical dilemma of consequence. Skill-Building Exercise 15-3 gives you an opportunity to practice using the eight steps for ethical decision making.

Developing Strong Relationships with Work Associates

A provocative explanation of the causes of unethical behavior emphasizes the strength of relationships among people.[23] Assume that two people have close professional ties to each other, such as having worked together for a long time or knowing each other both

---

SKILL-BUILDING EXERCISE 15-3

Ethical Decision Making

Working in small groups, take one or more of the following ethical dilemmas through the eight steps for screening contemplated decisions. If more than one group chooses the same scenario, compare your answers for the various steps.

Scenario 1: To Recycle or Not. Your group is the top management team at a large insurance company. Despite the movement toward digitizing all records, your firm still generates tons of paper each month. Customer payments alone account for truckloads of envelopes each year. The paper recyclers in your area claim that they can hardly find a market any longer for used paper, so they will be charging you just to accept your paper for recycling. Your group is wondering whether to recycle.

Scenario 2: Charitable Giving by Company. You are the chief financial officer at a large company that manufactures T-shirts, among other types of clothing. A particularly popular line of T-shirts contains drawings of wild animals such as wolves, polar bears, whales, and eagles. In-store promotion of these T-shirts includes the statement that the company will give back 5 percent of net revenue from these animal-themed T-shirts to local

charities. However, this year you notice that the company may not make a profit, so every dollar saved counts. You calculate that if you do not donate the five percent of revenues on these T-shirts, the company might make a profit or at least break even. Your group must decide whether the company should hold back on donating part of the proceeds from the sale of these T-shirts to charity.

Scenario 3: The High-Profit Toys. You are a toy company executive starting to plan your holiday season line. You anticipate that the season's hottest item will be Robo-Woman, a battery-operated crime fighter and superheroine. Robo-Woman should wholesale for $25 and retail for $45. Your company figures to earn $15 per unit. You receive a sales call from a manufacturing broker who says he can produce any toy you want for one-third of your present manufacturing cost. He admits that the manufacturer he represents uses prison labor in China, but insists that his business arrangement violates no law. You estimate you can earn $20 per unit if you do business with the manufacturing broker. Your decision is whether to do business with him.

---

on and off the job. As a consequence, they are likely to behave ethically toward one another on the job. In contrast, if a weak professional relationship exists between two individuals, either party is more likely to engage in an unethical relationship. The owner of a hair salon is more likely to behave unethically, such as recommending the purchase of a high-priced hair conditioner that a customer doesn't need, toward a stranger passing through town than toward a long-time customer. (The section in Chapter 13 about building relationships with coworkers and work associates provides suggestions for developing strong relationships.) The opportunity for unethical behavior between strangers is often minimized because individuals typically do not trust strangers with sensitive information or valuables.

The ethical skill-building positive consequence of information about personal relationships is that building stronger relationships with people is likely to enhance ethical behavior. If you build strong relationships with work associates, you are likely to behave more ethically toward them. Similarly, your work associates are likely to behave more ethically toward you. The work associates referred to are all your contacts, both internal and external customers.

Self-Assessment Quiz 15-2 provides an opportunity to think about the ethical aspects of your relationships with coworkers.

Using Corporate Ethics Programs

Many organizations have various programs and procedures for promoting ethical behavior. Among them are committees that monitor ethical behavior, training programs in ethics, and vehicles for reporting ethical violations. The presence of these programs is designed to create an atmosphere in which unethical behavior is discouraged, and reporting on unethical behavior is encouraged.

Ethics hotlines are one of the best established programs to help individuals avoid unethical behavior. Should a person be faced with an ethical dilemma, the person calls a toll-free line to speak to a counselor about the dilemma. Sometimes employees ask questions to help interpret a policy, such as, "Is it okay to ask my boss for a date?" or "Are we supposed to give senior citizen discounts to customers who qualify but do not ask for one?" At other times, a more pressing ethical issue might be addressed, such as, "Is it ethical to lay off a worker just five months short of his qualifying for a full pension?"

Although ethics hotlines are widely used, a study released by the Ethics Resource Center indicates that an immediate supervisor, not a hotline, is the most likely point of contact for reporting job misconduct.[24] (But not if the supervisor is the source of the misconduct!) A most likely explanation of this finding is that most employess are more comfortable discussing an ethical problem with their supervisor rather than via a telephone call to an anonymous person.

Human resource professionals contend that no amount of training will ensure that employees will act ethically in every situation, particularly because ethics deals with subtle matters rather than strictly right or wrong. Deborah Haliczer, director of employee relations at Northern Illinois University, explains, however, that training is valuable in starting a useful dialogue about right and wrong behavior that employees could remember in murky situations.[25]

The link between the programs just described and individual ethical skills is that these programs assist a worker's skill development. For example, if you become comfortable in asking about ethical issues, or turning in ethical violators, you have become more ethically skilled.

Being Environmentally Conscious

Another ethical skill is to be *green* or to do your job in helping sustain the physical environment. (*Green* derives from the idea that green vegetations such as trees and forests are a plus for the environment.) The reasoning behind this statement is that it is morally responsible to protect the environment. Do not be concerned with taking sides on the issue of global warming. Whether or not humans and the carbon dioxide emissions they create have contributed to global warming, the physical environment needs your help.

The Ethical Workplace Relationships Inventory

Directions: Describe how well you agree with each of the following statements, using the following scale: Disagree Strongly (DS); Disagree (D); Neutral (N); Agree (A), Agree Strongly (AS). Circle the number in the appropriate column.

No.		DS	D	N	A	AS
1.	I would give a sexually suggestive hug to a team member who I thought was physically attractive.	5	4	3	2	1
2.	If I were asked to purchase pizza and soft drinks for the group, I would be willing to ask for more in reimbursement than I actually paid.	5	4	3	2	1
3.	If I were the manager of my group, I would be willing to put pressure on group members to purchase direct sales items from me, such as beauty and health products.	5	4	3	2	1
4.	I would be willing to recommend for promotion to my supervisor a worker from a different racial group than my own.	1	2	3	4	5
5.	If I didn't get along with my manager or team leader, I would be willing to start a rumor that he or she was undergoing bankruptcy.	5	4	3	2	1
6.	To damage the reputation of a coworker I didn't like, I would be willing to write a negative social media post about the company and indicate that I was quoting him or her.	5	4	3	2	1
7.	I like the idea of encouraging a coworker to complain about a mutual boss and then reporting those negative comments back to the boss.	5	4	3	2	1
8.	If I were the team member who made a serious error on a project, I would quickly inform our team leader before the blame was placed on another team member.	1	2	3	4	5
9.	If I heard that a company executive was arrested in a domestic violence incident, I would immediately inform other employees.	5	4	3	2	1
10.	Stealing an idea from a coworker, and then taking credit for that idea is totally unacceptable under any circumstance.	1	2	3	4	5

Total Score _____

Scoring and Interpretation: Add the numbers you have circled to obtain your total score.

45–50: You are strongly ethical in your relationships with coworkers.

30–44: You show an average degree of ethical behavior in your workplace relationships and should therefore become more sensitive to ethical issues.

10–29: Your ethical values could lead you to develop a negative relationship with work associates, assuming that your unethical behavior is caught. Begin a serious study of business ethics.

The skill of being environmentally conscious has two major components. First is to take as many steps as you can individually to help preserve the environment, even in such small steps as carrying a reusable cloth bag to the grocery store and not throwing a plastic bottle on a lawn. Second is to be an advocate for the environment by mentioning its importance at work. You might, for example, present data to management about how solar heating can save the company money in the long run, and how benches and walkways made from recycled tires and plastics are attractive and economical. Figure 15-2 gives you a starting point for contributing to a sustainable environment. You might want to add to this list with suggestions of your own, or those you find in the media and scientific articles.

You may need to use your communication persuasion skills to make an impact on the environment. And you will also need to use your positive political skills so that you will not be perceived as an environmental, tree-hugging pest.

You are invited to do Skill-Building Exercise 15-4 to get started right away in improving the physical environment.

FIGURE 15-2 Representative Suggestions for Helping a Company Contribute to a Sustainable Environment

1. Conserve energy by adjusting thermostats to keep working areas cooler during cold months and warmer during warm months.

2. Do what you can to encourage your company and coworkers to send to recycling centers electronic devices that are no longer in use, such as desktop computers, laptop computers, cell phones, and personal digital assistants.

3. Spread the word about the environmental good that can be accomplished from making new products from recycled goods, such as paving stones and park benches made from recycled bottles and tires. The entire remanufacturing industry relies on the reuse of manufactured materials.

4. Do what you can to create a buzz about the possibilities of photovoltaic technology that is used to convert sunlight into clean energy. Alert influential people to energy-saving and money-saving solar heating systems, such as solar buildings that provide solar hot water and solar heating.

5. Place a lawn on the roof that can reduce its surface temperature by 70 degrees F and internal temperatures by 15 degrees F.

6. Carpool to work with at least three coworkers, and provide preferred parking spaces for carpoolers and hybrid or electric cars.

7. Campaign for a four-day, 40-hour workweek, which can save enormous amounts of energy by less commuting along with less heating and cooling of the workplace. (However, if the employees drive considerably on their day off and use more heating and cooling at home, much of the energy savings will be lost.)

8. Encourage employee use of mass transportation, and provide company shuttle busses from locations convenient to where employees live.

9. Offer employees at least $2,000 toward the purchase of a hybrid vehicle or electric car.

10. Turn off electronic machines when not in use unless starting and stopping them frequently uses more energy than leaving the machines turned on during working hours. Encourage the replacement of incandescent bulbs with fluorescent ones (if the replacement bulb provides enough light for the purpose).

11. Recycle as many packages as possible, and install driveways and purchase products such as office furniture made from recycled products including recycled vehicle tires. When possible, use old newspapers for packing material instead of new paper and plastic.

12. Use mugs instead of Styrofoam, and set up bins to recycle aluminum cans and plastic bottles.

13. When constructing a new building, seek Leadership in Energy and Environmental Design (LEED) certification from the US Green Building Council.

14. Provide bicycle racks and showers that enable employees to bike to work. Biking to work will save considerable energy as well as decrease carbon dioxide emissions.

15. Construct a system that captures rainwater to be reused for irrigation.

16. Grow as much vegetation on company premises as feasible, including celebrating special events by planting another tree. Use plants that are native to the region, because native vegetation does not require as much maintenance, fertilizer, chemical sprays, or water.

17. Drink as much tap water as possible to minimize the use of bottled water, or filter tap water to one's specifications.

18. Purchase clothing with a lower negative impact on the environment, as indicated by the label. For example, some clothing is manufactured in production facilities powered by sustainable, renewable energy. And some textile mills install processes for recycling and reclamation of cloth.

19. Combat litter and clutter in your work area and on company premises to help attain a pleasant, environmentally friendly atmosphere. Take such actions as alerting the company to exposed, rusted pipes, broken concrete in the parking lot, peeling paint, and broken fences.

20. Encourage people in your network not to drive at high speeds or sit in an idling vehicle while making phone calls or sending text messages. Encourage safe driving in general, because vehicular accidents consume enormous amounts of energy, including tow trucks, salvage operations, and life-sustaining hospital stays. Also encourage them to walk to errands instead of driving, whenever feasible.

21. Invest some of your shopping budget into making purchases at used-merchandise stores. Recyling helps the environment, but avoiding the purchase of all new merchandise fosters unemployment and even the eyesore of vacant stores and buildings.

21. A general guideline is to use less physical objects and less energy.

22. My suggestions:

Sources: Several of the ideas are from David Kreutzer, "The Countless Shades of Green Jobs," http://www.philly.com, March 30, 2012, pp. 1–2; Ben Elgin and Brian Grow, "The Dirty Secret of Recycling Electronics," *Business* Week, October 27, 2008, pp. 40–44; Letita M. Aaron, "The Big Payback," *Black Enterprise*, May 2009, pp. 64–66; Yvon Chouinard, Jib Ellison, and Rick Ridgeway, "The Sustainable Economy," *Harvard Business* Review, October 2011, pp. 52–62; David Roberts, "Another Inconvenient Truth," *Fast Company*, March 2008, p. 70; Tom Szaky, *Revolution in a Bottle* (New York: Portfolio, 2009).

Conducting an Environmental Audit

To create an environmentally friendly workplace, somebody has to take the initiative to spot opportunities for change. Organize the class into groups of about five, with one person being appointed the team leader. You might have to do the work outside of class, because your assignment is to do an environmental audit of a workplace, including a nonprofit setting such as a place of worship, a school, or an athletic facility. If the audit is done during class time, evaluate a portion of the school, such as a classroom, an athletic facility, or the cafeteria. Your task is to conduct an environmental audit with respect to the energy efficiency and healthfulness of the workplace. Make judgments on a 1-to-10 scale plus comments about the following factors:

1. How energy efficient is the workplace in terms of such factors as building insulation, use of fluorescent lighting, heating and cooling, and use of solar panels?

2. How safe is the environment in terms of pollutants, and steps to prevent physical accidents?

3. How aesthetic is the environment in terms of protecting against sight and sound pollution?

Summarize your findings and suggestions in a bulleted list of less than one page. Present your findings to classmates and perhaps to a manager of the workplace. Classmates might comment on whether your findings will really improve the planet from an ecology standpoint.

Following an Applicable Professional Code of Conduct

Professional codes of conduct are prescribed for many occupational groups, including physicians, nurses, lawyers, paralegals, purchasing managers and agents, and real estate salespeople. A useful ethical guide for members of these groups is to follow the code of conduct for their profession. If the profession or trade is licensed by the state or province, a worker can be punished for deviating from the code of conduct specified by the state. The code of conduct developed by the profession or trade is separate from the legal code, but usually supports the same principles and practices. Some of these codes of conduct developed by the professional associations are 50 and 60 pages long; yet all are guided by the kind of ethical principles implied in the ethical decision-making guide described earlier. For example, the National Association of Purchasing Management tells members to refrain from accepting gifts or favors from present or potential suppliers which might influence, or appear to influence, purchasing decisions.

Be Ready to Exert Upward Ethical Leadership

A politically delicate situation can arise when a worker wants to behave ethically, yet he or she works for an unethical manager. He or she might worry that being ethical will lead to being reprimanded or job loss. The ethical person working for an unethical boss might feel that his or her values are being compromised, such as a virtuous credit card specialist being told to approve credit cards for people who will probably wind up paying many late fees. **Upward ethical leadership** is leadership displayed by individuals who take action to maintain ethical standards, although higher-ups engage in questionable moral behaviors.[26]

At the extreme, an employee might blow the whistle on the boss, and report the unethical behavior to top management or a government agency. An example would be telling the Consumer Protection Agency that your company was selling cribs that could trap a baby's head after your boss refused to accept your complaint. As mentioned in the survey reported earlier in the chapter, about one-fifth of whistle-blowers are retaliated against, including physical attacks against the reporter's property.[27] Another problem with blowing the whistle, particularly in a bigt company, is that your complaint is likely to be ignored.[28] It might therefore be in your best interest to attempt to resolve the problem by exerting upward leadership.

The upward leadership approach attempts to resolve the problem before going to the extreme of whistle-blowing. The employee who spots the immoral or unethical behavior would use problem-solving and communication skills, along with conflict resolution skills. For example, the employee who spotted the potential head-trap problem might say to the boss, "I have a problem, and I would like to discuss it with you." The employee would therefore be engaging the boss in helping to solve the problem. Recognizing that you have less power than your boss, you would have to be diplomatic and nonaccusatory.

upward ethical leadership

The leadership displayed by individuals who take action to maintain ethical standards, although higher-ups engage in questionable moral behaviors.

Confronting the Unethical Boss

One student plays the role of Fred, a manager who makes frequent business trips by airplane. Fred also likes to fly frequently on vacation, and appreciates accumulating frequent-flyer miles. Company policy allows employees to keep the frequent-flyer miles they accumulate for work. So Fred will often take indirect trips to a destination to accumulate more air miles. For example, to fly to San Francisco, he flew from Boston to Atlanta and then to San Francisco. In this instance, he could have made a shorter trip by flying directly from Boston to San Francisco, or from Boston to Chicago to San Francisco. In general, the longer, indirect flights are more expensive.

Another person plays the role of Kelly, the office administrative assistant who sometimes helps Fred prepare his travel vouchers. Kelly, who has good knowledge of geography, notices this strange pattern of Fred taking indirect flights. She is also aware of company policy that permits employees to

accumulate frequent flyer miles that are earned on business trips. Kelly is disturbed about what she perceives to be an inappropriate use of company resources and therefore an ethical violation.

Kelly decides to discuss with Fred this most likely ethical violation. The role-play takes place in Fred's cubicle, and you can imagine how defensive Fred is going to be.

Run the role-play for about five minutes. For both scenarios, observers rate the role players on two dimensions, using a 1-to-5 scale from very poor (1) to very good (5). One dimension is "effective use of human relations techniques." Observers look to see if Kelly can preserve her sense of ethics while not doing too much damage to her relationship with her boss, Fred. The second dimension is "acting ability." A few observers might voluntarily provide feedback to the role players in terms of sharing their ratings and observations. The course instructor might also provide feedback.

It would be important to point to the problem (the possibility of an infant getting his or her head stuck) rather than accusing the boss of being unethical or immoral.

Skill-Building Exercise 15-5 gives you an opportunity to practice upward leadership skills for correcting unethical behavior.

Concept Review and Reinforcement

Key Terms

character traits 385
moral intensity 377
conflict of interest 381

defining moment 382
honesty 384
integrity 384

ethical screening 385
upward ethical leadership 391

Summary

Ethics refers to moral choices, or what is good and bad, right and wrong, just and unjust, and what people should do. Ethics turn values into action. A person's ethical code has a significant impact on his or her interpersonal relationships.

Understanding ethics is important for a variety of reasons. First, people are motivated by self-interest and a desire to be morally right. Second, good ethics can enhance business and avoid illegal acts and unsafe practices. Third, having high ethics improves the quality of work life.

Being ethical isn't always easy for many reasons, including the following: complexity of ethical decisions, a predisposition to be unethical, self-interest, level of moral development, moral disengagement, goals that reward unethical behavior, and motivated blindness. Ethical violations by workers at all job levels are widespread, even if decreasing from years past. Active social networkers report many negative experiences in their workplace.

Commonly faced ethical problems include illegally copying software, treating people unfairly including cronyism, sexually harassing coworkers, facing a conflict of interest, abusing confidential information, misrepresenting employment and educational history, misusing corporate resources, ethically violating computers and information technology, wasting company time, and engaging in unethical behavior to benefit the company.

A challenging twist to ethical decision making is to sort through your values when you have to choose between two morally sound choices. A defining moment is when you have to choose between two or more ideals in which you deeply believe.

One strategy for behaving ethically is to develop virtuousness that includes honesty and integrity. Seeing the big picture can help a person behave ethically. A key strategy for behaving ethically is to follow the eight steps in making a contemplated decision:

1. Gather the facts.
2. Define the ethical issues.
3. Identify the affected parties.
4. Predict the consequences.
5. Identify the obligations (such as to customers and society).
6. Consider your character and integrity.
7. Think creatively about potential actions.
8. Check your intuition.

Another way to raise the level of ethical behavior is to form strong professional relationships with work associates. This is true because people tend to behave more ethically toward people who are close to them. At times, using a corporate program such as an ethics hotline can help a person resolve ethical dilemmas. Being environmentally conscious contributes to ethical behavior. Following an applicable code of professional conduct, such as that for purchasing specialists, is another guide to behaving ethically. Upward leadership behavior can help you deal with the situation of maintaining ethical standards when the boss engages in questionable moral behavior. If upward leadership does not work, the person might become a whistle-blower, while understanding that retaliation is possible.

Questions for Discussion and Review

1. What possible conflicts of interest do you see when a manager and subordinate become Facebook friends?

2. How can behaving ethically improve a person's interpersonal relationships on the job?

3. Assume that you are walking by a lake and you witness a person throwing a few plastic bottles into the water. How would you deal with the situation?

4. What is your opinion of the ethics of using the wi-fi access of other people, including business firms when you are not a customer, without asking permission?

5. International companies often say that they need to pay huge salaries to attract the best executives. Do you agree that this is necessary in view of the widening pay gap between lowest and highest paid employees at many top companies?

6. Do you think the prime function of a company is to make money for shareholders? If not, then what other groups should it be satisfying?

7. In recent years several CEOs at major companies have been forced to resign after it was discovered that they faked at least one college degree on their résumé. What is your opinion of the fairness of firing these executives for having lied about their academic credentials?

8. Based on your knowledge of human behavior, why do professional codes of conduct—such as those for doctors, paralegals, and realtors—not prevent all unethical behavior on the part of members?

9. Check out the Web sites of a couple of major business corporations. What conclusion do you reach about whether an environmentally conscious (or green) person would fit in those companies?

10. Some companies have fired employees who have blown the whistle on practices they consider unethical. Do you believe whistle-blowing is justified, or that employees who divulge private company affairs are guilty of disloyalty?

The Web Corner

http://www.ethics.org
(Ethics Resource Center)

http://www.sustainability.com
(Includes brief case histories of what was done to make well-known business corporations improve sustainability)

http://globalethicsuniversity.com
(An examination of many phases of business ethics)

Internet Skill-Builder: Learning from Ethical Role Models

One of the many ways of learning ethical skills is to get good ideas from ethical role models. For example, you might observe a professor who takes the initiative to change a grade upward because she later discovered a calculation error. This Internet skill-builder is more abstract than some others, so you might find it a little frustrating. Search for a few specific ways in which you can learn from an ethical role model. To illustrate, you might learn from a business executive, sports figure, or public servant you admire.

Developing Your Human Relations Skills

Interpersonal Relations Case 15.1

The One-Cent Ethical Dilemma

Rajah majored in business administration and marketing at college, and looked forward to a career in retail management. While attending community college, he worked an average of 30 hours per week at retail stores, thereby taking him an additional year and one half to attain his degree. Still only 23 years old, Rajah received a job offer as the manager of a branch of a discount general store. He thought this would be a fine opportunity to begin his career in retail management. Although the store was referred to as a dollar store, the prices of individual merchandise ran as high as $30.

About three months into the job, his regional manager Lauren explained that cashiers were from here on not to give customers back change of only one cent. For example, if a customer's bill were $2.99 and he gave the cashier a $5.00 bill, the cashier was supposed to give the customer change of $2.00 and smile at the same time. Yet if the customer demanded the penny in change, the cashier should grant the request.

Rajah asked Lauren, "Why should our store do something that nasty? It's like stealing pennies from customers."

Lauren replied, "We have approximately 1,200 stores across the country, and all our stores are busy. Few customers care about one penny, but if we add up all those pennies, the company's profit for the years has a nice bump up."

Rajah was not happy with the new policy, but agreed to go ahead and encourage his cashiers to withhold the penny change unless a customer objected. Yet after a week, this new policy began to disturb Rajah. He felt he was forcing his cashiers into unethical if not illegal behavior. He did not want to lose his job by complaining about or not complying with company policy.

Case Questions

1. What actions do you recommend Rajah take about his concerns with respect to the new one-cent-in-change policy?
2. Explain whether you think Rajah shuld blow the whistle on his employer?
3. What is your opinion of the ethics of the new policy about withholding one-cent in change?

Interpersonal Relations Case 15.2

Am I Paid to Be My Manager's TV Repair Technician?

Karen worked for a division of a pharmaceutical company as a member of the technical support team. Among her many responsibilities were keeping the division's desktop computers, laptop computers, printers, and smartphones in working order. Gus, her manager, who had been with the company for about 10 years, had a general understanding of what the tech support staff was doing, but he was more of an administrator than a specialist in communication technology.

Several times in recent weeks, Gus complained to Karen and a few other team members about a problem he was having with a digital television set connected to an internal (rabbit ears) antenna. During a lunch break, he explained to Karen, "I'm going a little crazy. I have four television sets at home. The two big ones are satellite connected and they work just fine. I have a small set in the family room in the basement connected to rabbit ears, and the reception is reasonably good. I am picking up the digital signals with a few halts here and there, but I am getting the reception I need."

"The problem I have is with a relatively new set connected in our upstairs bedroom. I did the channel scan about one year ago, and I was getting the network channels I needed. A few weeks ago, I stopped receiving the channels I needed. All that was left was HSN (Home Shopping Network). I must have done a channel scan twenty times to try to fix the problem. Plus, I rotated the antenna a few times. I called tech support at the manufacturer of my set, and the rep couldn't help. He told me to telephone the FCC (Federal Communication Commission). I did that, followed the rep's instructions, and still no signal."

Karen agreed that Gus was facing a frustrating problem, but noted that many people using antennas on their TV sets have lost reception since the conversion from analog to digital in 2009.

A week later, Gus spoke to Karen again about his TV reception woes. He then asked Karen, "How about you coming over after work some night to help straighten out my TV problem? My wife and I would really appreciate your help. You're a great tech fixer."

Karen pondered for a moment, thinking that Gus was making an unreasonable demand. She replied, "Gus, let me think about your request. I really don't know a lot about TV reception. Also, I am pretty much tied up after work for a couple of weeks."

With a frown on his face, Gus said, "Karen, I know you can help. Please don't let me down."

Case Questions

1. What do you see as any potential ethical issues in Gus's request that Karen attempt to fix his TV set reception problem?

2. What advice might you offer Karen for dealing with this problem?

3. How do Gus's demands fit into the category of expecting Karen to exhibit strong organizational citizenship behavior?

Interpersonal Skills Role-Play

Dealing with an Unusual Request from the Boss

The case about the manager's request for tech support for his television set provides the background information for this role-play. The scenario is another meeting between Gus and Karen. One student plays the role of Gus, who is now increasingly frustrated that he cannot get the reception he wants. Just last week he telephoned a television repair service, and was told politely that he should simply hook up the set to cable or satellite TV. But Gus and his wife do not want any more wires running through their house. So this time, Gus is more insistent that Karen come over to his house to fix the problem.

Another person plays the role of Karen, who has thought through Gus's request some more, and she feels that his demand is both inappropriate and unethical. However, Karen still wants to maintain a good professional relationship with Gus.

Run the role-play for about five minutes. For both scenarios, observers rate the role players on two dimensions, using a 1-to-5 scale from very poor (1) to very good (5). One dimension is "effective use of human relations techniques." The second dimension is "acting ability." A few observers might voluntarily provide feedback to the role players in terms of sharing their ratings and observations. The course instructor might also provide feedback.

References

1. Quoted and adapted from "FDA Takes Action against Thousands of Illegal Internet Pharmacies," *http://www.fda.gov*, October 4, 2012, pp. 1–3.
2. Linda K. Treviño and Katherine A. Nelson, *Managing Business Ethics: Straight Talk about How to Do It Right* (New York: Wiley, 1995), pp. 24–35; O. C. Ferrell, John Fraedrich, and Linda Ferrell, *Business Ethics: Ethical Decision Making and Cases,* 4th ed. (Boston: Houghton Mifflin, 2000), pp. 13–16; Anita Bruzzese, "Tools Take Ethics to the Real World," Gannett News Service, May 16,

2005; Roger Parloff, "Wall Street: It's Payback Time," *Fortune*, January 19, 2009, pp. 56–69.

3. Thomas Cata and Amir Afrati, "New Heat for Google CEO," *The Wall Street Journal*, August 27–28, 2011, p. B1.

4. Thomas M. Jones, "Ethical Decision Making by Individuals in Organizations: An Issue Contingent Model," *Academy of Management Review*, April 1991, p. 391.

5. Jennifer J. Kish-Gephart, David A. Harrison, and Linda Klebe Treviño, "Bad Apples, Bad Cases, and Bad Barrels: Meta-Analytic Evidence About Sources of Unethical Decisions at Work," *Journal of Applied* Psychology, January 2010, pp. 1–31; Linda Klebe Treviño and Michael E. Brown, "Managing to Be Ethical: Debunking Five Business Ethics Myths," *Academy of Management Executive*, May 2004, pp. 69–72.

6. Scott J. Reynolds, "Moral Awareness and Ethical Predispositions: Investigating the Role of Individual Differences in the Recognition of Moral Issues," *Journal of Applied Psychology*, January 2006, p. 234.

7. John C. Bogle, "A Crisis of Ethic Proportions," *The Wall Street Journal*, April 21, 2009, p. A19.

8. Simona Covel, "Small Businesses Face More Fraud in Downturn," *The Wall Street Journal*, February 19, 2009, p. B5.

9. Celia Moore et al., "Why Employees Do Bad Things: Moral Disengagement and Unethical Organizational Behavior," *Personnel Psychology*, Number 1, 2012, pp. 1–48.

10. Max H. Bazerman and Ann E, Tenbrunsel, "Ethical Breakdowns," *Harvard Business Review*, April 2011, p. 58.

11. *2011 National Business Ethics Survey* ® (http://www.ethics.org/topic/national-surveys); *National Business Ethics Survey*, Ethics Resource Center, Arlington, Virginia, 2009 survey (http://www.ethics.org).

12. The basic outline for this section is from Treviño and Nelson, *Managing Business Ethics*, pp. 47–64.

13. Data reported in Dina Bass, "Software Piracy Jumps to $59 Billion in 2010, Report Says," *http://www.Businessweek.com/new*, May 12, 2011, p. 1.

14. "FTC: Bloggers Must Disclose Payments for Reviews," Associated Press, October 5, 2009.

15. Keith J. Winstein, "Inflated Credentials Surface in Executive Suite," *The Wall Street Journal*, November 13, 2008, p. B1;

Chad Brooks, "Yahoo CEO Not Alone: 7 Execs Busted for Résumé Lies," *Business News Daily*, May 15, 2012, pp. 10–14.

16. Joseph L. Badaracco Jr., "The Discipline of Building Character," *Harvard Business Review*, March–April 1998, pp. 114–124.

17. Elizabeth E. Umphress, John B. Bingham, and Marie S. Mitchell, "Unethical Behavior in the Name of the Company: The Moderating Effects of Organizational Identification and Positive Reciprocity Beliefs on Unethical Pro-Organizational Behavior," *Journal of Applied Psychology*, July 10, pp. 769–780.

18. Edwin A. Locke, "Business Ethics: A Way Out of the Morass," *Academy of Management Learning & Education*, September 2006, pp. 328–330.

19. Robert Hurley, "Trust Me," *The Wall Street Journal*, October 24, 2011, p. R4.

20. Melissa Korn, "Columbia Dean Wants Students to Connect Dots," *The Wall Street Journal*, July 7, 2011, p. B6.

21. The general outline is from Treviño and Nelson, *Managing Business Ethics*, pp. 71–75.

22. Scott Sonenshein, "The Role of Construction, Intuition, and Justification in Responding to Ethical Issues at Work: The Sensemaking-Intuition Model," *Academy of Management Review*, October 2007, p. 1030.

23. Daniel J. Brass, Kenneth D. Butterfield, and Bruce C. Skaggs, "Relationships and Unethical Behavior: A Social Network Perspective," *Academy of Management Review*, January 1998, pp. 14–31.

24. "Willingness to Report Misconduct is Key in Building an Ethical Workplace," http://ethics.org/news, September 7, 2010, pp. 1–2.

25. Cited in Jean Thilmany, "Supporting Ethical Employees," *HR Magazine*, September 2007, p. 106.

26. Mary Uhl-Bien and Melissa K. Carsten, "Being Ethical When the Boss Is Not," *Organizational Dynamics*," Issue 2, 2007, p. 197.

27. "Retaliation: When Whistleblowers Become Victims," *Ethics Resource Center* (http://www.ethics.org/nbes), September 4, 2012, pp. 1–2.

28. Jack and Suzy Welch, "Whistleblowers: Why You Should Heed Their Warnings," *Fortune*, June 11, 2012, p, 86.

Stress Management and Personal Productivity

Isabelle is the supervisor of a group of medical equipment repairers whose purpose is to install, maintain, and repair patient care equipment. An example of their activity is to maintain x-ray equipment in a dental office. Although most of the work is performed during the day, Isabelle's group is also on call at night and on weekends. As the demand for health services grew in her community, so did the demand for the service her group provides.

As Isabelle explains, "I love what I'm doing, but the work pressures became overwhelming. The fellows and gals in my group were forever calling or texting me. Customers kept coming at me with demands for service they wanted right away. And my own manager was forever asking me for something. I had so much stress that I was getting dizzy on the job. Almost as horrible, my mother told me that my hair was thinning."

After carefully studying a book and a few articles about time management and job work stress, Isabelle took two major steps to make her position feel less overwhelming. First, she dedicated two hours per night, two nights a week, and two hours most Saturday mornings to take care of work-related e-mails and complete forms. Although this technique added six hours more to her workweek, Isabelle now felt much less overwhelmed by e-mails and filling out required forms. Isabelle also began a program of jogging for fifteen minutes every day and sleeping one more hour per night. The jogging and extra sleep gave Isabelle an energy boost that made it easier to cope with the many demands she was facing. "I'm a revitalized work warrior, on top of my job," said Isabelle.

The supervisor just described become more productive by adding more time to her work week to take care of administrative tasks. At the same time, she overcame the stressor of feeling overwhelmed. Although this book is primarily about interpersonal skills, information about managing stress and enhancing personal productivity is relevant. Having your work under control and not being stressed out enables you to focus better on interpersonal relationships.

After reading and studying this chapter and completing the exercises, you should be able to

1. Explain many of the symptoms and consequences of stress, including burnout.
2. Describe personality factors and job factors that contribute to stress.
3. Manage your own stress effectively.
4. Reduce any tendencies you might have toward procrastination.
5. Identify attitudes and values that will enhance your productivity.
6. Identify work habits and skills that will enhance your productivity.
7. Pinpoint potential time wasters that drain your productivity.

The first half of this chapter deals with the nature of stress and how it can be managed, whereas the second half describes various approaches to improving personal productivity. The two topics are as closely related as nutrition and health. When you effectively manage stress, you can be more productive. And when your work is under control, you avoid the heavy stress of feeling overwhelmed. A useful thought to keep in mind is that many readers of this book will become or are already **corporate athletes**, workers who engage in high-level performance for sustained periods.[1] To be a corporate athlete, you have to manage your energy and stress well, in addition to having good work habits and time management.

corporate athletes

Workers who engage in high-level performance for sustained periods.

UNDERSTANDING AND MANAGING STRESS

A major challenge facing any worker who wants to stay healthy and have good interpersonal relationships is to manage stress effectively. Although *stress* is an everyday term, a scientific definition helps clarify its meaning. **Stress** is an adaptive response that is the consequence of any action, situation, or event that places special demands on a person. Note that stress, as used here, refers to a reaction to the situation, not the situation or force itself. A **stressor** is the external or internal force that brings about the stress. When workers deal effectively with stress, they also make a dent in a major challenge facing employers. Work stress causes more long-term absences than physical conditions such as back pain, neck pain, and reptitive-motion injury among workers performing physical work. Stress also causes more long-term absences than ilnesses such as cancer or heart attacks among office workers.[2]

Individual differences in the perception of an event play a key role in determining what events are stressful. Giving a presentation to management, for example, is stressful for some people but not for others. Some people perceive a presentation as a threatening and uncomfortable experience, while others might perceive the same event to be an invigorating challenge.

The term *special demands* is also critical because minor adjustments, such as a laser cartridge that runs dry, are usually not perceived as stressful. Yet piling on of minor adjustments, such as having 10 small things go wrong in one day, is stressful. This is true because stress is additive: A series of small doses of stress can create a major stress problem.

This textbook's approach to understanding stress centers on its symptoms and consequences, personality and job factors that contribute to stress, and methods and techniques for stress management. Managing stress receives more emphasis because the same techniques can be used to combat a variety of stressors.

Symptoms and Consequences of Stress

The physiological changes that take place within the body in response to stress are responsible for most stress symptoms. These physiological changes are almost identical for both

LEARNING OBJECTIVE 1

positive and negative stressors. Marathon racing, romantic attraction, and being downsized can make you feel about the same physically; however, positive experiences create a sense of joy that makes the stress symptoms more tolerable. The experience of stress helps activate hormones that prepare the body to run or fight when faced with a challenge. This battle against the stressor is referred to as the **fight-or-flight response**. It helps you deal with emergencies.

The brain is the organ that decides whether a situation is stressful and produces the behavioral and physiological responses. Yet, the brain's response is based on personal experience and culture. Eating seal meat would rarely be stressful for an Eskimo, yet might be for a Floridian. The brain senses stress as damage to wellbeing and therefore sends out a signal to the body to cope. The brain is thus a self-regulating system that helps us cope with stressors.

Physiological Reactions. The activation of hormones when the body has to cope with a stressor produces a short-term physiological reaction. Among the most familiar reactions is an increase in heart rate, breathing rate, blood pressure, and blood clotting. The stress hormone cortisol and other chemical responses to a stress can increase the cardiovascular function and the immune system in the short term. To help you recognize these symptoms, try to recall your internal bodily sensations the last time you were almost in an automobile accident or heard some wonderful news. Less familiar changes are a redirection of the blood flow toward the brain and large muscle groups and a release of stored fluids from places throughout the body into the bloodstream.

If stress is continuous and accompanied by these short-term physiological changes, annoying and life-threatening conditions can occur. Damage occurs when stress levels rarely subside. Eventually the immune system is suppressed, and memory is impaired. When the immune system is impaired, the severity of many diseases and disorders increases. With the rest of the body on alert, our ability to create immune cells diminishes. For example, people whose stress level is high recover more slowly from colds and injuries, and they are more susceptible to sexually transmitted diseases.

A stressful life event usually leads to a high cholesterol level (of the unhealthy type) and high blood pressure. Other conditions associated with stress are cardiac disease, migraine headaches, ulcers, allergies, skin disorders, irritable-bowel syndrome, and cancer. People under continuous negative stress, such as having severe family problems or having a life out of control, also age more quickly partially because of cell damage. Research suggests tht psychological stress leads to shorter telomeres, which are the protective caps on the ends of chromosomes. The explantion is that telomere shortening is an indicator of celluar aging and health.[3] (Have you ever observed that stressed-out friends of yours appear older than their chronological age?)

Stress symptoms vary considerably from one person to another. A general behavioral symptom of intense stress is for people to exaggerate their weakest tendencies. For instance, a person with a strong temper who usually keeps cool under pressure may throw a tantrum under intense pressure. Some common stress symptoms are listed in Figure 16-1.

Job Performance Consequences. Stress has both negative and positive consequences. **Hindrance stressors** are those stressful events and thoughts that have a negative effect on motivation and performance. Many of these have already been mentioned. In contrast, **challenge stressors** have a positive direct effect on motivation and performance.[4] A study with 215 employees across 61 offices of a state agency showed that when faced with challenge stressors, employees performed better on their regular tasks, citizenship behavior, and customer service. In contrast, performance on the three dimensions decreased when employees experienced hindrance stressors. An example of a challenge stressor was having high responsibility; having to deal with a lot of red tape to get the job done was an example of a hindrance stressor.[5]

The right amount of stress prepares us for meeting difficult challenges and spurs us on to peak intellectual and physical performance. An optimum level of stress exists for most people and most tasks. In general, performance tends to be best under moderate amounts of stress. The optimum amount of stress is a positive force that is the equivalent of finding excitement and challenge. Your ability to solve problems and deal with challenge is enhanced when the right amount of adrenaline flows in your blood to guide you toward peak performance. In fact, highly productive people are sometimes said to be hooked on adrenaline.

fight-or-flight response

The body's physiological and chemical battle against a stressor in which the person tries to cope with the adversity head-on or tries to flee from the scene.

hindrance stressors

Those stressful events that have a negative effect on motivation and performance.

challenge stressors

Stressful events that have a positive direct effect on motivation and performance.

FIGURE 16-1   A Variety of Stress Symptoms

Mostly Physical and Physiological

Heart beats faster, raising blood pressure and pulse; heart palpitations

Increased sweating

Dizziness

Difficulty breathing

Chest pains

Nerves become more sensitive, leading to increased perception of pain

Weight gain or weight loss

Trembling or shaking

Immune system weakens, making person more susceptible to illness

Breathing rate increases to pull in more oxygen to certain muscles

Upper and lower back pain

Low energy and stamina

Frequent craving for sweets

Increased alcohol or cigarette consumption

Frequent need to eliminate

Frequent teeth grinding

Mostly Emotional and Behavioral

Difficulty concentrating

Nervousness and worry about negative outcomes of events facing the person

Crying

Declining interest in sex

Frequent nail biting or hair tugging

Emotional exhaustion as stress continues over time (burnout)

Anxiety or depression

Forgetfulness based on poor concentration

Restlessness

Frequent arguments with others

Decrease in daily happiness

Anger outbursts

Note: Anxiety is a general sense of dread, fear, or worry not linked to a specific event, such as being anxious about your future.

If the stress is too great, people become temporarily ineffective; they may freeze or choke. Under too little stress, people may become lethargic and inattentive. The optimum amount of stress varies with individuals, with each person having a different stress threshold.[6] For example, in the same bank an investment specialist might welcome more stress, whereas a bank teller might welcome less stress.

Figure 16-2 depicts the relationship between stress and job performance. An exception to this relationship is that certain negative forms of stress are likely to lower performance even if the stress is moderate. For example, the stress created by an intimidating supervisor or worrying about radiation poisoning—even in moderate amounts—will not improve performance.

Burnout and Stress.   One of the major problems of prolonged stress is that it may lead to **burnout,** a condition of emotional, mental, and physical exhaustion in response to long-term stressors. Burnout is also referred to as work exhaustion because fatigue is usually involved. Burned-out people are often cynical. Two other examples of burnout symptoms

burnout

A condition of emotional, mental, and physical exhaustion in response to long-term stressors.

FIGURE 16-2   Relationship between Stress and Job Performance

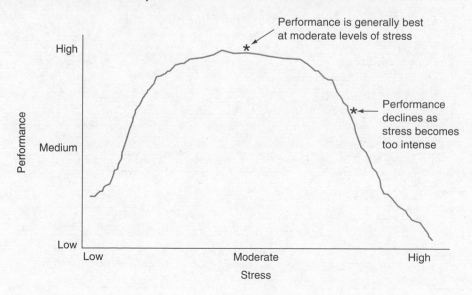

Performance is generally best at moderate levels of stress

Performance declines as stress becomes too intense

are irritability and impatience. Burnout victims also face other symptoms of heavy stress, such as cardiac disease.

Burnout is a complex phenomenon, with its causes centering on five factors. First is a feeling of limited autonomy or control in the workplace. Not being able to decide how to accomplish a task is significant, as well as having little say in choosing what tasks to do. Second is receiving insufficient recognition for accomplishments. Third is not having advancement opportunities and feeling stifled on the job. Fourth is having poor relationships with coworkers, including not getting much respect. Fifth is working in an organizational culture that is incompatible with your belief system, such as a vegetarian working for a poultry producer.[7] A study with Dutch workers suggests that having a charismatic leader can help reduce some of the problems that lead to burnout.[8] For example, a charismatic leader is likely to give ample recognition.

The key symptom of burnout is the distancing that occurs in response to work overload. Burnout sufferers shift into a mode of doing the minimum as a way of protecting themselves. They start leaving work early and dehumanizing their clients, patients, or customers. People experiencing burnout may do their jobs, but their heart is not in it anymore.[9] An example of a profession with many burnout victims is investment banking. Although still lavishly compensated, many of the bankers in their 30s have come to believe that there are too many sacrifices, such as 80-hour workweeks and some people still blaming investment bankers for past financial crises. Many of these investment bankers have left the field, including becoming entrepreneurs and franchiser operators.[10]

Personality and Job Factors Contributing to Stress

LEARNING OBJECTIVE 2

Workers experience stress for many different reasons, including personal predispositions, factors stemming from the job, or the combined influence of both. If a person with an extreme negative predisposition has to deal with irate customers, he or she is most likely to experience substantial stress. Here we describe a sampling of important individual and organizational factors that contribute to job stress. Keep in mind, however, that a large number of potential stressors exist and that many of them overlap. Fighting about money harms relationships, and worrying about money can create health problems. Figure 16-3 lists some stressors facing the general population, and these sources of stress duplicate some of the stressors described in the following pages.

Personality Factors Predisposing People toward Stress.   Individuals vary considerably in their susceptibility to job stress based on their personality traits and characteristics. Four such factors are described next.

perceived control

The belief that an individual has at his or her disposal a response that can control the negative aspects of an event.

Low Perceived Control   A key factor in determining whether workers experience stress is how much they believe they can control a given adverse circumstance. **Perceived control**

FIGURE 16-3   Cause of Stress among the General Population

Source of Stress	People Affected
Money	69%
Work	66%
The economy	61%
Family responsibilities	57%
Relationships (spouse, kids, girl/boyfriend)	56%
Family health problems	52%
Personal health concerns	51%
Health problems affecting my family	52%

Source: Based on data presented in the APA (American Psychological Association) Stress in America Survey, published in Sophie Bethune, "Healthy-Care Falls Short on Stress Management," *Monitor on Psychology,* April, 2013, p. 24.

is the belief that an individual has at his or her disposal a response that can control the negative aspects of an event. A survey of over 100 studies indicated that people with a high level of perceived control had low levels of physical and psychological symptoms of stress. Conversely, people with low perceived control are more likely to experience work stress.[11]

Low Self-Efficacy   Self-efficacy, like perceived control, is another personal factor that influences susceptibility to stress. (Note that because self-efficacy is tied to a specific situation, it is not strictly a personality trait.) When workers have both low perceived control and low self-efficacy, the stress consequences may be much worse; however, having high self-efficacy softens the stress consequences of demanding jobs.[12] If you believe that you can successfully resolve a difficult problem, such as troubleshooting the reason for packages being sent to incorrect addresses, you will be less stressed.

Type-A Behavior and Hostility   A person with **Type-A behavior** is demanding, impatient, and overstriving, and is therefore prone to negative stress. Type-A behavior has two main components. One is the tendency to try to accomplish too many things in too little time. This leads the Type-A individual to be impatient and demanding. The other component is free-floating hostility. Because of this sense of urgency and hostility, trivial things irritate these people. People with Type-A behavior are aggressive and hardworking.

Type-A personalities frequently have cardiac diseases, such as heart attacks and strokes, at an early age, but only certain features of the Type-A personality pattern may be related to coronary heart disease. The heart attack triggers are hostility, anger, cynicism, and suspiciousness, as contrasted to impatience, ambition, and being work driven. In fact, hostility is more strongly associated with coronary heart disease in men than smoking, drinking, overeating, or high levels of bad (LDL) cholesterol.[13] A review of studies confirms that there is no significant association between Type-A personalities and heart disease; however, there is a strong association between hostility and coronary heart disease. Hostility of the sort seen in habitual angry driving is also a heart-disease risk factor.[14] Note that the heart attack triggers also make for strained interpersonal relationships.

Negative Affectivity and High Reactivity   A major contributor to being stress prone is **negative affectivity**, a tendency to experience aversive emotional states. In more detail, negative affectivity is a pervasive disposition to experience emotional stress that includes feelings of nervousness, tension, and worry. The same disposition also includes such emotional states as anger, scorn, revulsion, guilt, self-dissatisfaction, and sadness.[15] Such negative personalities seem to search for important discrepancies between what they would like and what exists. Poor interpersonal relationships often result from the frequent complaining of people with negative affectivity.

Closely related to negative affectivity is that some people who have extreme reactions to stress may be hard wired to do so. People who have difficulty calming down after experiencing a stressor exhibit a highly reactive, vigilant pattern. Bruce J. Ellis, a professor of family and consumer sciences at the University of Arizona, Tuscon, explains the problem in this way: "A vigilant person is hypersensitive, reacting at a biological level and putting more effort and energy into warding off threats real or perceived."[16] So now you have a scientific explantion for a hothead who goes ballistic in your presence.

Job Sources of Stress.   Almost any job situation can act as a stressor for some employees, but not necessarily for others. As just described, certain personality factors make it more likely that a person will experience job stress. Furthermore, other personal life stressors may spill over into the workplace, making it more likely that a person will experience job stress. For example, a worker facing a severe relationship problem might be more susceptible to being stressed by even mild conflict with coworkers. Seven frequently encountered job stressors are outlined in Figure 16-4 and described ahead.

Role Overload Including Extreme Jobs   Having too much work to do, **role overload**, can create negative stress in two ways. First, the person may become fatigued and thus be less able to tolerate annoyances and irritations. Second, a person subject to unreasonable work demands may feel perpetually behind schedule, a situation that is itself a powerful stressor. Downsizing often creates overload because fewer people are left to handle the

Type-A behavior
A behavior pattern in which the individual is demanding, impatient, and overstriving and therefore prone to negative stress.

negative affectivity
A tendency to experience aversive emotional states.

role overload
Having too much work to do.

FIGURE 16-4   Seven Significant Sources of Job Stress

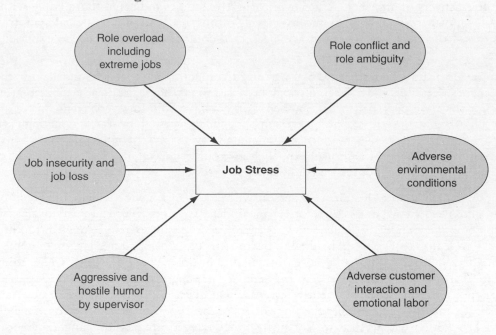

same workload as before. One stressful consequence of downsizing is the *work-more economy* in which many workers take on additional responsibilities and sometimes are asked to assume two jobs yet receive the wages of one worker.[17]

Work overload often takes the form of an **extreme job** in which the incumbent works at least 60 hours per week in a position that usually requires tight deadlines and heavy travel. Many of these jobs with long hours are found in information technology and financial services fields; yet many business owners work comparable hours. As implied in relation to burnout, many investment bankers have an extreme job, with some working 100 hours per week. A researcher from the University of Southern California shadowed two-dozen entry-level investment bankers who recently graduated from business school. Among the stress symptoms she observed in the group were insomnia, alcoholism, heart palpitations, eating disorders, and an explosive temper.[18]

Role Conflict and Role Ambiguity   Role conflict, described in Chapter 9 as an important workplace conflict, is also a major workplace stressor. People experience stress when they have to choose between two sets of expectations. Suppose an accountant is asked by her manager to state company earnings in a way that conflicts with the professional norms of accountants. If she complies with her manager, she will feel that she is betraying her profession. If she does not comply with her manager, she will enter into dispute with the manager. The woman is likely to experience job stress.

Role ambiguity is a condition in which the jobholder receives confusing or poorly defined expectations. Workers in many organizations are placed in situations in which they are unsure of their true responsibilities. Some workers who are placed on a work team experience role ambiguity because they are asked to solve many problems by themselves. It is less ambiguous to have the manager tell you what to do. Many people experience stress symptoms when faced with role ambiguity.

A quantitative review of many studies indicated that when workers experience role conflict and role ambiguity they are less likely to engage in organizational citizenship behavior. The problem appears to be that experiencing role conflict and role ambiguity interferes with a worker achieving worthwhile activities outside of his or her ordinary job responsibilities. Furthermore, workers not sure of which task to perform may cope with the role ambiguity by engaging in tasks they know are most likely to be evaluated favorably.[19]

Adverse Environmental Conditions   A variety of adverse organizational conditions are stressors, as identified by the National Institute for Occupational Safety and Health

(NIOSH). Among these adverse organizational conditions are unpleasant or dangerous physical conditions, such as crowding, noise, air pollution, or ergonomic problems. Enough polluted air within an office building can create a *sick building* in which a diverse range of airborne particles, vapors, molds, and gases pollute the indoor environment. The result can be headaches, nausea, and respiratory infections as well as the stress created by being physically ill.[20]

Tetra Images/Alamy

Ergonomic problems refer to a poor fit between the physical and human requirements of a job. The demands of the modern workplace contribute to the development of musculoskeletal disorders. Working at a computer monitor for prolonged periods of time can lead to adverse physical and psychological reactions. The symptoms include headaches and fatigue, along with eye problems. The computer vision syndrome includes that fact that one out of six patients requiring eye examinations have a computer-related eye problem. Also, the frequency of occular symptoms among computer users is 25 to 93 percent. Common visual problems are dry eyes and blurred or double vision. Another vision-related problem is that people lean forward to scan the monitor, leading to physical problems such as back strain.[21]

The repetitive-motion disorder most frequently associated with keyboarding and the use of optical scanners is **carpal tunnel syndrome**. The syndrome occurs when repetitive flexing and extension of the wrist causes the tendons to swell, thus trapping and pinching the median nerve. Carpal tunnel syndrome creates stress because of the pain and misery. About one in five computer users will suffer from carpal tunnel syndrome at some point.[22] A less publicized problem is a sore thumb (overuse syndrome) related to continuous use of the space bar and mouse while texting.

If ergonomic principles, such as erect posture, are incorporated into computer usage, these stress symptoms diminish. Modern office chairs allow for more flexibility of movement as workers shift rapidly between tasks such as moving toward the computer screen, placing feet on the desk, and turning for a face-to-face conversation. [23]

carpal tunnel syndrome

A condition that occurs when repetitive flexing and extension of the wrist causes the tendons to swell, thus trapping and pinching the median nerve.

Adverse Interaction with Customers and Clients and Emotional Labor   Interactions with customers can be a major stressor. Part of the problem is that the sales associate often feels helpless when placed in conflict with a customer. The sales associate is told that "the customer is always right." Furthermore, the store manager usually sides with the customer in a dispute with the sales associate. Unreasonable demands by clients and customers can also be stressful, such as customers who offer to buy a product or service below cost. Being subjected to sexual harassment by clients and customers is another stressor widely experienced by store sales associates, especially young women.

Related to adverse customer interaction is the stressor of having to control the expression of emotion to please or to avoid displeasing a customer. Imagine having to smile at a customer who belittles you or your employer. Alicia A. Grandey, associate professor of psychology at Penn State University, defines **emotional labor** as the process of regulating both feelings and expressions to meet organizational goals.[24]1 The process involves both surface acting and deep acting. Surface acting means faking expressions, such as smiling, whereas deep acting involves controlling feelings, such as suppressing anger toward a customer you perceive to be annoying.

emotional labor

The process of regulating both feelings and expressions to meet organizational goals.

A study with 285 pairs of employees and customers suggests that deep acting, rather than maintaining an artificial smile, leads to better customer service.[25] As a result of the better customer service, it is possible that the customer will treat the associate better, resulting in less stress for the latter.

Sales workers and customer service representatives often experience emotional labor because so often they have to fake facial expressions and feelings so as to please customers. Nevertheless, according to one study, the top five occupations in terms of emotional labor demands are (1) police and sheriff's patrol officers, (2) social workers, (3) psychiatrists, (4) supervisors of police and detectives, and (5) registered nurses. Bill and account collectors ranked 15![26]

Engaging in emotional labor for prolonged periods of time can lead to job dissatisfaction, stress, and burnout. Surface acting creates more dissatisfaction. A contributing cause is that faking expressions and emotions takes a physiological toll, such as the intestines churning. Workers who engage in emotional labor may also develop cardiovascular problems and weakened immune systems. The good news is that being extraverted helps reduce some of the stress associated with both surface acting and deep acting.[27] (Perhaps if you like people, you can better tolerate their unruly behavior.)

Aggressive and Hostile Humor by Supervisor   A supervisor who directs aggressive, hostile, mean-spirited humor at an employee, particularly when the humor recipient is singled out, can create considerable stress. An example of such malicious humor is a supervisor who told a dietician, "The next time you visit a hospital, why don't you get a brain transplant?" A study of the effects of aggressive humor by supervisors was conducted with 243 frontline employees at four manufacturing companies in China. Aggressive humor was defined as a joke used intentionally to tease, disparage, embarrass, or ridicule one employee or a group of employees. It was found that a supervisor's mean-spirited humor was associated with negative stress symptoms among the employees affected. Employee strain was worse when the supervisor focused the agressive humor on one employee and not his or her coworkers. Among the employee stress symptoms were Internet addictions, problem drinking, and excessive cigarette smoking.[28]

Job Insecurity and Job Loss   Worrying about losing your job is a major stressor. Even when jobs are plentiful, having to search for another job and facing the prospect of geographic relocation are stressors for many people. Downsizing and corporate mergers (which usually result in downsizing) have contributed to job insecurity. The anticipation of layoffs among employees can increase negative stress and lower job performance.

Job loss is usually a more intense stressor than worrying about losing one's job. Losing a job often leads to the stressors of financial problems and relationship conflict. Some people who lose their jobs become so stressed and depressed that they commit suicide. An unfortunate example is that between 2006 and 2008, France Télécom laid off approximately 22,000 workers. Twenty-four laid off workers committed suicide, with the labor union blaming the layoffs for most of the suicides.[29] We hypothesize here that workers with good resources, such as supportive friends and family, good professional contacts, and effective job search skills are the least likely to commit suicide after job loss.

Methods and Techniques for Stress Management

LEARNING OBJECTIVE 3   Unless stress is managed properly, it may lead to harmful long-term consequences, including disabling physical illness and a slowing of career growth. Managing stress refers to controlling stress by making it a constructive force in your life; however, the distinction between methods of preventing and reducing stress is not clear-cut. For example, physical exercise not only reduces stress, it also contributes to a relaxed lifestyle that helps you prevent stress.

A key principle about managing stress is that you are less likely to experience distress from stressors if you have the right resources. Having the right personality characteristics such as high perceived control, high self-efficacy, and not being hostile helps ward off stress. External resources to help ward off negative stress include having a network of friends who provide support, an encouraging manager, and programs for helping distressed employees.[30] Assume, for example, that a worker is heavily stressed by a long rush-hour commute. If the company provides flexible working hours that help decrease commuting during rush hour, the worker experiences less of a hindrance stressor.

Coping with, or managing, stress includes hundreds of activities, with substantial individual differences in which technique is effective. Running is a case in point. For many people, running or jogging is an excellent method of stress reduction. Others find that running creates new stressors, such as aching knees, shin splints, dizziness from breathing in vehicle exhausts, and worrying about being hit by vehicles. The following subsections describe eight methods for managing stress, including a list of everyday stress busters.

Eliminate or Modify the Stressor.   The most potent method of managing stress is to eliminate or modify the stressor giving you trouble. One value of relaxation techniques and tranquilizing medication is that they calm a person enough so that he or she can deal constructively with the stressor. A helpful way to attack the cause of stress is to follow the steps in problem solving and decision making. You clarify the problem, identify the alternatives, weigh the alternatives, and select one alternative. One difficulty, however, is that your evaluation of the real problem may be inaccurate. There is always a limit to self-analysis. For example, a person might think that work overload is the stressor when the true stressor is low self-efficacy.

A major strategy for modifying a stressor is to rethink your belief about a challenging situation. According to the **cognitive behavioral approach to stress management**, people learn to recognize how pessimistic and distorted thoughts of gloom and doom create stress. After recognition of the problem, the person learns to replace the overly pessimistic thinking with more realistic or optimistic thinking. Assume that Mandy is stressed about the prospects of losing her job. Using a cognitive-behavioral approach to stress management, she begins to think, "Would losing this job really be that bad? If this job folds, I could move to Denver where I've always wanted to live, and restart my career." Mandy is right on target, because a synthesis of many studies found that cognitive-behavioral approaches are the most effective method of combating workplace stress.[31]

cognitive behavioral approach to stress management

A method by which people learn to recognize how pessimistic and distorted thoughts of gloom and doom create stress.

Another application of the cognitive-behavioral approach to managing stress is to cope in advance with an upcoming stressor by aspiring for a positive future. If you create an optimistic picture of your ability to deal with an upcoming challenge, you may be less stressed when the challenge arrives. Aspiring for a positive future is more effective in preventing stress than attempting to prevent the possible stressor.[32] This technique works in this manner: You have to drive to visit an important customer tomorrow morning, and the weather forecast calls for a snowstorm. You regard driving in the snow to be a stressor. To cope with the situation, you imagine how you will drive slowly and perhaps follow in the path of a semi-trailer to give you extra safety. You also imagine how pleased the customer will be when you arrive to fix the problem. As a result, you are less stressed during your drive in the snowstorm.

Get Appropriate Physical Exercise.   A moderate amount of physical exercise is a cornerstone of managing stress and achieving wellness. To manage stress, it is important to select an exercise program that is physically challenging but does not lead to overexertion and muscle and bone injury. Competitive sports, if taken too seriously, can actually increase stress. Walking is highly recommended as a stress reducer, because it is inherently relaxing and offers many of the benefits of other forms of exercise with a minimum risk of physical danger. Doing housework, yard work, and washing and waxing a vehicle are examples of everyday forms of gentle exercise that offer the side benefits of getting tasks accomplished. A major mental and emotional benefit of physical exercise stems from endorphins produced in the thalamus portion of the brain. The endorphins are associated with a state of euphoria referred to as "runner's high." Endorphins also work like pain killers, adding to their stress-reduction value.

As researched by the American College of Sports Medicine, among the benefits of exercise are (a) a 50 percent reduction in the incidence of diabetes, (b) a 40 percent reduction in the incidence of high blood pressure, (c) a 40 percent reduction in the risk of developing Alzheimer's disease, and (d) a decrease in depression as effective as Prozac or behavioral therapy.[33]

Rest Sufficiently.   Rest offers benefits similar to those of exercise, such as stress reduction, improved concentration, improved energy, and better tolerance for frustration. The current interest in adult napping reflects the awareness that proper rest makes a person less stress prone and enhances productivity. A study was conducted of 23,681 healthy Greek adults over a six-year period, many of whom napped for about 30 minutes three times a week. Study participants who napped had a 37 percent lower risk of dying from a heart attack than the people who did not. A criticism offered of this study is that the people who napped may also take better care of their bodies and minds in general.[34] The connection of this study to stress management is that many heart attacks are stress induced.

Naps of about 15 minutes duration taken during the workday are used both as energizers and as stress reducers. Napping can help a worker become less stressed as well as more productive. A rested brain is a more effective brain. According to researcher David F. Dingess, who has studied astronauts, cognitive ability depends on how much sleep a person accumulates over a 24-hour period, not just overnight.[35] The indirect link to

FIGURE 16-5 Dietary Guidelines for Americans Developed by the United States Department of Agriculture

Source: US Department of Agriculture, Center for Nutrition Policy and Promotion, www.ChooseMyPlate.gov.

stress is that being cognitively sharp reduces errors, thereby reducing the stress that stems from making errors.

Maintain a Healthy Diet. Nutritious food is valuable for physical and mental health, making it easier to cope with frustrations that are potential stressors. Some non-nutritious foods, such as those laden with caffeine or sugar, tend to enhance a person's level of stress. According to the Dietary Guidelines of the US Department of Agriculture, a healthy diet is one that

- Emphasizes fruits, vegetables, whole grains, and fat-free or low-fat milk and milk products
- Includes lean meats, poultry, fish, beans, eggs, and nuts
- Is low in saturated fats, *trans* fats, cholesterol, salt (sodium), and added sugars

These recommendations are for the general public over two years of age. They are similar to a wealth of scientific research supporting the idea that healthy nutrition depends on a balanced diet consisting of the basic food groups of fruits, vegetables, grains, protein, and dairy.[36] Consult *www.ChooseMyPlate.gov*, as shown in Figure 16-5. Also, nutritionists highly recommend fibers found in whole-grain breads, rolls and cereals, and brown rice.

Build a Support Network. A **support network** is a group of people who can listen to your problems and provide emotional support. Members of your network can provide you with a sense of closeness, warmth, and acceptance that will reduce your stress. Also, the simple expedient of putting your feelings into words can be a healing experience. The way to develop this support network is to become a good listener so that the other person will reciprocate. A support network is, therefore, a method of stress management based squarely on effective interpersonal skills.

Practice Visualization and Meditation. Perhaps the most effortless and enjoyable relaxation technique for managing stress is to visualize a pleasant experience. Visualization, like so many stress-reduction techniques, including meditation, requires concentration. Concentrating helps slow down basic physiological processes, such as the heartbeat, and dissipates stress. Visualization, meditation, prayer, and chanting all appear to offer such advantages as lowering heart rate, blood pressure, and oxygen consumption. These techniques also alleviate symptoms associated with such conditions as hypertension, insomnia, depression, and anxiety.[37] Forcing yourself to concentrate is also valuable because a key stress symptom is difficulty in concentrating.

Meditation is a relaxation technique used to quiet the mind, as well as to relieve stress, and is more complicated than simple visualization. A typical meditation technique proceeds as follows: Hold your back straight, and relax the body. Take three gentle breaths, breathing

support network

A group of people who can listen to your problems and provide emotional support.

in and out through the nostrils. Let the respiration follow its natural flow. Your body breathes as if it was fast asleep, yet you remain vigilant. If you become distracted, simply let go of the thought, and return to the breath. It is helpful to count each inhale up to about 7. Each time your mind wanders, return back to one. Practice meditating about 20 minutes a day, and meditate on the spot after a stressful event or thought.[38] The breathing part of meditation is so important that it is an everyday method of stress reduction itself.

Participate in Resilience Training   A time-consuming yet robust method of reducing and preventing stress is to participate in resilience training. The purpose of much resilience training is to help people steel themselves against difficult situations instead of becoming overly stressed. At the same time, trainees are taught how to learn from the situation.[39] Part of steeling yourself against a highly challenging situation is to think of what skills you have in your repertoire that will help you work your way out of the problem. Suppose that restaurant manager Gary is witnessing a customer go ballistic in the restaurant. Instead of being overwhelmed by the problem, Gary reflects, "What conflict-resolution technique do I know that will help me conquer this problem? [Refer back to Chapter 9] Maybe disarm the opposition will work here." If Gary is able to calm down the customer, he will have learned from the stressful situation.

Practice Everyday Methods of Stress Reduction.   The simple expedient of learning how to relax is an important method of reducing the tension and anxiety brought about by both challenge and hindrance stressors. Visualization of a pleasant experience is one such method. A sample of everyday suggestions for relaxation and other methods of stress reduction are presented in Figure 16-6. Your stress symptoms will ordinarily return, however, if you do

FIGURE 16-6 Stress Busters

- Take a deep breath and exhale slowly. Inhale and your heart beats faster. Exhale and your heart beats more slowly, and slows down the cardiac muscle.

- Give in to your emotions. If you are angry, disgusted, or confused, admit your feelings. Suppressing your emotions leads to stress.

- When you feel stress coming on, replace negative or fearful thoughts with positive ones.

- Engage in enjoyable exercise in your daily life.

- Take a break from the stressful situation, and do something small and constructive, such as washing your car, emptying a wastebasket, or getting your hair cut or styled.

- Get a massage because it can loosen tight muscles, improve your blood circulation, and calm you down.

- Cuddle with someone you care about.

- Have a quiet place at home, and spend a brief idle period there every day.

- Finish something you have started, however small. Accomplishing almost anything reduces some stress.

- Stop to smell the flowers, make friends with a young child or elderly person, or play with a puppy or kitten—assuming that you like domestic animals.

- Strive to do a good job, but not a perfect job.

- Work with your hands, doing a pleasant task.

- Find somebody or something that makes you laugh, and have a good laugh.

- Minimize drinking caffeinated or alcoholic beverages and energy drinks. Drink fruit juice or water instead.

- Visit a Web site, including social media, that you perceive to be relaxing.

- Focus on the moment instead of thinking about the past, the future, or distracting thoughts.

- Help somebody less fortunate than you. The flood of good feelings will act like endorphins.

Personal Stress Management Action Plan

Most people face a few powerful stressors in their work and personal life, but few people take the time to clearly identify these stressors or develop an action plan for remedial action. The purpose of this exercise is to make you an exception. Here is an opportunity to develop an inventory of your stressors, think through the problems they may be causing you, and develop action plans you might take to remedy the situation. Use the form ahead, or create one with a word processor table or a spreadsheet.

Work or School Stressor	Symptoms This Stressor Is Creating for Me	My Action Plan to Manage This Stressor
1.		
2.		
3.		
Personal Life Stressor	Symptoms This Stressor Is Creating for Me	My Action Plan to Manage This Stressor
1.		
2.		
3.		

not eliminate and modify the stressor. If the stress is an emotional conflict you do not see or understand, assistance from a mental health professional is recommended.

Now that you have studied various methods of managing stress, reinforce your thinking by doing Skill-Building Exercise 16-1. Seven days after preparing this worksheet, observe if any of your stress symptoms have diminished. Also, identify those stressors for which only a long-term solution is possible.

IMPROVING PERSONAL PRODUCTIVITY

Achieving personal productivity is more in vogue than ever. Companies strive to operate with smaller staffs than in the past by pushing workers to achieve higher productivity. In the zeal to avoid time wasting, many companies are imposing rigorous performance quotas, forcing many people to work longer hours.[40] At the same time, there is a movement toward simplifying personal life by reducing clutter and cutting back on tasks that do not add much to the quality of life.

personal productivity

The amount of resources, including time, you consume to achieve a certain level of output.

Personal productivity refers to the amount of resources, including time, you consume to achieve a certain level of output. In measuring productivity, it is important to take into account quantity and quality of work as well as how the work was accomplished.[41] A customer service representative might spend more than an average amount of time with customers, thereby appearing to be unproductive. Yet the rep might be building good relationships with customers that result in customer loyalty and repeat business. Another example is that a safety inspector might be getting an above-average number of inspections accomplished in part because the inspector is not very thorough.

We approach productivity improvement from four perspectives: (1) dealing with procrastination, (2) attitudes and values that enhance personal productivity, (3) work habits and skills that enhance personal productivity, and (4) overcoming time wasters.

Dealing with Procrastination

LEARNING OBJECTIVE 4

procrastination

Delaying action for no good reason on tasks that need to be done.

The person who procrastinates delays action for no good reason on tasks that need to be done. **Procrastination** results in a gap between intention and action. A major reason why people procrastinate is that they want to feel good at the moment rather than reap future rewards. As such, procrastination is a form of impulsivity.[42] *Why bother getting in touch with my boss to discuss my prospects for promotion when I can send a tweet to 500 people right now?*

Procrastination lowers productivity because it wastes time, and many important tasks never get done. Another serious problem is that undone tasks rumble around in the back of your consciousness, thereby decreasing your concentration.

Many people regard procrastination as a laughable weakness, particularly because procrastinators themselves joke about the problem. Yet procrastination has been evaluated as a profound, debilitating problem, with between 20 and 25 percent of working adults identifying themselves as chronic procrastinators.[43] Approximately 90 percent of college students report problems with overdue papers and delayed studying. About 25 percent are chronic procrastinators, and many of them drop out of school.[44] The enormity of the procrastination problem makes it worthwhile to examine methods for bringing it under control. Take Self-Assessment Quiz 16-1 to think through your own tendencies toward procrastination—and don't wait until tomorrow.

Choose from among the following eight suggestions for controlling procrastination, based on those that appear to best fit your type of procrastination. A combination of techniques is likely to be the most effective.

1. **Commit to what you want in life.** If you are not committed to something you want in life, you are likely to be a chronic procrastinator. The reason is that it is difficult to prioritize and take action. (See the later discussion about a personal mission and work habits.) Your commitment to what you want in life will often translate into forgoing short-term pleasure, such as stopping by a café, in order to finish a project due today.

2. **Calculate the cost of procrastination.** You can reduce procrastination by calculating its cost. You might lose out on obtaining a high-paying job you really want by not having your résumé and cover letter ready on time. Your cost of procrastination would include the difference in compensation between the job you do find and the one you really wanted. Another cost would be the loss of potential job satisfaction.

3. **Follow the WIFO principle, which stands for "worst in, first out."**[45] If you tackle the worst task on your list first, doing the other tasks may function like a small reward.

SELF-ASSESSMENT QUIZ 16-1

Procrastination Tendencies

Directions: Circle yes or no for each item.

1.	I usually do my best work under the pressure of deadlines.	Yes	No
2.	Before starting a project, I go through such rituals as sharpening every pencil, straightening up my desk more than once, and reading and responding to all possible e-mail.	Yes	No
3.	I crave the excitement of the "last-minute rush," such as researching and writing a paper right before the deadline.	Yes	No
4.	I often think that if I delay something, it will go away, or the person who asked for it will forget about it.	Yes	No
5.	I extensively research something before taking action, such as obtaining three different estimates before getting the brakes repaired on my car.	Yes	No
6.	I have a great deal of difficulty getting started on most projects, even those I enjoy.	Yes	No
7.	I keep waiting for the right time to do something, such as getting started on an important report.	Yes	No
8.	I often underestimate the time needed to do a project, and say to myself, "I can do this quickly, so I'll wait until next week."	Yes	No
9.	It is difficult for me to finish most projects or activities.	Yes	No
10.	I have several favorite diversions or distractions that I use to keep me from doing something unpleasant, such as a difficult homework assignment.	Yes	No

Total Yes Responses _____

Scoring and Interpretation: The greater the number of "Yes" responses, the more likely it is that you have a serious procrastination problem. A score of 8, 9, or 10 strongly suggests that your procrastination is lowering your productivity.

You get to do what you dislike the least by doing first what you dislike the most. WIFO is particularly effective when faced with a number of tasks simultaneously.

4. **Break the task into manageable chunks.** To reduce procrastination, cut down a task that seems overwhelming into smaller projects that seem less formidable. If your job calls for preparing an enormous database, begin by assembling some readily available information. Then take the next step by assembling another small segment of the database—perhaps all customers whose last names begin with Z. Think of your task as pulling together a series of small databases that will fit into a master database.

5. **Make a commitment to other people.** Try to make it imperative that you get something done on time by making it a commitment to one or more other people. You might announce to coworkers that you are going to get something accomplished by a certain date. If you fail to meet this date, you are likely to feel embarrassed.

6. **Satisfy your stimulation quota in constructive ways.** If you procrastinate because you enjoy the rush of scrambling to make deadlines, find a more constructive way of using busyness to keep you humming. If you need a high level of stimulation, enrich your life with extra projects and learning new skills. The fullness of your schedule will provide you the stimulation you had been receiving from squeezing yourself to make deadlines and reach appointments on time.[46]

7. **Eliminate tangible rewards you are giving yourself for procrastinating.** If you are procrastinating through socializing with coworkers, taking a walk to obtain a beverage, surfing the Internet, or any other pleasant experience—stop rewarding yourself. Just sit alone in your work area doing nothing while procrastinating. If you remove the pleasant activities from your stalling routine, you may be able to reduce procrastination.

Enhancing Personal Productivity through Attitudes and Values

LEARNING OBJECTIVE 5

Developing good work habits and time-management practices is often a matter of developing the right attitudes toward your work and toward time.

Begin with a Mission and Goals.   A mission, or general purpose, propels you toward being productive. Assume that a person says, "My mission is to be an outstanding professional in my field and a loving, constructive spouse and parent." The mission serves as a compass to direct your activities, such as being well organized in order to accomplish more work and be highly valued by your employer. Goals are more specific than mission statements; they support the mission statement, but the effect is the same. Being committed to a goal also propels you toward good use of time. If you know that you can obtain the position in international business that you really want by mastering a second language, you are likely to work diligently on learning that language.

Skill-Building Exercise 16-2 gives you the opportunity to establish a mission statement and supporting goals.

Work Smarter, Not Harder.   People caught up in trying to accomplish a job often wind up working hard, but not in an imaginative way that leads to good results. Much time and energy are, therefore, wasted. A working-smart approach also requires that you spend a few minutes carefully planning how to implement your task. An example of working smarter, not harder, is to invest a few minutes of critical thinking before conducting a telemarketing campaign for home replacement windows. Develop a list of homeowners of houses that are at least 15 years old. People with relatively new homes are poor prospects for replacing their windows.

A new perspective on working smarter, not harder, is to keep perfecting your skills through **deliberate practice**—strong effort to improve target performance over time. Practice alone does not lead to nearly as much improvement as thinking through what you have done to look for areas for improvement.[47] Feedback from others is also helpful.

deliberate practice
Strong effort to improve target performance over time.

Value Orderliness and Cleanliness.   Being surrounded by a collection of small, unfinished tasks interferes with your ability to focus on major tasks. Also, less time is wasted and less energy is expended if you do not have to hunt for information that you thought you had on hand. A compelling reason for being neat and orderly is that a *CareerBuilder* survey indicated that 28 percent of employers are less likely to promote a worker who has a disorganized or messy workplace.[48]

Using a Mission Statement and Goals to Power Work Habits

People with a well-defined mission statement and supporting goals tend to have better work habits and time management than those who do not. The following exercise is designed to help you establish a mission statement and goals so that you will be energized to be more productive.

A. *Mission Statement:* To help develop your mission statement, or general purpose in life, ask yourself, "What are my five biggest wishes in life?" These wishes give you a hint to your purpose because they point toward an ideal purpose in life. Feel free to think big, because mission statements tend toward being idealistic.

B. *Long-Range Goals to Support the Mission Statement:* Now write down what long-range goals would support your mission statement. Suppose your mission statement related to "creating a better life for people who are disadvantaged." Your long-range goals might include establishing a foundation that would fund your efforts. You would also need to be successful enough in your career to get the foundation started.

C. *Intermediate-Range Goals to Support Long-Range Goals:* Write down the intermediate-range goals needed to support the long-range goals. You will probably need to complete your education, obtain broad experience, and identify a lucrative form of self-employment.

D. *Weekly Goals to Support Intermediate-Range Goals:* Write down what you have to do this week to help you complete your education, such as researching and writing a paper for a particular course, registering for courses for next term, and inquiring about career opportunities in your field.

E. *Today's Goals to Support Weekly Goals (My To-Do List):* Here's where your lofty purpose in life gets translated into reality. What do you have to do today to get that paper written? Do you need to get your car battery replaced, so you can get to the library, so you can write your paper, so you can graduate, so you can become rich, so you can ultimately help all those people who are disadvantaged? Get going.

The central message of the best-seller *Getting Things Done* by David Allen is that to achieve maximum efficiency and relaxation is to clear clutter both outside and inside your mind.[49] One way of clearing clutter from your mind is to write down your tasks on to-do lists. If you are orderly, you clear clutter.

As with any suggestions about human behavior, individual differences exist with respect to the impact of clutter on productivity. It has been argued that focusing too much on tidiness might detract from creative thinking and that many messy people, such as Albert Einstein, believe that a messy work area facilitates their creative thinking. To quote the great man, "If a cluttered desk is a sign of a cluttered mind, of what, then, is an empty desk a sign?"[50]

Value Good Attendance and Punctuality. Good attendance and punctuality are expected of both experienced and inexperienced employees. You cannot be productive unless you are physically present in your work area. The same principle applies whether you work on company premises or at home. One exception is that some people can work through solutions to job problems while engaged in recreation. Keep in mind, too, that being late for or absent from meetings sends the silent message that you do not regard the meeting as being important. Also, being late for a meeting, whether face-to-face or virtual, is regarded quite negatively by many managers. Some managers even lock the door to the meeting room after the meeting has begun. Whether the person is late or absent for work or just for a meeting, the behavior is interpreted by many as demonstrating irresponsibility.

Attain a Balance in Life, and Avoid Being a Workaholic. A productive attitude to maintain is that overwork can lead to negative stress and burnout. Proper physical rest and relaxation can contribute to mental alertness and an improved ability to cope with frustration. Many people do not achieve enough rest and relaxation, as inferred from the avoidance of vacations. A strategy for preventing overwork is to strive for a balance in which you derive satisfaction from various spheres of life. Major spheres in addition to work include family life, romance, sports, the arts and music, faith, and intellectual growth.

A strongly recommended technique for attaining balance between work and other spheres of life is to learn how to say no diplomatically to your boss and family members. For example, your boss might ask you to take on a project when you are already overloaded. It would be necessary to *occasionally* explain that you are so overloaded that you could not do a good job with the new assignment. And you might have to *occasionally* turn down your family's or friend's request to take a weekend vacation when you face heavy work demands.

Neglecting the normal need for rest and relaxation can lead to **workaholism**, an addiction to work in which not working is an uncomfortable experience. Some types of

workaholism

An addiction to work in which not working is an uncomfortable experience.

workaholics are perfectionists who are never satisfied with their work, therefore, find it difficult to leave work behind, and have no real hobbies outside of the office. In addition, the perfectionist-type workaholic may become heavily focused on control of people and information, leading to rigid behavior and strained interpersonal relationships. Many workaholics take laptops to bed, and leave their smartphones on during the night to catch any potential calls from distant time zones. Fifty percent of workers polled by Good Technologies, a mobile-security specialist, said they read or responded to work e-mails from bed. Some workers now have Wi-Fi mattresses.[51]

Leslie Perlow, a Harvard Business School professor of leadership, conducted an experiment with consultants who worked an average of 65 hours per week, not including approximately 20 hours per week spent monitoring their smartphones. During the experiment, the consultants took a full night off per week! Productivity actually increased as team members were forced to improve coordination.[52]

Despite the potential negatives of overwork, some people who work long and hard are classified as achievement-oriented workaholics who thrive on hard work and are usually highly productive.[53] For example, a person with strong family values might nevertheless work 65 hours per week for one year while establishing a new business.

Increase Your Energy.   According to Tony Schwartz, the founder of the Energy Project in New York City, increasing your energy is the best way to get more done faster and better. Becoming more energetic leads to more productivity gains than merely working longer hours. Rituals can be established to build energy in several spheres, with body and mental energy being the most relevant for personal productivity.

Body energy. Increasing body energy closely follows some of the guidelines for stress management described earlier. Proper nutrition, moderate physical exercise, adequate rest, and taking brief breaks from work all enhance a person's energy level. Naps, as previously described, are also key energy boosters.

Mental energy. To enhance mental energy, it is particularly important to minimize distractions that lead to constant multitasking. Switching to another task increases the amount of time required to complete the primary tasks by up to 25 percent, a phenomenon know as *switching time*.[54] We recognize, however, that you still have to live in a modern world. If you are preparing a report, and your boss sends you an urgent IM, or your sick parent or child sends you a text message, it is natural to be distracted away from your primary task.

A study about vitality and fatigue among professional workers provides new insights into enhancing energy to improve productivity. It was found that the strategies most related to having more vitality on the job focused on three areas: learning job-related skills and information, the meaning of one's work, and positive workplace relationships. Examples are (1) learning something new, such as how to cope with currency fluctuations; (2) reflecting how a person might make a difference at work; and (3) doing something that will make a coworker happy. The general point is that taking short breaks during the workday does not boost your energy unless you do something job-related and positive, such as praising a colleague or learning something new.[55]

Enhancing Personal Productivity through Work Habits and Skills

LEARNING OBJECTIVE 6

Overcoming procrastination and developing the right attitudes contribute to personal productivity. Effective work habits and skills are also essential for high productivity. Six key work habits and skills are described next. They represent a mixture of traditional productivity boosters and those geared toward information technology.

Prepare a To-Do List and Set Priorities.   At the heart of every time management system is list making, whether the list is placed on an index card, in a leather-bound planner, or in a smartphone. The to-do list is the basic tool for achieving your daily goals, which in turn helps you achieve bigger goals and your mission. Almost every successful person in any field composes a list of important and less important tasks that need to be done. A stellar example is the famous Sheryl Sandberg, the number two executive at Facebook, who uses a paper notebook to organize her super-charged workdays. Before you compose a useful list, you need to set aside a few minutes of quiet time every day to sort out the tasks at hand. This is the most basic aspect of planning.

As is well known, it is helpful to set priorities for items on the to-do list. A typical system is to use A to signify critical or essential items, B to signify important items, and C for the least important ones. Although an item might be regarded as a C (e.g., emptying the wood shavings from the electronic pencil sharpener), it still makes a contribution to your management of time and sense of wellbeing. Accomplishing anything reduces some stress. Also, many people obtain satisfaction from crossing off an item on their list, however trivial. If you are at all conscientious, small, unaccomplished items will come back to interfere with your concentration.

A to-do list may have to be revamped to meet the changing demands of the day. As a result, you should quickly prepare a new to-do list. For example, if you are alerted that a fire broke out in the warehouse, your to-do list as a production supervisor might change on the spot.

Preparing to-do lists should not become an end in itself, with so much time devoted to list making that accomplishing some of the tasks are neglected. The compulsive list maker sometimes neglects seeing the big picture of what needs to get done. Another danger is filling the to-do list with items you would have to accomplish anyway, such as "check e-mail" or "handle customer inquiry." The to-do list can become so long that it becomes an overwhelming task.

Streamline Your Work and Emphasize Important Tasks.   Getting rid of unproductive work is part of *business process improvement,* in which work processes are radically redesigned and simplified. Every employee is expected to get rid of work that does not contribute to productivity or help customers. In general, to streamline your work, look for duplication of effort and waste. An example of duplication of effort would be to routinely send people e-mail, intranet, and voice mail messages covering the same topic. An example of waste would be to call a meeting for disseminating information that could easily be communicated by e-mail.

Emphasizing important tasks means that you make sure to take care of A items on your to-do list. It also implies that you search to accomplish a few work activities that, if done well, would make a big difference in your job performance. Although important tasks may take less time to accomplish than many routine tasks, they can represent the difference between success and failure. Five minutes of telephone conversation with a major customer might do more good for your company than three hours of arranging obsolete inventory in the warehouse.

Concentrate on One Important Task at a Time Instead of Multitasking.   While working on important tasks, concentrate on what you are doing. Effective executives and professionals have a well-developed capacity to concentrate on the problem or person facing them, however surrounded they are with other obligations. Intense concentration leads to crisper judgment and analysis and also minimizes major errors. Another useful by-product of concentration is that it helps reduce absentmindedness. If you really concentrate on what you are doing, the chances diminish that you will forget what you intended to do.

Both experimental evidence and opinion have accumulated that show that multitasking while performing important tasks leads to problems in concentration, along with significant errors—for most people. The information about mental energy described earlier applies here. Multitasking on routine tasks has less negative consequences and can sometimes be a legitimate time saver. For example, waiting in line at the airport during business travel provides a good opportunity to review company documents or catch up on work-related news.

David E. Meyer, the director of the Brain, Cognition, and Action Laboratory at the University of Michigan, notes that when people attempt to perform two or more related tasks at the same time or alternating rapidly—instead of doing them sequentially—two negative consequences occur. Errors increase substantially, and the amount of time to perform the task may double.[56] Also, according to brain research, few people can concentrate on more than four tasks at once. The more workers switch back and forth between tasks, the less they accomplish, particularly with respect to professional and technical tasks.[57]

Multitasking has enormous potentially negative consequences when the lives of others are at stake, such as when driving a car or truck or flying an airplane. In a well-publicized case in

2013, texting by the pilot of a medical helicopter contributed to to a crash that killed four people on board, including himself. (He was also fatigued and had ignored pre-flight safety checks.) The pilot exchanged 20 text messages during the hour and 41 minutes preceding the crash. After the tragedy, federal accident investigators approved a safety alert advising pilots against using cell phones or other distracting electronic gadets during critical operations.[58]

Place the potential dangers of multitasking on a personal level. Would you want a cardiac surgeon to operate on a loved one while she was receiving personal calls on her cell phone? Would you want your commercial airline pilot to be sending text messages to "friends" on a social network while he was flying through a storm? (Using a tablet computer while in flight is not reassuring either.)

Stay in Control of Paperwork and Electronic Work.   Although it is fashionable to complain about paperwork in responsible jobs, the effective career person does not neglect paperwork. (Paperwork includes electronic work, such as electronic mail and voice mail.) Paperwork involves taking care of administrative details such as correspondence, invoices, human resource reports, expense reports, and inventory forms. A considerable amount of electronic work results in paperwork, because many e-mail messages and attachments wind up being printed. (Check out the reams of copying paper stacked high in your local office supply store.) Unless paperwork and electronic work are attended to, a person's job may get out of control. A small amount of time should be invested in paperwork every day. Nonprime time (when you are at less than your peak of efficiency, but not overfatigued) is the best time to take care of paperwork.

An effective technique is to respond quickly to high-priority e-mail messages, and permanently delete those you will most likely not need to refer to again. File only those e-mail messages of high importance to avoid being overwhelmed with piles of old messages. For many types of work, it is important to be able to access old e-mails; however, some workers complain (brag?) of having 6,000 e-mails in their inboxes. In addition to clogging the servers, this large accumulation of e-mails is distracting, thereby lowering productivity. Old e-mails should be archived, and others moved to appropriate folders.

Work Productively from Your Home Office or Virtual Office.   A growing segment of the workforce works either full or part time from home or from a **virtual office**. Estimates vary considerably, but it appears that about 5 percent of all workers in nonfamily businesses work at home at least one day per week.[59] Such an office is a place of work without a fixed physical location from which the worker or workers communicate their output electronically. A virtual office might be in a car, train, airplane, or hotel room; on a park bench; or wherever the worker happens to be at the time. Many people adapt well to working at home and from virtual offices because they are self-starters and self-disciplined. Many other workers lack the self-discipline and effective work habits necessary to be productive outside of a traditional office. The following is a list of representative suggestions for being productive while working independently.[60]

- Act as if you work in a traditional office. Set specific working hours, get dressed, go outside the house for a few minutes, then return and get to work. A frequent recommendation is not to work in your pajamas. Close your office at home or the virtual office at some regular time. Otherwise, you are open for business all the time. If you work at home, establish a specific workspace whether it be a den, bedroom, kitchen, attic, or basement. Let your family and friends know when you cannot be disturbed.

- Stay in touch with teammates to enhance your team player skills and not lose out on important information that could lower your effectiveness (such as missing an appointment at the traditional office). Stay in touch with other workers also, such as visiting an office supply store or attending networking meetings. In this way, you will feel less isolated from the workforce—assuming feeling isolated is a problem for you.

- Minimize the distraction of conducting your personal life at the same time as working (e.g., working while watching television, talking to neighbors, or shopping over the Internet).

- To avoid getting in a rut, switch your work environment from time to time, such as spending part of one day working from a library or quiet café.

virtual office

A place of work without a fixed physical location, where the output is communicated electronically.

Productivity Boosting through Work Habits

The chapter has already given you ideas about using work habits to increase productivity. Here is a chance to make some personal applications of your own. Gather into small teams or work individually to identify 10 ways in which good work habits, as well as using the Internet, can increase personal productivity either on the job or at home. To supplement your own thinking, you might search the Internet for ideas on how the Internet is supposed to boost productivity.

The practice of working at home or from virtual offices is increasing rapidly, so these suggestions merit careful consideration. Several of the productivity ideas also fit the conventional office. Also, if part of your job is to help other workers in person, or answer their spontaneous questions, a virtual office is not an effective option.

Enhance Your Internet Search Skills. An important job skill is searching the Internet for a variety of information. It follows that if you develop your Internet search skills, you will be more productive by obtaining the results you need within a reasonable time. First, it is helpful to rely on several search engines to seek needed information. Several metasearch engines claim to be so comprehensive that no other engine is required. Such claims are exaggerated, because the same search word entered into several different comprehensive engines will reveal a different list of sources. Millions of people believe that conducting an Internet search means only that you "google" your search term.

Second, give careful thought to the search word or phrase you use. The more specific you are, the better it is. Assume that you wanted to find software to enhance your productivity, and you enter the word "software" into a search engine. You will probably receive a message indicating that approximately one billion entries have been located in response to your personal inquiry. You are better advised to use the search phrase "Software for increasing personal productivity."

Third, for many searches, framing the query as a phrase by enclosing it in quotation marks refines the number of hits (or sites) returned. Place quotation marks before and after the search word, such as "software for improving work habits." Fourth, if you don't find what you want in your initial search, reframe your question in another way or change the terms. How about "software for time management" or "computer programs for increasing personal efficiency"? Skill-Building Exercise 16-3 will help you make better use of the Internet to enhance your personal productivity.

Overcoming Time Wasters

Another basic thrust to improve personal productivity is to minimize wasting time. The average US worker wastes 28 percent of the day with interruptions, such as checking e-mail, responding to an instant message, clicking on YouTube, or posting a personal message on Twitter or Facebook.[61] Preoccupation with the Internet is becoming such as problem that *Internet Addiction Disorder* is now listed in the offical psychiatrist's diagnostic manual. The wasted time includes doing the task and recovery time, with the combination resulting in an estimated productivity drain of $650 billion per year.[62] Recognize, however, that answering the phone or responding to an e-mail with a legitimate work purpose is not an interruption—it is part of your job.

Many of the techniques already described in this chapter help save time, such as eliminating nonessential work. Whether or not an activity is a time waster depends on the purpose of the activity. Suppose you play computer solitaire for 10 minutes to reduce stress, and then return to work refreshed and more productive. In contrast, another worker who spends 10 minutes playing solitaire just for fun is wasting time.

Figure 16-7 presents a list of common time wasters. Being aware of time wasters will help sensitize you to the importance of minimizing them. Even if you saved just 10 minutes per workday, the productivity gain over a year could be enormous.

To analyze whether you might be wasting time, do Skill-Building Exercise 16-4.

LEARNING OBJECTIVE 7

FIGURE 16-7   Ways to Prevent and Overcome Time Wasting

1. Minimize procrastination, the number-one time waster for most people.

2. Get your desk, as well as your work space (could be a cubicle, open work area, or office) in order, because sorting through disorder wastes so much time. Also, keep track of important names, places, and things to avoid wasting time searching for them.

3. Complete as many projects on time as possible so you do not have to invest time communicating with others about why you are late, and when you will get the work done.

4. Attempt to resolve personal problems, such as dealing with a relationship breakup, so that you will not be so distracted on the job.

5. Avoid the computer as a diversion from work, such as sending jokes back and forth to other workers, playing video games, and checkiing out recreational Web sites during working hours. Be particulalry alert to avoid Twitter unless it is being used for a legitimate work purpose, such as employee recruitment or brand building.

6. Cluster together tasks such as returning phone calls or responding to e-mail messages. For example, in most jobs it is possible to be polite and productive by reserving two or three 15-minute periods each day for taking care of e-mail correspondence.

7. Be prepared for meetings by, for example, having a clear agenda and sorting through the documents you will be referring to.

8. Set a time limit for tasks after you have done them once or twice.

9. Prepare a computer template for letters and documents that you send frequently.

10. When you arrive at work, be ready to get started working immediately. Greet people quickly, avoid checking your personal e-mail, and shut off your personal phone.

11. Avoid perfectionism, which leads you to keep redoing a project. Let go and move on to another project.

12. Overcome being a control freak so you will not have to spend so much time criticizing the work of coworkers and subordinates. Also, you will decrease the amount of time you spend giving detailed instructions to others.

13. Make use of bits of time—for instance, five minutes between appointments. Invest those five minutes in sending a work-related e-mail message or revising your to-do list.

14. Avoid spreading yourself too thin by doing too many things at once, such as having one project too many to manage. When you are overloaded, time can be wasted because of too many errors.

15. Manage interruptions by letting coworkers know when you are available for consultation, and when you need to work independently. Emergencies are an exception. Repond to instant messages and text messages only if your job requires responding immediately.

16. Think through carefully whether the work you are doing at the moment has any relevance. If what you are doing adds no value for anyone, stop performing the task unless your boss demands otherwise.

Sources: Toddi Gutner, "Beat the Clock," *Business Week*, February/March 2008, p. 58; Joe Queenan, "Lack of Sleep Costs Billions? How About Cats? " *The Wall Street* Journal, January 26–27, 2013, p. C121;Vince Thompson, "Make the Most of Your White Space," *up.theladders.com*, October 3, 2007; Claire Studdath, "My Life As An Efficiency Squirrel," *Bloomberg Businessweek*, October 29–November 4, 2012, pp. 88–90; Leigh Gallager, "How I Managed My Time—the Covey Way," *Fortune*, March 21, 2011, pp. 39–40.

SKILL-BUILDING EXERCISE 16-4

Maintaining a Time Log

An effective starting point to avoid wasting time is to identify how you spend the 168 hours you have each week (24 hours × 7 days). For two weeks, catalog all the time you spend, down to as much detail as you can tolerate. Include the large obvious items, as well as the small items that are easy to forget. Keep track of any activity that requires at least five minutes. Major items would include working, attending class, studying, reading, watching television, sleeping, eating, going places, and time with loved ones and friends (hanging out). Small items would include visiting the coffee shop or vending machine, purchasing gum, and clipping your nails.

If you multitask, such as walking and listening to music, do not double-count the time.

When your time logs have been completed, search for complete wastes of time, or activities that could be shortened. You might find, for example, that you spend about 45 minutes per day in the pursuit and consumption of coffee. If you reduced that time to 30 minutes, you would have an additional 15 minutes per day that you could invest in your career. If, however, coffee time includes forming alliances with people or maintaining relationships, maybe the 45-minute-per-day investment is worthwhile.

Concept Review and Reinforcement

Summary

A major challenge facing any worker who wants to stay healthy and have good interpersonal relationships is to manage stress effectively. Individual differences play a big role in determining whether an event will lead to stress. The physiological changes that take place within the body in response to stress are responsible for most of the stress symptoms. The fight-or-flight response is the battle against the stressor.

The activation of hormones, such as cortisol, when the body has to cope with a stressor produces short-term physiological reactions, including an increase in heart rate and blood pressure. When stress levels rarely subside, the physiological changes create damage. People under continual negative stress age quickly. Hindrance stressors have a negative effect on motivation and performance; however, the right amount of stress (challenge stressors) prepares us for meeting difficult challenges and improves performance. An optimum level of stress exists for most people and most tasks. In general, performance tends to be best under moderate amounts of stress.

One of the major problems of prolonged stress is that it may lead to burnout, a condition of emotional, mental, and physical exhaustion in response to long-term stressors. Feelings of having limited control and not being recognized are major contributors to burnout. Burnout also creates cynicism and a distancing from tasks and people. Workers who perceive the cause of burnout to be external are more likely to become less committed to the firm and more cynical.

Four personality factors predisposing people toward stress are low perceived control, low self-efficacy, Type-A behavior and hostility, and negative affectivity and high reactivity. The heart attack triggers associated with Type-A behavior are hostility, anger, cynicism, and suspiciousness, with hostility having the biggest impact. Frequently encountered job stressors are role overload including extreme jobs, role conflict and ambiguity, adverse environmental conditions including carpal tunnel syndrome and long commutes, environmentally induced attention deficit disorder, aggressive and hostile humor by the supervisor, and job insecurity and job loss. Another frequent job stressor is adverse interactions with customers and clients and emotional labor.

Managing stress refers to controlling stress by making it become a constructive force in your life. Coping with, or managing, stress includes hundreds of activities, with substantial individual differences in which technique is effective. Eight representative stress management methods are to eliminate or modify the stressor, get appropriate physical exercise, rest sufficiently, maintain a healthy diet, build a support network, practice visualization and meditation, participate in resilience training, and practice everyday methods of stress reduction.

Achieving high personal productivity on the job is more in demand than ever. A starting point in improving productivity is to minimize procrastination, an enormous problem for many people that can be approached as follows: Commit to what you want in life; calculate the cost of procrastination; follow the worst in, first out (WIFO) principle; break the task into manageable chunks; make a commitment to other people; remove some clutter from your mind; satisfy your stimulation quota in constructive ways; and eliminate rewards for procrastinating.

Developing good work habits and time management practices is often a matter of developing the right attitudes toward your work and toward time, as follows: (1) Begin with a mission and goals; (2) work smarter, not harder, including the use of deliberate practice; (3) value orderliness and cleanliness; (4) value good attendance and punctuality; (5) attain a balance in life and avoid being a workaholic; and (6) increase your energy, including both the body and the mind.

Effective work habits and skills are essential for high productivity, including the following: (1) Prepare a to-do list and set priorities, (2) streamline your work and emphasize important tasks, (3) concentrate on one important task at a time instead of multitasking, (4) stay in control of paperwork and electronic work, (5) work productively from your home office or virtual office, and (6) enhance your Internet search skills.

Another basic thrust to improved personal productivity is to minimize time wasting. Whether or not an activity is a time waster depends on its purpose. Being aware of time wasters such as those presented in Figure 16-6 will sensitize you to the importance of minimizing them.

Questions for Discussion and Review

1. Why might it be true that people who love their work live much longer than people who retire early because they dislike working?

2. Why might having your stress under control improve your interpersonal relationships?

3. Why do companies make unreasonable demands of their employees in terms of workload?

4. Give three examples of how technology has made work more stressful.

5. Provide an example from your own or somebody else's life of how having a major goal in life can help a person be better organized.

6. Executives at Toyota, among many other Japanese companies, emphasize that clean work areas in the factory enhance productivity. What might explain this relationship between cleanliness and productivity?

7. Suggest one suitable job for type A personality and one for type B.

8. Use the information in this chapter to explain how a person might be well organized, yet still not get very far in his or her career.

9. An increasing number of professional workers take their smartphones and laptop computers to bed so they can respond to e-mails, make phone calls, and do other work whenever they want. What do you see as the pros and cons of taking electronic gadets to bed?

10. With millions of workers making regular use of smartphones throughout the world, why hasn't productivity in organizations taken a dramatic leap forward?

The Web Corner

http://www.stress.org
(Institute for Stress Management—includes video)

http://stress.about.com
(Considerable information about stress, plus several self-quizzes)

http://ub-counseling.buffalo.edu/stressprocrast.shtml
(Overcoming procrastination for students)

Internet Skill Builder: Getting Personal Help from Your Employer

Use your favorite search engines to learn about Employee Assistance Programs (EAPs). After visiting several sites, answer these questions: (1) What type of help can an employee expect to receive from an EAP? (2) How does an EAP help with stress management? (3) Does the EAP counselor typically tell the company the nature of the problem facing the employee who sought assistance? (4) What benefits do companies expect from offering an EAP to employees? (5) What would I tell the company if I needed help with problems that are causing me severe stress?

Internet Skill Builder: What Do Employees Do with Their Time?

To learn about how time studies can improve productivity, visit http://getmoredone.com. The TimeCorder is an easy way to measure how employees spend their time. Watch a two-minute video about a user-friendly time and motion study. After watching the video and related information, ask, "What have I learned that will enhance my personal productivity?"

Developing Your
Human Relations Skills

Interpersonal Relations Case 16.1

The Overwhelmed Medical Billing Specialist

Sasha looked into the storeroom mirror and thought to herself, "You're looking bad, kid. Somehow you've got to get your life straightened out. You're on a treadmill, and you don't know how to get off. But it's a bad time to be thinking about myself right now. It's time to meet with my boss, Francesca. I wonder what she wants."

Francesca began the meeting with Sasha in her usual open manner: "Sasha, I'm concerned about you. For a long time you were one of the best medical billing specialists in our hospital. You received compliments from me and other department heads who had contact with your department. Now you're hardly making it. You've so irritable, so lacking in enthusiasm. And a lot of your work contains glaring errors and is also late. The reason I'm bringing up the subject up again is that your performance has gotten worse. What's your problem?"

"I wish it were only one problem, Francesca. I feel like the world is caving in on me. I work here about 35 hours per week. I'm trying to upgrade myself in life. As you know, I'm taking two courses in a business administration program. If I can keep up the pace, I'll have an associate's degree by next spring. But it's a grind."

"How are things at home, Sasha?"

"Much worse than they are here. My husband works, also, and he's getting fed up with never seeing me much when he comes home. I'm either working late at the office, in class, or studying at the library. Thursday is the one weekday night I'm home for sure, and that's Tony's bowling night."

"Our son Deon isn't too happy either. He's only five, but the other day he asked me if Daddy and I were getting divorced. Deon doesn't see us together much. When he does see us, he can feel the tension between us."

"So, you're under pressure at the office and at home," said Francesca.

"Add school to that list. I'm having a dreadful time getting through my business statistics course. If I flunk, my chances of getting a degree are set back considerably."

"Do the best you can, Sasha. I'm sympathetic, but I need better performance from you."

As Sasha left Francesca's office she said, "Thanks for being candid with me. My problem is that my boss, my husband, my child, and my professors all want better performance from me. I wish I knew how to give it."

Case Questions

1. What suggestions can you offer Sasha for working her way out of her problems?
2. Why is this case included in a chapter about improving productivity and managing stress?
3. How well do you think that Francesca handled the interview?

Interpersonal Skills Role-Play

Francesca Attempts to Help Sasha

This role-play provides an opportunity to practice one of the most frequent constructive interactions in the workplace, a supervisor attemptng to help a subordinate overcome a problem. One student plays the role of Francesca, who wants to help Sasha overcome her productivity problems, but there are limits to her patience. Another student plays the role of Sasha, who wants help and wants to improve, yet she feels overwhelmed. Run the role-play for about eight minutes. Observers will note whether the meeting will likely result in a useful outcome for Sasha. Also the observers might comment on Francesca's coaching skills.

Interpersonal Relations Case 16.2

Rob Naps to Boost His Personal Productivity

Nina, the director of marketing, was in a hurry early one afternoon to get back to the office to finalize her proposed budget for the upcoming fiscal year. Instead of entering the building through the front door, she chose a side door. Shortly after she entered the building, she noticed a man lying still under the concrete stairwell. Frightened, she thought the person might be ill or dead. As Nina was about to call 911 from her smart phone, she noticed that the person on the floor was Rob, the social media marketing specialist.

Nina nudged Rob with her foot, and he quickly awoke. "Rob, you frightened me. Why are you sleeping under the stairwell? Are you ill? Drunk? What's your problem? You are behaving very unprofessionally."

"Sorry to frighten you, Nina," said Rob. "As you know, my work is highly demanding and stressful. I have seen quite a few articles about how taking a nap during the working day can boost a person's productivity and reduce

stress. It's so nice and quiet out here for napping. Also, the concrete is nice and cool."

"I'm only half-convinced that daytime naps make a worker more productive, and you can work on reducing your stress after hours. But can't you find a better place to nap?"

Rob replied, "I tried napping in my cubicle, but my manager said I looked lazy and unprofessional. I tried napping in the storeroom, but I got a few nasty looks from my coworkers. My decision was to nap in the stairwell. It's been very comfortable, and I am usually more productive and less stressed for the rest of the day."

"I'll have to think about this," said Nina, as she proceeded into the building.

Case Questions

1. What do you recommend that Rob do about his productivity naps for the future?
2. How should Nina deal with the situation of Rob taking naps for productivity and stress reduction?

References

1. Cait Murphy, "The CEO Workout," *Fortune*, July 10, 2006, pp. 43–44.
2. Jennifer Schramm, "Manage Stress, Improve the Bottom Line," *HR Magazine*, February 2013, p. 80.
3. Research reported in Allie Mendoza, "What Are the Effects of Stress on Aging?" *Examiner.com* (http://www.examiner.com),September 12, 2001, pp. 1–4.
4. Jeffery A. Lapine, Nathan P. Podsakoff, and Marcie A. Lepine, "A Meta-Analytic Test of the Challenge-Stressor-Hindrance-Stressor Framework: An Explanation for Inconsistent Relationships among Stressors and Performance," *Academy of Management Journal*, October 2005, pp. 764–775.
5. J. Craig Wallace et al., "Work Stressors, Role-Based Performance, and the Moderating Influence of Organizational Support," *Journal of Applied Psychology*, January 2009, pp. 254–262.
6. Thea Singer, "The Perfect Amount of Stress," *Psychology Today*, March/April 2012, p. 82.
7. Christina Maslach and Michael Leiter, *The Truth about Burnout* (San Francisco: Jossey-Bass, 1997). Research updated in interview, Emily Waters, "Burnout on the Rise: Recognizing the Unconventional Telltale Signs," *NY Workplace Examiner* (http://www.examiner.com), June 18, 2009.
8. Annebel H. B. De Hoog and Deanne N. Den Hartog, "Neuroticism and Locus of Control as Moderators of the Relationships of Charismatic and Autocratic Leadership with Burnout," *Journal of Applied Psychology*, July 2009, pp. 1058–1067.
9. Maslach and Leiter, *The Truth About Burnout*.
10. Leslie Kwoh, "Taking Early Exits Off Wall Street," *The Wall Street Journal*, October 26, 2012, pp. C1, C2.
11. M. Afalur Rahim, "Relationships of Stress, Locus of Control, and Social Support to Psychiatric Symptoms and

Propensity to Leave a Job: A Field Study with Managers," *Journal of Business and Psychology,* Winter 1997, p. 159.

12. Steve M. Jex, Paul O. Bliese, Sheri Buzell, and Jessica Primeau, "The Impact of Self-Efficacy on Stressor-Strain Relations: Coping Style as an Explanatory Mechanism," *Journal of Applied Psychology,* June 2001, pp. 401–409.

13. Jeffrey R. Edwards and A. J. Baglioni, Jr., "Relationships between Type A Behavior Pattern and Mental and Physical Symptoms: A Comparison of Global and Component Measures," *Journal of Applied Psychology,* April 1991, p. 276; related research reported in Etienne Benson, "Hostility Is among Best Predictors of Heart Disease in Men," *Monitor on Psychology,* January 2003, p. 15.

14. Research reviewed in Nadja Geipert, "Don't Be Mad: More Research Links Hostility to Coronary Risk," *Monitor on Psychology,* January 2007, pp. 50–51.

15. Peter Y. Chen and Paul E. Spector, "Negative Affectivity as the Underlying Cause of Correlations between Stressors and Strains," *Journal of Applied Psychology,* June 1991, p. 398.

16. Research reported in Sue Shellenbarger, "Are You Hard-Wired to Boil Over from Stress," *The Wall Street Journal,* February 13, 2013, p. D3.

17. Ed Frauenheim, "Stress & Pressed," *Workforce Management,* January 2012, p. 19.

18. Leslie Kwoh, "Hazard of the Trade: Banker's Health," *The Wall Street Journal,* February 15, 2012, p. C1.

19. Erin M. Eatough, Chu-Hsiang Chang, Stephanie A. Miloslavic, and Russell E. Johnson, "Relationship of Role Stressors With Organizational Citizenship Behavior: A Meta-Analysis," *Journal of Applied Psychology,* May 2011, pp. 619–632.

20. William Atkinson, "Causes of Workplace Stress," *HR Magazine,* December 2000, p. 107; Michele Conlin, "Is Your Office Killing You?" Business Week, June 5, 2000, pp. 114–128; "Sick Building Syndrome," *http://www.doctorfungus.org,* accessed January 22, 2007, p. 1.

21. Natiolio J. Izsquierdo, "Computer Vision Syndrome," *Medscape* (http://emedicine.medscape.com), May 30, 2012, pp. 1–4.

22. Christine A. Spring et al., "Work Characteristics: Musculoskeletal Disorders, and the Mediating Role of Psychological Strain: A Study of Call Center Employees," *Journal of Applied Psychology,* September 2007, pp. 1456–1466.

23. Christina Binkley, "Sitting Pretty When You're Hard at Work," *The Wall Street Journal,* June 11, 2009, pp. D1, D7.

24. Alicia A. Grandey, "Emotion Regulation in the Workplace: A New Way to Conceptualize Emotional Labor," *Journal of Occupational Health Psychology,* 5; 1, 2000, pp. 95–110;

Grandey, "When the 'Show Must Go On:' Surface Acting and Deep Acting as Determinants of Emotional Exhaustion and Peer-Related Service Delivery," *Academy of Management Journal,* February 2003, pp. 86–96.

25. Markus Groth, Thornsen Henning-Thurau, and Gianfranco Walsh, "Customer Reactions to Emotional labor: The Roles of Employee Acting Strategies and Customer Detection Accuracy," *Academy of Management Journal,* October 2009, pp. 958–974.

26. Theresa M. Glomb, John D. Kammeyer-Mueller, and Maria Rotundo, "Emotional Labor Demands and Compensating Wage Differentials," *Journal of Applied Psychology,* August 2004, p. 707.

27. Timothy A. Judge, Erin Fluegge Woolf, and Charlice Hurst, "Is Emotional Labor More Difficult for Some than Others? A Multilevel, Experience-Sampling Study," *Personnel Psychology,* Spring 2009, pp. 57–88.

28. Yuanyuan Huo, Wing Lam, and Ziguang Chen, "Am I the Only One this Supervisor Is Laughing At? Effects of Aggressive Humor on Employee Strain and Addictive Behaviors," *Personnel Psychology,* Number 4, 2012, pp. 859–885.

29. "Executive Quits after Suicides at France Télécom," The Associated Press, October 6, 2009.

30. Jan de Jonge and Christian Dormann, "Stressors, Resources, and Strain at Work: A Longitudinal Test of the Triple-Match Principle," *Journal of Applied Psychology,* November 2006, pp. 1359–1374.

31. Katherine M. Richardson and Hannah R. Rothstein, "Effects of Occupational Stress Management Intervention Programs: A Meta-Analysis," *Journal of Occupational Health Psychology,* January 2008, pp. 69–93.

32. Stephanie Jean Sohl and Anne Moyer, "Refining the Conceptualization of an Important Future-Oriented Self-Regulatory Behavior: Proactive Coping," *NIH Public Access* (http://www.ncbi.nlm.nih.gov) July 1, 2009, pp. 1–9.

33. Data reported in Laura Landro, "The Hidden Benefits of Exercise," *The Wall Street Journal,* January 5, 2010, p. D1.

34. Lisa Belkin, "Some Respect, Please, for the Afternoon Nap," *The New York Times (http://nytimes.com),* February 25, 2007, p. 1.

35. Research cited in David Wescott, "Do Not Disturb," *Bloomberg Businessweek,* April 23–April 28, 2012, p. 90.

36. Nancy Rodriguez, "Would We Be Healthier With a Vegan Diet? No: It's a Question of Balance," *The Wall Street Journal,* September 18, 2012, p. B11.

37. Research reported in Sara Martin, "The Power of the Relaxation Response," *Monitor on Psychology,* October 2008, p. 33.

38. Katherine Ellison, "Mastering Your Own Mind," *Psychology Today,* October 2006, p. 75.

39. "Resilience Training" (http://www.mayoclinic.org/resilience-training), 2012; William Atkinson, "Turning Stress into Strength," *HR Magazine*, January 2011, pp. 49–52.

40. Alan Semuels, "As Employers Push Efficiency, the Daily Grind Wears Down Workers," *Los Angeles Times* (http://www.latimes.com), April 7, 2013.

41. "Productivity in the Office: A Matter of Impact," *Knowledge@Wharton* (http://www.knowledge.wharton.upenn.edu), May 8, 2013, pp. 1–4.

42. Stephen Kotler, "Escape Artists," *Psychology Today*, September/October 2009, pp. 73–75.

43. Data reported in Kotler, "Escape Artists," p. 75.

44. Maia Szalavitz, "Stand & Deliver," *Psychology Today*, July/August 2003, p. 50.

45. Shale Paul, as cited in "Tips to Keep Procrastination Under Control," Gannet News Service, November 9, 1998.

46. Dru Scott, *How to Put More Time in Your Life* (New York: New American Library, 1980), p 1.

47. Christopher Percy Collier, "The Expert on Experts," *Fast Company*, November 2006, p. 116.

48. Kaitlin Madden, "Get Organized for the New Year: Clear the Clutter from Your Desk," *CareerBuilder*, January 8, 2012.

49. David Allen, *Getting Things Done* (New York: Penguin, 2001, 2007).

50. Quoted in Adrian Wooldridge, "Why Clean Up Your Desk? Delight in Disorder Instead," *The Wall Street Journal*, January 2, 2007, p. D7. Book review of Eric Abrahamson and David Freedman, *A Perfect Mess* (New York: Little, Brown & Co., 2007).

51. Sue Shellenbarger, "More Work Goes 'Undercover': Bringing the Office To Bed for 3.a.m. Emails to China; Wi-Fi Mattresses," *The Wall Street Journal*, November 14, 2012, p. D1.

52. Cited in Joe Robinson, "Workaholics Anonymous," *Entrepreneur*, February 13, 2013, p. 26.

53. Brenda Goodman, "A Field Guide To the Workaholic," *Psychology Today*, May/June 2006, p. 41.

54. Tony Schwartz, "Manage Your Energy, Not Your Time," *Harvard Business Review*, October 2007, pp. 63–74.

55. Charlotte Fritz, Chak Fu Lam, and Gretchen M. Spreitzer, "It's the Little Things that Matter: An Examination of Knowledge Worker's Energy Management," *Academy of Management Perspective*, February 2011, pp. 28–39; Fritz, "Coffee Breaks Don't Boost Productivity After All," *Harvard Business Review*, May 2012, pp. 34–35.

56. The scientific information about multitasking is reviewed in Claudia Wallis, "The Multitasking Generation," *Time*, March 27, 2006, pp. 48–55. See also Joshua S. Rubinstein, David E. Meyer, and Jeffrey E. Evans, "Executive Control of Cognitive Processes in Task Switching," *Journal of Experimental Psychology— Human Perception and Performance*, Vol. 26, January 2000, No. 4, pp. 763–769.

57. Research from the University of Oregon reported in "The Problem with Extreme Multitasking," *The Wall Street Journal*, February 12, 2008, p. B4; "The Multitasking Paradox," *Harvard Business Review*, March 2013, pp. 30–31.

58. Joan Lowy, "NTSB: Pilot's Texting Contributed to Copter Crash," Associated Press, April 9, 2013.

59. Rick Hampson, "The Work-from-Home Tug of War," *USA Today*, March 12, 2013.

60. Debra Auerback, "Getting the Most from Telecommuting," *CareerBuilder*, August 26, 2012; Michelle Conlin, "Out of Sight, Yes. Out of Mind, No," *Business Week*, February 18, 2008, p. 60; Sue Shellenbarger, "When Working at Home Doesn't Work: How Companies Comfort Telecommuters," *The Wall Street Journal*, August 24, 2006, p. D1.

61. Survey cited in Maggie Jackson, "May We Have Your Attention Please?" *Businessweek*, June 23, 2008, p. 055.

62. "Internet Addiction: An ADA-Protected Disability?" *The HR Weekly*, April 8, 2013, p. 1.

Job Search and Career Management Skills

Tyler, age 27, was doing well in his position as an assistant purchasing manager in the Cleveland division of a company that manufactured and installed elevators, escalators, and moving walkways. To save money, the company decided to consolidate the Cleveland division into the Kansas City division. Tyler was told he would most likely have an opportunity to transfer to Kansas City. Because Tyler's wife had a satisfying position and he had family and close friends in Cleveland, he decided that he did not want to relocate. Instead, he initiated a job search in the Cleveland area.

Tyler carefully planned his job search, including informing his professional contacts that he was hoping to land a position as a purchasing manager, thereby upgrading his job status. After about 30 days of searching, Tyler had an interview for a position with a farm equipment

Ariel Skelley/Getty Images

After reading and studying this chapter and completing the exercises, you should be able to

1. Acquire new insights into conducting a job search, including writing an impressive cover letter, preparing a résumé, and being interviewed.
2. Identify a handful of career-enhancing strategies and tactics you intend to use.

manufacturer. Although the interview went well, the hiring manager decided to hire a candidate with more direct experience in the farm equipment industry. Two weeks later, Tyler had an interview for a purchasing manager position at a manufacturer of high-performance racing bicycles. Tyler decided he was going to really stand out in his upcoming interview.

Tyler decided that when the moment was appropriate he was going to ask a question that well-known career-placement specialist Marc Cenderella says is his best career tip. He recommends that when you get to the portion of the interview where the interviewer asks if have any questions for him or her, respond by asking, "How do I help you get a gold star on your performance review next year?"[1]

Tyler said that after he asked that question, the interviewing manager seemed shocked, but then broke out into a warm smile, and said "Lower our bike parts purchasing cost by 10 percent without sacrificing quality, and we will both get gold stars." From that point on, the interview got better and better, and Tyler was offered a position as a purchasing manager at a salary 7 percent higher than he was making before.

Tyler was well qualified and self-confident when he initiated a job search, yet he also was perceptive enough to follow some professional advice about conducting a successful job interview. Our approach to achieving career success is divided into two major segments: conducting a job campaign, and using career advancement strategies and tactics. The previous 16 chapters also dealt with topics and skills that facilitate success; however, the information presented in this chapter is more specifically about managing your career.

CONDUCTING A JOB SEARCH

The vast majority of workers have to conduct a job search at various times in their careers. Job searches are conducted to find employment in a firm the job seeker is not already working for or sometimes to find a new position within one's own firm. When job openings are on short supply, job search skills are especially important. Even during the most prosperous of times, when jobs are in ample supply, learning more about conducting a job search is useful. It can help you land an excellent position. Included in the job search are job-hunting tactics and preparing a résumé and cover letter.

LEARNING OBJECTIVE 1

Job-Hunting Tactics

Most people already have usable knowledge about how to find a job, and information about job hunting is abundant. Some of the ideas discussed next will therefore be familiar; some will be unfamiliar. We recommend using this list of tactics as a checklist to ensure that you have not neglected something important. Also, it is important to search for employment systematically. It is easy to overlook the obvious when job hunting, because your emotions may cloud your sense of logic.

Identify Your Job Objectives.   An effective job search begins with a clear perception of what kind of position (or positions) you want. If you express indecision about the type of work you seek, the prospective employer will typically ask in a critical tone, "What kind of work are you looking for?" Your chances of finding suitable employment increase when several different types of positions will satisfy your job objectives. Assume that one person who majored in business administration is only willing to accept a position as an office manager in a corporation. Another person with the same major is seeking a position as (1) an office manager; (2) a management trainee in a corporation; (3) an assistant manager in a retail store, restaurant, or hotel; (4) a sales representative; (5) an assistant purchasing agent; or (6) a social media marketing specialist. The second person has a much better chance of finding a suitable position.

In addition to identifying your job objectives, it is helpful to match your skills to the job you want. For example, if a person is seeking a position as an assistant manager at a hotel, that person should refect on all the relevant skills he or she might possess. Among these would be (1) an ability to deal with a variety of personalities including resolving conflicts, (2) information technology skills, (3) advanced telephone communication skills, and (4) adapatibility to long and irregular working hours.

Be Aware of Qualifications Sought by Employers.   What you are looking for in an employer must be matched against what an employer is looking for in an employee. If you are aware of what employers are seeking, you can emphasize those aspects of yourself when applying for a position. For example, applicants for almost any type of position should emphasize their information technology skills. Job interviewers and hiring managers do not all agree on the qualifications they seek in employees. Nevertheless, a number of traits, characteristics, skills, and accomplishments are important to many employers.

Self-Assessment Quiz 17-1 summarizes these qualifications in a way that you can apply to yourself as you think about your job hunt. Skill in a second language (item 21) is based on an analysis by *Brazen Careerist* that having command of a second language increases your job competitiveness now and down the road. Mandarin Chinese and Arabic have become more important on a global scale, with demand for people competent in these languages outstripping supply.[2] (And what an asset for our potential assistant hotel manager!)

Identify Your Skills and Potential Contribution.   The job market is skill based. Employers typically seek out job candidates with tangible skills (including interpersonal skills) that can be put to immediate use in accomplishing work. Job-relevant skills you might identify include all of those listed in Self-Assessment Quiz 17-1. The cornerstone of a job search should be a thorough list of assets and accomplishments, because they point to useful skills and abilities you can use to help the employer.

A successful candidate for a customer service position at a telecommunications company told the interviewer, "I know I can help your customers with their software and hardware problems. I worked at the technical support center at college, and my friends and family members are forever coming to me with their computer problems. I even get phone calls and text messages for help. Give me a chance to help your customers." (Notice that the candidate implied that he or she had good listening skills.)

Develop a Comprehensive Marketing Strategy.   A vital job-finding strategy is to use multiple approaches to reach the right prospective employer. This is particularly true when the position you seek is in short supply. A comprehensive marketing strategy is also useful because the job search can be framed as a plan for marketing yourself to prospective employers. The more channels you use, the greater the probability of being successful.

Among the many approaches employers use to recruit candidates are employee referrals, newspaper ads, job boards, employer Web sites, social networking Web sites, college and professional school recruitment, job fairs, temporary help firms, walk-ins, unsolicited résumés and phone calls, and government employment services. Even if some approaches to job finding are not the most effective, they all work some of the time. For example, some people think that newspaper ads are obsolete, yet all big-city newspapers, as well as *The Wall Street Journal,* advertise many interesting and high-paying positions. Some graduates are even finding jobs on Craigslist, particuarly with small companies.

Qualifications Sought by Employers

Directions: The following is a list of qualifications widely sought by prospective employers. After reading each qualification, rate yourself on a 1 to 5 scale by circling the appropriate number: 1 = very low, 2 = low, 3 = average, 4 = high, 5 = very high.

1.	Appropriate education for the position under consideration and satisfactory grades	1	2	3	4	5
2.	Relevant work experience	1	2	3	4	5
3.	Communication and other interpersonal skills	1	2	3	4	5
4.	Motivation and energy	1	2	3	4	5
5.	Problem-solving ability (intelligence) and creativity	1	2	3	4	5
6.	Judgment and common sense	1	2	3	4	5
7.	Adaptability to change, including ability to take on tasks not directly part of your field of expertise	1	2	3	4	5
8.	Emotional maturity (acting professionally and responsibly)	1	2	3	4	5
9.	Teamwork (ability and interest in working in a team effort)	1	2	3	4	5
10.	Positive attitude (enthusiasm about work and initiative)	1	2	3	4	5
11.	Emotional intelligence (ability to deal with own feelings and those of others)	1	2	3	4	5
12.	Customer service orientation (wanting to meet customer needs)	1	2	3	4	5
13.	Information and communication technology skills	1	2	3	4	5
14.	Willingness to continue to study and learn about the job, company, and industry	1	2	3	4	5
15.	Likableness and sense of humor	1	2	3	4	5
16.	Dependability, responsibility, and conscientiousness (including good work habits and time management)	1	2	3	4	5
17.	Willingness and ability to work well with coworkers and customers from different cultures	1	2	3	4	5
18.	Behaves ethically toward customers and company employees and obeys laws and regulations	1	2	3	4	5
19.	Relates well to customers (even if not in formal customer contact position)	1	2	3	4	5
20.	Able to use social networking sites for business purposes	1	2	3	4	5
21.	Speaking and writing fluency in a second language	1	2	3	4	5

Interpretation: Consider engaging in some serious self-development, training, and education for items on which you rated yourself low or very low. If you accurately rated yourself as 4 or 5 on all the dimensions, you are an exceptional job candidate.

Part of a comprehensive marketing strategy is to use a multi-track approach to job finding. Executive coach Donna Rawady suggests that you might prepare three different résumés focused on the contribution you would bring to each position.[3] You could then use the multiple-résumé approach for each approach to job finding, such as employer Web sites and job fairs.

Multiple approaches to finding a job can also include **extreme job hunting**, an offbeat way of attracting an employer's attention with a small probability of success. One approach, now apparently used by many extreme job hunters, is to post your need for a job and the type of job you are seeking on a sandwich board. You then stand in a busy area such as downtown or next to a highway. Wearing a T-shirt with similar information while working out in an athletic club frequented by business executives would be another extreme possibility. Extreme job hunting can lead to publicity, which in turn can lead to landing a job through personal contacts.[4]

Skill-Building Exercise 17-1 provides an opportunity to think through the realities of extreme job hunting.

extreme job hunting

An offbeat way of attracting an employer's attention, with a small probability of success.

Extreme Job Hunting

Assemble into brainstorming groups of about five people. The task is to dream up extreme approaches to job hunting that could possibly work for someone. It is best to choose a target position that would be in the realm of possibility for many members of the class. For example, it would probably be more useful to extreme job hunt for a marketing assistant position than for one as an astronaut or movie actor. After you have assembled a list of about six methods of extreme job hunting, appoint a team leader who will present your findings to the class. The team leader can also be the person in the group who records the ideas.

As you listen to all the team leaders present, including the person from your own group, think through which of these techniques might actually be helpful in a job hunt.

Go Where the Jobs Are.   One of the most practical strategies for finding a job is to apply to organizations within industries that are experiencing growth. The subtle point to recognize is that most industries have room for a variety of specialities. Assume that Jennifer is a skilled accounts receivables specialist in need of a job. Her speciality would be needed in almost any industry. As a result, she searches the Internet for accounts receivable specialists in several of the industries listed in Figure 17-1, including construction, hospitals, and truck tansportation. The basic principle is to enhance your chances of finding employement by attempting to apply your speciality to fields where the demand for workers is high.

Stay Organized During Your Job Search.   A major challenge for many people in conducting a job search is to not become overwhelmed by all the applications, Web sites, and job-finding suggestions you have amassed. It is necessary to keep track of all the jobs you have applied for, the e-mails you have sent, the companies you have researched, and the people you have spoken to. It is particularly embarrassing to apply for the same position two or three times. Many of the suggestions for improving personal productivity made in Chapter 16 are applicable.

A starting point is to create several folders for the job search. One folder might include all the places you have contacted, and another folder might contain any feedback you have received, positive or negative. A third folder might include people in your network as well as the extent of your contact with each one. A fourth folder might contain the several résumés you are using, along with cover letters.

Another approach is for the job seeker to create a spreadsheet with the following seven columns: employer name and contact, geographic location, job title, date the application

FIGURE 17-1   Business-Related and Health-Related Industries with High Projected Income and Employment Growth through 2020

- Construction
- Energy, including alternative energy such as solar and wind power
- Information technology
- Offices of health practitioners
- Hospitals
- Food services and drinking places
- Nursing and residential care facilities
- Management, scientific, and technical recruiting services
- Service to buildings and dwellings
- Child daycare services
- Truck transportation

Source: US Bureau of Labor Statistics, *Economic News Release,* updated February 2012; A few entries are from Evan Rod, "How Today's High-Demand Jobs Impact Salaries," *http://JournalStar.com,* April 16, 2013

was submitted, industry of the company, date of last contact, and whether the application is still pending.[5]

Use Networking to Reach Company Insiders. The majority of successful job campaigns stem from personal contacts. Employers rely heavily on referrals from employees to fill positions, even though many good positions are also announced publicly, such as through Web sites, classified ads, and employment agencies. Big companies realy heavily on their other workers to find new hires, thereby saving time and money. Workers without any connections therefore have a more difficult time finding employment.[6] The ideal is to have an experienced, credible professional vouch for your skills, thereby facilitating you receiving an interview.[7]

In regard to job hunting, networking is contacting friends and acquaintances and building systematically on these relationships to create a still wider set of contacts that might lead to employment. Formal mechanisms to develop network contacts have been introduced in recent years, such as bar parties in metropolitan areas devoted just to making job contacts. Social networking sites sometimes lead to useful contacts, and some people join social networking sites so that they can help strangers find a suitable position. Nevertheless, most of the contacts one develops on social media sites such as Twitter, Facebook, and Tumblr are much weaker than in-person contacts. The social networking contact becomes more useful if it leads to an in-person contact.

The networking technique is so well known today that it suffers from overuse. It is therefore important to use a tactful, low-key approach with a contact. For example, instead of asking a person in your network to furnish you a job lead, ask that person how someone with qualifications similar to yours might find a job. Or ask the person if you could use him or her as a reference. In addition, guard against taking up a large portion of a busy person's workday, for instance, by insisting on a luncheon meeting.

Another way of reaching company insiders is to write dozens of e-mail messages or hard-copy letters to potential employers. A surprisingly large number of people find jobs by contacting employers directly. Most large company Web sites have a section allocated to inviting job inquiries as part of the employee recruitment program. Prepare a prospective employer list, including the names of executives to contact in each firm. The people who receive your letters and e-mail messages become part of your network. A variation of this approach is to develop a 30-second telephone presentation of your background. After you have researched firms that may have opportunities for you, call them and make your pitch; however, voicemail systems usually make it difficult to speak directly to your target person.

Use Multiple Online Approaches. The Internet is a standard avenue for job hunting, even for middle-management and executive positions. Sources of job leads on the Internet include general job boards, specialty job boards, company Web sites, and social networking sites. Many employers search directly for candidates by scanning social media sites, with LinkedIn often favored because of its professional nature. With a job board (or job search site), the job seeker can post a résumé or scroll through hundreds of job opportunities. A number of job board Web sites are résumé database services because they give employers access to résumés submitted by job hunters. Most position announcements on the Internet require the job seeker to send a résumé by attached file. A few position announcements still request that the résumé be sent in the body of an e-mail, by fax, or paper mail because they prefer to avoid opening e-mail attachments.

Andrew J. DuBrin

Job boards post positions both by field and geographic region. Specialty job boards are preferred by some job seekers and employers because these boards are less flooded with positions and applicants. An Internet search will quickly reveal any specialty job site in your field, such as those for sales or finance. The simplest approach to finding a job lead on the Internet is to enter into the browser of a search engine the position you are seeking. For example, a person seeking a position as a dental office manager in Denver might enter into Bing, "Dental office manager, Denver."

Many managers prefer the employment section of their Web site over commercial job boards. Some of the more advanced company job sites, such as GE, present possible career paths for people who enter the company in the position sought. Many employers believe that the best way to find good job candidates is to advertise on Web sites where these candidates are likely to be spending considerable time, such as Facebook, LinkedIn, or Twitter. Job boards also have a presence on social networking sites, as do recruiting firms. Monster has an application form on the social networking site Facebook. The potential applicant can send an e-mail or instant message to a particular posting. A large number of employers have developed versions of their career Web sites suitable to hand-held devices. A job application can be filled out using a smartphone.

Hundreds of people every day land jobs they first learned about through a job board or company Web site, so this approach offers some promise. A caution is that job hunting on the Internet can lead to a false sense of security. Using the Internet, a résumé is cast over a wide net, and hundreds of job postings can be explored. As a consequence, the job seeker may think that he or she can sit back and wait for a job offer to come through e-mail. In reality, the Internet is just one source of leads that should be used in conjunction with other job-finding methods, especially personal contacts that might lead to an interview. Remember also that thousands of other job seekers can access the same job opening, and many of the positions listed have already been filled. Be aware also that scam artists posing as employment agencies might post job openings on the Internet. After making you a tentative offer, the scammer writes that you must now send him or her your social security and bank account numbers so that your application can be processed completely. You then become a victim of identity theft.

Establishing your own Web site or blog, with résumé included, will sometimes attract an employer who conducts an Internet search for potential candidates. For example, recruiting specialists often spend several hours per week scanning blogs for new talent or additional information about candidates already interviewed. A blog is most likely to attract a recruiter's attention if it relates to work in your contemplated field, such as explaining how you helped your employer save energy.

Smile at Network Members and Interviewers, and Be Enthusiastic. Assuming that you have the right qualifications, the simple act of smiling can be an effective job-hunting technique. Remember to smile as you hand your business card to a potential network member. One reason that smiling is effective at any stage of the job search is that it helps build a relationship, however brief. If you use a webcam or video as part of your job search, smile on camera. Closely related to smiling is to display enthusiasm and excitement when speaking to people who can help you land a position. Conducted properly, a job search should be exciting and invigorating, and you should express these emotions to your contacts. The excitement and invigoration stem from each small step you take leading to your goal of finding suitable employment.

A key way of projecting a positive image during the job search is to avoid negativity. Appearing desperate, including the candidate explaining how much he or she needs the job to pay back debt, creates a poor image. Complaining about former employers or managers is another frequently observed way to project a negative image.

Smooth Out Rough Spots in Your Background. About 95 percent of employers routinely conduct background investigations of prospective employees. A background investigation by a firm hired for the purpose could include speaking to neighbors and coworkers about your reputation. In addition, the investigator may delve into your driving record, check for criminal charges or convictions, survey your credit record, and find out whether you have had disputes with the government about taxes. The information just mentioned is used to supplement reference checks, because so many employers are hesitant to say anything negative about past employees. The information uncovered through the background check is often compared to the information presented on your résumé. A discrepancy between the two sends up an immediate red flag.

Another way to learn about what public information exists about you is to place your own name into a couple of search engines. Sometimes another person with the same name as yours—particularly if many people have the same name as you—might have been involved in criminal activity, so be prepared to defend yourself! *Googling* candidates has become standard practice to uncover both positive and negative information about job applicants. Going one step further, many employers search social Web sites like MySpace and Facebook to see if the candidate has engaged in outrageous behavior such as swimming in a public fountain while under the influence of alcohol—and then bragged about the episode on the social networking Web site. Employers also use professional online search services because they have the know-how to search police records and financial information not revealed by ordinary search engines.

A standard recommendation for guarding against prospective employers seeing information about you on social networking sites is to set your accounts to private so that only your friends and followers can see them.[8]

The Job Résumé and Cover Letter

A résumé is usually an essential part of the job hunt. Yet you can sometimes join a family business for a friend's enterprise without submitting a résumé. In some instances, you will be asked to complete a job application form instead of, or in addition to, a résumé. Résumés are also important for job hunting within your own firm. You may need one to be considered for a transfer with a large firm, or to be assigned to a team or project.

Résumé Purpose. Regard your résumé as a marketing tool for selling your skills and potential to handle new responsibilities. The most specific purpose of a résumé is to help you obtain an interview that can lead to a job. In rare situations in which a person of your skills is under such heavy demand, you will be hired based on your résumé, and the interview will be skipped. Your résumé, whether electronic, paper, or video, must therefore attract enough attention for an employer to invite you for an interview. A poorly prepared résumé often leads to an immediate rejection of the candidate. Recognize that you are competing against many carefully prepared résumés, some of which have been prepared with assistance from others. If the demand for your skills is high enough, it is conceivable that you will be hired without an interview.

Résumé Length and Format. Opinions vary about the desirable length for a résumé. For a recent graduate with limited work experience, a one-page résumé may be acceptable. One page might seem too short for more experienced workers. Employers today demand considerable detail in résumés, particularly about the candidate's skills, accomplishments, and teamwork and leadership experience. Nevertheless, a three-page or longer résumé may irritate an impatient reader. Two pages are therefore recommended for early stages in your career.

A résumé for a recent graduate is presented in Figure 17-2. Especially for experienced workers, it is now recommended that a professional qualifications summary be substituted for the job objective. A professional summary highlights the job seeker's best assets and positions the person for the job sought. It also summarizes your accomplishments and points to what your are offering the prospective employer.[9] Another change in job résumés in recent years is that references are rarely included, yet they might be asked for at another stage of job selection.

Recognize that hiring managers and human resource professionals have widely different perceptions of what constitutes an effective résumé. Both résumés include job duties performed as well as a chronological history. A résumé that focuses on work performed rather than a job chronology is referred to as a *functional* résumé. This type of résumé can be helpful in directing attention toward skills and away from employment gaps.[10] A résumé that does not list the candidate's skills and accomplishments is considered insufficient today. Whether references are listed on the résumé or presented in another format, it is preferable to use professional contacts rather than personal friends. A personal friend might attest to your good character, but would usually be hard pressed to describe your job competence. Check at least two résumé guides before preparing a final version of your résumé. Microsoft Word includes several templates for job résumés.

FIGURE 17-2   A Job Résumé for a Recent Business Graduate

Jennifer A. Koster
700 Anderson St., Apt. B • Fairfax, VA 22033 • (703) 555-2121 • Email: jakerwin@yahoo.com

Qualifications	Entrepreneurial and self-employment experience in addition to restaurant work and multimedia communication capabilities. Good at generating revenue.

Education

B.A., Business Administration, Marketing Major, Advertising Minor, December 2015
George Mason University, Fairfax, VA
GPA: In-major: 3.4/4.0 Overall: 2.7/4.0
Earned 40% of educational expenses

Accomplishments and Skills

Marketing/Sales/Promotion
- Grossed $16,000 in three months with summer landscaping business
- Raised $750.00 in advertising space for environmental-club folder project
- Raised $500.00 for sorority-sponsored car show
- Cold-canvassed community for potential clients
- Created informational brochure for apartment-leasing company
- Developed advertising campaign for class project

Management/Training/Organizational Ability
- Managed daily activities of own landscaping business including renting/purchasing equipment and supplies, hiring assistants, budgeting, payroll
- Arranged client contracts for landscaping business
- Coordinated sales presentation strategy for sorority car show and trained others in sales techniques
- Trained new fast-service restaurant employees
- Aided in refurbishing and renovating a restaurant
- Performed restaurant duties ranging from server to night manager

Communications/Language/Creative Projects
- Created multimedia presentation using slides, music, and narration to brief incoming George Mason students during orientation
- Developed sales presentations and assisted with advertising campaigns including radio spots, newspaper ads, billboards, posters, and brochures
- Designed and distributed flyers for landscaping business
- Conversational Spanish skills; write reasonably well in Spanish

Work Experience

Self-Employed, (Partnership) Whole Earth Landscaping, Reston, VA, Summer 2013
Waiter, Rainbow's of Washington, Washington, DC, Summers 2012, 2013, 2014

Activities

Theater Arts, George Mason, several roles in dramas and musicals, regularly participate in clothing and fund drives for homeless people in Washington, DC

Key Words and Past Tense of Verbs.   In writing your résumé, keep in mind that certain key words attract the attention of managers and specialists. Key words are particularly important for online submission of your credentials because software is used by human resource departments of large companies to reduce a large stack of candidates into a manageable list of finalists. The job description provides the starting point for choosing your key words. For example, if the job description uses the term *client* satisfaction rather than *customer* satisfaction, an effective résumé would contain the key term *client satisfaction*. Among the key words that might go beyond those mentioned in the job description or role are as follows: *languages, analytical skills, mobile devices, global outsourcing, insourcing, hands-on, results-driven, communication skills, online marketing, cultural diversity, social networking Web sites,* and *sustainable environment*. You can also find the key words that apply to your field by studying relevant ads.

In addition to key words, it is helpful to sprinkle your résumé with the past tense of verbs connoting accomplishments, action, and forcefulness. Among the possibilities are as follows: *achieved, contributed, discovered, managed, overcame, transformed,* and *won*. Powerful adverbs are also useful, including the following: *assertively, creatively, decisively, energetically, rapidly,* and *successfully*.[11]

Easy Access for Employers. When submitting your résumé and cover letter electronically, make it easy for the employer to access, such as attaching a Word file. Furthermore, concerns about computer viruses have prompted some employers to refuse to open any attached file. So you might send an attached word processing file, plus insert your résumé into the e-mail message. Make sure that the formatting is not lost when cutting and pasting your document into e-mail. Send your cover letter and résumé to yourself to check for lost formatting. Many employers will refuse to open a link to your Web site or a PowerPoint presentation, while many others will welcome a link to a personal Web site or LinkedIn profile. As a result, it pays to make it known on your résumé that the links relating to you are available, should the prospective employer be interested.

Error Minimization. Much has been written and said about making job résumés as error-free as possible, especially with respect to errors in spelling, grammar, and capitalization. Nevertheless, many employers complain about finding these types of errors on résumés. Use abbreviations sparingly, because they are visually jarring to many people. False abbreviations are particularly annoying, such as "accnt" for accounting and "mkt" for marketing. Spell checkers are helpful, but not sufficient for eliminating spelling errors, because the checker leads to many misused words such as "weather" for "whether" and "cubical" for "cubicle." A major caution is not to use the writing style popular in e-mails and text messaging for the purposes of preparing a professional résumé.

A problem with small errors in a résumé is that they may lead some prospective employers to be concerned about the applicant's focus on detail. It is helpful to have a knowledgeable person review your résumé for small errors—and perhaps large ones also. A frequent type of large error is to make vague statements without documentation. An example of a vague statement that requires clarification is stating that you are "highly knowledgeable and talented." It is better to specify what you are highly knowledgeable about and what specific talents you possess.

Video Résumés and Creative Formats. A rapidly growing approach to résumé construction is the online video résumé. Turning the camcorder or webcam on yourself, you present much of the basic information that would be found on a written résumé. The video approach is good for capturing your appearance, personality, and oral communication skills. Some job seekers place their video on their Web site or on YouTube, or simply send it as an attachment.

Unless you are highly skilled at video presentation, it is best to get professional help in constructing your video résumé. Careful editing might be needed to eliminate vocalized pauses and inadvertent distracting expressions. Another potential problem with the video résumé is that it focuses too much attention on soft skills for a candidate who wants to emphasize hard skills. Because some employers do not wish to spend the time watching a video, it is a good human relations tactic to also include a more conventional résumé. Or you can mention that your video résumé is available on your Facebook page or personal Web site. If an employer uses a video on its job site, the climate is probably right for you to submit a video résumé.

A trending format is to prepare your résumé in the form of a tweet, using 140 characters or less. A key purpose of the Twitter résumé is to attract the attention of companies who search Twitter for potential candidates.[12] The Twitter résumé is similar to the accomplishments section of your résumé or a cover letter and should only be used as a supplement to a more traditional résumé. Here is a tweet-format résumé for a person seeking a managerial position at an athletic club.

Five years of experience in athletic clubs, toned body, great personality, good grades, keeps members happy. Sam is ready for management job.

Skill-Building Exercise 17-2 gives you an opportunity to practice tweeting for your job hunt.

Honesty is Essential. Whatever type of résumé you choose, and whatever mode of transmission, honesty is important. It is generally acceptable to glamorize your accomplishments, yet inserting false statements crosses the line into unacceptable behavior.[13]

Many managers believe that a person who lies on a résumé might also behave unethically once on the job. Also, when lies are detected after a worker is hired, the worker is subject to immediate dismissal even if he or she is performing well. The Society of Human Resource Management reports that approximately 53 percent of job candidates lie to some extent on their résumés.[14]

The Cover Letter. A résumé should be accompanied by a cover letter explaining who you are and why you are applying for a particular position. Many companies now require a cover letter as part of the application process, as do many city and county governments. Sometimes the cover letter can be used as an introductory e-mail. The cover letter customizes your approach to a particular employer, whereas the résumé is a more general approach. (Be aware, however, that it is often recommended to modify your résumé to suit a particular position or positions of a similar type.) The cover letter can be as influential as a résumé in deciding who receives an interview offer.[15]

According to Bruce Hurwitz, a staffing professional, an effective cover letter is between 200 and 250 words, and should answer the question of why the person reading it should dig into your résumé.[16] Highlighting one success is attention-getting, such as "Increased clicks into sales 45% on our Web site in a six-month period."

Sometimes it is helpful to prepare an attention-getting cover letter in which you make an assertive statement about how you intend to help the employer deal with an important problem. A person applying for a credit manager position might state, "Let me help you improve your cash flow by using the latest methods for getting customers to pay on time, or even early."

The cover letter should contain a few short paragraphs and should focus on the skills and background you'll bring to the job. Follow this with a brief bullet-point list of your accomplishments. If possible, mention a company insider in your network, and then close the cover letter with appreciation for any consideration your qualifications might be given. If you do not have the name of the contact person, use an approach such as, "Dear Purchasing Manager." The ubiquitous "Hi" is best used for e-mails, text messages, and social networking sites.

Performing Well in a Job Interview

After a prospective employer has reacted favorably to your cover letter and résumé, the next step is a telephone-screening interview or a more comprehensive job interview. The purpose of the telephone-screening interview is generally to obtain some indication of the candidate's oral communication skill. Such an interview is most likely when one applies for a customer contact position or one that requires knowledge of a second language. Having passed the screening interview, the candidate is invited for an in-person job interview. Most of the suggestions for attaining success in an in-person interview, described in this section, also apply to the phone interview, but a few specific points are worth considering.

Some job candidates overlook the fact that the phone interview is a serious contact with their employer, and do not differentiate between a social interview and a professional one. Attempt to project excitement in your voice, thereby communicating the fact that you are seriously interested in the position.[17]

Typically one person at a time interviews the job candidate, yet team interviews are becoming more commonplace. In this format, members of the team or department with whom you would be working take turns asking you questions. One justification for team interviews is to observe how the candidate fits in with the team. A panel interview is particularly challenging because you have to make eye contact with more than one person.

Another variation on the traditional interview is that you meet for a brief interview with a series of interviewers. The process is referred to as *speed interview,* because of its similarity to speed dating in which the relationship seeker meets briefly with a series of prospective dates or mates at a planned event. Busy employers like speed interviews because they can quickly screen several candidates for the same position.[18]

A general guide for performing well in the job interview is to present a positive but accurate picture of yourself. Your chances of performing well in a job increase if you are suited for the job. Tricking a prospective employer into hiring you when you are not qualified is therefore self-defeating in terms of your career. What follows is a list of some key points to keep in mind when being interviewed for a job you want:

1. **Be prepared, look relaxed, and make the interviewer feel comfortable.** Coming to the interview fully prepared to discuss yourself and your background and knowing key facts about the prospective employer will help you look relaxed. Use the company Web site to gather background information about the prospective employer. Check out stories found on the Web site about the employer. Looking relaxed is also important because it helps prevent the impression of appearing desperately in need of employment. The other extreme to avoid is being so relaxed that you appear apathetic.[19] A subtle way of being prepared is to demonstrate that you know how to dress for the workplace, including a sensitivity to the type of clothing appropriate for the company you are seeking to join. Even if jeans are the preferred pants for that employer, it is important to wear jeans that create a positive impression.

2. **Avoid talking too much during the interview.** It is natural to think that during a job interview, you will be expected to talk; however, talking too much, including the presentation of your thoughts in a rambling, disorganized manner, will be perceived quite negatively by experienced interviewers. Being perceived as a compulsive talker will often lead to immediate rejection. Display effective communication skills by presenting your ideas in depth, yet concisely.

    Rehearsing answers to typical interview questions beforehand can help you present your ideas more concisely. Also, if the interviewer looks bored or fatigued, you may be rambling.

3. **Establish a link between you and the prospective employer.** A good way to build rapport between you and the prospective employer is to mention some plausible link you have with that firm. To illustrate, if being interviewed for a position at a Sears store, one might say, "It's fun to visit the office part of Sears. Our family has been shopping here for years. In fact, I bought a dehumidifier here last month. It works great."

4. **Ask perceptive questions.** The best questions are sincere ones that reflect an interest in the content of the job (intrinsic motivators) and job performance, rather than benefits and social activities. A good question to ask is "What would you consider to be outstanding performance in this job?" (Recall the opening case in this chapter.) If the issue of compensation is not introduced by the interviewer, ask about such matters after first discussing the job and your qualifications. Another useful line of questions reflect knowledge of the company, showing that you have conducted research.[20] For example, a person seeking a job with Amazon.com might ask the interviewer, "I have read that Amazon has plans to create more physical stores. How might a person with my background contribute to that direction of the company?"

5. **Be prepared to discuss your strengths and weaknesses (developmental opportunities).** Most interviewers will ask you to discuss your strengths and developmental opportunities. (These and other frequently asked questions are presented in Figure 17-3.) Knowledge of strengths hints at how good your potential job performance will be. If you deny having areas for improvement, you will appear uninsightful

FIGURE 17-3   Questions Frequently Asked of Job Candidates

An effective way of preparing for job interviews is to rehearse answers to the types of questions you will most likely be asked by the interviewer. The following questions are a sampling of the types found in most employment interviews. Rehearse answers to them prior to going out on job interviews. One good rehearsal method is to role-play the employment interview with a friend who asks these typical questions or records a video of you.

1. Why do you want to work for us?
2. What would be your ideal job?
3. What are your career goals?
4. What are your salary requirements?
5. What new job skills would you like to acquire in the next few years?
6. Give me an example of how you displayed good teamwork.
7. Describe how you have shown leadership on the job or off the job.
8. What are your strengths (or good points)?
9. What are your weaknesses (or areas for needed improvement)?
10. What would a former boss say about you?
11. How well do you work under pressure?
12. What positions with other companies are you applying for?
13. What makes you think you will be successful in business?
14. What do you know about our company?
15. Here is a sample job problem. How would you handle it?
16. How would you use the Internet to perform better in this job?
17. What questions do you have for me?
18. Why did you leave your last job?
19. What salary do you have in mind?
20. How long will you stay with us?
21. If I googled you, what positive and negative information would I find?

Source: Questions 1, 19, and 20 are from Tim Bearden, "Top 5 Interview Questions," *http://philly.com*, December 29, 2009, pp. 1, 3; Questions 2 and 9 are from "Questions Job Interviewers are Asking Most," *http://www.csmonitor.com/2003/0317/pl5s01-wmno.html*, April 20, 2003.

or defensive. When describing your weaknesses, it is helpful to also describe your action plan for dealing with the problem.

6. **Be prepared to respond to behavioral interview questions.** A behavioral interview includes direct questions about the candidate's behavior in relation to an important job activity. The job candidate is expected to give samples of important job behaviors. The behavioral interview is therefore more applicable to candidates with substantial work experience. Two behavioral inquiries are, "Tell me about a time in which your ability to work well on a team contributed to the success of a project" and "Give me an example of a creative suggestion you made that was actually implemented. In what way did it help the company?"

   Statement 7 and question 15 in Figure 17-3 are also behavioral interview questions. To prepare for such questions, think of some examples of how you handled a few difficult job challenges. The idea is to document specific actions you took or behaviors you engaged in that contributed to a favorable outcome.

7. **Show how you can help the employer.** A prospective employer wants to know whether you will be able to perform the job well. Direct much of your conversation

toward how you intend to help the company solve problems and get important work accomplished. Whatever the question, think about what details of your skills and experiences will be useful to the employer. Before your interview, think of an answer to the question, "What value do I bring to a company and why should they hire me?"

8. **Use nonverbal communication that projects confidence and decisiveness.** A job interviewer will often carefully observe the candidate's body language. Monitor your body language to appear confident and decisive. Some candidates look down at their hands during the interview because they feel lost without their smartphones. Such behavior is likely to be interpreted as being sad or having low self-confidence. Being carefully groomed, looking crisp and fresh, and having clean, unbroken nails also help project self-confidence. Dressing appropriately for the interview also reflects good emotional intelligence. For example, if the interviewer tells you in advance that business-casual dress is recommended, do not wear the same jeans you would wear to do yard work or wash your car.

9. **Practice good etiquette and manners during the interview and meals.** Under the pressures of applying for a job, it is easy to let etiquette slip. To display poor etiquette and manners, however, could lead to a candidate being rejected from consideration. The mistakes noted by at least 60 percent of managers in a survey were (1) answering a cell phone or texting, (2) appearing uninterested, (3) dressing inappropriately, (4) appearing arrogant, (5) talking negatively about current or previous employers, and (6) chewing gum.[21]

   Most of the suggestions made about etiquette in Chapter 13 apply to the job interview, but be particularly sensitive to allowing company officials to talk without interrupting them and practicing good table manners. Interviewers who are rude themselves, such as taking phone calls or typing on their computer while interviewing you, still expect *you* not to do the same. Offering to shake hands is generally good etiquette, yet be on guard for people who do not want to shake hands for cultural reasons, arthritis, or fear of catching unwanted bacteria. The best approach is to gently extend your hand and see if the interviewer is receptive.[22]

10. **Be low key about salary.** In general, it is best to discuss salary or other compensation only after the interviewer brings up the subject. Usually you have a good chance of the starting salary coming into the interview. Web sites such as Salary.com and Payscale.com will provide useful information about representative salaries for the position in question. The reason for not focusing too much on salary during the interview is that you want to demonstrate that you are more driven by results and the excitement of the job than by compensation.

11. **Minimize the use of utterances that annoy many interviewers.** A poll taken by Marist College found that five words and phrases are particularly annoying, and should therefore be minimized while interviewing (and in networking also). Starting with the worst, the utterances plus the percent of people saying the word is annoying, are: "Whatever" (47%), "You know" (11%), "It is what it is" (11%), "Anyway" (7%), and "At the end of the day" (2%).[23]

12. **Send a follow-up (or thank-you) letter.** As part of displaying good manners, mail a courteous follow-up (or thank-you) letter or send an e-mail message several days after the interview, particularly if you want the job. The most effective thank-you notes forward the discussion that took place in the interview.[24] A follow-up letter is a tip-off that you are truly interested in the position. You should state your attitudes toward the position, the team, and the company, and summarize any conclusions reached about your discussion. The follow-up letter might also include a key point about yourself that was not mentioned in the interview or that you want to emphasize.

Now do Skill-Building Exercise 17-3 to practice the job interview.

The Job Interview

As described in Figure 17-3, a good way to prepare for a job interview is to rehearse answers to frequently asked questions. In this role-play, one student will be the interviewer and one will be the interviewee (job applicant). The job in question is that of a property manager for a large apartment complex in Phoenix, Arizona.

Assume that the applicant really wants the job. The interviewer, having taken a course in human resource management, will ask

many of the questions in Figure 17-3. In addition, the interviewer will ask at least one behavioral question, perhaps about teamwork. The interviewer might also have other questions, such as "Why do you want to live in Phoenix?"

Before proceeding with the role-play, both people should review the information in this chapter about the job interview and in Chapter 4 about listening.

CAREER ADVANCEMENT STRATEGIES AND TACTICS

LEARNING OBJECTIVE 2

The many ways of improving interpersonal relationships described in this book can help advance and enhance a person's career. People who enhance their relationships with others are laying a foundation for career advancement. The following section discusses 14 other key strategies and tactics for career advancement, whether the advancement relates to a promotion, or growth at the same organizational level, or a combination of the two. The methods described are divided into controlling your own characteristics and behaviors and dealing more with interacting with the outside world.

Strategies and Tactics for Controlling Your Own Characteristics and Behaviors

One major thrust in advancing one's career is to regulate as best as possible one's own characteristics and behaviors.

Develop Career Goals. Planning your career inevitably involves some form of goal setting. Your career goals should have the same characteristics as other goals, as described in Chapter 1. Because organizations change so frequently, along with positions, today it may be better to establish general goals that focus on the type of work you want to do in the future. For example, "Within five years I plan to be leading a group of people toward improving the supply-chain management in a business firm."

Before establishing career goals, it is helpful to clarify your values, or prioritize what is important to you. These are probably the same values that enabled you to choose a career in the first place. While sketching out a career, you should also list your personal goals. They should mesh with your work plans to help avoid major conflicts in your life. Some lifestyles, for example, are incompatible with some career goals. You might find it difficult to develop a stable home life (spouse, children, friends, community activities, garden, etc.) if you aspire to holding field positions in international marketing.

career path

A sequence of positions necessary to achieve a goal.

For young professionals, today's **career path** often means having a series of jobs at the same level and acquiring valuable skills along the way. The series of jobs could be in the same company, across different companies, or even in different industries. The median number of years US workers have been in their current job is 4.4 years. A factor contributing to these series of jobs is that many employers value long-term employees less than they did in years past. [25]

Capitalize on Your Strengths and Build Your Personal Brand. A long-established principle of getting ahead in your career, as well as managing others, is to capitalize on strengths rather than to focus solely on overcoming areas for improvement. Visualize Sam, who has excellent interpersonal skills, but is mediocre in quantitative skills. Sam will go far as a manager or sales representative if he continues to hone his interpersonal skills. Yet as hard as he tries to strengthen his quantitative skills, he probably would become only a mediocre accountant, research analyst, or actuary.

Understanding your basket of strengths forms the basis for developing your **personal brand.** Your personal brand makes you unique, thereby distinguishing you from the competition. An important part of your personal brand is consistency. For example, if you are mature and professional in almost all work situations, while at the same time displaying a sense of humor, this combination of characteristics becomes part of your brand. Perhaps your brand will not reach the recognition of Nike or Rolex, but it will help develop your reputation. Your personal brand also helps you attract employers and perhaps potential clients—your identity as shown on the Internet including social networking sites is part of your personal brand, with LinkedIn being more closely tied to your professional image. Your online presence is also referred to as your online brand.

Your personal brand will be more effective if it is authentic in the sense of accurately reflecting who you are. You might add a little drama to your strengths, but the strengths should still be true. Another caution about personal branding is that it should not be used as a method of bragging. Marco Mattiacci, president and CEO of Ferrari North America, explains that if you want your personal brand to resemble a Ferrari, "stop bragging and focus on simply becoming the best at what you do."[26]

You begin developing your personal brand by identifying the qualities or characteristics that distinguish you from coworkers. Almost all the ideas in this chapter will help you develop your personal brand. Three useful questions to ask in formulating your personal brand are as follows:[27]

- What kind of work activities am I passionate about?
- What are my greatest strengths and personal assets?
- How can my strengths be applied to support my passion?

Developing a personal brand statement requires considerable work, and might require some professional coaching; however, here is the personal brand statement Mike developed:

I am a hard-hitting package of strengths who can be a real asset to an employer. Few people combine superb analytical, information technology, and people skills the way I do. The help I give the homeless shows that I really care about the welfare of others. In school, as well as on the job, I have established a record of high performance and dependability.

Sukhinder Singh Cassidy, founder and chairman of JOYUS, offers good advice about building your personal brand. She says that when you start a new job, work hard to get your professional momentum going so that you can start building a brand for yourself.[28]

Skill-Building Exercise 17-4 gives you an opportunity to start working on creating your brand.

Be Passionate about and Proud of Your Work.   Successful people in all fields are passionate about their work. Without passion, you rely too heavily on external rewards to sustain effort. Passion contributes to both your career growth and company productivity. Effective leaders and business owners are usually passionate about their work, and group members expect their leader to be passionate. For example, a joyous small-business owner is so excited about a product or service that it makes a difference. The owner of a company that makes safety goggles said, "I'm thrilled about preventing so many sports enthusiasts from losing their eyesight from being hit with a ball." Being passionate is also important because it is linked to developing expertise and high job performance. Taking pride in your work stems naturally from passion. If you invest the emotional energy into having passion, you are likely to be proud of your work.

SKILL-BUILDING EXERCISE 17-4

Creating a Personal Brand Statement

The guidelines presented in the text provide some workable ideas for creating a personal brand statement, yet there are still hundreds of other possibilities for developing a personal brand statement. The requirements of this exercise are for you to write a personal brand statement of a maximum of 50 words. Keep in mind that your personal brand statement is not simply a summary of your education and experience, but is instead a brief explanation of what makes you unique in comparison to other people doing your kind of work.

It may prove helpful to compare your personal brand statement with those written by several other class members. If your personal brand statement is unique, it will not read almost the same as those prepared by other students.

Recent research suggests that being passionate about your career is similar to having a **calling**—a consuming, meaningful passion people experience toward their field. You are probably familiar with the term *calling* used in reference to religious leaders, and perhaps to some physicians, nurses, and other medical personnel. If you perceive your work to be a calling, you are more likely to stay focused on your goals and be successful. You can discover if your work is a calling by answering the following research questions:[29]

- Would you sacrifice everything to be in business?
- When you describe yourself to others, do you first think about being in business?
- Would your existence be much less meaningful without your involvement in business?

The surest path to career success is to identify your area of expertise and then build a career around it, as in building a personal brand. The more passionate and proud you are about your area of expertise, the better. Becoming wealthy and achieving recognition are by-products of making effective use of your talents. Expertise combined with passion helps you attain high job performance. Consistently good job performance is the foundation on which you build your career. Job competence is still the major success ingredient in all but the most political organizations (those where favoritism outweighs merit).

Develop a Code of Professional Ethics and Prosocial Motivation. Another solid foundation for developing a career is to establish a personal ethical code. An ethical code determines what behavior is right or wrong and good or bad, based on values. The values stem from cultural upbringing, religious teachings, peer influences, and professional or industry standards. As implied in Chapter 15, a code of professional ethics helps a worker deal with such issues as accepting bribes, backstabbing coworkers, and sexually harassing a work associate.

A part of many workers' ethical codes is **prosocial motivation**, the desire to expend effort to help other people. Wharton School professor and industrial psychologist Adam Grant has conducted several experiments indicating that when the purpose of one's work is to help others, the worker tends to perform better or at least be better committed to their employer.[30] The practical implication for your career is that if you focus on helping clients or coworkers, you might perform better, thereby enhancing your own career.

Develop a Proactive Personality. If you are an active agent in taking control of the forces around you, you stand a better chance of capitalizing on opportunities. Also, you will seek out opportunities such as seeing problems that need fixing. A **proactive personality** is a person who is relatively unconstrained by situational forces and who brings about environmental change. The proactive personality has high perceived control over situations. Self-Assessment Quiz 17-2 offers you an opportunity to learn about your tendencies toward having a proactive personality.

People who are highly proactive identify opportunities and act on them, show initiative, and keep trying until they bring about meaningful change. A health and safety specialist with a proactive personality might identify a health hazard others had missed. She would identify the nature of the problem and urge management to supply funding to control the problem. Ultimately, her efforts in preventing major health problems would be recognized. Having a proactive personality facilitates being a good organizational citizen because you have a natural inclination to look around to accomplish worthwhile activities. For example, the employee with a proactive personality might take the initiative to help a coworker without being asked or report a leaking faucet to the maintenance department. Being a proactive personality can also help you protect your job in a recession, because management likes the team player attitude of the proactive worker.[31]

Two studies conducted with close to 700 male and female workers in diverse occupations examined the relationship between career success and a proactive personality. Proactive personality, as measured by a test, was related to salary, promotions, taking the initiative in one's career, and career satisfaction.[32] Another reason that being proactive facilitates career success is that employees are expected to be self-managing, more so than in the past. The proactive employee will identify and resolve many problems without being directed to

calling

A consuming, meaningful passion people experience toward their field.

prosocial motivation

The desire to expend effort to help other people.

proactive personality

A person who is relatively unconstrained by situational forces and who brings about environmental change.

My Tendencies toward Being a Proactive Personality

Indicate the extent of your agreement with the statements below by circling the number under the correct category: Agree Strongly (AS), Agree (A), Neutral (N), Disagree (D), Disagree Strongly.

No.		AS	A	N	D	DS
1.	I plan carefully for things that might go wrong.	5	4	3	2	1
2.	I don't worry about problems until after they have taken place.	1	2	3	4	5
3.	If I see something that is broken, I fix it.	5	4	3	2	1
4.	I have been told several times that I am good at taking the initiative.	5	4	3	2	1
5.	I often let things like a computer password expire without making the necessary changes.	1	2	3	4	5
6.	When something important needs doing, I wait for somebody else to take the initiative.	1	2	3	4	5
7.	I think that having a home security system is a good investment in money.	5	4	3	2	1
8.	I look around for good opportunities that would help me in my career or personal life.	5	4	3	2	1
9.	I don't give much thought to the future because there is not much I can do about it.	1	2	3	4	5
10.	It is a good idea to start saving or investing for retirement at the beginning of your career.	5	4	3	2	1
11.	I begin projects and tasks by myself, without requiring prompting from somebody else.	5	4	3	2	1
12.	The old saying, "The early bird gets the worm" doesn't make much sense in real life.	1	2	3	4	5
13.	I let the future take care of itself without giving it much thought.	1	2	3	4	5
14.	I set my own goals rather than have others set them for me.	5	4	3	2	1
15.	I create a lot of change both in work and personal life.	5	4	3	2	1
16.	I have often asked for feedback on my job performance.	5	4	3	2	1
17.	If your job is going well, it is a bad idea to explore new job possibilities from time to time.	1	2	3	4	5
18.	Once you have chosen a satisfactory career, it is a bad idea to explore the possibilities of another career from time to time.	1	2	3	4	5
19.	I readily express my opinion about the effectiveness of a work process.	5	4	3	2	1
20.	It is best to stick carefully to your job description rather than create responsibilities for yourself.	1	2	3	4	5
21.	I regularly take positive steps to increase the chances that I will stay healthy and physically fit.	5	4	3	2	1
22.	I am quite innovative both in work and personal life.	5	4	3	2	1
23.	When I have a day with nothing on my schedule, I take the opportunity to think of something useful to do.	5	4	3	2	1
24.	I sometimes stare at my desktop computer or mobile device waiting for my next e-mail or text.	1	2	3	4	5
25.	I sometimes fake being busy so nobody will ask me to do something.	1	2	3	4	5

Scoring and Interpretation: Total the numbers corresponding to your answers.

100–125: Scores in this range suggest that you have strong tendencies toward being a proactive personality. Such proactivity should be (or already is) an asset to you in your career and personal life. Yet scoring 115 points or more could suggest that you sometimes annoy people with your constant need for taking on new responsibility and creating change.

70–99: Scores in this range suggest that you have about average tendencies toward being proactive. To enhance you success and have more fun in life, you might attempt to become more proactive.

25–69: Scores in this range suggest that you have a problem with proactivity. Both your work and personal life would probably be enhanced if you became more proactive.

Source: The idea for this scale and several of its statements stem from Thomas S. Bateman and J. Michael Crant, "The Proactive Component of Organizational Behavior: A Measure and Correlates," *Journal of Organizational Behavior*, March 1993, p. 112.

do so by the manager. Another study indicated that a proactive personality influenced job search success among 180 graduating college students. The students took a test of proactive personality similar to the one presented in Self-Assessment Quiz 17-2. Search success was measured in terms of being offered follow-up interviews and receiving offers.[33]

An advantage of being proactive on the job is that it may enhance your reputation because you are likely to be perceived favorably by others, including many people who think that the good results you attain are the result of positive inner qualities. Finding a good way to be proactive may require creative thinking, particularly because it may not be easy to develop a proactive personality. In addition, keep the following suggestions in mind.

1. A basic starting point in showing signs of having a proactive personality in the workplace is to perform well in areas outside your job description. The caution, however, is not to grab responsibility that belongs to a coworker, thereby creating conflict between you and that person.

2. Another way to get started is to take more initiative to fix problems and attempt to be self-starting. Asking for permission to assume responsibility for a project that needs doing is also helpful. Many newcomers to an organization have enhanced their reputation by asking for permission to organize this year's office party.

3. Taking charge at work, or intending to bring about functional changes, is a particularly constructive way of demonstrating proactivity on the job. Taking charge facilitates organizational effectiveness, thereby enhancing the reputation of the person who has taken such initiative.

4. A way of expressing proactivity on a grand scale is to seek new opportunities, such as developing a new product or service, establishing a new company, or finding a new market for one's employer.

Keep Growing through Continuous Learning and Self-Development. Engaging in regular learning can take many forms, including formal schooling, attending training programs and seminars, and self-study. Some company executives regard the continuous learning of their employees as part of developing their organization, so the company will sponsor training and tuition assistance.[34] An everyday method of continuous learning is to ask intelligent questions about processes or procedures that will help you understand the business. For example, a manager might say that she checks out the competition every week by going to the Internet. You might ask, "Specifically how do you get the information? Where do you look? The process sounds fascinating."

It is particularly important to engage in new learning in areas of interest to the company, such as developing proficiency in a second language if the company has customers and employees in other countries.

Document Your Accomplishments. An accurate record of what you have accomplished in your career can be valuable when being considered for reassignment, promotion, or a position outside your company. The same log of accomplishments is useful for résumé preparation and to bring to a performance review. Sending e-mail updates to your manager about your noteworthy accomplishments is effective if not done to the point of being an annoyance. It is preferable to point to tangible, quantifiable accomplishments rather than to another person's subjective impression of your performance. Let's assume that a retail store manager reduced inventory shrinkage by 30 percent in one year. It would be better to state the fact than to record a statement from the manager saying, "Kelly shows outstanding ability to reduce inventory shrinkage."

Career coach Peggy Klaus recommends that you weave your accomplishments into an interesting story to tell other people.[35] The story approach has more appeal than a straightforward list of your accomplishments. Here is a fragment of a story that a man who worked for a food supplier to restaurants, schools, and hospitals used to document his accomplishments:

Our area was hit with a vicious lightning storm last March 12. Our computer and telephone systems went haywire because of power outages. We had to be in touch with our customers. I rounded up 10 people in the company who had smartphones with them. Using all the battery power we had left in our phones, we were able to contact all our customers. My manager said my cell phone rescue effort saved the day.

Documenting your accomplishments in a business field is similar to a person in the arts such as a photographer, interior designer, or architect developing a portfolio of work. When the person applies for a job or assignment, he or she carries along the portfolio of representative work.

Project a Professional Image.   In the workplace you are judged not only by your accomplishments and abilities, but also by your clothes, style, and grooming.[36] Your clothing, desk and work area, speech, and general knowledge should project the image of a professional, responsible person if you seek career advancement. A positive scent also contributes to a person's professional image, with light perfume, toilet water, or cologne *often* contributing to a positive image. Good grammar and sentence structure can give you the edge because so many people use highly informal patterns of speech. Being a knowledgeable person is important because today's professional businessperson is supposed to be aware of the external environment. Also, projecting a professional image hastens the development of trust and rapport in business relationships.

A subtle part of projecting a professional image is to have a positive attitude. Assume that things are not going well in the office, such as the CEO announcing that no year-end bonuses will be forthcoming this year. Instead of joining the complainers, you might say to your coworkers, "A bonus would be wonderful, but I am happy to know that by giving no bonuses there will be no layoffs." Joining in the negativity makes you appear unprofessional. Yet offering constructive criticism can be quite professional.

A challenge in projecting a professional image is to figure out what constitutes a professional image in your particular environment. Less restrictive dress codes have made it more confusing to select clothing that will create a favorable appearance.

For the last several years business formal attire for both men and women has been making a strong comeback. Business casual dress for everyday wear is losing popularity in many firms. Many firms have introduced Formal Fridays, during which professional workers are expected to dress elegantly.[37] A high-end example of formal business attire being required for professionals is real estate sales in Manhattan. For instance, agents at the large firm Halstead Property aim for a professional, polished look that matches the style of their clientele.[38]

Hairstyle is a superficial part of appearance that the career-minded person must ponder, whether or not standards forcoiffure border on being discriminatory. Some employers prefer that men in customer contact positions do not wear shoulder-length hair. The short-hair stereotype is also pronounced for women. Research suggests that both sexes perceive women with short, highlighted hairstyles as smart and confident, but not sexy, finds Marianne LaFrance, a psychologist at Yale University.[39] LaFrance is explaining stereotypes, not endorsing them as being true.

A general guideline is to dress somewhat like the successful people in your firm or the customer's firm. It might pay to contact a company you plan to visit in advance and inquire about the dress standards for key people in the company. Skill-Building Exercise 17-5 is designed to sensitize you to what constitutes a professional image in a specific environment.

SKILL-BUILDING EXERCISE 17-5

The Professional Image Investigation

Find out what constitutes a *professional image* in a specific job environment, either where you work or at another employer. Ask a handful of people, "What makes for a professional image here?" Speak to or correspond by e-mail with a top-level manager, as well as a few workers without managerial responsibility. Another approach to this assignment is to make some observations directly in a retail establishment like Safeway, a Toyota dealership, Macy's, or Nordstrom. How do the people in supervisory positions appear to dress, behave, and talk? Maybe you can conduct a one-minute interview with a service worker or two.

Share your observations with classmates, and see what conclusions can be drawn. For example, how does the type of company influence what constitutes a professional image? Are there different standards for men and women?

Perceive Yourself as a Provider of Services. A useful perspective for upgrading your professional self-image and enhancing your feelings of job security is to perceive yourself as something other than a traditional employee. According to career specialist John A. Thomson, everyone should see himself or herself as a personal service business entity. Basically you are a business, offering the company (also your client from this perspective) a valuable service. You keep offering the service so long as the company keeps you on the payroll and you enjoy the work. Note the similarity to a high-level professional, such as a dentist or information technology consultant. You are offering a service that many people need. Part of the same perception is that you own your skills, and that these are the service your business (you) offers to others.[40]

Perceiving yourself as a provider of services supports the strategy of developing a personal brand. Not being a traditional employee becomes part of your brand.

Strategies and Tactics for Interacting with the Outside World

The focus in this section is advancing your career mostly through creating circumstances in the external world to your advantage.

Develop Depth and Breadth. A continuing concern about career management is whether to acquire substantial depth in a specialty or to obtain broader experience. Is it better to be a specialist or a generalist? Typically it pays to have good depth in one area of expertise, yet also acquire broad experience. A distribution specialist who helped set up shipping systems in an automobile supply company, an office supply company, and a hospital supply company would have excellent credentials. Yet some career specialists would argue that knowing one industry well has its merits.

Rely on a Network of Successful People. Networking has already been described as a major assist to building relationships and finding a job. Members of your network can also help you by assisting with difficult job problems, providing emotional support, buying your products or services, and offering you good prices on their products or services. On the negative side, being excluded from informal networks in your company can block your career advancement. The starting point in face-to-face networking is to obtain an ample supply of business cards. You then give a card to any person you meet who might be able to help you now or in the future. Business cards, especially those with a creative flair, have made a strong comeback recently. The business card is perceived by many as a refreshing change from technology, and it also helps promote your personal brand.[41]

While first developing your network, be inclusive by inviting any plausible person into your network. Later, as your network develops, you can strive to include a greater number of influential and successful people. Professional and trade groups, such an association of bankers or sales professionals, are ideal for networking and are found in virtually every city. One reason that playing golf persists as a networking technique is that so many influential and successful people play golf. A general point about places to network is to stay alert to opportunities, such as networking with people in airport waiting areas and on airplanes.

Social networking sites such as Facebook, LinkedIn, and Twitter can often be used to find members for your professional network despite their social emphasis. A strictly professional site such as LinkedIn is directly targeted toward making professional contacts. Millions of professionals turn to LinkedIn to swap job details and contact information, often for recruiting purposes. To use these social networking sites for professional purposes, you will need to create an online profile, including your résumé.

Hard data exist that networking really does contribute to career success. A three-year study conducted with more than 200 German workers from a variety of industries found that networking was associated with both a higher salary and a higher growth rate of salary over time. Furthermore, people who networked more frequently were more satisfied with their careers.[42]

People may vary in how many social connections they can manage. Yet as you build your network over time, it is helpful to keep in mind Dunbar's number. British anthropologist Robin Dunbar contends thatn a person can only maintain 150 close social connections.[43] Even if Dunbar's number is only approximate, it is helpful to keep in mind

Building Your Network

From a career standpoint, networking involves developing a list of personal contacts who can help you achieve goals and to whom you offer something of value in exchange.

Networking is a career-long process, but the time to begin is now. Quite often the people who have been in your network the longest become your most valuable contacts. To begin networking, or systematize the networking you are now doing, implement the following steps:

Step 1: Write down the type of assistance you are seeking for the next several months. Perhaps you need leads for a job, advice about getting ahead in your industry, or help with a difficult computer problem.

Step 2: List all the people who might be able to provide you the assistance you need. Among them might be fellow students, former employers, neighbors, and faculty members. Prepare a contact card or database entry for each person on your list as if they were sales prospects. Include relevant details, such as name, position, major, e-mail address, phone numbers, postal address, and favorite pastimes. (Setting up a table with a word processor would work quite well for listing entries, or you can use a spreadsheet.)

Step 3: Identify an action step for making contact with the potential network members. Quite often the initial contact will be by e-mail. Gently mention that you would enjoy a telephone conversation or face-to-face meeting if it fit the contact's interest and schedule. You might also be able to think of creative ways to make the initial contact in person, such as attending professional meetings or talking to a neighbor while he or she is washing a car or doing yard work.

Step 4: Identify how you might be able to help each person in your contact list, or how you can reciprocate. For example, if a marketing person gives you an idea for a job lead, you can become part of his or her company's *guerilla marketing team* (you say nice things about the company's product to friends and in public or use the product in public). Sometimes the best approach is to ask the person who becomes part of your network what you can do to reciprocate.

Step 5: Maintain a log of all the contacts you make and what took place, such as an agreed-upon face-to-face meeting or specific assistance received. Indicate how you responded to the assistance, such as "I visited my contact's company Web site, went to the career section, and included her name as a person who is familiar with my work." Write down carefully your plans for reciprocity. Make a checklist as to whether you remembered to thank the person for any courtesy he or she extended to you.

Step 6: Update your log weekly, even if the activity requires only a few minutes of your attention. A network of helpers is a dynamic list, with people entering and exiting your network frequently. Each week, ask yourself, "Whom can I add to my network this week?"

that to have a network of meaningful contacts, avoid having so many contacts that they become superficial.

Skill-Building Exercise 17-6 provides suggestions for systematically building your network.

Work with a Mentor. In Chapter 12, mentoring was presented as a way of helping people grow and develop. Having a mentor can also facilitate career advancement. Ideally, a person should develop a small network of mentors who give advice and counsel on different topics, such as job advancement opportunities and how to solve a difficult problem. Many people who receive exceptional promotions within their own firms or receive excellent job offers from other companies are chosen by their mentors. At the root of mentoring is the ability to attract and build a relationship with a person who is more experienced and talented than you.

Networking is often used to find a mentor or mentors. As mentioned in Chapter 12, the current trend is to have multiple mentors, as facilitated by social networking sites. Among the suggestions for building and sustaining a network of mentors are as follows: (1) Take the initiative to strike up and maintain relationships with mentors, (2) reach beyond immediate coworkers and managers to others in your company and the community, (3) lend mentors a hand on their projects when feasible, and (4) do your best to be positive and personable.[44]

BananaStock/Thinkstock

In her best-selling book, *Lean In*, Facebook chief operating officer Sheryl Sandberg explains that an effective way of attracting a mentor is to impress a higher-up with how well you are performing in your job.[45] She believes this approach is far superior to asking an executive, "Will you be my mentor?" To project this impression, a person would have to use some version of the technique "document your accomplishments." When you do meet a prospective mentor, a good starting point in developing a relationship is to ask about the nature of his or her work, including what path led to his or her present position.

A mentor can help the career beginner overcome hurdles such as being disappointed about the first job, not being listened to, or not receiving enough feedback. Another disappointment might occur when a recent grad anticipates that all workers will be fired up and eager to help the company. Yet on the job, the grad might encounter workers who are bored with their work. The newcomer might ask a mentor in a senior position, "Did you go through this? Is this normal? When does it all change, if at all?"[46]

Find a Good Person–Organization Fit.   Assuming that you have the luxury of selecting among different prospective employers, it is best to work for a company in which your personality, values, and style fit the organizational culture. As implied at several places in the text, an **organizational culture** is a system of shared values and beliefs that influence worker behavior. You have to study the culture through observation and questioning to understand its nature. A good starting point is to ask, "In order to succeed, what is really expected of workers?" You might find out, for example, that pleasing customers and being honest is the path to success. Asking network members what they know about the prospective employer might be revealing, such as asking a former classmate, "You have worked at the corporate office of PepsiCo; what is it really like working there?"

A **person–organization fit** is the compatibility of the individual and the organization. Job interviews represent a good opportunity for evaluating a person–organization fit for both the applicant and the employer. During a visit to the company to learn whether a culture tended to be formal or informal, you might observe the formality of the people and the emphasis on procedures, such as a lengthy document to obtain a travel reimbursement. You might also look for a value match.

The compatibility in question often centers on the extent to which a person's major work-related values and personality traits fit major elements of the organization culture. Following this idea, a person who is adventuresome and risk taking would achieve the highest performance and satisfaction in an organization in which adventuresome behavior and risk taking are valued. Conversely, a methodical and conservative individual should join a slow-moving bureaucracy. How much an organization emphasizes individual effort versus teamwork is another important area for person–organization fit. Workers who enjoy teamwork would fit better in a teamwork-oriented culture.

Person–organization fit can also include superficial aspects of behavior such as physical appearance and dress. For example, a person who dresses like a Wall Street investment banker might not feel comfortable working in a high-tech firm in California where jeans and sandals are standard work attire. As a consequence of not feeling comfortable in your work environment, you might not perform at your best.

The consequences of a person fitting both the organization and the job have been systematically researched based on 25 studies. One of the conclusions reached was that commitment to the organization (a willingness to stay) was strongly associated with the person–organization fit. The study cautioned that it is not always easy for the job applicant to diagnose the fit in such areas as the conformance between the ethics of the individual and the company. When the topic arises, the hiring manager might be less than candid in explaining the company's true ethics.[47]

Take Sensible Risks.   People who make it big in their careers usually take sensible risks on their journey to success. Sensible risk taking means about the same thing as *moving outside your comfort* zone, because you stretch your capabilities but do not plunge recklessly into a new venture. Among these risks would be to work for a fledgling company that offers big promises but a modest starting salary, or to take an overseas assignment with no promise of a good position when you return. Purchasing stock in start-up companies is sometimes a sensible risk, if you do not absolutely need the funds for living expenses.

An approach to taking sensible risks worth considering is to enter a field or an industry that others might overlook because the field or industry does not receive much publicity or is not perceived as being glamorous. The so-called basic industries, however, often

organizational culture

A system of shared values and beliefs that influence worker behavior.

person–organization fit

The compatibility of the individual and the organization.

offer excellent growth opportunities. Also, some of these basic industries are more recession-resistant than glamour industries such as telecommunications, with low-price food companies and rapid-service restaurants leading the way. The waste-management industry, including garbage pickup, is another low-glamour industry with plenty of opportunity even if you are not a waste-management specialist. All big companies hire accountants, office administrators, IT specialists, and so forth.

Emphasize Relationships to Combat Being Outsourced. A major concern of many workers is that their job will be *outsourced* or *offshored* to a lower-paid worker in a country where a competent worker will perform the same job at lower pay. (Ousourcing to a region of one's own country where workers receive lower pay is also possible.) As companies throughout the world struggle to stay competitive in a global economy, more and more jobs are outsourced. Call center and information technology positions are the most frequently outsourced, but so is a variety of design work, some legal research, and medical diagnostic work. The positions least likely to be outsourced are those that require the physical presence of the worker and cannot easily be done remotely. Examples include nursing, real estate selling, teaching, funeral technician, massage therapist, and hair stylist. Managing people requires a physical presence, but not if your workers' positions have been outsourced.

Another way to decrease the chance of your job being outsourced is to make relationship building a key part of your job, whether or not you are performing mostly technical work. An obvious part of relationship building is to be physically present in the workplace, so working from home might make you more susceptible to your job being outsourced. A real estate agent with hundreds of personal contacts cannot be replaced by a Web site. And an information systems specialist who performs hands-on work with internal clients cannot be replaced by an IT specialist working 7,000 miles away in another country.

In short, good interpersonal relationships will not only advance your career, but will also help you preserve your position through the turmoil of technological change.

Concept Review and Reinforcement

Key Terms

extreme job hunting 429
calling 442

proactive personality 442
organization culture 448

prosocial motivation 442
person–organization fit 448

Summary

Recommended job-hunting tactics include the following:

1. Identify your job objectives.
2. Be aware of qualifications sought by employers.
3. Identify your skills and potential contribution.
4. Develop a comprehensive marketing strategy.
5. Go where the jobs are.
6. Stay organized during your job search.
7. Use networking to reach company insiders.
8. Use multiple online approaches.
9. Smile at network members and interviewers, and be enthusiastic.
10. Smooth out the rough spots in your background.

Job hunting almost always requires a résumé. A length of one page is recommended for a less experienced person and two pages for a more experienced person. Résumés should emphasize skills and accomplishments. Make good use of key words and past tense of verbs. Be aware of the problems of identity theft and scams associated with online résumés. Make your submissions easy to access for employers and minimize résumé errors. Video résumés can be important, as well as creative formats. A Twitter résumé can possibly attract an employer. Honesty about your credentials is important. A résumé should almost always be accompanied by a cover letter explaining how you can help the organization and why you are applying for this particular job.

Telephone screening interviews often precede a full job interview. A general guide for performing well in an interview, whether with one person or a panel, is to present a positive but accurate picture of yourself. More specific suggestions include the following:

1. Be prepared, look relaxed, and make the interviewer feel comfortable.
2. Avoid talking too much during the interview.
3. Establish a link between you and the prospective employer.
4. Ask perceptive questions.
5. Be prepared to discuss your strengths and weaknesses (developmental opportunities).
6. Be prepared to respond to behavioral interview questions (examples of job behaviors).
7. Show how you can help the employer.
8. Use nonverbal communication that projects confidence and decisiveness.
9. Practice good etiquette during the interview and meals.
10. Be low key about salary.
11. Minimize utterances that annoy many interviewers.
12. Send a follow-up (or thank-you) letter.

Improving interpersonal relationships assists career advancement, in addition to implementing strategies and tactics. Strategies and tactics aimed mostly at controlling your own characteristics and behaviors are as follows:

1. Develop career goals.
2. Capitalize on your strengths, and build your personal brand.
3. Be passionate about and proud of your work.
4. Develop a code of professional ethics and prosocial motivation.
5. Develop a proactive personality.
6. Keep growing through continuous learning and self-development.
7. Document your accomplishments.
8. Project a professional image.
9. Perceive yourself as a provider of services.

10. Develop depth and breadth.
11. Rely on a network of successful people.
12. Work with a mentor.

13. Find a good person–organization fit.
14. Take sensible risks.
15. Emphasize relationships to combat being outsourced.

Questions for Discussion and Review

1. During a labor shortage (when there are more positions open than qualified applicants), why is it still important to have good job search skills?
2. With all the emphasis on online job hunting, how do you demonstrate that you have effective interpersonal skills?
3. In what ways might video résumés both help and hinder a company to attain the goal of having a diverse workforce?
4. To what extent do you think it is still realistic for a person in his or her early twenties to join a large company and stay employed there for 40 or more years? Explain your reasoning.
5. Identify three sources for finding your strengths and weaknesses.

6. How do you find out about the organizational culture of a company if you do not know anyone that works there?
7. How does talent and expertise contribute to career advancement?
8. How would a knowledge of the business strategy of the company you work for help you in your career?
9. Which sport or pastime in addition to golf do you think would be useful for building a professional network? Why?
10. What is the most useful idea you picked up from this chapter about either conducting a job campaign or managing your career? Explain your reasoning.

The Web Corner

http://www.jobhuntingadvice.com
(Advice on all phases of job hunting, plus information about stable fields of employment)

http://www.Vault.com
(A wealth of information about career advancement, job finding, and occupational profiles)

http://www.careercast.com
(Finding the right professional mentor, including the attributes you should look for)

Internet Skill Builder: Finding a Job Efficiently

So many job boards exist on the Internet that conducting a Web-based job search can be baffling. A direct approach is to visit Monster (on the front page of www.Yahoo.com)

and enter three specific job titles of interest to you. You will be directed to loads of job opportunities closely matching the job titles you entered. It may be helpful to enter variations of the same job title, such as both "office manager" and "administrative assistant." Your assignment is to identify five jobs for which you appear to be qualified. Even if you have no interest in conducting a job search, it is informative to be aware of job opportunities in your field. Seek answers to the following questions:

1. Do I appear to have the qualifications for the type of job I am seeking?
2. Is there a particular geographic area where the job or jobs I want are available?
3. How good are opportunities in my chosen field?

Developing Your Human Relations Skills

Interpersonal Relations Case 17.1

Sharon Tackles a Job Interview

Sharon is a professional in the building construction field. Up until four months ago, she held a position as a construction supervisor for a large development company. Her employer faced a severe downturn in business and was forced to lay off 75 percent of its staff, including Sharon. She threw herself into a job search, carefully following several guides to conducting a job search. Sharon did get to the interview stage for two positions, but neither interview led to a job offer.

Today Sharon has another interview as a construction supervisor for a large building construction company in Houston, Texas. Sharon really wants to be hired for this position. An excerpt from her interview follows:

Interviewer: Why should we hire you as a construction supervisor?

Sharon: I've been out of work for four months, and I really need a job. I just started receiving unemployment insurance, and it is not enough to cover my bills. Also, you could also hire me because you need a construction pro to get the job done.

Interviewer: What position do you hope to have five years from now?

Sharon: Right now I'm thinking of the present. I want to get started working again. I'm not so sure about an exact job in the future, but I think that maybe your job would be a good one for me.

Interviewer: What are your strengths as they relate to this position?

Sharon: I'm not one to brag, so maybe you should ask my references. I know a lot about constructing buildings, and I get along well with people. I have lots of friends.

Interviewer: What are your weaknesses as they relate to this position?

Sharon: I don't like to sell myself short, but I do get a little lazy at times. It isn't easy for me to concentrate on my work all day. I tend to access online stores on my Samsung when I am bored.

Interviewer: Now that our interview is almost complete, what questions do you have for me?

Sharon: I know I would like to work for your company. If I do get hired, do you think I could get a hiring bonus or one month's salary in advance? I'm terribly short on cash.

Case Questions

1. What interviewee errors does Sharon appear to be making?
2. What has Sharon done right as an interviewee?
3. What advice can you offer Sharon about conducting herself in a job interview, should she fail to get an offer based on this job interview?

Interpersonal Skills Role-Play

What Sharon Should Have Done

One student plays the role of the interviewer, asking the same five questions as asked in the above case. Another student plays the role of Sharon, but this time she interviews in a more thoughtful manner that would more likely create a favorable impression and lead to a job offer. As you regard the role players, observe both what is said with words and their nonverbal communication.

Interpersonal Relations Case 17.2

Networking in Evanston

Jason, age 31, is an office administrator at a medical supplies company in Evanston, Illinois, located outside Chicago. He enjoys the medical supply field because he perceives the business as an efficient method of distributing medical supplies to settings such as hospitals, medical clinics, and hospices where they are vitally needed.

Jason has long been interested in advancing his career by making contacts that could help him in such ways as being recommended for a bigger position, learning new skills and technology, and bringing in business for his company. Although Jason is not working in sales, he believes that all professional employees have a responsibility to promote the company. One Sunday morning while reading the business section of the newspaper, he learned that a newly formed networking group, the Evanston Professionals, would be holding its first meeting that Friday at an upscale restaurant, starting at 5 p.m. Admission was $15.

Jason thought, "Here is an opportunity made for me. I'll send the event organizer an e-mail this morning, and pay at the door. I'll bring loads of business cards, and wear my sharpest business casual attire." (The announcement specified business casual as the dress code.) Jason showed up precisely at 5 p.m. for the event, and registered at the door. He told the woman at the front table, "I'm Jason, and I'm here to meet some great folks."

Jason purchased a glass of Chardonnay and then made his first move. He spotted a woman wearing a Coach bag, leading him to conclude that she must have a good position. Jason's opening line was, "Hi, I'm Jason, a key office administrator in the medical supply field. Here's my card with a condensed résumé on the back. I'm not specifically looking for a job, but I would never turn down a great opportunity. Be in touch with me if you want to learn more."

The woman wearing the Coach bag replied, "Thanks for coming over, I hope you have a nice evening."

Jason then spotted a hospital administrator, Baxter, whom he recognized from the past. He approached the administrator and said, "Hello, Baxter. I'm glad we're both attending the opening event for this networking group. Here's how you can help me. If you know about any really interesting job openings, let me know. Also, if you are using any new business processes for your hospital that work well, let me know. I can visit you at work to learn all about them."

Baxter replied, "I hear you, Jason. See you later."

Jason then thought, "So far, my networking approach is not working so well. Maybe I should try the personal touch before I get into professional areas." He next approached a woman dressed in a red blouse, slacks, and high heels. Jason's opening line was,

"Hello there, stylish Evanston professional. You look fabulous. I love red on a woman, and high heels please me also. Are you married? Here's my card."

With an icy stare, the woman replied, "I thought this was a professional networking event, not a place to hit on people."

Case Questions

1. What suggestions can you offer Jason for improving his networking effectiveness?
2. What important ground rule for networking is Jason violating?
3. What, if anything, is Jason doing right in terms of career networking?

References

1. Question from "Marc's Monday Morning Newsletter" (*marc@UpLadder.com*), May 2, 2011. p. 1
2. Christian Arno, "One Skill that Will Instantly Make You a Better Job Candidate," *Brazen Careerist*, November 14, 2012, pp. 1–2.
3. Donna Rawady, "Market Yourself Across Multiple Tracks," *Democrat and Chronicle* (Rochester, New York), October 18, 2009, p. 2E.
4. Joann S. Lublin, "Lessons of Extreme Job Hunting," *The Wall Street Journal*, September 1, 2009, pp. D1, D4.
5. Debra Auerbach, "Keep Organized During Job Hunt," *CareerBuilder*, November 4, 2012,
6. Nelson D. Schwartz, "In Hiring, a Friend in Need Is a Prospect, Indeed," *The New York Times* (http://www.nytimes.com), January 27, 2013, p. 1.
7. Jason Lee, "Build a Better Job Search Network," *Tribune Media Services* (http://www.chicagotribune.com), January 26, 2013. p.1.
8. Susan Ricker, "Refresh Your Job Search with Spring Cleaning." *Career Builder*, March 31, 2013.
9. Debra Auerbach, "Pack Your Résumé for Success," *CareerBuilder*, May 20, 2012; Jacqui Barrett-Poindexter, "How to Write the Perfect Resume Hook," *U.S. News and World Report* (http://www.finance.yahoo.com/news), June 19, 2012, p. 1.
10. Joann S. Lublin, "Silence Is Golden Rule for Résumés of People Who Have Broken It," *The Wall Street Journal*, October 2, 2007, p. B1.
11. "A Word on Résumés," *Philly.com*, July 13, 2009.

12. Rachel Emma Silverman and Lauren Weber, "The New Résumé: It's 140 Characters," *The Wall Street Journal*, April 10, 2013, p. B8.

13. Cindy Krischer Goodman, "Lying On Résumé as Really Bad Idea," *The Miami Herald* (http://www.miamiherald.com), May 15, 2012, p. 1.

14. Data presented in "Fake It and You're Busted," *http://TimesJobs.com*, January 23, 2009, p. 1.

15. Greg Faherty, "Cover Letter Secrets," *NY Resume Writing Examiner* (http://www.sanfranciscoexaminer.com), December 10, 2009.

16. Cited in Sindhu Sundar, "The Ten Worst Things to Put in Your Cover Letter," *Fins Finance* (http://www.fins.com), August 9, 2011, pp. 1.

17. Cited in Debra Auerbach, "Take Phone Interview Seriously," *CareerBuilder*, March 24, 2013.

18. Sarah E. Needleman, "Speed Interviewing Grows as Skills Shortage Looms," *The Wall Street Journal*, November 6, 2007, p. B15.

19. The suggestion about desperation is from Deb Koen, "How to Avoid Sounding Desperate in Your Next Job-Search Interview," *Democrat and Chronicle*, February 5, 2012, p. 2E.

20. "Career Advice: Be Ready to Ask Questions at Interviews," *Washington Post*, October 7, 2012, p. H1.

21. Survey cited in Rachel Louise Ensign, "Selling Yourself in 45 Seconds or Less," *The Wall Street Journal*, June 11, 2012, p. R2.

22. Amy Lindgren, "Job Search Etiquette," *The Atlanta Journal Constitution* (http://www.ajc.com/business), 26, 2012, p. 1.

23. Dawn Klingensmith, "5 Most Annoying Interview Phrases," *http://www.philly.com,* January 22, 2010.

24. Susan Ricker, "Don't Forget the 'Thank-You,'" *CareerBuilder*, August 19, 2012, p. 2F.

25. Anya Kamentz, "The Four-Year Career," *Fast Company*, February 2–12, p. 74.

26. Quoted in Vickie Elmer, "The Perils of Self-Promotion," *Fortune*, November 21, 2011, p. 38.

27. Judy Martin, "Aligning Your Passion with Your Personal Brand," *San Francisco Examiner (http://www.examiner.com),* March 7, 2009.

28. Sukhinder Singh Cassidy, "The Best Advice I Ever Got," *Fortune*, July 6, 2009, p. 47.

29. Shoshana R. Dobrow, and Jennifer Tosti-Kharas, "Calling: The Development of a Scale Measure," *Personnel Psychology*, Number 4, 2011, pp. 1001–1049.

30. Susan Dominus, "Is Giving the Secret to Getting Ahead?" *The New York Times* (http://www.nytimes.com), March 27, 2013.

31. Janet Banks and Diane Coutu, "How to Protect Your Job in a Recession," *Harvard Business Review*, September 2008, p. 114.

32. Scott E. Seibert, Maria L. Kraimer, and J. Michael Crant, "What Do Proactive People Do? A Longitudinal Model Linking Proactive Personality and Career Success," *Personnel Psychology*, Winter 2001, pp. 845–874; Scott E. Seibert, J. Michael Crant, and Maria L. Kraimer, "Proactive Personality and Career Success," *Journal of Applied Psychology*, June 1999, pp. 416–427.

33. Douglas J. Brown et al., "Proactive Personality and the Successful Job Search: A Field Investigation with College Graduates," *Journal of Applied Psychology*, May 2006, pp. 717–726.

34. Pamela Babcock, "Always More to Learn," *HR Magazine*, September 2009, p. 51.

35. Cited in Cheryl Dahle, "Showing Your Worth without Showing Off," *http://nytimes.com,* September 19, 2004; http://www.bragbetter.com.

36. Carlin Flora, "Personal Packaging," *Psychology Today*, July/August 2009, p. 61.

37. Andy Jordan, "If You Really Want to Defy Conformity, Dress Up Today," *The Wall Street Journal*, January 4, 2013, p. A1.

38. Robin Kawakami, "To Sell a Penthouse, Polished Attire Preferred," *The Wall Street Journal*, January 3, 2013, p. D3.

39. Cited in Louise Dobson, "Skirting the Line: In the Office, Wardrobe Mistakes Can Be Disastrous," *Psychology Today*, July/August 2006, p. 13; Flora, "Personal Packaging," p. 61.

40. Cited in "Taking Charge in a Temp World," *Fortune*, October 21, 1998, pp. 247–248.

41. Harriet Barovick, "The Return of the Calling Card," *Time*, August 11, 2008, p. 57.

42. Hans-Georg Wolff and Klaus Moser, "Effects of Networking on Career Success: A Longitudinal Study," *Journal of Applied Psychology*, January 2009, pp. 196–206.

43. Cited in Chris Brogran, "The Network is Everything," *Entrepreneur*, October 2010, p. 56.

44. Dawn E. Chandler, Douglas T. Hall, and Kathy E. Kram, "How to Be a Smart Protégé," *The Wall Street Journal*, August 17, 2009, p. R5.

45. Sheryl Sandberg, *Lean In* (New York: Knopf, 2013).

46. Erin White, "The First Job Blues: How to Adjust, When to Move On," *The Wall Street Journal*, July 25, 2006, p. B7.

47. Amy L. Kristof-Brown, Ryan D. Zimmerman, and Erin C. Johnson, "Consequences of Individuals' Fit at Work: A Meta-Analysis of Person-Job, Person-Organization, Person-Group, and Person-Supervisor Fit," *Personnel Psychology*, Summer 2005, pp. 281–342.

GLOSSARY

acceptance of power and authority The degree to which members of a society expect, and should expect, power to be distributed unequally.

action plan A series of steps to achieve a goal.

active listener A person who listens intensely, with the goal of empathizing with the speaker.

assertiveness Being forthright in expressing demands, opinions, feelings, and attitudes. In relation to cultural values, the degree to which individuals are (and should be) assertive, confrontational, and aggressive in their relationships with one another.

authentic leader A leader who is genuine and honest about his or her personality, values, and beliefs, as well as having integrity.

backstab An attempt to discredit by underhanded means, such as innuendo, accusation, or the like.

behavioral feedback Information given to another person that pinpoints behavior rather than personal characteristics or attitudes.

blind spots Areas of unawareness about our attitudes, thinking, and behaviors that contribute to poor decisions.

brainstorming A group problem-solving technique that promotes creativity by encouraging idea generation through noncritical discussion.

brainwriting Brainstorming by individuals working alone.

bullies People who verbally, and sometimes physically, attack others frequently.

burnout A condition of emotional, mental, and physical exhaustion in response to long-term stressors.

business etiquette A special code of behavior required in work situations.

carpal tunnel syndrome A condition that occurs when repetitive flexing and extension of the wrist causes the tendons to swell, thus trapping and pinching the median nerve.

casual time orientation A cultural characteristic in which people view time as an unlimited and unending resource and therefore tend to be patient.

challenge stressors Stressful events that have a positive direct effect on motivation and performance.

charisma A special quality of leaders whose purposes, powers, and extraordinary determination differentiate them from others. (However, people besides leaders can be charismatic.)

coaching A method of helping workers grow and develop and improve their job competence by providing suggestions and encouragement.

cognitive behavioral approach to stress management A method for people learning to recognize how pessimistic and distorted thoughts of gloom and doom create stress.

cognitive fitness A state of optimized ability to remember, learn, plan, and adapt to changing circumstances.

cognitive restructuring Mentally converting negative aspects into positive ones by looking for the positive elements in a situation.

cognitive style A mode of problem solving.

collective efficacy A group's belief that it can handle certain tasks.

collectivism A feeling that the group and society should receive top priority, rather than the individual.

commitment A perceived psychological bond that employees have with some target associated with their jobs, often another person.

communication The sending, receiving, and understanding of messages.

compromise Settlement of differences by mutual concessions.

concern for others An emphasis on personal relationships and a concern for the welfare of others.

conflict A situation in which two or more goals, values, or events are incompatible or mutually exclusive.

conflict of interest A situation that occurs when a person's judgment or objectivity is compromised.

confrontation Taking a problem-solving approach to differences and identifying the underlying facts, logic, or emotions that account for them.

consensus General acceptance by the group of a decision.

constructive gossip Unofficial information that supports others, is based on truth, and respects confidential information.

corporate athletes Workers who engage in high-level performance for sustained periods.

cross-functional team A work group composed of workers from different specialties, and about the same organizational level, who come together to accomplish a task.

cultural fluency The ability to conduct business in a diverse, international environment.

cultural intelligence (CQ) An outsider's ability to interpret someone's unfamiliar and ambiguous behavior the same way that person's compatriots would.

cultural sensitivity An awareness of and willingness to investigate the reasons why people of another culture act as they do.

cultural training A set of learning experiences designed to help employees understand the customs, traditions, and beliefs of another culture.

customer-centric sales process An approach to sales that emphasizes a low-pressure environment in which the sales staff acts as consultants, offering information and explaining how the product or service can help solve a customer's problem.

cycle-of-service chart A method of tracking the moments of truth with respect to customer service.

defensive communication The tendency to receive messages in such a way that our self-esteem is protected.

defining moment Choosing between two or more ideals in which one deeply believes.

deliberate practice A strong effort to improve target performance over time.

denial The suppression of information we find uncomfortable.

developmental need A specific area in which a person needs to change or improve.

difficult person An individual who creates problems for others, even though he or she has the skill and mental ability to do otherwise.

diversity training Training that attempts to bring about workplace harmony by teaching people how to get along better with diverse work associates.

effort-to-performance expectancy The probability assigned by the individual that effort will lead to performing the task correctly.

emergent leaders Group members who significantly influence other group members even though they have not been assigned formal authority.

emotional intelligence Qualities such as understanding one's own feelings, empathy for others, and the regulation of emotion to enhance living.

emotional labor The process of regulating both feelings and expressions to meet organizational goals.

empathy In communication, imagining oneself in the receiver's role and assuming the viewpoints and emotions of that individual.

employee network (or affinity) group A group composed of employees throughout the company who affiliate on the basis of group characteristics, such as race, ethnicity, gender, sexual orientation, or physical ability status.

empowerment The process of managers transferring, or sharing, power with lower-ranking employees.

ethical screening Running a contemplated decision or action through an ethics test.

ethics The moral choices a person makes. Also, what is good and bad, right and wrong, just and unjust, and what people should do.

expectancy theory A motivation theory based on the premise that the effort people expend depends on the reward they expect to receive in return.

extreme job One in which the incumbent works at least 60 hours per week in a position that usually requires tight deadlines and heavy travel.

extreme job hunting An offbeat way of attracting an employer's attention, with a small probability of success.

feedback In communication, messages sent back from the receiver to the sender.

fight-or-flight response The body's physiological and chemical battle against a stressor in which the person tries to cope with the adversity head-on or tries to flee from the scene.

formality A cultural characteristic of attaching considerable importance to tradition, ceremony, social rules, and rank.

frame of reference The fact that people perceive words and concepts differently because their vantage points and perspectives differ. Also, a lens through which we view the world.

g (general) factor A factor in intelligence that contributes to the ability to perform well in many tasks.

Galatea effect A type of self-fulfilling prophecy in which high expectations lead to high performance.

gender egalitarianism The degree to which a culture minimizes, and should minimize, gender inequality.

group decision making The process of reaching a judgment based on feedback from more than one individual.

group norms The unwritten set of expectations for group members.

groupthink A deterioration of mental efficiency, reality testing, and moral judgment in the interest of group solidarity.

hindrance stressors Those stressful events that have a negative effect on motivation and performance.

humane orientation The degree to which a society encourages and rewards, and should encourage and reward, individuals for being fair, altruistic, caring, and kind to others.

impression management A set of behaviors directed at enhancing one's image by drawing attention to oneself.

incivility In human relations, employees' lack of regard for each other.

individual differences Variations in how people respond to the same situation based on personal characteristics.

informal learning The acquisition of knowledge and skills that take place naturally outside a structured learning environment.

information overload A phenomenon that occurs when people are so overloaded with information that they cannot respond effectively to messages.

in-group collectivism The degree to which individuals express, and should express, pride, loyalty, and cohesiveness in their organizations and families.

integrity (a) Consistency of words and deeds, and (b) being true to oneself.

intelligence The capacity to acquire and apply knowledge, including solving problems.

intermittent reward A reward that is given for good performance occasionally, but not always.

interpersonal skill training The teaching of skills in dealing with others so they can be put into practice.

intuition An experience-based way of knowing or reasoning in which the weighing and balancing of evidence are done automatically.

leader-exchange model A theory explaining that group leaders establish unique working relationships with group members, thereby creating in-groups and out-groups.

leadership The ability to inspire support and confidence among the people who are needed to achieve company goals.

leadership efficacy A form of efficacy associated with confidence in the knowledge, skills, and abilities associated with leading others.

learning style The way in which a person best learns new information.

locus of control The way people look at causation in their lives.

mentor An individual with advanced experience and knowledge who is committed to giving support and career advice to a less experienced person.

message A purpose or idea to be conveyed.

metacommunication To communicate about your communication to help overcome barriers or resolve a problem.

microinequity A small, semiconscious message we send with a powerful impact on the receiver.

micromanager One who closely monitors most aspects of group members' activities, sometimes to the point of being a control freak.

mirroring Subtly imitating someone.

mixed message A discrepancy between what a person says and how he or she acts.

moments of truth Situations in which a customer comes in contact with a company and forms an impression of its service.

moral intensity In ethical decision making, how deeply others might be affected by the decision.

motivation An internal state that leads to effort expended toward objectives; an activity performed by one person to get another to accomplish work.

motivational state Any active needs and interests operating at a given time.

multiple intelligences A theory of intelligence contending that people know and understand the world in distinctly different ways and learn in different ways.

multitasking (a) You have two or more projects that you are working on, but you do not work on these projects at the same time. (b) The person does two or more things simultaneously.

narcissism An extremely positive view of the self, combined with limited empathy for others.

negative affectivity A tendency to experience aversive emotional states.

negative reinforcement (avoidance motivation) Rewarding people by taking away an uncomfortable consequence of their behavior.

negotiating Conferring with another person to resolve a problem.

networking Developing contacts with influential people, including gaining their trust and confidence. Also, contacting friends and acquaintances and building systematically on these relationships to create a still-wider set of contacts that might lead to employment.

noise Anything that disrupts communication, including the attitudes and emotions of the receiver.

nominal group technique (NGT) A group problem-solving technique that calls people together in a structured meeting with limited interaction.

nomophobia The fear of being without a mobile phone.

nonverbal communication The transmission of messages through means other than words.

nurturing person One who promotes the growth of others.

organization culture A system of shared values and beliefs that influence worker behavior.

organizational citizenship behavior The willingness to go beyond one's job description without a specific reward apparent.

organizational politics Gaining power through any means other than merit or luck.

paraphrase To repeat in your own words what the sender says, feels, and means.

participative leadership Sharing authority with the group.

peak performance Exceptional accomplishment in a given task.

peer coaching A type of helping relationship based on qualities such as high acceptance of the other person, authenticity, mutual trust, and mutual learning.

perceived control The belief that an individual has at his or her disposal a response that can control the negative aspects of an event.

performance orientation The degree to which a society encourages, or should encourage, and rewards group members for performance improvement and excellence.

performance-to-outcome expectancy The probability assigned by the individual that performance will lead to outcomes or rewards.

personal brand For career purposes, what makes you unique, thereby distinguishing you from the competition.

personality Persistent and enduring behavior patterns that tend to be expressed in a wide variety of situations.

personality clash An antagonistic relationship between two people based on differences in personal attributes, preferences, interests, values, and styles.

personality disorder A pervasive, persistent, inflexible, maladaptive pattern of behavior that deviates from expected cultural norms.

personal productivity The amount of resources, including time, you consume to achieve a certain level of output.

person–organization fit The compatibility of the individual and the organization.

person–role conflict The situation that occurs when the demands made by the organization clash with the basic values of the individual.

political correctness Being careful not to offend or slight anyone and being extra civil and respectful.

political decision-making model The assumption about decision making that people bring preconceived notions and biases into the decision-making situation.

positive psychological capital A positive psychological state of development in which you have hope, self-efficacy, optimism, and reslience.

positive self-talk Saying positive things about yourself.

positive reinforcement Increasing the probability that behavior will be repeated by rewarding people for making the desired response.

positive visual imagery Picturing a positive outcome in your mind.

power The ability or potential to control anything of value and to influence decisions.

practical intelligence An accumulation of skills, dispositions, and knowledge, plus the ability to apply knowledge to solve everyday problems.

proactive personality A person who is relatively unconstrained by situational forces and who brings about environmental change.

procrastination Delaying action for no good reason on tasks that need to be done.

prosocial motivation The desire to expend effort to help other people.

protégé The less experienced person in a mentoring relationship who is helped by the mentor.

Pygmalion effect The phenomenon that people will rise (or fall) to the expectations that another person has of them.

rational decision-making model The traditional, logical approach to decision making based on the scientific method.

relationship conflict Conflict that focuses on personalized, individually oriented issues.

role A tendency to behave, contribute, and relate to others in a particular way.

role ambiguity A condition in which the job holder receives confusing or poorly defined expectations.

role conflict The situation that occurs when a person has to choose between two competing demands or expectations.

role overload Having too much work to do.

role-person conflict A situation that takes place when the role(s) your organization expects you to occupy is in conflict with your basic values.

s (special) factors Specific components of intelligence that contribute to problem-solving ability.

self-compassion Treating yourself kindly.

self-efficacy The confidence in your ability to carry out a specific task.

self-esteem The overall evaluation people make about themselves, whether positive or negative.

self-respect How you think and feel about yourself.

self-sacrificing personality A tendency to be more concerned about the welfare and interests of others than of oneself.

sexual harassment Unwanted sexually oriented behavior in the workplace that results in discomfort and/or interference with the job.

social intelligence An understanding of how relationships with bosses and colleagues and family and friends, shape our brains and affect our bodies.

social loafing The psychological term for shirking individual responsibility in a group setting.

social support seeking The degree to which people seek out others to help them with difficult problems through such means as listening, offering sympathy, and giving advice.

stress An adaptive response that is the consequence of any action, situation, or event that places special demands on a person.

stressor The external or internal force that brings about stress.

strong customer orientation A set of individual predispositions, and an inclination to provide service and to be courteous and helpful in dealing with customers and associates.

support network A group of people who can listen to your problems and provide emotional support.

synergy A situation in which the group's total output exceeds the sum of each individual's contribution.

task conflict Conflict that focuses on substantive, issue-related differences related to the work itself.

team A small number of people with complementary skills who are committed to a common purpose, set of performance goals, and approach for which they hold themselves mutually accountable.

time orientation The importance nations and individuals attach to time.

toxic person One who negatively affects others because he or she dwells on the negative.

training The process of helping others acquire a job-related skill.

Type-A behavior A behavior pattern in which the individual is demanding, impatient, and overstriving, and therefore prone to negative stress.

universal training need An area for improvement common to most people.

unwritten boundaries Dividing lines of behavior appropriate to different roles.

upward ethical leadership The leadership displayed by individuals who take action to maintain ethical standards, even though higher-ups engage in questionable moral behaviors.

urgent time orientation A cultural characteristic of perceiving time as a scarce resource and tending to be impatient.

utilitarian predisposition A belief that the value of an act's outcomes should determine whether it is moral.

valence The value, worth, or attractiveness of an outcome.

value The importance a person attaches to something.

virtual office A place of work without a fixed physical location, where the output is communicated electronically.

virtual team A small group of people who conduct almost all of their collaborative work by electronic communication rather than face-to-face meetings.

win–win The belief that after conflict has been resolved, both sides should gain something of value.

workaholism An addiction to work in which not working is an uncomfortable experience.

work engagement High levels of personal investment in the work tasks performed in a job.

work–family conflict A state that occurs when an individual's roles of worker and active participant in social and family life compete with each other.

work orientation The number of hours per week and weeks per year people expect to invest in work versus leisure or other nonwork activities.

INDEX